Marx Worldwide

Historical Materialism Book Series

The Historical Materialism Book Series is a major publishing initiative of the radical left. The capitalist crisis of the twenty-first century has been met by a resurgence of interest in critical Marxist theory. At the same time, the publishing institutions committed to Marxism have contracted markedly since the high point of the 1970s. The Historical Materialism Book Series is dedicated to addressing this situation by making available important works of Marxist theory. The aim of the series is to publish important theoretical contributions as the basis for vigorous intellectual debate and exchange on the left.

The peer-reviewed series publishes original monographs, translated texts, and reprints of classics across the bounds of academic disciplinary agendas and across the divisions of the left. The series is particularly concerned to encourage the internationalization of Marxist debate and aims to translate significant studies from beyond the English-speaking world.

For a full list of titles in the Historical Materialism Book Series
available in paperback from Haymarket Books, visit:
https://www.haymarketbooks.org/series_collections/1-historical-materialism

Marx Worldwide

*On the Development of the International
Discourse on Marx since 1965*

Jan Hoff

Translated by Nicholas Gray

Haymarket Books
Chicago, IL

First published in 2016 by Brill Academic Publishers, The Netherlands
© 2017 Koninklijke Brill NV, Leiden, The Netherlands

Published in paperback in 2017 by
Haymarket Books
P.O. Box 180165
Chicago, IL 60618
773-583-7884
www.haymarketbooks.org

ISBN: 978-1-60846-832-4

Trade distribution:
In the US, Consortium Book Sales, www.cbsd.com
In Canada, Publishers Group Canada, www.pgcbooks.ca
In the UK, Turnaround Publisher Services, www.turnaround-uk.com
All other countries, Ingram Publisher Services International, ips_intlsales@
ingramcontent.com

Cover design by Jamie Kerry of Belle Étoile Studios and Ragina Johnson.

This book was published with the generous support of Lannan Foundation
and the Wallace Action Fund.

Printed in Canada by union labor.

10 9 8 7 6 5 4 3 2 1

Library of Congress Cataloging-in-Publication data is available.

Contents

Preface   IX

Introduction   1

1   The Development of Varying Marx-Oriented Conceptual Approaches
between the Poles of Politics and Theory from the 1960s to the
Present   18
　1   Dogmatic Marxism before the Political and Theoretical Upheaval   19
　　1.1   *Soviet Marxism-Leninism before De-Stalinisation*   19
　　1.2   *A Brief Insight into the Current State of Research into Chinese
Marxism before 1978*   23
　2   Marxism's Resurgence between the Inception and Highpoint of
Political Movements of Emancipation (Circa 1960/65–77)   26
　　2.1   *Western Europe and the Anglo-Saxon World*   27
　　2.2   *Latin America and Asia*   39
　　2.3   *'Heretical Marxism' in Eastern Europe*   50
　3   From the Proclamation of the 'Crisis of Marxism' to the Decline of
Marxism as a Mass Ideology (Circa 1974–90)   51
　　3.1   *Europe and North America*   52
　　3.2   *Latin America, Africa and Asia*   57
　4   The Global Situation after the End of Marxism as a Mass Ideology
(Circa 1990–2008)   63

2   The Further Development of the Marx Debate since the 1960s:
A Survey   73
　1   West Germany   74
　2   Japan   92
　　2.1   *The Situation before 1945*   92
　　2.2   *The Evolution of the Japanese Debate from the Postwar Period to
the Present*   97
　3   Other Asian Countries   115
　　3.1   *South Asia*   115
　　3.2   *East Asia*   118
　4   The Former Socialist Countries in Europe   123
　　4.1   *The Soviet Union*   123
　　4.2   *The GDR and Other Former Socialist Countries in Europe*   136

5   Italy, France and Other Western European Countries   142
       5.1   *Italy*   142
       5.2   *France*   153
       5.3   *Other Western European Countries*   162
6   Latin America and Spain   166
       6.1   *Latin America*   166
       6.2   *Spain*   180
7   The Anglo-Saxon World   182
             Critical Excursus *on Perry Anderson's* In the Tracks of Historical
             Materialism   196

3 **In-Depth Analyses: Central Discourses within the German and
   International Discussions of Marx from the 1980s to the Present**   200
       1   The Understanding of the Object of Critique and Value-Theory   202
              1.1   *On the Understanding of the Object of the Critique of Political
                    Economy*   202
              1.2   *A Survey of the International Debate on Marx's Theory of Value,
                    with a Particular Focus on the Analysis of the Value-Form*   211
              1.3   *Summary*   226
       2   The Problematic of Enquiry and Exposition in the Critique of Political
              Economy   227
              2.1   *A 'Mont Blanc' of Research Material*   227
              2.2   *The Ascent from the Abstract to the Concrete and the 'Problem of
                    the Beginning' in Marx's Presentation*   233
              2.3   *The Relation of Marx's Critique of Political Economy to Hegel's
                    Philosophy as Reflected in the International Debate*   248
              2.4   *Summary*   265
       3   The Six-Volume Plan and the Concept of 'Capital in General'   265
              3.1   *The Structure of the Critique of Political Economy in Six
                    Volumes*   265
              3.2   *The Problematic of 'Capital in General'*   282
              3.3   *Summary*   292
       4   Crisis Theory in and after Marx   293
              4.1   *Approaches to the Interpretation of Marx's Crisis Theory*   293
              4.2   *An Insight into the Marx-Oriented Discussion of Crisis in South
                    Korea following the Asian Financial Crisis of 1997*   307
                    Excursus on the World Market and Crisis   311
              4.3   *Summary*   313

Conclusion   314

Postface   321

Bibliography   323
Index   383

Preface[*]

The present study is a revised version of my doctoral thesis, which bore the title 'The Globalisation of the Critique of Political Economy: On the Development of the International Discourse on Marx from the 1960s to the Present'.[**]

As a comprehensive worldview, Marxism is historically obsolete. Yet Marx's theoretical approach, which consists in a detailed exposition of the internal interconnection of economic categories and relations, and effects a 'disenchantment'[***] of the 'inverted world' of the economy, is still of great theoretical significance. Marx's goal of theoretical enquiry into, and exposition of, the economic laws of motion of modern bourgeois society has lost none of its relevance. Internationally, over the last 50 years in particular, generations of researchers have engaged with Marx's insights.

The object of the present study, which is composed of three central chapters, is to outline the historical development within this international discourse. In chapter 1, an exposition is undertaken of the development of Marx-oriented conceptual approaches between the poles of politics and theory. Chapter 2 deals with the further development of the reception of Marx and of Marx-oriented critical social theory, providing a survey of the historical development of the discussion in various regions of the world, especially since circa 1965. Finally, chapter 3 engages in more depth with central discourses within the German-language and international scientific discussion of Marx from the 1980s to the present.

The above doctoral thesis was accepted by the Department of History and Cultural Studies at the Free University of Berlin in the summer semester of 2008; it was successfully defended on 22 December 2008.

My special thanks go to my primary supervisor, Professor Dr. Wolfgang Wippermann, and my secondary supervisor, Professor Dr. Frieder Otto Wolf, both of whom consistently supported and accompanied my doctoral research project. I would also like to thank the participants of the research colloquia of both professors for their fruitful contributions to the discussion.

---

[*] The symbol * throughout the book indicates the translator's footnotes.
[**] Thanks are due to Frank Engster, William Lewis, Gary Roth, Christoph Lieber, Nate Hawthorne, Riccardo Bellofiore, Tommaso Redolfi Riva, Simon Mussell and others for bibliographic assistance provided during the preparation of the English-language edition of this book.
[***] [*Entzauberung*] – i.e. demystification.

In addition, I would like to express my gratitude to Dr. Mischka Dammaschke for his commitment to my work in his role as publishing editor at Akademie Verlag.

Dr. Michael Heinrich, Professor Dr. Rolf Hecker, Professor Dr. Thomas Sekine, Dr. José María Durán, Martin Birkner, Rafael Carrión and Ken Kubota deserve my thanks for the valuable support they provided.

Last but not least, I am grateful to the *Berliner Verein zur Förderung der MEGA-Edition e. V.* for a financial grant towards the publication of this book.

Jan Hoff
Berlin, April 2009

Introduction

In the first volume of *Capital*, Karl Marx located the 'homeland of political economy' in 'Western Europe'.[1] He likewise ascribed a relatively limited geographical space to his own theory – i.e. the critique of political economy. At least he did so in his letter to Ferdinand Lassalle of 12 November 1858, in which he referred to his theoretical project of the critique of political economy as a contribution to science 'in the German sense':

> In your letter from Frankfurt you said nothing about your economic work. As far as our rivalry is concerned, I don't believe that the German public suffers from an *embarras de richesses* in this field. In fact economics as a science in the German sense of the word has yet to be tackled and to that end not just the two of us but a dozen will be needed.[2]

Likewise, in his famous review of Marx's *A Contribution to the Critique of Political Economy* (1859), Engels wrote the following:

> While in this way in Germany the bourgeoisie, the schoolmasters and the bureaucrats were still making great exertions to learn by rote, and in some measure to understand, the first elements of Anglo-French political economy, which they regarded as incontestable dogmas, the German proletarian party appeared on the scene. Its theoretical aspect was wholly based on a study of political economy, and *German political economy* as an independent science dates also from the emergence of this party. The essential foundation of this German political economy is the *materialist conception of history* whose principal features are briefly outlined in the Preface to the above-named work [i.e. *A Contribution to the Critique of Political Economy* – J.H.].[3]

---

1   Marx 1976a, p. 931.

2   Marx 1983i, p. 355. It is an open question as to what Marx actually meant by his statement that the study of 'economics as a science in the German sense' was yet to be undertaken – it is possible that he was making an implicit reference to Hegel, or perhaps to the underdeveloped state of contemporary German economics in comparison to British economics. What is clear in any case is that Marx situated his theoretical project within a specific national context.

3   Engels 1980, pp. 466–9 (italics in the original).

Marx considered the critique of political economy to be a contribution to economic science 'in the German sense'; Engels regarded it as German political economy. Thus both thinkers explicitly added a national epithet to the critique of political economy.

Nonetheless, Marx's critique of political economy was received, discussed and further developed beyond national, linguistic and continental boundaries. This process has occurred in a more intensive form in the period spanning from the 1960s to the present than at any previous time. Accordingly, a kind of globalisation in the sphere of theory and science* can be said to have taken place. It is important to note here that the focus of the present study is explicitly placed on the history of the international interpretation and discussion of Marx's 'mature' critique of political economy, rather than on the international publishing history of Marx's works. More precisely, the object of the present work is the international reception of the critique of political economy in the period from the 1960s to the present.

The globalisation of Marxian theory was already underway in the nineteenth and early twentieth centuries. Various studies of this early process of dissemination have been published in the intervening period.[4] By the time of the October Revolution (and perhaps earlier), this phenomenon also encompassed the countries of the 'global South and East' in a consolidated way. However, Marx's doctrine was frequently propagated in a form heavily inflected by the Marxisms of the Second and Third Internationals. The 1960s and 1970s represent a watershed in the history of the globalisation of Marxian theory, for reasons which are both political and immanent within the theory itself. Firstly, the new 'wave of globalisation' which was generated at this time came after the de-Stalinisation of the Soviet Union, and it was at the forefront – or at least occurred within the context – of the formation of new emancipatory and social revolutionary movements on a worldwide scale. Secondly, the new era of globalisation of Marxian theory which began in the 1960s was accompanied by the emergence and development of an innovative (and, as such, novel) theoretical potential in the interpretation and further elaboration of the Marxian critique of political economy. This process developed (and continues to develop) in sev-

---

* [*Wissenschaft*] – Marx's allusion to 'science "in the German sense"' should be borne in mind in the context of the present work: 'science' and 'scientific' should be taken as referring to the dialectical theory as exhibited in Marx's critique of political economy (with its debt to Hegelian dialectic, as acknowledged by Marx), in contrast to what might justifiably be characterised as the Anglo-American, positivist understanding of science which holds sway within the 'scientific community' today.

4 Cf. for example, Uroeva 1978, pp. 180 ff.

eral areas of the world almost simultaneously, occasionally with a high degree of interdependence between the various local processes, with the result that a complex web of mutual theoretical references, international transfer of theory and intellectual exchanges now stretches across the globe.

In the last two decades, an enormous transformation took place which generated the conditions for a genuine globalisation of Marxian theory and the related discussion. After the fall of the 'Iron Curtain' in 1989/90, the opportunities for a lively and open exchange of ideas between researchers from East and West were much improved. The second *Marx-Engels-Gesamtausgabe* (*MEGA²*), formerly under the aegis of party-affiliated institutes in East Berlin and Moscow, has been continued as a publishing project with an increased international orientation since the 1990s (with cooperation between researchers in the 'West', 'East' and 'far East'). With its highly rigorous editorial principles, *MEGA²* not only affords access to (previously virtually unknown) sources in relation to Marx's critique of political economy, among other things, thus providing new material for source-oriented research, but also connects the scientific work of numerous historians, social and political scientists, economists and philologists in different countries and continents. Likewise, since the 1990s, the internet has enabled the rapid worldwide dissemination of the results of research, and facilitated communication between researchers.

The present work is a study in the history of theory, and examines several aspects of the broad and variegated field of international processes of theory formation in connection with the Marxian critique of political economy within the period from circa 1965 to the present. With this focus on the period since 1965, and the simultaneous emphasis on the specifically international and intercontinental dimensions of the process of theoretical development in relation to the critique of political economy, this work fills a gap in research, despite the multiplicity of existing approaches to the historiography of Marxism.

Some two decades after the collapse of 'actually existing socialism', the question which might be asked of a study of the development of certain theoretical currents which have taken up, interpreted or further developed Marx's critique of political economy on a worldwide scale over the last 50 years is the following: how is such a study of contemporary relevance? It is so in at least two regards. Firstly, in the case of many of the currents thematised in my enquiry, these represent forms of thought which draw on Marx, but which cannot be placed under the rubric of an anachronistic 'science of legitimation' in the context of an authoritarian party dictatorship; on the contrary, these currents were mainly forms of a 'dissident' Marxism, often emerging in opposition to the orthodox Marxist-Leninism of the communist parties, from which they dissociated themselves. Secondly, the historic failure of 'actually existing social-ism' in no way negated the most important aspects of the Marxian critique of political economy, since the object of this critique was not socialism, but cap-italism. Thus an exposition such as the present one – situating itself within the history of theory, and exploring the various readings and currents of interpret-ation of Marx's project of a critical theory of capitalism that have developed over recent decades – is of undiminished contemporary significance and relev-ance.

In the following, Marx's critique of political economy is to be grasped as a critical theory oriented to the investigation of the structure and laws of motion of the modern capitalist economy. Marx's critique of political eco-nomy can also be described as a 'critical theory of capitalist society'. Thus, if the present study undertakes the exploration of the history of the globalisa-tion of Marxian theory (or of Marxism more broadly) as a critical social theory from the 1960s to the present, it does so by significantly restricting the relev-ant thematic field within the history of the formation of Marxist theory in the sense outlined above. The historical development of dialectical materialism, of historical materialism, and of the various approaches to 'concrete' Marx-ist historiography and to Marxist political theory (in a narrow sense) do not fall within the scope of this work, and are not considered here. The dissoci-ation of Marxism as a critical social theory from these fields of Marxist theory formation is itself the result of a process of historical development. Other ele-ments which have long moulded the understanding of Marxism – for example as a 'dialectics of nature', drawing on the late Engels, or as a specific determ-inistic conception of history, through a construal of the work of both Marx and Engels – withdrew into the background within the historical process of the development of theory, or were increasingly regarded critically, at the same time as there was a growing interest in Marxism as a critical social theory, at least in some areas within the international reception of Marx. A more precise explanation of how Marxism can be characterised as a 'critical social theory' cannot be given in advance, however. Rather, this will emerge from the expos-ition of the historical processes within the development of Marx-related the-ory.

In apparent opposition to the virtually global dimension in which the form-ation of Marx-oriented theory has occurred, a theoretical provincialism has remained a regrettable characteristic and something of a tradition within the history of thought inspired by Marx and within that of the reception of his theory. This is the case not least with regard to the German-language discus-sion of Marx. It is precisely due to this theoretical provincialism, and in view of the corresponding vacuum in research and knowledge in German-speaking countries, that the task of analysing the historical development of theory on an international scale since the 1960s is of such significance, particularly in these countries themselves.[5]

In the introduction to his comprehensive study of the Latin American thinkers, Adolfo Sánchez Vázquez and Bolívar Echeverría, both of whom take up Marx's work, Stefan Gandler writes – exaggerating somewhat, but identifying a real problem – as follows: 'While, for example, in Mexico every theoretical "innovation" in Europe or the United States is followed and commented upon with care – not only are translations prepared, but they are also published and read – in Frankfurt the simple discovery that two philosophers living in Mexico are worth reading arouses exclamations of delight or commotion, both expressions of the same phlegmatic self-satisfaction'.[6]

In actual fact, the problem is not merely that there is only a very limited German body of knowledge on, for example, the Latin American theoretical discussion (this in itself is a deficit which ought to be eradicated, or at least reduced); weighing even more heavily are the lack of openness to, and disinterest in, the Latin American debate and its history. Gandler's reference to 'exclamations of delight' might be expanded upon by adding that a euphoric, uncritical reception of the history of processes of theory formation in the 'global South and East' would be no more constructive than the currently prevailing indifference. This would merely be the other side of the coin of theoretical provincialism.

An example of theoretical provincialism – again, within the context of the German discussion – is to be found in Christoph Henning's important monograph on the development of Marx-related philosophical thought after Marx. Henning justifies the predominant focus on literature in the German language with the argument that an approach specifically oriented to philosophy is bound to refer especially to the discussion in the German language. This, he contends, is because the three sources of Marxism identified by Lenin in his famous thesis of 1913 (French socialism, English political economy and German philosophy) have since drifted in different directions. Already for Lenin, the third 'source of Marxism' was not simply philosophy, but *German* philosophy:

---

5 Nevertheless, the problematic of the relation between Marx and/or Marxism and interculturality has been the subject of discussion within the discipline of philosophy in recent times in Germany. Marco Iorio has arrived at the ambivalent conclusion that the 'antiinterculturalist traits, which can be unequivocally demonstrated in Marx and his work' contrast 'with a whole series of characteristics which definitely indicate the presence of some interculturalist trace elements' (Iorio 2005, p. 110).

6 Gandler 2015, p. 6.

'... Germans, a metaphysical people, have their problems with politics, and thus Marx was soon read in an "intellectual" way once again – he was *rephilosophised*.[7]

Henning's argument in relation to his particular concentration on the German-language philosophical discussion is questionable. A decidedly philosophical approach to the critique of political economy is not specifically (and certainly not exclusively) a characteristic of the German (or German-language) debate. Thinkers such as the Latin American, Enrique Dussel, the Briton, Christopher Arthur, or the Russian, Viktor Vazjulin, immediately spring to mind as counterexamples in this regard. All three figure later in this study; in the case of Dussel, it can be stated in advance that his original approach to Marx's work is taken precisely from the 'peripheral', Latin American (and decidedly non-Eurocentric) perspective of the philosophy of liberation – i.e. simultaneously from a specifically philosophical, and a specifically Latin American, standpoint.

An exemplary case of provincialism in Germany (and especially in the Western part of the country) is provided by the preface to a commemorative volume for Helmut Reichelt, written by some of his students and their associates.[8] The historical development of the interpretative orientation labelled by Hans-Georg Backhaus as the '*Neue Marx-Lektüre*' (or 'New Marx-Reading'), which focuses in a specific way on Marx's understanding of object and method, is traced by these authors aptly enough on some points. Yet at a second glance (at the latest) it is striking that they not only concentrate on Germany; worse still, their scope is limited to the former Federal Republic of Germany, and in fact they identify one unambiguous central locus: Frankfurt am Main. This claim is not tenable with regard to the facts of the matter – i.e. with regard to the historical development of the *Neue Marx-Lektüre* as a reception of Marx. In the course of the present study, it will become evident that it is thoroughly appropriate to understand important theorists 'from all over the world' precisely as the protagonists of a New Marx-Reading – and indeed, in the sense that their approaches to the interpretation of Marx are, in decisive aspects, extremely similar to those of the West German discursive constellation around Hans-Georg Backhaus, Helmut Brentel, Michael Heinrich, etc.

The present work aims to overcome theoretical provincialism. The task here is to provide an exposition of the international historical development of a specific current of Marx-related thought over the last five decades. Nevertheless,

---

7   Henning 2005, p. 22.
8   Kirchhoff, Pahl, Engemann, Heckel and Meyer 2004, pp. 7 ff.

such an undertaking requires critical self-reflection on the part of its author regarding his or her own criteria, evaluations and level of expertise. The present study is an 'international history of the reception' of Marx's critique of political economy. It should be noted, however, that it is written from a specific (West) German perspective – i.e. it is permeated by the author's point of view, which has been arrived at through the West German *Neue Marx-Lektüre*. Moreover, my familiarity with non-German-language debates (and particularly those in Asian or Slavic languages, which are inaccessible to me) is necessarily limited.

A number of attempts – some of them very elaborate – at a historicisation of Marxism have been published in which the specifically international character of the processes of the formation of Marxist theory is taken into account. At the same time, it can be demonstrated that there is room for improvement with regard to the treatment, by some of the historians of Marxism referred to here, of the specifically global dimension of the reception of Marx's theory and of processes of the formation of Marx-related theory.

An important work on the history of Marxism as a theory is that of the Yugoslav philosopher Predrag Vranicki.[9] The first edition of his *Historija marksizma* [*The History of Marxism*], published in 1961, contains the development up to the end of the 1950s, while the second edition from 1971 also takes into account the progression up to 1968.* The author was involved with the Praxis Group, and as such can be considered as a representative of a specifically Yugoslav Marxism which was independent of the Soviet orthodoxy. Vranicki was close to the current of humanist Marxism. The first part of Vranicki's comprehensive work deals with Marx and Engels themselves; the second part covers the Marxism of the period of the First and Second Internationals; the third part is dedicated to Lenin; the fourth part treats the Marxism of the period of the Third International; the fifth and final part, which is of most interest here, engages with the Marxism of the contemporary period. Under this heading, the Yugoslav philosopher includes, firstly, Marxism in the 'socialist camp'; secondly, Chinese Marxism; thirdly, Marxism in the capitalist world (especially in West Germany, France, Italy and the Anglo-Saxon countries); and finally, Marxism in his own country. Vranicki's wide-ranging study in the history of theory is indispensable as a significant standard work in the historiography of Marxism. Yet, in his concluding observations, Vranicki makes the following remarks on Marxist thought:

---

9   Vranicki 1971.
*   Vranicki's work has been published in German (see Vranicki 1985).

It emerged and developed as the expression of European culture, and it is on European soil that it has achieved its greatest and most fruitful victories. The other centres of modern civilisation … did not represent suitable terrains for the further development of such complex thinking. Whether this was due to their historically backward situation, or to their lack of certain cultural and intellectual traditions, the other parts of the world were only able thus far to contribute to this development in the periods of the most intense practical revolutionary action, and indeed especially with regard to the socio-political problematic and to revolutionary praxis.[10]

On the basis of the results of research presented in this study, it can be demonstrated not only that Vranicki's judgement is inappropriate in view of the contemporary situation in the early twenty-first century, but also that the Eurocentric verdict of the Yugoslav historian of Marxism is also problematic in relation to the period up to 1968, as dealt with in the second edition of his work.

The exiled Polish non-Marxist philosopher and historian of ideas, Leszek Kołakowski, authored a further important work on the history of Marxism (this work was conceived by him as a handbook).[11] The first volume principally covers Marx and Engels and locates them within the history of theory. The second volume deals with the period spanning from the Marxism of the Second International to Leninism. Finally, the third volume encompasses the development from early Soviet Marxism to the Marxism-Leninism of the postwar period; it also details the Marxisms of Gramsci; Lukács; Korsch; Goldmann; the leading exponents of the Frankfurt School; Marcuse; Bloch; lastly, it provides an overview of the most recent developments in Marxism at the time it was composed (this final volume, which covers part of the period which is the focus of the present study, dates from 1975/6). Like Vranicki's study, Kołakowski's comprehensive standard work is characterised by Eurocentrism. The names of such significant Latin American or Asian theorists as Adolfo Sánchez Vázquez, Marta Harnecker, Hajime Kawakami, Kōzō Uno or Samezō Kuruma do not figure in the index of names in Kołakowski's compendium. However, Kołakowski himself states the following at the beginning of the third volume: 'The present volume deals with the evolution of Marxism in the last half-century. Writing it has involved especial difficulties, one of which is the sheer bulk of the available

---

10   Vranicki 1985, p. 1071.
11   See Kołakowski 2008, p. xxiii.

literature: no historian can be fully acquainted with it, and it is therefore, so to speak, impossible to do everyone justice'.[12]

Alongside the historian E.P. Thompson, one of the most important protagonists of the intellectual New Left of the 1960s and 1970s in the UK was Perry Anderson, not merely on account of the latter's editorial activity for *New Left Review* (formerly a significant journal in the area of Marxist theory). Anderson's attempt at a historicisation of a determinate domain of Marxist thought in the twentieth century, which he published in his *Considerations on Western Marxism* in 1976,[13] had a relatively large impact, reaching beyond the borders of the Anglo-Saxon world. One sign of this impact, among others, is the fact that Anderson has contributed considerably to the dissemination of the concept of 'Western Marxism' (it should be noted, however, that the French philosopher, Maurice Merleau-Ponty, had already employed this concept before Anderson's book was published). According to Anderson, Western Marxism originated in the 1920s with Lukács, Korsch and Gramsci. Among others ranged within this current alongside these thinkers are the main exponents of the Frankfurt School. A distinctive feature attributed by Anderson to Western Marxism consists in its structural separation from political praxis (this is its 'most fundamental' characteristic);[14] he also considers that it is characterised by an obsessive engagement with methodology.[15] According to Anderson, Western Marxism retraced Marx's own development, but in the opposing direction: Marx moved away from philosophy and towards politics and economics, whereas Western Marxism progressively turned back from economics and politics to the terrain of philosophy.[16]

The theoretical and political heterogeneity of the thinkers subsumed under the concept of 'Western Marxism' in Anderson's study presents a problem, however. In general, the meaningfulness of assigning thinkers as heterogeneous as Adorno and Korsch, for example, to one and the same category of Marxism is questionable (even, in part, on the basis of Anderson's own criteria). This problem cannot be dealt with in more depth here; the term 'Western Marxism' is used – with reservations – in the present study because it has become established within this field of research.

---

12   Kołakowski 2008, p. 787.
13   Anderson 1976. For Anderson's critical engagement with E.P. Thompson, see Anderson 1980.
14   Anderson 1976, p. 29.
15   Anderson 1976, p. 53.
16   See Anderson 1976, p. 52.

According to Anderson, the events of May 1968 in Paris altered the conditions for a Marxist-inspired development of theory: 'The advent of a new period in the worker's movement, bringing to an end the long class pause that divided theory from practice, is now however visible. The French Revolt of May 1968 marked in this respect a profound historical turning point. For the first time in nearly 50 years, a massive revolutionary upsurge occurred within advanced capitalism ...'.[17]

With this development, Anderson argues, new possibilities are opened up for a new generation of Marxist thinkers. The significance of this is that there is to be a shifting of priorities within the production of theory away from philosophy and towards the political and economic domains. Anderson, who at the time harboured certain sympathies for Trotskyism, particularly emphasises the role of Trotskyist intellectuals such as Isaac Deutscher or Roman Rosdolsky, to a certain extent posing them as an alternative to so-called Western Marxism. Anderson writes as follows: 'Western Marxism ... was always magnetically polarized towards official Communism as the only historical incarnation of the international proletariat as a revolutionary class. It never completely accepted Stalinism; yet it never actively combated it either. But whatever nuance of attitude successive thinkers adopted towards it, for all of them there was no other effective reality or milieu of socialist action outside it'.[18]

For Anderson, then, it is precisely here that an important difference between Western Marxism and Trotsky is to be found (although Anderson would have done well to realise that Korsch's political and theoretical opposition to Bolshevism and Stalinism totally contradicts this schema).

Anderson's basic conception from 1976 can be represented as follows: so-called Western Marxism should in no way be ignored by a new generation of socialists. It is rather a question of 'settling accounts' with it. A basic condition for the renewal of Marxist thought is, according to Anderson, to learn from this tradition of thought, but also to overcome it. Ultimately, for Anderson, the fact that this tradition – a tradition which is in Anderson's view to be superseded – is geographically bounded is also a cause of its weakness: 'Marxism aspires in principle to be a *universal* science – no more amenable to merely national or continental ascriptions than any other objective cognition of reality.'[19]

In his study on so-called Western Marxism, Anderson focuses primarily on thinkers from continental Europe. However, a question which arises is whether

---

17   Anderson 1976, p. 95.
18   Anderson 1976, p. 96.
19   Anderson 1976, p. 94.

non-European thinkers, such as Kazuo Fukumoto or Adolfo Sánchez Vázquez, might not also be ranged under the category of so-called Western Marxism. If this current were defined according to content-related criteria, rather than geographical ones, there would be substantial arguments for locating these theorists in the lineage of so-called Western Marxism. Unfortunately, neither thinker figures in Anderson's account. Elias José Palti writes that 'in his survey of Western Marxism, Anderson fails to mention any Latin American current'.[20] A subsequent book published by Anderson in 1983, *In the Tracks of Historical Materialism*, which is considered later in the course of this study, represents a *nadir* of theoretical provincialism.

Between 1978 and 1982, a five-volume history of Marxism was published in Italian.[21] This project was characterised by a consistently international orientation, both in terms of the authors involved and in relation to its thematic scope. In addition to its focus on the Marxism of Marx's time, and the Marxism of the Second and Third Internationals, this project paid close attention to contemporary developments in the area of Marxist theory. Alongside the 'official' and 'heretical' Marxisms in Eastern Europe, it encompassed not only significant West European currents such as the Della Volpe School and the Althusser School, but also non-European theoretical orientations such as the Japanese Uno School, which was familiar to only a limited number of people outside Japan at the time. This five-volume project affords important insights into the globalisation of Marx-oriented theory formation up to circa 1980, but a corresponding exposition spanning the last three decades remains a *desideratum*. It is by no means in Europe alone that approaches to the historiography of international Marxism have been developed. As is demonstrated by the comments of Su Shaozi, a Chinese researcher of Marxism (and a representative of the Institute of Marxism-Leninism-Mao Zedong Thought at the Chinese Academy of Sciences at the time), Chinese research in the 1980s engaged with Vranicki and with Western historians of Marxism, among others, and pursued the aim of launching a specifically Chinese historiography of international Marxism: 'the proposal for writing and publishing a *History of the Development of Marxism* of several volumes by researchers of Marxism in our country through concerted effort is an important event for Chinese social scientists'.[22] Su Shaozhi formulates the position to be adopted in such an undertaking as follows: 'It is understood that to write a history of the development of Marxism it is neces-

20   Palti 2005, p. 55.
21   Hobsbawm et al. (eds.) 1978–82.
22   Shaozhi 1985, p. 3.

sary to take Marxism-Leninism and Mao Zedong Thought as the guide and to adhere to the proletarian stand of the Party'.[23] It should be noted, however, that Su Shaozhi himself was the protagonist of an opening up of Chinese Marxism in the post-Mao Zedong era and that the Institute of Marxism-Leninism-Mao Zedong Thought was subjected to criticism by dogmatic ideologues and ultimately even state repression in the 1980s. Su Shaozhi can be considered to a certain extent to represent the opening up of Chinese Marxism *vis-à-vis* the external world of international Marxism – a process which occurred extremely cautiously at first, and which was not without setbacks.

In the mid-1990s, the (West) German social scientist, Michael Krätke, engaged with the history of Marxism, distinguishing four historical phases. The first of these spans from 1842 to 1883, the year of Marx's death; the second, that of 'classical Marxism', from 1883 to the First World War; the third phase is characterised by Krätke as follows: 'It is not so much a phase of "Western" Marxism that is inaugurated by the October Revolution and the declaration of the creation of the Soviet Union during the civil war, but rather a phase of the great schism between, on the one hand, a party- and state-ideology, *Marxism-Leninism*, which was very much present in both East and West, and, on the other, a variety of Marxisms which are more or less loosely associated with the socialist workers' movement outside the Soviet Union, but which no longer play the role of official organisation doctrine in these countries'.[24] According to Krätke, this historical phase stretches to the end of the 1960s. Krätke then outlines a fourth, contemporary period: the phase of a specific social-scientific Marxism, with its basis in the Marx renaissance of the 1960s. Krätke asserts that the *MEGA*² edition represents a 'constant source of energy' for this social-scientific Marxism. However, it is striking that, in his exposition of currents of thought since the 1960s (an exposition undertaken from the standpoint of the history of theory), Krätke refers primarily to Europe and North America, and the development of theory in Asia and Latin America is rather neglected.

At the end of the 1990s, the (West) Berlin political scientist and interpreter of Marx, Michael Heinrich, published an annotated bibliography on the reception and discussion of Marx's critique of political economy; Heinrich's notes contain a thorough historicisation of the debate.[25] Heinrich's procedure in this historicisation is to separate off a strand of reception oriented to social theory and methodology from the history of the narrowly 'economistic' debate,

---

23   Shaozhi 1985, pp. 3–4.
24   Krätke 1996, p. 82.
25   Heinrich 1998, pp. 188 ff.

and to accord the former rather more attention – especially to its development from 1960 onwards. With regard to the readings of Marx which are oriented to social theory and methodology, Heinrich refers to interpretations which, according to him, 'explicitly do not reduce the critique of political economy to an undertaking within the specialist area of economics, grasping it instead as the analysis and critique of a determinate relation of socialisation and of the forms of everyday and scientific consciousness that are generated by the latter'.[26] In his historical literature survey, Heinrich draws mainly on approaches from Western Europe (including the Federal Republic of Germany), Central and Eastern Europe (including the German Democratic Republic), as well as the Anglo-Saxon world. Important Japanese contributions are discussed at the margins of Heinrich's survey.

In France, several approaches to the history of Marxism have been developed covering the period that is the focus of the present study. In the form of a synopsis transcending national and continental boundaries, Jacques Bidet draws a broad arc over the various interpretative currents oriented towards Marx's critique of political economy from the 1960s almost to the present day. He considers the analytic Marxism of the English-speaking countries, the Japanese Uno School (including its 'Canadian wing'), the West German approaches stemming from the tradition of the Frankfurt School (Schmidt, Backhaus, Reichelt), the Latin American Marx-interpreter influenced by liberation philosophy, Enrique Dussel, but also theoretical currents from Italy, France and Eastern Europe. However, Bidet lacks the space to provide a thoroughgoing and detailed elaboration of the complexities of the international debate that he touches upon.[27]

André Tosel's central focus is a periodisation of the history of theory. He divides the development of the debate on Marx and Marxism from the 1960s to 2005 into three different stages: the first stage (1968–75) is determined by the end of Marxism-Leninism and by the last contributions of the 'great heretics' of Marxism (he names Lukács and Bloch as examples). The second period (1975–89) is characterised as the crisis years of Marxism. The third stage, which begins in 1989, is conceived of by Tosel as a period of theoretical pluralism, as a 'period of a thousand Marxisms'. Tosel's overwhelming focus is on France, Italy, Central Europe (especially West Germany) and the Anglo-Saxon world. The historical development of theory in Asia, and in particular in Japan, is excluded, despite the fact that this development is so theoretically rich and of such significance

---

26   Heinrich 1998, p. 205.
27   See Bidet 2005a.

for the history of the formation of theory drawing on Marx's critique of political economy. However, Tosel does mention Enrique Dussel in relation to the Latin American debate.[28,*]

Contributions to research into the history of Marxism have also been made in Latin America. As far as the history of Latin American Marxism is concerned, the first body of work to cite would be that of the Brazilian Trotskyist and Marx researcher, Michael Löwy. A further point of reference in this regard is a work by the South American, Javier Amadeo; the latter's exposition transcends the boundaries of his own continent.[29] Amadeo traces the historical development of Marxism up to the recent past. He directs his attention especially to French Marxism (Althusserianism, among other variants); Italian Marxism; the critical theory of the Frankfurt School; the Budapest School; and Marxism in the Anglo-Saxon world ('analytic Marxism' and other currents). In relation to Marxist thought in Latin America, Amadeo focuses above all on the Marxism of liberation theology, although he is conscious of the fact that while the latter constitutes – on his own assessment – 'one of the most important theoretical currents of our own continent',[30] it in no way represents the entire bandwidth of Latin American Marxism. Amadeo thus concentrates especially on the historical development traversed by Marxism in the second half of the twentieth century in Western and Central Europe, the Anglo-Saxon world and Latin America. It is a shortcoming of his wide-ranging study that the historical development of Marxism in other countries – i.e. Chinese and Japanese Marxism, among others – scarcely comes into the author's field of vision, if at all.

An innovative approach to the historicisation of the formation of Marxist theory is that undertaken by Ingo Elbe and sketched in his essay, 'Between Marx, Marxism and Marxisms – Ways of Reading Marx's Theory'.[31] Elbe identifies as core elements of 'traditional Marxism' the transformation of Marxian theory into a 'closed ... proletarian worldview and doctrine of the evolution of nature and history',[32] the central significance accorded to ontology, as well as the historicist reconstrual of the form-genetic method of Marx's critique of political economy. Elbe regards the leading theoretical figures of the Second and Third Internationals as important representatives of 'traditional Marxism',

---

28   Tosel 2008a. An earlier French exposition of the history of Marxism is given in Favre and
      Favre 1970.
*   See also an abridged version of Tosel's text published in English translation (Tosel 2008b).
29   See Amadeo 2006.
30   Amadeo 2006, p. 92.
31   Elbe 2013.
32   Ibid.

such that it becomes evident that this type of Marxism – according to Elbe – dominated the theory formed by both the Social Democratic and Communist movements. Elbe contends that so-called Western Marxism, which emerged after the First World War and the failure of revolution in the 'West', promoted an increased sensibility for the subjective mediatedness of the object and grasped Marxism as a 'critical revolutionary theory of social praxis'.[33] Elbe's argument is that since the category of praxis and the subjective mediatedness of the object were hardly considered adequately within the paradigm of 'traditional Marxism', Western Marxism should be conceived of as an essentially different type of Marxism *vis-à-vis* the 'traditional' variant. According to Elbe, then, Lukács, Korsch, Gramsci, the Frankfurt School and the Yugoslav Praxis Group, among others, can be considered important protagonists of Western Marxism.

One of the merits of Elbe's work is to have devised a systematising approach in relation to the type of Marxism represented by the New Marx-Reading, which first began to develop in the 1960s and 1970s (if early precursors are disregarded, such as Isaak Ill'ich Rubin and Evgeny Pashukanis in the Soviet Union of the 1920s). According to Elbe, this New Marx-Reading refers to Marxian theory as a 'deciphering and critique of the forms of capitalist socialization'. Elbe is concerned to show how the references to the works of Marx and Engels vary according to the respective types of Marxism, and how the latter focus their interest on different texts or parts of texts from these works as central points of reference.

The present study can be held to supplement Elbe's pioneering work: a considerable part of the thinkers presented in the present study can be attributed to the New Marx-Reading, or at least stand in close proximity to it. Moreover, as this study will make clear, this type of theory is not only to be found in West Germany, but represents an international phenomenon.

In the meantime, Elbe has produced a comprehensive standard work which goes into great depth on the emergence and development of the New Marx-Reading in West Germany from the middle of the 1960s, and which points the way for future debates on the recent reception of Marx.[34] In this work, Elbe refers to the fundamental value-theoretical and methodological reflections which have been developed in the recent history of the reception of Marx's critique of political economy, and also to the so-called state-derivation debate and to interpretations of Marx's theory of revolution.

---

33   Ibid.
34   Elbe 2010.

Although Elbe restricts himself in his monograph mainly (but not exclusively) to the West German debate, his work is demonstratively characterised, in two respects, by an openness to an 'internationalist perspective' and by its capacity to establish connections in this regard. Firstly, Elbe considers early Soviet thinkers such as Rubin and Pashukanis as precursors to the New Marx-Reading[35] and concedes that various later authors from the countries of 'actually existing socialism' stand in a certain proximity to the New Marx-Reading.[36] Elbe also traces the possible influence of Louis Althusser on the West German reception of Marx, and observes that many of the motifs and insights 'which would characterise the debate in the Federal Republic of Germany in the 1970s' are already anticipated in a contribution by the French Marx-exponent, Jacques Rancière.[37] Secondly, despite his concentration on the New Marx-Reading in the Federal Republic of Germany,[38] Elbe establishes a determination of this special type of theory which can ultimately be extended to the range of problems with which the *international* reception of Marx is engaged. In this connection, the criterion which proves particularly decisive, according to Elbe, is that this type of theory is characterised by a perspective on Marx's theory which is sharply focused specifically on form-theory and form-critique. (Elbe consequently locates the international 'Open Marxism' current, on the basis of its references to Rubin, Pashukanis, and form- and fetish-theory, within the New Marx-Reading). In this way, Elbe's project can form a point of reference for the present study, provided the horizon of the investigation is more rigorously and consistently broadened beyond a West German point of reference.

The historian Wolfgang Wippermann has also published an engagement with the history of Marxism.[39] Wippermann's exposition revolves around the thought that Marx led 'four lives'. Accordingly, the first life of Karl Marx was Marx's own, which was especially determined by his existence as the author of *Capital* and through his activity as a political revolutionary. Marx led a kind of

---

35   Elbe 2010, pp. 32 ff.

36   Elbe 2010, p. 30.

37   Elbe 2010, p. 58. However, Rancière's contribution 'was not translated into German until 1972, and since then it has hardly been noted in Germany, let alone given the praise it deserves' (ibid).

38   That the New Marx-Reading in Germany cannot be reduced to the Frankfurt strand of Marx-reception around Hans-Georg Backhaus and Helmut Reichelt (even though this current represented and continues to represent an important component of the New Marx-Reading in this country) ought to be clear, once and for all, to anyone who has read Elbe's book.

39   Wippermann 2008.

'second life' in the tradition of the Marxist workers' movement of the Second and Third Internationals. Wippermann grasps the corresponding development in terms of an increasing deformation of Marxian theory. According to the German historian, Marx was given a 'third lease of life' through a renaissance of Marxist thought shaped by 'dissident' Marxist theorists. Wippermann contends that in the most recent past, Marx, having been falsely written off, has once again made a comeback or been brought back to life. Wippermann argues that Marx deserves to be read once more in the contemporary world, not only as an economist, but also – and particularly – as a historian and as a philosopher. Wippermann attributes an importance to Marx in relation to the discussion on globalisation, concentrates attention on his theories of 'Asian despotism' and Bonapartism, and focuses on Marx as a 'critic of religion and philosopher', who can offer an orientation 'in the struggle against, and overcoming of, fundamentalism, and in the creation of a better world'.[40]

The present study draws upon the above-mentioned attempts at a historiography of Marxism. However, the aim here is also to go beyond them, first and foremost in view of the virtually global dimension characterising the development of a determinate current drawing on the thought of Marx over the last decades. Not least, it can be demonstrated that the non-European world of the last 50 or 60 years has produced not only 'revolutionary praxis' (see Vranicki above) but also theoretical innovations of great interest from the standpoint of the history of theory.

---

40   Wippermann 2008, p. 133.

CHAPTER 1

The Development of Varying Marx-Oriented Conceptual Approaches between the Poles of Politics and Theory from the 1960s to the Present

This part of the present study deals with the historical development undergone by the international debate on Marxism from the 1960s to the present; more precisely, this development is considered in connection with determinate historical and political processes. Following on historically from the late Stalin-period and the subsequent de-Stalinisation within Soviet Marxist-Leninism, three phases can be distinguished in relation to the historical development of Marxism – a development which occurred on a world scale between the poles of politics and theory.

Firstly, there was a period (circa 1960/65–77) characterised by the rise of an innovative Marxism which broke free from the shackles of dogmatic Marxism-Leninism, especially the dogmatic Marxism-Leninism of Soviet provenance. This occurred in the course of the formation and development of worldwide political movements inspired by Marx and Marxism. The subsequent phase (circa 1974–90) was inaugurated by the registering of a kind of 'crisis of Marxism' (particularly in Western Europe) when revolutionary political upheavals failed to materialise, culminating in the decline of 'Marxism as a mass ideology' (John Milios)* in the wake of the 'transition' in Eastern Europe and the collapse of Soviet Marxism-Leninism. The third phase (circa 1990–the present) can be designated as a period of new approaches within a largely marginalised Marxism. Intellectual forms of resistance drawing on Marx – these could be described as 'attempts to think against the *Zeitgeist*' – existed before the historic demise of Marxism as a mass ideology, and such forms continue to exist to the present day.

---

* John Milios is also known as Yannis/Giannis Milios.

1 Dogmatic Marxism before the Political and Theoretical Upheaval

1.1 *Soviet Marxism-Leninism before De-Stalinisation*

The framework of the present study permits no more than a cursory presentation of the theoretical side of Soviet Marxism-Leninism of the late Stalin-period in some of its aspects; it is not possible here to consider all of its fundamental characteristics. It is important to note, first of all, that Stalinism, which went under the name of Leninism or Marxism-Leninism,[1] was not formed historically by direct reference to Marxian thought; rather, it emerged from determinate theoretical developments in the Marxisms of the Second and Third Internationals. The conception of the unity of the theories of Marx and Engels played a considerable role here, as did the conception of a later development of this theory, first through Lenin, and subsequently through Stalin. Engels's 'dialectics of nature' and Lenin's text, *Materialism and Empiriocriticism*, were thereby canonised. The development of Marxism to a comprehensive and self-contained '*Weltanschauung*',[2] a process begun before Lenin, and taken up and pursued further by Lenin himself, also formed a core element of theoretical Stalinism. Dialectical and historical materialism were elevated to the status of mandatory precepts for all Marxist thought. Historical materialism was thereby understood by the Stalinists in the sense of an extension of the axioms of dialectical materialism to the investigation of social life, to the investigation of the history of society. An abstract schematism of the opposition between materialism and idealism was established as a decisive criterion for the evaluation of previous thinkers in terms of the history of philosophy. On the epistemological level, the position advanced corresponded to the theory of reflection. In turn, the Marxian critique of political economy was reinterpreted as a proletarian political economy.

On the level of Marx-interpretation, Stalinism entailed a massive restriction of scientific freedom. Elements of the theory of Marx and Engels were misused for the purposes of the legitimation of domination. Research was to be subordinated to politics, under the threat of repression. Accordingly, Rolf Hecker has theorised the termination of the project to publish the first *Marx-Engels–*

---

1 On theoretical Stalinism, see also Negt 1974. David McLellan provides a more concise overview in McLellan 1979, pp. 134ff.

2 'The Marxist doctrine is omnipotent because it is true. It is comprehensive and harmonious, and provides men with an integral world outlook ...' (Lenin 1977, p. 23); Lenin's dictum dates from 1913.

Gesamtausgabe as a result of the politics of the Stalin-period. Following Hecker, two different levels of Stalinist reaction to Marx-oriented thinking might be distinguished:

> *Stalinism* in the social structures of domination, which led to political 'purges' and thus to the elimination of critical-thinking and argumentative personalities; *Stalinism* also as a reduction of the Marxian doctrine to a rigid ideological dogma that could tolerate no 'deviations' and that was instrumentalised *qua* Marxism-Leninism for the legitimation and consolidation of the claim to absolute power.[3]

The research undertaken by Hecker and other researchers for the anthology *Stalinismus und das Ende der ersten Marx-Engels-Gesamtausgabe* (*1931–1941*) provides the basis for a historical reconstruction of the brutal state persecution (and even murder) of researchers focusing on Marx and Engels, and of editors of the works of Marx and Engels during the Stalin-period.

A distinctive feature of *Capital*-exegesis after the imposition of theoretical Stalinism was the interpretation of Marx's main work as providing proof of a historical inevitability or necessity of the transition from capitalism to the dictatorship of the proletariat or to socialism. Thus the Soviet philosopher, Mark M. Rosental, wrote the following in 1952:

> If the utopian socialists put forward socialist theories which offered no explanation of the objective mechanism of capitalism, whose own development leads to its own demise, it is to Marx's credit that he showed socialism arising not from the wishes of people, but as the necessary, law-governed result of social development. For this reason, there is no scientific socialism without *Capital*.[4]

The interpretation offered by P.S. Trofimov in 1951 points in a similar direction; he saw *Capital* as propounding 'the inevitability of proletarian revolution and dictatorship of the proletariat'.[5] With regard to Marx, however, it is problematic that interpretations of this kind can certainly find a textual warrant in Marx's *magnum opus*. In the seventh section of the chapter in *Capital* on so-called original accumulation,* Marx does indeed refer to capitalist production

---

3   Hecker 2001a, p. 10.

4   Rosental 1953, p. 332.

5   Trofimov 1953, p. 579. I. Blyumin advances a similar position (see Blyumin 1953).

*   [*ursprüngliche Akkumulation*] – often rendered in English as 'primitive accumulation'.

as inducing its own negation with the inexorability of a natural process.[6] There is an ambiguity in Marx's work with regard to historical determinist thinking. While the Stalinist tradition took up the *topos* of the lawlike necessity of the transition to socialism, it is precisely this dimension that anti-Stalinist interpreters seek to call into question in their critical reappropriation of Marx.

Stalinism also had an impact on the discussion of abstract, theoretical questions, which at first sight had little to do with politics. For example, a negative view of the philosophy of G.W.F. Hegel was officially prescribed, at least during the latter phase of Stalinism.[7] The negative representation of Hegel, which bore the imprint of theoretical Stalinism, coincided with the common, superficial tendency of reducing the history of philosophy to an opposition between idealism and materialism. In considering the historical background to the current engagement with the Hegel-Marx relation, it is worth noting that, at least in the late-Stalinist period in the Soviet Union (i.e. until the time of the 'Khrushchev Thaw'), and also in the late-Stalinism of the GDR of the 1950s, any objective and reasonable discussion of Hegel's philosophy risked coming up against intense ideological resistance. According to the guidelines issued by Stalin, the dominant image of Hegel in official Marxism-Leninism was one in which the philosopher hailing from Stuttgart was portrayed as a political reactionary and precursor to German fascism.[8] Camilla Warnke reports the following:

> At a secret conference of the Central Committee of the Communist Party of the Soviet Union in 1944, Stalin passed a motion according to which Hegel was also to be held responsible for German nationalism and chauvinism, and thereby became a precursor of fascism (a typical interpretation at the time, not only for Stalin!) The significance of this judgement is undoubtedly to be sought in political ideology.[9]

---

6 See Marx 1976, p. 929.

7 A consideration of the debate between 'dialecticians' and 'mechanicists' (and their varying evaluations of Hegel) is beyond the scope of the present study.

8 See Warnke 2000, pp. 523 and 544. On the image of Hegel in late Stalinism, see, among other works, Zimmerli 1984, pp. 27 ff. For a general treatment of the various aspects of the understanding of Marxism in the early GDR, see, among other works, Prokop 2006, pp. 359 ff.

9 Warnke 2000, p. 523. Elsewhere, Warnke reproduces an anecdote (itself transmitted by a historian who is not always reliable, it should be added): 'D. Volkogonov's Stalin biography from 1990 contains new material on Stalin's relation to Hegel. We learn that Stalin had difficulties dealing with dialectic. For this reason, at the end of the 1920s Stalin was apparently given instruction in philosophy by the philosopher and old Bolshevik, Jan Sten (the then deputy director of the Marx-Engels Institute), following a programme of study especially

Warnke's interpretation is that the corresponding defamation of Hegel was intended as a contribution to the ideological buttressing of the 'anti-German attitude' of Stalinist politics. In addition, it was a case of 'countering the great influence traditionally exerted on Soviet philosophy by the German classics, and particularly by Hegel'.[10] Theoretical Marxist-Leninism in the late Stalinist period declared Hegel – in the face of resistance by Marxist philosophers such as György Lukács or Wolfgang Harich – to be a *persona non grata*. In the post-Stalinist period, however, Hegel's philosophy came to be discussed again. From this point on, references to Hegel would occasionally take on a comparatively more positive character.

The ideological atmosphere of late Stalinism is clearly illustrated by a passage, chilling alone in its diction, from a book by the Soviet philosopher Mark M. Rosental that first appeared in Russian in 1955. Here Rosental polemicises against the theoretical current of the Soviet exponent of Marx, Isaak Ill'ich Rubin, who was one of the most significant Marx-oriented thinkers of the inter-war period and who had been murdered during the great 'purges' of the 1930s:

> The supporters of Rubin and the Menshevising idealists who were at large in the fields of economics and philosophy in the 1920s and 1930s wrote a great deal on the 'dialectic of *Capital*', but they treated Marx's method in the spirit of the Hegelians, they turned it into a scholastic play of concepts, a complicated system of sophistries and casuistries that was worlds apart from science. The idealist-scholastic treatment of Marx's dialectic by Rubin, for example, was intended to disorientate Soviet economists and to entangle them in abstract problems ... A conspicuous example of the idealist-Hegelian treatment of the method of *Capital* can be found in the work of Kushin, a student of Rubin ... the Communist Party has smashed these tendencies which are alien to Marxism, and has helped Soviet philosophers and economists to expose their nature.[11]

---

devised for him by the latter: this programme included the study of Hegel, Kant, Feuerbach, Fichte and Schelling, and also covered Plekhanov and Kautsky. According to Volkogonov, Sten attempted twice weekly to bring Hegel's philosophical world closer to his high-ranking student. Yet the "abstractness enraged Stalin" and prompted him repeatedly to interrupt his tutor with splenetic questions: "what significance does all this have for the class struggle?" and "how is anyone supposed to use this nonsense in practice?"' (Warnke 2001, p. 199). Warnke then proceeds to note (again citing Volkogonov) that Jan Sten did not survive the great 'purges'.

10   Warnke 2000, p. 524.

11   Rosental 1957, p. 19.

The first steps towards de-Stalinisation were taken in the Soviet Union shortly after Stalin's death in 1953, at the beginning of the period of the so-called 'Khrushchev Thaw'. Khrushchev's secret speech criticising Stalin at the Twentieth Congress of the Communist Party of the Soviet Union (CPSU) in 1956 played an important role in this process. Five years later, at the Twenty-Second Congress, the turn away from the Stalin-period was further intensified. In the People's Republic of China, it was not until 1978 that a process began that could be compared, within certain limits, to Soviet de-Stalinisation. De-Stalinisation in the Soviet Union is to be understood as a historical turning point with regard to the international communist movement. Indirectly, it opened up a new space in which the formation of Marxist theory, which until this point had largely ossified into dogma, could unfold. The various dogmatisations which characterise the Marxism of the Second and Third Internationals frequently went hand-in-hand with a vulgarisation of Marxian theory.[12] During the course of de-Stalinisation, and in the subsequent period, the various new theoretical approaches which elaborated a novel understanding of Marx and Marxism – an understanding at least partially freed of dogmatic ballast – were in many cases no longer compatible with coarse simplifications.

1.2   A Brief Insight into the Current State of Research into Chinese Marxism before 1978

The present framework permits no more than a cursory consideration of the complex and widely ramified history of Chinese Marxism before the watershed year of 1978 in order to draw out key points in relation to the current state of international research. Nick Knight, one of the most prominent Western experts on the history of early Chinese Marxism, considers it to be evident that 'Marxist philosophy in China during its formative years was heavily influenced by European and Soviet Marxist philosophy' with regard to the theoret-

---

12   Incidentally, Marx himself was infuriated when acquaintances of his preferred to avoid theoretical difficulties rather than displaying any resolve to engage with them. A letter from 1851 reveals Marx's attitude: 'I am usually at the British Museum from 9 in the morning until 7 in the evening. The material I am working on is so damnably involved that, no matter how I exert myself, I shall not finish for another 6–8 weeks ... The democratic "simpletons" to whom inspiration comes "from above" need not, of course, exert themselves thus. Why should these people, born under a lucky star, bother their heads with economic and historical material? It's really all so simple, as the doughty Willich [a political opponent – J.H.] used to tell me. All so simple to these addled brains! – Ultra-simple fellows!' (Marx 1982a, p. 377).

ical aspects of determinism, ontology, epistemology and logic.[13] It can be seen from Knight's study on the Chinese philosopher, Li Da, that, as far as the interpretation of Marxian theory was concerned, a transfer of ideas via and from Japan was one of the conditions for the emergence and development of early Chinese Marxism. In the interwar period, Li Da translated Hajime Kawakami, one of the founders in terms of the formation of Japanese Marxist theory, into Chinese.[14] The transfer of theory from Europe to China also occurred, at least in part, via Japan, or via translations from the Japanese.[15] Wolfgang Lippert maintains that the categories and concepts of Marx's and Engels's social theory were introduced into the Chinese intellectual culture almost without exception through Japanese mediation.[16]

Knight engages with the history of Marxist philosophy in China from 1923 to 1945, with a central focus on the theorists Qu Qiubai, Ai Siqi, Li Da and Mao Zedong, who were of great significance for the Chinese reception of Marx. Despite Qu Qiubai's earlier endeavours to introduce Marxist philosophy into China, Knight considers that the work of Ai Siqi, Li Da and others towards the 'introduction ... of the Soviet Union's New Philosophy' in the 1930s represented a more important development.[17] In Knight's account, the years between the late 1930s and the Seventh Congress of the Chinese Communist Party in 1945 form the period in which Mao Zedong's thought was able to rise to the status of party ideology. As central elements of Mao's philosophical thought, the theory of contradiction and the theory of praxis were, according to Knight, 'clearly not his own invention'. Rather, Knight argues that '[t]he immediate inspiration for Mao's understanding of these foundational dimensions of Marxist philosophy was the New Philosophy [from the Soviet Union – J.H.]'. Knight continues as follows: 'This philosophy described the law of the unity of opposites (or contradictions) as "the fundamental law of dialectics", and provided a detailed explanation of its logical structure and examples of its manifestation. Similarly, in its discussion of epistemology, the New Philosophy asserted that practice is the touchstone against which claims to knowledge are evaluated'.[18] According to Knight, Mao constructed his philosophical theory on the foundations of the doctrines of contradiction and praxis.

---

13   Knight 2005, p. 222.
14   See Knight 1996, p. 130.
15   See Knight 1996, p. 117 f.
16   See Lippert 1979, p. 393.
17   Knight 2005, p. 216.
18   Ibid.

Chenshan Tian, a historian of traditional Chinese philosophy and of Chinese Marxism, has presented an interpretation of the history of the latter in which he grants a significant role to traditional Chinese philosophy. He refers to a sinicisation of dialectical materialism, which, on his account, occurred in the 1920s and 1930s. According to Tian, intellectuals such as Qu Qiubai and Ai Siqi engaged with the Marxist dialectic against the background of classical Chinese philosophy. Tian claims that the sinicisation of Marxism was further intensified by Mao Zedong. On the one hand, according to Tian, the latter received Marxist texts through the lens of a specifically Chinese philosophy, namely the *tongbian* tradition of thought (translated by Tian as 'continuity through change'). On the other hand, Tian argues that Mao also read elements of traditional Chinese thought through dialectical materialism. Tian infers that 'the form taken by Marxism in its encounter with China was no longer the one inherited from the tradition of Marxian dialectic in Europe'. What now emerged was a version that 'in fact expressed *tongbian*, a traditional Chinese way of thinking, in a language' that was based on the terminology of Western Marxism, 'but in Chinese translation'. Ultimately, on Tian's account, it is possible to refer in this case to 'a modernised form of traditional thought'.[19] David Salomon has raised the following objection to Chenshan Tian's historico-philosophical interpretation: 'Tian's thesis that the "sinicisation of Marxism" consists in detaching it from the Western tradition and integrating it into the Chinese tradition as a variety of *tongbian* fails to take into account the *critical* content of Marxist thought in Europe, especially given that "Western Marxism" has been characterised as the "philosophy of praxis" (Gramsci)'.[20] For Salomon, the decisive aspect of praxis and the characteristic Marxist criteria for social emancipation are not sufficiently considered in Tian's interpretation. The following qualification can be added here: precisely the category of praxis was, in my opinion, of decisive significance for the philosophical thought of Mao Zedong. It is not possible within the present framework to go into more detail on the putative sources of Chinese Marxism (whether Soviet, West European, Japanese, or traditional Chinese). However, some developments relating to the Chinese engagement with Marxism during the period after Mao's death – i.e. the period shaped politically by Deng Xiaoping – will be referred to later.

---

19   Tian 2006, p. 192.
20   Salomon 2006, p. 193.

2   **Marxism's Resurgence between the Inception and Highpoint of
         Political Movements of Emancipation (Circa 1960/65–77)**

There was a specifically international dimension to the political revolts of the
1960s. The Vietnam War; the Japanese movement against the Security Treaty
between the USA and Japan in 1960 (and again in 1970); the ever advancing
development of the Cuban Revolution; the Latin American guerrilla movements in the countryside as well as in the cities;[21] the US movement against
the Vietnam War; the Indian Naxalite insurgency; the student movements in
Mexico, West Germany, Japan, Spain and numerous other countries in the
second half of the 1960s; May 1968 in Paris; the strike wave of the 'Hot Autumn'
in Italy: these were all political events or movements which had an international discursive resonance, and in some cases they became important sources
of political inspiration across national borders. The specifically international
dimension of the political revolts of the 1960s should not be presented as a historical novelty, however, since the transmission of revolutionary influences and
ideas across national borders has occurred previously in history (one need only
think of the international revolutionary events in 1848–9 or 1917–19). Yet the
revolts of the 1960s transcended not only national boundaries, but also, to a
greater extent, continental ones.

   The revolts of the 1960s were bound up with a growing interest in an intensive engagement with Marxian theory. At the same time as the political revolts
were occurring, there was a developing wave of appropriation of Marxian theory, especially of his critique of political economy. This latter process also had
an international character. There developed a lively transfer of theories and
interpretations beyond linguistic and national boundaries. In the words of
Miloš Nikolić: 'The new wave of dissemination of Marxism and its more intensive political and theoretical re-affirmation began … in the early 1960s. This wave
brought a re-affirmation of Marxism in West Germany, it spread Marxism for
the first time in Great Britain and the USA, it advanced Marxist theory in Latin
America, and took the first significant steps in the development of Marxism in
Africa'.[22] Nikolić adds that Marxism was able to anchor itself in the academic
sphere in the 1960s. A critical qualification ought to be made here in relation
to Nikolić's account: the international wave of Marxism that he sketches cannot actually be so precisely dated. It would be more accurate to say that it did

---

21   Although the Marxist forces in Latin America endured a setback with the right-wing
        putsch in Brazil.
22   Nikolić 1983, p. 20.

not develop simultaneously in all countries: in Japan, for example, this had already occurred in the 1950s.[23] According to Nikolić, an important moment in the development of this postwar Marxism was the initiation of a process of revision and supersession in relation to the Marxism of the Third International. Nikolić writes that this process, which has been described as a renaissance of Marxism, began with a return to Marx's original texts.

Within the timeframe thematised here (circa 1960/65–77), there was thus a burgeoning interest in Marxism as a critical social theory; this was the case on an international scale. In the following historical exposition, it should be borne in mind that it will be necessary time and again to consider individual theorists in whose thinking currents of ideas or political events were reflected, and to refer to intellectuals from all over the world whose thinking accompanied processes of development both in the political sphere and within the history of ideas.

2.1   *Western Europe and the Anglo-Saxon World*

In West Germany, there was at first little indication of a renaissance of Marx-oriented thought in the early 1960s: the KPD (*Kommunistische Partei Deutschlands*)* had been proscribed in 1956 and the SPD (*Sozialdemokratische Partei Deutschlands*)** had renounced its last points of reference to Marxism in its Godesberg Program of 1959. Yet in West Germany there were a few lone intellectuals who at least endeavoured to ensure that interest in Marxian and Marxist theory was sustained. In this context it would be appropriate to mention Leo Kofler,[24] but also the political scientist, Iring Fetscher, and not least a philosopher coming from the tradition of critical theory, namely Alfred Schmidt.

In the 1960s, the SDS (*Sozialistische Deutsche Studentenbund*)***,[25] underwent a process of political radicalisation, including in West Berlin and Frankfurt – the bastions of the student movement. This movement experienced its highpoint in 1968. This political process was accompanied by a burgeoning

---

23   Nikolić does not mention Japan at this point in his exposition.

*   Communist Party of Germany.

**   Social Democratic Party of Germany.

24   On Leo Kofler's person, see Jünke 2000, pp. 7 ff.; Kessler 2002, pp. 43 ff. On Kofler's understanding of Marxism, see Kofler 2000, pp. 40 ff. For a closer consideration of Kofler within the milieu of the postwar West German Left, see Jünke 2007, pp. 271 ff. On the precarious situation of Marxist intellectuals in the postwar period in West Germany, see Deppe 1999.

***   The Socialist German Student Federation.

25   Probably the best-known work on the history of the SDS remains Fichter and Lönnendonker 1977.

interest in theoretical engagement with Marx. In 1966, Rudi Dutschke compiled a kind of Marxist literary canon in order to provide his comrades with a guide for a renewed understanding of the emergence, development and reception of Marxist theory. The theoretical horizon of a determinate part of the Berlin SDS can be inferred from this canon,[26] and in this regard it is striking that, according to Dutschke's understanding of Marxism, 'the attempt to "reestablish" Marxism through an unmediated and direct recourse to the "pure" Marx' misconstrues 'the essence and method of Marx'.[27] Indeed, the reception of Marx within the SDS, not only in Berlin, but also in Frankfurt, was undertaken in both a direct and a mediated way. The latter approach was characterised by a critical engagement with thinkers inspired by Marx – in particular with Karl Korsch, but György Lukács and Herbert Marcuse were likewise read and discussed in both Frankfurt and Berlin.[28]

The most significant theorist of the Frankfurt SDS was Hans-Jürgen Krahl. According to research into the SDS, 'there had already been a reception of the Frankfurt School by other groups within the SDS beyond the Frankfurt group towards the end of the 1950s'.[29] However, the theoretical influence of the Frankfurt School was especially present in the Frankfurt group of the SDS.[30] Krahl was personally a student of Theodor W. Adorno. During the course of the student movement, Krahl chose to ignore Adorno's reservations with regard to revolt,[31] but his theory did not lose its Adornian stamp. Shortly after Adorno's death, Krahl paid tribute to his mentor, whose 'micrological power of exposition' had brought to light 'the submerged emancipatory dimension of Marx's critique of political economy, the self-conscious character of which as a revolutionary theory, and thus as a doctrine whose propositions construe society from the perspective of its radical transformation, is mostly lost on contemporary Marxist economic theorists'.[32] According to Krahl, Adorno's legacy was

---

26   The theoretical protagonist of an earlier generation of the West Berlin SDS was Michael Mauke (see Mauke 1970). Mauke died in 1966.

27   Dutschke 1966, p. 2.

28   Students from the milieu around the SDS also sought personal contact with Lukács. In this connection, there is also a 1967 letter by Dutschke to Lukács which was published by Frieder Otto Wolf (Dutschke 2000). On the famous encounter between Marcuse and students in the main auditorium of the Free University of Berlin in the summer of 1967, see Lefèvre 2005, pp. 71 ff.

29   Becker 2002, p. 17.

30   On the general problematic of 'critical theory and the student movement', see Wiggershaus 1995, pp. 609 ff.

31   On Adorno's relation to the student revolts, see also Adorno 2000, pp. 42–116.

32   Krahl 1999, p. 79.

the transmission of the consciousness of emancipation characteristic of the Western Marxism of the interwar period through his specific reference to the categories of reification, fetishisation, mystification and second nature.

Adorno's intervention against the invocation of a unity of theory and practice – a postulate which was characteristic of Marxism-Leninism – was nothing if not consistent, given the position he had taken. Already in *Negative Dialectics*, which was written before the student movement, he had criticised a corresponding conception:

> The demand for the unity of theory and praxis has irresistibly debased the former to a mere underling, eliminating from it what it was supposed to have achieved in that unity. The practical visa-stamp demanded from all theory became the stamp of the censor. In the famed unity of theory-praxis, the former was vanquished and the latter became non-conceptual, a piece of the politics which it was supposed to lead beyond; delivered over to power.[33]

Significantly, it was precisely Adorno's student, Krahl, who, despite his political engagement, opposed potential tendencies inimical to theory within the student movement.[34]

Krahl engaged intensively with Marx's critique of political economy. Hans-Georg Backhaus (who studied alongside Krahl under Adorno in the 1960s and was subsequently a pioneer of the New Marx-Reading in the Federal Republic of Germany) maintains that it was his (Backhaus's) own engagement with Marx's critique of political economy that spurred Krahl to 'turn his attention to the texts on Marx's value theory with which he was unfamiliar at the time'.[35] Within the German-language debate, Krahl figures as the protagonist of a

---

33   Adorno 2001, p. 91.

34   Detlev Claussen regards Krahl as being considerably influenced by Adorno's social critique, and characterises him as a protagonist of the 'third generation' of critical theory whose contribution in the course of the student movement also consisted precisely in the articulation of 'opposition to tendencies in the movement which were inimical to theory and thus to emancipation' (see Claussen 1998, pp. 69 f.). On Krahl, see also Reinicke 1973.

35   Backhaus 1997b, p. 31. It should be borne in mind that Backhaus is somewhat critical towards Krahl in his retrospective view of the latter. Backhaus asserts that the title of Krahl's famous essay – 'Zur Wesenslogik der marxschen Warenanalyse' (Krahl 1971) ['On the Essence-Logic in Marx's Commodity-Analysis'] – is 'misleading: in Krahl's essay there is by no means any essence-logical concretisation of the commodity-analysis pointing beyond what I have set out in relation to the category of doubling [*Verdopplung*], for instance vis-à-vis the problem of the commodity as "immediate contradiction". The title

'Hegelianising' interpretation of the Marxian critique of political economy. Thus, he states the following: 'The transfer of the categories of Hegelian logic, these having been extracted from their metaphysical context, to the categories of political economy is, according to Marx, that which defines the critique of political economy. In Marx's view, Hegelian logic is the self-movement of capital dressed in metaphysical garb'.[36] Accordingly, the subsequent critique of 'Hegelian Marxism' was directed against Krahl in particular.[37]

Between 1968 and 1969, the fractional tensions within the SDS became increasingly intense. The organisation was finally dissolved in 1970 following the death of Hans-Jürgen Krahl in an accident. In the meantime, the student movement had left an important legacy in the FRG: a completely novel kind of intense and widespread interest in an engagement with Marx's *oeuvre* in general, and with his critique of political economy in particular; this interest was sustained into the second half of the 1970s.[38]

---

was presumably added by Krahl's editors. Krahl merely repeats in various formulations the category of "doubling" [*Verdopplung*]; by contrast, it is rather his essay, *Bemerkungen zum Verhältnis von Kapital und Hegelscher Wesenslogik* ["Observations on the Relation between Capital and Hegel's Logic of Essence"] that represents a step forwards. Yet the almost simultaneous elaboration of the same problem by Helmut Reichelt, and, with certain reservations, by Klaus Hartmann, was far more rigorous: the function of the "dialectical exposition" completely escaped Krahl' (Backhaus 1997b, p. 40).

36   Krahl 1970, p. 141. This passage is formulated differently in another published version (see Krahl 1984, p. 160).

37   Michael Heinrich makes the following criticism of Krahl: 'Such a transfer [as the one referred to by Krahl in the above quotation] does not correspond to Marx's own self-understanding. Above all, however, Hegelian philosophy itself precludes such a procedure. Thus, the proposition that the specific form of Marx's exposition is to be sought in Hegel's logic presupposes something that is assumed by all Hegelian-Marxist authors without giving grounds for such an assumption: that it is at all *possible* to separate out the figures of argumentation of Hegelian logic from their speculative premises, without destroying them in the process. Hegel's logical categories, however, are precisely not mere forms that were applied to a content distinct from them and that could therefore be applied to any given content' (Heinrich 1986, p. 147).

38   George Katsiaficas, an American writer who focuses on the international dimension of the protest events of 1968, states the following: 'The German New Left was among the most theoretically inclined ... members of the global movement' (Katsiaficas 1987, p. 49). Incidentally, contact with the student movement of the 1960s coincided with a heightened interest in Marx and Marxist theory within the milieu around the West Berlin journal *Das Argument*, which itself had its origins in the anti-nuclear movement of the 1950s. Wolfgang Fritz Haug comments as follows: 'By the time the student movement had become a mass movement, the group around *Das Argument* had already crossed the threshold to

In Italy, the situation in the postwar period was considerably different from that in West Germany, for, in contrast to the KPD, which was proscribed in 1956, the PCI (*Partito Comunista Italiano*)* remained an influential mass party in the 1950s and 1960s. Two dimensions were initially of particular importance in relation to the context within which Marx- and Marxism-related theory was formed (i.e. the context defined by the tension between politics and science): first, the emergence of a political line that was partially independent vis-à-vis Moscow, and that was especially connected to the activity of Palmiro Togliatti; second, the renewed interest that in particular the philosopher Galvano Della Volpe (1895–1968) was able to arouse in an intensive engagement with Marxian theory and with Marx's original texts.

Under Togliatti, the PCI of the postwar period pursued a new path that was to lead to socialism via 'structural reforms', such that the programmatic orientation to revolution slipped into the background. At the Eighth Congress of the PCI, in 1956, Togliatti had already anticipated the thesis of an independent Italian path to socialism (i.e. independent vis-à-vis Moscow). On a theoretical level, it was above all the theoretical interpretation of Della Volpe that provided a central impetus: here it can be noted that the influence of Della Volpe in inspiring the formation of a school of thought gradually became evident over the course of the 1950s and 1960s. Lucio Colletti has suggested that Della Volpe's standing within the PCI was temporarily boosted due to the fact that he remained in the party at a time when many intellectuals had turned their backs on it in the wake of the international events of 1956.[39] At the beginning of the 1960s, there were reproaches within the party of fraction-building around the Della Volpe School.[40] The second part of this study will focus more closely on the Della Volpe School.

Around the beginning of the 1960s, a new political and theoretical current emerged in Italy and evolved its own grasp of Marxian theory independently of 'academic Marxism'. As a result, there is a distinction to be made in relation to the Italian engagement with Marx's critique of political economy between, on the one side, a theoretical current oriented to the theory of struggle and more strongly geared toward political and revolutionary praxis, and, on the other, the

---

Marxism' (Haug 1978, p. 486). The study of *Capital* was significant in this process. In 1972, Haug, the editor of *Das Argument*, insisted on what he presumed to be the internal connection between the critique of political economy and Marxian socialism. See Haug 1972, pp. 561 ff.

*   Italian Communist Party.

39   See Colletti 1974, p. 5.

40   See Fraser 1977, p. 15.

more markedly 'academic' debate around Marx. According to Giacomo Marramao, the distinction between 'academic' and 'militant' Marxism was at its sharpest in Italy in the second half of the 1960s.[41],* Within this context, the so-called *operaismo*** of the 1960s is of special relevance: this was a revolutionary communist movement which originated in Italy and had its greatest effect there, but its influence certainly radiated outwards to other countries.[42] Politically, the *operaista* movement stood – in contrast to the established workers' organisations – for resolute struggle *against* labour, in which the comparatively new figure of the 'mass worker' served as an important reference point.[43] The journal, *Quaderni Rossi*, founded by Raniero Panzieri, played an important role in the development of *operaista* theory. Claudio Pozzoli describes the engagement with Marx's works as being central for the theorists in the milieu around this journal. In this process, the critique of political economy became a decisive point of reference, according to Pozzoli. He writes that 'the interpretative categories for an analysis of Italian society with revolutionary intent were taken from *Capital* and the *Grundrisse*'.[44]

Between 1963 and 1964, following a split in the group around *Quaderni Rossi*, a new journal, *Classe Operaia*, came into existence, with the collaboration of Mario Tronti (who had also contributed to *Quaderni Rossi*). Within *operaismo*, it was in particular these two thinkers – i.e. Tronti and Panzieri (the latter died in 1964) – who stood for an intensive engagement with Marx's critique of political economy. Tronti sought to appropriate Marx's thought from a revolutionary, class standpoint. The labour theory of value cannot be separated from the political, according to Tronti: 'For Marx, labour value is a political thesis, a revolutionary watchword; it is neither an economic law nor a means for the scientific interpretation of social phenomena; or, better: it contains these two latter determinations, but on the foundation of the first, and as its consequence'.[45],*** Tronti elaborates on this point by asserting that labour is the

---

41   See Marramao 1973, p. 217.

*   See also Marramao 1975.

**   A literal English translation of *operaismo* would be 'workerism', although this term has tended to have a different, pejorative connotation in English-language Marxist discourse.

42   On the reception of Italian *operaismo* by parts of the West German Left of the 1970s, see Ebbinghaus 2003, p. 241.

43   For a detailed account of the history, and especially the history of the theory, of *operaismo*, see Wright 2002.

44   Pozzoli 1972, p. 7.

45   Tronti 2006, pp. 225. This text originates from 1965.

***   An English-language edition of Tronti's work, *Operai e Capitale*, is forthcoming (Mayfly Books, translation by Peter Thomas).

measure of value *'because the working class is a condition for capital*. This political conclusion is the true, presupposed starting point of Marx's economic
analysis itself'.[46] In the 1970s, the *operaista* movement would undergo a further process of political and theoretical development in which the reference to
Marxian theory was of fundamental significance.

The events of May 1968 in France can be considered (perhaps alongside
the Italian 'Hot Autumn' of 1969) as the highpoint of the revolts in Western
Europe – and here it should be noted that, in France and Italy, these revolts
were not merely student rebellions, but also workers' insurgencies. The May
events themselves and the first years thereafter were characterised by the rising
strength of Trotskyist and Maoist groupings.

On a theoretical and political level, the 'internal French' development of
the discussion around Marxian and Marxist theory was of more significance
than external influences on the reception of Marxism in France.[47] While the
PCF (*Parti Communiste Français*)* had opposed any thoroughgoing de-Stalinisation, to an extent even after 1956, a broad and heterogeneous field of emancipatory philosophy and social theory had already evolved in France before
May 1968,[48] in which Marx sometimes represented an important point of reference. Prior to 1968, there already existed an intellectual atmosphere in which
various tendencies within French Marxism directed their efforts towards a new
appropriation, liberated from any dogmatism, of Marxian theory in general,
and *Capital* in particular.

On the theoretical level, the most significant intellectual processes occurring in France between the poles of theory and politics were those carried
out by Louis Althusser and his school.[49] With regard to Althusser's theoretical approach, it is significant that his theoretical interventions in the early and

---

46   Tronti 1974, pp. 225–6.

47   On the historical development of French Marxism in the twentieth century, see Khilnani
      2003, pp. 299 ff. On the development up to the beginning of the 1970s, see Bandyopadhyay
      1972, pp. 129 ff.

*   French Communist Party.

48   This field comprises, among others, the Marxist philosopher Lucien Goldmann, the Situ-
      ationist Guy Debord, the *Arguments* group, the non- or anti-Marxist 'anarcho-socialist'
      Cornelius Castoriadis, Jean-Paul Sartre, the sociologist and Marx researcher Henri Lefeb-
      vre, who was expelled from the PCF in 1958 (see, among other sources, Lefebvre 1985), as
      well as the 'Marxologist' Maximilien Rubel.

49   The process of development of the theory formed by Althusser, in its various phases in the
      1960s and 1970s, cannot be adequately presented within the framework of the treatment
      here. Nor do the constraints of space permit any discussion of Althusser's pre-1960 writings
      in the present study.

mid-1960s were undertaken within a historical situation in which Marxist theory was confronted by the antagonism between post-Stalinist dogmatism and a de-dogmatisation which supposedly de-rigidified Marxist thought. Althusser created an alternative to this opposition within Marxist theory by opening up Marxist theory formation to a greater complexity through his reception of the concept of overdetermination from psychoanalytic theory, without however renouncing the claim to theoretical rigour and Marxist orthodoxy. In this way, he made a decisive contribution to the theoretical and political 'renovation' of Marxism in the 1960s. Althusser aimed in particular to separate Marxian from Hegelian dialectic.

An interpretation of Althusser is possible which contends that he also pursued distinctly political aims in his engagement with Marx's work. Althusser's approach to theory and thus also to Marx's texts is in no way to be understood as a renunciation of political praxis. Decisive for Althusser were the struggle (including within the PCF, or perhaps especially in this context) over a new Marxist orthodoxy, and the project of elaborating a new kind of approach to truly revolutionary theory. Althusser's endeavours are thus certainly to be understood in a pedagogical sense. He functioned as the teacher of the up-and-coming elite of a new generation of revolutionary theoreticians whose role was to provide the theory to accompany the revolutionary process in politics. Althusser insisted on the pre-eminent position of leading Marxist theoreticians.

It should be noted that Althusser operated theoretically within two prominent institutions. Within the academic sphere, Althusser worked at the *École Normale Supérieure*, which was one of the most distinguished university institutions within France. Althusser's seminar on Marx in 1965 at the *École Normale Supérieure* attracted a circle of students that would subsequently have a decisive influence on the intellectual (and, in part, also the political) life of the French Left. On the other hand, within the politico-intellectual sphere, the PCF was at least as important as an institutional point of reference, and here Althusser attempted to influence its political and theoretical orientation.[50]

Althusser's theoretical work of the 1960s can also be understood as a political intervention in a more specific sense, namely insofar as one of his aims in this work, among others, was to provide an alternative to a determinate interpretation of Marxism – i.e. the one which prevailed at the time within the PCF. Althusser wrote in 1968 that the critique of Stalinism following the Twentieth

---

50   It is not possible within the constraints of the present study to go into more detail on the various phases of development of Althusser's relation to the PCF.

Congress of the CPSU in 1956 had revived a 'petty bourgeois' ideology within the communist parties which – according to Althusser – corresponded to an interpretation of Marxism as 'humanism' and a focus on Marx's early writings, as well as on concepts such as 'human being', 'alienation', 'appropriation of the human essence' and 'freedom'. Althusser makes his point as follows: 'Up to that point, the interpretation of Marxism as "humanism" – i.e. the ethical, idealist interpretation of Marxist theory, the recourse to Marx's early writings – had been the affair of bourgeois intellectuals, social democratic ideologues or avant-garde theologians (among them some Catholics). From this point on, it was now the affair of numerous Marxists and communists themselves'.[51] Following the Twentieth Congress of the CPSU, the attempt at a 'de-Stalinisation' of French communism – partly resisted by the PCF – was bound up with the emergence of a 'humanist' interpretation of Marx within the PCF (such an interpretation, it should be noted, was also promoted outside the party). It was precisely this tendency that Althusser criticised and against which he oriented his diametrically opposed ('anti-humanist') interpretation of Marx. Althusser's position was especially counterposed to that of Roger Garaudy, an important protagonist of a humanist-oriented Marxism within the PCF of the post-Stalinist era; Althusser refused to deviate from his 'theoretical anti-humanism'.[52]

In the second half of the 1960s, around 1967, Althusser moved more strongly than previously in a direction which ultimately amounted to taking a standpoint characterised by the 'primacy of politics'. Althusser's position, which had previously stood in proximity to the principle of an autonomy of theory vis-à-vis politics, now shifted in an 'over-politicising' direction.[53] Lenin now became a centrally important point of reference in Althusser's thinking. Althusser emphasised the role of the class struggle, especially retrospectively. Thus, he wrote in 1971: the 'whole *theory* of Marx, i.e. the *science* founded by Marx' – by which Althusser understands historical materialism – 'and the *philosophy* inaugurated by Marx' – by which Althusser understands a newly defined dialectical materialism – 'has the *class struggle* at its heart and at its centre'.[54]

---

51   Althusser 1974, p. 318.

52   On Garaudy and Althusser, see Geerlandt 1978. On the discussion held by the Central Committee of the PCF in Argenteuil in 1966, as well as the reaction to it, see Judt 1896, p. 192 f.; Schoch 1980, p. 223 f.; and Khilnani, p. 162 ff.

53   On the shift in Althusser's political and theoretical position around 1967, see, among other works, Elliott 1987, pp. 197 ff.

54   Althusser 1985, p. 12. In Althusser's theoretical interventions around 1970, it was especially his theory of 'ideological state apparatuses' that assumed a central importance; this cannot be further addressed here.

However, political implications were manifest not only in Althusser's own theoretical work, but also in the critique by others of the theoretical corpus that he developed. Jacques Rancière, in theoretical terms one of the most significant students of Althusser and a co-author in the *Lire le Capital* project,* would subsequently denounce the 'reactionary political foundations'[55] of this theoretical project, of which his own study 'The Concept of "Critique" and the "Critique of Political Economy" from the "Paris Manuscripts" to *Capital*' formed a part, having been published in *Lire le Capital*. Rancière's critique came after he had dissociated himself from the Althusser School and turned towards Maoism; he performed his political and theoretical volte-face against Althusser and the Althusserian School in the 1960s.[56]

According to the historian of Marxism, Montserrat Galcerán Huguet, 'despite the fact that censorship still prevailed' in the final years of the Franco dictatorship in Spain, 'the books, studies and essays on what Perry Anderson calls' Western Marxism 'came ever more into the foreground'.[57] One of the best-known Marxist thinkers in Spain was the philosopher Manuel Sacristán Luzón (1925–85). Politically, Sacristán could be located within the context of the PCE (*Partido Comunista de España*)** for a long period during the Franco dictatorship. From 1965 to 1970, he was a member of the party's central committee. Towards the end of the 1960s, the May 1968 events in Paris and the Prague Spring became sources of inspiration for his political thought.

Sacristán's work can also be considered as playing an important role in establishing the presuppositions for a theoretically advanced Marxism (which had to a great extent long remained a desideratum), insofar as he endeavoured to contribute, through translation and reception, to the process whereby awareness of the contemporary state of the international debate on Marxism could be transferred to Spain, and to elevate the Spanish discourse on Marx and Marx-

---

*   Rancière's contribution – along with those of Roger Establet and Pierre Macherey – was omitted from the abridged second edition of *Lire le Capital*, and likewise from the English-language edition, *Reading Capital* (see Althusser and Balibar 1970). An unabridged English-language edition which restores the original contributions is forthcoming (Verso).

55   Rancière 1989, p. 181.

56   For Rancière's critique of Althusser, see Rancière 2011, pp. 125 ff. On the theoretical and political confrontation between Althusser and John Lewis (a theorist from the ranks of the Communist Party of Great Britain), which took place at the beginning of the 1970s, see Arenz, Bischoff and Jaeggi 1973. For E.P. Thompson's critique of Althusser, see Thompson 1978.

57   Galcerán Huguet 1987, p. 263.

**   Communist Party of Spain.

ism to the level of the international debate. In this regard, he engaged with the theories of Marx, Engels, Gramsci, Lukács, the Frankfurt School, the Della Volpe School, as well as those of the contemporary Czech philosopher and interpreter of Marx, Jindřich Zelený. Sacristán related critically to Althusserianism, which was widely received in Spain in the 1970s.[58]

A recently published collection of Sacristán's writings on Marx's critique of political economy affords an insight into his reading of the *Grundrisse*, *Theories of Surplus-Value* and *Capital*. This is notable insofar as it demonstrates that a reception of Marx's blueprints for the construction of the critique of political economy has occurred within the Spanish engagement with Marx: Sacristán endeavoured to retrace the sequence of Marx's structural outlines of the critique of political economy with meticulous attention to detail.[59] Considered as a whole, Sacristán's work represented an important contribution to the development of an advanced Marxism in a country with a historically weaker Marxist tradition than Italy or France (which remains the case today).

In the Anglo-Saxon countries, Marx-oriented intellectuals moving within the context of the charged relationship between theory and politics encountered a greater level of resistance than did their Italian or French comrades; this was due to the fact that such intellectuals were confronted in the Anglo-Saxon world both by a more widespread militant anti-communism, and by a more pronounced tradition of pragmatism (which is also to be encountered on the political Left) with its hostility towards theory.

In the United Kingdom,[60] a 'first New Left' emerged in the wake of the political events of 1956, and aimed to renovate socialist politics beyond the orthodoxy of the Communist Party. The 'first New Left' in the UK, whose best-known representative is perhaps the historian and 'socialist humanist', E.P. Thompson, who had resigned from the Communist Party, can in turn be distinguished from a 'second New Left' of the 1960s and 1970s. One of the most important intellectual protagonists of this 'second New Left', Perry Anderson,[61] was concerned to make continental theoretical currents – i.e. so-called Western Marxism – known to the British public. Not only did British Marxists originally have no great part in 'Western Marxism' (not one of the prominent exponents of 'Western Marxism' was British), but as a rule most British Marxists had neither an adequate knowledge of these 'alien' theorists, nor any great interest in their thought until the intercultural mediation undertaken by Anderson and the *New*

58   Sacristán's relation to Althusser is dealt with by Salvador López Arnal (López 2007).

59   See Sacristán 2004, pp. 138 ff. On Sacristán, see also Muntaner and Buey 1998.

60   On the New Left in the UK, see Chun 1993.

61   For a closer consideration of Anderson, see Elliott 1998.

Left Review, which he edited. The transfer of theory which did then occur from the continent to the UK in the 1960s and 1970s, and the initiation and intensification of the reception of 'Western Marxism', were regarded with suspicion by E.P. Thompson, who remained to a large extent blinkered by an insular provincialism, and aimed criticism at Althusser in particular.

In the 1960s, a New Left emerged in the US.[62] A typical characterisation is given by Herbert Marcuse's 1967 assessment of the American New Left, which he claims is, with the exception of a few small groups, 'not orthodox Marxist or socialist. It is characterised by a deep mistrust of all ideology, even socialist ideology ...'.[63] However, it ought to be noted that the hostility to ideology designated by Marcuse was a concealing and euphemistic characterisation, disguising a deep-seated hostility to *theory*. James William Chesebro cites Tom Hayden, one of the most important precursors of the New Left in the US, who asserted that the New Left was based 'more on feeling than on theory'.[64] Such an attitude was not exactly conducive to an intensive engagement with Marx's critique of political economy. While George Katsiaficas attributes 'theoretical strengths' to the (West) German New Left in his retrospective historical appraisal, he refers to the 'militant pragmatism' of the American New Left.[65] Yet from the end of the 1960s onwards, parts of the American New Left moved towards different variants of Marxism or Marxism-Leninism.

In fact, it was precisely a representative of the Frankfurt School, Herbert Marcuse (1898–1979), who became a mentor to parts of the student opposition in the US, accompanying them theoretically and politically. During the student revolts, Marcuse acted as a constant point of reference for the radical students.[66],* This was the case not least because his thought represented an

---

62   The processes of theory formation within the New Left in the USA are investigated by Richard Guarasci (see Guarasci 1980).

63   Marcuse 1967, p. 398.

64   Chesebro 1972, p. 96.

65   Katsiaficas 1987, p. 181.

66   Other contemporary Marxist intellectuals of the English-speaking world are nowadays eclipsed by Marcuse in terms of the prominence accorded to them: these include, in the US, the economist, Paul Sweezy, and the Marxist-Humanist, Raya Dunayevskaya, and, in the UK, the Trotskyist historian, Isaac Deutscher. Also worth bearing in mind in this context is the German-American economist and council communist, Paul Mattick, even though he remained an intellectual and political outsider. Important works by Mattick include a collection of essays entitled *Kritik der Neo-Marxisten: Baran, Gillman, Hook, Mandel, Sweezy*, in which he critically engages with bourgeois and Marxist economists (Mattick 1974), and *Marx and Keynes: The Limits of the Mixed Economy* (Mattick 1969).

*   See Mattick 1935, Mattick 1959, Mattick 1978, Mattick 1981, Mattick 1941, Mattick 1967,

alternative to Marxist or Marxist-Leninist orthodoxy of Soviet provenance.[67] Although Marcuse did not see in the oppositional students and protesting ethnic minorities a new subject of the revolutionary process – i.e. a subject that could 'replace' the working class in the proper sense – he did accord them a kind of 'precursor' function within a possible liberatory and transformative process. Marcuse considered that the formation of emancipatory theory had to react to the significant alterations in the social and political situation – the point of departure for the formation of theory – since Marx's time, and that theory had to be renewed accordingly. Marcuse's own theoretical approaches are located within this context.

2.2 Latin America and Asia

The best-known and most influential Marxist thinker in Latin America in the first half of the twentieth century was the Peruvian, José Carlos Mariategui. According to Raúl Fornet-Betancourt, this thinker attempted, in the 1920s and until his death in 1930, to use the Marxist approach as a 'guide to creative thinking – i.e. to a thinking which sees its historical task as that of adequately analysing the concrete reality which determines its own context'.[68] Mariategui's thought forms an important stage within a theoretically productive line of development of Marxist thought of Latin American provenance. This innovative Latin American theoretical tradition was of renewed relevance in the 1960s.[69]

The Brazilian historian of Marxism, Michael Löwy, maintains that the Cuban Revolution, which took place in 1958–9 and underwent a process of political and ideological radicalisation in the subsequent years, favoured an intellectual atmosphere which was conducive to a renewal of Latin American Marxism and which influenced its emancipation from the model of Marxism-Leninism of the Soviet kind. Löwy expands on this point as follows: in the 1960s, Cuba saw 'a flourishing of sociological, historical, and philosophical research – a witness

---

Mattick 1968, Mattick 1972 and Mattick 1962 for the corresponding English-language versions of the essays contained in *Kritik der Neo-Marxisten* (thanks are due to Gary Roth for bibliographic assistance provided in relation to Mattick's writings).

67   On Marcuse's own critical engagement with Soviet Marxism, see Marcuse 1958.

68   Fornet-Betancourt 1994, p. 106.

69   Space does not permit a consideration here of Latin American dependency theory, which developed in particular from the 1960s onwards, and relied at least in part on elements of theory from the Marxist tradition. Parallels between dependency theory and the thought of Enrique Dussel, which will be considered in more detail later, cannot be dismissed out of hand.

to the existence of a creative and open Marxism',[70] which found expression in the Cuban journal *Pensamiento Crítico*.[71] The decisive circumstance here is that the Cuban Revolution provided a stimulus in theoretical and political terms in relation not only to the situation in Cuba, but also to that in Latin America as a whole.

Also worthy of consideration within the context of the tension between theory and politics is the thought of one of the most important Latin American Marx-inspired philosophers of the 1960s, who collaborated in the development of an undogmatic Marxism in Central and South America: the Mexican, Adolfo Sánchez Vázquez. Sánchez Vázquez was born in 1915 in Spain and fled to Mexico after the Spanish Civil War. However, insofar as it was particularly subsequent events in Latin America that formed an important frame of reference for his political and philosophical thought, he is to be understood more as a Latin American philosopher than as a European one. This is particularly true in relation to the Cuban Revolution. In 1978, Sánchez Vázquez responded to the question as to what the Cuban Revolution had signified for him as follows: 'Without my first live and direct encounter with the men and the accomplishments of the Cuban Revolution in 1964, my book *Las ideas estéticas de Marx* [Published in English as: *Art and Society*] would not have been possible, and nor would my effort to make my way through Marxism, in my *Philosophy of Praxis*, casting aside the crutch of the instruction manuals'.[72]

A significant political movement that formed the backdrop to the theoretical discussion of the subsequent years was the Mexican student movement of the 1960s, whose decisive turning point came with the massacre in the *Plaza de las Tres Culturas* in October 1968. Stefan Gandler quotes Sánchez Vázquez's retrospective evaluation of those events: 'Although it was crushed, the movement of '68 changed the political physiognomy of the country, and from that point onward the Universidad Nacional was never the same again. Marxism with a critical and anti-dogmatic edge became one of the most vigorous currents of thought in the institutions of the UNAM [the *Universidad Nacional Autónoma de México* – one of the most important academic institutions in the whole of Latin America – J.H.] and especially in the humanities'.[73]

---

70   Löwy 1992, p. xlvii.
71   Yohanka León del Río goes into more detail on the development of Marxist-oriented philosophy in Cuba in the 1960s (see León del Río 2000).
72   Cited in Gandler 2015, p. 15.
73   Cited in Gandler 2015, p. 37.

Alongside Gandler, Wolfgang Fritz Haug is one of the few Germans to have engaged with these Mexican thinkers. Already at the beginning of the 1980s, Haug emphasised the undogmatic character of Sánchez Vázquez's philosophy. According to Haug, Sánchez Vázquez binds 'Marxist philosophers to the incontrovertibility of discussion and argument *within* Marxism, counter to any claim to a monopoly'.[74] Sánchez Vázquez identifies Marx's turn to the category of praxis as the decisive moment of the latter's thought. Sánchez Vázquez's interpretation of Marx remains problematic, however, insofar as he relies first and foremost on Marx's early work (the *Theses on Feuerbach* among others), and only engages with the mature Marxian critique of political economy to a limited extent – even though, in his view of Marx's work as a whole, he rejects the idea of a radical rupture in Marx's development (as is emphasised by Gandler).[75] Sánchez Vázquez's book *The Philosophy of Praxis* must be considered one of his most important works; here he attempts, from the perspective of a philosophy of praxis, to go beyond traditional Marxist orthodoxy and to open the way for a different understanding of Marxism. This book first appeared in 1967, i.e. before the highpoint of the Mexican student movement, and in subsequent years became an important point of reference in the Latin American discussion on Marxism.[76]

In Japan, interest in Marx's theory intensified in the postwar period. For an adequate presentation, within their historical setting, of important Marxist theoretical approaches located within the context of the tension between theory and politics, it is necessary first to go back further in time and to touch upon a significant theoretical and political controversy in the Japanese Marxism of the interwar and immediate postwar period. In 1922, a communist party was constituted under the aegis of the Comintern. The party received directives from the Comintern in the 1920s and 1930s in the shape of various draft theses, with the theses of 1932 finally being regarded as definitive.[77] According to the latter Comintern directive, the revolution was to be thought of as occurring in two phases: it was a question first of eliminating the Tenno system by means of a bourgeois revolution; once this had taken place, the socialist revolution could then be organised. In the early 1930s, a group of Marxist researchers,

---

74   Haug 1981, p. 529.

75   See Gandler 2015, p. 130. 'Distinguishing himself vehemently from Althusser's Marxism, Sánchez Vázquez insists that Marx's work is indivisible' (Gandler 2015, p. 177).

76   In a preface, written in 1972, to the English-language edition of his book, Sánchez Vázquez himself refers to the 'enthusiastic reception of this study' by the public (Sánchez Vázquez 1977, p. xii).

77   See Furihata 1987, p. 78.

the so-called 'Lectures School' (*Koza-ha*),* published a multi-volume work on the development of Japanese capitalism in which they set out the conceptions that seemed adequate to the task of undergirding the Communist Party strategy prescribed by the Comintern.[78] According to Setsuo Furihata, a central thesis of the Lectures School was that, as a whole, the Meiji Reform merely constituted a transformation in which 'purely feudal land ownership had been reorganised into semi-feudal land ownership'.[79] Hiroshi Mizuta underscores the significance in this context of the theorist Moritaro Yamada (1897–1980). Yamada, 'an associate professor of Tokyo Imperial University and the most influential of those authors [of the Lectures School], published a book based on his contributions [to the above-mentioned multi-volume work]. The book was entitled *Analysis of Japanese Capitalism* ... and called, ironically, a bible for his disciples'.[80]

The ultimate judgement of the Lectures School as to the previous and contemporary economic structure and development in Japan contrasted with the thesis put forward by Marxist researchers from the milieu around the journal *Workers and Farmers* (*Rono-ha*)** and the communist politician Hitoshi Yamakawa (1880–1958). The latter's faction had opposed the steering of the communist movement in Japan by the Comintern, and had split from the party.[81] The thesis of the Worker-Farmer Faction*** amounted to the following point of view: the *Rono-ha* understood the Meiji era as a quasi-bourgeois transformation and grasped contemporary Japanese society as one which was already developing primarily in a capitalist direction. The Worker-Farmer Faction diverged from the conceptions of the Lectures School on a decisive point: the latter considered that the process of social transformation was less advanced in a capitalist direction than could be surmised from the positions of the former. Accordingly, a further development of the theses of the Worker-Farmer Faction implied that political strategy was to be focused directly on the socialist revolution, rather than on a revolution in two phases.[82] According to Tessa Morris-Suzuki, Itsuro Sakisaka, one of the important theorists of the Worker-Farmer Faction, made a critical intervention against the supposed tendency

---

*   Also referred to in English as the 'Symposium School'.

78   See Furihata 1987, p. 79.

79   Furihata 1987, p. 79.

80   Mizuta 2006, p. 116.

**   Also referred to in English as 'Workers and Peasants'.

81   See Sekine 1980a, p. xi.

***   Also referred to in English as the 'Worker-Peasant Faction'.

82   See Furihata 1987, pp. 79 f.

of the Lectures School to regard the Japanese society of the post-Meiji era as a static formation. Morris-Suzuki writes that Sakisaka's criticism of the approach of the Lectures School was that the latter 'entirely ignores the profound changes that have occurred, and continue to occur, within the system – above all the gradual transformation of the peasantry into a modern proletariat'.[83] The theoretical (and also, in a secondary sense, political) controversy between the Lectures School and the Worker-Farmer Faction shaped the Japanese Marxist milieu of the 1930s,[84] which was nonetheless subjected to increasingly brutal state repression until 1945.

In the postwar period, both a 'neo'-Lectures-School and a 'neo'-Worker-Farmer-Faction approach were constituted. The former remained consistent in its proximity to the official party line of the Japanese Communist Party, thus forming a continuity with the Lectures School of the interwar period. Following a brief phase of radicalisation towards the beginning of the 1950s (the period of the so-called 'Molotov Cocktail Programme'), the JCP switched in the second half of the 1950s to a more moderate course, gradually orienting itself towards the political perspective of 'structural reform'. A parallel can certainly be drawn here with the Italian Communist Party: both parties demonstrated certain characteristics which anticipated the subsequent emergence of Eurocommunism. The 'neo'-Worker-Farmer-Faction moved within the orbit of the non-CP, left-socialist spectrum. Itsuro Sakisaka (1897–1985), one of the important theorists of the Worker-Farmer-Faction in the 1930s, became a leading protagonist of a politically and theoretically oriented group with its roots in the Worker-Farmer-Faction. This was the Socialist Association, which was active within the Socialist Party. Sakisaka demonstrates that Marxism-Leninism was also embraced by leftwing Japanese intellectuals outside the JCP: 'Although Sakisaka argued that Japan's revolution would pursue its own peaceful course, he did not criticize the shortcomings of the Soviet experience; nor did he limit the validity of Marxism-Leninism to the Soviet Union. He envisaged the JSP [the Japanese Socialist Party] as a party ideologically based on Marxism-Leninism ...'.[85] Yet Sakisaka was equally active politically and theoretically – also in Marx research – in the postwar period.[86] Sakisaki translated all three volumes of Marx's *Capital*; the first of these translations was published in 1947, and the others subsequently.

---

83   Morris-Suzuki 1989, p. 87.
84   On the controversy between the Lectures School and the Worker-Farmer Faction, see Hoston 1986, pp. 35 ff.; Sugihara 1987, pp. 24 ff.; Itoh 1980, pp. 22 ff.; Gayle 2003, p. 24 f.; Gayle 2006, p. 92 f.
85   Hoston 1986, p. 281.
86   See Itoh 1980, p. 35 f.

Although the predominant Marxist-Leninist theoretical orthodoxy within the orbit of the JCP was of great influence among Japanese leftist intellectuals in the postwar period, it is also appropriate here to consider Japanese intellectuals with an orientation towards Marxism whose political and theoretical work presented an alternative to the theoretical orthodoxy of the JCP and contributed to the 'de-Stalinisation' of the intelligentsia of the Japanese Left. An example of an 'alternative' (and, moreover, fairly influential) current of thought within Japanese Marxism which developed in clear demarcation from theoretical Stalinism from the 1960s onwards is the 'Civil Society' School; within this theoretical orientation, Kiyoaki Hirata elaborated a critique of actually existing socialism which drew on Marx himself. However, it was not only within this theoretical tendency that critiques of real socialism or theoretical Stalinism were developed.

An intellectual who exerted a notable influence in the course of the attempted 'de-Stalinisation' of the Japanese Left as early as the 1950s was Tadayuki Tsushima (1901–79). Tsushima had an extremely critical attitude towards the political and social system of the USSR in particular, and disputed its socialist character. To this convinced anti-Stalinist, the USSR was a state-capitalist country under the rule of a bureaucratic dictatorship. Tsushima held that within a socialist society there is no law of value, the labour objectified within a product does not take the form of value, and value itself and the value-form are non-existent. Tsushima's conception can be supplemented as follows: if Marxian theory is extended in a certain direction, it becomes apparent that the products of labour in a socialist society result from immediately socialised labour, rather than from private labour which first assumes the character of universal social labour within the process of exchange (as is the case in capitalist society). The value-character and the commodity-form of the products of labour within the capitalist mode of production are the necessary result of a determinate, historically specific mode of the socialisation of labour. This mode is to be abolished in socialist society. By contrast, Stalin's conception implied that the law of value could also exist in a socialist society. Stalin proceeded from this assumption in his late text, *Economic Problems of Socialism in the USSR* (1952). Tsushima criticised this text in his 1956 work, *Myths of the Kremlin*, in which he denounced Stalin's theoretical incomprehension. For the Japanese theorist, the existence of the law of value meant that Soviet society could by no means be considered a socialist one. The non-existence of the categories of value and money within the socialist mode of production was a necessary implication of Marx's value theory.[87]

---

87   See Tsushima 1956. Marx himself wrote in the *Critique of the Gotha Programme*: 'Within

A further critic of Stalinism deserves a somewhat more detailed consideration. In the 1950s and 1960s, an economic school of thought developed in Japan
which is referred to as the Uno School after its founder and 'doyen', Kōzō Uno
(1897–1977), and which attracted numerous intellectuals with an interest in the
formation of Marxist theory. It should be pointed out, in order to prevent any
misunderstanding, that Uno can in no way be described as a *political* leading
figure. He himself eschewed any great political engagement. For many young
intellectuals, however, Uno and his school represented a compelling theoretical alternative to Marxism-Leninism, from which Uno consistently distanced
himself. Uno's thought thus served as a point of reference for a portion of those
Marx-oriented intellectuals who felt no affinity towards orthodox Marxism-
Leninism and its Japanese adepts. To this extent, his thought also had an effect
precisely within the field defined by the charged relationship between theory
and politics.

An important criterion which distinguishes Uno's theory from Marxism-
Leninism consisted in Uno's critical opposition to the doctrine of dialectical
materialism. His revision of the traditional understanding of Marxism within
the Japanese and international orthodoxy also extended to the postulate of
the 'unity of theory and practice'. Uno broke with this authoritative doctrine
of Marxism-Leninism.

Uno himself attached great importance to the separation of the process
of theory formation from any direct political engagement. For this reason,
affiliation to the Uno School by no means implied the adoption of a determinate political position; this remains the case today. In fact, in his own self-
understanding, Uno did not at all consider himself to be a Marxist, even though
he located himself theoretically within Marx's tradition. For Uno, the term
'Marxist' denoted an intensive participation in political practice, for which
reason he rejected this description for himself, despite his affinity with Marx
and socialism.[88] Despite his inclination towards a supposed abstinence in practice and the separation of the process of theory formation from immediate
political engagement, Uno by no means shied away from openly criticising Stalinism. He expressed his criticisms already in the 1950s. Contrary to Stalin's
conception, according to which the law of value would continue to apply in

---

the co-operative society based on common ownership of the means of production, the
producers do not exchange their products; just as little does the labour employed on the
products appear here as the *value* of these products, as a material quality possessed by
them, since now, in contrast to capitalist society, individual labour no longer exists in an
indirect fashion but directly as a component part of the total labour' (Marx 1989a, p. 85).

88   See Joe 1995, p. 139.

socialism, Uno advanced the view that a socialist economy 'should aim at
the abolition of economic laws, such as the law of value, dominant in capitalist society'.[89] Uno's theory was in turn the object of vehement critique on
the part of orthodox Marxist-Leninists with the intelligentsia of the Japanese
Left.

Within the context of the tension between theory and politics, another
important aspect of Uno's work consists in his attribution of a 'scientific' character to Marx's critique of political economy – in contrast to his evaluation of
historical materialism, which he accords the status of a mere 'ideological' hypothesis. This 'heretical' proposition is to be considered against a background in
which historical materialism was held to be of considerable scientific significance within the theoretical understanding of intellectuals close to the JCP.
The Uno-scholar Thomas Sekine reflects the Uno School conception as follows:

> Socialism never becomes a science; it remains an ideology. Socialism
> does not become even more defensible because of the formulation of the
> materialistic conception of history. The conception (otherwise known as
> historical materialism) [is] an ideological hypothesis.[90]

Political economy, according to Sekine, is the scientific basis of Marxism. Yet
Marxism (including socialism) is not a science; it is an ideology based on scientific achievements.[91] Uno, one of the most influential thinkers with an orientation towards Marxian theory in Japan, clearly broke with the traditional
orthodox Marxist conception of 'scientific socialism', without however renouncing his advocacy of socialism in the sense of a political standpoint.

The historian of Marxism, Hiroomi Fukuzawa, maintains that the impact of
Uno's *magnum opus* from the beginning of the 1950s, *Keizai Genron*, can be in
part attributed to Uno's assertion that it is necessary to separate political economy as a science from the question of the political utility of theory formation.
Fukuzawa adds the following: 'The explosive character of his assertion is only
imaginable on the basis of a familiarity with the Marxist camp at that time: any
criticism of Marx would immediately entail the critic being branded as anti-
Marxist, and Marxist theory was understood as the handmaid to politics for
the sake of the revolution'.[92]

---

89   Itoh 2006, p. 23.
90   Sekine 1975, p. 850 f.
91   Ibid.
92   Fukuzawa 1981, p. 140.

Uno's views by no means caused him to be discredited in the eyes of the entire politically active intellectual Left in Japan, however. One of the most important points of reference of the Japanese student movement of the 1960s, alongside the protest against the Vietnam War, was in particular the rejection of the military 'security policy' alliance between Japan and the US, which found its expression in the militant protests against the 'security treaties' of 1960 and 1970. The left-wing student umbrella organisation *Zengakuren* (All-Japan Federation of Student Self-Government Associations) had already been founded in 1948. In subsequent years it underwent a process of radicalisation, having first stood more or less under the control of the JCP until the emergence of the Japanese New Left in the second half of the 1950s. From the late 1950s onwards, a New Left was formed amid a continual process of regrouping – i.e. a Left beyond the classical Moscow-oriented party communism and beyond the Marxism of the Japanese Socialist Party. In the late 1960s, the spectrum of the student Left had developed into a complex structure of rival communist party, left socialist, Trotskyist, Maoist and anarchist groupings, with violent struggles erupting between the various factions in some instances.[93]

Despite his distinction between 'science' on the one hand and socialist 'ideology' on the other, and despite his own 'academic' abstinence from practice, Uno's theoretical approach exerted a certain magnetic effect on parts of the Japanese New Left. Andrew Barshay depicts the situation as follows: 'This same combination of a demonstrated anti-Stalinism (Stalin being portrayed as willfully distorting Marxism) with a powerful systematizing drive that provided Uno's economics its academic bona fides may also have made it attractive to elements of the radical student movement and a leftwing fraction of the Socialist Party'.[94] This is especially true of the processes of theory formation within the Japanese Communist League (not to be confused with the JCP), one of the best-known organisations of the New Left, founded in 1958.

Uno's theory was critically acclaimed not least by Kan'ichi Kuroda.[95] In the period of the formation of the New Left, Kuroda was a leading theorist of the Japan Revolutionary Communist League, which had emerged from the Japan Trotskyist League.[96] Kuroda's interpretation of the exposition of Marx's critique of political economy is noteworthy insofar as he formulated a critique of the reading of Marx's commodity theory as a theory of (historical, pre-capitalist)

---

93   A detailed overview of the various groupings and organisations can be found in McCormack 1971, pp. 37 ff.

94   Barshay 2004, p. 124.

95   See Kuroda 2000.

96   See Derichs 1995, p. 63.

'simple commodity production' as early as the 1960s. In Kuroda's work, the
political bearing of his interpretation of *Capital* is immediately evident. Kuroda
wrote in the 1960s that *Capital* is 'a mental weapon for the self-liberation of the
proletariat all over the world, as well as being the monumental achievement
of Marxism'.[97] In political and theoretical terms, Kuroda was concerned to
distance contemporary European and Asian 'actually existing socialism' from
the thought of Marx and Lenin:

> The socialist Soviet Union, realized through the Russian revolution in
> 1917, has undergone Stalinist degeneration. It exists as something alike
> in appearance but quite different in nature from the socialism envisaged
> by Marx and Lenin. This is not restricted to the contemporary Soviet
> Union. The so-called 'socialist countries' in Eastern Europe and Asia exist
> as something different from socialist societies or states under proletarian
> dictatorship clarified theoretically by Marx and Lenin.[98]

But now let the account return to Uno himself, and to his relation to Marxian
theory. In the famous subchapter on the historical tendency of capitalist accumulation within the chapter on original accumulation* in *Capital*,** Marx
refers to the supposed necessity of the transformation from capitalism to socialism. Marx writes as follows:

> The capitalist mode of appropriation, which springs from the capitalist
> mode of production, produces capitalist private property. This is the first
> negation of individual private property, as founded on the labour of its
> proprietor. But capitalist production begets, with the inexorability of a
> natural process, its own negation. This is the negation of the negation.
> It does not re-establish private property, but it does indeed establish
> individual property on the basis of the achievements of the capitalist era:
> namely co-operation and the possession in common of the land and the
> means of production produced by labour itself.[99]

---

97   Kuroda 2000, p. 221.
98   Kuroda 2000, p. 126.
*   [*ursprüngliche Akkumulation*] – often rendered in English as 'primitive accumulation'.
**   English-language editions of *Capital* are structured differently to the fourth German
      edition: the chapter on original accumulation in the original corresponds in English-
      language editions to Part Eight, and the subchapter on the historical tendency of capitalist
      accumulation to Chapter 32.
99   Marx 1976a, p. 929.

Uno felt compelled to take a position with regard to this point in *Capital*. His central thesis is as follows: although Marx refers to a 'necessity' of the transition from capitalism to socialism, 'I do not believe that this necessity follows from the economic laws which Marx discusses in *Capital* of the motion of capitalist society'.[100] Uno continues by asserting that the 'pure' theory of capitalism has to present the capitalist commodity economy 'as if it were a self-perpetuating entity in order to divulge the laws of its motion. It, therefore, seems to me quite impossible for economic theory to demonstrate at the same time a transformation which involves the denial of these laws'.[101] Neither a theory of 'pure' capitalist society, nor a theory of the various stages of capitalism, nor empirical studies of a concrete, historical capitalist economy can provide an economic explanation of the process of transition to socialism, according to Uno. He states his core conception as follows: 'In any case, whether or not the victory of socialism is necessary depends on the practice of socialist movements, not directly on the economic laws of motion of capitalist society'.[102] For Marxist-Leninist theorists in Japan, who were oriented towards the Moscow orthodoxy, the opportunity thus presented itself to object to Uno's theory on the grounds that in the latter, Marx's allusion to the necessity of the transition to socialism plays no positive role, but is rather problematised.[103]

Setsuo Furihata – himself one of the best-known members of the Uno School – reports that the influx of Marxist scientists into the Uno School increased under the impact of the loss of authority of the JCP as a result of the international events of 1956, and that, somewhat later, 'of the approximately one thousand members of the association of Marxist economists in Japan ("The Scientific Association for Economic Theory" – *Keizai Riron Gakkai*), circa 20 percent could be numbered among the Uno tendency'.[104]

---

100 Uno 1980, p. 125.

101 Ibid.

102 Uno 1980, p. 126.

103 A similar critique was formulated, for example, by Samanosuke Omiya (Omiya 1980, pp. 371 ff.).

104 Furihata 1987, p. 83. The dissemination of Marxism in the various Asian countries varied very widely in the 1960s, but nowhere else was there a comparable scientific intensity and theoretical depth of the discussion of Marx. In contrast to Japan, it is possible to refer to other Asian countries in which Marxist politics and theory have never exerted any significant influence. This applied, and still applies, to Turkey, for example, which can be described as a historical paradigmatic case in all matters relating to anti-Marxism. Yet even here, there were attempts to introduce Marxian theory, although these were largely unsuccessful. According to Yakub Demir, the first volume of *Capital* appeared in Turkish

2.3   'Heretical Marxism' in Eastern Europe

One of the best-known 'heretical' tendencies in Eastern European Marxism in the 1960s and 1970s was represented by a Yugoslav group of theorists around the journal *Praxis* – i.e. by thinkers such as Mihailo Marković, Danko Grlić, Gajo Petrović and Predrag Vranicki. This rather heterogeneous current stood, at least in part, for a 'theoretical humanism' especially oriented to the young Marx. Within the Yugoslav interpretation of Marx,[105] a great deal of attention was paid to Marx's early work.[106] In particular, the *Economic and Philosophical Manuscripts* (first published in 1932) played a role in the Yugoslav discussion of the 1960s and 1970s around Marx's early writings. Hans-Georg Conert, who provides an exhaustive treatment of the Yugoslav discussion on Marxism in this period, states the following:

> The unmistakably enthusiastic reception of the conception of alienation in the *Economic and Philosophical Manuscripts* is in the first instance an expression of a corresponding need to catch up on the part of those Yugoslav philosophers who were not confronted with this aspect of Marxism during their studies in the USSR in the early post-war years or subsequently in Yugoslavia, and who presumably had no access to the interpretations and discussions which followed the first publication of these manuscripts in 1932.[107]

Due to its focus on Marx's early works in particular and its emphasis of the alienation problematic, the approach of parts of the Yugoslav discussion towards Marx's work is reminiscent of a general tendency in parts of the West European discussion of Marx in the postwar period. However, the fact that there was a significant turn towards Marx's early work within the Praxis Group does not mean that no attention was paid to *Capital* or to Marx's mature critique of political economy in general in the Yugoslav discussion of Marx. Although a translation of the *Grundrisse* was first published in Yugoslavia in 1979, one of

---

translation in full for the first time in 1966–7 – i.e. 100 years after the first German edition. (See Demir 1968, pp. 357 ff.). Demir relates that the book 'met with a silence laden with fear and fury on the part of reactionary Turkish journalists' (Demir 1968, p. 366). In the early 1980s, Wolfgang Fritz Haug reported the torture and assassination of a Turkish publisher of Marx (see Haug 1983, p. 426).

105   A survey of the engagement with Marx and Marxism in Yugoslavia, although it mainly refers to the debates up to 1963, can be found in Vrtačič 1975.

106   See Conert 1974, pp. 76 ff.

107   Conert 1974, p. 76.

the best-known representatives of the Praxis Group, the philosopher Gajo Pet-rović, had previously presented research into these manuscripts by Marx which date from 1857–8.[108]

The work of the Praxis Group was widely received internationally. An international edition of the journal *Praxis* appeared intermittently in addition to the Yugoslav edition. From 1963 to 1974, an international summer school initiated by the Praxis Group was held on the Croatian island of Korčula in the Adriatic; among other purposes, this served to facilitate intellectual exchange between Yugoslav and foreign thinkers. However, the representatives of the Praxis Group were criticised by the official Yugoslav party orthodoxy and were ultimately confronted by state repression – the *Praxis* journal was discontinued in 1975.[109]

A further 'heretical' orientation within Eastern European Marxism was the so-called Budapest School – i.e. the circle around György Lukács (1885–1971). Lukács succeeded in gathering a circle of theorists around him, among whose most prominent members figured the philosophers György Márkus and Agnes Heller.[110] Marx's early work played an important role in Márkus's philosophical reading of Marx, as it did in the discussions of the Yugoslav Praxis Group.[111] A core aspect of Márkus's thought consisted in bringing Marxism and anthropology into relation with each other. After Lukács's death, Heller would follow a trajectory from protagonist of a critical Marxism to resolute opponent of Marxist thought.

3   From the Proclamation of the 'Crisis of Marxism' to the Decline of Marxism as a Mass Ideology (Circa 1974–90)

The interest in an intensive and differentiated engagement with Marxian theory began to decline once again in the ensuing period, after the anticipated revolutionary political transformations had failed to materialise. This was particularly the case in Western Europe. In parts of Latin America and Asia, by contrast, a situation of open development presented itself on both a political and a theoretical level.

---

108   See Veljak 2008, p. 262.

109   See Grebing 1977, p. 235 f.

110   Yet Lukács stated the following in an interview: 'Márkus is not a student of mine. Márkus returned from Moscow 75 percent a complete human being, and I am not saying that I had no influence on him, but he cannot be described as my student' (Lukács 1981, p. 232).

111   See Márkus 1969, p. 18 ff.

3.1   *Europe and North America*

Within the period from the mid-1970s up to 1989–90, the various Marxist-oriented political forces in the countries outside the sphere of control of actually existing socialism were ever more on the defensive, at least when the political balance of forces is considered on a world scale (Central America and South Korea certainly represent exceptions to this rule). This political development was accompanied by a change in the intellectual *Zeitgeist*. In France, a '*nouvelle philosophie*' evolved in the circle around Bernard-Henri Lévy and André Glucksmann, who a few years previously still figured as part of the radical Left and who now adopted an 'anti-totalitarian' and anti-communist position. The intellectual climate was transformed, and interest in a sophisticated and differentiated engagement with Marx continually receded.

The years between 1973 and 1979 can be considered as marking a kind of turning point. On a political level, this assertion can be backed up by referring to the decline of radical socialist movements in Western Europe and North America (most notably, Autonomia was smashed in Italy) and the failure of attempts at socialist transformation in Chile and other countries within this period. The communist parties of Italy and France – the most significant in Europe – turned politically to the right at this time. In the 1970s, the PCI embarked on a path of so-called 'historical compromise', while the PCF dropped its demand for the establishment of the 'dictatorship of the proletariat' during its Twenty-Second Party Congress in 1976. On the other hand, there is also a further reason to characterise the years between 1973 and 1979 as a turning point. Two 'leading theoretical figures' of Western European Marxism attempted, through sensational interventions, to draw the attention of their audiences to a supposed 'crisis of Marxism'. While it is true that references to a 'crisis of Marxism' can be traced back to Karl Korsch and even earlier, such a proposition regained its currency in the 1970s.

In 1974, the Italian philosopher Lucio Colletti, whose origins were in the Della Volpe School, spoke, in a interview which gained a great deal of attention, of the fact that Marxism was in crisis. He argued as follows: 'Not only has the falling rate of profit not been empirically verified, but the central test of *Capital* itself has not yet come to pass: a socialist revolution in the advanced West. The result is that Marxism is in crisis today, and it can only surmount this crisis by acknowledging it'. Yet, Colletti argued, numerous Marxists consciously refused to recognise that there was any such crisis. According to Colletti, such a refusal was understandable on the part of apologist intellectuals within the communist parties, 'whose function is merely to furbish a Marxist gloss for the absolutely unMarxist political practice of these parties'. However, the matter weighed much more heavily in the case of intellectuals who were of real theoretical significance, 'who systematically hide the crisis of Marxism in their work, and thereby contribute to prolonging its paralysis as a social science'.[112] Colletti's own intellectual and political biography illustrates why the period up to 1990 delineated here can be interpreted as a time of crisis at least as far as West European Marxism was concerned. Once one of the most important prot-agonists of Italian Marxism in the context of the Della Volpe School, Colletti subsequently turned ever more to the right. In the 1980s, he drew closer to the Socialist Party. Later, he was even elected to the Italian parliament as a repres-entative of Berlusconi's *Forza Italia*.

In autumn 1977, Louis Althusser issued a call for a conference on 'The Crisis of Marxism' organised by the group around the Italian newspaper, *Il Manifesto* (which represented a position independent of the PCI).[113] The reverberations generated in Western Europe by Althusser's provocative thesis can hardly be overestimated. For Althusser, the crisis of Marxism was a 'phenomenon which must be grasped at the historical and world level, and which concerns the difficulties, contradictions and dilemmas in which the revolutionary organisa-tions of struggle based on the Marxist tradition are now involved'.[114] Accord-ing to the French philosopher, the crisis also affected Marxist theory forma-tion. At the same time, for Althusser the crisis of Marxism was in no way a new type of problem, even though it had not previously come to light: it had already emerged 'for us'[115] in the 1930s, but was simultaneously blocked dur-ing Stalinism. Yet Althusser understood the crisis of Marxism not merely as something purely negative or immutable, but also as a challenge. It forced Marxists to modify Marxism. Althusser held that it was of great importance to acknowledge the difficulties, contradictions and *lacunae* which indeed exis-ted within the Marxist theoretical tradition. If Marxists were in a position to carry out such a change, the crisis would open up a historical opportun-ity.

The expression 'crisis of Marxism' soon became a buzzword. The centre of the debate over the 'crisis of Marxism' was Western Europe,[116] not least due to the sensational interventions by Colletti and Althusser, although the corres-

---

112   Colletti 1974, p. 21.

113   See Goshgarian 2006, p. xxii. See Elliott 1987, pp. 275 ff., for a detailed consideration of Althusser's thesis of the 'crisis of Marxism'.

114   Althusser 1978a, p. 215.

115   Althusser does not make clear at this point whom precisely he means by 'us': Marxists in general as opposed to non-Marxists, French or Western European Marxists as opposed to others, or an entirely different grouping.

116   The West Berlin journal *Prokla* also addressed the 'crisis of Marxism' (see *Prokla* 1979).

ponding debate was also received outside Europe (for example in Mexico).[117] The thesis of the 'crisis' was not taken up by all Marxist theorists in Western Europe, however. The philosopher Lucien Sève, a long-time leading intellectual of the PCF, opposed the thesis as follows: 'In my opinion, to refer to a "crisis of Marxism" amounts to giving a false answer to real problems. We live in the age of revolutions, and living Marxism is their simultaneously critical and creative soul'.[118]

In hindsight, it would be appropriate to make a critical distinction in relation to the references to a 'crisis of Marxism' which were in vogue in the late 1970s. It would have to be asked *which* variant of Marxism was in a situation of crisis in Western Europe at the time. Most plausibly, it was Marxism in the sense of a unity of theory and political practice that was afflicted by crisis from the mid-1970s on. This did not apply, or at least not to the same extent, to the historical development of Marxist theory in the sense of the formation of theory related to Marx's critique of political economy. However, a development began in the late 1970s which can be understood as a decoupling of the sophisticated scientific discussion of Marx (which continued its positive evolution) from the progressively receding broad interest in Marxian theory.

In the 1970s, Italy was still one of the countries in Western Europe where political confrontation still took a militant form. However, a reorientation took place within the revolutionary movement as it reorganised: the concept of the 'socialised worker' as the emancipatory subject took the place of the 'mass worker' of the classical *operaismo* of the 1960s. The sphere of struggle was thereby extended from the factory to society. In 1978, one of the intellectual protagonists of the struggles of the 1970s, the philosopher Antonio Negri, produced an attempt at a new reading of Marx which was systematically based on the *Grundrisse* (and which he incidentally presented at a seminar at the *École Normale Supérieure* at the invitation of Althusser). In the guise of this initiative, the struggle-oriented theoretical engagement with Marx's critique of political economy that had evolved within the intellectual culture of the Italian *operaismo* of the 1960s underwent a specific further development.[119] Negri attributed

---

117   For a more recent Brazilian contribution to the discussion of Althusser's thesis of the 'crisis of Marxism', see Limoeiro-Cardoso 2002, pp. 107 ff.

118   Sève 1980, p. 523. On the 'crisis of Marxism', see also a presentation by Guido Liguori, who outlines the development of Italian Marxism between the poles of theory and politics in the period between 1963 and 1991 (Liguori 2006, p. 34).

119   Negri was arrested in 1979 as part of the repressive measures taken by the Italian state against the radical Left, and was subsequently sentenced to more than 30 years in prison. After a period spent in exile in France and in prison, Negri is now free and has risen

enormous theoretical and political significance to the *Grundrisse* manuscript, which he considered to be 'the summit of Marx's revolutionary thought'. A core element of Negri's perspective on the *Grundrisse* consists in his stated intention to investigate this text 'for itself'[120] – in contrast to other readings of the *Grundrisse*, which reduce this manuscript to a mere developmental step in Marx's intellectual process that would ultimately lead to *Capital*. According to Negri, however, the *Grundrisse* also opens up the possibility of an adequate reading of *Capital*.

At around the same time that Negri presented his reading of the *Grundrisse*, in the USA, Harry Cleaver was developing an extremely similar perspective in relation to the reading to be made of Marx's critique of political economy.[121] In political and theoretical terms, Cleaver could be located in the current of 'autonomist Marxism', which was influenced by Italian *operaismo*, and which was also represented in the USA. He emphasised the necessity of a political reading of capital, and counterposed the decidedly political reading of Marx to the economic and the philosophical readings. Cleaver states his aims as follows: 'to bring out the political usefulness of the analysis of value by situating the abstract concepts' of the first chapter of *Capital* 'within Marx's overall analysis of the class struggles of capitalist society'.[122] The American theorist claims that his approach to interpreting Marx facilitates a return to the original purpose of Marx's process of theory formation: Marx 'wrote *Capital* to put a weapon in the hands of workers'.[123] This quotation from Cleaver could be supplemented by recalling that Marx himself described *Capital* as the 'most terrible missile that has yet been hurled at the heads of the bourgeoisie (landowners included)'.[124]

---

to the position of leading theoretician (in collaboration with the US literary theorist, Michael Hardt) of a post-*operaista* theoretical current. This current is influenced by French poststructuralism, and places its revolutionary hopes in a nebulous 'multitude'. The post-*operaista* approach to the formation of emancipatory theory developed by Hardt and Negri since the 1990s and finally presented particularly in the shape of their book, *Empire* (Hardt and Negri 2000), generated much resonance in circles of the Left and among left intellectuals just after the turn of the millennium, but also (and not least) criticism. It seems indisputable that, while the reference to Marx's critique of political economy is still present in Negri's more recent theory formation, it now ranks alongside (or perhaps even behind) other essential theoretical references.

120   Negri 1984, p. 15.
121   See Cleaver 1979.
122   Cleaver 1979, p. 3.
123   Cleaver makes a similar argument to that in his book in an essay entitled 'Karl Marx: Economist or Revolutionary' (Cleaver 1986, p. 144).
124   Marx 1987i, p. 358.

At approximately the same time – towards the end of the 1970s – as the last large-scale attempt by the radical Left to bring about political and social transformation failed in Italy, numerous Western European Leftists progressively lost their previously close connection to Marxian or Marxist theory under the impact of the rise of the so-called New Social Movements (the ecological movement, feminism, etc.). An additional problem was engendered by the fact that the crisis of Marxism (widely referred to among the intelligentsia of the West European Left) was in no way restricted to the Western part of Europe. Following the waves of protest that were unleashed against the socialist regime in Poland in 1956 and 1968, anti-communist dissent attained a new high point with the *Solidarność* movement in the early 1980s. By this time, Marxism had become marginalised not only among the masses of the Polish population, but also within the Polish intelligentsia. It was against this backdrop that Adam Schaff, who numbered among the very few internationally renowned Marxist thinkers in Poland as Director of the Institute for Philosophy and Sociology at the Polish Academy of Sciences, published his intervention in the first half of the 1980s. With regard to the interpretation of Marx's works, the Polish philosopher insisted upon the unity of Marx's early and mature work. Schaff opposed the reduction of the theory of alienation to the doctrine of the young Marx alone. According to Schaff, the theory of alienation had shaped Marx's entire creative process – including the formation of theory in his mature period.[125] At first sight it might appear paradoxical, but Schaff placed himself in the position of an outsider vis-à-vis the intelligentsia of his socialist native country with his defence of Marxism (which he understood as an open and undogmatic system). The Polish philosopher was forced to concede at the time that 'in Poland, the myth of the "end of Marxism" … is very widespread'.[126] Indeed, Schaff modified the thesis of a crisis of Marxism to the 'crisis of the Marxists'. This was not only a contemporary problem, in Schaff's view: there had also been such a crisis in 1956, when it was 'in fashion to be anti-Marxist'.[127] According to Schaff, in the early 1980s there was a higher level of interest in Marxism in the West (he himself held a professorship in Vienna and visiting professorships at various American universities) than in his home country.[128]

---

125   See Schaff 1984a, p. 137.
126   Schaff 1984b, p. 171.
127   Schaff 1984c, p. 152.
128   See Schaff 1984d, p. 160.

3.2   *Latin America, Africa and Asia*

Politically, Latin American Marxism was forced onto the defensive in the 1970s through right-wing military coups supported by the USA, such as in Chile and Argentina. However, as far as the formation of emancipatory and critical social theory was concerned, a new approach soon coalesced in the shape of a specific wing of the Latin American 'philosophy of liberation'. The philosophy of liberation has developed alongside liberation theology since the 1970s and shares several commonalities with the latter, although the two should not be automatically identified. Within the extremely heterogeneous current of thought that is the philosophy of liberation, one tendency, represented by Enrique Dussel, developed an emphatic and innovative relation to Marxian thought.

The philosopher and theologian, Dussel,[129] who hails originally from Argentina and has been resident in Mexico since the mid-1970s, ranks – within the context of the tension between politics and theory – among the most important interpreters of Marx south of the Río Grande. This is true of the contemporary Latin American debate, and was already the case in the 1980s. Although Dussel forms his theory from a specifically Latin American perspective, his significance reaches far beyond this continent. He ranks among the protagonists of the ethics of liberation, and as such he moves within a determinate intellectual orientation within Latin American liberation philosophy. A feature of Dussel's theory is that it is shaped by the study of the French philosopher Emmanuel Levinas, and also by an intense engagement with Marxian theory, in particular with the various drafts of the critique of political economy. A crucial point of reference in Dussel's conceptual approach is the division of the contemporary world into centre and periphery. Dussel brings together periphery with the category of exteriority, thus drawing on a central category from Levinas's thought. For Dussel, it is a question of understanding the peoples and cultures of the so-called 'Third World', and Latin America in particular, as a historical-concrete exteriority in the sense of an 'other' vis-à-vis the capitalist totality. The relationship between totality and exteriority is of decisive importance for Dussel with regard to both his interpretation of the contemporary capitalist world system and his reading of Marx's critique of political economy, since he grasps as a determining theorem in Marx the fact that the totality of capital stands counterposed to the exteriority of 'living labour'. According to Dussel, the economic relationship between centre and periphery is one of dependency, whose hallmark he identifies as the transfer of surplus value. Dussel's core thought

---

129   On Dussel's biography, see Schelkshorn 1992, pp. 16 ff.

can be sketched as follows: the 'vertical' social relation of capital and labour is characterised by exploitation. Labour produces surplus value within this relation. However, for Dussel, there also exists a 'horizontal' social relation, which has an international character; in this relation, economic competition between the bourgeoisie of economically more developed world regions and that of less developed ones plays a decisive role. This international relation is not one of direct exploitation, although it is an international relation of domination. Surplus value is not produced within this relation; rather it is partially transferred between different world regions. It flows from the periphery to the centre.

Dussel's political and philosophical perspective amounts to the advocacy of a social emancipation in the countries of the periphery (the countries of the so-called 'Third World'), whereby it is conceived of as a kind of 'popular emancipation'. An important point of reference in emancipatory theory for Dussel is the category of 'the people'. With this term, Dussel refers to the oppressed masses, to whom an exteriority corresponds in the sense that they represent the peripheral 'other' vis-à-vis the totality. For Dussel, this proposition is to be made more concrete by the acknowledgement that the centre of the capitalist world system is counterposed to the 'peoples' of the oppressed periphery. This theory forms the political context of Dussel's intensive engagement with the various Marxian texts on the critique of political economy, which is considered in more detail in Part 2 of this work. At the present juncture it should be noted that it was only a considerable time after his development as a philosopher of liberation (i.e. only from the end of the 1970s or beginning of the 1980s) that Dussel clove a path to a positive relation to Marx's theory; he had initially considered Marx as a theorist in the European tradition of a certain totality-thinking.* It was only in the course of an intensive new reception of Marx's writings that Dussel came to identify Marx as a thinker of exteriority.[130] Dussel's philosophical development, which led from a critical to a positive attitude towards Marx and Marxism, ran counter to the trend in Western Europe as exemplified by the trajectories of Colletti and other thinkers.[131]

In a report on an international Marx conference which took place in the early 1980s, Wolfgang Fritz Haug states that Marx 'is still only in the process of "arriving", or becoming linguistically accessible, in various regions of the

---

*   [*Totalitätsdenken*] – thinking (in terms of) totality.

130   On Dussel's re-evaluation of Marx, see Peter 1997, pp. 72 ff.

131   Another work worthy of mention within the context of the Latin American debate on Marx in the 1980s, and one which caused something of a stir, is Aricó 1980. Here it was claimed that Marx was occasionally somewhat uncomprehending when confronted by the social and political reality of Latin America.

world, and that this arrival incurs brutal persecution in many places'.[132] The same could be said in relation to various regions of the world in the 1960s and 1970s. In considering the question of the accessibility of Marx's work, it should be borne in mind that it was not until the 1980s that the *Marx-Engels Collected Works* (*MECW*) edition, which was conceived in part also with the English-speaking countries of the so-called 'Third World' in mind, was initiated. The Soviet Marx-researcher, Lew Golman, wrote the following in relation to the *MECW* in 1978: 'The English-language edition is intended for an extraordinarily large readership. It has been distributed not only in England and the USA, but also in all English-speaking countries – in Ireland, Australia, New Zealand, Canada, India, Burma, Sri Lanka – as well as in a series of other Asian and also African countries which have only recently freed themselves from the colonial yoke of British imperialism'.[133] In some regions of the so-called 'Third World', a theoretically sophisticated methodological discussion oriented to Marx was (and continues to be) hardly existent, for various economic, political or politico-ideological reasons. This applied (and continues to apply) to Arab countries,[134] for example, but also to Sub-Saharan Africa. In the 1980s, Paulin J. Hountondji, who originates from Benin and has become one of the best-known African philosophers, explained the African perspective as follows: 'We still have no real, consistent, intellectual Marxist tradition. We still continue to learn and teach our Marxism out of popular handbooks written elsewhere, especially in the Soviet Union'.[135] In another text dating from 1976, the West African philosopher expanded on the point as follows: 'We must promote positively a *Marxist theoretical tradition* in our countries – a contradictory scientific debate around the work of Marx and his followers. For let us not forget this: Marxism itself is a tradition, a plural debate based on the theoretical foundations laid by Marx'. Hountondji deplores the fact that there still exists a theoretical 'vacuum' in relation to Marxist discussion in Africa. He continues as follows: 'We learned our Marxism from popular works, and having swallowed it in little pills, we used to enjoy whispering about it in tightly closed circles'. According to Hountondji, a solution would consist in the following: 'here and

---

132   Haug 1983, p. 428.

133   Golman 1978, p. 436.

134   See Mchaurab 1984, for a contribution from the 1980s which deals with the situation regarding editions of Marx's work in the Arab language. On Marxism in the Arab world, see also Hafez 1969. The best-known critical social theorist of African-Arab origins drawing on Marx is the Egyptian, Samir Amin, who lives in Senegal: Amin engaged extensively with Marx's critique of political economy in the 1970s (see, among other works, Amin 1978).

135   Hountondji 1984, p. 107.

now, in the semi-silence in which we are compelled to work, we should set about broadening our knowledge of Marx and the rich tradition he inaugurated and thus stamp out once and for all our unanimist and dogmatic prejudices: we must restore to theory its birthright'.[136]

With regard to the situation in Korea, the South Korean Marx-researcher, Moon-Gil Chung, claims that, before 1945, 'the interest of Korean intellectuals in Marx and in Marxism, and their contacts to this ideology, were similar in level to those of the Japanese intelligentsia'.[137] The question as to whether or not Chung's view is to be endorsed cannot be answered here. Nevertheless, it is a fact that the division of the country into a capitalist Southern part and a Stalinist Northern part as a consequence of the Second World War and the 1950–3 Korean War represented a fundamental point of rupture in this regard. In the South, any engagement with Marx and Marxism, whether politically motivated or primarily scientific, had to contend with repressive measures on the part of the state. Beyond the oppositional underground movement, there was hardly any space for an engagement with Marx and Marxism that transcended anti-communist indoctrination. In the Stalinist North, the dogmatism of the ruling '*Juche*' ideology suffocated any emancipatory theoretical potential.

After the Gwangju massacre in 1980, in which hundreds of protesters were slaughtered by the military, a strong oppositional protest movement developed in South Korea; the latter was more strongly radicalised in comparison to previous protest movements, and more ideologically oriented towards Marxism. Of significance in this context was the development of an intellectual 'counter-' and 'underground' culture, in which a movement of reading circles interested in Marxian and Marxist literature played an important role. The South Korean Left of the 1980s, which was compelled to operate underground as the result of state repression, drew for the most part on forms of dogmatic Marxism. The two most significant currents within the South Korean Left of the 1980s were an orthodox Leninism on the one hand, and the North Korean '*Juche*' ideology on the other (by contrast, Trotskyism was pretty much insignificant at the time). An important theoretical debate within the Marxist underground milieu in South Korea of the 1980s revolved around the specific socio-economic character of South Korean society.[138]

It was not until the 1990s, when both the militant protest movement and interest in Marxian and Marxist theory were already in decline in South Korea,

---

136   Hountondji 1996, p. 183.
137   Chung 1998, p. 269.
138   The term 'social formation debates' is sometimes used to describe this discussion. For a detailed account, see Shin 2002, pp. 359 ff.

that a kind of South Korean counterpart to the New Left in the West could gain a foothold.[139] With the reduction (although not complete disappearance) of state repression in the same decade, the research situation improved for South Korean scientists with an orientation towards Marxian theory. However, the present relatively scant interest in Marx on the part of the new generation can hardly be compared with the intensive reception of Marx and Marxism by the protest generation of the 1980s. Nevertheless, Althusserianism and (post-) *operaismo* have recently found a positive resonance among a few intellectuals in South Korea (more precisely: Althusserianism represented something of a fashionable current within the South Korean Left above all in the 1990s, whereas in the 2000s, the same could be said of post-*operaismo*).[140]

In the People's Republic of China, Mao's death in 1976 and Deng Xiaoping's subsequent rise to a leading position marked the beginning of a new era not only politically, but also in the ideological sphere. Surveying the time under Mao, the philosopher Fangtong Liu explains in retrospect that 'both Marxism and other cultural fields were confined to a closed situation for a long time, which cut them off from the development of the rest of the world. It obstructed their growth and enrichment'.[141] The intellectual situation had changed since the political and social upheavals at the end of the 1970s. The philosopher Li-Quan Chou perceived a new intellectual openness in this context. In the 1980s, he wrote that the classical works of Marx, Engels, Lenin, Stalin and Mao were no longer regarded as the ultimate criterion of truth. In addition, a transfer of various philosophical ideas from Eastern Europe, Western Europe and America to China was now taking place. An important theme of Chinese research in this new period was the question of the relationship between Marxism and humanism; in this context (and against the backdrop of the new openness), a genuine philosophical discussion was able, somewhat diffidently, to unfold.[142] Thus, according to Chou, the exponents of the conception that 'humanism is

---

139   In this paragraph I rely above all on the work of a Korean sociologist and historian of the protest movement in her country, who lives and lectures in the Anglo-Saxon world: see M. Park 2002 and Park 2005. The Marxist economic scientist, Seongjin Jeong, criticises both the '*Juche*' wing of the South Korean Left of the 1980s, and the latter's Leninist wing, which he regards as 'Stalinist' (see Jeong 1996).

140   On (post-) *operaismo* in South Korea, see, among other works, Kim 2007, pp. 170 ff.

141   Liu 2004, p. 187.

142   On the occasion of the centenary of Marx's death, Shaozhi wrote the following: 'There is … the relationship between Marxism and humanism to consider. For a long period, this question remained a forbidden area of study in China. Today, fewer and fewer people still refuse to admit that there is humanism in Marxism' (Shaozhi 1983, p. 39).

indeed an essential ingredient of Marxism' found themselves confronted by those thinkers who represented the view that 'humanism cannot be incorporated into Marxism'.[143] In the early 1980s, Shaozhi, then a high-ranking representative of the Institute of Marxism-Leninism-Mao Zedong Thought at the Chinese Academy of Sciences, was able to report that there was a new understanding of Marxism in China. According to Shaozhi, the potential connections and differences between Marx's early and mature work, the relation between Marxism and humanism, the relationship between science and ideology, as well as 'the connection and/or differences between Marx on the one hand, and Engels and Lenin on the other',[144] all represent important questions that the Chinese debate on Marxism had to pose. Shaozhi wrote elsewhere that Marxism cannot be handled like a religion or a compulsory ideology: it is 'a branch of the social sciences, but it is not an all-encompassing "science of sciences"'.[145]

The 'ideological struggles' around reform-based attempts to foster an openness within Chinese Marxism in the period of the late 1970s and the 1980s can be illustrated by the example of the history of the Institute of Marxism-Leninism-Mao Zedong Thought, which was founded in 1979.[146] To all appearances, this institute was characterised by a strong interest in determining the contemporary state of the international discussion on Marxist theory: 'The Institute regularly published *Reference Materials on the Study of Marxism* (distributed internally) to introduce Chinese readers to the various schools of Marxism and socialism in the contemporary world, commentary on Marxism abroad, criticisms and revisions of Marxism in the West and Eastern Europe, and descriptions of the reforms under way in the Soviet Union and Eastern European countries'.[147] However, there were repeated setbacks to contend with in the form of repression, as Shaozhi reports. An example is the campaign against 'intellectual pollution' which was led by dogmatic hardliners in 1983. Shaozhi writes that following the death in 1989 of the reformist politician, Hu Yaobang, and the massive student protests that this triggered, the Institute of Marxism-Leninism-Mao Zedong Thought was subjected to state repression. Members of the institute were arrested and later released. Shaozhi found himself compelled to emigrate.

---

143   Chou 1988, p. 61. On the development of Chinese Marxism since Mao's death, see also Kha 1987, pp. 113 ff.

144   Shaozhi 1984, p. 78.

145   Shaozhi 1993a, p. 111.

146   On this institute, see Shaozhi 1993b, pp. 335 ff.

147   Shaozhi 1993b, p. 342.

It is also worth noting that the thesis of a crisis of contemporary Marxism was also developed by a Chinese theorist – namely by Shaozhi himself – in the latter half of the 1980s. Shaozhi outlined the historical process which had led to the crisis of Marxism as follows: 'For a long period, approximately since the end of the 1920s or the beginning of the 1930s, Marxism has been simplified, petrified and dogmatised. The scientific spirit and innovating power of Marxism was destroyed. The practice of socialism and the world communist movement were damaged, and Marxist theory regressed far behind practice – it no longer had the power to further develop itself'.[148] According to Shaozhi, Stalin had expedited the development of Marxism into a dogma. By contrast, Shaozhi advocated a pluralist and open Marxism, and took up in this context the dictum of letting a hundred schools of thought contend.[149,*]

4   The Global Situation after the End of Marxism as a Mass Ideology (Circa 1990–2008)

If a distinction is made, following the Greek social theorist, John Milios** (see below), between 'Marxism as an ideology of the masses' and 'Marxism as a theoretical system', it can be said in relation to the latter that the systematic theoretical and scientific engagement with Marx was affected by the collapse of actually existing socialism, insofar as this entailed the extensive 'winding down' of institutionalised Marx-research in the former countries of actually existing socialism and especially in the GDR. However, theoretical and scientific engagement with Marx's *oeuvre*, and with Marx's critique of political economy in particular, continues to the present in both East and West and in some

---

148   Shaozhi 1989, p. 747.

149   Shaozhi 1989, p. 752.

*   '"Let a hundred flowers blossom, let a hundred schools of thought contend" and "long-term coexistence and mutual supervision" – how did these slogans come to be put forward? They were put forward in the light of China's specific conditions, in recognition of the continued existence of various kinds of contradictions in socialist society and in response to the country's urgent need to speed up its economic and cultural development. Letting a hundred flowers blossom and a hundred schools of thought contend is the policy for promoting progress in the arts and sciences and a flourishing socialist culture in our land' (Mao 1977, p. 408). Mao's 'Hundred Flowers Campaign' of 1956–7, in which criticism of the regime was encouraged, was followed by the repressive crackdown on dissent during the 'Anti-Rightist Campaign'.

**   John Milios is also known as Yannis/Giannis Milios.

countries of the so-called 'Third World'. In the eyes of numerous researchers worldwide, the Marxian project of a critique of political economy has in no way been rendered obsolete by the political collapse of the system of states of actually existing socialism in Central and Eastern Europe, or by the transformation of the People's Republic of China into a modern capitalist society (a process which has steadily intensified since the 1990s). The continuation, under the aegis of the *Internationale Marx-Engels Stiftung*, of the *Marx-Engels Gesamtausgabe* ($MEGA^2$)* – the most representative international project in terms of research into, and publication of, the works of Marx and Engels – exemplifies the fact that engagement with Marx continues to be of contemporary scientific relevance after 1990.

Yet mainstream interest in Marxian theory – beyond merely superficial engagement – has further receded in this period. It must thus be acknowledged that, in comparison with the 1970s, the attractiveness of Marx's works has considerably subsided as far as the new stream of scientific researchers, but also the younger generation of political activists, is concerned. Adorno's reference to the 'neuroticisation that consciousness has experienced in relation to Marx'[150] would seem to be of contemporary relevance once more.

Historically, the collapse of actually existing socialism signified the end of Marxism as a political and ideological mass movement. Here it is to be noted, however, that previously the Marxisms of the mass parties of the Second and Third Internationals and of their historical successors were mostly accessible to the masses only in their vulgarised form, meaning that, for the most part, there was no intensive engagement with Marx's critique of political economy on the part of the masses. Following the political and economic processes of transformation which began in 1989 in Central and Eastern Europe, even the vulgarised variants of Marxism have definitively lost all 'compatibility with the masses' – at least in most countries of the world. Marxist thought appears to be fundamentally discredited (although the objection could be made that this is not the case to the same extent in all countries).

Beyond the narrow confines of the intensive scientific engagement with Marx and with Marxism that has continued undiminished since 1989, the 'requiem' for Marxism became a commonplace of intellectual discourse. Francis Fukuyama's conjectures concerning the end of history – his speculation that liberal democracy marks the endpoint of the ideological development of humanity – were broadly received in the 1990s. Even if such hyperbole is to be

---

* The critical edition of the complete works of Marx and Engels.

150   Adorno 1974, p. 272.

dismissed, it remains the case that the collapse of actually existing socialism and of Marxism-Leninism in theory and practice represents a historical turning point: it forms the historical background to the subsequent further development, between the poles of politics and theory, of theoretical approaches to social criticism since 1989/91.

The collapse of Eastern European Marxism-Leninism had far-reaching consequences for Marxists worldwide, regardless of whether they were sympathetic to the Soviet variant of Marxism or distanced themselves from it. Yet it was Marxism in those countries in which it had previously constituted the official ideology of the ruling party that was most immediately affected by these political and ideological transformations. The Soviet Union constitutes a striking example in this context. Alexander Litschev and Dietrich Kegler draw a distinction between two differing interpretations of the Soviet philosophy of this period of upheaval and the way that it related to Marx.[151] On the one hand, they identify theoretical 'attempts to rescue' Marxism which militated in favour of a return to the original – and, it might be added, unadulterated – Marx. On the other hand, another tendency which joined the debate pushed for a complete overcoming and elimination of Marxism. A more differentiated study than that of Litschev and Kegler in relation to the understanding of Soviet philosophy in the late phase of *perestroika* is provided by the South Korean, Seong-Paik Lee.[152] He identifies a certain 'Marxist humanism' as a fundamental guiding principle of those forces who were in favour of a philosophy of reform and who struggled for a renewal of Marxist thought within *perestroika*. According to Lee, Marxist humanism had had 'its decisive origin in the discussion on the "young Marx" in the 1960s'.[153] Lee's study enables a parallel to be drawn between the strands of Marxist thought which strove for a renewal during the Soviet *perestroika* period and the theoretical openings and developments within Chinese Marxism which came to light – however tentatively, and against stern resistance on the part of the dogmatists – during the Deng Xiaoping era. In China, too, a 'Marxist humanism' was developed.

Although instances of a differentiated engagement with Marxian or Marxist theory can still be found in Russia today (in the context of the $MEGA^2$ project, for example),[154] these represent a marginal phenomenon within Russian philosophy and social science. For example, Alexander Buzgalin and Andrej Kolganov are working to form a school of thought of post-Soviet Marxism in

---

151   See Litschev and Kegler 1992, pp. 9 ff.
152   See Lee 1998.
153   Lee 1998, p. 45.
154   See for example Mayer 2007; see also Mayer and Küttler 2007, pp. 740 ff.

Russia: this school is to be characterised by the critique of theoretical Stalinism, with currents of humanist Marxism forming its central point of reference.[155]

From the 1990s onwards, the critique of so-called 'globalisation'[156],* marked the emergence of a new social movement on a world scale; points of reference for this movement were the *Zapatista* uprising of 1994,[157] the protests against the meeting of the World Trade Organisation in Seattle in 1999, and against the G8 Summit in Genoa in 2001. The international counter-globalisation movement is a politically and theoretically variegated protest movement. Marx-oriented currents have a presence within this movement, although as yet only in a marginal form. Opinions are divided within the counter-globalisation movement on the question of Marxian theory. It can safely be assumed that Marxian theory has little significance for the majority of the 'more pragmatic' critics of globalisation, and yet a newly reconfigured context of the tension between theory and politics emerged with the counter-globalisation movement. Moving within this new context are various thinkers from different countries who can certainly be said to have engaged intensively with Marxian theory. Although these theorists have not as yet succeeded in exerting an influence on broad circles of globalisation critics, it is worth casting a glance at the profile of several of the thinkers with an orientation towards Marx who also relate to the counter-globalisation movement.

In Japan, intensive engagement with Marx continued after the upheavals in Central and Eastern Europe.[158] Against the backdrop of globalisation since the end of the Cold War, the Asian Financial Crisis of 1997 and global migration flows, the Japanese philosopher and Marx-researcher, Tomonaga Tairako, deals with suggestions for possible solutions and attempts to deliberate the role of philosophy in this context. Tairako expands as follows: 'The most critical goal of globalization studies is to construct resistant discourse against capitalist globalization without falling into the pitfall of nationalism'.[159] The Japanese

---

155   See Buzgalin and Kolganov 2007.

156   On the problematic of 'Marx and the critique of globalisation', see Henning 2006, pp. 29 ff. Nevertheless, one of the internationally best-known intellectuals to have criticised globalisation, the Filipino sociologist Walden Bello, describes Marx as a formative influence on his own thought (see Bello 2004).

*   See also Pradella 2015.

157   This was an uprising by the indigenous population which began in the Southern Mexican region of Chiapas in 1994. The designation *Zapatista* derives from one of the leading figures of the Mexican Revolution of the early twentieth century, Emiliano Zapata.

158   See for example Ito 1994, pp. 323 ff.

159   Tairako 2005, p. 59.

philosopher's projected goal consists in the creation of a global safety net to protect all individuals from direct violence and oppression, as well as from the 'structural' violence associated with capitalist globalisation. Regarding the role that philosophy can play, Tairako writes that it should take seriously 'the needs and demands of people suffering from today's globalization'. He adds that it is important 'to keep supporting the social movements for empowering them and to equip them with the sense of human dignity and ethical meaningfulness which grounds on historical necessity'.[160] Tairako's interpretation of Marx – an interpretation which is of great significance with regard to Japanese research into Marx on account of the original reading that Tairako makes of the critique of political economy via the theory of reification – will be considered later in this study.

One of the best-known intellectual critics of globalisation in the People's Republic of China is currently the economist Han Deqiang; however, the latter also relates critically to Marxism (or what he understands by Marxism). He presented some of his theses to a non-Chinese audience at an international Marx conference in Havana: according to Deqiang, the People's Republic of China is characterised by 'the emergence of [a] new exploiting class and the return in reality of capitalism'. Deqiang asserts that China is a 'new economic colony of the United States'.[161] Deqiang's theoretical approach points in a different direction from that of Shaozhi, referred to above, who was close to the reform wing of Chinese Marxism in the 1980s. Deqiang refers to Mao Zedong and even ultimately evaluates the basic approach of the Cultural Revolution positively. He insists on a fundamental revision of Marxism. His critique is expressed in his proposition of inverting the traditional base-superstructure schema: 'So, this Marxist statement would be rewritten as: "the superstructure of a society dominates its economic basis while the latter restrains the former"'.[162] Deqiang's radical voluntarism is expressed in this inversion, as well as the leading role that he ascribes to an 'ideological revolution'. According to Deqiang, it must be conceded that the writings of Marx and Engels 'leave too much room for revisionists. What is more, Marxism is likely to become detached from revolutionary practice since it does not fully recognize the importance and complexity of ideological revolution'.[163] This, in Deqiang's

---

160 Tairako 2005, p. 60. Incidentally, Tairako has also published a contribution on the problematic of 'Marx and globalism' (Tairako 2003, p. 11 ff.).

161 Deqiang 2003.

162 Deqiang 2003, p. 7.

163 Deqiang 2003, p. 10.

view, is a key limitation of Marxism. The solution to the problem that he proposes is 'to admit the limitation of Marxism, innovate and integrate Marxist theory through a summary of international communist revolutionary practice under the guidance of Marxism in the last 150 years, and consequently establish new theories that are more fitting to revolutionary practices and historical rules, thus laying a solid theoretical foundation for the final elimination of capitalism and for true liberation of humanity'.[164] In political terms, Deqiang's ultimate partisan defence of Mao Zedong and the Cultural Revolution is catastrophic. Nevertheless, it is important to consider his thinking here to the extent that it is an expression of the social and ideological tensions which traverse contemporary Chinese society in its colossal process of transformation in the context of capitalist globalisation.

In his 1970 work, *Marx's Theory of Alienation*, the Hungarian philosopher, István Mészáros, who preferred to remain in his homeland rather than to emigrate to the West after the 1956 uprising, regards the concept of alienation as the key to understanding both the early and the mature Marx.[165] This work, in which the trajectory of Marx's further intellectual development is not contested, even though Mészáros resolutely opposes any interpretation which establishes a strict dichotomy between the 'young' and the 'mature' Marx, was of great significance for the discussion of Marx in the Anglo-Saxon world (and, to a certain extent, beyond). In a more recent book, *Beyond Capital* (published in 1995),[166] Mészáros retains his emancipatory socialist perspective; this work was received not only in the Anglo-Saxon world, but also in Latin America.[167] Dorothea Melcher has written that *Beyond Capital* was even 'translated and published by the Venezuelan government in 2001'.[168] Mészáros himself argues that the title, *Beyond Capital*, is to be understood in three ways. One meaning of this formulation refers back to Marx himself: 'In this sense it means going beyond *capital as such* and not merely *beyond capitalism*'.[169] Secondly, it is a question of going beyond the three volumes of *Capital* (and also the *Grundrisse*

---

164   Ibid.
165   See Mészáros 1970.
166   See Mészáros 1995.
167   Two interviews (from 1992 and 1999) also afford insight into Mészáros's political thought in the 1990s: Mészáros 1993, pp. 9 ff. and Mészáros 2000, pp. 26 ff.
168   Melcher 2005, p. 511. This information cannot be verified here. Incidentally, one of the best-known Venezuelan interpreters of the critique of political economy was the philosopher and economist, José Rafael Núñez Tenorio. See, among other works, Núñez Tenorio 1969 and Núñez Tenorio 1985.
169   Mészáros 1995, p. xxi.

and *Theories of Surplus-Value*). Thirdly, the Hungarian theorist adds that it is a question of going beyond the Marxian project itself, as the latter 'could be articulated under the circumstances of commodity society's global ascendancy in the nineteenth century, when the possibilities of adjustment for capital as a "hybrid" system of control – which became fully visible only in the twentieth century – were as yet hidden from theoretical scrutiny'.[170] Nevertheless, Marx remains a crucial point of reference for Mészáros's thought.

Alongside Mészáros and the above-mentioned Argentinian-Mexican philosopher, Enrique Dussel, whose theoretical output continues to be received in Latin America (and beyond), there are further intellectuals worth registering here as exerting a certain influence on the contemporary Marxist discussion in Latin America. Thus the German social scientist, Heinz Dieterich, who lives in Mexico, deserves mention at this point: he is considered the visionary behind the project for a 'socialism of the twenty-first century' (according to Dieterich, such a project is to have a grassroots democratic configuration);[171] such a project is also invoked by the President of Venezuela, Hugo Chávez.[172]

Another thinker worthy of mention is Marta Harnecker, a philosopher originating from Chile. Harnecker made a significant contribution to the dissemination and development of Marxist thought in Latin America in the 1960s and 1970s by publishing a textbook on the fundamental concepts of historical materialism; Harnecker's work was considerably influenced by Althusser's 'structuralist Marxism'.[173] Numerous editions of Harnecker's book were produced, and in total approximately one million copies are in circulation in the Spanish-speaking world. Reception of this work continues to this day. After Pinochet's military coup in 1973, Harnecker fled to Cuba and worked as a historian of the Latin American Left and as an observer of its political development.[174] The thrust of her thinking in relation to Marxism can be encapsulated in the proposition that the updating of Marxist theory represents an important theoretical challenge.

---

170   Ibid.

171   See Dieterich 2006, pp. 65 ff.

172   One of the fiercest critics of Dieterich is the British Trotskyist, Alan Woods, who is evidently attempting to gain political and theoretical influence within the process of the 'Bolivarian Revolution' in Venezuela. For the critique of Dieterich, see Woods 2008.

173   See Harnecker 1969. Harnecker also produced a popular guide to *Capital* (Harnecker and Lapidus 1972). This book consists of three parts, two of which are authored by Harnecker; the third part is a translation of a Soviet textbook from 1929, which addresses the fundamental concepts of *Capital*.

174   See Harnecker 1999.

A further theorist to be cited here is the Irishman, John Holloway, who lives and lectures in Mexico. Holloway's approach is oriented towards a theory of revolution.[175] The Irish thinker draws on Marx's critique of political economy[176] as well as on *operaismo* in the context of his own distinctive combination of critical perspectives: Holloway's theory is informed by both the theory of fetishism and a theory of struggle. Holloway is engaged in a reorientation of Marxist thought, as is given expression in his critique of the 'tradition of "scientific Marxism"'; Holloway contends that the latter is blind to the fetishism problematic. A decisive factor influencing Holloway's thought is his background in the circle of theorists involved in the international 'Open Marxism' project.[177] This international Marxist theory project developed in the 1990s with a programmatic orientation towards the interconnection between theory and practice, and was characterised by an emancipatory perspective.[178] (The 'Open Marxism' project was at least in part influenced by the West German New Marx-Reading, or more precisely, by the works of Backhaus and Reichelt).[179] Holloway's intellectual approach, which is informed by a theory of emancipation, has certainly resonated with a minority within the counter-globalisation movement.

Some of the Marx-interpreters who can be grouped under the rubric of international Trotskyism[180],* also relate to the counter-globalisation movement.

---

175 See Holloway 2002. On Holloway, see also Elbe 2006.

176 For Holloway's view of Marx's critique of political economy, see also Holloway 2001.

177 On the 'Open Marxism' project, see, among other works, Altamira 2006, pp. 181 ff.

178 See Bonefeld, Gunn, Holloway and Psychopedis 1995.

179 This becomes evident from a consideration of, among other writings, Bonefeld's study on the significance of the Marxian concept of critique. See Bonefeld 2001, pp. 53 ff. Among the aspects foregrounded by Bonefeld, a German representative of the 'Open Marxism' project, in his approach to reading Marx, are those of form theory and fetish critique.

180 The Belgian economist, Ernest Mandel (1923–95), ranked as one of the best-known Trotskyist interpreters of Marx's critique of political economy in the 1960s and 1970s; his work was widely disseminated internationally (see, among other works, Mandel 1962; Mandel 1970; Mandel 1976a; and Mandel 1991). Jan-Willem Stutje recently produced a biography of Mandel, which also deals with the Belgian theorist's contacts to the West German and French student movements of the 1960s (see Stutje 2007). As one of the leading protagonists of Western European Trotskyism, Mandel stood critically opposed in political terms both to the 'Moscow orthodoxy' and to the communist parties in Western Europe, and explicitly understood himself as a representative of an undogmatic, open Marxism (see Mandel and Agnoli 1980). In the FRG, however, there were vehement criticisms of Mandel's economic theory formation from an early stage (see Bader, Bischoff, Ganssmann, Goldschmidt, Hoffmann and Riehn 1970).

* Mandel 1991 contains German translations of Mandel's introductions to the three volumes

These include the French philosopher, Daniel Bensaïd (a member of the *Ligue Communiste Révolutionnaire*), the Brazilian or Franco-Brazilian philosopher, eco-socialist and Marxism researcher, Michael Löwy (also a member of the *Ligue Communiste Révolutionnaire*), as well as the British social scientist, Alex Callinicos (member of the Socialist Workers' Party). Callinicos engaged with the counter-globalisation movement in the form of his *Anti-Capitalist Manifesto*.[181] As he declared in 1983, his underlying concern in his engagement with Marx is to rescue the latter 'from the distortions he has suffered'.[182] In the context of his engagement with Marxian theory, Callinicos more recently criticised the 'New Dialectic' approach of the British Marx-interpreter, Christopher Arthur (see below).[183] For his part, Bensaïd grasps Marxian theory neither in the sense of a philosophy of history, nor in the sense of a sociological theory of class or an economic science, but rather as a kind of critical theory of social struggle and transformation of the world.[184] As regards Löwy: beyond his research into the historical development of Latin American Marxism, the Brazilian Trotskyist has engaged with Marx's theory of revolution, among other themes.[185] In relation to the recent development in Latin America, Löwy maintains that the *Zapatista* movement has inherited the historical legacy of Che Guevara and liberation theology, among other traditions. In Löwy's assessment, the 'Bolivarian Revolution' under Hugo Chávez draws on not only Símon Bolívar (the liberator of South America from the colonial yoke and visionary thinker who strove to unify the continent), but also Marx and Engels, Luxemburg, Trotsky, Mariategui and Guevara. The question of whether and to what extent this is true cannot be addressed here. What is clear, however, is that the Marx-interpreters referred to here cannot be reckoned to have exerted more than a slight influence on the international counter-globalisation movement overall.

To conclude this section, a brief summary: the historical point of departure of the present exposition was the international rise of socialist movements, particularly in the 1960s. During the course of this political ferment, there was probably a more intensive reception of Marxian theory than ever before. Marx-

---

of *Capital* (see Mandel 1976b, Mandel 1978 and Mandel 1981), along with a foreword and afterword.

181   See Callinicos 2003.

182   Callinicos 2004a, p. 11. There is also a shorter, general introductory presentation of Marxian theory in Callinicos 2007, pp. 78 ff.

183   See Callinicos 2005a, pp. 41 ff.

184   See Bensaïd 2002, p. 12.

185   See Löwy 2003.

ism was to large extent de-dogmatised. From the mid- to late 1970s onwards, a debate developed – particularly in Western Europe – over the (alleged) 'crisis of Marxism'. From the 1980s onwards, however, new opportunities arose for Marxist thought to have an impact in other parts of the world (Latin America, South Korea). In the People's Republic of China, certain tendencies towards de-dogmatisation emerged within Marxist theory formation during the Deng Xiaoping era. Since the end of 'Marxism as a mass ideology' that was signalled by the epochal watershed of 1989–90, Marx-oriented thought has been marginalised to a large extent within the sphere defined by the tension between theory and politics, but it is still present: since the 1990s, it has retained a presence in the milieu around the international counter-globalisation movement.

The Further Development of the Marx Debate since the 1960s: A Survey

The intensive reception of Marx's critique of political economy in the postwar period was prefigured by the work of significant historical precursors in the period before the Second World War. Notable contributions in this context include: Rubin's research into value theory in the Soviet Union in the 1920s; Samezō Kuruma's discussion in interwar Japan of the problematic of Marx's plans for the architectonic of his critique of political economy, among other themes; the theoretical disputes around Hajime Kawakami and Kazuo Fukumoto; and finally, during the period of the Weimar Republic, Henryk Grossmann's treatment of various issues including the problematic of Marx's plans for the architectonic of his critique of political economy. Numerous other examples could doubtlessly be cited here. Disregarding these historical precursors, however, it can be established that there was a significant upturn in terms of theoretically sophisticated, systematic and differentiated discussion of the critique of political economy, particularly in the postwar period: this was the case in Japan, in Western Europe, in the socialist countries of Europe (in the Soviet Union in particular, and somewhat later in the GDR), and finally, also in West Germany, as well as in the Anglo-Saxon world (from the 1960s and above all from the 1970s on) and, more markedly than ever before, in Latin America from the 1960s and 1970s on.

A survey is given here, from the perspective of the history of theory, of the development of the international reception and further elaboration of the Marxian critique of political economy from the 1960s to the present. In this survey, reference is made to the existence of determinate research fields and to theses which have played an important role in the formation of theory in different countries; various theoretical currents and schools of thought in individual regions of the world are presented; and, within this context, it is crucial to address the international transfer of theory and the way in which theories refer to each other across national and linguistic boundaries.

1   West Germany[1]

Since West German theoretical approaches after 1980 are considered in detail within the in-depth thematic examination of the historical development of the international discussion on Marx which is undertaken in the third part of the present study, I concentrate here primarily on the exposition of the West German debate of the 1960s and 1970s. So as not to pre-empt the later exposition, the later theoretical development is merely briefly outlined and periodised here. However, the particular emphasis on the 1960s and 1970s at this juncture should in no way be read as an indication that little or no progress has been made in the theoretical debate in the subsequent period up to the present. On the contrary, it was only later – from the point of view of the history of theory – that the West German debate experienced its highpoint.

The rediscovery and reappropriation of Marx's 'mature' critique of political economy was the most important task that presented itself in the 1960s – the discussion of Marx having been brutally terminated by National Socialism, and having been subsequently neglected to a large extent in favour of the focus on Marx's early writings that typified the postwar period in West Germany. West German engagement with Marx received an effective impetus towards further development from outside the FRG – namely from an exile in the USA, Roman Rosdolsky, who composed a widely-read commentary on Marx's *Grundrisse*.[2]

Rosdolsky – a Marx-researcher originating from Galicia, who was aware of the destruction of the Rubin current in the Soviet Union in Stalin's time,[3] and who was nearly killed himself as an anti-fascist resistance fighter in the concentration camps of Auschwitz, Ravensbrück and Oranienburg – disclosed the motivation behind his *magnum opus* as follows: he himself was by profession neither an economist, nor a philosopher. He would not have dared to

> write a commentary on the Rough Draft if a school of Marxist theoreticians still existed today – as it did for the first thirty years of this century – which would have been better equipped to carry out this task. However, the last generation of notable Marxist theoreticians for the most part fell

---

1   In the present study, the Western part of Berlin is included within the concept of 'West Germany'.

2   See Rosdolsky 1977.

3   See Rosdolsky 1977, p. 570.

victim to Hitler's and Stalin's terror, which interrupted the further development of the body of Marxist ideas for several decades. Given these
circumstances I feel obliged to offer this work to the reading public – as
defective and incomplete as it might be – in the hope that a new generation will follow for whom, once more, Marx's theory will be a living source
both of knowledge and the political practice which this knowledge directs.[4]

This hope of Rosdolsky's was to be fulfilled, not least as a result of his own
theoretical contribution. (He himself did not live to experience this, as he
died in 1967 in exile in Detroit, whereas his major work was only published
posthumously the following year in West Germany).

Whereas in Japan, a differentiated discussion around Marx's method in his
critique of political economy had soon begun to develop again a short time after
1945 (not only drawing on the state of the discussion of the interwar period, but
also going beyond it), a comparable development failed at first to materialise
in West Germany. Here it was a matter of bringing to life a debate about *Capital*
which had reached no more than a preliminary stage before 1933,[5] and which
had then been violently broken off and had remained largely non-existent in
the intervening period.

In the 1950s, during the peak of Rosdolsky's work on his monograph which
was published in 1968, a correspondence developed between Rosdolsky and
Korsch. The latter ranked among the most important representatives of a critical Marxism in opposition to the 'official' Marxism-Leninism of the interwar
period, and likewise had access to one of the few copies of the *Grundrisse* to
have reached the West after it was first published in the Soviet Union in 1939/41.
Michael Buckmiller writes of the discussion between Rosdolsky and Korsch: 'In
December 1950, Rosdolsky was so advanced in his treatment of the *Grundrisse*
that he intended to start drafting his commentary and his "recomposition" and
requested that Korsch ... act as a critical proofreader and discussant – above

---

4 Rosdolsky 1977, p. xiv.
5 In the 1920s, Grossmann had identified the task of reconstructing the underlying method
   in *Capital*. However, he drew up a sobering balance sheet in relation to the contemporary
   state of research: 'My view is that the unsatisfactory state of the literature on Marx is ultimately rooted in the fact – which will appear strange to some – that until today no one
   has proposed any ideas at all, let alone any clear ideas, about Marx's *method* of investigation. There has been a general tendency to cling to the results of the theory ... In all this
   the *method* has been totally ignored' (Grossmann 1992, p. 29). On Grossmann, see Kuhn
   2007.

all in relation to providing support in the interpretation of Hegel'.[6] Rosdolsky's lament – that he was merely able to address the problematic of the Marxian relation to Hegelian logic, which he himself considered to be very important, but was unable to theorise it in any greater depth – rings true in the published version of Rosdolsky's monograph.

Rosdolsky's study on the *Grundrisse* was almost completed by the turn of the year 1953/4. In 1953, an investigation into the problematic of 'capital in general' in Marx, which was included in the monograph, was published in the Swiss journal, *Kyklos*.[7] This aroused little sustained attention, in contrast to the publication of his book in 1968. It would appear that the German-language – and particularly the West German – Marx discourse of the 1950s was not yet ripe for a broad and intensive discussion of methodological problems of this kind. The left-socialist political scientist, Wolfgang Abendroth, to whom Rosdolsky had given the manuscript for his book in the 1950s, characterised the situation as follows in a 1957 letter: 'The Marx discussion ought to be restarted in Germany in a serious manner, and not in a merely philosophically or theologically meditative way'.[8] Thus the question can be posed as to whether, against the backdrop of the dominance of the West German discourse on Marx's early writings and in particular of the Marx debate within the milieu of the Evangelical Academies, Rosdolsky's study could have had such an inspirational and sustained effect in the 1950s and early 1960s as it did from 1968 onwards. In any case, Rosdolsky only revised his almost-finished monograph and made it ready for printing shortly before his death in 1967. Core substantive theses from Rosdolsky's work will be considered in part three of the present study; here, it is sufficient to note that Rosdolsky's monograph contributed to the opening of new thematic horizons for West German engagement with Marx in the following decades and to the demarcation of important problem areas for further research. This is especially the case vis-à-vis the debate on the 'problematic of Marx's planned architectonic of his critique of political economy' in relation to the six-volume structure he originally conceived; it also applies to the debate on the structuring concept of 'capital in general', but also to the discussion around the genesis of Marx's *magnum opus*.

The *Capital*-debate associated with the student movement of the late 1960s must be considered in part against the backdrop of the interpretations of Marx that were developed within the milieu of the Frankfurt Institute for Social

---

6   Buckmiller 2006, p. 310.

7   Rosdolsky 1953, pp. 153 ff.

8   Wolfgang Abendroth, in a letter cited in Buckmiller 2006, p. 316.

Research at the end of the 1950s and beginning of the 1960s.[9],* Of note in this context is first and foremost the dissertation on the concept of nature in Marx written between 1957 and 1960 by Alfred Schmidt, a student of Horkheimer; this work was widely disseminated in the years following its publication in 1962. Although Schmidt's study cannot be characterised thematically as an intensive critical engagement with the specifics of Marx's critique of political economy comparable to those subsequently undertaken by Backhaus and Reichelt, it represented an important impetus for the ensuing debate on Marx, as is reflected in Schmidt's 1971 postscript:

> It was one of the first attempts to draw on the politico-economic writings of middle-period and mature Marx, in particular Capital and the

---

9   It is worth mentioning in connection with the engagement with Marx within the milieu of the Frankfurt Institute for Social Research that two different sources highlight the theoretical influence of Adorno's reading of Marx independently of one another. Ernst-Theodor Mohl writes the following: 'In an exclusive tutorial at the beginning of the 1960s, he [Adorno] explained to me the section on fetish and the subject-object inversion which follows from it in such a way that I was subsequently able to avoid taking an economistically foreshortened perspective on Marx's critique of capitalism' (Mohl 2002, pp. 18 f.). Hans-Georg Backhaus states the following in relation to his notes from a lecture by Adorno which were published in 1997 (see Backhaus 1997c): 'The notes from the summer of 1962 published in the appendix to this volume might afford an insight into the intellectual and political atmosphere which gave the impetus to a new Marx-reading in the early to mid-1960s, and which also played a part in shaping the intellectual background to the protest movement' (Backhaus 1997b, p. 29). In 1974, Backhaus made the following criticism of the Frankfurt School: 'The fact that the Frankfurt School's concept of society and ideology can only be understood on the basis of Marx's labour theory of value, whereas this value-theoretical dimension was completely neglected in the German positivism dispute as well as in the way this dispute is presented in the literature, indicates however that Adorno and Horkheimer themselves reflected the foundations of critical theory in the labour theory of value in a way that was methodologically inadequate. Although, in Adorno and Horkheimer's opinion, the basic concepts of Marxian value theory transcend value theory as a specialist economic discipline, it is astonishing how little care was taken in the interpretation of these concepts which were fundamental for the sociology and philosophy of the Frankfurt School. Taking into account the extraordinary function that is attributed to a single concept, namely value or social labour, it is all the more surprising that Adorno and Horkheimer should completely ignore the sociologically and philosophically relevant object lesson in the labour theory of value – i.e. the value-form analysis' (Backhaus 1997a, pp. 75 f.). In the meantime, a series of studies on the reception of Marx by Adorno and by Horkheimer has appeared (Hafner 2005; Ritsert 1998; Blank 2002).

*   On Adorno's reception of Marx's critique of political economy, see also recent studies by Werner Bonefeld (Bonefeld 2014 and Bonefeld 2016) and Dirk Braunstein (Braunstein 2011).

... Grundrisse, for a 'philosophical' interpretation of Marx's life-work. In doing this, the book opposed the widespread Western European, often neo-Existentialist, tendency of the 1950s to reduce Marx's thought to an unhistorical 'anthropology' centred on the alienation problematic of the early writings (in particular the Paris Manuscripts of 1844).[10],*

According to Schmidt, the focus on the 'philosophical depth' of the young Marx had served to keep the critic of the bourgeois economy at arm's length. The Marx-reading of the 1960s was indeed characterised in part by the attempt to overcome the deficits of the relatively one-sided interpretation centred on the early writings which had been predominant until that point.

One factor which set the course for the new Frankfurt interpretation of Marx which burgeoned in the 1960s, and which by the 1970s – if not sooner – had developed into an important theoretical configuration, was the theoretical legacy of the Frankfurt School. Whereas Engels's 'dialectic of nature' and in particular the development of Marxian or Marxist theory into a proletarian 'worldview' – a development prefigured by Engels's *Anti-Dühring* – were of decisive significance for traditional Marxism, the representatives of a younger generation attempted to tap *Capital*, long stylised as a classic and yet seldom given a rigorous reading, and especially the 1857–8 *Rohentwurf*,** which had previously been overlooked to a great extent. This occurred precisely under conditions in which a theoretical ballast that had encumbered most attempts to engage with Marxism up to that point was being shaken off: the ballast of the history of the reception of Marx under the worldview Marxisms of the Second and Third Internationals. In 1978, Backhaus wrote the following:

---

10   Schmidt 2014, p. 9. A further West German author to examine the *Grundrisse* in the 1960s, Friedrich Tomberg, could not be considered a genuine representative of the 'Frankfurt tendency' of Marx-interpretation (see Tomberg 1969, pp. 187 ff.).

*   In the English-language edition (Schmidt 2014), this quotation occurs in the preface (written 1970). It should be noted that Schmidt's formulation in his postscript to the 1971 German edition is slightly different: there, he characterises 'the tendency, widespread in the Western Europe of the 1950s, to reduce Marx's thought to an ahistorical "anthropology" centred on the alienation problematic of the early writings' as being 'tinted by Existentialism and also by theology' (see Schmidt 1993, p. 207).

**   The German title of the *Grundrisse* is *Grundrisse der Kritik der politischen Ökonomie (Rohentwurf). 1857–1858*. This is rendered in English as 'Outlines of the Critique of Political Economy (Rough Draft), 1857–58'.

The 'New Marx-Reading' emerged within the milieu of the Frankfurt School and is thus owed above all to [the latter's] critique of the theory of reflection, of the dialectic of nature, and of the base-superstructure theorem. It relates in an orthodox way only vis-à-vis Marx's critique of political economy, and in a thoroughly revisionist way vis-à-vis certain core philosophical conceptions of Marx and Engels. On account of this ambivalent position, the 'logical' current of *Capital* interpretation could be termed as *neo-orthodox*.[11]

It is thus a matter here of a selective appropriation of the classics on the part of the leading theoretical exponents of the Frankfurt reading of Marx of the 1960s and 1970s, and one which was influenced by the interpretative schema of the Frankfurt School around Adorno and Horkheimer. The formative influences exerted by an older theoretical current constituted a decisive precondition which enabled a 'neo-orthodoxy', which was simultaneously orthodox and revisionist, to position itself against the traditional Marxist theoretical orthodoxy of both Western and Eastern provenance. However, Backhaus abandoned this 'neo-orthodoxy' in the third part of his *Materialien zur Rekonstruktion der Marxschen Werttheorie*,* published in 1978, since he now considered an 'orthodox' position vis-à-vis Marx's critique of political economy to be inappropriate given the (alleged) problems that could be identified within it.

A further factor which influenced the Frankfurt *Capital* reading of the 1960s was a fortuitous discovery made by Backhaus in around 1963 – the doyen of the Frankfurt interpretation of Marx was a student at the time – in the library of Hermann Brill, a social-democratic politician who had died a few years previously. The discovery in question was the first edition of *Capital*, published in 1867, which was scarcely-known at the time (at least in West Germany);[12] 'even at first glance', wrote Backhaus in retrospect, 'categorial differences were apparent in the formation of concepts in, and also in the questions posed by, value theory – differences that are only hinted at in the second edition. This older text had been completely ignored in a hundred years of discussion of

---

11   Backhaus 1997a, p. 138.
*   'Materials towards the reconstruction of Marx's value-theory', republished in Backhaus 1997a.
12   In the GDR, the popularised appendix on the analysis of the value-form had been republished by 1955, and in Japan a reprint of the first edition of *Capital* had appeared in or before 1959. At the time, these events in publishing history did not attract the attention that they deserved within the reception of Marx in West Germany.

Marx's value theory ...'.[13] There are in fact notable differences between these two editions of the first volume of *Capital*. Eventually the Frankfurt political scientist, Iring Fetscher, became aware of the newly discovered 1867 first edition of *Capital*, and included an excerpt on value theory in the Marx-Engels study edition, published in 1966, that he edited.[14] What might appear at first glance to be a mere anecdote from the 1960s reveals, on closer inspection, far-reaching theoretical consequences. Backhaus's chance discovery inaugurated a development in which the interpretation of differences in terms of value theory and value-form theory between these two editions of the first volume of *Capital*[15] – notable interpretations being proposed by a number of theorists ranging from Backhaus himself, via Gerhard Göhler, to Winfried Schwarz,[16] Michael Heinrich[17] and Christian Iber –[18] became a virtually 'classical' field of enquiry for the West German interpretation of *Capital*, through which central questions (the logical and the historical in Marx's exposition, the problematic of form-analysis and the theory of action, or the question of the popularisation of Marxian theory undertaken by Marx himself) could be discussed or broached.

A first highpoint of the new Frankfurt engagement with Marx's critique of political economy was attained in 1967 at the Frankfurt Congress to mark the centenary of the publication of the first edition of the first volume of *Capital*. Alfred Schmidt was once again centre-stage, and here, he succeeded in identifying a number of important themes which are still being taken up within *Capital*-interpretation to this day. This is the case, on the one hand, vis-à-vis the relation between Marx's early and mature work, which Schmidt determined as follows:

> Marx's methodological principle is to be used in relation to Marx's life's work itself – we should explain the anatomy of the ape from the anatomy of the human, and not vice versa. Marx and Engels' early writings, which were long considered to contain the original philosophical and humanist

---

13   Backhaus 1997b, p. 29.

14   See Fetscher 2006, p. 464.

15   For a contribution by a researcher from the former GDR on Marx's reworking of his value theory in the context of his preparation of the second edition of the first volume of *Capital*, see Lietz 2000.

16   See Schwarz 1987.

17   See Heinrich 1999a, pp. 226 ff. On Marx's analysis of the value-form, see also Heinrich 2008, pp. 104 ff. and 259 ff.

18   See Iber 2006.

content of Marxism, can only be completely understood on the basis of the historical and economic analysis of *Capital*.[19]

On the other hand, Schmidt emphasised Marx's concept of critique with regard to his project of the critique of political economy. Importantly, too, Schmidt conceived of the thought that Marx-interpretation would have to go 'constructively' beyond the immediacy of Marx's texts and the necessary philological work associated with them. Elements of a procedure of this kind can certainly be found in subsequent research that has been carried out. In addition, Schmidt argued that Marx's self-understanding – as important as this might be – remains often enough far behind 'that which Marx offers theoretically in his material analysis'.[20] It is perhaps no overstatement to claim that Schmidt's paper represents a kind of 'birth document' for what was a new phenomenon in postwar West Germany: the intensive and sophisticated engagement with the critique of political economy.

Since the 1960s, Backhaus and his research colleague, Reichelt, have placed a central focus on a specifically 'qualitative' problematic in Marx's work – a problematic upon which the engagement with Marx's critique of political economy must be concentrated, they argue. Backhaus argues that although Marx's critique of economic categories transcends the specialist discipline of economics, in fact the analysis of the value-form accomplishes a sublation* of the antinomies of economics as a specialised discipline. With his treatment of the problematic of the value-form and fetishism, which was published in 1969 within the framework of his widely received essay, 'On the Dialectics of the Value-Form', Backhaus paved the way for a part of the subsequent (West) German discussion on the critique of political economy.[21]

In 1969, Reichelt had criticised a foreshortened mode of reading of Marx's critique of political economy – i.e. the reading of the critique of political economy through the specialist discipline of economics.[22] If the beginnings of the first 'wave' of the new Frankfurt engagement with Marx can be traced back to Schmidt's monograph on the concept of nature in Marx, Reichelt's 1970 interpretation of Marx's value theory, money and capital marks its end. Reichelt's dissertation deals with the exposition elaborated by Marx for the explication

---

19   Schmidt 1968, p. 33.

20   Schmidt 1968, p. 32.

*   *Aufhebung* – a dialectical supersession.

21   See Backhaus 1980, pp. 91 ff. This essay is based on a dissertation completed in 1968.

22   See Reichelt 1969, p. 17 ff.

of economic categories, and represents an attempt to retrace a part of the progression of this exposition – or, more precisely, the movement from commodity and money to the most abstract form of capital. According to Reichelt, Marx insists upon a strict derivation of the genesis of economic forms.[23] Reichelt's work locates itself within the context of the international wave of readings of the *Grundrisse* of the 1960s and 1970s. Reichelt argues that it is more evident in the *Grundrisse* that 'the abstruse Hegelian mode of expression' is actually an integral component of Marxian critique. The intrication is so narrow between, on the one hand, the material circumstances which are traditionally considered to lie within the domain of economic science and, on the other, a form of exposition of these material circumstances which is oriented towards Hegelian logic, that the one can no longer be thematised in isolation from the other.[24]

The emphatic reference to the *Grundrisse* would remain constitutive for Backhaus's and Reichelt's later critical engagement with Marx's critique of political economy. Marx's subsequent texts dedicated to the critique of political economy, starting with *A Contribution to the Critique of Political Economy* (published in 1859), were popularised by Marx himself,[25] and his method was 'concealed' – this is the general tenor of Backhaus's and Reichelt's research since the 1990s. In this process, according to Backhaus and Reichelt, Marx obscured essential moments of his critique of political economy. Conversely, this thesis implies a positive revaluation of the *Grundrisse* and the *Urtext* of 1858.[26]

Within the German-speaking countries, Backhaus's series of essays from the 1970s, *Materialien zur Rekonstruktion der Marxschen Werttheorie*, in particular the second part from 1975, founded the interpretative current of the 'monetary theory of value', or of the reading of Marxian value theory as a critique of pre-monetary theories of value. Backhaus stated his view succinctly as follows: 'Marx's value theory is conceived as a *critique* of pre-monetary theories of value – on the level of exposition corresponding to simple circulation, it is essentially the *theory of money*'.[27] Backhaus ascribed a strictly 'logical' character to Marx's exposition of his critique of political economy and criticised the

---

23   See Reichelt 2001, p. 22. The first edition of this book was published in 1970.

24   Reichelt 2001, p. 21. For Reichelt's later perspective on the *Grundrisse*, see Reichelt 2007, pp. 87 ff.

25   This is known as the 'popularisation thesis of Backhaus and Reichelt'.

26   Dieter Wolf has undertaken an extensive attempt to refute Reichelt's more recent approaches to value theory and the theory of money (Wolf 2004).

27   Backhaus 1997a, p. 94.

'logical-historical' reading of Marx's exposition (which dates back to Engels),[28] although subsequently in 1978 he called his own views into question in this regard in the third part of *Materialien zur Rekonstruktion der Marxschen Werttheorie*.

In West Germany, including West Berlin, as Frieder Otto Wolf, Alexis Petrioli, Ingo Stützle and I have already shown elsewhere, a lively critical engagement 'could be registered not only with the Marxist "classics", but also with the contemporary understanding of *Capital* at home and abroad. Within the review columns of the journals *Sozialistische Politik*, *Internationale Wissenschaftliche Korrespondenz zur Geschichte der deutschen Arbeiterbewegung*, *Das Argument* and *Neue Kritik*, there were critical engagements'[29] with interpretations of Marx's critique of political economy which had been advanced by the Marburg sociologist Werner Hofmann, the Belgian Marxist and Trotskyist Ernest Mandel, the Halle-based Marx-researcher Wolfgang Jahn, the Czech philosopher Jindřich Zelený, the Marx-researcher Roman Rosdolsky, the Soviet/East German Marx-interpreters Vitaly Vygodsky and Walter Tuchscheerer, but also by Jürgen Habermas.[30] 'It is noticeable from the way that the works of Vygodsky, Tuchscheerer, Jahn and Zelený were taken up, that the *Capital*-reading by the student movement in the FRG, despite the latter's innovative potential, was not a purely "domestically cultivated" affair; rather, there was also a fruitful theory transfer from East to West which occurred parallel to the "internal" processes of theory formation'.[31] Furthermore, the question can be posed as to the possible influence of the Althusser School on the West German reception of Marx.[32] The West German Marx debate, which developed above all in the wake of the student movement, is not to be regarded as an isolated phenomenon. Within the international discussion – a discussion held on both sides of the 'Iron Curtain' – it rather represented an important intersection between its own theoretical approaches and those emanating from East and West.

An essential aspect of the engagement with the critique of political economy that took place during or immediately after the student movement was the reception of texts by Marx that had previously been neglected in West Ger-

---

28   Backhaus was not alone in researching Engels's engagement with Marx's critique of political economy in the FRG in the 1970s: compare Kittsteiner 1977.

29   Hoff, Petrioli, Stützle and Wolf 2006b, p. 26.

30   The following contributions exemplify the series of critical confrontations which are to be found in the above-cited periodicals between 1968 and 1970: Müller 1969a and Müller 1969b.

31   Hoff, Petrioli, Stützle and Wolf 2006b, p. 26.

32   Ingo Elbe comments on this question in Elbe 2010, pp. 48 ff.

many. Of particular note in this connection, alongside the republication in 1966 of the opening part of the above-mentioned 1867 first edition of *Capital*, is the considerable interest in the *Grundrisse* – an interest which burgeoned after 1968, not least due to the publication of Rosdolsky's monograph.[33] A further example that can be cited in this context is the *Results of the Immediate Process of Production*. After this text by Marx was first published in 1933 (in German and Russian), it was republished at the end of the 1960s in West Germany.

An intensive debate on *Capital* had developed in West Berlin with a brief time lag relative to the initially somewhat more advanced discussion in Frankfurt. Joachim Bischoff ranked as one of the most influential Marxist theorists in West Berlin in the 1970s; among the questions that Bischoff addressed in the context of his critical engagement with the problematic of dialectic was that of enquiry and exposition in Marx. While Bischoff ascribed a dialectical form to the exposition of the critique of political economy, he could not identify any indications of a contribution by the dialectical method in relation to the process of enquiry, which is concerned with the detection of an internal interconnection between economic forms.[34] The *'Projektgruppe Entwicklung des Marxschen Systems'* (*PEM*)* was formed within the milieu around Bischoff at the beginning of the 1970s. In addition to its interpretation of various drafts of Marx's theory of money,[35] the *PEM* would subsequently produce commentaries on *Theories of Surplus-Value* and other texts.[36]

Of great significance was the theoretical controversy over the fundamental status of *Theories of Surplus-Value* within Marx's *oeuvre* which was argued out in the 1970s between the West Berlin *PEM* and Marx researchers from the GDR, or more specifically from the milieu of the *Marx-Engels-Werke* (*MEW*) and *Marx-Engels-Gesamtausgabe* (*MEGA²*) publishing projects. As is well known, the *Theories of Surplus-Value* – which form a component of Marx's *1861–63*

---

33   Incidentally, a discussion of the *Grundrisse* is still taking place to this day – see Hafner and Huckenbeck 2008, pp. 267 ff.

34   See Bischoff 1973.

*   'Project Group: Development of Marx's System'.

35   See *Projektgruppe Entwicklung des Marxschen Systems* 1973. Elbe surmises that in this text the 'insertion of the money-form into the analysis of the value-form' was 'explicitly thematised and interpreted with regard to its significance for the course of the exposition in *Capital*' probably for the first time within the West German New Marx-Reading (see Elbe 2008, p. 214).

36   See, among other works, *Projektgruppe Entwicklung des Marxschen Systems* 1975 (this study will be engaged with below) and *Projektgruppe Entwicklung des Marxschen Systems* 1978.

Manuscripts (in the shape of Notebooks VI to XV, supplementary material being contained in subsequent notebooks, in particular Notebook XVIII) – represent Marx's most significant and best-known critical engagement with the history of political economy. Given that from the summer of 1865 (and perhaps earlier), Marx planned to divide his main work of critique of political economy into four volumes – the fourth of which was to contain his historiography of the-ory –[37] *Theories of Surplus-Value* has since come to be known within certain interpretations of Marx as the fourth volume of *Capital*. Indeed, *Theories of Surplus-Value* is given a corresponding subtitle in the *MEW* edition.[38] Research-ers in the milieu around the *MEGA²* project defended in principle the view according to which *Theories of Surplus-Value* did actually represent a text that, taking into account its character as a 'rough draft', corresponded (more or less) to the fourth volume envisaged by Marx in his later plans. The *PEM* advanced a different conception, which indicated that the designation of *Theories of Surplus-Value* as 'the fourth volume of *Capital*' was inappropriate, given that the text had an essentially different character. According to the *PEM*, *Theories of Surplus-Value* is to be regarded not least as a document of Marx's process of enquiry in the context of his critical engagement with the history of polit-ical economy; by working on *Theories of Surplus-Value*, Marx had deepened his knowledge both of the history of this science and, crucially, of the structure of the object itself. The general significance of this textual treatment by the *PEM* for the historical development of the reception of Marx in the FRG resided in the approach taken by the theory-collective: a given text by Marx was inter-rogated with regard to its specific character; this allowed the *PEM*, within its critical interpretative engagement with the Marxian *oeuvre*, to go beyond the dubious practice of reducing Marx's texts to a repository of quotations.

Alongside those of Bischoff and the *PEM*, other orientations and projects were represented within the Marxist debate on *Capital* which took place in West Berlin in the 1970s. In 1974, Wolfgang Fritz Haug's introductory lectures to *Capital* were published for the first time;[39] these were originally conceived of as events organised at the university to accompany the reading groups that were the expression of an innovative 'reception of *Capital* which was taking place on a massive scale'.[40] Among the core aspects focused on by Haug in his lectures were the problem of the beginning of Marx's exposition and the prob-lematic of the value-form. One of Haug's concerns was 'to demonstrate that

---

37   See Marx 1987a, p. 173.
38   See Marx 1965, Marx 1967, and Marx 1968.
39   See Haug 1985.
40   Haug 1985, p. 6.

the unity of "the logical" and "the historical" is fundamental for the method of the critique of political economy".[41] A similar motif was also of crucial importance in the reception of Marx's critique of political economy by a further well-known representative of West Berlin Marxism in the 1970s: the psychologist Klaus Holzkamp drew on the traditional 'logical-historical' reading of Marx's critique of political economy within the context of his theoretical argument with Bischoff, thus pursuing what is in my opinion an approach which is highly problematic in objective terms.[42]

Another West Berlin group project consisted in a critical engagement with the critique of political economy that was tailored to a reconstruction of Marx's approaches to crisis theory.[43] Despite their assessment that Marx's critique of political economy 'has a broad scope and a high level of explanatory power', Bader et al. represent the view that there are certainly also deficiencies in *Capital* with regard to the way that determinate economic laws of motion and their internal interconnection are grounded. On their view, Marx in no way arrived at a systematic exposition of crises beyond his wide-ranging initial approaches. Bader et al. endeavoured to provide a methodological foundation to their study of Marx's various approaches to crisis theory. In this context, core elements of the Marxian method were to be explained with reference to the philosophy of Hegel. Bader et al's emphatic reference to Hegel is in line with a general tendency among sections of the West German debate on Marx.

Alongside the two centres of West German engagement with the Marxian critique of political economy (Frankfurt and West Berlin), corresponding reading movements were also formed in several 'sub-centres' in the 1970s. The interpretation of Marx in Konstanz (around Volkbert Roth)[44] was influenced by the theoretical discussion in Frankfurt around Backhaus and Reichelt, and soon established connections with the Anglo-Saxon debate on Marx (the 'Sydney-Konstanz Project').[45] In Hannover, there emerged a *Projektgruppe zur Kritik der*

---

41   Haug 1985, p. 9.

42   See Holzkamp 1974. Elmar Altvater was considered to be a further protagonist of West Berlin Marxism in the 1970s and 1980s, which as a whole was relatively heterogeneous. For many years, Altvater organised Marx seminars at the Otto Suhr Institute for Political Science at the Free University of Berlin, and eventually summarised the results of this academic activity (see Altvater 1998).

43   See Bader et al. 1975a and Bader et al. 1975b.

44   See von Holt, Pasero and Roth 1974.

45   The orientation, in terms of its content, of research in Konstanz and Sydney will be addressed below in the context of the survey of the historical development of the Anglo-Saxon debate.

politischen Ökonomie'.* According to this group's interpretation, *Capital* investigates the form-determinacies of the capitalist mode of production, and these
are to be characterised as historically specific. Marx's argumentation is accordingly to be grasped as a form-analysis of capital. Furthermore, this group of
authors refers to the high level of abstraction of Marx's exposition in *Capital*,
pointing out that the latter is exposition of the general, lawlike structures of
capitalism.[46] According to the 'Hannoverian' interpretation of the progression
of Marx's exposition, the economic categories within it are not to be 'incorporated externally on the basis of empirical observation, rather they are to be
developed from one another in the ascent from the abstract to the concrete'.[47]
Responding to the impact of the sharp increase in interest in Marx in the wake
of the West German student movement, some 'professional philosophers' haz-
arded a 'guest performance' in Marx-interpretation. Alongside studies by Hans
Friedrich Fulda[48] and Michael Theunissen,[49] a notable contribution in this
context is that of Rüdiger Bubner, according to whom two logical elements
speak in favour of a convergence between Hegel's *Logic* and Marx's *Capital*. In
this connection, Bubner refers to the problem of presupposition and the question of the determination of relations between categories.[50]

In the mid-1980s, Egbert Dozekal proposed the thesis that a development
had taken place within the West German theoretical debate from the late 1960s
into the 1980s: this evolution had led from the project of the reconstruction of
Marxian theory to the proclamation of a 'crisis of Marxism' and the debates
associated with the latter.[51] However, it should be noted that on closer inspection, Dozekal's thesis of the development of the West German debate on Marx
and Marxism in this direction alone proves to be overstated. The 'spectacular'
proclamation of a 'crisis of Marxism' by French and Italian Marxists from the
mid-1970s were not without a certain resonance in the West German discussion
of Marxism, yet here there was still a whole series of theorists who continued
to work assiduously, and in a theoretically productive way, on detailed research
into Marx's critique of political economy, and on opening it up for further elaboration. In relation to the period between the end of the 1970s and the beginning of the 1980s, the monographs of Gerhard Stapelfeldt, Winfried Schwarz,

---

*   'Project Group on the Critique of Political Economy'.

46   See *Projektgruppe zur Kritik der politischen Ökonomie* 1973, p. 13.

47   *Projektgruppe zur Kritik der politischen Ökonomie* 1973, p. 24.

48   See, among other works, Fulda 1974.

49   See Theunissen 1974.

50   See Bubner 1973, p. 73.

51   See Dozekal 1985.

Fred Schrader and Gerhard Göhler in particular deserve a cursory consideration here (some aspects of their approaches to the interpretation of Marx are
referred to in more detail in Part 3 of the present study).

Towards the end of the 1970s, Winfried Schwarz presented a structural-
theoretical investigation into the genesis of Marx's *opus* on the critique of
political economy, and attempted a critical 'examination' of Rosdolsky's interpretation of the destiny of the concept of 'capital in general' through the various
iterations of Marx's critical project.[52] Schwarz arrived at the conclusion that
Marx did in fact retain this concept, with the qualification that it was now
placed under the dominance of a new structuring principle. Probably the most
meticulous West German investigation into the period from 1850 to 1858 within
Marx's process of enquiry and elaboration of the critique of political economy
is that presented by Fred Schrader in 1980,[53] at a time when Marx's London
notebooks (1850–3) had not yet been published in *MEGA*[2] (indeed, at the time
of publishing, this process still remains to be completed).* Schrader focused
particularly on Marx's research notebooks and the critical engagement with
political economy on questions relating to the theory of money, among others,
that these contain; he also attempted to demonstrate the effect that Marx's critical engagement with political economy in these notebooks had on his elaboration of the *Grundrisse* manuscripts. In addition, he provided an interpretation
of Marx's 'solutions' to the 'problem of the beginning of the exposition' both in
the run up to composing *A Contribution to the Critique of Political Economy* and
in the latter text itself. Within this context, Schrader ascribes a decisive significance to Marx's excerpts from Benjamin Franklin in 1858. At almost the same
time as Schrader, Gerhard Stapelfeldt grappled with 'the problem of the beginning' (of the exposition) in Marx.[54] Stapelfeldt attempted a reconstruction of
Marx's value theory, or value-form theory, and an interpretation of the structure
of the value-theoretical argumentation in Marx's critique of political economy.
Here, in turn, there is a thematic parallel to Gerhard Göhler's monograph. The
latter undertakes an enquiry into the different types of dialectical exposition
in Marx's theory of the commodity, value, the value-form and the process of
exchange.[55] To summarise, the development that the West German debate on
Marx underwent in the late 1970s and early 1980s deserves to be understood –

---

52   See Schwarz 1978.
53   See Schrader 1980.
*   This remains the case at the time of the publication of the present English-language
      edition.
54   See Stapelfeldt 1979.
55   See Göhler 1980.

beyond the thesis of a 'crisis of Marxism' – as representing considerable progress in theoretical terms (i.e. progress immanent within the theory itself); this is true in the sense that further research was carried out into Marx's texts on the critique of political economy, and these were opened up for further elaboration.

A further stage in the engagement with Marx's critique of political economy – and one which signalled the way for the current debate – spans from approximately the middle of the 1980s to the early 1990s. Within this period, Dieter Wolf presented a comprehensive investigation into the dialectical contradiction in *Capital*,[56] while a work by Helmut Brentel located the core content of Marx's understanding of his object in a specific form-theory.[57] Michael Heinrich also presented an understanding of Marx's critique of political economy above all in the sense of a scientific revolution.[58,*] Heinrich's reception and redefinition of the concept of 'theoretical field', which originates from the Althusser School, played a decisive role in this context. According to Heinrich's interpretation, Marx broke with the theoretical field of political economy; in carrying out this break, Marx was largely (but not entirely) successful. The approaches of Brentel and Heinrich will be considered in detail in Part 3 of the present study.

Since its foundation in 1992, important debates around the critique of political economy have been carried out within the *Marx-Gesellschaft*.[59,**] Discussions within this society facilitated an understanding of the dissensus in relation to content between the various lines of interpretation within the German-language debate on Marx; no consensus could be reached over central questions, however.[60] The question of whether it is possible to speak of a dimension

---

56 See Wolf 2002. This is a revised edition of a book originally published in 1985 under the title *Ware und Geld: Der dialektische Widerspruch im 'Kapital'*.

57 See Brentel 1989. On Brentel's theoretical approach, see also Behrens 1993.

58 See Heinrich 1999a. This is an expanded and revised edition of a text which was first published in 1991.

*   A sixth edition of Heinrich's work was published in 2014. An English edition is forthcoming, to be published in the Historical Materialism Book Series by Brill and Haymarket Books under the title *The Science of Value: Marx's Critique of Political Economy between Scientific Revolution and Classical Tradition* (translated by Alexander Locascio).

59 See Hafner 1999.

** The *Marx-Gesellschaft*, or Marx Society, was established in Frankfurt in 1992 as an initiative by Hans-Georg Backhaus, Diethard Behrens and Hans-Joachim Blank, and has provided a forum for critical Marx-related theoretical discussion over the following decades.

60 In any case, the purpose of the debates was not to dispel all scientific dissension. In one of the discussions, Michael Heinrich made the following comments: 'I also doubt whether we

corresponding to a philosophy of history in Marx's thinking (in the critique of political economy, as well as elsewhere) led to a controversy within the *Marx-Gesellschaft* in the 1990s. In this context, Thomas Lutz Schweier represented the view that Marx, in his own self-understanding, was no philosopher of history. Schweier rejected as inapposite the point of view according to which Marx was construed as a philosopher of history.[61] Heinrich adopted a more deliberative position: 'Today, the assertion of a historical determinism appears rather as a cause for embarrassment (at least within scientific discussion)'.[62] Heinrich adds that undogmatic Marxists are therefore keen to ascribe historical determinism to a foreshortened reception of Marx, thus absolving Marx himself of any defect. However, Heinrich reached the conclusion that in Marx's post-1857 work on the systematic critique of political economy, there are also points of view which can be identified that correspond to a philosophy of history or to a historical determinism. 'Such passages cannot lay claim to a scientific content corresponding to that of the critique of political economy, however'.[63] According to Heinrich, the excerpts in question are merely isolated statements or additions to declamatory parts of Marx's texts. In Heinrich's view, these historico-philosophical passages do not represent 'any premise for substantive arguments' within the framework of Marx's critique of political economy – they are not constitutive for scientific analysis.[64]

------

will be able to find the lowest common denominator at all, but that is not strictly necessary. At one time, when this *Marx-Gesellschaft* was first established, there was much talk of achieving consensus about dissensus. This means that when a consensus is not reached on certain questions, there is at least a consensus over *this* fact: the disagreement lies in such and such points. In this way, the situation can be avoided where people are constantly batting objections back and forth: "you haven't understood me, I meant it in a completely different way". Instead, an understanding is reached, and there is simply a disagreement on such and such points, a dissensus that is allowed to stand as such' (Heinrich 2002a, p. 11).

61   'To interpret him in this way is either something one would associate with the *Marxist-Leninist tradition*, or with that of *bourgeois humanism*, or else it is due to a conception which attempts to play off Marx's hopes for a social revolution against his claims to scientific rigour' (Schweier 1999, p. 149, emphasis in original). The Marxian self-understanding referred to by Schweier is given expression in a letter written in 1877 to the editors of the Russian journal *Otecestvenniye Zapisky*. At least in this context, Marx states explicitly that he in no way claims to possess the 'universal passport of a general historico-philosophical theory, the supreme virtue of which consists in being super-historical' (Marx 2001, p. 201).

62   Heinrich 1999b, p. 136.

63   Heinrich 1999b, p. 138.

64   Ibid.

The theoretical intervention by Nadja Rakowitz is also to be located within the context of the debates within the *Marx-Gesellschaft*. In a work published in 2000, she drew on Backhaus's value-theoretical reading of Marx of the 1970s, despite the fact that she underlined certain differences vis-à-vis Backhaus and Reichelt, above all in the interpretation of the key Marxian category of 'abstract labour'. According to Rakowitz, Marxian value theory is to be understood as a 'monetary theory of value'. In addition, Rakowitz criticises the misinterpretation of Marx's theory of 'simple circulation' as a theory of a historical, pre-capitalist 'simple commodity production', and delivers a corresponding critique of Engels; on this point, Rakowitz is in agreement with Backhaus. However, she also presented a further elaboration of the further ramifications of this 'Frankfurt' discourse specifically with regard to the critique of ideology.[65]

A further discussion has continued in recent years concerning dialectic.[66] In a 1998 essay, Dieter Riedel called into question the virtually endless attempts to decipher the 'dialectical exposition' in *Capital* insofar as these were based – according to Riedel's explanation – on the assumption that Marx's method remained in principle the same throughout the history of the development of his critique of political economy (at least from the *Introduction* of August 1857 onwards). On Riedel's view, this assumption fails to recognise a crisis in Marx's understanding of his method. In this connection, Riedel refers to the fact that Marx broke off the process of drafting the *Urtext* of *A Contribution to the Critique of Political Economy* in the autumn of 1858. According to Riedel, Marx's method underwent a profound alteration after he had come to recognise the limits of the dialectical form of presentation. It is worth recalling in this context the now-familiar Marxian *topos* from the *Urtext* of 1858: 'the dialectical form of presentation is correct only when it knows its own limits'.[67] Riedel argues as follows: 'In a complicated and contradictory process characterised by non-simultaneities, Marx had recognised that the dialectical form was not adequate to his object, that it was not suitable for the exposition of the emergence and self-reproduction of the capitalist mode of production. The

---

65   See Rakowitz 2000.

66   The problematic of the 'limits of the dialectical form of exposition' has played a central role in this discussion: see Riedel 1998. For a response to Riedel's text, see Reichelt 2003. Frieder Otto Wolf provides a critical commentary on the debate between Reichelt and Riedel (Wolf 2006). More recently, Dieter Wolf has also intervened within this debate (see Wolf 2007).

67   Marx 1987b, p. 505 [translation modified – N.G.].

method that Marx applied in *Capital* was no longer bound by the pretension to a dialectical development of the concept'.[68] Yet Riedel's assessment of this circumstance is evidently far from a negative one: if the reader also drops this pretension, then a 'complex, but surprisingly clear and transparent structure of argumentation emerges'.[69]

Other well-known points of contention within research on Marx's critique of political economy in recent years include the following: the critical engagement by the circle around Michael Heinrich with the 'traditional' interpretation of Marx in relation to the problematic of the money-commodity;[70] the debate involving Dieter Wolf and Helmut Reichelt on the specific interconnection between value-form, the emergence of money, and the exchange process; and finally, the confrontation between Wolfgang Fritz Haug and Michael Heinrich on the problematic of the 'monetary theory of value', among other themes.[71] From these debates it can be seen that references to Marx's exposition of the commodity and money have retained their importance within the discussion of Marxian theory. It seems reasonable to assume that little will change in this regard in the future.

2   Japan

2.1   *The Situation before 1945*

In Japan, Marxism developed an extraordinarily large influence within economic science in particular, but also within Japanese intellectual life as a whole, in the course of the twentieth century.[72] Yet this development was unforeseeable at the beginning of the twentieth century. European economic science reached Japan during the Meiji period primarily in the shape of a German current, namely that centred around the '*Verein für Socialpolitik*'* (whose leading figures included Gustav von Schmoller, Adolph Wagner, Lujo Brentano); this

---

68   Riedel 1998, p. 40.

69   Ibid.

70   A synopsis of the current state of the discussion on the 'money-commodity problematic' is provided in Stützle 2006.

71   See Heinrich 2003 and Haug 2003. For a renewed critique of the 'monetary theory of value', see Haug 2007. A reaction to the controversy between Haug and Heinrich is given in Wolf 2008.

72   This is also true in relation to historical science. See Krämer, Schölz and Conrad 2006, pp. 17 f.

*   Social Policy Association.

current was inclined towards anti-Marxism.[73] Thus a theoretical orientation corresponding to the German model exerted a great influence in Japan in the early twentieth century, whereas Marxian theory, in all its complexity, was at first largely unknown. For example, one of the best-known non-Marxist theorists of the 'social question' to emerge in Japan in the first decades of the twentieth century, Tokuzō Fukuda, studied under Lujo Brentano, and gained his doctorate in Munich.

There follows a very brief survey of the historical development of the Japanese reception of Marx's critique of political economy before 1945. The first complete translations into Japanese of the three volumes of *Capital* were published between 1920 and 1924. In the period before 1920 in Japan, it had not been possible for a discussion that was differentiated in terms of its content and scientifically ambitious to develop properly in relation to Marx's economic theory, or his critique of political economy.[74] Hajime Kawakami (1879–1946) was one of the first economic theorists to succeed in distancing himself from the current which was inclined towards the *'Verein für Socialpolitik'*, and to orient himself in the direction of the Marxian critique of political economy.[75] In addition to his other scientific and political activities, Kawakami translated *Capital* into Japanese. In the early period of Japanese Marxism, he played an important role in enabling thought that was oriented towards the formation of Marxian theory to begin to gain purchase among Japanese intellectuals, and not least in Japanese universities. He was arrested on political grounds in the 1930s.

The economist and historian of Marxism, Makoto Itoh, reports that an animated discussion of Marx's value theory emerged in Japan between 1922 and 1930.[76] Kawakami and his critical star pupil, Tamizo Kushida (1885–1934), were among those who participated in the debates on the theory of value of the 1920s which had been provoked by the Böhm-Bawerk-inspired critique of Marx from the perspective of non- or anti-Marxist economic theory in Japan, among other catalysts. Importantly, Kushida was also concerned, despite his pupil-master relationship with Kawakami, to overcome the theoretical restrictions of the latter's interpretation of Marx's theory of value. Kawakami responded to the criticisms levelled at Marx's theory of value 'with a series of articles in which he criticised the neo-classical school and developed his own defence of the labour

---

73 See Sekine 1980a, pp. ixf. On the great influence of (non-Marxist) German economics on Japanese economics in the process of the latter's emergence, see also Yagi 2004, p. 12.

74 On the embryonic state of the Japanese reception of Marx's critique of political economy before 1920, see Lippert 1979, pp. 75 ff., especially p. 83.

75 This process is outlined in Bernstein 1976, pp. 103 ff.

76 See Itoh 1980, p. 17.

theory of value'.[77] Yet Kawakami's defence of Marx was itself theoretically deficient. Kawakami modified 'Marx's view – that exchange value is determined by the amount of labour required to produce a given commodity – into the statement that the value of any object reflects the amount of human effort and sacrifice involved in its production'.[78] Kawakami's student, Kushida, was able to go beyond the former's interpretation. Tessa Morris-Suzuki gives the following account: 'As Kushida Tamizo was quick to point out, Kawakami had tried to create a universal and immutable theory of value that applied to all things and all times'.[79] By contrast, Kushida recognised the historicity of the category of value: he considered that Marx had precisely demonstrated the historical character of value. Kawakami in turn soon corrected his own previous position on the theory of value. Further debates which were held in the interwar period revolved around the problematic of the reproduction and accumulation of capital and around the category of ground-rent. Kawakami also participated in these debates on Marx's critique of political economy.

Kawakami also commented on the 'problem of the beginning' in Marx's exposition. In a study published in 1928, Kawakami's theoretical approach amounted to the proposition that – to express it in Marxian terminology – science uncovers the essence of the object which is concealed beneath the form of manifestation. According to Kawakami, vulgar economics is content to seize upon the form of manifestation. Kawakami maintains that scientific enquiry does indeed begin with the form of manifestation and interprets the beginning of the exposition in *Capital* in this way: 'The wealth of societies in which the capitalist mode of production prevails appears as an "immense collection of commodities"; the individual commodity appears as its elementary form. Our investigation therefore begins with the analysis of the commodity'.[80] The Japanese theorist grasps the commodity as the contradictory unity of use-value and value. According to Kawakami, the commodity contains the germ of every contradiction within capitalist society.[81]

It was a critic of Kawakami who would provide an important link between so-called Western Marxism as it began to emerge after the First World War and Marxist thought in Japan. The theorist in question was Kazuo Fukumoto

---

77   Morris-Suzuki 1989, p. 79.

78   Ibid.

79   Morris-Suzuki 1989, p. 80.

80   Marx 1976a, p. 125.

81   See Kawakami 1928. On Kawakami's theoretical studies in the 1920s, see also Hoston 1986, pp. 46 f.

(1894–1983), who was influenced by György Lukács and Karl Korsch.[82] In 1923, Fukumoto had participated, along with Korsch and Lukács, in the renowned 'Marxist Working Week' in the Thuringian Forest; this event was closely bound up with the prehistory of the Frankfurt Institute for Social Research. Upon returning to Japan, Fukumoto became engaged in the communist movement in that country; for a short period, he even held a leading political position within this movement, but was ousted in 1927 on account of his political divergences with the Comintern. He was arrested the following year and was eventually sentenced to a lengthy term of imprisonment.[83]

Fukumoto enriched the Japanese discussion of Marx's critique of political economy. In the mid-1920s, he attempted to draw the attention of Japanese Marxists to a moment which had, on the whole, been rather neglected until then: Marx's methodology. Above all, Fukumoto posed the question of the object and scope of *Capital* (he held the object of the critique of political economy to be much more comprehensive than that of *Capital*). For Fukumoto, the 'chapter on method' – Marx's 1857 *Introduction to the Critique of Political Economy* – played an important role from a methodological point of view. According to Fukumoto's interpretation, the Marxian method contains a combination of analytic abstraction and synthetic construction. Fukumoto thus ranks among the earlier interpreters of Marx's critique of political economy who ascribed an important significance to the 'problem of the beginning of the exposition', thus anticipating a widely discussed dimension of the international debate on Marx in the second half of the twentieth century. Fukumoto's intervention marked a turning point in the historical development of Japanese Marxism, and called into question the position of Kawakami and Kushida as the leading theorists engaging with Marx in Japan.[84]

The Ōhara Institute for Social Research in Osaka, which was founded in 1919 and financed by the entrepreneur, Magosaburō Ōhara, and which would later engage in scientific cooperation with the Marx-Engels Institute in Moscow, played a certain role in the development of Marxist thought in Japan. This was a research institute in which younger Marxist researchers could find a position, including Samezō Kuruma[85] (1893–1982) and Kawakami's student,

---

82   See Sakuramoto 2000. For more detail on Fukumoto's role in linking German-language and Japanese Marxism in the 1920s, see Yagi 2011.

83   For an account of the events of 1927–8, see Sakuramoto 2000, p. 184.

84   For a critical appraisal of Fukumoto from an orthodox Marxist-Leninist standpoint, see Iwasaki 1987, p. 21. Fukumoto is considered in detail in Yagi 2005. As early as 1929, a review of an important work by Fukumoto was published in German (see Hirano 1929).

85   Kuruma's interpretation of Marx's theory of value and of money will be considered below.

Kushida. Although the director of the institute in the 1920s, Iwasaburo Takano (1871–1949), favoured empirical research over engagement with abstract methodological questions on Marx's critique of political economy (incidentally, he had studied under Lujo Brentano), he moved ever closer to Marx. Rolf Hecker has written that the researchers of the Ōhara Institute considered it one of their tasks 'to contribute to the dissemination of the Marxist body of thought on scientific foundations in Japan'.[86] The Ōhara Institute is still in existence to this day; it is now affiliated to the Hosei University in Tokyo.

There was already a scientific exchange between Japanese and Western interpreters of Marx before 1945. This is evidenced by the example of the Japanese economist, Shigeto Tsuru (1912–2006),[87] who lived for a period in the USA, where he collaborated with the Marxist economist, Paul Sweezy, among others, in the early 1940s. In an article published in a British journal in 1938, the Japanese researcher, who had previously engaged in detail with Marx's theory of fetishism and with Marx's methodology,[88] criticised the interpretation of Marx's theory of value by the Marxist economist, Maurice Dobb. In his critique, Tsuru referred to the specifically 'qualitative' dimension of the problematic of value.[89] In his own *Theory of Capitalist Development*, published in 1942, Sweezy in turn made positive references to the engagement with Marx's theory of value by Tsuru in the latter's critique of Dobb,[90] and furthermore published an appendix on Marx's reproduction schemata which originated from the Japanese economist.[91]

The discourses enumerated above were somewhat overshadowed, however, by the development of the two competing Marxist schools of thought in the 1930s referred to earlier: the Lectures School* and the Worker-Farmer Faction.** Moreover, the situation of Marxist researchers became ever more pre-

---

86   Hecker 1997, p. 90. Also of interest in relation to the Ōhara Institute is Kubo 2006.

87   For a biography of Tsuru, see Suzumura 2006.

88   See Tsuru 1994a.

89   See Tsuru 1994c.

90   See Sweezy 1972, p. 39.

91   According to Kotaro Suzumura, Tsuru would eventually become 'one of the greatest political economists and influential opinion leaders in post-war Japan' (Suzumura 2006, p. 613). From 1972 to 1975, Tsuru was president of the Hitotsubashi University in Tokyo. Although Tsuru's intellectual field of activity extended far beyond Marx research in a more narrow sense, he also continued to engage with Marxian theory in the period after the Second World War: see Tsuru 1994b and Tsuru 1993, pp. 3 ff.

*   [*Koza-Richtung*] – occasionally referred to in English as the 'Symposium School'.

**   [*Rono-Richtung*] – occasionally referred to in English as the 'Worker-Peasant Faction'.

carious as a result of the repressive measures taken by the Japanese state. Nonetheless, the Japanese reception of Marx and Marxism before 1945[92] had served to establish a substantial basis, behind which the Japanese debate of later years would no longer be able to regress. Yet Japanese research would not fulfil its potential until the period after the Second World War. It was above all in this period that Japan successfully established itself as an intellectual centre of international research into, and further development of, Marxian theory.

2.2   The Evolution of the Japanese Debate from the Postwar Period to the Present

It is fair to say that in Japan, an innovative potential was developed in the shape of various conceptual approaches within the field of the interpretation of Marx, and within critical social theory that was substantially inspired by Marxian theory. Part of the background to this development is the extraordinarily wide dissemination of Marx's writings in Japan. Taking into account all the various editions of *Capital* that have been published in that country, several million copies are in circulation.[93]

Already in the immediate postwar period, there was a new surge in the intensive reception of *Capital*. Various leading theorists and interpreters of Marx, including Itsuro Sakisaka, Kōzō Uno and Samezō Kuruma, participated in the debates that took place in Tokyo in 1947–8. Kiyoshi Nagatani enumerates several questions and thematic fields that were debated during this period as follows: '[the question] whether a commodity in the opening chapter of Capital 1 is a commodity in simple commodity production or one in capitalist production; the law of value in a socialist economy; the relevancy of the method by which to abstract value as congealed labor leaving aside both use-values

---

92   Restrictions of space do not permit a closer consideration here of two thinkers who occupied a position between Marxism and the Kyoto School (the latter being oriented towards Kitaro Nishida [1870–1945], one of the best-known Japanese philosophers): Kiyoshi Miki (1897–1945) and Tosaka Jun (1900–45).

93   An overview of the publication history of *Capital* before 1980 is given by Ōmiya 1980, p. 366. In addition, it is worth noting that the complete translation of the *Grundrisse* into Japanese, which, according to Rolf Hecker, was published between 1958 and 1965, was one of the first complete translations of this work to appear in any language. Hecker reports that the first complete translation into Russian was not published until 1968/9 (see Hecker 2001b). For a detailed account of the publication and reception of the *Grundrisse* in Japan, see Uchida 2008, p. 213 ff.

in an exchange relation between two commodities; the connection of the value form with the exchange process of commodities (Chapter 2), and so on'.[94] The debates at this time formed a foundation for determinate theoretical developments of the subsequent period, even though the latter pointed in different directions, as, for instance, in the contrasting approaches to value theory of Uno and Kuruma.

Not only was the Japanese engagement with Marx's critique of political economy carried out in greater depth following the Second World War, but it also became broader. Two North American researchers with a specialism in the theory formed in Japan estimate that 'at its height in the late 1960s perhaps as many as 50% of all professors of economics in Japanese Universities were primarily oriented towards Marxian economic theory'.[95] Although it can be taken for granted that this intellectual balance of forces no longer obtains, it is still safe to assume that there is scarcely another capitalist country in the world where scientific interest in the Marxian critique of political economy is greater than in Japan. According to Izumi Omura, almost 4,000 scientific studies engaging with the critique of political economy were published in Japan within the period from 1975 to 1998.[96]

In his 1980s survey of the various theoretical currents within contemporary Japanese Marxism,[97] Toshio Yamada highlights three main orientations: firstly, the theoretical approach of the Uno School (which is considered in detail below);[98] secondly, the 'Civil Society' current, which investigates, among other things, the specific characteristics of Japanese capitalism; and thirdly, the critical theory of reification, which can be traced back to the philosopher, Wataru

---

94   Nagatani 1997.

95   Albritton and Bell 1995, p. 3. Thomas Sekine provided concrete statistical data in the mid-1970s: 'There are approximately 2,300 academic economists in Japan, most of whom belong either to the Economic Theoretical Association, with a 100 percent Marxian membership of 950, or to the Theoretical-Economic and Econometric Association, with a 100 percent non-Marxian membership of 1,000. Those who do not belong to either of these associations are specialists in economic history, finance, and other applied fields and can be of either Marxist or non-Marxist persuasion. Thus, it can be safely concluded that, outside the communist world, Japan probably possesses the largest group of Marxian political economists who are professionally engaged in teaching and/or research' (Sekine 1975, pp. 847 f.).

96   See Omura 2006, p. 75.

97   See Yamada 1987. An important article surveying the reception of Marx in Japan is available in German: see Otani and Sekine 1987.

98   On Uno, see also Kubota 2009, among other works.

Hiromatsu (1933–94),[99] whose work inspired a school of thought. In the latter theoretical current, a specific concept of reification is strictly differentiated from the concept of alienation.

Of crucial significance in Hiromatsu's interpretation of Marx is the assumption that a theoretical break occurred in connection with the development of Marx's thought from the *Economic and Philosophical Manuscripts* to *The German Ideology*. According to Hiromatsu, Marx's turn away from the theory of alienation is to be located within this development. Hiromatsu maintains that, following this break, Marx turned to the theory of reification. Ryoji Ishizuka, the Hiromatsu specialist of the *Historisch-Kritischen Wörterbuchs des Marxismus*,* offers an interpretation in relation to this theoretical break that the Japanese philosopher thematises and discerns in Marx's work: according to Ishizuka, Hiromatsu considers that the theory of alienation implies a subject-object schema. The concept of alienation 'originally [describes] the process in which the "human essence" passes over into the object (objectification), and in which the latter counterposes itself to the subject as an alien, hostile power (alienation)'.[100] In making his theoretical break, Marx discards this subject-object schema, and develops in its place a theoretical approach oriented towards social relations and their reification. It is worth noting in relation to Hiromatsu in general that he ranked among the most important theorists of the Japanese New Left, and that his philosophy can by no means be reduced, with regard to its primary sources and its thematic breadth, to the reception of Marx in a narrower sense.[101]

Beyond the currents enumerated by Yamada, there also existed an orthodox Marxist-Leninist theoretical strand which wielded considerable influence within the postwar Marxist discussion in Japan, as well as a broad field of research oriented to the history of the emergence and elaboration of Marx's works and to methodological questions in Marx in a narrower sense. It is debatable whether a 'further development' of the Uno School since the 1960s – the 'World Capitalism' current that was substantially influenced by Hiroshi Iwata –[102] ought to be regarded as a school of its own or as a branch of the

---

99   Little of Hiromatsu's work has been published in Western languages. See, for example,
      Hiromatsu 1987.

*   The *Historical-Critical Dictionary of Marxism*, serialised in English translation in the *Historical Materialism* journal.

100   Ishizuka 2004.

101   An impression of Hiromatsu's philosophy is given in Kobayashi 1998.

102   A closer consideration of Iwata and the 'World Capitalism' current is given in Mitsunobu
      2002, pp. 233 ff.

Uno School. The Uno-critic and former director of the Ohara Institute, Samezō Kuruma, whose theses in relation to Marx's theory of value and of money exerted a great influence on the Japanese debate, will be considered in depth later. Although there was a circle of emulators around Kuruma, he refused to found a school of his own.[103]

One of the schools of thought identified by Yamada can be presented here in more detail: the Uno School, which emerged in the 1950s.[104] The devotion of more space to the Uno School than to the other schools of thought is certainly warranted on several grounds. Firstly, of the Japanese schools of thought inspired by Marxian theory, the Uno School was by far the most successful in gaining a profile beyond Asia.[105] Notice was – and still is – taken of this school on an international level, beyond Japan and Asia, and it continues to exert an influence on this scale. This is true at least with regard to fundamental questions of methodology in critical social theory. This current's best-known exponents have become firmly established within the international discussion, in particular the Anglophone one. Secondly, the Uno School polarised the Japanese discussion over a long period. Participants could either associate themselves with this current, or else vehemently reject it, but it could not be ignored. Anyone engaging with Marx in Japan was obliged to position themselves in relation to this school of thought. Thirdly, Uno made a decisive contribution to the repudiation of the orthodox Marxism-Leninism of a Stalinist stamp which was widely disseminated among the intelligentsia of the Japanese Left in the postwar period. This would seem to be extremely significant, even if Uno was not the only Japanese intellectual to render such a service. Fourthly, Uno could marshal a large number of scholars who either took up his approach or further developed it independently. According to Andrew Barshay, Uno's theory garnered support among 'hundreds of adepts, particularly among economists with ties to Tokyo University, where Uno had moved shortly

---

103   Alongside the currents enumerated here, the 'mathematical-economic' line of interpretation of Nobuo Okishio (1927–2003) might also be mentioned. See Okishio 1963. Another 'mathematical-economic' interpreter to engage intensively with Marx was Michio Morishima (1923–2004). See Morishima 1973.

104   In engaging with Uno, this study will focus on the *freestanding* theory formed by the latter in connection with Marx, rather than on his reception of Marx in a narrower sense.

105   Although it is true to say that there is now also an awareness of Hiromatsu's work in the People's Republic of China, the Hiromatsu School is less well known in the West than Uno and his school of thought.

after the war had ended'.[106] Barshay writes the following of the most important Uno scholars: 'These scholars in their turn trained their own students, so that over the two decades from the mid-1950s through the mid-1970s, Marxian economics in Japan came to be dominated by, or at least to assume its strongest academic "personality" in, the Uno school'.[107] The term proposed by Barshay here (albeit not without reservations) – 'dominance' – is a little exaggerated, since the Uno School also found itself confronted by numerous Marxist critics in Japan, including some theoretically influential ones (e.g. Samezō Kuruma). Furthermore, the influence of the Uno School in Japan has rather tended to decline in recent times. Nevertheless, the enduring merit of the Uno School is that it achieved a considerable prominence beyond national and continental boundaries as a Japanese school of thought focusing on fundamental methodological questions of critical social theory, and oriented to Marx's *magnum opus*. This consideration alone justifies the space granted here – i.e. in a study presenting the *globalisation* of Marxist theory – to Uno and his school (including the Japanese Uno scholars, Makoto Itoh and Thomas Sekine, to whom the transfer of Uno School theory to the Anglo-Saxon world can largely be attributed).

Kōzō Uno can be considered one of the most important and influential critical social theorists of the twentieth century. For Uno and his school, it was crucial to refer precisely to Marx's major work (i.e. to his mature critique of political economy), rather than to his early writings. Furthermore, the posing of specifically methodological questions was central to the independent formation of theory by Uno. When Japanese engagement with Marxist theory was given an unforeseen impetus in the period following the Second World War, Uno endeavoured to usher in a new epoch in Marx-oriented political economy in Japan.

A decisive factor in setting the course of Uno's life as a young man was the time he spent studying in Germany at the beginning of the 1920s, where he first undertook an intensive reading of *Capital*. Having been appointed Professor of Economics at the University of Sendai in 1924, and subsequently removed from the university system at the end of the 1930s following his imprisonment on political grounds, Uno took up a professorship again in Tokyo in 1947. It was approximately at this time that he began his career as a significant heretic of Japanese Marxism. From Tokyo, Uno was able to develop a considerable influence on the Marxist theoretical discussion in his country through the

---

106   Barshay 2004, p. 123.
107   Barshay 2004, pp. 123 f.

publication between 1950 and 1952 of his two-volume *magnum opus*, which was entitled *Keizai Genron* (the title is rendered in English as *Principles of Political Economy*). A significant text by Uno on the theory of value had already appeared in 1947.[108]

The English translation of the 1964 abridged edition of *Keizai Genron* contributed substantially to the reception of the Uno School in the Anglophone world.[109] Incidentally, alongside the three versions of Uno's major work (the two-volume edition of 1950/2, the abridged edition of 1964 and the 1967 seminar edition), several works by Uno scholars either share its title or have terminological variations as their title,[110] reflecting these scholars' conscious intention to locate themselves and their theoretical production in the tradition of their master. It should be noted here that, in his *Principles of Political Economy*, Uno scarcely engages in research into, or interpretation of, Marx – at least if the numerous footnotes are disregarded which refer to Marx and virtually form a kind of subtext. Instead, Uno is concerned with the exposition of the 'matter itself', namely the presentation of a 'pure' capitalist society. This is the explanation for the title and subtitle (*Theory of a Purely Capitalist Society*) of the English-language edition. However, since Uno saw Marx as a precursor in precisely this theoretical approach (even if, according to Uno, certain deficiencies remained in Marx's approach), he positioned himself in the tradition of Marx.

Located at the centre of Uno's thought is a 'three-levels-theory',[111] which was of defining importance for his scholars and belongs to the core content of his school. For Uno, *Capital* is not an exposition of the capitalist mode of production in a particular country at a particular point in time, but rather the analysis of a 'pure' capitalist society (even if Marx was not always consistent in this regard). Such a theory is to be established at a high level of abstraction. The 'theory of a purely capitalist society' corresponds to the first level in Uno's three-level schema. A decisive moment in Uno's exposition of a 'pure' capitalist society is the system concept – i.e. the exposition of such a society as system. The second, or intermediate, level within the 'three-levels-theory' is that of a stages theory; on this level, the object of investigation is the determinate historical stages of capitalist society. Uno distinguished the stages of mercantilism, liberalism and imperialism within the development of the capitalist

---

108 Thomas Sekine writes of this study that its publication 'set against him [Uno] not only the Marxian professors of Tokyo University but virtually the whole profession of Marxian political economy in Japan' (Sekine 1975, p. 848).

109 The following presentation relies on this translation.

110 See Mawatari 1985, p. 407.

111 See also MacLean 1981, pp. 213 ff., Bidet 1987, p. 56, and Bidet 1990, pp. 241 ff.

mode of production. If Uno's approach were expanded upon, an example of theory formation on this level of abstraction could be found in Lenin's text on imperialism,[112] for instance. The analysis of the concrete historical situation of a concrete capitalist economy is to be carried out on the third and most concrete level within Uno's schema. It is evident, then, that the distinction between different levels of abstraction within Marxist theory constituted a core principle in Uno's methodology.

In Uno's conception, 'historical materialism' is merely accorded the status of an 'ideological hypothesis' rather than that of a 'scientific theory'. Uno insisted on the primacy of the science of political economy.[113] In order to understand Uno's approach, it is crucial to recognise that he was not so much concerned in his *Principles of Political Economy* (i.e. in his theory of a 'pure' capitalist society) with an interpretation of Marx's various drafts of his critique of political economy; rather, he intended to construct a theory of a 'pure' capitalist society according to its immanent logic. Parallels to, and deviations from, Marx are thus the result of Uno's understanding of the 'matter itself', rather than of his understanding of Marx. Although Uno recognised his debt to Marx's basic approach, the former's thought cannot be reduced to a mere appropriation of Marx's critique of political economy (as it has been bequeathed in Marx's various drafts). Uno is to be characterised as an essentially independent thinker who intends to go beyond Marx, even though he stands in the Marxian tradition. To criticise Uno's theory of a 'pure' capitalist society for failing to correspond to Marx's critique of political economy on this or that point would be to miss the essence of Uno's theory and to fail to recognise its independent character.

From the point of view of the Uno School, there are specific Marxian 'deficits' to be overcome, however. Shoken Mawatari states the following from just such a perspective: 'In order to locate *Capital* as the principles of the capitalist economy, we must purify Marx's *Capital*, by setting aside Marx's references to historical changes, by eliminating his ideological forecasts and prejudices, and by removing his logical inconsistencies'.[114] The Uno scholar Thomas Sekine criticises Marx for having failed to distinguish adequately between 'the theory of a purely capitalist society, capitalism in its liberal stage of world-historic development, and the economic history of England up to the middle of the nineteenth century'.[115] It should be noted that Uno's theory of a 'pure' capitalist

---

112   See Lenin 1964.

113   See Joe 1995, pp. 30 f.

114   Mawatari 1985, p. 406.

115   Sekine 1980b, p. 151.

society forms a self-contained theoretical system. This implies the presupposition that the economic life of the 'pure' capitalist society corresponds entirely to a commodity-economy: all products take on the commodity-form.[116]

It is worth considering more closely two points on which Uno deviates from Marx's conceptions. The first of these is Uno's view that Marx's theory of abstract labour as the substance of value is misplaced. According to Uno, the exposition of abstract labour as the substance of value does not belong in the theory of circulation, but rather in the subsequent theory of production:[117] that is to say, its adequate place is much later within the systematic exposition. The theory of the value-form is to be developed prior to, and independent of, the theory of abstract labour as the substance of value. Uno writes that Marx underlines the significance of the commodity-form of products at the beginning of his exposition in the first volume of *Capital*, and yet 'after stating that use-value and value are the two elements of a commodity, he immediately attributes the substance of value to labour that is required to produce the commodity. But the production-process of a commodity is not yet analyzed at this stage'.[118] In his *The Dialectic of Capital*, a work written following the precepts of Uno's *Principles of Political Economy*, the Uno scholar Thomas Sekine does not systematically expound the substance of value until he develops his doctrine of production.[119,*] The background to Uno's reflections on where to locate the exposition of abstract labour as the substance of value within his theory is given by his endeavour to establish a strict separation between the 'Doctrine of Circulation', the subsequent 'Doctrine of Production', and the 'Doctrine of Distribution', which is the last to be expounded in this series. This strict separation and sequence is virtually constitutive for his exposition of the 'pure' capitalist society. It is thus clear in this context too – i.e. with regard to the inner structure of *Principles of Political Economy* – how the distinction between different levels of abstraction was of crucial importance for Uno's methodology.

A second important point to consider is that Uno effects alterations in the logic of the exposition vis-à-vis the structure of the third volume of Marx's *Capital* – i.e. within the sphere that Uno, within the context of his tripartite divi-

---

116   In a 2007 study, the Canadian Uno scholar, Robert Albritton, emphasises the crucial significance of Marx's theory of the commodity-form (see Albritton 2007, p. 21 ff.).

117   See Joe 1995, pp. 67 ff.

118   Uno 1980, p. xxviif.

119   See Sekine 1986, pp. 199 and 297. More recently, a revised and shortened new edition of this book has been published (see Sekine 1997).

*   Sekine's *The Dialectic of Capital* is due to be republished by Brill in the Historical Materialism Book Series.

sion between circulation, production and distribution, assigns to the doctrine of distribution.[120] It is particularly striking that Uno positions the treatment of ground rent logically before the exposition of interest. Uno elaborates on the structural division of his doctrine of distribution as follows: 'The theory of interest including the account of commercial profit must follow the theory of rent which directly supplements the general theory of profit because rent originates in the direct participation of landed property in the production-process of capital'.[121] It should be borne in mind here that Uno agreed with Marx that the structural division of the exposition should not be made following external considerations; rather, it should adequately express the interconnection of economic categories, and as such is itself given by the structure of the object. Uno's structural division of the doctrine of distribution contrasts with that of the third volume of Marx's *Capital* as follows:[122]

Uno's Doctrine of Distribution
Introduction
1. Profit
    – The formation of the general rate of profit: the transformation of values into prices of production.
    – Market prices and market values (or market prices of production): the relation between supply and demand and the formation of surplus profit.
    – The tendential fall in the general rate of profit: the increase in productive forces and business cycles.
2. Ground rent
3. Interest
    – Credit capital and banking capital.
    – Commercial capital and its profit.
    – Capital as an automatic interest-bearing force.
    – The class structure of capitalist society.

The alterations made by Uno within the structure of the exposition vis-à-vis the Marxian one are considerable. The structural division of the third volume of Marx's *Capital* is reproduced as follows:[123]

---

120   On Uno's modification of the structure of the third volume of *Capital*, see Joe 1995, pp. 117 f.
121   Uno 1980, p. 75.
122   It should be kept in mind here that this structural division is drawn from the 1980 edition of *Principles of Political Economy*, which corresponds to the 1964 edition of *Keizai Genron*.
123   Marx 1981a, pp. 5–8.

Capital, Volume Three

Part One:	The Transformation of Surplus Value into Profit, and of the Rate of Surplus Value into the Rate of Profit.*
Part Two:	The Transformation of Profit into Average Profit.
Part Three:	The Law of the Tendential Fall in the Rate of Profit.
Part Four:	The Transformation of Commodity Capital into Commercial Capital and Money-Dealing Capital (Merchant's Capital).
Part Five:	The Division of Profit into Interest and Profit of Enterprise. (Industrial and Commercial Profit). Interest-bearing Capital.**
Part Six:	The Transformation of Surplus Profit into Ground Rent.
Part Seven:	The Revenues and their Sources.

Some Uno scholars, while remaining true to the spirit of their mentor, felt justified in going beyond Uno, in the same way that the latter had gone beyond Marx. A decisive criterion for affiliation to the Uno School is normally held to be the acceptance of the three-levels method and the associated evaluation of the level of *Principles of Political Economy* as in a certain sense constituting the foundation of theory formation on the intermediate level (i.e. that of stages theory) as well as on the third, most concrete level. Yet, within the tradition deriving from Uno, there is also a current which takes critical aim at the theoretical fundament of the Uno School – i.e. the three-levels method. This tendency is made up of theorists from the 'World Capitalism' current around Hiroshi Iwata and others, which was formed in the 1960s. According to the Uno scholar, Mawatari, this theoretical tendency favours a two-level method over the three-level one, with the level of stages theory being discarded.[124] By contrast, Uno's tripartite division of levels of abstraction, including a level of stages theory, retains its validity in the eyes of other Uno scholars.[125]

The Uno School was in no way homogeneous, and this remains the case to this day. Uno scholars are divided not only on the question of how to evaluate Uno's fundamental method, but also on the question of how to further elabor-

---

*   The German and English versions do not correspond here.

**   The German and English versions do not correspond here.

124   See Mawatari 1985, pp. 413 f. A caveat should be included here: it is not clear that this characterisation by Mawatari represents a correct interpretation of the 'World Capitalism' current's critique of Uno.

125   This applies, for instance, to Thomas Sekine in *The Dialectic of Capital* (Sekine 1986, pp. 64 ff.).

ate his theory. Numerous Uno scholars have attempted to further develop Uno's approaches – be it on the level of *Principles of Political Economy*, on the level of stages theory, or on the level of concrete and empirical analysis. The assumption underlying these endeavours was that Uno's approaches were to be found in a less developed form, the more concrete the corresponding level of theory. Nonetheless, further research was also carried out within Uno scholarship in relation to the most abstract theoretical level (that corresponding to *Principles of Political Economy*), on the theories of value, rent, credit and crises, among others.[126] As indicated by Thomas Sekine, there was no theoretical unanimity in the way that Uno's theory of value was referred to within the Uno School.[127]

The theorist Kan'ichi Kuroda (already mentioned above) deals extensively with the discourse on the theory of value within Japanese Marxism in the 1950s and 1960s. In his treatment, Kuroda counterposes the interpretation of the opening sections of *Capital*, which reads these as corresponding to 'simple commodity production' – an interpretation vehemently rejected by Kuroda himself, and one which was (also) represented within the context of theoretical Stalinism – to Uno's position on the theory of value. According to Kuroda, Uno's conception is incompatible with the 'simple commodity production' interpretation:

> In opposition to the Stalinist distortion of Marx's theory of commodities into a theory of simple commodity production, he [Uno] proposes the 'theory of circulation' merely as a theory of circulation forms (unrelated to the process of production), by abstracting from the issue of the *substance* of commodities (the so-called 'dual character of labour') *to be corroborated later* (i.e. in the theory of production process).[128]

It might be added that, in actual fact, Uno considers that the theory of 'pure' capitalism must begin with the theory of circulation, 'in which the forms of circulation alone are to be examined'.[129] Kuroda himself was a vehement critic of Stalin's economic theory, which he held to be fundamentally different from the theory set out by Marx.

To the survey provided here of Kōzō Uno's theoretical approach, it might be added that the interpretation of the opening sections of *Capital* which reads these as corresponding to a historical, pre-capitalist era of 'simple commodity

---

126   See Mawatari 1985, p. 414.

127   See Sekine 1984, p. 419.

128   Kuroda 2000, p. 55.

129   Uno 1980, p. xxiv.

production' can be traced back to Friedrich Engels. Moreover, there is a long tradition in Japan of engagement with the problem of the relation between Marx and Engels; according to Akira Miyakawa, this tradition 'dates back to the period following the Second World War'.[130]

A divergent position with respect to the so-called 'logico-historical' interpretation of Marx's method (which originally derives from Engels) was apparently advanced by Sekisuke Mita.[131] In the 1960s and 1970s, Mita ranked among the best-known interpreters of Marx's critique of political economy in Japan. In his consideration of Marx's procedure, Mita refers to a dialectical method in the sense of a method of development, and argues that Marx added such a method to the analytic one that he retained. On Mita's view, the analytic method was also that of classical political economy; this method represented the foundation, which Marx supplemented by the dialectical method. Thus, according to Mita, Marx's procedure relies on the analytic method and additionally pursues the dialectical method.[132] Incidentally, Mita numbered among the outspoken opponents of Uno within Japanese Marxism.

In his 1970s survey of the Marxist discussion of dialectic in Japan, Chikatsugu Iwasaki refers to a research controversy regarding the relation between the dialectical contradiction and the principle of consistency, or freedom from contradiction, deriving from formal logic. Iwasaki comments as follows: 'All Marxist philosophers of course concur that the dialectical contradiction cannot be grasped with the help of formal logic alone. However, their opinions are divided on the question as to whether the dialectical contradiction can be expressed without infringing the logical principle of consistency'.[133] It might be added that this problem must be understood as a significant one for any adequate comprehension of Marx's critique of political economy.

A great deal of attention has been paid in the Japanese discussion both to the theoretical relation between Marx and the classical political economists and to that between Marx and Hegel. According to Kan'ichi Kuroda, a Hegelian-influenced reading of *Capital* was already undertaken in Japan shortly after the

---

130   Miyakawa 1999, p. 254.

131   See Otani and Sekine 1987, p. 249. In relation to Mita, the question remains open as to whether his critique of the logic-historical interpretation of Marx's method was merely directed at an 'idealist, mystificatory' *version* of this mode of interpretation of the critique of political economy, or against the logico-historical interpretation *in general*. On Mita, see, among other works, Kakuta 2009.

132   See Mita 2006.

133   Iwasaki 1979, p. 363.

Second World War.[134] It is apparent from the studies published in the 1980s and 1990s that the Marx-Hegel relation has been an object of focus in later times. Hirochi Uchida posed the question of whether the relation between Marx's *Grundrisse* and Hegel's *Logic* was not 'more profound and more systematic than hitherto appreciated'.[135] Uchida presented a 'Hegelianising' interpretation of the *Grundrisse*, in which parallels are drawn between the 1857 *Introduction* and the Doctrine of the Concept in Hegel's *Logic*, between the chapter on money in the *Grundrisse* and Hegel's Doctrine of Being, and finally between the chapter on capital in the *Grundrisse* and Hegel's Doctrine of Essence. The Marx and Hegel researcher Yoshihiro Niji has attempted to demonstrate that there is an essential parallel between Hegel's logic of judgement on the one hand, and Marx's analysis of the value-form on the other, or that certain elements of Hegelian logic are to be regarded as a source of Marx's theory of value.[136] Niji's position has been noted, and criticised, within the German discussion.[137]

It is worth emphasising that Niji's approach ought to be considered within a specific context within the history of the reception of Marx. The interpretation of Marx's analysis of the value-form (as well as of his theory of money)[138] represents a virtually 'classical' field of Japanese engagement with Marx, to which a great deal of attention was devoted already in the 1950s (at a time when the analysis of the value-form was on the whole rather neglected within the West German debate on Marx). This has remained the case in the more recent past in Japan. Thus, for example, the analysis of the value-form is accorded a central place in Susumu Takenaga's examination of Marx's theory of the commodity.[139] A defining circumstance to be considered in this case is that Takenaga grasps Marx's theory of the commodity as the foundation of Marx's entire economic theory. (A positive side effect or after-effect of the intensive engagement with Marx's theory of value by Japanese scientists is the fact that in Japan a great deal of attention is devoted to the manuscript Marx wrote for self-clarification in the process of revising *Capital* between the first and second editions of the first volume, namely the *Ergänzungen und Veränderungen zum ersten Band des 'Kapitals'** composed at the turn of the year 1871–2).

---

134   See Kuroda 2000, pp. 35 and 232 ff.
135   Uchida 1988, p. 1.
136   See Niji 1983 and Niji 1995.
137   These criticisms are reproduced in Hafner 1999, p. 28.
138   A more recent interpretation of Marx's theory of money has been proposed by Masao Ishikura (see Ishikura 2004).
139   See Takenaga 1985, pp. 127 ff.
*   ['*Additions and Alterations to the First Volume of Capital*'].

In the 1980s, the interpreter of Marx, Tomonaga Tairako, grasped a specific inversion as a structural peculiarity of modern bourgeois society. According to Tairako, this inversion consists in the fact that an essence necessarily takes on an inverted form of appearance, such that this essence is no longer immediately transparent. For Tairako, a core content of Marx's dialectical method consists in the 'genetic development, from essence itself, of the stages of the process by means of which essence is inverted and thus necessarily assumes forms of appearance which seemingly contradict it'.[140] In his consideration of Marx's theory of inversion, Tairako makes a basic distinction between *Sache* and *Ding*, and between *Versachlichung* and *Verdinglichung*:*

> Firstly, the commodity production reverses the human interaction of pro-
> ducers to the reified interaction of things (*Sachen*). Secondly, it further
> reverses the social characteristics of this reified interaction itself to the
> natural attributes which pertain to the natural things (*Dinge*). The first
> reversal is termed *Versachlichung* in the sense of the reversal of the human
> relations of production to the reified (*versachlicht*) ones. The second
> reversal is termed *Verdinglichung* in the sense of the reversal of the rela-
> tions of things to the natural properties of things.[141]

With Tairako's interpretation, a new point of departure has been established in Japan for the reading of Marx informed by the theory of reification.

In the 1990s, Akira Miyakawa provided a contribution which addressed Marx's critical engagement with classical political economy. His interest here was in the problematic of the total social reproduction process in the history of the formation of economic theory. The arc drawn by Miyakawa in the history of theory within this context spans from François Quesnay's *Tableau économique*, via Adam Smith's dogma according to which the value of the annual social product resolves into the revenues of wages, profit and ground rent – a theory that Marx held to be deficient – to Marx's own exposition of the total social reproduction process. According to Miyakawa, Marx devised his theory of reproduction through his critical engagement with the Smithian dogma, and it was especially in the *1861–63 Manuscripts* that the Trier-born thinker made

---

140   Tairako 1987, p. 105.

*   *Sache* and *Ding* can both be translated into English as 'thing'. *Sache* can also have the sense
       of 'matter' (as in 'the matter in hand'), or 'affair'. *Verdinglichung* and *Versachlichung* are
       both rendered in English as 'reification'.

141   Tairako 2002, p. 51. The German concepts and emphases are given in the original. On the
       distinction between *Versachlichung* and *Verdinglichung*, see also Tairako 1997, p. 45.

progress in overcoming Smith's erroneous doctrine. Yet, as Miyakawa argues, Marx in no way subsequently abandoned his critical interrogation of the Smithian dogma: 'its critical overcoming extends like a red thread through the history of the origins of Marx's theory of reproduction'.[142]

A significant study by Takahisa Ōishi, bearing the title *The Unknown Marx: Reconstructing a Unified Perspective*, was published in English in 2001.[143] Ōishi defends the thesis that Marx is to be considered a largely unknown thinker to the extent he has previously been interpreted above all under the influence of Soviet Marxism-Leninism. This perspective has yielded a problematic image of Marx, according to Ōishi. The Japanese researcher is concerned to demarcate Marx's theory, which he considers to be centred upon the critique of political economy, from Engels on the one side, and also from the theories of the classical political economists on the other. Ōishi locates the core content of Marx's critique of political economy both in the method of dialectical exposition of economic categories and in its specificity as a critique of the categories of political economy. Drawing a parallel with the notorious 'Adam Smith Problem', which concerns the relation between the *Theory of Moral Sentiments* and *Wealth of Nations*, Ōishi dubs the internationally much-discussed question of the relation between Marx's early and late work the 'Karl Marx Problem'. Yet Ōishi argues that no methodological break, no really profound rupture can be identified between the young and the mature Marx. Instead, Ōishi discerns a continuity in the historical development of Marx's work. With regard to the difference between Marx and classical political economy, Ōishi argues that Marx rejected David Ricardo's ahistorical understanding of the capitalist economy in his 1847 *The Poverty of Philosophy* – a text to which Ōishi makes copious references.[144]

A more recent approach to the reading and reconstruction of Marxian theory, but one which draws rather less on Hegel than on Kant, is that proposed by the philosopher Kōjin Karatani. Karatani's is an ambitious project to devise a reading of Kant informed by Marxian thought, and likewise a reading of Marx informed by Kantian philosophy, in which the specific moment of critique is recognised as being central to both thinkers. Karatani comments on his undertaking as follows: '*Capital* is commonly read in relation with Hegelian philosophy. In my case, I came to hold that it is only the *Critique of Pure*

---

142   Miyakawa 1994, p. 40. On Marx's various drafts for the second volume of *Capital*, see
        Miyakawa 1996, p. 46f.
143   See Ōishi 2001.
144   See also Ōishi 1995, p. 164.

Reason that should be read while cross-referencing *Capital*.[145] At a later point, Karatani elaborates further: 'In fact, Marx sought to describe the capitalist economy as if it were a self-realization of capital *qua* the Hegelian Spirit' – yet *Capital* differs from Hegelian philosophy with regard to its motivation. 'The end of *Capital* is never the "absolute Spirit". *Capital* reveals the fact that capital, though organizing the world, can never go beyond its own limit. It is a Kantian critique of the ill-contained drive of capital/reason to self-realize beyond its limit'.[146] Karatani discerns a decisive break in Marx's mature work – more precisely, between the *Grundrisse* and *Capital*. On Karatani's view, Marx remained within the Ricardian horizon in terms of his theory prior to this break (even if in a radically critical way). Karatani argues that it was this break that enabled Marx to rid himself of these limitations through the elaboration of his theory of the value-form, thus achieving a decisive theoretical breakthrough. In this, so runs Karatani's argument, Marx was certainly inspired by Samuel Bailey's critique of Ricardo. Karatani maintains that Marx subsequently developed his theory of value between the poles of Ricardo and Bailey, but overcoming both.

Crucially, the ongoing *MEGA*[2] critical edition has continued to serve as a stimulus not only for the German-language discussion of Marx, but also particularly for the corresponding Japanese discussion. In Akira Miyakawa's view, research into *Capital* in Japan has gained a recent and essentially qualitative impetus as a consequence of the publication of the previously unpublished original draft for volume three of *Capital* which is contained in the *1863–65 Manuscripts*.[147] Over many years, Japanese Marx and Engels researchers and editors have been carrying out an important part of the work on the *MEGA*[2] critical edition.[148] Japanese scholars have participated since the 1980s in the discussion around this publishing project. In certain cases, Japanese philologists[149] specialising in Marx have even attempted to correct potential errors or inaccuracies on the part of the *MEGA*[2] editors. One point of contention consisted in the question as to whether or not the third edition of the first volume of *Capital*, which was published in *MEGA*[2], Volume II/8, could be described as

---

145 Karatani 2005, p. ix. The Japanese original was published in 2001.

146 Karatani 2005, p. 9.

147 Miyakawa 1999, p. 251.

148 See Omura 2005, pp. 35 ff.

149 This description is by no means used in a pejorative sense, but rather in a positive one: it indicates a great knowledge of Marx's texts. As Alfred Schmidt once commented: 'The ever-changing history of Marx-interpretation teaches us that whenever the so-called letter was sacrificed in favour of the spirit, it was the latter itself that suffered the damage' (Schmidt 1981, p. 83. Translation amended – N.G.).

the 'final edition authorised by Marx' (Izumi Omura answered this question in the negative);[150] another contested issue revolved around the difficulties in dating certain sections of Marx's *1861–63 Manuscripts*.[151]

Scientific exchange between Japanese researchers on the one hand, and (East) German Marx researchers and editors of *MEGA*[2] on the other, had already taken place prior to 1989, and has been steadily intensified since the 1980s. The Japanese 'Marx-Engels Researchers' Association' has played a certain role in this context.[152] According to Thomas Marxhausen, before the 'transition' in 1989, a fifth of the print-run of each *MEGA*[2] volume published was sold in Japan. When the *MEGA*[2] project was in acute danger of being discontinued at the beginning of the 1990s, approximately 1,500 Japanese researchers signed a petition in favour of its continuation.[153] Recently, the cooperation between Japanese and German *MEGA*[2] researchers has been more intensive than ever.

In recent years, the Uno School is seemingly attracting fewer Marx-oriented researchers. Yet its international profile is growing. The Japanese scholars Makoto Itoh and Thomas Sekine have disseminated Uno's theory and their own respective further elaborations of the latter both within and beyond Japan more or less independently of one another since the 1970s and particularly since the 1980s. It was in this way that the Uno School reached the Anglophone sphere in particular.[154] Within the Anglo-Saxon debate, Itoh and Sekine met with both approbation[155] and criticism.[156] Sekine's approach,[157] which relied on Uno's theory, reached Canada in particular, where Sekine taught as Professor of Economics at York University, Toronto.

In his major work (published in English in the 1980s), Sekine was concerned with the exposition of a 'dialectic of capital'[158] on the level of abstraction corresponding to a theory of the 'pure' capitalist society. Like his mentor, Uno, Sekine

---

150   See Omura 1995.

151   See Omura 1995, pp. 66 f.; see also Miyake 1993.

152   See Hashimoto 1991.

153   See Marxhausen 2006, p. 600.

154   There has also been a reception of works by Makoto Itoh in China.

155   A positive evaluation of the approach to value theory of the Uno-Sekine tendency is offered by Robert Albritton (see Albritton 1984).

156   A critique aimed particularly at Itoh's theoretical roots in Uno's thought is provided by Simon Clarke (see Clarke 1989).

157   Itoh's theoretical approaches will be considered in more depth in Part 3; Sekine can be treated in more detail here.

158   See Sekine 1986. Sekine affords an insight into his specific concept of dialectic in two essays: Sekine 1998 and Sekine 2003.

structures the exposition of the 'pure' capitalist society according to the principle of a tripartite division in which the exposition of circulation precedes the exposition of production, which itself precedes the exposition of distribution. Furthermore, on essential points he follows Uno's restructuring and modification of the third volume of *Capital*. Sekine concludes that for Marx, logic coincides with political economy, whereas for Hegel, logic coincides with metaphysics. Sekine writes that Uno 'never related his approach to economic theory to Hegel's *Logic*. Nor did he, unlike Lenin, ever recommend his students to familiarize themselves first with the Hegelian *Logic* in order to understand correctly Marx's *Capital*'.[159] However, in his *The Dialectic of Capital*, Sekine argues the following: 'It is my belief that the dialectic operates essentially in the same way whether in idealism or in materialism, and that therefore Marx's thought can never be understood as it was intended to be without a full comprehension of the significance of the Hegelian dialectic'.[160] According to Sekine, 'the materialistic substitute for Hegel's Absolute' can be found in Marx's *Capital*. The dialectic of capital 'replaces the dialectic of the Absolute; with Marx "capital" plays the same role as Hegel's Absolute'.[161]

Uno's theory, or Sekine's interpretation of this theory, and in particular the corresponding methodology, was taken up by researchers in the Anglo-Saxon debate.[162] One instance is the work of Robert Albritton, who attempted to familiarise the Anglophone readership with Uno's (and Sekine's) methodological conceptions.[163] A more recent monograph by Albritton likewise draws on the theoretical tendency moulded by Sekine with the Uno School. In this work, the Canadian also refers to the methodological dimension of the Uno-Sekine tendency.[164] Albritton and John R. Bell even suggested in the mid-1990s that the Uno School was in decline in Japan, while – in their opinion – the 'Canadian branch' of this school was 'doing the most to develop the legacy of Uno'.[165]

159   Sekine 2003, p. 120. Mawatari claims, however, that Uno had made a careful reading of
        Hegel's *Logic* (see Mawatari 1985, p. 405).

160   Sekine 1986, p. 26.

161   Sekine 1986, p. 35.

162   Alongside Robert Albritton, this is (or was) true of John R. Bell, Brian MacLean and Colin
        A.M. Duncan. See Bell 1995, Bell 2003, Maclean 1981 and Duncan 1983.

163   See, for example, Albritton 1986.

164   See Albritton 1999.

165   Albritton and Bell 1995, p. 1. In any event, the 'Canadian wing' of the Uno School has
        also been acknowledged approvingly by researchers in this school's country of origin (see
        Ishibashi 1995).

Further aspects of the Japanese debate on Marx are considered in Part 3 of this study. These include the interpretation of Marx's theories of value and money that Samezō Kuruma expounded in the 1950s, and the discussion of the problematic of Marx's plans for the architectonic of his critique of political economy – a problematic which Japanese researchers addressed in the period following the Second World War, thus further elaborating a theme which had already been an object of Japanese research into Marx's critique of political economy in the interwar period.

3   Other Asian Countries

3.1   *South Asia*

The South Asian reception of Marx with regard to the critique of political economy remains to this day relatively narrowly bound to the Anglo-Saxon debate. In Germany, relatively little is known of the reception of Marx's critique of political economy on the Indian subcontinent.[166] Towards the end of the 1970s, an approach to the interpretation of Marx advanced by the Indian intellectual, Jairus Banaji, gained a certain prominence within the Anglo-Saxon sphere; in his interpretation of Marx, Banaji broached important problems of value theory and methodology.[167] In a sense, the Indian interpreter of Marx takes a kind of counter-position to those currents which establish a primary separation between Marx's method and Hegel's philosophy. For Banaji, there is no doubt that 'the method that Marx followed was a method "which *Hegel* discovered"'.[168] There is also a parallel between Banaji's position and a part of the West German interpretation of Marx in the 1970s, insofar as the Indian theorist interprets Marx's theory of value as constituting a unity of the theory of value and the theory of money (what is more, with explicit reference to Backhaus). In

---

166   Specialist circles in Germany are acquainted with a comprehensive Indian introduction to *Capital*: Ranganayakamma 1999. A further example of an Indian contribution to the reception of Marx's critique of political economy is Bose 1980. According to Eric Hobsbawm, *Capital* is available to Indians not only in English translation: a 'major linguistic extension of *Capital* occurred in independent India, with editions in Hindi, Bengali and Malayalam in the 1950s and 1960s' (Hobsbawm 1982, p. 343). By contrast, an East German author wrote in the 1970s that of all the Indian languages, a 'complete translation of the three volumes of Karl Marx's *Capital* ...' was only available 'in Malayalam' (see Krüger 1975, p. 277).

167   See Banaji 1979.

168   Banaji 1979, p. 19.

addition, in his study Banaji addresses the 'problem of the beginning' (which numbers among the virtually classical thematic fields within the international reception of *Capital*). Banaji apprehends the 'problem of the beginning' by distinguishing between an 'analytic' and a 'synthetic' point of departure in Marx. On Banaji's view, the 'analytic' point of departure is the commodity, as it is expounded at the beginning of *Capital*; from here, we arrive at value. Value is in turn qualified as the 'synthetic' point of departure in *Capital*.

The Iranian, Ali Shamsavari, contributed to the international discussion with a monograph on the method of the critique of political economy and Marx's relation to Hegel's philosophy.[169] The starting point for Shamsavari's attempt to reconstruct both the methodology of Marx's critique of political economy and the link that connects Marx's methodological perspective to Hegel's philosophy and logic is a critical engagement with interpretative approaches that try to distance Marx's thought from Hegel's philosophy. In this context, Shamsavari has in his sights economists inspired by neo-Ricardianism, such as Ian Steedman, as well as 'analytic Marxism' (see below), alongside the 'usual suspects', namely Althusser and Colletti. The formation of 'anti-Hegelian' currents of thought into the 1980s forms the background within the history of theory from which Shamsavari aims to distance himself with his alternative interpretation: 'As opposed to the anti-Hegelian trends ... it is the central contention of this book that the dialectical method as developed by Hegel constitutes a central influence on Marx's economic and historical studies, and that, furthermore, that method in itself is valid and essential for social theorizing'.[170]

Shamsavari understands Marx's theory of value to represent a scientific breakthrough; the Iranian theorist argues that this is the case in particular because Marx is able, through his value-form analysis, to transcend the value-theoretical horizon of classical political economy in a theoretically decisive way. The failure of classical political economists to conduct an analysis of the value-form is interpreted by Shamsavari as a consequence of their deficient method. Nevertheless, Shamsavari also criticises Marx's theory of value. Shamsavari's criticism engages with a similar point to that already addressed by Backhaus in the German discussion;[171] the Iranian theorist writes as follows:

---

169 See Shamsavari 1991.

170 Shamsavari 1991, p. 14.

171 'The inadequate mediation of the substance and form of value is already expressed in the fact that a break can be identified in the development of value: it is no longer obvious that the transition from the second to the third section of the first chapter is a *necessary* one' (Backhaus 1980, p. 101). Although Backhaus wrote this in 1969, he advised me in a conversation in 2002 that he still held this view, at least in its fundamentals.

The central problem with Marx's presentation of his theory of value in Chapter One of *Capital 1*, as I see it, concerns the curious isolation of the value-form analysis both from the question of the essence and the measure of value (which precedes the analysis of value-form) and from the fetishism of commodities (which follows the section on value-form).[172]

Shamsavari's thesis might be supplemented here by noting that, in the appendix to the first edition of *Capital* in 1867, the problematic of commodity fetishism is at least partially integrated with the fourth peculiarity of the equivalent form in the value-form analysis itself under the rubric, 'The fetishism of the commodity-form is more striking in the equivalent form than in the relative form of value'.[173]

At virtually the same time as Shamsavari developed his approach, the Thai, Pichit Likitkijsomboon, critically engaged with the Marxian relation to Hegelian dialectic, and proposed a theoretical approach that can be described as a 'Hegelianising' reading of Marx.[174] On Likitkijsomboon's view, a sustainable interpretation of Marx's theory must be based on an adequate understanding of both Hegelian dialectic and its reception by Marx. Likitkijsomboon grasps the Marxian theoretical project as being concerned with identifying all relevant economic categories and investigating their logical interrelation, in order to adequately expound the 'pure form' of the capitalist economy. According to Likitkijsomboon, Marx aims to present the logic of the process of capital's self-unfolding – the Thai theorist apprehends capital as subject. More precisely, Likitkijsomboon holds that Marx traces this logic of the process of capital's self-unfolding from the most abstract and simple categories right up to the fully developed totality of the 'pure' capitalist economy. Likitkijsomboon's manner of referring to a 'dialectic of capital' and a 'pure capitalist economy' might at first sight suggest a theoretical proximity to the Uno School, and in particular to Thomas Sekine, but in fact the Thai theorist exposes the latter to a pointed critique. According to Likitkijsomboon, Sekine's conception of dialectic, which the Thai theorist characterises as 'an interpretation of "dialectic" from the standpoint of formal logic', in no way corresponds to Marx's or Hegel's understanding of dialectic.[175]

---

172   Shamsavari 1991, p. 246.

173   See Marx 1994, pp. 21–3.

174   See Likitkijsomboon 1992.

175   Likitkijsomboon 1992, p. 418.

Likitkijsomboon critically engaged with Marx's value-form theory in a further text from the 1990s.[176] A central thesis of the Thai theorist consists in the
assumption that 'a systematic overview of Marx's theory of value-form, with
its dialectical method, reveals a theory consisting of both social and quantitative aspects. The two aspects are logically integrated within the dialectical
structure of the theory'.[177] Likitkijsomboon regards Marx's theory of money as
being logically grounded in his labour theory of value and value-form theory. In
the light of his considerations on Marx's value-form analysis, the Thai theorist
criticises value-form theory as developed by the Uno School, among others.[178]
It should be recalled that the Uno School proposes to defer the theorisation
of abstract labour as the substance of value from the doctrine of circulation
to the doctrine of production, whose exposition is only to be undertaken at a
later stage – i.e. the Uno School proposes the immediate separation of the theorisation of abstract labour as the substance of value from the theory of the
value-form. Likitkijsomboon's criticism is that 'Unoist adventure in the sphere
of value-form only mystifies the categories of value and value-form and obliterates the utmost significance of the necessity to verify private, individual labor
as social labor, which is' – here Likitkijsomboon puts his finger on a very important point – 'at the root of Marx's value theory'.[179]

3.2   East Asia

Aspects of the interpretation of Marx in China and South Korea in the more
recent past are briefly surveyed here.[180] Wei Xiaoping, Director of Marxist
Studies at the Institute for Philosophy, Chinese Academy of Social Sciences,
reports that there are currently three main lines of engagement with Marxism
in the People's Republic of China: firstly, 'official' Marxism in the sense of
the ideological guidelines of 'Socialism with Chinese characteristics' – i.e. in
the sense of the ideology of the leadership of the Chinese Communist Party;
secondly, 'academic Marxism' (which, it might be added, holds most promise

---

176   See Likitkijsomboon 1995.
177   Likitkijsomboon 1995, p. 74.
178   A further theorist criticised by Likitkijsomboon is the Dutchman, Geert Reuten (although
      the latter is not associated with the Uno School). For Reuten's response to this criticism,
      see Reuten 1995.
179   Likitkijsomboon 1995, p. 89.
180   As far as the interpretation of Marx is concerned, the People's Republic of China and South
      Korea are, after Japan, the most important East Asian countries in which an engagement
      with Marxian theory has occurred. On the situation with regard to publishing in Mongolia,
      for example, see the report given in Birwa 1989.

for a further development of the methodological discussion around *Capital*); and thirdly, the reception of what can be described as 'Western Marxism'.[181] Xiaoping states that the latter theoretical tradition has been acknowledged in the People's Republic of China in particular since the 1980s. Recently, the philosopher, He Ping, believed that it was possible to observe a 'return to Marx' in Chinese Marxist philosophy.[182]

A first Chinese edition of the collected works of Marx and Engels, comprising some 50 volumes, was already published in the People's Republic of China between 1956 and 1985 (primarily on the basis of the second Russian edition of the works of Marx and Engels). The fact that 'the first German edition and the French edition of the first volume of *Capital* (1867 and 1872–75, respectively)'[183] are also available in Chinese translation alongside the three volumes of *Capital* would seem to indicate that the publishing situation in China permits a differentiated debate on *Capital* (at least to a certain degree). Indeed, the situation is set to improve further in the future from a publishing point of view. With its plans for a second Chinese edition of the collected works of Marx and Engels, this time based on $MEGA^2$, the Institute for the Publishing and Translation of the Works of Marx, Engels, Lenin and Stalin of the Central Committee of the Chinese Communist Party aims to ensure a qualitative improvement of editorial standards in relation to both the translation and the scientific apparatus. This edition is oriented to a scientific readership, and, following the structural division of $MEGA^2$, will comprise four series (works and drafts; *Capital* and preparatory works; correspondence; and excerpts/notes/marginalia), making up approximately 70 volumes in total.[184] The first volume of this new edition appeared in 1995. The second Chinese edition of the collected works of Marx and Engels is remarkable on account of its scope and by virtue of the attention paid to the $MEGA^2$ edition in its elaboration. There is no indication yet of when it will be completed; work on this large-scale publishing project is proceeding at rather a slow rate. A

---

181   See Xiaoping 2006, pp. 384 ff.

182   See Ping 2007. A Japanese Marx-researcher has written the following: 'In China, a tendency has emerged since the beginning of the 1990s' which has resulted in 'increasing numbers of Chinese Marx-researchers no longer orienting themselves to the dogmatic theories of orthodox Marxism-Leninism, but to Marx's original texts' (Tairako 2009–12, p. 50; Tairako's text is also due to be published in *Wissenschaftliche Mitteilungen des Berliner Vereins zur Förderung der MEGA-Edition, Heft 7*).

183   Renxiang 1998, p. 263.

184   See Chai 2006; Chai's text is also due to be published in *Wissenschaftliche Mitteilungen des Berliner Vereins zur Förderung der MEGA-Edition, Heft 7*.

smaller, 10-volume edition of the works of Marx and Engels, originally scheduled for publication in recent years, is to include the three volumes of *Capital*.[185]

Furthermore, Marx's *Grundrisse* is also available in Chinese translation, along with a compilation of excerpts with commentaries by Marx which forms a part of the background to this manuscript which he wrote in 1857–8. The first issue of a periodical dedicated to research into Marx and Engels, published in 1989 by the Marx-Engels Department of the Institute for the Publishing and Translation of the Works of Marx, Engels, Lenin and Stalin of the Central Committee of the Chinese Communist Party,[186] contained the first Chinese translation of Marx's *Bullion* manuscript.* The latter is a compilation of excerpts revised and edited by Marx and used by him during the winter and spring of 1851 as he systematically reorganised the materials he had collected to that date relating to the theory of money. Since *Bullion* belongs to the materials Marx used as he completed the *Grundrisse*, its publication affords access to a better understanding of the research background behind the latter manuscript, and indeed to an enhanced appreciation of the 1857–8 *Rohentwurf* itself.**

Within Chinese engagement with Marx, there has been a detailed focus, since the 1980s at the latest, on the history of the origins of his economic *magnum opus*. Within this process, Chinese researchers have devoted attention not least to the *Grundrisse*.[187] Zhongpu Zhang reports that the results of Chinese research into Marx's six-volume plan were published in 1995;[188] on this point it seems that there is a thematic parallel between the Chinese and the international reception of Marx's critique of political economy.

Here a brief glance can be cast at an example from recent Chinese interpretation of Marx. References to a 'capital-logic' are no longer limited to the German, Danish or Anglo-Saxon discussion of Marx, but also play a role in recent Chinese engagement with Marx's critique of political economy. The thrust of Haifeng Yang's interpretative approach is to profile three central aspects of

---

185   On the new edition of the collected works of Marx and Engels in the People's Republic of China, see also Lu 2006 and J. Yang 2006.

186   See Skambraks and Haixian 1991.

*   *Bullion. Das vollendete Geldsystem* [*Bullion: The Consummate Monetary System*] (Marx 1986). This text has not yet been published in English translation.

**   The German title of the *Grundrisse* is *Grundrisse der Kritik der politischen Ökonomie (Rohentwurf). 1857–1858*. This is rendered in English as 'Outlines of the Critique of Political Economy (Rough Draft), 1857–58'.

187   See Zhang 2008, pp. 220 f.

188   Ibid.

Marx's philosophy: firstly, the critique of metaphysical philosophy; secondly, the exposition of 'capital-logic'; and thirdly, the dimension of social criticism, in which Marx's theory of fetishism is a significant moment.[189]

Yang is a former student of the philosopher Yibing Zhang, who belongs to the 'academic' tendency within engagement with Marx and Marxism in China. Zhang is also one of the protagonists of the Chinese critical involvement with so-called Western Marxism, and has come to represent the trend of a 'return to Marx' in China since the 1990s. It is worth mentioning with regard to the question of the theory transfer from Japan to China that Zhang has been a driving force in the Chinese reception of the theory of the Japanese interpreter of Marx and philosopher, Wataru Hiromatsu, whose work inspired a school of thought in Japan (as noted above).

In the People's Republic of China there exists a network of scientific institutions oriented to Marxism, which includes among others the Marxism Research Institute at the Shanghai University of Finance and Economics and the Academy of Marxism at the Chinese Academy of Social Sciences. One institution in which the project of the reception of modern non-Chinese Marxism is being pursued is the Center for Studies of Marxist Social Theory. The World Association for Political Economy (WAPE) – an association founded a few years ago whose headquarters is located in Hong Kong and whose chairperson, Enfu Cheng, holds a leading position at the Academy of Marxism at the Chinese Academy of Social Sciences – can be considered an example of the attempt to promote international cooperation in Marxist economic research.

Under the impact of increasing oppositional activity in South Korea from 1980 onwards, there was a wave of editions of the writings of Marx and Engels in the subsequent period. Although a new edition of *Capital* was impeded in 1987 by the organs of state repression and the publishers were arrested,[190] as a rule the activity of editors and scientific interpreters of Marx's works has subsequently been able to continue to a large extent unchecked. It is striking that many significant research contributions originate from South Korean researchers who were educated in Europe. The overseas education of numerous South Korean interpreters of Marx has been a contributing factor which has facilitated their critical engagement with theoretical approaches of European Marxism. Alongside this factor, the reception of Japanese Marxism has also played a role, however. Of the older generation of researchers with an orientation towards the Marxian critique of political economy, Soo-Haeng

---

189   See H. Yang 2006.
190   See Chung 1999, pp. 279 f.

Kim had studied in London, Young-Ho Park in Frankfurt am Main, and Woon-Young Jeong in Leuven (Belgium), before they could establish themselves at universities in their home country in the 1980s. Of the South Korean Marx-researchers to have completed their doctorates in the recent past, No-Wan Kwack, Young Bin Hahn, Lee Jun Kim, Kyung-Mi Kim[191] and Dae-Won Park were educated in Germany (the study on Isaak Ill'ich Rubin and Kōzō Uno authored by the South Korean, Hyeon-Soo Joe, who was also educated in Germany, has already been referred to above). Significant results of research undertaken by theorists from this circle will be considered in detail later in this study, for instance the sophisticated conceptual approaches oriented towards the interconnection between the theories of money, credit and crisis, or towards epistemological problems. A further South Korean researcher, Chai-On Lee, carried out research and was awarded a doctorate in the United Kingdom. Lee scrutinised the charges of redundancy, inconsistency or lack of realism levelled against the Marxian theory of value by neo-Ricardian economists or 'analytic Marxists', among others, and attempted to defend Marx against these objections.[192] Cheong-Lip Chu's study, *Ideologie und Kritik*, came into existence as a doctoral thesis at the Goethe University of Frankfurt.[193] Chu opened up a form-theoretical perspective on Marx's critique of political economy, and, influenced by Hans-Georg Backhaus, grasped Marx's value-form analysis as the unity of the theories of value and money.

Methodological questions also play a role within South Korean research engaging with Marx. This can be demonstrated with an example: one of the problematics considered within the South Korean research of the 1990s was that of the categorial transitions within Marx's exposition of his critique of political economy. The explanation of the Marxian transition from money is accorded a significant status in the enquiry by Seung-Wan Han, who incident-ally also obtained a doctorate in Germany.[194] Han writes, with regard to the categorial transition to money within Marx's exposition – a transition which must necessarily occur before the transition from money to capital – that in the *Grundrisse* Marx drew on Hegelian logic as a resource in the construction of this transition. Han argues that although a passage of the *Grundrisse* that recalls Hegel's logic of the determinations of reflection is omitted in *A Contri-bution to the Critique of Political Economy*, there is still a similarity between the

---

191   Kyung-Mi Kim was originally associated with the Marburg '*Forschungsgruppe Politische Ökonomie*' ('Research Group on Political Economy'). See Kim 1999.

192   See Lee 1993.

193   See Chu 1998.

194   See Han 1995.

development of money in the latter work and the way this is expounded in the *Grundrisse*. Han states that '[h]ere too, the immanent contradiction within the commodity develops into an external contradiction between the commodity and money'.[195] The South Korean researcher advances the thesis with regard to the transition from money to capital that Marx executes a dual transition in the *Grundrisse*. Thus, on the one hand, a transition is constructed from the sphere of circulation to productive activity; yet this is not the transition to capital itself. According to Han, the dual transition from money to capital consists in the fact that 'in this transition, a shift occurs in one instance between spheres from circulation to production; in another instance, but simultaneously, the categorial development from money to capital takes place'.[196] With his treatment of the problematic of the categorial transitions to money and to capital, Han engaged with a range of problems that also occupies a certain space within Japanese and European research. A thematic parallel between Han's enquiry and later studies carried out in South Korea consists in the attention devoted to the Hegel-Marx relation.[197]

4   The Former Socialist Countries in Europe

4.1   *The Soviet Union*[198]

Marx's *Capital* reached Russia at an early stage. In fact, its introduction into Russia was so early as to be almost anachronistic, given that the theory which aimed to expose the economic laws of motion of modern capitalist society arrived in Russia before this form of society itself. The first Russian translation of the first volume of *Capital* was published in 1872.[199] Thus, as Marx observed, 'the first foreign nation to translate *Kapital* [was] the Russian'.[200] After the socialist October Revolution, resources were made available for the foundation of the Marx-Engels Institute in Moscow (in 1921) and for the publication of the first historical-critical edition of the complete works of Marx and Engels (the

---

195   Han 1995, p. 99.

196   Han 1995, p. 110.

197   See Kim 2007.

198   As is the case with the reception of Marx in the Asian countries, the Soviet reception of Marx can only be partially considered in the present study – to the extent, that is, that it is documented in West European languages.

199   See Uroeva 1978, p. 190. Valeri Tschechowski considers an interesting dimension of the translation of Marx into Russian (see Tschechowski 2007).

200   Marx 1988a, p. 130.

first *MEGA*) under the aegis of the institute's director, David B. Ryazanov.[201] For
the elaboration of the first *MEGA*, connections were successfully established
with the Frankfurt Institute for Social Research, whose director at the time was
Carl Grünberg (Max Horkheimer would only later become director).[202]

A sophisticated discussion of Marx's theory of value had already developed
in the Soviet Union in the 1920s. A central figure in this discussion was Isaak
Ill'ich Rubin, whose major work *Essays on Marx's Theory of Value* was first published in 1923.[203] Following the republication of this work in several languages
in the 1970s, and the publication of further texts by Rubin outside the Soviet
Union, his theoretical output has been the focus of much interest in the debate
on value theory in Western Europe, Japan, and North and South America. Rubin
gave expression to deliberations whose content can to a certain extent 'be interpreted as anticipating the conception of Marx's theory of value as a monetary
theory of value – a conception which was developed from the 1970s on, particularly in West Germany'.[204] According to Rubin, Marx's theory of value contains the synthesis of the theory of the substance of value and the theory of
the form of value (i.e. the 'form of value' not in the sense of the value-form,
but of 'value as form'), and the synthesis of the qualitative and quantitative
aspects of the theory of value.[205] With regard to the category of 'equal labour',
Rubin distinguishes between three determinations: (1) physiologically equal
labour, which exists in all historical epochs; (2) socially equated labour, which
is characteristic of all systems with a social division of labour; (3) abstract or
abstract-universal labour, which characterises commodity production. Rubin
emphasises that 'Marx links the category of abstract labour inseparably with
the concept of the universal equivalent',[206] and elucidates as follows: 'In reality we defined abstract labour as labour which was made equal through the
all-round equation of all the products of labour, but the equation of all the
products of labour is not possible except through the assimilation of each one

---

201   See Hecker et al. 1997, p. 10 ff. On the life and works of Ryazanov, see, among other works,
      Külow and Jaroslawski 1993, pp. 10 ff. More recent literature to have appeared on Ryazanov
      and the first *MEGA* includes Hecker 2010. Readers of Russian can consult a comprehensive
      biography of Ryazanov by Jakov Rokitjanskij (see Rokitjanskij 2009).

202   See Hecker et al. 2000.

203   See Rubin 1972. This work underwent four editions in the Soviet Union until 1930. The
      changes between the second and third editions are discussed in detail in Takenaga 2007.

204   Hoff, Petrioli, Stützle and Wolf 2006b, p. 17.

205   See Rubin 1972, pp. 107 ff.

206   Rubin 1994, p. 49.

of them with a universal equivalent'.[207] According to Rubin, then, the concept of abstract labour necessarily leads to that of money. The problematic of commodity fetishism was of particular significance for the Soviet theorist,[208] which demonstrates that he accorded a central status to the specifically qualitative dimension of Marx's critique of political economy, in contrast to potentially reductionist, quantitative, economistic interpretations of Marx.[209]

In the 1930s, scientific engagement with Marx in the Soviet Union suffered setbacks at the hands of Stalinism. The Marx-Engels Institute was 'purged' and reorganised in 1931, researchers were persecuted and subsequently even murdered, and the publication of the first *MEGA* was discontinued in 1935.[210] It was under difficult conditions that the worldwide first edition of the *Grundrisse* was successfully published (outside the framework of the *MEGA*) in 1939/41; this was a milestone in the publishing history of the works of Marx.[211] The *Grundrisse* was thus first published in the Soviet Union, but in the original German: the complete Russian translation first appeared in 1968/9. Rolf Hecker reports that two essays by the editor of the *Grundrisse*, Paul Weller, were published in 1940/1 as 'practically the first signal of the impending first publication of the *Grundrisse*'.[212] The early reception of the *Grundrisse* – a reception thoroughly informed by methodological deliberations – was undertaken before the Stalinist era had ended.[213] A Russian researcher relates that a monograph published in 1946 by the Marx-interpreter, Lev Leontiev, aroused 'much interest in the *Grundrisse* amongst a new generation of scholars'. In celebration of the 100th anniversary of the *Grundrisse*, articles by A.G. Achundov (1957) and Igor A. Boldyrev (1958) were published.[214] In 1963, the Soviet Marx-researcher, Alexander Malysch, considered that the significance of the 1857–8 manuscripts

---

207   Rubin 1994, p. 48.

208   See Joe 1995, pp. 142 ff.

209   Although Rubin's extensive critical engagement with Marx's theory of commodity fetishism is contained in the North American edition of *Essays on Marx's Theory of Value* (Rubin 1972, pp. 5–60), it is omitted in the German edition of this work. However, the section of Rubin's text dealing with commodity fetishism was recently published in German for the first time (see Rubin 2010). On the other hand, it remains the case that Rubin's comprehensive study on the history of economic thought has been published in English (see Rubin 1979), but not in German.

210   See Hecker 2001a.

211   See Hecker 2001b for a detailed account of the 1939/41 edition of the *Grundrisse der Kritik der politischen Ökonomie*.

212   See Hecker 2001b.

213   See Müller 1978a, p. 116.

214   Vasina 2008, p. 205.

'could hardly be overestimated'. In his study, he examined the *Grundrisse* with a focus on the theories of value and money, as well as the theory of surplus value.[215] To summarise, the history of the development of Marx's critique of political economy – or, in J.P. Kandel's orthodox formulation, the history of 'the formation of the economic doctrine of Marxism' – constituted a branch of research within the Soviet discussion on Marx and Marxism of the interwar and postwar periods.[216]

Neither Isaak Ill'ich Rubin nor David B. Ryazanov survived the Stalin period, however. They were arrested and removed from their posts, and were both executed during the 'Great Purges' of 1937–8.[217] Whereas Ryazanov was subsequently rehabilitated in 1958, Rubin remained *persona non grata* right up to the *perestroika* period. During this time, little objective discussion of Rubin's works was possible, as access to these had been removed. Nevertheless, there was a certain latitude for critical scientific engagement with Marx's economic theory in the Soviet Union even before de-Stalinisation. Worthy of mention here, alongside M.M. Rosental (the Marx-researcher referred to above in connection with his opposition to Rubin), who presented a methodological enquiry into the critique of political economy in 1955,[218] is David I. Rosenberg, who left behind a detailed investigation of Marx's and Engels's engagement with political economy in the 1840s as part of a comprehensive research project.[219] Rosenberg's planned *oeuvre* on the history of the origins and development of Marx's economic theory remained unfinished due to his death in 1950.

The 'thaw' which followed Stalin's death (1953) and the Twentieth Congress of the CPSU (1956) granted the Soviet discussion of Marx a theoretical margin which went far beyond the mere brief of providing legitimation to the Soviet regime. One of the best-known monographs from the Soviet debate after de-'Stalinisation', which received a great deal of attention, not only in the former GDR, but also in the FRG, was a work by Vitaly Vygodsky published in 1965.[220] Vygodsky's focus in this work was particularly centred on the interpretation

---

215   See Malysch 1963.
216   See Kandel 1960/1, p. 239 f.
217   See Vasina 1994 and Rokitjankskij 1993.
218   See Rosental 1957.
219   See Rosenberg 1958.
220   See Vygodsky 1974. In an expanded version of this work, published in 1970, Vygodsky provided a systematic overview of the various stages in the development of Marx's work on the critique of political economy (see Wygodski 1976). On Vygodsky's profile as a researcher, see Vasina 2002. The same author has recently published a detailed account of the life and work of Vygodsky (see Vasina 2010).

of the formation and development of Marx's economic *oeuvre*; accordingly, Vygodsky refers to Marx's preparation and processing of a broad range of materials, to his research studies and to the excerpts made by him, all of which form part of the background to the history of the origins and development of *Capital*. Marx's reception of the corpus of economic theory is accorded a significant status in Vygodsky's study. The method of the ascent from the abstract to the concrete in the critique of political economy, which was also thematised by Vygodsky, formed one of the objects of a study by the philosopher, Evald Ilyenkov, during the period of the 'Khrushchev Thaw'.[221] Ilyenkov considered that the method of the ascent from the abstract to the concrete could be identified not only in the *Grundrisse* and in *A Contribution to the Critique of Political Economy*, but also in *Capital*.[222,*]

A further study to be noted in this context is that by the philosopher Viktor Vazjulin on the logic of Marx's exposition; this study was first published in 1968. Vazjulin engages with the question of a reconstruction of the dialectical logic of *Capital*. Vazjulin considers it possible 'to identify a universal system of materialist dialectic through the analysis of a special case of materialist dialectic, namely the dialectic of capitalism'.[223] According to Vazjulin, Marx theoretically developed the system of economic categories in the course of his critical engagement with Hegel's logic, and in the process of extracting the 'rational kernel' of Hegelian philosophy. The movement of the ascent from the abstract to the concrete consists in a spiralling movement of thought which encompasses all three volumes of *Capital*, and which passes from 'immediate knowledge to essence taken for itself, and then from essence as such to appearance and reality'.[224] A determinate section of this great spiral itself in turn represents a smaller spiral – namely 'that stage of immediate knowledge which corresponds to the exposition of the doctrine of the commodity and money in *Capital*'.[225]

---

221   See Ilyenkov 1982. A part of this study, which first appeared in Russian in 1960, was also published in a West German edited volume (see Iljenkow 1969).

222   Theorists from various countries have also engaged with Ilyenkov in recent times. On Ilyenkov's interpretation of Marx's critique of political economy, see for instance Behrens 2007, pp. 23 ff.

*   See also the edited collection by Alex Levant and Vesa Oittinen (Levant and Oittinen 2014), especially the chapter by Oittinen and Paula Rauhala (Oittinen and Rauhala 2014) which situates Ilyenkov's *The Dialectics of the Abstract and the Concrete in Marx's Capital* in relation to the recent value-form debate and that around Marx's method.

223   Vazjulin 2005a, p. 204.

224   Vazjulin 2005a, pp. 217 f.

225   Vazjulin 2005a, p. 218. In his monograph on the logic of Marx's *Capital*, Vazjulin gives a

In the course of the work on *MEGA*² (the critical edition of the complete works of Marx and Engels, the publication of which was begun in 1975 by the Institute of Marxism-Leninism of the Central Committee of the Communist Party of the Soviet Union in Moscow, and by the Institute of Marxism-Leninism of the Central Committee of the Socialist Unity Party of Germany in East Berlin), a portion of Soviet research into Marx and Engels took on the character of accompanying studies to the *MEGA*² edition, and became accessible also to a German-speaking readership through its publication in East German companion periodicals to the *MEGA*² edition. Within this context, Soviet researchers also worked on methodological problems relating to Marx's critique of political economy.

Some clarification is in order here: although the second *MEGA* edition was published up to the collapse of the Soviet Bloc by the respective institutes of the ruling parties in East Berlin and Moscow, and although these latter emphasised that this edition was to serve 'the further dissemination of the ideas of scientific communism',[226] the *MEGA*² edition and the accompanying research – especially the methodological research on Marx's critique of political economy – were ultimately scientific projects that went far beyond mere exercises in ideological legitimation on the part of official Marxism-Leninism in the Soviet Union and the GDR. Rolf Dlubek, who was himself involved in the *MEGA*² project for many years, expands on this point as follows:

> In the state socialist countries ... the intended function of Marx-Engels research was to underpin Marxism-Leninism as the ideology of the ruling parties. The publishing of editions of the works of Marx and Engels was the domain of central Party Institutes. A historical-critical edition of the complete works of Marx and Engels required a huge amount of effort and resources, whereas politically it would only have an indirect effect, or indeed it might even cause a certain amount of erosion to the canonised ideological edifice of Marxism-Leninism. For these reasons, it was contested within the Party Institutes. It was only possible to push forward with and realise a historical-critical edition of the collected works of Marx and Engels on an altered foundation thanks to the tenacious endeavours of scientific researchers, who all too frequently

---

more detailed treatment of the commodity and money within the whole formed by Marx's exposition, and of the 'small spiral' as a section of the 'large spiral' (see Vazjulin 2005b, pp. 172 ff.).

226   Redaktionskollegium des Marx-Engels-Jahrbuchs 1978, p. 11.

had to contend with narrow-minded political utilitarianism and incompetent bureaucratism.[227]

It should be noted in relation to the history and pre-history of the second *MEGA* edition that the original initiative to resume the project of an edition of the complete works of Marx and Engels came from Soviet researchers. However, it soon appeared that there was a growing commitment to the new *MEGA* edition in the GDR,[228] and hesitancy on the Soviet side. Dlubek reports that, for a certain period of time, the Soviet editors of Marx were confronted by a situation in which the projected new historical-critical *MEGA* edition met with rejection within the leading party structures of the CPSU.[229]

Initially the Soviet editors needed to work on a second Russian edition of the works of Marx and Engels. In its time, this edition served as an important point of reference and orientation for the compilation of multi-volume editions of the works of Marx and Engels in languages other than Russian, similar to the role that the *MEGA*[2] edition would subsequently play vis-à-vis the English-language *Marx-Engels Collected Works*, the second Chinese edition of the works of Marx and Engels, and, in future, the French-language *Grande Édition Marx-Engels*.[230] The second Russian edition of the works of Marx and Engels (*Sochineniya*) was published in 50 volumes (including the supplementary volumes) from 1954 to 1981, and represents the most important Russian-language edition of the works of Marx and Engels to have been published to date.[231]

It is worth noting with regard to the *MEGA*[2] edition that, on the basis of a comparison between the numbers of volumes edited in the Soviet Union and the GDR respectively, the editorial contribution made by researchers from the GDR can be reckoned as being proportionally somewhat greater than that by Soviet researchers. Since the 'transition' in the GDR and German reunification,

---

227 Dlubek 1994, pp. 62 f.

228 'At the beginning of the 1960s, the initiative vis-à-vis the new *MEGA* project was transferred to the Berlin Institute of Marxism-Leninism, although the latter had at its disposal neither the requisite scientific personnel and resources nor the original source material that it would have needed in order to take over the leading role in such a project' (Dlubek 1994, p. 65).

229 See Dlubek 1992, p. 43.

230 According to Lew Golman and Richard Sperl, 'multi-volume editions in Bulgarian, Japanese, Korean, Polish, Romanian, Serbo-Croat, Czech, Ukrainian, Hungarian and other languages' rely on the second Russian edition and the East German *Marx-Engels-Werke* (Golman and Sperl 1976, p. 59).

231 See Miskevitsch 2006.

the collapse of the Soviet Union, and the resulting 'dissolution' of the Institutes of Marxism-Leninism in East Berlin and Moscow (i.e. the 'dissolution' of the institutions which had previously been publishing the $MEGA^2$ edition), the International Marx-Engels Foundation ($IMES$) has functioned as the institution responsible for publishing the $MEGA^2$ edition.[232] Researchers from Russian institutions have participated in the continuation of the $MEGA^2$ project since the 1990s under the umbrella of the $IMES$, alongside the International Institute for Social History in Amsterdam, the Berlin-Brandenburg Academy of Sciences, the *Karl-Marx-Haus* in Trier and various working groups at different universities (including in Japan). The unparalleled significance of the $MEGA^2$ edition within the context of international publication of the works of Marx and Engels is recognised by researchers all over the world: the editorial principles behind the $MEGA^2$ edition (completeness; fidelity to the originals; reproduction of all stages of textual development; and the provision of commentaries) qualify it as *the* scientific and historical-critical edition of the works of Marx and Engels.[233] The great contribution made by Soviet or Russian researchers within the framework of the $MEGA^2$ edition and accompanying research is beyond question.

At this point it is appropriate to leave the present situation and go back approximately three decades. An important methodological discussion in the 1970s led to a dispute at the Department of Political Economy at the Lomonosov Moscow State University. The point of contention in the debate between the researchers N. Chessin and V.P. Shkredov was over the methodological status of the opening sections of *Capital*.[234] While Chessin proceeded from the assumption that Marx expounds a pre-capitalist 'simple commodity production' in the corresponding sections of his text, thus insisting on a reading which draws on Engels, Shkredov regarded a completely different interpretation as being more accurate. According to the latter, Marx does not present an alleged pre-capitalist simple commodity production at the beginning of his exposition in *Capital*, but rather the 'capitalist process of commodity exchange in its first, immediate, abstract form'.[235]

Of course, other Soviet researchers also expressed their views on the methodological status of the 'beginning' of Marx's exposition. Vitaly Vygodsky, one of the best-known Soviet interpreters of Marx, presented the point of view that the relations of capitalist commodity production are investigated in an *abstract form* in the first section of the first volume of *Capital*, but that an analysis of

---

232   See Rojahn 1994.

233   On the editorial principle of completeness in the $MEGA^2$ edition, see Sperl 2004a.

234   See Hecker 2002.

235   Cited in Jahn 1978, p. 69.

real pre-capitalist commodity relations is undertaken simultaneously.[236] Rolf Hecker, who, in his capacity as doctoral candidate at the Lomonosov Moscow State University at the end of the 1970s, was briefed first-hand on the state of the discussion within Soviet research, gives the following account of the contemporary Soviet (and East German) debate on the object of investigation in the first section of the first volume of Marx's *magnum opus*: 'The predominant opinion on this question is that Marx investigates the historical process of development of simple commodity production. In recent times, however, a series of studies has appeared in which this interpretation is not shared, and which deem that Marx places the simple circulation of capitalistically produced commodities before the analysis of the theory of surplus value in his exposition'.[237] With his characterisation of the latter tendency within research, Hecker had a number of researchers in mind, not least Shkredov. To Hecker himself, Chessin's assertion that Marx investigates 'simple commodity production' appeared 'groundless'.[238] It is also worth noting that the debate around Shkredov and Chessin was received in the GDR and stimulated the discussion of these issues there, and also that this debate clearly exhibited parallels to the *Capital* discussion that was being held virtually simultaneously in the FRG.

This methodological debate in the Soviet Union was hindered in due course by political pressure on Shkredov,[239] who, furthermore, in his process of theoretical self-clarification had also drawn on the theoretical work of the still unrehabilitated Rubin.[240] In the 1970s, the situation had changed unmistakeably vis-à-vis the Stalin period with regard to the way in which 'alternative' interpretations of Marx and those deviating from the official credo were dealt with – it suffices to recall that Rubin was executed during the 'Great Purges'. Nonetheless, Shkredov's scientific interventions had repercussions on a political level. Hecker and Chepurenko write that 'above all during his years at the university, [Shkredov] was confronted not by scientific discussions in themselves, but by ideological campaigns on the part of the heads of department and the party committee against his alleged Hegelian-idealist interpretation of *Cap-*

---

236   See Hecker 1987, p. 190.

237   Hecker 1979, p. 79.

238   See Hecker 1979, p. 82.

239   See Hecker 2002, p. 82. See also an editorial postscript by Rolf Hecker and Alexander Chepurenko to Shkredov's article on Engels's historicism in his interpretation of *Capital* (Hecker and Tschepurenko 1998).

240   It is also worth noting in this connection that Hecker reports that Hans-Georg Backhaus's approach to the interpretation of Marx's theory of value formed part of the obligatory reading in Shkredov's seminars in the 1970s.

ital.[241] In a subsequent retrospective contribution to the Soviet debate of the
1970s, Shkredov openly criticised the 'historicist' interpretation of Marx's critique of political economy by Engels.[242] The debate demonstrates that, *contra*
the Marxist-Leninist ideologeme of the unity of the thought of Marx and Engels,
and despite the prevalence of a not unproblematic politico-ideological atmosphere, researchers were to be found in the Soviet Union by the 1970s at the
latest who were prepared to call into question the 'traditional' Engels-inspired
interpretation of the opening sections of *Capital* which read these as an exposition of a pre-capitalist 'simple commodity production'. The same can be said in
relation to researchers in the GDR, where the Soviet discussion formed a point
of reference.

Accordingly, the Soviet debate around the methodological status of the
'beginning' of the first volume of *Capital* was not without echo in the GDR.
Wolfgang Jahn regarded the object of initial analysis in *Capital* as 'simple circulation' in the sense of an abstract sphere of the capitalist mode of production,
and thus diverged from the traditionalist interpretation, deriving from Engels,
of this initial object of analysis as 'simple commodity production'.[243] Viewed as
a whole, a certain kind of 'Western' retrospection on the question of the plurality of the post-Stalinist Soviet discussion of Marx, and of the corresponding
debate in the GDR, appears questionable: typically, such retrospective standpoints characterise the Marx debate in the East as tending towards theoretically
sterile, unitary thought, and overlook the fact that plurality, although restricted,
did in fact exist in this context. The significance of Marx-interpretation in the
'East' should by no means be underplayed.[244]

---

241   Hecker and Tschepurenko 1998, p. 130.

242   See Schkredov 1998, pp. 114 ff. Shkredov argued as follows: 'The interpretation of the logic of
       Capital as a historical reflection of the transformation of simple commodity production
       into capitalist commodity production leads invariably to an abbreviated understanding
       of the dialectical method employed by Marx, and to the reduction of the latter to the
       historical process of the emergence and development of given economic forms. The blame
       for this tragic misconception can be said not to lie with Engels alone, but also with the
       subsequent commentators on, and defenders of, Marx's theory of value' (Schkredov 1998,
       p. 122).

243   See Jahn 1978.

244   Thus, the following assertion by Backhaus is problematic: 'Since *Capital* was accorded
       above all a legitimatory function within Soviet Marxism, and the *Critique of Political
       Economy* was misappropriated as a Bible and instrumentalised as a tool of the political
       struggle, scarcely anyone was interested in a serious reprocessing of its theoretical content'
       (Backhaus 1997b, p. 18).

Yet nor did the *MEGA*² edition remain free from the problematic theorem of the fundamental theoretical unison between Marx and Engels. The following statement can be read in the introduction of the *MEGA*² volume II/2, which was edited by Soviet researchers (under the overall editorial control of Larisa Mis'kevich) and published in 1980:

> A comparison of the most important theses of Engels' review [referred to here is Engels's review of *A Contribution to the Critique of Political Economy*, a review which is highly problematic precisely from a methodological point of view – J.H.] with the 'Introduction' Marx wrote in 1857 ... shows that many of Engels' deliberations and assessments are, in terms of content, in accordance with Marx's exposition, and that this review is essentially a supplement to Marx's book. This represents further confirmation of the fact that there was a constant exchange of opinions and a prevailing theoretical congruence between the two friends, and that Marxist political economy is the collective result of the theoretical deliberations of the founders of scientific communism.[245]

Likewise, Viktor Vazjulin wrote the following in 1987 in relation to the theoretical debate in his country: 'In Soviet philosophy, and particularly in the economic literature, the hitherto dominant conception of the historical and the logical has been the one based on *Engels'* propositions in his review of *Marx's* A Contribution to the Critique of Political Economy and in the former's preface to the third volume of *Capital*. Marx's views on this problem are *de facto* identified with Engels' propositions'.[246] It might be added that such a conception of the theoretical unison between Marx and Engels had already been superseded by the state of research as it existed at the time.

Several thematic domains and ranges of problems can be identified within scientific research on Marx in the Soviet Union before the *perestroika* period by drawing on the literature survey undertaken by Rolf Hecker, in which he reports on Soviet dissertations from the 1980s. In these studies, the following aspects were thematised: the development of Marx's theory of ground rent, the formation of Marx's labour theory of value in the 1840s and 1850s, the elaboration of the problem of the circulation of capital in the manuscripts of the 1860s, the development of Marx's theory of money in the 1840s and

---

245   Marx 1982b, p. 22*.
246   Vazjulin 1987, p. 238.

1850s, and Marx's conception of alienated labour.[247] Moreover, the extensive consideration of the history of the origins and development of Marx's critique of political economy represents one of the general strengths of the Soviet research into Marx.

With *perestroika* and the collapse of the Soviet Union, theoretical approaches emerged which were no longer compatible with Marxism-Leninism, nor indeed with Marx's theory.[248] Other contributions also pointed to the need for an innovative procedure in the formation of Marxist theory which went beyond Marx's *Capital* – an example is Albert Kogan's approach to the question of the problematic of the money commodity;[249] here there is an obvious parallel to parts of the contemporary discussion in the 'West'. Vygodsky's attempt to critically interrogate certain dogmas of the orthodox interpretation of Marx also deserves to be mentioned in this context.[250] The opening up of the scientific discussion of Marx during the *perestroika* period was demonstrated by the fact that representatives of the Marx-Engels Department of the Institute of Marxism-Leninism of the Central Committee of the CPSU wished to collaborate more intensively with researchers from the FRG 'even if our assessments should diverge' (this willingness was articulated by Alexander Chepurenko in the summer of 1988).[251]

It is worth noting that Chepurenko also places emphasis on 'such "outsiders" as Shkredov, Kogan, Boldyrev and others' when considering the history of the origins and development of *Capital*, or when considering the method in *Capital*.[252] Igor Boldyrev, the third of the 'outsiders' referred to by Chepurenko here, is known within the context of research on Marx's work in the critique of political economy between 1861 and 1867 for having surmised, towards the end of the 1970s at the latest, that the so-called *1863–65 Manuscripts* did not in fact contain a lost draft of the first volume of *Capital*. Boldyrev suggested that Marx wrote no such text at that time. According to Boldyrev, Marx relied on earlier material, namely the *1861–63 Manuscripts*, in elaborating the first volume of *Capital*, which was published in 1867.[253] Boldyrev's hypothesis was rejected by

---

247   See Hecker 1982, pp. 95 ff.

248   See, for example, Burtin 1991.

249   See Kogan 1991.

250   See Vygodski 1993.

251   See Tschepurenko 1989, p. 32. Naturally, Soviet researchers had collaborated with Marx-researchers from the GDR for longer and much more closely. See Mtschedlow 1978, p. 28.

252   Tschepurenko 1989, p. 32.

253   See Galander and Galander 1979, p. 1260.

other Soviet researchers, including by Chepurenko himself.[254] Boldyrev's suggestion is incompatible with the conceptions of the Soviet editors of $MEGA^2$, Volume 11/4.1, which was published in 1988 under the direction of Vitaly Vygodsky. The latter proceed from the assumption that Marx 'prepared the final version of the text of the first volume of *Capital* on the basis of the manuscript of Book One that he drafted in 1863–64'.[255] By the beginning of the 1990s, Boldyrev had himself discarded this controversial hypothesis. Nonetheless, it remains to his credit that he provided an important stimulus to the debate on Marx's critique of political economy between the years of 1861 and 1867. No conclusion can be reached here as to whether the problem was correctly solved by the editors of $MEGA^2$, Volume 11/4.1.

At the beginning of the new millennium, Russian research into Marx still retains a presence in the international theoretical debate.[256] Russian researchers continue to collaborate in the $MEGA^2$ edition. Since the collapse of the Soviet Union, Russian and German Marx-researchers have dedicated themselves to the historical examination of the political 'purges' and persecution to which numerous Marx-researchers and Marx-publishers fell victim during the Stalin period. The new situation since the 1990s has not only caused source material to be unearthed, permitting the history of the persecution of Marx-oriented researchers to be reconstructed, but is also affording new insights into the results of theoretical research undertaken during the early Soviet debate on Marx, to which public access was severely restricted over a long period. For instance, largely unknown research by Isaak Ill'ich Rubin has recently been published – more than 70 years after he was murdered by Stalin's *régime* of terror.[257]

---

254   See Miskewitsch, Ternowski, Tschepurenko and Wygodski 1982, pp. 295 f.

255   Marx 1988d, p. 445.

256   A recent methodological research contribution is that by Antonova 2006.

257   A special issue, *Beiträge zur Marx-Engels-Forschung: Neue Folge, Sonderband 4*, was recently published to fulfil this purpose (see Vollgraf et al. 2012). This issue includes a manuscript by Rubin on Marx's theory of money which had remained unpublished for a long time (see Rubin 2012); Rubin's considerations on Marx's theory of value and money in this work also permit a reading according to which the Soviet theorist goes some way towards anticipating the standpoint which would now be termed the 'monetary theory of value'.

4.2   The GDR[258] and other Former Socialist Countries in Europe

In the part of Europe where 'actually existing socialism' prevailed, it was Marx-interpretation in the GDR which was particularly prominent alongside Soviet research as far as the investigation of the history of the origins, and the method, of Marx's critique of political economy was concerned. An inventory of Marx-research in the GDR up to the early 1960s[259] reveals that methodological questions and the problematic of Marx's plans for the architectonic of his critique of political economy were already the subject of discussion in the 1950s.[260] Yet, in 1962, the East German Marx-researcher, Walter Tuchscheerer, complained that research into Marx and Engels was being largely neglected in the GDR. Tuchscheerer made a case for the significance of research into the history of the origins and elaboration of Marx's critique of political economy – in the 1850s and 1860s in particular – as a potential perspective for GDR research. This perspective would indeed come to define parts of subsequent GDR research. However, for Tuchscheerer, a further aspect was decisive: 'We will ... only have taken a step forwards in Marx-Engels research when preconditions, both in terms of cadre and institutions, have been met for a systematic, planned, targeted and all-round investigation into the emergence and development of Marxist political economy'.[261] Precisely this came to pass subsequently, and here the decisive role of the MEGA[2] project should be emphasised, for it was in this context that the most fertile reception of Marx in scientific terms was carried out in the GDR.[262]

The MEGA[2] edition was buttressed by a variety of research projects, whose results were published in companion periodicals and thus made publicly avail-

---

258   In this section of the present study, the reception of Marx in the GDR will only be briefly addressed; by contrast, a prominent research project undertaken by researchers from the GDR engaging with the problematic of Marx's plans for the architectonic of his critique of political economy will be extensively considered later.

259   See Tuchscheerer 1962.

260   Of importance in this context is a study by Fritz Behrens (Behrens 1952); incidentally, Roman Rosdolsky engaged with Behrens's study (albeit critically). Behrens was apparently one of the first researchers in the GDR to deal with the history of the origins and development of Marx's economic theory. In 1953, he wrote: 'The question of the development of political economy by Marx himself has not yet been investigated' (Behrens 1953, p. 444). Alongside Behrens, another GDR researcher to engage at an early stage with methodological questions was Hermann Ley (see Ley 1954). On the discussion of the *Grundrisse* in the GDR in the 1950s, see Paragenings 2006.

261   Tuchscheerer 1962, p. 98.

262   The fact that the MEGA[2] project also has an extended prehistory is documented by Dlubek 1993, among other studies.

able to a scientific readership both within and beyond the GDR. The numerous research studies in the context of the *MEGA*[2] edition mark a qualitative leap in GDR research when compared to the previous engagement with Marx. The *MEGA*[2] edition itself and the emergence of the corresponding companion periodicals from the 1970s onwards thus can be seen to mark a historical watershed, although Walter Tuchscheerer's monograph (see below), which was posthumously published in 1968, already represented an anticipation of this new level of research. With the exception of the situation of research in the USSR, this dimension of intensive research accompanying the *MEGA*[2] edition also distinguishes research in the GDR from investigation into Marx in the other countries of 'actually existing socialism'.

The monographs by Walter Tuchscheerer and Manfred Müller, each of which focuses on a particular period of the historical development of Marx's work on the critique of political economy, provided important impulses to the debate; incidentally, it should be noted that these works were also received in the West at the time.[263] Among other questions, Tuchscheerer retraced the development of Marx's conceptions of the theory of value and the relation of these to David Ricardo. In addition, Tuchscheerer's monograph contains one of the relatively early engagements with the *Grundrisse* in the German-language discussion. For its part, Manfred Müller's monograph addresses, among other themes, the history of the development of the structure of the critique of political economy; here, the question of the different levels of exposition in Marx's critique of political economy plays an important role. In general, Müller's work places great emphasis on research into Marx's *1861–63 Manuscripts* and the corresponding preparatory studies.[264]

Manfred Müller belonged to the 'Halle' fraction of GDR Marx-research (alongside Wolfgang Jahn, Dieter Noske, Thomas Marxhausen and many others). In this context it is worth noting the assessment by the West German, Ernst Theodor Mohl, according to whom Halle is to be considered the 'secret capital' of GDR Marx-Engels research, with its thematic focus on the 'history of Marx's *Capital*';[265] in my opinion, Mohl's assessment is well-founded. A particular focus of Halle-based research was the development of the critique of political economy in the period from 1850 to 1863; in this research, attention

---

263   See Tuchscheerer 1968 and Müller 1978b.

264   See, among other works, Müller 1977 and Müller 1983.

265   Mohl 1991, p. 118. Researchers based or educated in Halle made up a considerable portion of the authors of two edited volumes: Nietzold, Skambraks and Wermusch 1978 and Jahn et al. 1983.

was directed precisely to methodological considerations in Marx. The ambitious venture of a reconstruction of Marx's six-volume project, which was to be informed by methodological research undertaken by the circle of Halle-based researchers, will be considered in detail later. For now, it is sufficient to draw attention to the productivity of the Halle-based researchers in their research into Marx's method and their indexing of the development of Marx's work on the critique of political economy. In this context, the research activities of a subsequent generation also made an impact in the 1970s and 1980s.

While the main focus of Halle-based research was unambiguously centred on detailed enquiries into Marx's manuscripts on the critique of political economy and the accompanying mass of excerpted material, the approaches of young researchers such as Ulrike Galander, Thomas Marxhausen and Marion Zimmermann exhibited a perspective which was not overly restricted to Marx alone. A hallmark of Halle-based research consisted in a commitment to a scientific engagement with Marx's texts on the critique of political economy that was to be closely coupled with the exploration of the source material used by the Trier-born theorist.[266]

In the intervening period, it seems that Marx's critical theory of fetishism has become a central point of reference for a 'modern' understanding of Marxism which is represented by, among others, intellectuals who wish to distance themselves from the antiquated dogmas of 'traditional Marxism'. One of these intellectuals, John Holloway, is critical of the fact that the category of fetishism, which was so important for Marx, has been almost completely overlooked in mainstream Marxism.[267] Yet a caveat is in order here: care should be taken to avoid prematurely pronouncing a corresponding sweeping verdict against the Marx discussion in the GDR, for the problematic of fetishism was certainly present in the reception of Marx in the GDR, as can be demonstrated by referring to the theoretical output of Thomas Marxhausen.[268]

Of particular importance for scientific engagement with Marx in the GDR from an institutional point of view was the 'Wissenschaftliche Rat für Marx-Engels Forschung',* established in 1969; this body enabled the coordination of

---

266   See, for example, Galander, Marxhausen and Zimmermann 1983. An earlier study by Zimmermann focuses on Marx's reception of Ricardo in 1851 (Zimmermann 1979). Thomas Marxhausen addressed the question of Marx's reception of Ricardo and/or classical economics on several occasions: see Marxhausen 1987a, Marxhausen and Schattenberg 1978, and Marxhausen 1980.

267   See Holloway 2005, p. 118.

268   See Marxhausen 1988 and Marxhausen 1987b.

*   'The Scientific Council for Marx-Engels Research'.

scientific activity in the various research facilities.[269] In a 1988 lecture, Erich Kundel argued that the activity of this council had facilitated a process in which there was increasing success in 'clustering specific Marx-Engels research in the GDR around the MEGA edition, thus enabling a corresponding identification of specific foci, the constitution of long-term lines of development, and the establishment of an immediate connection between research and editorial practice'.[270] It is no surprise, then, that the most important East German publishing organs for research on Marx (and their successors in the FRG after reunification) were (and continue to be) conceived as companion periodicals to the MEGA² edition.[271] In these companion periodicals, contributions are also to be found which engage with methodological questions related to Marx's critique of political economy; in part, these contributions are by researchers from the GDR. East German Marx-research was confronted by radical changes through the political and social upheavals in 1989 and 1990 and the ensuing 'winding down' of facilities in the academic and institutional sphere. In 1990, East Berlin Marx-researchers founded the MEGA-Stiftung e. V.[272],* In 1991, this organisation changed its name to Berliner Verein zur Förderung der MEGA-Edition e. V.,** and continues to represent an important forum for Marx-Engels research in the context of the MEGA² edition.

---

269   See Kundel 1989.

270   Kundel 1989, p. 26.

271   These include the following: the Marx-Engels-Jahrbuch, published by the Central Committee of the CPSU and the Central Committee of the SED (13 issues between 1978 and 1991); Beiträge zur Marx-Engels-Forschung, published by the Marx-Engels Department of the Institute of Marxism-Leninism of the Central Committee of the SED (almost 30 issues between 1977 and 1990); Arbeitsblätter zur Marx-Engels-Forschung, published by the Marxism-Leninism Department at the Martin Luther University of Halle-Wittenberg (more than 20 issues between 1976 and 1988); Marx-Engels-Forschungsberichte, published during the 1980s at the Karl Marx University in Leipzig; Beiträge zur Marx-Engels-Forschung: Neue Folge, published by Rolf Hecker, Carl-Erich Vollgraf and Richard Sperl (more than 20 issues, including special volumes, since 1991). Additionally, the results of research by scholars from the former GDR found, and continue to find, a forum in Wissenschaftliche Mitteilungen, published by the Berliner Verein zur Förderung der MEGA-Edition e. V. (several issues since 2002); in the MEGA-Studien, published by the Internationale Marx-Engels Stiftung (approximately 10 issues between 1994 and 2001); as well as in the new version of the Marx-Engels-Jahrbuch, also published by the Internationale Marx-Engels Stiftung (several issues since 2003).

272   See Vollgraf 1991.

*   'MEGA Foundation (Registered Association)'.

**   'Berlin Association for the Promotion of the MEGA Edition (Registered Association)'.

It was not only in the Soviet Union and the GDR that theoretical engagement with Marx took place partly within a context of legitimation of domination; this was also the case in the other Warsaw Pact countries, as well as in Yugoslavia. In these countries, just as in the Soviet Union and the GDR, a differentiated and elaborate scientific engagement with Marx's critique of political economy was nonetheless possible.

Important contributions from the Czechoslovak discussion of Marx in the 1960s include a monograph on philosophy of science and methodology by Jindřich Zelený and the theoretical approach of the philosopher, Karel Kosík.[273] Zelený's study[274,*] was translated into German and widely received both in the GDR and in West Germany in the 1960s and 1970s, and played an important role in the international discussion of *Capital*.[275] In Zelený's interpretation, a significance is accorded to, for example, the relation between essence and appearance in Marx's economic theory, the 'problem of the beginning' in Marx's exposition, and the theoretical relationship between Marx and Hegel's philosophy on the one hand, and that between Marx and Ricardo's classical political economy on the other. Zelený attempts to draw out central theoretical differences between Marx and Ricardo. One of the conclusions that the Czech theorist arrives at is that Marx was able to overcome the one-sided focus on quantitative aspects characteristic of Ricardo's economic theory (Zelený refers to a quantitativism in Ricardo's theory). Zelený identifies a structural-genetic analysis at work in Marx's *Capital*. An important conclusion drawn by Zelený is that Marx sets out a novel kind of scientific thinking. For his part, Karel Kosík was one of the authors who, like Alfred Schmidt in West Germany,[276] drew attention to the emphatically critical character of Marx's project of a critique of political economy at an early stage.[277]

In the 1970s, the Polish philosopher, Marek Siemek, focused his attention on a similar problematic in his attempt to fathom the specific concept of critique in the critique of political economy. According to Siemek, *Capital*

---

273   In the ČSSR, there were high circulation figures for editions of *Capital*. See Dvořáček 1983, p. 387.

274   See Zelený 1980.

*   It should be noted that Zelený's work in the original Czechoslovak edition is entitled 'The Logical Structure of Marx's *Capital*'.

275   An example of the reception of Zelený's study in the FRG is Ritsert 1973. Ingo Elbe has recently engaged critically with Zelený (see Elbe 2008, pp. 211 ff.).

276   See Schmidt 1968, pp. 33 f.

277   See Kosík 1967. Another Czech contribution (Svetly 1993) remains to a large extent on a rather general level.

should in no way be ranged under the category of political economy. In Siemek's view, the author of *Capital* was a philosopher and thus moved on a different level of theory from that of economic science. Siemek grasps the 'critique of political economy' as an epistemological project, and argues that this is not to be equated with the immediate epistemic 'knowledge' which characterises political economy. According to Siemek, it is not the 'method', but rather the *object* and the *level of theory* that most sharply distinguish Marx's critique of political economy from political economy itself. That is to say, in Marx, we find the epistemological level on which the actual object appears not as 'the object of economics', but as economics itself. More precisely, Siemek argues that Marx takes economics as his object of critique within the structural relationship that economics has to its object – i.e. to the reified form of objectivity of social being. According to the Polish philosopher, economics simultaneously expresses and disguises this reified form of objectivity.[278] At any rate, Siemek's interpretation is opposed to the simplifying reduction of the critique of political economy to an 'alternative' political economy.

That the problem of the beginning of Marx's exposition and Marx's analysis of the commodity continued to define a field of interpretation for Eastern European Marx-research in the 1980s can be demonstrated by referring to two examples. Within the framework of his critical engagement with Marx's analysis of the commodity, the Yugoslav philosopher, Davor Rodin, presented an interpretative approach which consisted in reading Marx's theory as a critical demystification of reified social relations and of commodity fetishism. According to Rodin, the commodity structure obtains a fundamental significance: 'Just as, in Hegel, the essence of logic purely formally pervades and governs the whole philosophy of right, aesthetics, the philosophy of history and the philosophy of nature, so too the commodity structure pervades and governs all spheres of life – including the state and bourgeois society'.*,[279] Rodin grasps the commodity as the essence-structure of political economy, and he argues that it is the perspective of the analysis of the commodity which first makes possible the critique of political economy. For his part, the Hungarian philosopher, Imre Tagai, draws attention to a central difference between Hegel and Marx:

---

278   Siemek 2002, p. 30. Further Polish research was carried out in the 1970s by the philosopher of science, Leszek Nowak, who attempted, among other things, to identify a specifically Marxian 'model of explanation' (see Nowak 1976), and to draw out methodological differences between the approaches of Marx and Weber (see Nowak 1978).

*   [*bürgerliche Gesellschaft*] – it should be noted that within the context of Hegel's philosophy of right, *bürgerliche Gesellschaft* is customarily translated as 'civil society'.

279   Rodin 1988, p. 45.

'Hegel begins with the *Concept*, or *Being-in-General*; by contrast, Marx begins with a concrete category, the *determinate* concept: the commodity. Furthermore, the relationship between use-value and exchange-value does not follow the "schema" of Hegelian determinations of reflection'.[280] In the context of his research, Tagai took the view that Marx not only turned Hegel's logic the right way up, but that he also completely transformed it.

5   Italy, France and Other Western European Countries

5.1   *Italy*

As far as the Western European discussion of Marx is concerned, the discourses in Italy and France constitute the most important points of reference, if by no means the only ones. Within the present framework, however, the discussions in Italy and France can only be considered selectively. Thus, the whole range of the extremely variegated and theoretically rich history of Italian Marxism from the postwar period to the recent past (encompassing thinkers such as Ludovico Geymonat, Sebastiano Timpanaro, Gianfranco la Grassa) cannot be presented here; rather, attention is focused on a few of the authors who have distinguished themselves with their interpretation of Marx's critique of political economy and have gained a certain international prominence as a result.[281]

The philosophers, Galvano Della Volpe[282,*] and Lucio Colletti[283] (both of whom have already been mentioned above), exerted a decisive influence on the Italian Marx discussion of the postwar period;[284] among other questions,

---

280   Tagai 1989, p. 173. On the various Hungarian editions of *Capital* up to the 1960s, see Hay 1968. On Marxist thought originating in Hungary, see Gabel 1975.

281   The sequence in which the authors presented in this subchapter are considered is not always a chronological one.

282   See Della Volpe 1973. See also Graf 1995. An introduction to Della Volpe's methodological engagement with Marx, which goes into the historical circumstances in which Della Volpe's thought developed, is given in Montano 1971.

*   See also Della Volpe 1979a, 1979b, 1979c and 1979d.

283   See Colletti 1973 and Colletti 1975. Martin Jay devotes much attention to both Della Volpe and Colletti in his well-known study, *Marxism and Totality* (see Jay 1984, pp. 423 ff.). Ingo Elbe gives a detailed consideration of Colletti (see Elbe 2010, pp. 139 ff.).

284   On earlier discussion of Marx in Italy, see Bravo 1989. On Italian editions of Marx and Engels up to 1926, see Gianni 2007. On editions of Marx and Engels after the Second World War, see Bravo 1992. See Corradi 2005 for a comprehensive work dealing in detail with the history of Italian Marxism from the late nineteenth century, from Labriola to the recent past, via Gramsci, the postwar Marxism of the Della Volpe School and *operaismo*. On

the clarification of Marx's relation to Hegel played an important role for both of these philosophers. The following can be considered central aspects of Della Volpe's reception of Marx's theory: the insistence on the specific scientific character of Marx's thought and on the latter's break with Hegel's philosophy, and particularly the interpretation of Marxian abstraction as a 'determinate abstraction' that stands opposed to Hegelian abstraction. Della Volpe conceived of Marx's method as a movement from the concrete to the abstract, and then back from the abstract to the concrete. Generally speaking, Della Volpe is to be credited within Italian Marxism for having considerably contributed to the process whereby a methodologically oriented Marx-reading could establish itself in the postwar period. The emergence of the Della Volpe School[285] in the 1950s marked a watershed in the history of Italian Marxism, in particular with regard to the systematic engagement with Marxian theory that was brought to the fore by Della Volpe.[286]

Following its publication in 1950, Della Volpe's important philosophical work, *Logica come scienza positiva*,[287] gradually gained in influence. Lucio Colletti has since claimed that Marx's theory (and above all *Capital*) only exerted a rather slight influence on the intellectual life of the Italian Left until around 1955 or 1956. Colletti formulates the point as follows:

> The essential lesson I learnt from contact with the writings of Della Volpe was the need for an absolutely serious relationship to the work of Marx – based on direct knowledge and real study of his original texts. This may sound paradoxical, but it is important to remember that the penetration of Marxism in Italy in the first post-war decade, from 1945 to 1955, was intellectually and theoretically very superficial and exiguous.[288]

Italian Marxism in the twentieth century, see also Bellofiore 2007. A perspective on the history of Italian Marxism is also given by Costanzo Preve (see Preve 1993). (For Preve's interpretation of Marx, see, among other works, Preve 1984 and Preve 2007. It is not possible within the present framework to go into Preve's political conceptions).

285   Alongside Lucio Colletti, Nicolao Merker and others, the philosopher Mario Rossi deserves mention as one of the best-known theorists to have come from this school. On Rossi, see Bufalo and Alcaro 1990.

286   It goes without saying, however, that Della Volpe's thematically multi-faceted *oeuvre* cannot be reduced to his reception of Marx (in the narrow sense).

287   The 1969 edition appeared under a different title: *Logica come scienza storica* ('Logic as a Historical Science').

288   Colletti 1974, p. 8.

Whether or not Colletti's assessment is held to be accurate, it remains the case that an important step in the direction of a more intensive reception of Marxian theory was taken in the 1950s.

In this context, Della Volpe's reading of Marx will now be considered more closely. There is an important similarity between Della Volpe's interpretation of Marx and that of Louis Althusser: both philosophers insist on an irreconcilable theoretical difference between Hegel and Marx.[289] Both Della Volpe and Althusser considered that the development of Marx's thought was marked by a radical 'break' or 'turning point' that had a decisive effect on the latter's theoretical *oeuvre*. Nevertheless, an important distinction ought not to be overlooked here: these two thinkers locate the decisive break in Marx's *oeuvre* – from the point of view of this *oeuvre*'s genesis or formation – at different chronological points. Althusser dates Marx's break with his earlier 'humanist' or 'ideological' thought in 1845 at the earliest, and argues that the *Theses on Feuerbach* and *The German Ideology* document this rupture. By contrast, for Della Volpe, Marx's 1843 *Critique of Hegel's Doctrine of the State* already marks his decisive break – i.e. with Hegel. It might be added here that this implies a completely different evaluation of Marx's thought in the period between 1843 and 1845 on the part of Della Volpe and Althusser respectively. The dimensions of this difference become apparent if the great significance of the year 1844 in particular – the evaluation of which is so fiercely contested by Della Volpe and Althusser – is borne in mind: 1844 was the year in which Marx crucially intensified his engagement with political economy, after which there would be no going back as far as this new field of theoretical work was concerned.[290] Incidentally, it is not only in the comparison between Della Volpe and Althusser that differences – beyond superficial similarities – should be borne in mind; this also applies to the comparison between Della Volpe and a further philosopher whose work inspired the formation of a school of thought, and who also emphasises the decisive significance of a break in Marx's *oeuvre* – namely the Japanese theorist and interpreter of Marx, Wataru Hiromatsu. The latter, whose approach focuses on the theory of reification, also dates the break in Marx's thought as occurring at a later point than that identified by Della Volpe.

Through his translations and interpretations of Marx's writings from 1843 and 1844, Galvano Della Volpe succeeded in familiarising the Italian public with this phase in the history of the development of Marx's *oeuvre*. Della Volpe attributed a decisive significance to precisely this period within Marx's pro-

---

289   See also Althusser's critical appraisal of Della Volpe (Althusser 1979, pp. 37–8).
290   On Marx's reception of political economy in 1844, see, among other works, Musto 2007a.

cess of development: here, according to the Italian philosopher, Marx laid the foundations for a new methodology which contrasted with the Hegelian one. In Della Volpe's conception, however, the *Critique of Hegel's Doctrine of the State* of 1843 was even more important than the *Economic and Philosophical Manuscripts* of 1844. Yet the Italian philosopher in no way restricted himself to concentrating on Marx's early writings before 1848; in particular, his study of the 1857 *Introduction* played a crucial role in the shaping of his perspective on Marx's understanding of his method.[291] Della Volpe regarded the methodological movement from the concrete to the abstract, and then back to the concrete, as having been thematised in the *Introduction* and applied in *Capital*.

Like Della Volpe, another philosopher, Lucio Colletti, who was influenced by the former and had his origins in the Della Volpe School, also proposed an anti-Hegelian interpretation of Marx. In the 1970s, Colletti's further theoretical development, based on a new reading of Marx, became manifest. For Colletti's interpretation of Marx, Kant's philosophy represented an important point of reference; he drew a fundamental distinction between 'dialectical contradiction' and 'opposition devoid of contradiction' – the latter being understood in the sense of the Kantian real opposition [*Realopposition* or *Realrepugnanz*], and being completely compatible with the principle of non-contradiction. For Colletti, the principle of non-contradiction was a basic axiom of materialism and science: 'Reality cannot contain dialectical contradictions but only real oppositions, conflicts between forces, relations of contrariety. The latter are *ohne Widerspruch*, i.e. non-contradictory oppositions, and not dialectical contradictions'.[292] Yet Colletti maintains that for (the mature) Marx, the oppositions in capitalist society were dialectical contradictions, and not mere real oppositions.

An important point to note is that in the course of his disengagement from Della Volpe, Colletti revised the latter's thesis of Marx as a scientist who corresponded to the paradigm set by Galileo Galilei, and now established a distinction between a scientific discourse and a kind of 'philosophical' discourse in Marx. Consequently, Colletti saw in the mature Marx a thinker with two different faces. Colletti's image of Marx had been shaken. Finally, the Italian thinker turned his back on Marx and Marxism. Yet Colletti was by no means

---

291   See Della Volpe 1979d. See also Merker 1975, pp. 14 f. The 1857 *Introduction* has remained an important point of reference for the Italian reception of Marx from Della Volpe, via Mario Dal Pra (see Dal Pra 1977, pp. 283 ff.), to, more recently, Marcello Musto (see Musto 2008, pp. 3 ff.).

292   Colletti 1975, pp. 28 f.

the only one within the Italian reception of Marx to reflect upon the latter's 'two faces'. The economist, Claudio Napoleoni, distinguished himself as one of the most significant Italian interpreters of the critique of political economy in the 1960s and 1970s, and drew a distinction between two different discourses in connection with Marx's critique of political economy (in a way not dissimilar to Colletti's central thesis). Napoleoni argued that Marx developed on the one hand a philosophical discourse; in this context, Marx crucially transcended the problems posed by traditional economic science. On the other hand, according to Napoleoni, Marx's 'other' discourse – his economic one – found itself more or less in continuity with classical political economy. On the Italian economist's view, both discourses were present in Marx's deliberations on the theory of value.[293]

It goes without saying that the Marx debate of the 1950s to the 1970s was in no way limited to the trio of Della Volpe, Colletti and Napoleoni.[294] For instance, the Della Volpe-influenced Italian economist and interpreter of Marx, Giulio Pietranera, posed the question in the 1950s of the difference between Marx's method and that of classical political economists.[295] Given a context in which there had long been a much more intensive reception of the first volume of *Capital* than of the second and third volumes,[296] it is worth noting that, in the 1950s, Pietranera was instrumental in broadening interest in Marx's

---

293   On Napoleoni, see, among other works, Potier 1989, pp. 63 and 67f. Riccardo Bellofiore also gives a consideration of Napoleoni (see Bellofiore 1997, pp. 5ff.). Bellofiore's essay is dedicated to the Italian debate on Marx's theory of value, particularly in the 1970s. Space does not permit a consideration of the details of this debate or of Napoleoni's process of development in individual theoretical questions. Further relevant references in the present context are Napoleoni 1975 and Napoleoni 1983.

294   A volume edited by Franco Cassano gives an overview of the discussion on Marx and Marxism that took place in Italy from the 1950s to the 1970s (see Cassano 1973). It is not possible within the limits of the present subchapter to reflect the individual facets of the discussion documented in Cassano's volume. On Italian Marxism in the 1960s, see also Badaloni 1971.

295   See Pietranera 1973, p. 31. The Italian theorist wrote this text in 1956.

296   The Mexican interpreter of Marx, Raúl Rojas, even writes the following: 'The second and third volumes of *Capital* ... never achieved the popularity of the first volume. The only people who were eager to obtain a copy of the final two volumes of *Capital* were professional economists ... By contrast, workers and political activists never attached any great significance to the second and third volumes of *Capital*. From a historical perspective, it was only the first volume of *Capital* that was read. Even though Marx himself always emphasised that *Capital* formed a theoretical whole, it was never read accordingly' (Rojas 1989, p. 253).

critique of political economy beyond the engagement with the first volume of *Capital* alone. In the 1970s, the Della Volpe-influenced philosopher, Mario Rossi, produced a study in the history of philosophy, *Da Hegel a Marx*, in which he dealt extensively with the development of Marx's thought up to 1848, including reflections on the *Economic and Philosophical Manuscripts* (first published in the interwar period)[297] and *The German Ideology*.[298]

A significant postwar Marx-interpreter in Italy was the philosopher, Cesare Luporini, who attempted to supersede Galvano Della Volpe's methodological interpretation. To the latter's interpretation of the Marxian method as a movement first from the concrete to the abstract, and then back to the concrete, Luporini counterposed a conception of the trajectory of Marx's thought which begins with the abstract and ends with the abstract. In his essay, 'La logica specifica dell'oggetto specifico', he relied on Marx's postface to the second edition of the first volume of *Capital*.[299] Here, Marx addresses his own method, and includes considerations of its relation to Hegel. The corresponding passage from the postface is, on Luporini's view, to be interpreted literally and analytically. According to the Italian philosopher, Marx had identified the rational kernel from Hegel's dialectic and extracted it from its mystical shell. Thus, the critical peculiarity of the dialectic, which reveals itself in this core, consists in the circumstance that the positive understanding through the dialectic of the existing *status quo* simultaneously contains the understanding of the negation of this *status quo*.

Yet Marx left an important point incomplete, according to Luporini. As is well known, Marx recognised in his postface that Hegel had been 'the first to present [the dialectic's] general forms of motion in a comprehensive and conscious manner'.[300] For Luporini, however, the following problem arises in this context: if 'one proceeds from the starting-point of the rational kernel, how are the general forms of motion to be reconstructed in the dialectic which has been turned the right way up? It has to be said immediately that Marx never solved this problem – that is, he never filled the gap between the "rational kernel" and the "general forms of motion" of dialectic'.[301] Yet Marx did have a feeling for the problem, according to Luporini, who poses the following question: 'If the dialectic has been turned the right way up and de-mystified,

297   See Rossi 1974, pp. 456 ff.
298   See Rossi 1975, pp. 20 ff.
299   See Luporini 1976. Further works by Luporini also include an extensive interpretation of Marx's conception of history (see Luporini 1983).
300   Marx 1976a, p. 103.
301   Luporini 1976, p. 6.

can its "general forms of motion" continue to exist in the same way as in Hegel? Can they continue to exist at all? To put it another way: can they (or a modified configuration of them) be set out in a categorical continuum – i.e. systematically – on the terrain of materialist dialectic?'[302] At any rate – according to Luporini – Marx left behind a theoretical void.

With regard to the Italian reception of Marx in the postwar period, it should be borne in mind, however, that important texts by Marx only became available in Italian at a late stage (if the details provided by Umberto Cerroni are correct, the third volume of *Capital* and *Theories of Surplus-Value* were not published in Italian until the 1950s, and the *Grundrisse* did not appear in Italian until 1968–70).[303] In the 1960s and 1970s, however, there evolved an extremely intensive engagement with Marxian theory. A thinker to be noted in this context, alongside the aforementioned theorists, is the philosopher, Nicola Badaloni.[304] In his study, *Per il comunismo*, Badaloni explored Hegel's logic and also the logic of Marx's *Capital*.[305] A further Marx-interpreter of this period, the philosopher, Salvatore Veca,[306] engaged with Marx's scientific programme and grasped historical materialism as its 'metaphysical core'.[307]

Italian studies dating from the 1970s and 1980s deal with the problematic of the 'dialectical exposition'[308] and with the 'problem of the beginning'.[309] These thematic fields are of course also present in the German discussion. Luporini was one interpreter who paid a great deal of attention to the 'beginning' of the critique of political economy – i.e. Marx's analysis of the commodity, his analysis of the value-form and his exposition of the exchange process. In his reading, Luporini understands the value-objectivity of commodities – an objectivity which is, according to Marx, a spectral, supersensuous one – as a purely social dimension. Towards the end of the 1970s, the Marx-researcher, Alberto Gajano, published an investigation into Marx's commodity analysis in which he relied

---

302   Luporini 1976, pp. 6–7.

303   See Cerroni 1972, p. 40. The so-called 'Fragment on Machines' from the *Grundrisse* (see Marx 1981b, pp. 569–84), which was a reference point for *operaista* theoretical production, was published in Italian translation in 1964 in *Quaderni Rossi*. Examples of the Italian reception of the *Grundrisse* are to be found in Rovatti 1973 and Schiavone 1976. A closer examination of the reception of the *Grundrisse* in Italy is given in Tronti 2008.

304   On Badaloni, see, among other works, Kallscheuer 1986, pp. 150 ff.

305   See Badaloni 1972.

306   See, among other works, Veca 1971 and Veca 1977.

307   See Veca 1977, p. 99.

308   See Grassi 1976.

309   See Porcaro 1986.

systematically on the first chapter of *A Contribution to the Critique of Political Economy*.[310] With regard to Marx's method, Gajano distinguished between an analytic moment and a synthetic-genetic one.[311]

In the 1970s and 1980s, some interpretations emerged within Italian research on Marx's theory of value which implied a certain similarity with the approach of economists such as Ian Steedman, who himself was influenced by the neo-Ricardian economist, Piero Sraffa (1898–1983). From the latter's approach, Steedman inferred the redundancy of Marx's labour theory of value. The status of Marx's labour theory of value was also critically called into question by Italian interpreters. The Italian reception of Marx yielded an interpretation of Marx's theory of value that was also received internationally – namely the monograph by the economist, Marco Lippi; Lippis's approach moved in the direction of a possible disengagement from Marx's labour theory of value.[312] Another study which pointed in a similar direction was that by Massimo Mugnai.[313] The latter also provided an elucidation of Marx's concept of contradiction and thematised the relationship between Marxian and Hegelian dialectic.

Furthermore, a great deal of attention within the Italian debate was paid to the problematic of fetishism within Marx's critique of political economy.[314] In the 1970s, the philosopher, Alessandro Mazzone, engaged with the problematic of capital fetishism and ideology theory.[315] With regard to the problematic of fetishism, which was discussed in both Italy and Germany, Alfonso M. Iacono presented an approach in the 1980s which broadened the debate to include the question of the background of the sources for Marx's concept of fetishism. Iacono refers to the reception by Marx of an ethnological study by Charles de Brosses from 1760, entitled *Du culte des dieux fétiches*.[316]

More recently, Franco Soldani pursued an approach to the interpretation of Marx which has from time to time been rather neglected in the history of the reception of the critique of political economy. Like the South Korean, Seung-Wan Han, or the Swiss working group around Judith Jánoska, Soldani demonstrates an appreciation of the fact that Marx critically engaged with the natural

---

310 See Gajano 1979.

311 On Gajano, see also Fineschi 2002a, pp. 231f.

312 See Lippi 1979. Lippi's book has also been translated into Spanish.

313 See Mugnai 1984.

314 See, for example, Rovatti 1972.

315 See Mazzone 1977, Mazzone 1978a and Mazzone 1978b. Mazzone subsequently engaged in research into the specific temporality of the capitalist mode of production (see Mazzone 1988), and into Marx's concept of class (see Mazzone 2002a).

316 See Iacono 1987, p. 101.

science of his time.[317] The Italian interpreter of Marx enquires as to the stimulus that Marx might have gained from this engagement with natural science. According to Soldani, aspects of the rationality characterising natural science were reflected in Marx, firstly in the shape of his differentiation between the immanent laws of capitalist production from their form of manifestation as the coercive laws of competition, and secondly in the guise of the 'difference between the "internal organisation" of this society and its typical "modes of existence" in the phenomena or *Erscheinungsformen* of economic life'.[318]

The *MEGA*[2] edition has been a focus of attention in Italy for a considerable time; in part, this has also been the case vis-à-vis a broader readership through the theoretical journals, *Marxismo oggi* and *Critica marxista*.[319] The attention paid to the *MEGA*[2] edition in Italy is also attested to by, among other publications, a volume edited by Alessandro Mazzone in 2002, in which German, Italian and US authors inform an Italian readership about the history of the *MEGA*[2] edition and the restructuring and continuation of the project after the transition in Eastern Europe, but also about the debate within the German-language engagement with Marx's theory of value.[320,*]

For some time now, Riccardo Bellofiore and Roberto Finelli have ranked among the best-known representatives of a methodological discussion on Marx which has continued to be variegated. Bellofiore and Finelli regard the circle of presupposition and posit in the logic of Marx's exposition of the critique of political economy as a decisive point of reference. That which is presupposed, and which forms the starting point of the exposition, reveals itself in the course of the exposition of economic categories as posited. Bellofiore and Finelli develop the point as follows: 'At the beginning of *Capital*, abstract labour ... is hypothetically "presupposed" ... But in the course of the three volumes

---

317   See Soldani 2002.

318   Soldani 1998, p. 92.

319   See Cazzaniga 1987, p. 112; Fineschi 1999; Sylvers and Fineschi 2003; Musto 2004. Musto outlines the contents of *MEGA*[2], Volume III/9, but also gives his perspective on the history and pre-history of the *MEGA*[2] edition. Fineschi also goes briefly into the *MEGA*[2] edition within the context of an essay of his on the Hegel-Marx relation (see Fineschi 2006, pp. 70f.). In addition, an interview of the *MEGA*[2] editors, Manfred Neuhaus and Gerald Hubmann, carried out by Fineschi was published in *Marxismo oggi* (see Fineschi 2007). Most recently, Musto has given another view of the *MEGA*[2] edition in Musto 2007b.

320   See Mazzone 2002b. In this volume, see Fineschi's contribution on the German discussion of value theory in the 1970s and 1980s (Fineschi 2002b).

*   See Fineschi 2008 and Bellofiore and Fineschi 2009 for further examples of Italian scholarly (re-)interpretation of Marx in the light of the *MEGA*[2] edition (the latter volume also contains contributions by a number of international exponents of Marxian theory).

[of *Capital*], abstract labour turns out to be the "posit" of *capitalist* labour, that is, of "labour that is opposed to capital" or wage labour'.[321] Neither Bellofiore nor Finelli (nor indeed Fineschi) subscribe to the strictly 'anti-Hegelian' reception of Marx by probably the two best-known Italian interpreters in the postwar period: Della Volpe and Colletti. Bellofiore and Finelli identify an important 'Hegelian legacy' in Marx's logic in *Capital*. At any rate, the elucidation of Marx's relation to Hegel remains a traditional question in the Italian debate, even after the theoretical interventions by Della Volpe and Colletti. Indeed, the Hegel-Marx relation is a central focus of a recent work by Fineschi.[322]

A study by Fineschi from 2002 revolves around the question of the logical and the historical in Marx's critique of political economy, and more precisely with regard to the problematic of the analysis of the value-form and the exposition of the exchange process.[323] Fineschi's approach implies an understanding of the 'historical' moment in Marx's development of money in *Capital* itself in a 'logical' sense. Fineschi writes that 'a critical engagement with the traditional distinction between the "historical" and the "logical"' is possible on the basis of his interpretation of Marx. 'Under these definitions, it is possible to understand two different levels of the logic that is immanent within the concept of the commodity, rather than a relationship of opposition ...'.[324]

Roberto Fineschi has recently published an important contribution to research on Marx's concept of capital; in the questions it poses, this study is reminiscent of the German-language discussion around the different levels of abstraction in Marx's critique of political economy, or in the respective plans that Marx drafted for such a critique.[325] With regard to Marx's exposition, Fineschi distinguishes four levels of abstraction corresponding to the concept of capital: the level 'zero', namely the level of abstraction of simple circulation; the level of the universality of capital; the level of the particularity of capital; finally, the most concrete level of abstraction, which is that of the singularity of capital. In this context, Fineschi argues, it is clear that Marx draws on Hegel's logic of the concept. Fineschi takes it that Marx maintained a structural division in his theory of capital between universality, particularity and singularity corresponding to the Hegelian triad throughout the historical development

---

321 Bellofiore and Finelli 1998, p. 51. On the 'methodological circle of presupposition-posit', see, among other works, Bellofiore 2006, pp. 265 f., and Finelli 2006.

322 See Fineschi 2006a.

323 See Fineschi 2006b.

324 See Fineschi 2006b, pp. 132 f.

325 See Fineschi 2005. This text is based on a monograph by Fineschi (see Fineschi 2001).

and elaboration of his *oeuvre* on the critique of political economy – i.e. from the *Grundrisse*, right up to (and including) *Capital*.

Fineschi points out, however, that in further developing his theory, Marx undertook modifications with regard both to the respective scope of the universality, the particularity, and the singularity of capital, and also to the respective elements of the transitions between these. Thus, according to Fineschi, the problematic of accumulation, which Marx originally located on the level of abstraction corresponding to particularity, was finally assigned to the level corresponding to universality. Furthermore, the Italian theorist maintains that Marx gave up his original intention to locate capital as unity, or capital as a whole, on this latter level of abstraction, and to ascribe many capitals to the level of particularity rather than to that of universality. By contrast, in Marx's later manuscripts the plurality of capitals appears already at the level of universality, even if Marx still abstracts from competition at this level. Fineschi identifies a change in Marx's approach within the formative process of his critique of political economy: 'If, at the beginning, Marx tried to apply Hegel's scheme to a given matter to put it in order, going on he understood that the very theory of capital could be worked out only following its own inner logic. That's why changes occurred and that's why the final structure is *more* dialectic and consistent than the original one'.[326]

A remarkable feature of the Italian reception of Marx and of Marxism is the favourable situation regarding the translation of foreign research contributions. Important works of foreign research have long been available in Italian: from the former Soviet Union (at least two studies by Vitaly Vygotsky and one by Evald Ilyenkov, alongside Isaak Ill'ich Rubin's *Essays on Marx's Theory of Value*); from both German states (studies by Hans-Georg Backhaus, Helmut Reichelt and Walter Tuchscheerer); and from German-speaking exile (Roman Rosdolsky's major work). It can thus be inferred that the knowledge of standard works from, among others, the German- and Russian-speaking spheres represents part of the background to the Italian discussion. It is nonetheless above all home-grown approaches – such as those by Della Volpe, Colletti, Napoleoni, Luporini and other Italian interpreters of Marx's critique of political economy – that have been central within the Italian Marx discourse of the last decades. However, it is also the case that the Italian and French engagements with Marx have mutually inspired one another, with the discussion in each country being followed attentively in the other.[327]

---

326 Fineschi 2005, p. 23.

327 See, for example, Giacometti et al. 1986 and Potier 1986.

5.2   *France*

It must be emphasised with regard to the French debate that it is not possible within the present framework to give a comprehensive presentation of
the history of postwar French Marxism as a whole (in the same way that a corresponding exposition was not feasible in the Italian case). Even a debate as
important as the French one on the principal significance of dialectic – a discussion which was carried out between Jean-Paul Sartre, Roger Garaudy, Jean
Hyppolite and others, and with which German-speakers soon became acquainted –[328] cannot be gone into here. Instead, a few insights will be given into
various approaches within the debate around questions of methodology and
social theory in Marx's critique of political economy, with a focus on the way in
which this debate has developed since the 1960s in particular.

The first French edition of the first volume of *Capital* appeared while Marx
was still alive and was indeed edited by Marx himself.[329] It should thus come
as no surprise that the French reading of *Capital* has a long tradition; after
the Second World War, this was able to develop more strongly than at any
time previously.[330] Marx's *Capital*[331] and his theory of value[332] were already
discussed in the years shortly after the war. In the postwar period, a tendency within the French interpretation of Marx went by the self-description
'Marxology' (this term was also used in the GDR, although here it was not a
self-description: it was rather employed with polemical undertones to characterise parts of the 'Western' Marx discussion). The postwar current of French
Marxology is particularly associated with the scientific work of Maximilien
Rubel.[333] Rubel was one of the first authors in the 'West' to carry out research
into the *Grundrisse*, and, in fact, he did so before this manuscript was first
made available to a wider 'Western' circle of readers through the 1953 East German edition. In an essay published in 1950 – at approximately the same time
that Korsch and Rosdolsky were engaging in depth with the *Grundrisse* in their
respective American exiles, and at a time when this manuscript was still largely

---

328   See the volume edited by Alfred Schmidt (Schmidt 1965).

329   See Marx 1989f.

330   On the publishing history of *Capital* in France, see Badia 1981. On the relationship of
        French economic scientists to Marxism in the latter half of the nineteenth century, see
        Pouch 2001.

331   See Hippolyte 1973.

332   See Guihéneuf 1952 and Denis 1957.

333   See, for example, Rubel 1980. In one of his last essays, written in the mid-1990s, Rubel
        intervened in the debate around Friedrich Engels that was taking place at that time (see
        Rubel 1995).

unknown (at least outside the Soviet Union) – Rubel devoted his attention to a number of themes in this manuscript, one of which was the chapter on money.[334]

At the beginning of the 1960s, Maurice Godelier presented methodological investigations into *Capital*.[335] With regard to Marx's procedure, Godelier outlined the connection between two methods which complement one another and yet which must be distinguished: on the one hand, a hypothetical-deductive method, and on the other, a dialectical one. Godelier argues that the dialectical method presupposes the hypothetical-deductive one. Godelier's approach has since been eclipsed by the more influential theoretical approach of Louis Althusser. The emergence of the Althusser School, with its orientation towards 'structuralism', occurred in the 1960s.[336] The formation of this school marked an important watershed in the reception of Marx not only within France, but also internationally.

In the 1960s, Althusser pursued his project of establishing a new *Capital* reading movement[337],* together with his students, Étienne Balibar, Jacques Rancière,[338] Roger Establet and Pierre Macherey.[339] Althusser put forward the principle of a 'symptomatic reading'. According to the French philosopher, such a reading was intended to detect the 'absent presence' in Marx's discourse – i.e. to take into account the fundamental preconditions of Marx's thought which,

---

334 See Rubel 1950; at around the same time as Rubel, Auguste Cornu also undertook research into Marxian theory (see Cornu 1954–68). Cornu moved to what would become the GDR after the Second World War.

335 See Godelier 2012; a further methodologically oriented engagement with *Capital* in the 1960s was that undertaken by Pierre Naville (Naville 1968).

336 It is beyond the scope of the present study to address Althusser's writings in the period before the 1960s. On the Althusser School within and beyond France, see Wolf 1994.

337 See Althusser and Balibar 1970. The texts by Rancière, Establet and Macheret from the first edition of *Lire le Capital* were omitted in the German-language edition, (Althusser and Balibar 1972). Althusser's subsequent engagement with *Capital* has received somewhat less attention in the international Marx discussion (see Althusser 1978b).

*   The texts by Rancière, Establet and Macheret from the first edition of *Lire le Capital* were omitted from subsequent editions, and also from English-language editions. They are reinstated, however, in the forthcoming Verso English-language edition, and have already been restored in the recent German-language edition (Althusser, Balibar, Establet, Macherey and Rancière 2014).

338 See Rancière 1976. This text is Rancière's contribution to the first edition of *Lire le Capital*.

339 A further theorist who moved within the orbit of the Althusser School was Nicos Poulantzas; see his arguments in Poulantzas 1968.

although not manifested textually, instead remaining implicit, are nonetheless absolutely constitutive. In the context of his philosophical approach based on 'structuralism', Althusser was thus concerned to expose the theoretical presuppositions of *Capital*.

While Althusser himself engaged critically in *Reading Capital* with the problem of the object of *Capital*, Balibar addressed the basic questions of historical materialism in the same work, whereas Althusser's student, Establet, focused on the problematic of the plans for the architectonic of *Capital*. For his part, Rancière dealt with the critique of political economy as formulated in the 1844 *Economic and Philosophical Manuscripts* and then later in *Capital*. In his text on the problematic of Marx's exposition, Macherey broached the question of the starting point of Marx's exposition of the critique of political economy in his *magnum opus*, considering in this context Marx's analysis of the commodity and his theory of value.

To return to Althusser himself: an important idea of the French philosopher was the assumption of an epistemological rupture or break in Marx's work. Althusser thematised an (alleged) break in the history of Marx's *oeuvre* between the earlier 'ideological' or 'humanist' works, and the later 'scientific' works. In *For Marx*, Althusser, strictly speaking, distinguishes four phases of Marx's work: his early writings up to 1844;[340] the works dating from the turning point of 1845, which were decisive for the break (i.e. *Theses on Feuerbach*[341] and *The German Ideology*); the works during Marx's process of maturation up to 1857; and finally, Marx's mature works from 1857 up to his death.[342]

Subsequently, Althusser held the view – at least temporarily, in 1969 – that the process by which Marx overcame the influence of Hegel's philosophy did not reach its conclusion until the final years of his life. According to Althusser, it was only in Marx's late works – i.e. among other writings, in his *Notes on Adolph Wagner's 'Lehrbuch der politischen Ökonomie'*, which was his last work on the critique of political economy, written a short time before his death – that he definitively concluded the process of overcoming the influence of Hegel's philosophy.

---

340 There is an ongoing Francophone engagement with Marx's writings from 1843 and 1844, which Althusser assigns to the period before the so-called 'epistemological break'. The following examples can be cited: Mercier-Josa 1986; the various contributions in an edited volume (Balibar and Raulet 2001); Kouvelakis 2003, pp. 232 ff.

341 French contributions on Marx's *Theses on Feuerbach* include Labica 1987 and Macherey 2008.

342 See Althusser 1979, pp. 34–5.

The famous *Preface* of 1859 (to *A Contribution to the Critique of Political Economy*) is still profoundly Hegelian-evolutionist. The 'Grundrisse' ... are themselves profoundly marked by Hegel's thought, for in 1858 Marx had re-read the *Great Logic* with amazement.

When *Capital* Volume One appeared (1867), traces of the Hegelian influence still remained. Only later did they disappear completely: the *Critique of the Gotha Programme* (1875) as well as the *Marginal Notes on Wagner's 'Lehrbuch der politischen Ökonomie'* [which Althusser dates as having being written in 1882 – J.H.] are totally and definitively exempt from any trace of Hegelian influence.[343]

Alongside the inspirational effect that the Althusserian School had on the French debate, as well as on French theoretical currents beyond the interpretation of Marx in a narrow sense,[344] the influence that it exerted in Latin America and the Anglo-Saxon world was considerable; each of these regions formed their own respective branches of this current.[345] In West Germany, Althusser encountered resistance from an early stage, even though he also had his supporters there.[346] Among other factors, the dominance of 'autochthonous' readings of Marx in the 1960s and 1970s, and, to all intents and purposes, up to the present – readings in which, moreover, emphatic and positive references to Hegel played an important role at times – prevented Althusserianism from becoming hegemonic in the German-language discussion of Marx.

Regarded as a whole, it is fair to say that Althusser's reading of Marx, together with its broad international reception, had conflicting effects. On the one hand, Althusser directed attention to the oft-neglected epistemological problematic, and provided a concept – that of the 'theoretical field' – which would subsequently be received and further developed by the approaches of Michael Heinrich or the Heinrich-influenced South Korean, No-Wan Kwack. On the

---

343   Althusser 1971, pp. 93–4.

344   On the relationship between Althusserianism and the 'Regulation Theory' that emerged in the 1970s in France, see Lipietz 1992.

345   Grahame Lock provides a survey of British Althusserianism (see Lock 1977). The US reception of Althusser has also been registered in France (see Balibar 1990).

346   See Schmidt 1969. In general, Schmidt referred to Althusser in a way that was critical, but by no means exclusively negative. Ulrich Müller identifies a 'thoroughgoing revision of Marxism' at work in Althusser (see Müller 1975), and speaks of an 'attack on central components of Marx's thought' (Müller 1975, p. 85). Rather fewer German interpreters of *Capital* make positive reference to Althusser. However, two examples are Kocyba 1979 and Wolf 1983.

other hand, Althusser had a negative impact with regard to the way in which determinate problems were viewed. In this context, an obvious instance is Althusser's problematic take on Marx's theory of fetishism – a theory to which the French philosopher was critically opposed. The latter's instruction to readers of *Capital* that they should not start with the first section on commodities and money, but that they should rather skip ahead to the second section on the transformation of money into capital,[347] must surely be considered a curiosity in the international history of readings of *Capital*.[348] In relation to the undervaluation of Marx's theory of fetishism by Althusser, however, it should be added that the philosopher, Étienne Balibar, whose roots lie in the Althusserian School, cast Marx's theory of fetishism in a better light in a study of Marx published in 1993, characterising it in the following terms: 'It is not merely a high point of Marx's philosophical work, entirely integrated into his "critical" and "scientific" work, but one of the great theoretical constructions of modern philosophy'.[349] A few years after the publication of *Lire le Capital* (1965), the swelling wave of Western European reception of the *Grundrisse* also reached France.[350] This manuscript first appeared in French translation in 1967–8. However, Althusser's central focus was not this text, but rather *Capital*.[351] The philosopher, Lucien Sève, levels a serious charge against Althusser: 'Althusser never *read* the *Grundrisse* in the strong sense of the word, except for several texts from this manuscript, such as the 1857 Introduction of course, on which he wrote some notable sections'.[352] The veracity of Sève's assertion cannot be assessed here. In the more recent French debate on Marx, Jacques Bidet has critically engaged with a theoretical approach which he argues has been adopted by both French and international thinkers (including Italian, Japanese and German ones); for Bidet, this approach consists in these theorists

---

347 See Althusser 1969, pp. 7 ff.

348 Althusser restated his views on the beginning of the exposition in *Capital* in 1978 (see Althusser 2006).

349 Balibar 1995, p. 56. In 1974, Balibar had engaged extensively with Marx's theory of fetishism (see Balibar 1974, pp. 203 ff.). Space does not permit a consideration of the development of Balibar's conception of the problematic of fetishism here.

350 See, for example, Semprún 1968. In a later study, Henri Denis devoted a great deal of attention to the *Grundrisse* and to the *Urtext* of *A Contribution to the Critique of Political Economy*, which had become available in French translation by 1957, if not earlier (see Denis 1980, pp. 55 ff. and pp. 121 ff. respectively). On the French reception of the *Grundrisse*, see Tosel 2008c.

351 See Guibert 2006, p. 77.

352 Sève 2004, p. 29 (emphasis in original).

'seek[ing] the truth of *Capital* in the texts that precede it, these being character-ised by a far more intensive use of concepts drawn from the Hegelian tradition in Marx's elaboration of the theory of capitalism'.[353] It might be added that it is especially the *Grundrisse* manuscript, together with the latter's international reception and its significance for a 'Hegelianising' interpretation of Marx (with regard to this latter aspect, recall the work of the Japanese philosopher and eco-nomist, Hiroshi Uchida) which ought to be borne in mind in this context.

The discussion around Althusser's theoretical interventions developed soon after the publication of *Pour Marx* and *Lire le Capital*.[354] However, criticisms of Althusser's theoretical output were also voiced by French Marxists.[355] In his own interpretation of Marx, which he presented in the early 1960s, Paul Boccara addressed the problematic of Marx's plans for the architectonic of the critique of political economy.[356] Boccara preferred a logico-historical interpretation of the exposition in *Capital*: 'In order to explain the fact that both *Capital* and *A Contribution to the Critique of Political Economy* begin with the commodity, it is not sufficient to state that the commodity is the economic form of the product, and thus the connection between all economic relations – the "most funda-mental" entity in economic life'. Boccara continues as follows: 'Above all, it must be recognised that commodity production precedes capitalist production his-torically, and forms the latter's point of departure. Accordingly, the historical starting point also constitutes the logical starting point'.[357,*] In this context, Boccara's reading points in a direction similar to that taken by Engels's defi-cient interpretation of Marx's method – an interpretation which, despite its problematic content, exerted a great influence on traditional Marxism.

In the French debate on Marx of the 1970s, Michel Vadée engaged with the development of the critical theory of abstraction over the historical course of the elaboration of Marx's *oeuvre*, while François Ricci attempted, in his investigation into the logical structure of the beginning of the exposition in *Capital*, to distinguish between different levels in Marx's thought.[358] In 1967, Suzanne de Brunhoff had already published a much-cited study on the theories of money and credit in Marx's critique of political economy.[359] At the end of

---

353   Bidet 2005b, p. 124.

354   For an example of a contribution to the discussion before May 1968, see Forquin 1968.

355   See, for example, Avenas and Brossat 1972.

356   Boccara's study thus pre-dated *Lire le Capital*.

357   Boccara 1982, p. 35.

*   See also Boccara 1978.

358   See von Wroblewsky 1977.

359   An English-language version was published in 1976 (see de Brunhoff 1976).

the 1970s, the economist, Gérard Duménil, presented an interpretation of the critique of political economy in which he focused on elaborating the concept of economic law to be found in Marx's *magnum opus*. In his study, Duménil aims to identify the specific logic of Marx's thought in *Capital*.[360] Further, a two-volume work first published in 1976 by the non-Marxist philosopher, Michel Henry, contains an interpretation both of Marx's early works and of his mature critique of political economy; Henry establishes a fundamental separation between the thought of Karl Marx and Marxism.[361]

Following Jacque Rancière's presentation, in his 1965 contribution to *Lire le Capital*,[362] of a reading of Marx through the theory of fetishism, and Pierre Macherey's consideration of the problem of the beginning of the exposition in Marx, the intensive engagement with Marx's theory of fetishism, with his value-form theory and with the 'beginning' of *Capital*, gained fresh impetus in the 1970s. A significant contribution in this context came in 1977 from Paul-Dominique Dognin, who produced an edition of, and commentary to, the beginning of the first volume of *Capital* (including the value-form analysis) from the 1867 first edition of Marx's work.[363] Knowledge of this latter text is of decisive significance for the interpretation of the historical development of Marx's theory of value, yet it was little-known within the French debate until that point. From the 1970s to the 1990s in particular, an important current within Marx-interpretation began to develop. The theorist, Jean-Marie Vincent, who died in 2004, was one of the French interpreters of Marx to adopt a stance on Marx's theory of the fetish which sharply contrasted with that of Althusser (who, as indicated above, underrated this theory).[364] Vincent opened up a perspective on Marx's critique of political economy which was acutely focused on the theory of fetishism. Within the French reception of Marx, one of the most elaborate texts to be produced by the fetish- and form-theoretical interpretative current is a central work by Tran Hai Hac, which will be considered in more detail below. The emergence of this interpretative tendency ought to be understood as marking decisive theoretical progress in the French discussion

---

360   See Duménil 1978.

361   See Henry 1976a and Henry 1976b.

362   See Rancière 1976. Ingo Elbe gives an extensive and appreciative consideration of Rancière's contribution (see Elbe 2010, pp. 58ff.); Elbe credits the French thinker with having broken, in his interpretation of Marx, with the traditional understanding of Marx's exposition as a 'logico-historical' one (an understanding which can be traced back to Engels's interpretation).

363   See Dognin 1977.

364   Among Vincent's major works are Vincent 1973, Vincent 1991 and Vincent 2001.

of Marx. The recent approaches of Antoine Artous[365] and Alain Bihr[366],* attest to the fact that that the form- and fetish-theoretical interpretation continues to be pursued further within the French reception of the critique of political economy.

It is worth mentioning here that the publication of the $MEGA^2$ edition from 1975 onwards was noted within French engagement with Marx in the 1980s. To cite an example, the French specialist in German philology and translator of *Capital*, Jean-Pierre Lefebvre, addressed the $MEGA^2$ edition.[367] With regard to French engagement with Marx since the 1980s in general, however, it is above all the important contribution to the reception of Marx's critique of political economy in the shape of the theory developed by Jacques Bidet which merits consideration here.[368] In the 1980s, Bidet (together with Jacques Texier) founded the journal, *Actuel Marx*, a significant periodical which played an important role in familiarising the French public with the debate on Marxism in Japan, China, Italy, the Anglo-Saxon world and elsewhere; in this journal, attention was also (and continues to be) paid to the German discussion of Marx.[369] Although Bidet's own theoretical contributions have certainly been registered in Germany,[370] there has been a more intensive reception of them elsewhere.

Jacques Bidet's study, *Que faire du Capital?*, was first published in 1985. Despite its title, this work by no means refers to *Capital* alone; the object of this study by the French interpreter of Marx is the critique of political economy as presented in the form of Marx's texts from the period between 1857 and 1875. Of note in this context are, alongside the *Grundrisse*, the *1861–63 Manuscripts* (which contain *Theories of Surplus-Value*), the so-called *1863–65 Manuscripts*, the first and second German editions of the first volume of *Capital*, and the French edition of the latter, published in 1872–5. Although the chronological

---

365   See Artous 2006 and Artous 2004.

366   See Bihr 2007 and Bihr 2001.

*   See also Bihr 2010.

367   See Lefebvre 1985.

368   See, among other works, Bidet 1990, Bidet 1999, Bidet 2007 and Bidet 2004.

369   For instance, a recent contribution by Michael Krätke affords an insight into the latter phase of Marx's engagement with the critique of political economy (see Krätke 2005). An example of an important 'autochthonous' contribution is that by Emmanuel Renault (see Renault 2000). In the context of a consideration of the critical character of Marx's theory, Renault investigates the various critical perspectives and types of critique in the young and mature Marx.

370   See, for example, Reichelt 1992.

timeframe demarcated here falls within Marx's 'mature' period, Bidet finds that it is nonetheless marked by a series of breaks. Since its publication, *Que faire du Capital?* is considered within the international discussion of Marx to be a standard work, and has been published in Serbo-Croat, Japanese, Korean and English.[371]

Bidet's further theoretical development since the first edition of *Que faire du Capital?* cannot be considered here in any detail. It is sufficient to note that in the meantime Bidet's approach has evolved in the direction of an extension, and fundamental 'refoundation', of Marxian theory. A more recent text by the French theorist outlines his attempt, over the last few years, to draw on Marx himself in order to go beyond Marx.[372]

The logic of the exposition in *Capital* is interpreted by Bidet as a dialectic on three levels: firstly, the level of 'metastructure'[373] or presupposition; secondly, the level of 'structure'; and thirdly, the level of 'practices'. According to Bidet, the object of the first section of *Capital* is universal and abstract – i.e. it is itself the 'metastructure'. For the French theorist, this metastructure consists in a society which, in the final analysis, is formed by commodity producers, who mutually recognise each other as free, equal and rational agents in the exchange of their commodities.[374] Nonetheless, the 'metastructure' corresponding to the commodity form is ultimately posited and generalised by the capitalist 'structure'. The transition from money to capital which is executed in *Capital* is taken by Bidet to be one from 'metastructure' to 'structure'. The level of 'structure' encompasses the class relations of capitalist society; the latter were disregarded at the level of 'metastructure'. The 'structure' is in turn reproduced by 'practices', through the process of capitalist production.

In his 2006 essay, Bidet criticises the beginning of Marx's exposition. He argues as follows: 'As plausible as the beginning of the exposition might seem, it can be criticised for the "one-sided" or "unipolar" character that it exhibits, when in fact *two poles* are to be considered'.[375] Thus, Bidet refers to, on the one hand, the 'market form', and, on the other, the 'form of organisation': 'the "form of organisation" has a character which is equally as abstract as the

---

371   The English version of *Que faire du Capital?* was published under the title *Exploring Marx's Capital: Philosophical, Economic and Political Dimensions* (see Bidet 2007).

372   See Bidet 2006. This essay provides a summary of some important reflections contained in *Explication et reconstruction du 'Capital'*.

373   Bidet also elaborates on his central concept of 'metastructure' in earlier published work (see Bidet 1992 and Bidet 1991).

374   Bidet 2006, p. 147.

375   Bidet 2006, p. 149.

"market form", and which is likewise presupposed by the ensuing analysis. The fact that Marx only discovers organisation in the fourth section of the first volume of *Capital*, and deals with it under the rubric of "cooperation", is utterly disconcerting'.[376] Bidet maintains that the beginning of the exposition needs to be expanded so as to encompass both poles.

Bidet's 2004 monograph, *Explication et reconstruction du 'Capital'*, represents a continuation of his reading of *Capital*. The perspective opened up by Bidet in this work is that of, on the one hand, an explanation of *Capital*, and, on the other, a reconstruction of Marx's *magnum opus*.[377] Here, the French theorist sets out his critique of Marx for the latter's one-sided focus on the market dimension at the beginning of *Capital*, which leads him to somewhat neglect the dimension of organisation at this point. Bidet is not content merely to provide a reconstruction in the sense of a 'correction'; rather, his reconstruction envisages above all an 'expansion'. *Capital* can 'only tackle the questions it presents on condition of being reconstructed on an expanded basis, according to the twin "poles" of the metastructure [the poles of market and organisation – J.H.] and its twin "aspects", economic and legal-political'.[378] Within the German-speaking countries there has not as yet been a properly broad reception of the theory formed by Bidet over approximately the last decade.

5.3   *Other Western European Countries*

In Scandinavia, above all a Danish theoretical current deserves to be highlighted as an independent approach to the interpretation of Marx's critique of political economy, even though the effects of the West German discussion of Marx form the background to the emergence of this current in the 1970s. The 'capital-logic' tendency developed in Denmark at this time under the influence of the West German New Marx-Reading. For instance, Hans-Jørgen Schanz developed an independent theoretical position which was influenced by Reichelt's doctoral thesis (but also by Rosdolsky's monograph), and was marked by the impact of the wave of reception of the *Grundrisse* of the 1960s and 1970s.[379] The 'capital-logic' tendency adopted a critical stance towards

---

376   Bidet 2006, pp. 149 f.

377   See Bidet 2004, pp. 149 ff.

378   Bidet 2007, pp. xxif. This quotation is taken from a preface written in 2006.

379   See Schanz 1973. According to Vesa Oittinen, 'a further representative of Danish capital-logic [alongside Schanz – J.H.] was Anders Lundkvist, who, like Schanz, is also closely aligned to Reichelt' (Oittinen 2008); see also Lundkvist 1973.

another current within the Danish debate on Marxism which attempted to draw on Louis Althusser.[380] Foregrounded within the Danish 'capital-logic' discourse were the programmatic commitment to a project of reconstruction of Marx's critique of political economy, and the development of approaches to a form- and fetish-theoretical reading of Marx; in this way, the Danish 'capital-logic discourse' shared features of the West German debate around Hans-Georg Backhaus and others.[381] Formerly a sizeable intellectual constellation, 'capital-logic' went into decline from the 1980s on, even though Danish interpreters of Marx have continued to engage with Marx's method in his critique of political economy and with the problematic of the value-form until the recent past. In Germany, the discourse of Danish 'capital-logicians' has hardly been registered, despite its thematic intersections with parts of the West German Marx debate, and despite the fact that there is potential for connections to be established between these two discussions in terms of their content.[382] By contrast, the Danish 'capital-logic' tendency subsequently engaged in a reception of further approaches to research within the orbit of the West German 'New Marx-Reading', such as those by the German-Australian working group, the 'Sydney-Konstanz Project'.[383,*]

---

380 An insight into the Danish debate around Althusser and capital-logic is afforded by Schmidt 1977.

381 A relatively high level of familiarity with Backhaus's early works was in evidence in the Scandinavian discussion.

382 The East German philosopher, Peter Ruben, did at least mention Schanz's above-mentioned book in an article (see Ruben 1977, p. 41).

383 Finally, some general references to Scandinavian engagement with Marx can be provided here. On the publishing history of Marx's works in Denmark, see Callesen 1987; a more recent Danish study on Marx's critique of political economy has appeared in German (see Swing 2006). The question of the relation between the logical and the historical was also thematised in Finland in the 1980s (see Pietilä 1984). Since its establishment in Finland 1997, a 'Marx Society' (*Karl Marx-Seura*) has functioned as a scientific association. Probably the best-known work of Swedish research into Marx and Engels is *Motsatsernas spel: Friedrich Engels' filosofi och 1800-talets vetenskaper* ['The Play of Contradictions: Friedrich Engels's Philosophy and the Sciences of the 19th Century'] by Sven-Eric Liedman, which was the focus of much attention after it was first published in 1977 (see Liedman 1977). An abridged German version exists (see Liedman 1986). In this work, Liedman refers to Marx's 1857 *Introduction*, which contains the famous 'chapter on method' (see Liedman 1986, pp. 44 ff.). A Norwegian author, Jørgen Sandemose, also addresses Marx's 1857 *Introduction* (see Sandemose 2007).

*   For a sophisticated recent Swedish engagement with the *Neue Marx-Lektüre*, see Ramsay 2009.

In Switzerland, a critical engagement with Marx's method in his critique of political economy began shortly after the Second World War.[384] In the 1970 new edition of Otto Morf's study, an appendix was added on the *Grundrisse*, which had first been made accessible to a wider readership beyond the Soviet Union through the East Berlin edition of 1953.[385] Here, although he is aware of the provisional and experimental character of this rough draft, Morf understands the *Grundrisse* as 'methodologically the most revealing connecting link between the early and late works' of Marx.[386] The Swiss theorist especially thematises the specific interconnection between the categories of capital, landed property and wage labour, which were to be expounded in the first three volumes of Marx's Six-Volume-Plan; Morf considered these three to be the most important. In the 1970s, Anton Fischer, a further Marx-interpreter from Switzerland, produced a work in which he regarded Marx's analysis of the capitalist mode of production as a form-analysis. Fischer addressed the problematic of fetishism theorised by Marx, and devoted attention to Marx's analysis of the value-form, among other questions.[387]

A more recent Swiss contribution focuses on a section of the 1857 *Introduction*, a text which preceded Marx's work on the *Grundrisse*.[388] The Swiss commentary on Marx's 'chapter on method' presented by Judith Jánoska, Martin Bondeli, Konrad Kindle and Marc Hofer in the early 1990s has been noted in Germany, at least within specialist circles, and in general ranks among the most important German-language contributions to the methodological discussion of Marx. Arguably, this standard work represents the most ambitious investigation of the 'chapter on method', not only within German-language research, but within international research as a whole.[389] This historical and systematic commentary of Marx's text will be considered at greater length below.

Since the 1990s, a notable level of research activity on Marx's critique of political economy has been developed around the Greek theoretical journal,

---

384   See Morf 1970. With the exception of its expanded appendices, this edition is based on the original 1951 edition.

385   See Morf 1970, pp. 171 ff.

386   See Morf 1970, p. 221.

387   See Fischer 1978.

388   If the datings given in *MEGA*², Volume II/1, are correct, that is. Some research carried out in the Soviet Union has indicated that Marx had already begun work on the *Grundrisse* by the beginning of 1857. See Vasina 2008, p. 207.

389   See Jánoska, Bondeli, Kindle and Hofer 1994. The investigation of Marx's 'chapter on method' had already played an important role in Otto Morf's work (see Morf 1970, pp. 37 ff.).

Theseis; the specialist readership in German-speaking countries is no doubt acquainted with this research activity, at least to some extent, as a result of the contributions of its most important representatives to German-language publications. John Milios,* Dimitri Dimoulis and George Economakis compiled their most important studies in 2002, making them available to an international readership in the form of a monograph.[390] A number of the approaches presented in this work are influenced by the Althusserian School and particularly by Michael Heinrich's interpretation of Marx. In the interpretation by these Greek theorists, Marx's critique of political economy is fundamentally distinguished from political economy itself. On this reading, Marx transcended the 'theoretical field' of political economy, brought about 'the formation of a new theoretical domain',[391] and developed a specifically monetary theory of value centring on the internal interconnection between the theory of value and the theory of money. The status of money should be emphasised here: 'The Marxian analysis does not ... entail reproduction of the barter model ... since it holds that exchange *is necessarily mediated by money*. This amounts to a monetary theory of the capitalist economy (a monetary theory of value), since money is interpreted as an intrinsic and necessary element in capitalist economic relations'.[392] Milios understands Marx's labour theory of value as a monetary theory of value, which implies a radical break with, and a radical critique of, David Ricardo's theory of value.

Yet Milios et al. argue in their monograph that there are in fact ambivalences in Marx's work, despite the fundamental theoretical advances that he makes beyond classical political economy. On their view, Marx falls back into a Ricardian value-theoretical approach in dealing with determinate theoretical problems in his manuscripts dating from the period between 1861 and 1865 – i.e. he regresses to a kind of 'sophisticated version of the Ricardian Political Economy of value as "labour expended"'.[393] The Greek authors maintain that these theoretical weaknesses of Marx's cannot be disregarded: 'Every "sanctifying" attitude towards Marx, presenting him as the inculpable master ... practically blurs the scientific and heuristic kernel of Marx's analysis, as it identifies it

---

*   John Milios is also known as Yannis/Giannis Milios.

390   See Milios, Dimoulis and Economakis 2002. I have outlined their central theses with regard to Marx's relation to classical economic theory elsewhere (see Hoff 2004, pp. 115 f.).

391   Milios, Dimoulis and Economakis 2002, p. viii.

392   Milios, Dimoulis and Economakis 2002, p. 28. On the monetary theory of value in Marx, see also Milios 2006, p. 101.

393   Milios, Dimoulis and Economakis 2002, p. ix.

with the Ricardian element, present in some of his elaborations'.[394] The Greek
theorists identify a categorial confusion in Marx's treatment of the problematic of the transformation of values into prices of production.[395] Likewise, they
also consider Marx's theory of ground rent to be deficient: 'Marx's analysis on
ground rent and especially the part of it on absolute ground rent is one of the
weakest points in his whole economic work'.[396] Alongside their exposition of
the categorial structure of commodity–money–capital and their thoroughgoing critical engagement with the problematic of fetishism[397],* and with themes
from the third volume of *Capital*, Milios et al. devote a great deal of attention
to the crisis-theoretical dimension of the critique of political economy. This is
examined more closely in Part 3 of the present study.[398]

6   Latin America and Spain

6.1   *Latin America*

Within the history of the Latin American discussion of the critique of political
economy, the most important countries are Mexico, Argentina and Brazil.[399] In
Brazil, a *Capital* reading movement had developed from the late 1950s onwards,
in which young intellectuals participated, such as the philosopher, José Artur
Giannotti, or the future President, Fernando Henrique Cardoso.[400] With regard

---

394   Milios, Dimoulis and Economakis 2002, p. 208.

395   Milios, Dimoulis and Economakis 2002, p. 119.

396   Milios, Dimoulis and Economakis 2002, p. 140.

397   See Milios, Dimoulis and Economakis 2002, p. 67 ff. See also Dimoulis and Milios 2000,
      pp. 12 ff.

*   See also Dimoulis and Milios 2004.

398   A further Marx-oriented theorist from Greece with intellectual roots – at least to a cer-
      tain extent – in the West German discussion of Marx's critique of political economy was
      Kosmas Psychopedis. The latter thinker, who died in 2004, stood in close proximity to the
      international 'Open Marxism' project briefly presented above, and his theoretical concep-
      tion was influenced by Hans-Georg Backhaus and Helmut Reichelt (see Psychopedis 2000
      and also Psychopedis 1984). Stavros Tombazos can be considered an important protagon-
      ist of Marx-interpretation in Cyprus (see Tombazos 2014).

399   It is debatable whether Cuba should also be included in this list. However, it is worth
      noting that the Cuban periodical, *Marx ahora: Revista internacional* – a scientific journal
      dedicated to research into Marx and Marxism and edited by the philosopher, Isabel
      Monal – draws on an international circle of contributors, including German researchers
      involved with the *MEGA*[2] project.

400   An important volume has recently been published compiling the work of numerous

to the Argentinian reception of Marx in the late 1950s, a figure to be highlighted is Milcíades Peña (1933–65); at that time, Peña engaged with (among other questions) Marx's theory of alienation, which he saw as informing both Marx's early and mature works.[401] In Mexico, the *Universidad Nacional Autónoma de México* (*UNAM*) developed into one of the most important centres of Marx-oriented theory formation in the whole of Latin America, particularly from the 1960s onwards.[402]

In his 1987 survey of research into Marx and Engels in Mexico, Andrés Barreda reports that there was 'enormous' interest in Marx's *Capital* in Mexico up to the time of writing.[403] The Mexican reception of Marxism from the 1960s onwards was partly determined by an intellectual constellation in which an exiled Spanish representative of the philosophy of praxis inspired by Marx's early works – namely, Adolfo Sánchez Vázquez,[404] who was presented above – stood opposed to the Latin American exponents of the Althusser School.[405] A Spanish-language edition of *Lire le Capital* had been published in Mexico City by 1969 at the latest, and before long it had aroused great interest and was widely received, as was the famous Althusserian 'textbook' by the Chilean, Marta Harnecker.[406] Nevertheless, Sánchez Vázquez adopted a critical stance towards Althusser.

Bolívar Echeverría has been a further important participant in the Mexican Marx debate since the 1970s and 1980s.[407] Within the framework of his engagement with Marx's critique of political economy, the Ecuadorian-born Echeverría focused his interest on, among other questions, the 'problem of the beginning' of Marx's systematic exposition of this critique – i.e. on a problem

---

authors on the history of Marxist politics and thought in Brazil; this work affords an insight into the breadth and scope of Brazilian Marxism (see de Moraes et al. 1995–2007).

401   See Peña 2000.

402   Stefan Gandler reports that reading *Capital* over five semesters was part of the official curriculum for the UNAM's bachelor's degree in economics (see Gandler 2015, p. 66).

403   See Barreda 1987, p. 274.

404   Alongside Sánchez Vázquez, two further well-known representatives of Latin American Marxism originally came from Spain: firstly, the Spanish-Mexican theorist and translator of *Capital*, Wenceslao Roces (who died in 1992, and who, like Sánchez Vázquez, taught at the UNAM; for Roces's view on *Capital*, see Roces 1983); secondly, the Spanish-Venezuelan philosopher, Juan David García Bacca, who died in the same year. On the latter, see Fornet-Betancourt 1994, pp. 252 ff.

405   For Sánchez Vázquez's critique of Althusser, see Sánchez Vázquez 1978.

406   *Lire le Capital* had already been published in Spanish translation in Havana in 1966.

407   See Gandler 2015, pp. 195 ff. See also Gandler 2000 and Gandler 2007.

that has been the focus of much attention in the German-language discussion of Marx.[408] In general, the discussion of the 'beginning of the exposition' has played an important role in the Latin American discourse on Marx since the 1970s, and Enrique Dussel's interpretation in this regard has in the meantime been internationally received (see below). A further Latin American researcher, Mario L. Robles Báez, criticised Friedrich Engels's 'logico-historical' interpretation of Marx's method; Robles Báez argues that the original Marxian method and Engels's interpretation are to be sharply distinguished. With regard to the 'problem of the beginning' of the exposition, Robles Báez maintains that the first section of the first volume of *Capital* ought by no means to be understood as a historical stage prior to capitalist production.[409]

Although Sánchez Vázquez focused his research principally on Marx's early writings, while Bolívar Echeverría concentrated his research mainly – although not exclusively –[410] on Marx's mature work on the critique of political economy, both opposed Althusser's argument that there was a radical 'break' or turning point in Marx's work, and rejected Althusserianism.[411] Nevertheless, it should not be overlooked that Althusser and his Chilean student, Harnecker, played a significant role in the late 1960s and 1970s in the development of the critical Marxist theoretical discussion in Latin America. The Mexican, Fernanda Navarro, describes the situation at the time as follows: 'One could take up a stance for or against the position of the author of *Lire le Capital*, but this position could not be ignored. In Mexico, as in most of the universities of the metropoles (such as Buenos Aires, Sao Paulo, Rio, Lima, etc.), Althusser was studied and taught from 1969 to 1981, with one common feature uniting all these cases: the vehemence of the discussions'.[412]

---

408   See Echeverría 1979. In 1987, Andrés Barreda made the following claim with regard to Echeverría: 'Bolívar Echeverría ... is the first Marxist, and almost the only one, to have taken cognizance in an intensive way of the very rich Marxist discussion in Germany on the critique of political economy and on the legacy of Marxian thought contained in the new *MEGA* edition' (Barreda 1987, p. 278). It should be added here that Enrique Dussel has also made important contributions since the 1980s in terms of acknowledging the *MEGA*[2] edition and its accompanying research literature. Alongside Echeverría, Barreda also mentions the theologian, José Porfirio Miranda, as an expert on the *MEGA*[2] edition within the Mexican discussion of Marxism. On Porfirio Miranda, see, among other works, Kee 1990, pp. 203 ff., 249 ff., 271 ff.

409   See Robles 2000.

410   On the *Theses on Feuerbach* as part of Marx's early work, see Echeverría 1975.

411   See Gandler 2015, pp. 129–30 and p. 202.

412   Navarro 1992, p. 55. Another to have engaged with Althusser and his reading of Marx is the Argentine, Saül Karsz (see Karsz and Althusser 1974, pp. 25 ff.). An example of

At the end of the 1970s, a Latin American philosopher and Marx-interpreter who did not belong to the Althusserian School, Rafael Echeverría (not to be confused with Bolívar Echeverría), presented a critique of one of the most important methodological texts by Marx, namely the 1857 *Introduction*, which contains the famous 'chapter on method'.[413] Echeverría was not alone in focusing on Marx's 1857 *Introduction* at this time: the philosopher, Gabriel Vargas Lozano, founder of the important Mexican theoretical journal, *Dialéctica*, also referred to this key text by Marx in the 1976 first issue of this periodical.[414] Echeverría takes the opposite stance to that of a significant tendency within the international discussion: he considers that Marx's method in *Capital* ought by no means to be regarded in the light of the 1857 *Introduction* – on the contrary, the latter text is, on Echeverría's view, a highly problematic treatise from which Marx's method in *Capital* must be sharply distinguished. Although Echeverría examines all four sections of the *Introduction*, and not only the 'chapter on method', it is the latter which is the central focus of his critique. According to Echeverría, it is important 'to challenge the supposed identity of the criteria of the *Introduction* with those of *Capital*, and thus to demonstrate the profoundly problematic character of the *Introduction*'.[415] On Echeverría's view, the argumentation in the 'chapter on method' relies on the presence of two different concepts of abstraction: 'If the population is criticised as a starting point because it is abstract, it is not possible to conclude that the analysis should be initiated from abstract and general definitions without a resulting introduction of a new and completely different concept of abstraction'.[416]

Rafael Echeverría understands the *Introduction* as a single text in which Marx adopts an intermediate position between stances which can be traced back to Feuerbach and Hegel respectively, although 'without being able to conciliate both epistemological perspectives'.[417] According to Echeverría, the population is initially grasped by Marx as a *concretum*, since it is real in the

---

the engagement of Latin American authors with Althusser's theoretical production is provided by the third issue (1977) of a Mexican journal, *Dialéctica*, published by the School of Philosophy and the Humanities of the Autonomous University of Puebla (see Escuela de Filosofía y Letras, Universidad Autónoma de Puebla 1977). Further essays from subsequent issues of this journal also refer to the Althusser-reception in Mexico (see Morales 1983 and Vargas 1988).

413   See Echeverría 1989.
414   See Vargas 1976.
415   Echeverría 1989, p. 243.
416   Echeverría 1989, pp. 249 f.
417   Echeverría 1989, p. 251.

Feuerbachian sense. Ultimately, however, it is understood as an *abstractum*, since it is theoretically indeterminate according to the Hegelian paradigm. On Echeverría's view, Marx's argumentation is by no means unproblematic: 'The ambiguous presence of the concept of concrete totality in Marx's argument, clear in that of Hegel, impedes the distinction between the particular concrete and the concrete totality, as will be drawn later in his position, and this is the source of ambiguity in his argument'.[418] For the Latin American philosopher, it is obvious how Marx's subsequent overcoming of the 'Feuerbachian residue' in his methodological thinking is to be understood: 'It will be superseded not by a mere superposition of the Feuerbachian and the Hegelian epistemological standpoints, but by a critical and rectificatory appropriation of Hegel, which will produce an original Marxist distinction between the concrete and the abstract'.[419]

According to Echeverría, Marx's argumentation in the 'chapter on method' suffers from the absence of an adequate distinction between the concrete particular and the concrete totality. Echeverría holds that Marx identifies the determination of the 'simple' category with that of the 'abstract' category. According to Echeverría, Marx subsequently corrected this problematic identification, just as he later corrected the reduction of the concrete to the concrete totality which he had performed in the *Introduction*. The Latin American philosopher argues that Marx proceeded to determine the commodity as a simple *concretum*: 'The commodity is concrete, but also a simple concrete. In distinction to the position assumed in the *Introduction*, the identity between the abstract and the simple is broken'.[420] The 1859 preface to *A Contribution to the Critique of Political Economy*, which was to replace the *Introduction* – the latter, characterised by Echeverría as highly problematic, having been composed approximately 18 months previously – 'establishes the need to ascend from the particular to the general, from the concrete unit to the concrete totality, via the necessary course of abstraction'.[421]

The Latin American discussion of Marx entered into a new phase of development with the interpretation of the critique of political economy presented in the form of a trilogy by the Argentinian philosopher and theologian, Enrique Dussel, between 1985 and 1990. These three volumes are to be considered as the result of an intensive new reception of Marx developed over many years by Dussel, a process begun by the Argentinian at the UNAM after his relocation

418   Ibid.
419   Ibid.
420   Echeverría 1989, p. 266.
421   Echeverría 1989, p. 268.

to Mexico in the latter half of the 1970s. As is the case with regard to Sánchez Vázquez, Dussel cannot be included under the rubric of Latin American Althusserianism. As explained in Part 1 of the present study, Dussel's intellectual and political background consists in his status as a pioneer of the ethics of liberation, which represents a central contribution to the Latin American 'philosophy of liberation' which has evolved as a correlate to liberation theology on this continent since the 1970s. In order to understand Dussel's theory and his perspective on the critique of political economy, it is crucial to acknowledge that this background in the philosophy or ethics of liberation by no means remains extrinsic to Dussel's engagement with Marx. This is the political and theoretical background against which the Argentinian philosopher's engagement with Marx is to be understood.

Dussel's trilogy consists of a series of commentaries on texts by Marx. The first instalment[422] of the trilogy contains a commentary on the *Grundrisse*;[423] the second instalment is dedicated to *A Contribution to the Critique of Political Economy* (1859), but above all to the *1861–63 Manuscripts*, whose best-known component is *Theories of Surplus-Value*;[424] the concluding instalment of the trilogy deals with Marx's drafts for *Capital* from the period between 1863 until shortly before his death.[425] In this final work in the trilogy, Dussel focuses his attention on the so-called third (1863–5) and fourth (1866) drafts of *Capital*.

Dussel considers that the theoretical influence of Hegel on Marx in the *Grundrisse* is significant.[426] The Argentinian-Mexican philosopher argues that the reference to Hegel is also present in Marx's later manuscripts, and deems that there is also a Hegelian legacy immanent within the theory formed by the 'final' Marx (Dussel's expression for the post-1863 Marx). However, this recognition needs to be supplemented by the acknowledgment of another decisive dimension of the Marx-Hegel relation: according to Dussel, Marx's thought fundamentally distinguishes itself from Hegel's philosophy in that Marx, as a thinker of exteriority, goes beyond a Hegel-oriented thinking of totality. In Dussel's interpretation of Marx, the category of totality refers to capital, whereas the category of exteriority corresponds to the dimension of 'living labour'.

---

422   See Dussel 1985.
423   On the dissemination and reception of the *Grundrisse* in hispanophone countries, see Ribas and Plá 2008.
424   See Dussel 2001a. An Italian edition has also been published.
425   See Dussel 1990.
426   See Dussel 1985, p. 343.

At the point at which the category of exteriority comes into view, Schelling's philosophy becomes an important reference for Dussel, for whom Marx becomes transformed into a 'Schellingian'. 'Living labour', which is bound up with the subjectivity of the worker, is taken by Dussel to be capital's other, as something which is 'external' to the totality of capital, but which capital incorporates within itself. Thus, Dussel concludes that Marx's thought by no means coincides with a logic of the totality, such as that for which (on Dussel's view) Hegel stands. It is precisely this logic of the totality (in the sense given by Hegelian philosophy) which Dussel overcomes through his perspective on exteriority; the Argentinian-Mexican philosopher claims that he finds warrant in Marx for this position. A core component of Dussel's reading of Marx consists in his attempt to make Marx into a 'Schellingian' by referring to the creative power of 'living labour' as the source of value.[427] According to Dussel's interpretation, Hegel begins his logic with being itself, whereas, for Schelling, there is something prior to being, namely its creative source, which brings being into existence in the first place. Being does not create itself, but is itself constituted. Likewise, according to Marx, it is 'living labour' – as a moment which is external to capital, pertaining to the realm of exteriority, but which is incorporated into capital – which first creates the being of capital, namely value. On Dussel's interpretation of Marx, 'objectified labour' stands counterposed to 'living labour' – the latter forming the central point of reference for the Argentinian-Mexican philosopher. Thus, Dussel writes in *El Último Marx* that '[the] "absolute" and "originary" distinction of the whole dialectic in *Capital* is the one that opposes "living labour" and "objectified labour"'.[428] 'Living labour' is the creator of surplus value. Value does not create itself, but is itself constituted. Adumbrated here is the significance which, on Dussel's view, corresponds not to the Hegelian, but rather to a 'Schellingian' element in Marx's critique of political economy – i.e. to an element which is bound up with the category of exteriority.

On their own, these theses would be sufficiently controversial, but the way in which Dussel came to them – i.e. his own process of intellectual development – makes his approach even more contentious: in the 1970s, Dussel had initially been inclined towards a philosophy of liberation which was not oriented

---

427   It might not come as a surprise that Dussel's reference to Schelling has met with criticism within international research. In a review of the English-language translation of Dussel's commentary on the so-called second draft of *Capital*, Christopher Arthur writes that 'Schelling is ultimately unhelpful in solving problems present in Marx's theory' (Arthur 2003c, p. 255).

428   Dussel 1990, p. 420.

towards Marx. At this time, the category of exteriority, which Dussel adopted during the course of his reception of the French philosopher, Emmanuel Lévinas (1905–95), was already central to the Argentinian-Mexican's conceptual approach. Dussel understood both Hegel and Marx as thinkers of the 'logic of totality', and counterposed 'analectic' (in the sense of a kind of 'logic of exteriority') to the dialectical logic associated with the names Hegel and Marx. In Dussel's view, his own philosophy of liberation was (and remains) a thinking from a specifically Latin American perspective, a thinking from the perspective of the periphery, so to speak. And it was precisely in this context that the category of exteriority was given the role according to which it formed the decisive point of reference. However, this also implied that Dussel's liberation-philosophical approach was only possible as an alternative (or, to put it more acutely, in opposition) to Marx as a thinker of the 'logic of the totality'. Yet, following Dussel's subsequent, more intensive reception of Marx's theory, his relation to Marx's critique of political economy began to be transformed. From the late 1970s and early 1980s on, Dussel embarked on a path leading away from antagonism vis-à-vis Marx, and towards affinity with the latter, and ultimately he no longer counterposed analectic and dialectic. Instead, he grasped analectic as a central component of the specifically Marxian dialectic, in the following sense: analectic was a constitutive feature of Marx's dialectic, and one which crucially distinguished it from Hegel's philosophy. Dussel has since identified the category of exteriority as a central point of reference in Marx's critique of political economy. This new view of Marx as a thinker of exteriority implies the possibility, for and with Dussel, of a specifically Latin American perspective on Marx, of a liberation-philosophical thinking 'from the standpoint of the periphery'.[429]

Dussel's extensive commentaries on Marx's various manuscripts on the critique of political economy from 1857 onwards – incidentally, it is worth noting that Dussel takes the $MEGA^2$ edition into consideration, together with Soviet and East German research – represent, in general terms, a contribution of great significance, not least on account of the methodological and epistemological questions that the Argentinian-Mexican interpreter of Marx raises in relation to the latter's critique of political economy. Within the context of his engagement with the critique of political economy, Dussel distinguishes between various levels of the latter. He understands the level of production as a kind of 'deep

---

429   The basic features of Dussel's thought are outlined in detail in Fornet-Betancourt 1994, pp. 272 ff.

level', and the level of circulation as a kind of 'surface level'.[430] In addition, the philosopher and theologian underscores the emphatic concept of critique in Marx, and refers to Marx's fetish-critique and to the specifically critical bearing of Marx's critique of political economy vis-à-vis the question of epistemology. Dussel insists on the dual character of Marx's concept of critique: 'Marx performs a double critique: he not only performs the critique of *texts* (from the vulgar capitalist or classical political economy); but, and above all, the critique of capitalist *reality*'.[431] Dussel maintains that, according to Marx, the specifically scientific content consists, among other things, in reaching behind the surface phenomena in order to return to the essence itself. In the first book in his trilogy, Dussel draws the conclusion that Marx developed an ontology of capital. He argues that Marx's discourse is simultaneously economic *and* philosophical: it is a question of an ontology of the economy, or of an ontological economy.[432]

Marx's theory of fetishism must be accorded a central significance in Dussel's thought.[433] Yet Dussel is by no means alone in the Latin American debate in this regard. The Argentinian interpreter of Marx, Néstor Kohan, judges the critique of fetishism to be anything but pre-scientific; rather, he considers it to be the foundation which enables 'scientific enquiry'. According to Kohan, Marx's critique of political economy is based on a critique of the fetishism of this discipline, and Marx's theory of value stands in an internal and indissoluble relation to his theory of fetishism.[434] Kohan had already emphasised the importance of Marx's theory of fetishism in an earlier work.[435] Marx's theory of fetishism also constitutes a central point of reference in the theory formed by the Irishman, John Holloway, who lives and lectures in Mexico. According to Holloway, the concept of fetishism is of decisive significance within the framework of Marx's critique of capitalist society. Yet, as Holloway argues, 'the category of fetishism, so central for Marx, is almost entirely forgotten by the mainstream Marxist tradition'.[436] Holloway's approach stands opposed to this (alleged) traditional neglect. Furthermore, the theory of fetishism plays an important role in the reception of Marx by one of the most significant liberation theologians in Latin

---

430   See Dussel 1990, p. 408.

431   See Dussel 2001a, p. 190.

432   See Dussel 1985, pp. 347 f.

433   Dussel investigates the development of Marx's concept of fetishism in the four so-called drafts of *Capital* (see Dussel 1993, pp. 59 ff.).

434   See Kohan 2005.

435   See Kohan 1998.

436   See Holloway 2005, p. 118.

America, the German-born Franz Josef Hinkelammert.[437] Bolívar Echeverría held the deciphering of fetishism to be essential for Marx's programme of critique. As has been established, a whole series of authors from, or residing in, Latin America has laid great emphasis on the significance of precisely Marx's theory, or critique, of fetishism, underrated as this was by Althusser; in so doing, these authors operate within an interpretative orientation which is opposed to Althusser on this important point.

Within the Latin American research of the 1980s and 1990s, (presumed) ambivalences or deficits in the theory formed by Marx were certainly thematised, however. At the end of the 1980s, an investigation of the history of the emergence and development of Marx's *oeuvre* on the critique of political economy by the Mexican, Raúl Rojas, was published in German.[438] This study presents Marx's critical engagement with his economic sources, while simultaneously the attempt is made to gauge potential deficits in Marx's theory. Among the central theses of this monograph are the incompleteness of Marx's systematic critique of political economy, and the proposition that Marx nonetheless accomplished a scientific revolution. In particular, Marx's elaboration of the theory of ground rent and of the theory of international trade and exchange rates is problematic, or even altogether insufficient, according to Rojas. Among the issues thematised by a further interpreter of Marx, the Mexican philosopher, A. García de la Sienra, are the presumed ambivalences or deficits in Marx's theory of value.[439]

The recent, multifaceted reception of Marx by Brazilian researchers will only be addressed selectively here. As was the case in the hispanophone Latin American countries, Brazilian engagement with Marx has also been partially influenced by Althusserianism (and Marta Harnecker has played a considerable role in the dissemination of this theoretical orientation in Brazil, much as she has done in the hispanophone countries). In recent years, a different path has been taken by Alfredo Saad-Filho, who, alongside the above-mentioned Michael Löwy, is probably one of the better-known Brazilian interpreters of Marx. Saad-Filho orients himself towards methodological considerations of the Soviet theorist, Evald Ilyenkov, who was one of the best-known philosophers and Marx-researchers of the period of the 'Khrushchev Thaw'.[440] Saad-Filho's interpretation of Marx centres particularly on the theory of value. With regard to the Marxist theoretical discussion, the Brazilian theorist distinguishes between

---

437   See Kern 1992, pp. 186 ff.
438   See Rojas 1989.
439   See García 1992.
440   See Saad-Filho 2001.

a traditional 'labour-embodied' reading and a value-form theoretical reading of Marx's theory of value (the latter being partly influenced by I.I. Rubin).[441] Within the context of the question of the globalisation of the discussion of Marx, the fact that Saad-Filho belongs to those non-Anglo-Saxon researchers to have engaged intensively with the British 'New Dialectic' approach (see below) is of some relevance.[442]

Also important for the discussion of Marx in Brazil are the studies by the philosopher, Ruy Fausto; the latter engaged with the category of abstract labour, among other questions, in the 1980s.[443] A more recent study by Fausto relates to the problematic of the dialectic; here, the Brazilian philosopher endeavours to clarify both the connections and the differences between Hegelian and Marxian dialectic.[444] Thematically, this represents a point of contact with the international theoretical discussion. That the methodological problematic played a central role within the Brazilian engagement with Marx's critique of political economy in the 1990s can be demonstrated by referring, for example, to a debate between Francisco Teixeira[445] and Hector Benoit.[446] A further thematic parallel can be drawn between the German and Brazilian receptions of Marx's critique of political economy in terms of the investigation of the categorial interconnection between value and money.[447] In his approach to research into Marx's 'theory of money in capitalism', the Brazilian Marx-researcher, Claus Magno Germer, indicates the necessity of combining the theory of money with the theory of capital in order to go beyond Marx's theory of money, which remains at the level of simple circulation.[448]

A striking point of contact between the New Marx-Reading in Germany and the recent Brazilian reception of Marx can be identified in the content of the journal, *Crítica marxista*, which has provided a forum for the debate on the critique of political economy.[449] Parts of both the respective German and Brazilian debates have been characterised by the insight that Marx's the-

---

441   See Saad-Filho 2001, pp. 21 ff.

442   See Saad-Filho 1997.

443   See Fausto 1986, pp. 97 ff.

444   See Fausto 1997.

445   See Teixeira 1995 and Teixeira 1999.

446   See Benoit 1996 and Benoit 1999.

447   See Mollo 1991; see also Paulani 1994.

448   See Germer 1997. For Germer's perspective on Marx's 1857 'chapter on method', see Germer 2001.

449   This Brazilian journal should not be confused with the similarly named Italian periodical mentioned above.

oretical project is concerned not with an 'alternative political economy', but rather a *critique* of political economy, in which the specific character of critique is to be emphasised. (In the history of the reception of Marx – particularly in the countries of 'actually existing socialism' – the Marxian project has often been construed using terms such as 'Marxian political economy', the 'political economy of capitalism', the 'political economy of the working class', rather than the 'critique of political economy'. Such terminology failed to adequately reflect the peculiar critical character of Marx's endeavour).

For the Brazilian interpreter of Marx, Jorge Grespan, the Marxian *critique* of political economy goes far beyond a mere critical engagement with other theories.[450] According to Grespan, the aspect of critique is absolutely essential to Marx's theoretical endeavour – i.e. for the elaboration of his theory of capitalism. Grespan relies on a letter that Marx wrote to Lassalle on 22 February 1858, while working on the *Grundrisse*: 'The work I am presently concerned with is a *Critique of Economic Categories* or, if you like, a critical exposé of the system of the bourgeois economy. It is at once an exposé and, by the same token, a critique of the system'.[451] On Grespan's view, it is not a question, in Marx's thought, of two disparate discourses (one setting out his own theory, and another consisting in the critique of the ideas which had previously been expounded); rather, these two moments merge into one. Grespan maintains that Marx was obliged to distinguish himself in a specific way as a 'quasi-immanent' critic of political economy, since political economy was neither capable of transcending its limits within its own theoretical horizon, nor of removing its own aporias.[452]

Rolando Astarita ranks among Argentinian interpreters of the theory of value that is to be found in Marx's critique of political economy.[453] In forming his theory, Astarita foregrounds the form-theoretical aspect of Marx's critique of political economy. Thus, he engages in an interpretation of the critique of political economy in which he refers to themes including the distinction between 'social form' and 'material content'. The Argentinian explicitly points out the difficulties in comprehending the beginning of Marx's exposition. He understands value-objectivity in Marx as specifically social, and argues that

450   See Grespan 2000, Grespan 2001 and Grespan 2002.

451   Marx 1983k, p. 270.

452   For an attempt by another Brazilian author to establish a demarcation between Marx and political economy, and between Marx and the latter's inconsistencies, see Paulani 2002.

453   See Astarita 2004.

Marx's concept of form (which is of decisive significance for him) relates to the specifically social dimension of the commodity. Astarita writes that 'Marx distinguishes *social forms* from *material content or substance*'.[454]

Rolando Astarita emphatically refutes the idea that Marx first establishes a critical distinction between himself and bourgeois political economy in the context of his theory of surplus value; according to the Argentinian, there is already a fundamental difference between Marx and Ricardo with regard to the theory of value. Thus, Astarita maintains that Marx dialectically sublated – i.e. he simultaneously overcame and preserved – Ricardian theory with his theory of value. Astarita refers to the fact that Marx criticised the Englishman for failing to pay sufficient attention to the value-form and for neglecting the internal interconnection between value and value-form. Thus, according to the critique presented by Astarita, Ricardo reduces money to a mere means of exchange. On this view, Ricardo fails to grasp money as the 'incarnation of value', and instead maintains an open attitude to Say's Law and to the quantity theory of money.[455] Astarita further argues that Marx's theory of value is not a 'mere "development" of Ricardo's theory, but essentially its critique'.[456] The significance that Astarita attributes to Marx's form-theory – the sensitivity that the Argentinian demonstrates towards the form-theoretical dimension of

---

454   Astarita 2004, p. 63.

455   Marx's critique of Ricardo's theory of money – a critique brought to bear by the Trier-born theorist from the standpoint of the specific unity of his theory of value and theory of money – is formulated explicitly in *Theories of Surplus-Value*: 'Yet *Ricardo does not investigate* the form of this labour (the particular determination of labour as creative of exchange-value, or of labour which presents itself in exchange-value) – he does not investigate the *character* of this labour. Hence he does not grasp the interconnection of *this labour* with *money* or that it must present itself in *money*. Hence he completely fails to grasp the interconnection between the determination of the exchange-value of the commodity by labour-time and the fact that commodities must necessarily proceed to the formation of money. Hence his erroneous theory of money' (Marx 1989b, pp. 389–90 [translation modified – N.G.]). At a later point, Marx states that money is grasped by Ricardo 'merely as an intermediary in the exchange of products, and not as an essential and necessary form of existence of the commodity which must manifest itself as exchange-value, as general social labour' (Marx 1989c, p. 132). According to Marx, Ricardo 'does not understand the specific form in which labour is an element of value, and fails in particular to grasp that the labour of the individual must present itself as abstract general labour and, in this form, as *social* labour. Therefore he has not understood that the development of money is connected with the nature of value and with the determination of this value by labour-time' (Marx 1989c, p. 324).

456   Astarita 2004, p. 88.

the critique of political economy – allows an analogy to be drawn with those German interpretations of Marx which can be ranged under the rubric of the so-called New Marx-Reading.

A further interpretation of Marx's labour theory of value is that offered by the Mexican-born Begoña Gutiérrez de Dütsch. Her comprehensive study, first published in 2005, should rightly be considered the result of a long-standing research process, reaching back at least to the early 1980s. This author obtained her doctorate in Frankfurt am Main, and her work can be located, as regards its thematic content, within the context of the Frankfurt debate on value theory and value-form theory;[457] yet there is also decisive intersection in terms of content between her research and the recent Latin American debate on *Capital*.

The object of Gutiérrez's enquiry is the beginning of Marx's exposition in the various versions of the first volume of *Capital* (but also in *A Contribution to the Critique of Political Economy*), and in particular his value-form analysis. The Mexican author grasps Marx's exposition of the 'curiosity' of economic fetishism as a unique and revolutionary scientific discovery in the socio-economic domain. Gutiérrez writes:

> If there is anything to *Marx's exposition of economic categories* and the associated *theory of fetishism*, and if these can simultaneously be regarded as a kind of critical materialist procedure in order to demonstrate the *historical specificity of capitalist society* system-immanently, as it were, then it might well be said that this in effect constitutes a unique and revolutionary approach. For at issue here is the status of *economic categories* themselves; it is a question of their concealing function in *bourgeois society*, as it were, and, ultimately, a matter of calling them *radically into question and dismantling them*.[458]

It is precisely the fact that the fetishism problematic is at the centre of Gutiérrez's focus on Marx's critique of political economy which not only binds her interpretation to the Frankfurt discourse on Marx, but also allows connections to be drawn with the Latin American debate. The Mexican author insists on the

---

457   In an epilogue to Guttiérez's study, Egon Becker – a protagonist of the Frankfurt debate on Marx since the 1970s – writes that in the light of Guttiérez's work, it might prove difficult to 'continue the Frankfurt discourse on the value-form within the habitual patterns. In this sense, it is a concluding text. It can only be followed by something completely different' (Becker 2005, p. 396).

458   Gutiérrez 2005, pp. xxiif.

specificity of economic fetishism, and is extremely critical in her opposition to any potential attempts to transfer this 'unique' socio-economic dimension to other spheres of social life. At issue here, according to Gutiérrez, is a fundamental socio-economic condition *sui generis*.

Within the Latin American reception of the critique of political economy, there is certainly an engagement with interpretative approaches from other parts of the world; yet the independence and theoretical originality of the Latin American reception should be emphasised. Discussion of the theory formed by Isaak Ill'ich Rubin has played a certain role in the recent Argentinian debate in relation to the critique of political economy. Thus, for example, one of Juan Iñigo Carrera's contributions has been to provide an extensive treatment of this early Soviet approach to the interpretation of Marx's theory of value.[459] The recent Argentinian discussion has also yielded a study by Axel Kicillof and Guido Starosta which relates critically to Rubin.[460] A further study by Starosta aims, in the context of the interpretation of Marx's commodity theory at the beginning of the first volume of *Capital*, to supersede a large part of the Anglo-Saxon debate on Marx's dialectical method of exposition.[461] Starosta objects that the studies in question do not adequately take into account the particular role of the moment of analysis (as opposed to the moment of synthesis) within Marx's dialectical exposition, and furthermore that they neglect the specific form of the analytic process within dialectical thought.[462] Starosta aims to address these problems, and his contribution to research is evidence of the ongoing engagement by Latin American interpreters of Marx with the beginning of the exposition of the critique of political economy.

6.2   *Spain*

In Spain, interest in Marx and Marxism appears to have receded after the intermediate 'wave of Marxism' which peaked in the 1970s.[463] In a study dating from the 1980s, Monserrat Galcerán Huguet set out the view that the contemporary crisis of Spanish Marxism was to be interpreted as a side effect of the crisis of French and Italian Marxism. Traditionally, Marx-oriented thought in Spain was relatively highly dependent upon influences from abroad. Although (to

---

459   See Iñigo 2004, pp. 290 ff.

460   See Kicillof and Starosta 2007a. Kicillof and Starosta also criticise a value-theoretical current within the tradition of Autonomist Marxism (see Kicillof and Starosta 2007b).

461   See Starosta 2008.

462   See Starosta 2008, p. 297.

463   See Galcerán 1987, p. 268. On the earlier reception of Marx in Spain, see Ribas 1994.

cite an example) the Spanish philosopher, José María Ripalda,[464] took note of studies emerging from the discussion oriented towards Marxian theory in West Germany in the 1970s, it is reasonable to surmise that it was rather French theoretical influences, for instance, which stood in the foreground within the Spanish Marxist discussion.

Within this context, particular significance was accorded to Althusserianism. In 1977, Luis Crespo wrote the following: 'More concretely, in Spain, Althusser has facilitated the work of disseminating Marxism as a scientific theory among the masses (of militants as well as students), such that few would doubt today that Marxism has been taken note of as a theory of history – the multiple editions of Althusser's classic *oeuvre* [Crespo refers to *Lire le Capital* and *Pour Marx*, among other works – J.H.] bear witness to this fact'.[465] In the 1970s, a work by the theorist, Albert Roies, contributed to the familiarisation of the Spanish public with Althusserianism.[466] The philosopher, Gabriel Albiac, also participated in the reception of Althusser. In addition, it should be noted that the Chilean member of the Althusserian School, Marta Harnecker, had an effect on the Spanish Marx debate. A further theorist, César de Vicente Hernando, particularly emphasises two phases in the Spanish reception of Althusser: the first of these he locates in the period up to 1979, and the second from 1992 onwards. According to de Vicente, a great deal of attention was paid in the former phase to the epistemological problematic (among others), with works such as *Lire le Capital* playing an important role. De Vicente maintains that the Spanish reception of Althusser since 1992 has been characterised by the further exploration of Althusser's complete works.[467]

Spanish works of note from the 1970s and 1980s include contributions to the international wave of reception of Marx's *Grundrisse* which also reached Spain in the 1970s,[468] but also a study by Emilio Lamo de Espinosa which was published in 1981, and which addresses Marx's theory of reification, among other issues.[469] A study by Felipe Martínez Marzoa dating from 1983 is considered within the Spanish discussion to be a standard work on the critique of political economy. Martínez engages in a reading of *Capital* from a specifically philosophical standpoint.[470] One thematic similarity to discourses on *Capital* in

---

464   See, among other works, Ripalda 1978 and Ripalda 1981.
465   Crespo 1977, p. 61.
466   See Roies 1974.
467   See de Vicente 2004–5.
468   See, for example, Bueno 1973.
469   See Lamo 1981.
470   See Martínez 1983.

other countries which can be observed in Martínez's study consists in the great deal of attention paid to the 'problem of the beginning'. In his interpretation of Marx's analysis of the commodity, Martínez construes the question as to the commodity's being *qua* commodity – i.e. its specific mode of being *qua* commodity – as an ontological one. At issue, according to Martínez, is the analysis of the form assumed by products in modern capitalist society.[471] On Martinez's view, a theory of the capitalist mode of production presupposes the analysis of the commodity. It is an immanent necessity within such a theory that the analysis of the commodity should constitute its starting point.

A survey of critical economic thought in Spain in the period spanning from 1960 to 1990 is provided by Diego Guerrero. Although the theory formed by Guerrero himself is oriented to Marx's critique of political economy, the Spanish theorist emphasises that economic heterodoxy in Spain cannot be reduced to the adepts of Marx.[472] Nonetheless, Guerrero accords the 'Marxian/Marxist' current a central place in the exposition that he presents in his survey. However, the Spanish theorist establishes a fundamental distinction between 'Marxist' and 'Marxian' economics, according to which the latter is more narrowly defined theoretically and draws more closely on Marxian theory, whereas the former attempts to build a bridge towards social and historical reality (e.g. through the theory of imperialism or that of monopoly capitalism). On Guerrero's view, 'Marxist' economics proportionately outweighs the 'Marxian' variety. According to his own schema, a recent theoretical contribution by Guerrero – a résumé of the three volumes of *Capital* – would undoubtedly belong in the category of 'Marxian' economics.[473]

7   The Anglo-Saxon World

The Anglo-Saxon engagement with Marx's critique of political economy since the 1960s, and particularly since the 1970s and 1980s, constitutes a new phase of the debate in the corresponding countries to the extent that methodological problems and the specifically 'qualitative' content of Marx's critique of political economy have been more markedly foregrounded than at any time previously. Older thinkers, such as Ronald Meek[474] (1917–78) or Paul Sweezy,[475]

---

471   See Martínez 1983, p. 34.

472   See Guerrero 1997, pp. 160 ff.

473   See Guerrero 2008.

474   See Meek 1967.

475   See Sweezy 1970 (a work first published in 1942).

had already, before the 1970s, anticipated to a certain degree the subsequent engagement with Marx's method, or with the qualitative side of the problematic of value and with the theory of fetishism; yet, from the 1970s and 1980s onwards, research into these thematic fields became more intensive, and in part attained a new and higher level of critical engagement with this content.

One problem was that the state of affairs with regard to English-language editions of Marx's texts was anything but satisfactory up until the 1970s. Thus, for instance, a complete edition of the *Grundrisse* was first published in English in 1973 – i.e. at a time when this text had long since constituted an important foundation for widespread discussion in both German states.[476] It is also worth noting in passing that this English-language edition did not contain the *Urtext* (the original draft of *A Contribution to the Critique of Political Economy*), which the East German publishers of the 1953 edition had included in an appendix. This deficit with regard to the availability of English-language editions of Marx's work was at least partially rectified by the completion of the 50-volume edition of *Marx-Engels Collected Works*,[477] even if it remains the case that no scientific research can afford to dispense with the *MEGA²* edition.[478]

The *Grundrisse* was not completely unknown to the English-language readership before 1973, however: Martin Nicolaus had already presented this work to a broad public in 1968,[479] his tone openly enthusiastic at times ('the *Grundrisse* blows the mind').[480] Yet, above all, textual excerpts from the *Grundrisse* had already been translated and published before publication of the complete English-language edition. To cite the two best-known examples: Eric Hobsbawm had already engaged with the *Grundrisse* in 1964,[481] and had edited an

---

476 For a detailed assessment of the dissemination and reception of the *Grundrisse* in the Anglophone world, see Arthur 2008.

477 See Golman 1978.

478 Dissatisfied with the existing published English translations, Anglo-Saxon interpreters of Marx occasionally make their own independent translations of certain passages from the *oeuvre* of the Trier-born theorist. An example of the problems that can arise in this way can be seen in an absurd translation (published in the *Historical Materialism* journal) of a term from Marx's 'chapter on fetish' in the first volume of *Capital*: Jim Kincaid suggests that the translation of '*theologische Mucken*' (which is rendered as 'theological niceties' in the Penguin edition) could be improved by translating '*Mucken*' as 'small-biting insects, e.g. mosquitoes, midges' (Kincaid 2005b, p. 102). But perhaps this is merely an example of British humour.

479 Nicolaus 1968, p. 59.

480 In the same year, even the *Times Literary Supplement* acknowledged the existence of the *Grundrisse* (see Anonymous 1968, pp. 67 f.).

481 See Hobsbawm 1964.

excerpt from this text;[482] this was followed, in 1971, by the publication of a compilation of excerpts from the *Grundrisse* edited by David McLellan.[483]

In 1974, Keith Tribe presented an early Anglo-Saxon engagement with Marx's *Grundrisse* as part of the international wave of reception of this text, whose publication had attracted much attention from Marxist intellectuals.[484] However, Tribe emphasised the presumed incoherence and 'labyrinthine nature' of this work by Marx, which he took to be a transitional manuscript (he refers to the 'transitional nature of the work').[485]

In 1970, the Conference of Socialist Economists was founded in Britain; this would prove to be an important forum for the discussion of Marx's critique of political economy.[486] The 1970s and 1980s formed a turning point in the Anglo-Saxon engagement with Marx, not least due to a sharpened focus on, on the one hand, the development of the latter's plans for the architectonic of his critique of political economy through the various iterations of this project, and, on the other, his specifically form-theoretical approach. Marx's value-form analysis became a significant point of reference for the reception of his theory of value. The transfer of theory from the German-language discussion played a by no means unimportant role in the establishment of this new orientation for research.[487] In addition, *Pour Marx* and *Lire le Capital* were also received in the Anglo-Saxon world – incidentally, Eric Hobsbawm engaged with these works already in 1966.[488] The Althusserian School was to a certain extent positively received in the Anglo-Saxon countries. Worthy of mention in this context, alongside the British Althusserianism of the 1970s in particular, is an

---

482   See Marx 1964.

483   See Marx 1971.

484   It is worth noting here that the Anglo-Saxon discussion referred not only to the text of the *Grundrisse*, but also to the extended introduction by Martin Nicolaus. For a critique of Nicolaus's introduction, see Postone and Reinicke 1974/5. See also Keane and Singer 1974/5.

485   Tribe 1990, p. 735.

486   See Lee 2001.

487   One of the important elements of this theory transfer was the 1977 publication in English of Roman Rosdolsky's monograph on the *Grundrisse* and the problematic of the Marx's plans for the architectonic of his critique of political economy (see Rosdolsky 1977); a shorter, foundational text by Rosdolsky on methodological questions in Marx had already been published in English in 1974 (indeed, appearing in an early issue of the journal, *New German Critique*, it had a broad readership; see Rosdolsky, Bathrick and Rabinbach 1974). Hans-Georg Backhaus's 1969 *Zur Dialektik der Wertform* – a foundational text for the West German debate on value-form theory – was published in English as 'On the Dialectics of the Value-Form' in 1980 (see Backhaus 1980).

488   See Hobsbawm 1973.

Althusser-influenced current in the USA, grouped around Richard Wolff.[489] Furthermore, there was also a reception, at least in part, of the Italian discussion of Marx around Della Volpe, Colletti and others in the Anglo-Saxon world.[490] The value-theoretical approach of I.I. Rubin and various studies by South Asian researchers (Banaji and, later, Shamsavari) have acted as further stimuli to the Anglo-Saxon discourse on Marx.

Despite the considerable theory transfer from abroad, it would be wrong to reduce to external influences the attempts that were made in the Anglophone world during the 1970s to establish a discriminating and methodologically oriented discussion of Marxian theory, and of the critique of political economy in particular. In the 1960s and 1970s, the question of Marx's method was raised by Anglo-Saxon interpreters of the critique of political economy, with a discussion arising particularly around the problematic of fetishism.[491,*]

Since the 1970s, 1980s and 1990s, differentiated interpretative approaches have emerged in the Anglophone world which resemble the German-language discussion of the 1960s to the 1990s with regard to a number of questions posed: e.g. Marx's theory of form; Marx's relation to Hegel; the theoretical relation between Marx and Engels; the development of the plans for the architectonic of the critique of political economy; and the so-called monetary theory of value. Roman Rosdolsky's commentary on the *Grundrisse*, which thematised the problematic of Marx's six-volume plan and the structural concept of

---

489   See Wolff 2006. In my opinion, the 'overdeterminist' interpretation of *Capital* of Richard Wolff and those in his orbit does not rank among the most theoretically fertile currents within the Anglo-Saxon debate. For example, the following position taken by Wolff with regard to the 'problem of the beginning' in relation to the logic of Marx's exposition can, without polemical exaggeration, be described as simply erroneous: 'Marx is interpreted [by the overdeterminist reading of *Capital*, to which Wolff himself subscribes – J.H.] as beginning *Capital* with a discussion of commodities and exchange chiefly because that is what his contemporaries believed to be the core of "economics." He disagreed, but chose a strategy for his book that began with commodity exchange to engage readers and then quickly moved those readers, in *Capital*, volume one's first chapters, to the very different matter of identifying capitalism's unique mode of organizing the surplus. Thus, *Capital's* unique interpretation of the labour theory of value enables Marx smoothly and quickly to pass on to the theory of "surplus value"' (Wolff 2007, p. 31). On the theoretical current around Richard Wolff in general, see also Resnick and Wolff 2007.

490   Nevertheless, Gregory Elliott points out that important works of the Italian discussion of Marx and Marxism remain untranslated into English (see Elliott 2008, pp. 34f.).

491   See, among other works, Morris 1966, Hodges 1967, Hodges 1970, and Geras 1990. Another example of the Anglo-Saxon engagement with Marx's method is provided by Sayer 1979.

*   See also a important later work by Sayer (Sayer 1987).

'capital in general', among other questions, appeared in English translation in 1977, providing the Anglo-Saxon Marx debate with material for discussion.[492] John Rosenthal identifies Hans-Georg Backhaus's approach as a (West) German influence on the 'Hegelian-oriented' English-language engagement with Marx.[493]

The theory transfer from Germany can be demonstrated by referring to the 'Sydney-Konstanz Project': this was a collaborative project between Australian and German researchers (Michael Eldred and Marnie Hanlon; Volkbert M. Roth and Lucia Kleiber respectively), who elaborated a sophisticated interpretative orientation within the Anglo-Saxon debate. The 'Sydney-Konstanz Project' can be regarded as an important initial step towards a globalisation of intensive engagement with Marx's critique of political economy. In the 1970s, Konstanz had emerged as a sub-centre of German-language Marx-interpretation; within this same decade, a research community was founded with Australian researchers.[494] Within this process, the form-analytic Marx-reading of the 'Sydney-Konstanz Project' – a reading which ascribed a decisive significance to the problematic of the value-form – was inspired by the New Marx-Reading that had coalesced in the Federal Republic of Germany around the contributions by Hans-Georg Backhaus and others.[495]

Michael Eldred and Marnie Hanlon identify in Marx's value-form theory a decisive advance beyond the 'labour-embodied' theory of value of classical political economy: 'Marx's theory, however, constitutes a fundamental advance over classical and other embodied labour value theories in that it is able to grasp the peculiar characteristics of the form of value, namely, the commodity form and, most importantly, to develop money as a form of value. This

---

492   John Mepham gives critical arguments against Rosdolsky's interpretation (see Mepham 1979).

493   'Many of the earliest English-language writings in this vein [the author refers here to recent 'Hegelian Marxism' – J.H.] bear the influence of the West German Hegel-Marx scholar Hans-Georg Backhaus' (Rosenthal 1998, p. 225). By contrast, Jim Kincaid makes the following assertion: 'The revival of value-form readings of Marx in the Anglophone literature can be criticised for a too limited direct engagement with analogous work in German from the 1970s onwards' (Kincaid 2005a, p. 34).

494   See Eldred, Hanlon, Kleiber and Roth 1984, p. 26.

495   It is worth noting that reference is made in the 'Sydney-Konstanz Project' both to Marx's value-form analysis in a narrow sense (i.e. in the sense of the third section of the first chapter of the first volume of *Capital*), and in a broader sense. In this latter sense, the economic categories which are thematised at subsequent levels of the exposition in *Capital* are regarded, within the framework of an approach oriented towards a value-form theoretical reconstruction of *Capital*, as forms of value.

aspect of Marx's theory has generally been neglected'.[496] Given the emphasis on the project of a 'reconstruction of Marx', there is an obvious parallel to the emphatically reconstructive approach of Backhaus. One of the ways in which the latter's influence can be discerned is through recognition of the role played in Eldred's 1984 monograph by the reconstruction of Marx's theory of value as a critique of pre-monetary theories of value.[497]

Eldred refers to a widespread 'illusion of completeness' within the discussion of Marx's *Capital*.[498] Eldred's own programme consisted in a form-analytic reconstruction of the critique of political economy and in the thematic extension of Marx's system. The Australian philosopher's project was that of

> a systematic theory of the bourgeois form of society, which relates directly to Marx insofar as his writings on the critique of political economy form the indispensable theoretical raw material for a reconstructed capital-analysis. Marx's theory is the best in a long series of attempts to analyse capitalism. This reconstructed capital-analysis, in turn, serves as foundation for a theory of the surface of capitalist economy and of the bourgeois superstructure.[499]

Eldred is ultimately concerned with the structure of the whole system of the bourgeois form of society. To this extent, the scope of Eldred's reconstructive approach extends beyond that of Backhaus, which represented a source of inspiration for the Australian philosopher.

However, Eldred by no means stands alone in his view of the incompleteness of the Marxian project. Within the Anglophone world, a study by Michael Lebowitz registering the lack of the book on wage labour envisaged in Marx's six-volume plan points in a somewhat similar direction.[500] Returning to Eldred and the other participants in the 'Sydney-Konstanz Project', it must be recognised that there has either been a perceptible decrease in activity in relation to this project, or it has currently ceased functioning altogether. In the meantime, there has been a reception of its approach by another theoretical project. Among the results yielded by the latter in this context was an enquiry into the 'determination of economic policy' in capitalist society.[501] Within the frame-

---

496 Eldred and Hanlon 1981, p. 24.
497 See Eldred 1984.
498 Eldred 1984, p. ix.
499 Eldred 1984, pp. xif.
500 See Lebowitz 1992.
501 See Reuten and Williams 1989.

work of their project, Geert Reuten and Michael Williams advocate a 'value-form theoretic reconstruction of the abstract-labour theory of value', which they conceive of as a kind of synthesis of two theoretical approaches (on the one hand, the 'abstract-labour theory of value', and on the other, 'value-form analysis') which, according to them, had emerged in competition with the 'labour-embodied theory of value' that had prevailed until the 1960s.[502] With this work, Reuten and Williams locate themselves within the context of what can be considered, from the point of view of the history of theory, as an upturn in the critical engagement with Marx's theory of value.

Relatively well-known within the German-language discussion of Marx is a comprehensive monograph written in the 1980s and early 1990s by the American historian and interpreter of Marx, Moishe Postone;[503] in his intellectual approach, Postone seeks to draw a fundamental distinction between Marx's critical theory and the Marxist theoretical tradition.[504] Central to Postone's reading of the critique of political economy is a new interpretation of Marx's concept of labour. In the interpretation of Marx's analysis by the Chicago-based historian, it is not the market or private property in the means of production which constitutes the core of capitalism, but rather the dual character of labour. In accordance with this dual character of labour (i.e. the distinction between abstract and concrete labour), Postone introduces a corresponding distinction between abstract and concrete time.[505]

As in other countries, an important point of discussion in the Anglo-Saxon debate concerns the Hegel-Marx relation, with opinions divided on this matter. A number of Anglo-Saxon works of research have been produced which investigate the proposition that Marx draws on certain elements of Hegel's philosophy, or which interpret these as a valuable source of inspiration for the critique of political economy. An example is a study by Norman Levine tracing Marx's reception of Hegel's logic of essence and detecting corresponding

---

502   Reuten and Williams 1989, p. 55.

503   Since Postone studied at the Johann Wolfgang Goethe-Universität in Frankfurt am Main, which was one of the centres of the West German 'New Marx-Reading' of the 1970s and 1980s, it might plausibly be assumed that he was influenced by the theoretical discussion there. As is well-known, the latter discussion served to propagate an approach to a fundamentally new interpretation of Marxian theory (as is the case in Postone's work), and, indeed, posed questions which bore a strong similarity to those subsequently formulated by Postone.

504   See Postone 1993. A German edition was published in 2003 (see Postone 2003).

505   An example of the German engagement with Postone is provided by Schmieder 2005, especially pp. 125 ff.

influences in the *1861–63 Manuscripts*.[506] The philosopher, Scott Meikle, who, alongside his research into Marx, engages mainly in research into Aristotle, detects in Marx a legacy of the philosophical tradition of essentialist metaphysics, with which Meikle associates the philosophies of Aristotle and Hegel: 'It is from the categories of essentialist metaphysics that Marx's characteristic conceptions of law, form and necessity arise [these conceptions play a central role in Marx's critique of political economy according to Meikle – J.H.], and they are as different as chalk from cheese from the currently familiar conceptions, in use by many Marxists, which arise from empiricist or atomist metaphysics'.[507] For the philosopher, Tom Rockmore, Marx even ultimately reveals himself as a 'Hegelian'.[508]

Further interpretations of Marx's relation to Hegel have been published in the journal, *Capital and Class*. Thus, contrary to the tendency within research to foreground the *Science of Logic* as a point of reference for Marx, Robert Fine (not to be confused with a better-known Anglo-Saxon Marx-researcher called Ben Fine)[509] investigates the relation between *Capital* and Hegel's philosophy of right.[510] Ian Fraser is an exponent of an 'extreme' parallelisation between Hegel and Marx.[511] According to Fraser, the conceptions of dialectic of both thinkers are 'one and the same, two of a kind'. Fraser criticises Marx's critique of Hegel, which famously rests on the assumption (which Fraser rejects) of an essential distinction between the conceptions of dialectic of these two thinkers.

Within the contemporary discussion, Christopher Arthur, who engaged with Marx's value-form theory already in the 1970s,[512] is an exponent of an approach based on a 'Hegelianising' interpretation of the critique of political economy, namely the tendency which has been dubbed the 'New Dialectic'. This theoretical current focuses on a form-theoretical reading of the critique of political economy, and critically distances itself from the Engels-inspired historicist or logico-historical interpretation of Marx's method; in particular, it holds Engels's reading of the beginning of *Capital* as the exposition of a pre-capitalist 'simple

---

506   See Levine 2002.

507   See Meikle 1985, p. viii.

508   See Rockmore 2002.

509   See Fine and Saad-Filho 2003. This introduction to Marx's *magnum opus* has been widely disseminated in the Anglo-Saxon world.

510   See Fine 2001.

511   See Fraser 1997.

512   See Arthur 1979.

commodity production' to be untenable.[513] (Here, there is a certain concordance with the results of German research). Arthur identifies a 'systematic' dialectic in Marx's critique of political economy; his 'New Dialectic' approach[514] has generated an important controversy in the Anglophone world,[515] and has been registered in French, Italian, German and Latin American research. Arthur is engaged in a critical dialogue with a competing approach, namely that of the Canadian wing of the Uno School, represented by Robert Albritton.[516] A more exhaustive engagement with the interpretative approaches of Christopher Arthur, Tony Smith and Patrick Murray is presented in the third part of the present study.

Another participant in the complex of discussions in the Anglo-Saxon world that has developed around Christopher Arthur, Fred Moseley and others, is the Dutchman, Geert Reuten, who presents his reflections on the question of how to elaborate a theoretically adequate reconstruction of Marx's theory of value. One of Reuten's concerns is to develop a theory of specifically social value which is able to dispense with the use of the metaphors of 'physical-substance embodiment' that he finds irritating.[517]

A contrasting approach to that of Arthur is pursued by Bertell Ollman, one of the best-known experts on Marx and dialectic in the USA. His standard work, *Dance of the Dialectic*,[518] 'brings together the best of my life's work on dialectics';[519] this is a 'best of' compilation, so to speak, from his previ-

---

513   See Arthur 1996. Arthur directs criticism against not only Engels, but also Ernest Mandel (see Arthur 2000, pp. 5 f.).

514   See Arthur 2002a. An earlier influential book by Arthur focuses on Marx's 1844 *Economic and Philosophical Manuscripts* (see Arthur 1986).

515   The journal, *Historical Materialism*, dedicated a large part of its 13/2 issue to the debate around *The New Dialectic and Marx's Capital*. See Murray 2005 as well as other contributions to the discussion in the same issue.

516   See Arthur 2002b, p. 253. See also Albritton's response (Albritton 2002), in which he attempts to identify important differences between the Canadian wing of the Uno School and Arthur. Albritton has also formulated a critique of Arthur's *The New Dialectic and Marx's Capital*: 'It is my belief that his account gets stuck on two specific oppositions: the opposition between value and use-value and between capital and labour. It seems to me that a dialectical approach based on the work of Japanese political economists Uno and Sekine can deal with these oppositions in a much more effective way than does Arthur, a way that conceives Marx's theory of capital as a much more coherent dialectic, while, at the same time, presenting a potentially much more powerful way of theorising class struggle' (Albritton 2005, p. 167).

517   See Reuten 1993.

518   See Ollman 2003.

519   Ollman 2003, p. ix.

ous books and essays. One of the reasons why this work is important is that it reflects a line of questioning which focuses on the scope of Marx's dialectical method. Ollman directs his criticism against a series of authors whose approaches he subsumes under the rubric of 'systematic dialectics'. Here, Ollman identifies an interpretative orientation with regard to Marx's dialectical method which he sees as being represented by Christopher Arthur and Tony Smith, as well as by the exponents of the Uno School, Thomas Sekine and Robert Albritton. According to Ollman, this interpretative orientation exhibits the following characteristics: Marx's dialectical method is reduced to a method of exposition; this method of exposition is located in the first volume of *Capital*; Marx is held to have essentially adopted a corresponding logic from Hegel.[520] Ollman argues that Marx's exposition in the first volume of *Capital* cannot be reduced to the systematic dialectic which is indeed in evidence there: 'Systematic Dialectics can only be understood as a misguided attempt to reduce Marx's varied strategies of presentation to a single one, albeit one that does play a major role in expounding the systematic nature of the capitalist mode of production in *Capital* I'.[521] Furthermore, Ollman maintains that Marx's dialectical method cannot be reduced to a 'method of exposition'. The American theorist prefers a much more broadly defined concept of Marx's dialectical method; here, Ollman has in mind an ontological and an epistemological dimension, as well as further dimensions, i.e. 'inquiry'; 'intellectual reconstruction (or self-clarification)'; exposition; and, ultimately, praxis.

Towards the end of the 1970s and the beginning of the 1980s, a new current emerged, in part within the context of the reception of Gerald Cohen's attempted reconstruction of historical materialism;[522] this current was so-called 'analytical Marxism'.[523] The latter can be considered a genuinely Anglo-Saxon intellectual orientation. Although there are considerable differences between the approaches of various researchers subsumed under this label (which, incidentally, is also used as a self-description),[524,*] certain basic features can be iden-

---

520   See Ollman 2003, p. 182.

521   Ollman 2003, p. 186.

522   See Cohen 2000 (a work first published in 1978).

523   See, for example, Tarrit 2006. See also Niechoj 2003. On the whole, relatively few German-speaking authors have undertaken a truly intensive engagement with analytical Marxism; for one such engagement, see Müller 1988.

524   The heterogeneity within 'analytical Marxism' is also pointed out by a vehement critic of this tendency (see Roberts 1996, p. 213). On the heterogeneity between Gerald Cohen's 'functionalism' and Jon Elster's and John Roemer's individualism, see Callinicos 1989. The theoretical heterogeneity within 'analytical Marxism' is also referred to in Van Parijs 1994 and Callinicos 2004b.

*   See also Callinicos 2005b.

tified which are common to the approaches of two of the best-known major
exponents of this research orientation, Jon Elster and John Roemer. First and
foremost among these would be the rejection of dialectic. Another decisive
feature is the positive recourse to methodological paradigms of modern economics and social science of non-Marxist provenance. Thus, methodological
individualism is accorded a central significance within this theoretical current. John Roemer is candid in his expression of the issues as he construes
them: 'With respect to method, I think Marxian economics has much to learn
from neoclassical economics'.[525] In the early 1980s, John Roemer referred positively to a 'microfoundations approach' in methodology, explaining that '[t]he
microfoundations approach consists in deriving the aggregate behavior of an
economy as a consequence of the actions of individuals, who are postulated to
behave in some specified way'.[526] Methodological individualism thus holds a
central significance within Roemer's thought.

Upholding the theoretical rigour and clarity which they associated with
formal logic and with the methodology of modern non-Marxist social science, the major exponents of 'analytical Marxism' seem to have been concerned above all to distance themselves from a tradition of Marxist theory
'encumbered' by the legacy of dialectical thought, which they located – quite
coherently, according to their approach – in the proximity of obscurantism. In
this context, it is indicative that the 'September Group' (an internal discussion
forum of important exponents of 'analytical Marxism', named after the month
chosen for its regular conferences) bore the alternative name of 'Non-Bullshit
Marxism Group'. As a rule, the methodological approaches of 'analytical Marxists' were met by the same level of hostility from exponents of dialectical Marxism as characterised the former's attitude toward the latter.

Jon Elster does not merely relate critically to dialectic; he also rejects the
labour theory of value.[527] It should be noted here, however, that Elster's analytic
Marxism was by no means the only current within the Anglo-Saxon debate to
discard the labour theory of value (in its Marxian formulation). A similar move
also occurred within the neo-Ricardian theoretical corpus which drew on the
Italian economist, Piero Sraffa; neo-Ricardian theories had a certain resonance
in the Anglo-Saxon world in the 1960s and 1970s, and tended to imply, at least
in part, a rejection of Marx's labour theory of value. In turn, other theoretical
orientations vehemently defended Marx's theory of value. For his part, Elster

---

525   Roemer 1986, p. 191.

526   Roemer 1981, p. 7.

527   Although a Norwegian, Elster operates within the context of a specifically Anglo-Saxon
       discourse, and is thus included here within the Anglo-Saxon discussion.

emphasises what he understands by methodological individualism: 'all social phenomena – their structure and their change – are in principle explicable in ways that only involve individuals – their properties, their goals, their beliefs and their actions'.[528] Reacting to criticisms of his methodology by theorists with an orientation to Marx, Elster writes the following: 'I regard methodological individualism as trivially true, worth stating only because triviality notwithstanding it was regularly violated by Marx'.[529] Like John Roemer, Elster maintains an open attitude towards game theory.[530] The question is posed, then, as to what actually is supposed to qualify Elster as a 'Marxist'. For Elster himself, an essential dimension of Marx's thought consists in the critique of exploitation and alienation. Elster's intention is to draw on this element of Marx's thought, with an ethical dimension being considered at all times.[531]

The discussion (and dissemination) of 'analytical Marxism' occurred to a large extent within the Anglophone world. Thomas Mayer endorsed the approach, which he saw as making it possible 'to gain the power of bourgeois social scientific methodology'.[532] Others, such as Michael Lebowitz, vehemently criticised 'analytical Marxism': 'not only is there not much of Marx left in Analytical Marxism, but its essential thrust ... is *anti*-Marxist'.[533] From a terminological point of view, Lebowitz concludes that the appellation 'Marxism' was a misnomer for this approach. The Canadian interpreter of Marx points out that 'analytical Marxism' does not even provide a grounding for its premises (he refers to its 'unsupported premise'). With critical undertones, Lebowitz writes: 'It is not supported because it need *not* be: the power of Conventionalism in contemporary social science ensures that such a premise will be accepted

---

528   Elster 1985, p. 5.

529   Elster 1986, pp. 66 f.

530   'How should Marxist social analysis relate to bourgeois social science? The obvious answer is: retain and develop what is valuable, criticize and reject what is worthless. Marxist social science has followed the opposite course, however. By assimilating the principles of functionalist sociology, reinforced by the Hegelian tradition, Marxist social analysis has acquired an apparently powerful theory that in fact encourages lazy and frictionless thinking. By contrast, virtually all Marxists have rejected rational-choice theory in general and game theory in particular. Yet game theory is invaluable to any analysis of the historical process that centers on exploitation, struggle, alliances, and revolution' (Elster 1982, p. 453).

531   Significantly, the three best-known theorists commonly ranged under the rubric of 'analytical Marxism' – Elster, Roemer and Cohen – have all since turned their attention to ethical debates within social philosophy.

532   Mayer 1989, p. 439.

533   Lebowitz 1988, p. 212.

as the common sense of scientific practice'.[534] In recent years, however, the controversy around 'analytical Marxism' has increasingly faded into the background of the Anglo-Saxon discussion of Marx and Marxism.

In the meantime, a rich and differentiated methodological discussion of Marx has unfolded in the Anglo-Saxon world; this debate has long since begun to take on an independent character. If Fred Moseley remarked in 2002 that 'the level of Marxian scholarship is higher today than ever before',[535] this assessment is surely true of the Anglo-Saxon methodological discussion of recent years. Yet, in a text co-authored with the Australian, Nicole Taylor, the Italian, Riccardo Bellofiore, has referred to deficits in the Anglo-Saxon Marx debate: 'The immaturity of Marxist research in this language [i.e. in English – J.H.] can be measured by the fact that most of the new primary and secondary literature coming out from the $MEGA^2$ is almost unknown ... Testimony to the poor state of contemporary Marxian theory everywhere, but especially in the English-speaking world, is that after Rosdolsky's ... classic book, almost nothing is known of the following debates on Marx's method in Germany'.[536] According to Bellofiore, this is true both in relation to a 'first wave' of the German debate comprising contributions by Backhaus, Reichelt, Tuchscheerer, Alfred Schmidt and others, and with regard to a 'second wave', whose representatives include Jahn, Schwarz, and Manfred Müller. Bellofiore puts the point starkly as he admonishes the English-speaking readership: 'No informed discussion – either about the "form" of value in relation to the "substance" of value or about Marx having abandoned the category of capital "in general" – can be pursued very far without taking these works into account'.[537] Nevertheless, Bellofiore's criticism – even if it is essentially apposite to some extent, at least in relation to the younger generation of Anglo-Saxon recipients of Marx –[538] might be in need of relativising somewhat. It can be shown that there are numerous parallels between German and Anglo-Saxon research, implying that there are indeed potential points of contact for a common discussion. In my opinion, this circumstance is even more important than the deficits that can (correctly) be identified in the Anglo-Saxon reception of Marx.

---

534   Lebowitz 1994, p. 165.

535   Moseley 2002, p. 128.

536   Taylor and Bellofiore 2004, p. 4.

537   Ibid.

538   By contrast, it can easily be demonstrated that some of the older generation of Anglo-Saxon researchers have indeed engaged with the German-language debate. Alongside representatives of the 'Sydney-Konstanz Project', Norman Levine is worthy of mention here as an authority on German-language research.

A shortcoming characterising at least some parts of the Anglo-Saxon discussion of the critique of political economy consists in the fact that, to some extent, sufficient notice has still not been taken of the *MEGA²* edition, or of the way the latter adheres to the principles of completeness and reflects the various stages in the development of texts. However, there are also examples of an altogether 'enthusiastic' reception of the *MEGA²* edition – the description of it as the 'Dead Sea Scrolls of Marxism' by the American, Norman Levine, for instance. The *Marx-Engels Collected Works* (*MECW*), which is the most important and comprehensive English-language edition of the works of Marx and Engels, came into being on the foundations provided by the *MEGA²* edition and in cooperation with the latter's editors;[539] however, the *MECW* edition has not been produced in accordance with the principles adhered to in the *MEGA²* edition. Nevertheless, texts and versions of texts that were not included in the *MECW* edition have been registered in the Anglo-Saxon reception of Marx and Engels. In 1983, an Anglo-Saxon author, Kevin Anderson, undertook valuable pioneering work in engaging with the 1872–5 French edition of *Capital* which Marx himself revised.[540] To those with an interest in Marx, but who can read only English, a number of important texts or versions of texts by Marx remain inaccessible, namely those texts and drafts which were neither included in the 50-volume *Marx-Engels Collected Works*, nor published separately in English translation – not to mention the dedicated literature accompanying the *MEGA²* edition, which is available predominantly in Japanese, Russian or German.

A survey of the history of the methodological and social-theoretical discussion of Marx over the last decades in the Anglo-Saxon countries reveals that longstanding deficits were to a great extent successfully remedied through research contributions in the period between the 1970s and the 1990s. This occurred, on the one hand, through the reception of tendencies within non-Anglo-Saxon research, and, on the other, through the emergence of significant 'autochthonous' discourses. An important role has been played in this regard by the large number of scientific journals which have provided, or continue to provide, a forum for the formation of Marx-oriented theory. (A by no means exhaustive list would include the following: *Capital & Class*, *Science and Society*; *Historical Materialism*; *Rethinking Marxism*; *Critique*; *Studies in Marxism*; *Research in Political Economy*; *Review of Radical Political Economics*; *Thesis Eleven*; *New Left Review*; *Radical Philosophical Review*).* In recent times, the

---

539   See Golman 1978.
540   See K. Anderson 1983.
*   The journal *Telos* surely deserves to be included in this list, as it published a number of

Anglo-Saxon reception of Marx has matched the innovative potential displayed by international research, but for the most part has not yet been able to attain the level of familiarity with Marx's work as a whole (particularly in relation to Marx's complete economic *oeuvre*, or, more accurately, his complete *oeuvre* on the critique of political economy) that partially characterises Japanese and German research.

It was thus symptomatic that Anglo-Saxon research was certainly not 'first fiddle' within the debate on the theme of 'Marx, Engels and the third volume of *Capital*' that took place in the mid-1990s in connection with the edition of *MEGA²*, Volume II/4.2 (this important debate revolved around the edition of Marx's manuscripts for the third volume in his so-called 1863–5 draft of *Capital*, which were being published for the first time in their original version, as opposed to the version edited by Engels).[541,*] All in all, the Anglo-Saxon reception of Marx has not been as closely tied to the continuing progression of the *MEGA²* edition, or to the associated systematic exploration of new and important source material in relation to Marx and Engels's works, as is to a certain extent the case with regard to Japanese and German research. An impression is thus created that the Anglo-Saxon debate is less 'up-to-date', at least on this level.

Critical Excursus *on Perry Anderson's* In the Tracks of Historical Materialism

A reference was made at the beginning of the present study to Perry Anderson's much-received engagement with 'Western Marxism' – a phenomenon which he principally located in France, Central Europe and Italy. In 1976, Anderson hoped not only for a 'productive' overcoming of 'Western Marxism', but also that the Anglo-Saxon world would play an important role in the future further development of Marxist theory, despite the 'relative modesty to date of Marxist culture' in these countries.[542] In 1983, seven years after the publication of *Considerations on Western Marxism*, a short follow-up study appeared, in which Anderson indicated that the latter of these hopes had already been fulfilled.[543]

---

important and groundbreaking contributions relating to Marxian theory and method, particularly in the late 1960s and 1970s.

541   See, among other works, Behrens 1995; Hecker 1995; Jungnickel and Vollgraf 1995; Vollgraf and Jungnickel 1995.

*   See also Heinrich 1996.

542   Anderson 1976, p. 102.

543   See P. Anderson 1983.

In fact, Anderson makes a further claim that the 'geographical structure' of Marxist theory formation has fundamentally altered since the 1970s:

> Today the *predominant* centres of intellectual production seem to lie in the English-speaking world, rather than in Germanic or Latin Europe, as it was the case in the inter-war and post-war periods respectively. That shift in locus represents an arresting historical change. Very much as I had felt might happen, the traditionally most backward zones of the capitalist world, in Marxist culture [Anderson refers here to the Anglo-Saxon countries – J.H.], have suddenly become in many ways the most advanced.[544]

It would appear that Anderson's 'geographical' history of the development of (the then) recent Marxist thought boils down to the construction of an international hierarchy. The Briton places his compatriots at the top of this hierarchy: 'The traditional relationship between Britain and Continental Europe appears for the moment to have been effectively reversed – Marxist culture in the UK for the moment proving more productive and original than that of any mainland state'.[545] Ranked slightly below Britons are their 'cousins' across the Atlantic: in North America, according to Anderson, the corresponding shift has occurred as 'a more restricted but not dissimilar change'.[546] The British theorist has Germans continuing to stagnate in a consolidated, mid-table position: Germany 'saw neither a qualitative growth of Marxist culture of the Anglo-American type nor a precipitous fall-back of the Franco-Italian kind, but rather the consolidation of a traditionally strong production'.[547] From here, Anderson's account descends to the low-lying regions of the international theory landscape, namely to 'Latin Marxism', or to the 'Latin recession within the international map of contemporary Marxism'.[548] Anderson makes the following claim: 'At the very time when Marxism as a critical theory has been in unprecedented ascent in the English-speaking world, it has undergone a precipitous descent in the Latin societies where it was most powerful and productive in the post-war period. In France and Italy above all, the two leading homelands of a living historical materialism in the fifties and sixties, for anyone like myself who learnt much of their Marxism from these cultures, the massacre of ancestors has been

---

544   P. Anderson 1983, p. 24.
545   P. Anderson 1983, p. 25.
546   Ibid.
547   P. Anderson 1983, p. 68.
548   P. Anderson 1983, p. 32.

impressive'.[549] Yet here, too, there are subtle nuances. Anderson's verdict essentially applies even more to the French than it does to the Italians: according to the Briton, the former have undergone a particularly sharp decline. In Anderson's account, France could boast of 'a cosmopolitan paramountcy in the general Marxist universe' following the Second World War.[550] Other regions of the world are scarcely registered by Anderson, if at all. When speaking of 'Latin Marxism', he does not refer to Latin Americans (or, if so, scarcely), but rather to 'Latin Europeans'. When speaking of Germany, he refers exclusively to the FRG, since engagement with Marx by researchers in the GDR is apparently of little interest to him. Not even the Japanese interpretation of Marx is indicated on Anderson's world map of Marxist thought.

In fairness, it should be borne in mind that Anderson surveys a thematic bandwidth of Marxist thought which extends far beyond the actual interpretation of Marx's critique of political economy (in the narrow sense). Yet it is precisely the intensive engagement with the critique of political economy – i.e. with the texts left by Marx on this complex of problems – which in general forms a decisive element in all thought drawing on Marx. At any rate, a sharpened focus on engagement with Marx's critique of political economy reveals a different picture of the 1980s.

How, then, can the situation in the 1980s (the decade in which Perry Anderson formulated his theses) be characterised? In this decade, a positive further development, in various directions, of thought drawing on Marx's critique of political economy also occurred *outside* the Anglo-Saxon world. Within the Latin American debate, for example, Enrique Dussel elaborated extensive commentaries on the four 'drafts' of *Capital*; no equivalent work of this type has been undertaken within the Anglo-Saxon world.[551] To cite a Japanese example, Tomonaga Tairako developed his reification-theory-oriented approach to the interpretation of Marx's critique of political economy during this time. In the Federal Republic of Germany, there was no stagnation in the development of the reception of Marx's critique of political economy; if anything, there was a productive further development in this regard, as exhibited by the studies undertaken by interpreters such as Helmut Brentel and Dieter Wolf. What occurred in the country whose Marxist culture is most berated by Anderson – i.e. in France? Here, the 1980s were of decisive significance for the development of the *Capital*-reading of Jacques Bidet, for example, whose important

549   P. Anderson 1983, p. 30.

550   P. Anderson 1983, p. 32.

551   Dussel's noted trilogy was published between 1985 and 1990.

study, *Que faire du 'Capital'?*, which was published in 1985, has in the mean-time aroused much interest in the Anglo-Saxon world. Regarded as a whole, it is inappropriate to refer to a supposed theoretical decline in the French discourse on Marx in the 1980s. By contrast, this decade saw the emergence of 'analytical Marxism' – a theoretical tendency which has since largely sunk into oblivion, and which must ultimately be regarded as marking a theoretical regression pre-cisely from a methodological standpoint – as one of the best-known currents within Anglo-Saxon Marxism. In the end, what remains from Anderson's text is the underlying pretension of an author who is concerned to portray his own (i.e. the Anglo-Saxon) Marxist discourse as virtually definitive within the inter-national theoretical debate. The only conclusion to be drawn, then, is that *In the Tracks of Historical Materialism* fails to persuade in terms of its content.

In-Depth Analyses: Central Discourses within the German and International Discussions of Marx from the 1980s to the Present

In the following presentation, in which themes developed thus far are to be explored at greater depth, various approaches to the interpretation of the method of political economy will play a particular role. Here, the engagement with Marx's method within the historical reception of his works will be considered to the extent that this method is taken to relate to the object of economic science. Despite the extremely problematic bearing of Friedrich Engels's engagement with methodological questions in his famous review of Marx's *A Contribution to the Critique of Political Economy*, it is to the former's credit that, in 1859, as one of the very first interpreters of Marx, he drew attention to the significance of '[t]he working out of the method which underlies Marx's critique of political economy' (even if Engels's review is marked by errors of interpretation which were to have disastrous consequences for the history of the reception of Marx).[1] Thus, although the methodological problematic was already discussed within the reception of Marx's works during the latter's own lifetime (as is indicated by the survey of this reception provided by Marx in the postface to the second edition of the first volume of *Capital*),[2] the methodological discussion entered a new stage with the emergence of so-called Western Marxism after the First World War. The problematic of 'method' was a central focus in György Lukács's *History and Class Consciousness* of 1923.[3] However, where the

---

1   Engels 1980, p. 475.

2   Marx 1976b.

3   In the essay entitled 'What is Orthodox Marxism?', the Hungarian philosopher writes as follows: 'Let us assume for the sake of argument that recent research had disproved once and for all every one of Marx's individual theses. Even if this were to be proved, every serious "orthodox" Marxist would still be able to accept all such modern findings without reservation and hence dismiss all of Marx's theses *in toto* – without having to renounce his orthodoxy for a single moment. Orthodox Marxism, therefore, does not imply the uncritical acceptance of the results of Marx's investigations. It is not the "belief" in this or that thesis, nor the exegesis of a "sacred" book. On the contrary, orthodoxy refers exclusively to *method*. It is the scientific conviction that dialectical materialism is the road to truth and that its methods can be developed, expanded and deepened only along the lines laid down by its founders. It is

focus in the following is occasionally on the history of the development of the debate on the method of Marx's critique of political economy, attention will be directed to various historical approaches which, in the context of interpreting Marx's method, also formulate propositions about the object of Marx's theory. Ultimately, behind the approaches to the investigation of Marx's method discussed here lie a series of theoretical undertakings which are themselves also effective in the investigation of the capitalist mode of production itself – i.e. in the investigation of the very object of Marx's critical enquiry.

The goal of Marx's engagement with the object of his enquiry was to undertake an investigation into, and to elaborate an exposition of, the internal interconnections between economic categories and relations, and to reveal the economic laws of motion of modern bourgeois society. In general, the guiding insight here is that the methodological discussion – the discussion of Marx's method – must be oriented not least to the 'matter itself' – i.e. to the object to which Marx's method relates.

According to an adequate understanding of method, the Marxian one is not the result of arbitrary criteria, nor can it be applied externally to the object of enquiry, but must correspond to this object's own internal structure, as it were. Ultimately, in any adequate methodological reception of Marx, the object of his enquiry also becomes a central focus via the engagement with his method. The problematic of method cannot be isolated from the problematic of the object.

The period from approximately 1980 to the present has been marked by the emergence of new theoretical currents within the international reception of Marx. This new phase can be distinguished from the preceding one and its associated theoretical currents (the earlier phase having been initiated in the 1950s or 1960s). On the whole, there was a further deepening of the international Marx discourse during the more recent period. Important results yielded by the historical development of theory since 1980 will be evaluated here. However, the following exposition necessarily comprises two intertwining strands: on the one hand, it is a question of exploring in detail the state of the international discussion of Marx's critique of political economy with regard to several important problematics.[4] To this extent, the present exposition refers to the historical developments in the reception of Marx's critique of political economy. On the other hand, this exposition cannot avoid an extensive consideration of Marx's primary texts themselves, since these constitute the decisive point of refer-

---

the conviction, moreover, that all attempts to surpass or "improve" it have led and must lead to over-simplification, triviality and eclecticism' (Lukács 1971, p. 1).

4   Not all the centrally significant ranges of problems can be considered here, however.

ence for, and background to, the debate from the 1980s to the present. Such a treatment is simply indispensable for the present purposes. It follows from the nature of the object of the present study that these two strands must necessarily be continually interwoven. However, to make it patently clear: in the present study, it cannot (nor should it) be a question of 'solving' once and for all the problems thrown up by or resulting from Marx's approach itself – an example would be the much-discussed problem of Marx's relation to Hegel. No such pretensions are harboured here.

1   The Understanding of the Object of Critique and Value-Theory

1.1   *On the Understanding of the Object of the Critique of Political Economy*

Marx provides a statement of what he considers to be the object of his critique of political economy in the preface to the first edition of the first volume of *Capital*: 'What I have to examine in this work is the capitalist mode of production, and the relations of production and forms of intercourse [*Verkehrsverhältnisse*] that correspond to it'.[5] Later in the same preface, Marx maintains that 'it is the ultimate aim of this work to reveal the economic law of motion of modern society'.[6] The first thing to be noted here, with regard to Marx's terminology, is that he does not refer to 'capitalism' (a common concept in today's usage), even though the term did exist in his time. The Japanese researcher, Sumio Shigeta, has argued that international research has not yet succeeded in finding a definitive answer to the question as to who first introduced the concept of 'capitalism'. Shigeta further asserts that contemporaries of Marx did indeed use this term, but in a sense that diverges from today's usage: it had not yet been employed as an expression for the specific economic system and form of society corresponding to modern society.[7] It can be demonstrated that there are isolated occurrences of the concept 'capitalism' in Marx; as a rule, however, he describes the object-domain of *Capital* as the 'capitalist mode of production'. This latter term first occurs in the manuscripts Marx wrote from 1860 onwards, according to Shigeta.[8]

In working on his *magnum opus*, Marx was thus concerned to reveal the economic law of motion of modern bourgeois society, to investigate the internal

---

5   Marx 1976a, p. 90.
6   Marx 1976a, p. 92.
7   Shigeta 2006, p. 89.
8   Shigeta 2006, p. 89.

interconnection between economic categories and relations within the capitalist mode of production, and to provide a systematic development of this
interconnection within his exposition. Marx's form-theory of labour and his
theory of the specific economic form-determinacy of the products of labour
within the capitalist mode of production possess a virtually constitutive significance for the critique of political economy. Marx refers to the doubling of
the commodity into commodity and money in the process of value-exchange.
'It is not simply the exchange process as a mere "social metabolism" that Marx
presents; rather, it is the exchange process as a "social metabolism", in which –
and this is essential – the products of labour are commodities or money, i.e.
they assume or possess a specific form-determinacy. This corresponds to a
determinate historical form of the sociality of labours'.[9] Marx's concern to draw
attention to the decisive aspect of form-determinacy is characteristic not only
of his theory of the commodity and his theory of money, but also of his theory
of the capitalist mode of production on all levels of his exposition. According
to Marx, a shortcoming of previous economic theory formation lies precisely
in the insufficient sensitivity displayed by political economists to the moment
of form-determinacy. Marx expresses the following criticism in the *Grundrisse*:
'When it is said that capital "is accumulated (realized) labour (properly, objectified [*vergegenständlichte*] labour), which serves as the means for new labour
(production)", then this refers to the simple material of capital, without regard
to the formal character without which it is not capital. This means nothing
more than that capital is – an instrument of production ...'.[10]

The most important German-language study on the understanding of the
object of the critique of political economy was that presented by Helmut Brentel. However, Brentel's approach is located within a broader scientific context,
which must first be outlined. The context in question is formed by the 'Frankfurt' current of investigation into the understanding of the object and method
of the critique of political economy – a research orientation, which, although
it has yielded results that have occasionally diverged widely with regard to
detail, by and large proceeds on the basis of similar lines of enquiry. Hans-
Georg Backhaus and Helmut Reichelt can be considered early exponents of
this orientation, which played an important part in shaping the research controversies within the German *Marx-Gesellschaft*; an 'intermediate' generation
of researchers is represented by Helmut Brentel and Diethard Behrens; the
'younger' generation includes researchers such as Nadja Rakowitz. Common

---

9   Hoff 2008, p. 91.
10   Marx 1973, p. 257.

points of reference for these three generations of 'Frankfurt' researchers are the following: firstly, the critical distancing of their interpretation of Marx from Marxist-Leninist orthodoxy, and/or from Friedrich Engels's understanding of the Marxian critique of political economy; secondly, an insistence on the specific interconnection between the theory of value and the theory of money in Marx; thirdly, research into the specific interconnection between the sphere of simple circulation and capital. In particular, the approach taken by Hans-Georg Backhaus to research into the specific unity of the theory of value and the theory of money has exerted an influence far beyond the German-language discussion; this has also occurred indirectly, through the contribution made by the international research project in Sydney and Konstanz referred to above, which has elaborated a Backhaus-inspired approach to the theory of value from the late 1970s onwards and made this accessible to an international readership. More recently, the international 'Open Marxism' project has contributed to the dissemination within the Anglophone world of the results of research by Hans-Georg Backhaus and Helmut Reichelt.

Hans-Georg Backhaus and Helmut Reichelt raise the question of the specific mode of being of the object of economic science. According to these theorists, economic categories correspond to a 'reality *sui generis*' beyond the duality of the subjective and the objective. On this view, economic categories are to be reconstructed as 'subjective-objective' forms, or as 'objective forms of thought'. Backhaus aims to provide a fundamental theory of the economic object. His central focus here is not the questions posed by an economics that is understood as a primarily 'quantitative' science; rather, he is concerned first and foremost with essentially 'qualitative' problems. According to Backhaus, the economic science which currently predominates is not sufficiently sensitive to determinate, specifically qualitative lines of enquiry which would need to be pursued in the context of an adequate understanding of the object. In connection with his research into Marx's understanding of his object, Backhaus also aims to reconstruct both the conceptual content of Marx's concept of critique,[11] and Marx's original method; assessing the history of the development of Marx's *oeuvre*, Backhaus maintains that, after reaching a certain point in the course of the elaboration of his critique of political economy, Marx 'concealed' this original method, with the result that it became unrecognisable in its specificity.[12]

---

11   See Backhaus 2000a and Backhaus 2000b. One of the most significant Frankfurt-based exegetes of Marx, Alfred Schmidt, drew attention to the centrality of the Marxian concept of critique during the wave of *Capital*-reception of the late 1960s (see Schmidt 1968).

12   See Backhaus 1998, and Backhaus and Reichelt 1994. See also two responses to the latter article: Heinrich 1995a and Sperl 2000.

The most elaborate approach within the 'Frankfurt' reconstruction of the Marxian understanding of the object was developed in the 1980s by Helmut Brentel, and culminated in his 1989 monograph.[13] According to the latter, one of the characteristic features of the critique of political economy consists in the fact that Marx placed the actual object-domain of economic science – i.e. economic-social objects and forms – at the centre of his investigation. According to Brentel, 'the decisive critical perspective within Marx's conception of the object' lies 'in its significance as a *theory of form and a theory of fetish*'.[14] In Brentel's reading of Marx's critique of political economy, a form-theory of labour and value coincides in the work of the Trier-born theorist with a theory of the 'fetishism' of economic categories. According to Brentel, the Marxian understanding of economic-social objectivity has the following thrust: 'Marx consistently exhibits economic objectivity – *qua* the specific form-objectivity of labour whose socialisation is capitalist – in its character as *fetish-objectivity*, as the systematic occultation and veiling of the actual relations of socialisation'.[15] With regard to his reception of the Marxian theory of form, Helmut Brentel establishes a fundamental distinction between the two dimensions of the concept of form. The Frankfurt-based interpreter of Marx distinguishes between 'Form I' and 'Form II', setting out the distinction as follows:

> Economic objectivity *qua* 'value-objectivity' is social form – the specific social form of labour – in a twofold sense: as thing and as relation simultaneously. In the latter sense (as relation): the relation of equality between labours is constituted as the specifically social form of the sociality of labours (Social Form I). In the former sense (as thing): on the one hand, value itself gains an objective character and is manifested as the fetishistic natural feature of the products of labour in bourgeois society (Form I); on the other hand, such value must attain a form of existence in a value-form, in the natural form of another commodity as an equivalent form (Social Form II).[16]

Thus, value in turn possesses a form of existence in the shape of a value-form, which elicits a reference to Form II. According to Brentel, Marx grasps both value and the value-form as specifically social forms of social labour. For the Frankfurt-based interpreter of Marx, all categories of bourgeois economics are

---

13   See Brentel 1989.
14   Brentel 1989, p. 15.
15   Ibid.
16   Brentel 1989, p. 273.

to be deciphered as forms of abstract-universal labour. In sum, Helmut Brentel's approach must be regarded as the most considered attempt hitherto within the West German New Marx-Reading at an explication of the unity of the Marxian theories of object, form and fetish. It is thus unsurprising that, following the publication of Brentel's monograph, there has been a continuing engagement with the range of problems dealt with by him, with his work constituting a substantial point of reference for subsequent research in these areas.[17]

With regard to the Francophone discussion, a comprehensive project within the new reading of *Capital* undertaken by the Vietnamese-born researcher, Trai Han Hac, surely ranks as an important contribution.[18] Trai Han Hac's study affords an insight into the unity of the Marxian theories of object and form (and is comparable to Brentel's work in this regard). In his attempt at a new or re-reading of *Capital*, the author develops a differentiated value-theoretical approach which is informed by a form-theoretical perspective. Trai Han Hac does not grasp Marx's critique of political economy as merely 'another' political economy; instead, he emphasises precisely the *critical* character of the Marxian project. According to Trai Han Hac, Marx's critique of the science of political economy takes critical aim at the latter's very presuppositions. On this view, political economy prior to Marx – more precisely, both 'classical' and 'vulgar' variants – treats economic categories as 'naturally given', such that their existence requires no further explanation. Trai Han Hac regards the theory formed by political economy as beholden to fetishism. Like Helmut Brentel, the Vietnamese-born author also establishes a differentiation within the concept of form: he distinguishes value as form from the form of value. Thus, according to Trai Han Hac, Marx constructed 'two fundamental concepts of his problematic': 'value as form and the form of value'.[19] With regard to the former, Trai Han Hac cites *Capital*: 'Political economy has indeed analysed value and its magnitude, however incompletely, and has uncovered the content concealed within these forms. But it has never once asked the question why this content has assumed that particular form, that is to say, why labour is expressed in value, and why the measurement of labour by its duration is expressed in the magnitude of the value of the product'.[20] Trai Han Hac is

---

17   On the reception of Brentel's path-breaking work, see, among other works, Behrens 1993.

18   See Hac 2003. In 1993, Hac had already published an introduction to Marx together with Pierre Salama; in this work, Hac was the author of the section on the commodity and money, which in some regards anticipates his 2003 study (see Salama and Hac 1992, pp. 7 ff.).

19   Hac 2003, p. 206.

20   Marx 1976a, pp. 173–4.

concerned with value as the specific form taken by abstract universal social labour within the capitalist mode of production. With regard to the form of value, i.e. 'form' in the latter sense, Trai Han Hac underscores the significance of Marx's value-form analysis. Moreover, the Vietnamese-born interpreter of Marx points out the fundamental difference between the theory of money in Marx and Ricardo. According to Trai Han Hac, the latter reduced money to mere means of circulation. By contrast, the Vietnamese-born writes that '[f]or Marx, the critique of political economy will consist in demonstrating that the capitalist mode of production implies not only the commodity, but also money as the polar form of commodities'.[21] Trai Han Hac insists on the 'strategic significance' of the first section of the first volume of *Capital* for an adequate understanding of Marx.

Marx's theory of fetish is of central significance within the context of his understanding of the object.[22] The theory of fetish plays a prominent role within the German-language reception of Marx's critique of political economy; however, it is no longer a specificity of the German-language discussion that a great deal of attention is devoted to Marx's theory of fetish. It has already been shown above that the interpretation of, and reference to, Marx's theory of fetish is of great relevance for, for instance, representatives of the Latin American discussion who are not (primarily) influenced by Althusser (such as Enrique Dussel, Bolívar Echeverría and Néstor Kohan). Since the 1990s (and perhaps earlier), the interpreters of Marx associated with the Greek journal, *Theseis*, John Milios* and Dimitri Dimoulis, have engaged extensively with the fetish problematic; these theorists consider the theory of fetishism to be a central moment of Marx's critique of political economy, and one which is to be assessed positively.[23] Dimoulis and Milios strictly oppose the limitation of the discussion of fetishism to the first chapter of the first volume of *Capital*. These authors ascribe a central significance to Marx's theory of capital-fetishism, arguing that it cannot be ignored. Dimoulis and Milios charge Althusser with having fallen foul of a correspondingly foreshortened interpretation – a defect to be avoided at all costs.[24]

---

21 Hac 2003, p. 98.

22 Since it is possible to establish a distinction between fetishism and mystification, it might be added here that Marx's critical theory of mystification is likewise of central significance within the context of his understanding of the object.

* John Milios is also known as Yannis/Giannis Milios.

23 See Dimoulis and Milios 2000.

24 See Dimoulis and Milios 2000, pp. 34f. It should be noted that Milios is by no means generally hostile to Althusser's interpretation of Marx. Milios endorses Althusser's thesis

A decisive factor within the context of Marx's understanding of the object is his insistence on the historicity of the capitalist mode of production and the corresponding economic categories and relations. Marx's point might be expanded upon as follows: the particular mode of the socialisation of labours which predominates within the capitalist mode of production also possesses a historically specific character. To this particular mode of the socialisation of labours corresponds the commodity-form of the product of labour. Although the latter was present in some earlier modes of production, bourgeois society is the only one in which – to express it in Marx's words – 'the *commodity-form* is the universal form of the product of labour, hence the dominant social relation is the relation between men as *possessors of commodities*'.[25]

The Marxian conception of the historicity of the capitalist mode of production thus forms an essential element of his understanding of the object of the critique of political economy. This is by no means as trivial as it might appear against the background of the Marx debate, given the traditional emphasis placed, within the history of the reception of Marx's work, on the historicity of the capitalist mode of production. For Marx's highlighting of the historically specific character of the capitalist mode of production represents an important distinguishing criterion vis-à-vis the theory formed by political economists such as David Ricardo.

The capitalist mode of production is, for Marx, no 'eternal natural form' of social production. In a famous footnote in the 'chapter on fetish' of the first volume of *Capital*, Marx locates the reason for the theoretical neglect of the problematic of the value-form by certain economists not only in their focus on the magnitude of value. The reason lies deeper:

> The value-form of the product of labour is the most abstract, but also the most universal form of the bourgeois mode of production; by that fact it stamps the bourgeois mode of production as a particular kind of social production of a historical and transitory character. If then we make the mistake of treating it as the eternal natural form of social production, we necessarily overlook the specificity of the value-form, and consequently of the commodity-form together with its further developments, the money form, the capital form, etc.[26]

---

of Marx's radical break with classical political economy; nonetheless, despite the affinity shown towards Althusser by Milios, the latter stresses that it is important not to overlook certain theoretical weak points in the work of the French philosopher (see Milios 2007).

25   Marx 1976a, p. 152.
26   Marx 1976a, p. 174.

A few years previously, in the section on the history of economic thought in the chapter on the commodity in his *A Contribution to the Critique of Political Economy*, Marx had already criticised Ricardo as follows: 'Apart from bourgeois society, the only social system with which Ricardo was acquainted seems to have been the "parallelograms of Mr. Owen"'.[27] For Marx, Ricardo was 'trapped within the bourgeois horizon'. Ricardo regarded 'the bourgeois form of labour ... as the eternal natural form of social labour'.[28] Marx's critique of political economy stands absolutely opposed to any such ahistoricism.

Within the context of his fundamental thesis of the two different 'theoretical fields' (that of political economy on the one hand, and that of Marx's critique of political economy on the other), Michael Heinrich attempts to demonstrate that Marx overcomes the ahistoricism of political economy, albeit partially.[29] Together with this fundamental thesis, Heinrich also provided a contribution in the 1990s to the interpretation of Marx's understanding of the object of critique; this contribution was connected to Heinrich's reception and redefinition of Althusser's concept of 'theoretical field'. In Heinrich's reading of Marx, a fundamental significance is accorded to a (supposedly) essential feature of Marx's theory, namely its overcoming of individualism, anthropologism, ahistoricism, and – through an epistemological critique – empiricism. According to Heinrich, both classical economics and the vulgar economics so castigated by Marx share a common 'theoretical field' – i.e. they share determinate foundational conceptions (which form the presuppositions to their actual discourses) with regard to their object and the possibilities of reproducing the latter theoretically. For Heinrich, the constitutive moments of this 'theoretical field' of political economy are thus ahistoricism (whereby the capitalist mode of production is conceived of as the eternal natural form of social production); anthropologism (whereby the assumption of a fixed 'human essence' forms a point of reference for formation of theory); individualism (whereby it appears that individuals immediately constitute the social interrelation); and empiricism (whereby the social interrelation appears to be immediately transparent, with 'essence' and 'manifestation' directly coinciding).[30] Incidentally, it should be noted that

---

27   Marx 1987b, p. 300.

28   Ibid.

29   See Heinrich 1999a, p. 82 and p. 310.

30   For Marx, to take account of the difference between essence and manifestation is of decisive importance: in the third volume of *Capital*, he writes that 'all science would be superfluous if the form of appearance of things directly coincided with their essence' (Marx 1981a, p. 956). In a letter written to his friend, Ludwig Kugelmann, in 1868, Marx makes the critical observation that '[t]he vulgar economist thinks he has made a great

Heinrich's thesis of the common 'theoretical field' shared by classical and vulgar economics by no means implies that he levels out all the differences between them.

Heinrich argues that for his part, Marx broke with this 'theoretical field' – successfully, on the whole, although not entirely. Yet, on Heinrich's assessment, Marx did not possess an adequate conception of the 'theoretical field' that he had overcome, nor did he completely grasp the status of his own (scientifically revolutionary) theory. On Heinrich's view, these circumstances led to ambivalences in Marx's theory. To gloss Heinrich's approach: the break with the 'theoretical field' of political economy can be grasped as the core conceptual content of Marx's 'scientific revolution'. A decisive factor here is the way in which Heinrich construes the concept of scientific revolution: 'by *scientific revolution*, what is understood is not merely the transition to a new paradigm, but only to such a paradigm that has broken with the theoretical field of previous paradigms'. This implies that it is by no means sufficient, in order to qualify as a scientific revolution, that new questions are posed; rather, 'this science's concept of the object, its *concept of reality*, and also, in connection with this, the *concept of science* itself must have been transformed'.[31] It would seem – on the basis of Heinrich's arguments – that the theoretical difference between the classical economists and Karl Marx ought to be assessed as being even greater, and more fundamental, than Marx himself believed.

According to Heinrich, the classical economists – in contrast to Marx – do not have within their scope the non-empirical level of theory necessary for a sufficient theoretical penetration of the object of political economy. However, interpretations have also been put forward which at least tend to run counter to Heinrich's view that Ricardo was not able to marshal a non-empirical level of theory. Thus the Czechoslovak philosopher and Marx-researcher, Jindřich Zelený, offered the interpretation in the 1960s that 'in Ricardo's analysis of capitalism there is an implied conception of the scientific mode of explanation' which is characterised by, among other things, the moment of distinction between essence and the empirical surface.[32] The circumstance that the corresponding problematic has not been discussed as intensively as might have been hoped within the German-language interpretation of Marx can be attributed

---

discovery when, faced with the disclosure of the intrinsic interconnection, he insists that things look different in appearance. In fact, he prides himself in his clinging to appearances and believing them to be the ultimate. Why then have science at all?' (Marx 1988b, p. 69).

31   Heinrich 1999a, p. 25.

32   See Zelený 1980, p. 10 [translation modified – N.G.].

to the scarcely comprehensible reluctance on the part of many of those with
an interest in Marx to engage in detail with Ricardo's *magnum opus, Principles
of Political Economy and Taxation*.[33]

A further dimension of Michael Heinrich's interpretation of Marx's understanding of the object relates to the moment of the high level of abstraction
in Marx's exposition of the capitalist mode of production. According to Heinrich, the three volumes of *Capital* are to be characterised as an exposition of the
capitalist mode of production 'in its ideal average'. This implies that the object-
domain referred to by Marx is considerably restricted. On Heinrich's view, Marx
is concerned with

> that which makes capitalism what it is. If we can talk of there being
> capitalism both in nineteenth century England and in Germany at the
> beginning of the twenty-first century, then there must be something in
> common in these two cases which allows us to use this concept. Marx's
> exposition is oriented towards precisely this commonality which is to be
> found in *each and every* developed capitalism.[34]

Heinrich maintains that it is precisely owing to the high level of abstraction in
Marx's exposition that the latter is by no means restricted to the relations of
the nineteenth century. On this view, the object thematised by Marx is by no
means obsolete.

1.2   *A Survey of the International Debate on Marx's Theory of Value, with
       a Particular Focus on the Analysis of the Value-Form*

It goes without saying that it is impossible within the present framework even
to begin to delineate the international debate on Marx's theory of value in its
entirety, least of all with regard to the various interpretations of Marx's value-
form analysis – these being legion. Marx's value-form analysis represents a
central focus for a large proportion of international research into the critique
of political economy. Accordingly, the following exposition merely highlights a
few particularly prominent approaches to the interpretation of Marx's theory
of value and his theory of the value-form that have emerged in recent decades.

First, however, it is necessary to return once again to Marx himself, in order
to indicate the theoretical point of reference of the debate. The history of the
origins of Marx's critique of political economy shows that he by no means

---

33   I would exempt Michael Heinrich from this charge.
34   Heinrich 2008, p. 17.

planned a separate analysis of the value-form – such as the one given in *Capital* (in its various versions in the different editions) – from the outset. The value-form analysis in *Capital* is to be understood as the result of a protracted process of self-clarification and elaboration with regard to the theory of value and the theory of money. The *Grundrisse der Kritik der politischen Ökonomie* of 1857–8 begins with an extensive critique of Proudhonism.[35] Although Marx's critical engagement here is not with Pierre-Joseph Proudhon himself, but rather with a follower of the latter, Alfred Darimon, it is clear that the thrust of the critique is aimed at Proudhonism. From the *Grundrisse* onwards, Marx was increasingly concerned to develop an adequate understanding of the specific interrelation between the commodity, value and money. Accordingly, Marx was able to hone his critique of Proudhon in *A Contribution to the Critique of Political Economy* as follows: 'it was left to M. Proudhon and his school to declare seriously that the degradation of money and the exaltation of commodities was the essence of socialism and thereby to reduce socialism to an elementary misunderstanding of the inevitable correlation existing between commodities and money'.[36] Marx first expounded his theory of money in a truly comprehensive way towards the end of the 1850s, firstly in the *Grundrisse* and in the *Urtext*, and subsequently in a more elaborated form in *A Contribution to the Critique of Political Economy*. In the latter work, Marx grasps money as the immediate materialisation* of universal labour time – i.e. of abstract universal labour as the substance of the value of the commodity. In contrast to Marx, neither Smith nor Ricardo had managed to provide an adequate investigation into, and exposition of, the internal, necessary interconnection between the commodity, value and money. For Marx, the specific unity of the theory of value and the theory of money was of the greatest significance.

Although Marx was able to overcome the deficiencies within the theory of money of classical political economy in the *Grundrisse*, he was by no means completely satisfied with his exposition of the theory of money here. Furthermore, the path from the *Grundrisse* to *A Contribution to the Critique of Political Economy* certainly did not present itself as a simple one for Marx. Having broken off an intermediate draft, the so-called *Urtext*, Marx decided to restrict the scope of his work initially to the theory of the commodity, the theory of

---

35   On the *Grundrisse* and its reception, see Stützle 2008.

36   Marx 1987b, p. 323.

*   The German term employed by Marx in this context is '*Materiatur*', a term which occurs in Hegel. When used by Marx in his appendix to the first edition of the first volume of *Capital*, 'The Value-Form', it is translated by Mike Roth and Wal Suchting as 'material expression(s)' (see Marx 1994, p. 28).

value and the theory of money. The final version appeared in the early summer of 1859 under the title of *A Contribution to the Critique of Political Economy*. Here, in his first systematic exposition of the critique of political economy to be published, Marx ventures to address a complex of themes which he himself described as 'the most difficult because most abstract part of political economy'.[37]

In *A Contribution to the Critique of Political Economy*, Marx first considers the initial category, the commodity, in its two opposing dimensions, i.e. use-value and exchange-value, and undertakes an analysis of these two opposing determinations. In addition, he analyses the two opposing determinations of labour, and identifies the labour objectified in exchange-value as abstract universal, or equal, social labour, whereas the labour objectified in use-values is a concrete, particular activity.[38] At a later point in the text, Marx segues into the exchange process:

> So far two aspects of the commodity – use-value and exchange-value – have been examined, but each one separately. The commodity, however, is the direct *unity* of use-value and exchange-value, and at the same time it is a commodity only in relation to other commodities. The *exchange process* of commodities is the *real* relation that exists between them.[39]

Marx states that it is within this process that commodities must be realised, both with regard to their use-value dimension and in their capacity as exchange-values. Marx further argues that 'they must assume a new determinate form, they must evolve money, so as to be able to confront one another as *exchange-values*'.[40]

Marx thus develops a monetary theory of value, a specific unity of the theory of value and the theory of money. Subsequently in his 1859 text, he states that '[t]he principal difficulty in the analysis of money is surmounted as soon as it is understood that the commodity is the origin of money'.[41] If the various excurses on the history of economic thought in *A Contribution to*

---

37 Marx 1983b, p. 377.

38 It should be borne in mind that in *A Contribution to the Critique of Political Economy*, Marx had not yet established the precise terminological distinction between value and exchange-value (with the latter as the form of manifestation of the former) that he would subsequently apply in *Capital*.

39 Marx 1987b, p. 282.

40 Marx 1987b, p. 289.

41 Marx 1987b, p. 303.

the Critique of Political Economy are disregarded, the development of money and the exchange process from the structure of the commodity is followed directly by the exposition of the functions of money. *A Contribution to the Critique of Political Economy* comes to an end before the subsequent categorial transition – i.e. the transformation of money into capital. The corresponding continuation of the text published in 1859 is to be found at the beginning of the *1861–63 Manuscripts*. During his work on these manuscripts, Marx arrived at a new understanding of his theory of value through his critical engagement with Ricardo and Bailey, among others.

In *Theories of Surplus-Value*, Marx adopts a critical stance towards Ricardo's economic theory. Marx charges Ricardo with failing to investigate the specific determination of the labour which presents itself in exchange-value or in value: 'Ricardo does not *investigate* the character of this labour. He thus fails to grasp the interconnection between *this labour* and *money*, and fails to understand that it must present itself in money'.[42] As a consequence, the interconnection (which, it might be added, is a specifically necessary one) between the determination of value through labour time and the fact that 'commodities must necessarily proceed to the formation of money' escapes Ricardo. Marx adds the following comment: 'Hence his erroneous theory of money'.[43] Later in this same text, Marx makes the following critical observation of Ricardo: '[t]herefore he has not understood the interconnection between the formation of money and the essence of value – i.e. between the formation of money and the determination of value by labour-time'.[44] It might be added here that in *Capital*, Marx grasps money *qua* extrinsic measure of value as the necessary form of manifestation of the immanent measure of value of commodities, namely of abstract labour. Through his demonstration of the specific, necessary interconnection between, on the one hand, the substance of value – abstract labour – or value itself, and, on the other, the universal equivalent or money, Marx was able to go beyond the horizon of classical economics in terms of the theory of value and the theory of money. Value-form analysis thus has a key function within this context.

During the course of the 1860s, Marx thus further deepened his research into the theory of value/the theory of money, even though he had already published his theory of value/his theory of money at the level of abstraction of simple circulation in *A Contribution to the Critique of Political Economy*.

---

42   Marx 1989b, pp. 389–90 [translation modified – N.G.].

43   Ibid [translation modified – N.G.].

44   Marx 1989b, p. 324 [translation modified – N.G.].

Following the appearance of the latter work, however, it became clear to Marx that this already published version of his theory of value could not be the final one. On 13 October 1866, he wrote a letter to Ludwig Kugelmann in which he revealed his thinking with regard to the opening section of the first volume of *Capital*:

> It was, in my opinion, necessary to begin again *ab ovo* in the first book, i.e., to summarise the book of mine published by Duncker [*A Contribution to the Critique of Political Economy*] in one chapter on commodities and money. I judged this to be necessary, not merely for the sake of completeness, but because even intelligent people did not properly understand the question, in other words, there must have been defects in the first presentation, especially in the *analysis of commodities*.[45]

This illustrates that Marx was in retrospect not completely satisfied with the corresponding exposition in *A Contribution to the Critique of Political Economy*. In order to do justice to his own high standards, he was obliged to publish a new version of his analysis of the commodity.

The first edition of the first volume of *Capital* appeared in 1867 with two different sections of the text devoted to the analysis of the value-form. The first analysis of the value-form formed part of the main text; the second analysis, which represented a popularised version – and one which had been modified in terms of its content – was included as an appendix.[46] However, the further elaboration and revision of the analysis of the value-form in *Capital* which Marx subsequently undertook in the early 1870s represent clear evidence that Marx's endeavours to improve his exposition and efforts at self-clarification – as becomes apparent from the manuscript entitled *Ergänzungen und Veränderungen zum ersten Band des 'Kapitals'** which Marx wrote between the end of 1871 and the beginning of 1872 – had by no means been concluded with the two versions of the analysis of the value-form published in the first edition of *Capital* in 1867 (in the main text and in the appendix).[47]

---

45   Marx 1987c, p. 327 (emphasis in the original).
46   In an 1867 letter to Engels, Marx states the following: '1. I have written an appendix in which I set out the same subject again as simply and as much in the manner of a school text-book as possible, and 2. I have divided each successive proposition into paras. etc., each with its own heading, as you advised. In the Preface I then tell the "non-dialectical" reader to skip page x–y and instead read the appendix' (Marx 1987d, p. 384).
*   [*'Additions and Alterations to the First Volume of Capital'*].
47   On the various editions of *Capital*, see Marxhausen 2008.

At this point, the Marx-interpretation of the Australian, Anitra Nelson, can be critically interrogated. With regard to the analysis of the value-form, the latter author comments that the changes undertaken by Marx from one edition to the next principally relate to stylistic questions and clarifications, etc., rather than to substantial revisions of content.[48] Yet an adequate reception of Marx's various versions – i.e. the first edition of the first volume of *Capital*, published in *MEGA*², Volume II/5 (the analysis of the value-form in the main text, and the one contained in the appendix); the second edition, published in *MEGA*², Volume II/6; and the important revisions manuscript of 1871/2 – would demonstrate the unsustainability of Nelson's assessment, as would a careful engagement with German-language research in this area. Within this context, it suffices – in order to substantiate a critical objection to Nelson – to refer to one significant revision in terms of the content of the analysis of the value-form, namely the replacement of Form IV (including its inversion) in the first edition of the first volume of *Capital* by the money-form in the second edition (indeed, this revision is already present in the 1867 appendix).[49]

Located at the core of Marx's theory of value is in particular the specific interconnection between the substance of value, value and the value-form. 'What was decisively important, however, was to discover the intrinsic, necessary interconnection between value-*form*, value-*substance*, and the *magnitude* of value; i.e., expressed *ideally*, to prove that the value-*form* arises out of the value-*concept*'.[50] Marx was able to correctly grasp the substance of value as well as the value-form. It is against this background that Marx's verdict in the 'Marginal Notes on Adolph Wagner's *Lehrbuch der politischer Oekonomie*' is to be assessed; here, Marx's interpretation is that Ricardo had 'neither examined nor grasped the substance of value'.[51] A reference was made above to the assessment given by Marx in the section on fetish of the chapter on the commodity in the first volume of *Capital*, according to which Smith and Ricardo had neglected the problematic of the value-form. The fact that Marx went beyond Ricardo in his theory of the substance of value as well as in his theory of the value-form is of decisive significance. The specific interconnection between

---

48   See Nelson 1999, p. 161.

49   However, both versions of the analysis of the value-form in the 1867 edition of *Capital* (i.e. in the main text and in the appendix) have also been published in English in an edition to which Nelson refers (see Marx 1976c). The appendix to the 1867 first edition of *Capital* on the value-form analysis was also published in English translation in the *Capital & Class* journal: see Marx 1978a.

50   Marx 1976c, p. 34 [translation modified – N.G.].

51   Marx 1989d, p. 552.

the substance of value and value-form in Marx must be considered an important point of reference for an adequate interpretation of the Marxian theory of value.

Since the interpretation of Marx's analysis of the value-form represents a thematic domain that has been subject to intensive engagement within international research, it is only possible here, as has already been indicated, to go into a small proportion of the developments within this research. Japanese research has proven particularly active within this thematic field. Here, a Japanese approach from the 1980s will be considered in detail; first, however, it is necessary to survey the prehistory of the recent debates – a prehistory which reaches back at least to the late 1940s and the 1950s.

A few short years after the Second World War, Kōzō Uno presented a value-form analysis which both drew on, and deviated from, the Marxian one; Uno's analysis was widely received in Japan, and has also since been registered in the Anglo-Saxon sphere. Uno's conception of value-form analysis in *Principles of Political Economy* diverges from Marx to the extent that, in contrast to the latter, he is not concerned to establish a systematic separation between the analysis of the value-form and the behaviour of commodity owners in the sense of a distinction between two different levels of the exposition (for Marx, by contrast, the behaviour of commodity owners constitutes an element of the exposition of the exchange process). In his exposition, Uno systematically treats commodity owners as an element of the value-form analysis.

If linen finds itself at the pole of relative form of value, with the coat at the opposite pole of the equivalent form, this implies the following for Uno:

> Of course, this value expression is a subjective evaluation on the part of the linen-owner; it has nothing to do with a similar value expression of the owner of the coat. In the former expression, the coat is nothing more than a value-reflecting object in the mind of the linen-owner. Because of this expression, however, the use-value of the coat, no matter what the subjective evaluation of its owner turns out to be, already embodies the value of linen. In other words, the owner of the coat can at any moment obtain twenty yards of linen for his coat, if he so desires. He is placed in the position, without so asking, of being able to purchase twenty yards of linen with his coat at a moment's notice, whereas the linen-owner who actually desires the coat and is willing to pay for it with linen is in no position actively to realise the exchange.[52]

---

52   Uno 1980, p. 6.

It is apparent that commodity owners are accorded a different significance in Marx's and Uno's respective analyses of the value-form. Marx systematically abstracts from commodity owners and from their actions in his analysis of the value-form, and indeed only mentions them on a few isolated occasions within this context, for example in certain passages with an explanatory character in his popularising appendix to the first edition of *Capital*.[53] The opposite is true of Uno's value-form analysis, in which commodity owners play a systematic role. This is particularly true of the commodity owner whose commodity finds itself at the pole of the relative form of value. Accordingly, there is no counterpart in *Principles of Political Economy* to the (more or less strict) Marxian separation – in the sense of a distinction between two different levels – between the analysis of the value-form and the behaviour of commodity owners.

The British interpreter of *Capital*, Christopher Arthur, offers the following criticism of Kōzō Uno's value-form theory (which in fact represents a rework-ing of the Marxian analysis of the value-form): 'Whereas Uno interprets the forms of value in the context of the process of exchange, I argue that we must entirely abstract from owners and their proposals in deriving the forms of value at the level of abstraction of Marx's first chapter: the standpoint of the own-ers is appropriate only when the real process of exchange is to be concretely addressed as it is in his second chapter'.[54] Arthur's criticism against Uno, that the analysis of the value-form ought to abstract from commodity owners, is not new, however. The same criticism was levelled against Uno within the Japan-ese discussion shortly after the Second World War by Samezō Kuruma (incid-entally, no mention of Kuruma is made by Arthur). The differing conceptions represented by Kōzō Uno and Samezō Kuruma with regard to value-form the-ory formed the foundation of one of the most important controversies around Marx-inspired value theory in postwar Japan.

In my opinion, the decisive point here is not that Uno delivers a misinter-pretation of Marx; it is well known that Uno aspired to provide more than a mere interpretation of Marx in his *Principles of Political Economy*. Uno's inten-tion, as an independent theorist, was to provide an exposition of the 'matter itself' by drawing on Marx's approach, but correcting the (alleged) deficien-cies of the latter. In his exposition of the 'matter itself', Uno thus diverges from Marx. The systematic reference to commodity owners constitutes an element of Marx's exposition of the exchange process. It strikes me as questionable whether a convincing argument can be found that Marx's far-reaching separa-

---

53   See Marx 1994, pp. 13, 21–2, and 27.
54   Arthur 2006a, p. 33.

tion in his exposition – a separation between the analysis of the value-form on the one hand, and the analysis of the behaviour of commodity owners on the other – should be abandoned, as is done by Uno. In any case, the value-form can certainly be analysed without systematic reference to commodity owners; by contrast, such systematic reference is necessary in the exposition of the exchange process.

Through the treatment of value-form theory and the theory of the exchange process on two different levels, the exposition in *Capital* appears as clearly structured. It is also Michael Heinrich's reading that the form-analysis and the exposition of the exchange process (with the latter encompassing the exposition of the actions of commodity owners) are located on two different levels in Marx's theory. Heinrich is ultimately critical in his assessment of Marx's insertion of the money-form into the analysis of the value-form in *Capital* (a revision which first occurs in the popularised appendix to the first edition of 1867 and is maintained thereafter), since the strict separation between these two levels of exposition can no longer be maintained in this altered theoretical context.[55] In this new context, according to Heinrich, Marx's argument refers to the actions of commodity owners and abandons the purely form-analytic level. Yet this scenario must still be sharply distinguished from Uno's approach to the analysis of the value-form, in which commodity owners play a systematic role from the simple, isolated or accidental form of value onwards.

In the first edition of *Capital*, Marx frames his transition to the exposition of the exchange process as follows:

> The commodity is *immediate unity of use-value and exchange-value*, thus of two opposed entities. Thus it is an immediate *contradiction*. This contradiction must develop as soon as the commodity is no longer considered as hitherto in an analytic manner (at one time from the viewpoint of use-value and at another from the viewpoint of exchange-value) but is, as a whole, really related to other commodities. The *real* relating of commodities to one another, however, is their *process of exchange*.[56]

Here, Marx makes it clear that the following exposition will take place at a new level.

However, to return to the Japanese discussion: with regard to the interpretation of the opening section of the first volume of *Capital*, it should be borne

---

55 See Heinrich 1999a, pp. 227 f.

56 Marx 1976c, p. 40 [translation modified – N.G.].

in mind that the strict differentiation between Marx's value-form analysis and his exposition of the exchange process has played an important role not only in the German-language or Italian discussions (in the interpretations of Michael Heinrich, Dieter Wolf and Roberto Fineschi, among others), but also in parts of the Japanese discussion itself. Thus, the strict differentiation between these two levels of Marx's exposition was absolutely fundamental to Samezō Kuruma's reconstruction of Marx's theory of money.

The Japanese discussion – both within and beyond the Uno School – has yielded numerous research contributions on the set of problems associated with the theory of value and of money. In the mid-1980s, Masao Oguro described the intensive research activity in his native country as follows: 'In Japan, the analysis of the value-form has very frequently been the focus of discussion – particularly following the Second World War. Over 200 books or articles have been written on this topic alone. Over the last ten years or so, this problem has once again been discussed intensively, which has served to deepen the understanding of the analysis of the value-form in Japan'.[57] The specifically qualitative conceptual content of Marx's value-form analysis was also registered at an early stage in the Japanese discussion.

The specifically qualitative problematic of the value-form analysis was also a focus of research undertaken by Samezō Kuruma.[58] The latter's interpretation of Marx's value-form analysis and exposition of the exchange process – an interpretation which he set out in a book published in 1957 – exerted a great influence on the Japanese discussion of the first two chapters of *Capital* (as per the second edition of 1872/3), but remained virtually unknown in Germany (and especially in the Western part of the country). In his interpretation, Kuruma was concerned with the interconnection between the value-form analysis, the exposition of commodity fetishism and the exposition of the exchange process. A student of Kuruma, Teinosuke Otani, writes that Kuruma had come to the conclusion that 'Marx himself had briefly but clearly indicated both the content and the structure of the theory of the formation of money in *Capital*'[59] with the following proposition: '[t]he difficulty lies not in comprehending that

57   Oguro 1986, p. 24.

58   Kuruma was, for a time, Director of the Ohara Institute for Social Research. In addition, along with other researchers (including Teinosuke Otani) he was editor of an important resource for researchers, namely a Marx Lexicon, in which for each given thematic complex, the corresponding important passages from Marx's texts are compiled (see Kuruma 1977). Teinosuke Otani and Iichiro Sekine emphasise Kuruma's critical stance vis-à-vis Kōzō Uno (see Otani and Sekine 1987, pp. 248 f.).

59   Otani 1989, p. 177.

money is a commodity, but in discovering how, why and by what means a commodity becomes money'.[60] According to Kuruma, the 'how, why and by what means' in the latter part of the proposition corresponds to the respective sections of Marx's text, in the following sequence: 'Marx analyzes the *how* of money in the theory of the value-form and the *why* of money in the theory of the fetish-character, whereas in the theory of the exchange process he examines the question of *through what*'.[61] The early intensive engagement by Japanese researchers with the problematic of the value-form can serve as an exemplary demonstration of the extent to which the Japanese Marx discussion of the postwar period was further advanced than the corresponding West German Marx debate at that time. Within the latter debate, it would take until the mid- or late 1960s for an adequate sensitivity to be developed towards central qualitative aspects of the value-form problematic.

A more recent approach to research is that taken by Hachiro Masaki.[62] In the mid-1980s, Masaki presented the results of a lengthy research process, in which he interpreted Marx's theory of the value-form as being characterised by the configuration of two mutually exclusive logical procedures. According to Masaki, the widespread interpretation of Marx's value-form analysis consists in identifying its essential themes as being, on the one hand, the analysis of the structure of the value-form, and on the other, the tracing of the development of the value-form. In this interpretation, on Masaki's view, the concept of value is simply presupposed. According to the Japanese researcher, 'under the presupposition of the concept of value as a pre-established given ..., a logic which stands in contradiction with itself is continually applied to the matter in hand, and ever more adequate forms of expression for the concept of value can be put forward, one after the other'.[63] Masaki argues that a conception is thus represented according to which the development of the value-form resolves into the development of the contradiction between the concept of value and its form of existence. Yet – it might be added, to pursue Masaki's line of thought – this would be to misappropriate or overlook a decisive dimension of the conceptual content of the value-form analysis. According to Masaki, it is constitutive for Marx's value-form theory that two mutually exclusive methodological approaches exist alongside one another. On the one hand, within the framework of an analytic-genetic logic (Masaki himself concedes that this term

---

60   Marx 1976a, p. 186.

61   Kuruma 2008, pp. 65f. For a general treatment of Kuruma, but also of his controversy with Kōzō Uno, see Schauerte 2007.

62   See Masaki 1986.

63   Masaki 1986, p. 28.

is not entirely appropriate) the concept of value, of substance, is presupposed as a pre-established given. Within the context of this logic, the value-form analysis is concerned with forms of manifestation as opposed to the constitution of that which is already presupposed – i.e. the substance of value. The starting point here, according to Masaki, consists in a substantially grounded relation of equality. The Japanese theorist argues that Marx proceeds differently, however, within the context of his 'logic of the language of commodities', in which linen, as subject, relates itself to the coat. Masaki maintains that Marx's corresponding argumentation stands 'diametrically opposed to the standpoint which presupposes the concept of value and the substance of value as given in their abstractness and sociality, and then sets about tracing the development of their phenomenal forms'.[64] The constitution of that which is presupposed as given in analytic-genetic logic is thematised within the 'logic of the language of commodities'. By this, Masaki means that the linen which finds itself in the relative form of value first becomes a commodity in its relation to the equivalent, i.e. to the coat – 'value emerges simultaneously with the separation of value from the natural form'.[65] Masaki argues that in the 'logic of the language of commodities', passive commodities are no longer equated; instead, it is the commodity finding itself in the relative form of value which itself, *qua* subject, posits the relationship of equality. Masaki seems to be of the opinion that within the context of the analytic-genetic method, the distinction cannot adequately be maintained between the roles played by two commodities facing each other at opposite poles of the value expression – i.e. in which one commodity is to be found at the pole of the relative form of value, and the other at that of the equivalent form. Why – on Masaki's view – is the combination of these two mutually alien logics within Marx's value-form analysis necessary? In the exchange relation,

> a qualitative equalisation or abstraction occurs as the presupposition of exchange. However, the foundation of this equalisation cannot be posited through the logic of the 'language of commodities' itself. Although this logic involves the operation of an abstraction from the given properties of the commodity, this operation does not extend to the necessary selection of labour from these properties in order to highlight it (labour) as the substantial foundation of the value relation.

---

64   Masaki 1986, p. 29.
65   Masaki 1986, p. 36.

Thus, according to Masaki, Marx chose a mode of exposition in which a decisive role is, of necessity, not accorded to the 'logic of the language of commodities' alone – i.e. not without the latter being combined with a different kind of logic. 'Marx had first – and this is obviously incompatible with the logic of the "language of commodities" – to exhibit the substantially grounded "relation of equality" ... and then, following the logic of the "language of commodities", to investigate the structure of the expression of value, or abstraction through the value relation as a qualitative equalisation'.[66] For Masaki, then, this substantial foundation cannot be arrived at within the context of the 'logic of the language of commodities', but once it has been presupposed (and this occurs through the combination with the other, alien method), the substantial foundation can also be adequately abstracted within the 'logic of the language of commodities'.

In the 1980s, probably the most significant exponent of the Frankfurt value-form theory discourse initiated in the 1960s by Hans-Georg Backhaus was Helmut Brentel, whose basic premise was that Marx had elaborated a criticism of pre-monetary approaches to the theory of value within the course of his exposition.[67] According to Brentel, Marx's analysis of the value-form sets itself various tasks. In Brentel's interpretation of Marx's value-form theory, a characteristic feature of the latter consists in its unambiguous directional orientation (although this aspect of Marx's theory had already been emphasised by other authors before Brentel). The Frankfurt-based interpreter of Marx considers particularly important a theory of the constitution of value which, he argues, is implied by the theory of the value-form. According to Brentel, the equalisation of the labours contained in commodities as abstract universal and equal social labours occurs within the commodity relation. Brentel writes that the crucial point of Marx's theory of the constitution of value consists in his assertion of the 'positedness of value and exchange-value, of the substance of value and the value-form, *in each other and as one*, within the actual commodity *relation*'.[68] Form and substance are located within a co-originary relationship of positing. At the same time, Brentel discovers within Marx's analysis of the value-form an engagement with the aporias of merely 'simple' forms of value. 'Whereas the "simple" forms of value ultimately could not issue in a truly universal expression of value, and thus in a true constitution of value (the putative abstract-universal labour only ever being posited merely aporetically), it is ... only with

---

66   Masaki 1986, p. 32.
67   See Brentel 1989, p. 307.
68   Brentel 1989, p. 311.

the universal equivalent form ... that the level of the actuality* of the value-form is reached'.[69] The value-form first corresponds to the concept of value in the shape of the universal form of value. Brentel's interpretation coincides with Marx's theory here.[70] With regard to the theory of value, Brentel thus proves in a certain sense to be a successor to Hans-Georg Backhaus, who had interpreted Marx's theory of value as a critique of pre-monetary theories of value.

Parallel to the investigation of Marx's theory of value and of money, a question posed within international research pertains to the assessment of Friedrich Engels's reception of this theory. Although the 'problem of the beginning' in Marx's exposition by no means represents the only thematic area in relation to which a close scrutiny of Engels's engagement with Marx's critique of political economy is advisable,[71] particular attention has been paid to Engels's reception of Marx's theory of the commodity and of money within German, Japanese, Latin American and Anglo-Saxon research. This question has been discussed above all against the background of the following problematic: did Engels's 'historical' or 'logico-historical' interpretation of Marx's method and, in particular, his reading of the beginning of *Capital* as the exposition of a historical, pre-capitalist 'simple commodity production' do justice to Marx's theory?

In the 1970s, Heinz-Dieter Kittsteiner and Hans-Georg Backhaus, among others, had already addressed the aporias or deficiencies within Engels's reception of Marx's critique of political economy; Backhaus reprised his central ideas on this score together with Helmut Reichelt in 1994; Christopher Arthur subsequently expressed criticisms of Engels's view of Marx's critique of political economy in a contribution (published in 1996) marking the centenary of the former's death in 1895.[72] Arthur's critical engagement with Engels's reception of Marx's critique of political economy relies principally on the former's review

---

*   [*Wirklichkeit*] – also translatable as 'reality'.

69   Brentel 1989, p. 318.

70   'Only through this *universal* character does the *value-form* correspond to the *concept of value*' (Marx 1994, p. 28 [translation modified – N.G.]).

71   On Engels's view of the third volume of *Capital*, which Marx left unfinished, and which the former was to edit on Marx's request, see Vollgraf 2006. Michael Krätke counters the view that Engels 'adulterated' *Capital* (see Krätke 2006a). A critical response to Krätke's essay is provided by Ingo Elbe (see Elbe 2007).

72   See Arthur 1996. It should be borne in mind that there is also a tradition in the Anglo-Saxon world in which theoretical differences between Marx and Engels are emphasised or demonstrated. Works by Norman Levine can be cited within this context (see Levine 1975, Levine 1984 and Levine 2006–8); it should be noted, however, that Arthur critically distances himself from Levine.

of *A Contribution to the Critique of Political Economy* and on his preface and postface to the third volume of *Capital*. It is well known that the first of these texts by Engels is of decisive significance with regard to the conception corresponding to the so-called logico-historical reading of Marx's critique of political economy, whereas Engels's preface and postface to the third volume of *Capital* has the same status in connection with the conception of 'simple commodity production'.[73] Arthur correctly rejects Engels's interpretation that Marx's focus in the opening chapters of the first volume of *Capital* is on a historical, pre-capitalist 'simple commodity production': '[t]he truth is that *Marx never used the term "simple commodity production" in his life*'.[74] Arthur remarks upon the influence exerted on the history of the reception of Marx by the interpretation deriving from Engels as follows: 'Generations of students have been taught Marxist economics on the basis of a distinction between capitalist production and "simple commodity production". Yet this approach descends from Engels, *not Marx*'.[75] The British interpreter of Marx also comments on the problem of the law of value. Of relevance for Arthur in this context is not merely the textual argument that Marx's object is, from the beginning of his exposition, the capitalist mode of production; he also introduces another dimension, namely the thesis that no law of value in the Marxian sense can be held to prevail within 'simple commodity production': 'The law of value is not something lying at an *origin*, whether logical or historical; it is something that *comes to be* in the capitalist totality'.[76] According to Arthur, the starting point of *Capital* is to be understood as an 'immature', abstract moment of a complex totality: 'The exposition has to remedy the insufficiency of the starting point by showing how value, in its complete, finished form, does make good the promise of a law of value, by grounding it in the *developed* value forms – first money, then capital, then productive labour, finally circulation and accumulation of capital'.[77] There

---

73 An enigma within research on Marx consists in the following: why did Marx do nothing to prevent Engels's review (which, according to much research, fails to give an accurate representation of Marx's method) being published, even though *Das Volk* (i.e. the organ in which the review appeared) was 'effectively edited by Marx' at that time (Marx 1980, p. 403). Alexander Malysch, a Soviet Marx-Engels researcher, at one time speculated whether Marx might even have asked Engels to 'place special emphasis on the problem of the relation between the logical and the historical in economic research' (Malysch 1971, p. 58). The editors of *MEGA*[2], Volume II/2, published in 1980, even proceed on the assumption that 'Marx edited the review himself' (Marx 1980, p. 403).

74 Arthur 1996, p. 190 (emphasis in the original).

75 Ibid (emphasis in the original).

76 Arthur 1996, p. 195 (emphasis in the original).

77 Arthur 1996, pp. 198 f. (emphasis in the original).

would seem to be a puzzling omission in Arthur's interpretation of Engels's reception of Marx's critique of political economy, however: the British philosopher scarcely takes into account a central text in Engels's reception which refers, among other things, to Marx's theory and value and his theory of money. The text in question is Engels's 1868 synopsis of *Capital*, which received a certain amount of scrutiny within West German research already in the 1970s.[78]

1.3   *Summary*

With the research undertaken since the 1980s into the peculiar understanding of the object of the critique of political economy, benchmarks have been set for future interpretative approaches: theoretical regression behind the state that the debate has thus reached ought no longer to be possible. It is of course the case that recent approaches to research in this area also have an extended pre-history. To cite an example, the origins of a sophisticated reading of Marx's critique of political economy with a focus on the theory of fetishism can be traced back to Isaak Ill'ich Rubin in the 1920s; Rubin has posthumously (i.e. since the 1970s) become a 'classical' theorist within the international debate on Marx. Over the last two decades, there has been an increasing tendency for Marx's form-theory and fetish-theory to be emphasised within the international debate. Furthermore, it is now clear that any elucidation of Marx's understanding of the object of his critique must take into account both the high level of abstraction of Marx's exposition of the capitalist mode of production and his demonstration of the historicity of this mode of production.

In the discussion offered here of Japanese, German and Anglo-Saxon contributions to the interpretation and/or further development of Marx's theory of value, it has not been possible to address more than a tiny proportion of the extensive debate on this thematic complex within the critique of political economy. However, a few indispensable observations relating to the approaches presented in this section can be added here. It has proven necessary to establish a strict demarcation between the beginning of Marx's exposition and Engels's interpretation of the latter. It is also imperative to clearly differentiate between the various levels of exposition in Marx's theory of value. The question must also be posed whether Marx in fact used several 'methods' rather than a single one in his analysis of the value-form. Finally, a special significance must be attributed to the interpretation of Marx's theory of value as a 'monetary theory of value' (an interpretation which is suggested by Brentel, for example).

---

78   Engels 1985 pp. 263 ff.

Surveying the entirety of the international discussion of *Capital* beyond the approaches presented here, the emergence of a determinate interpretative tendency can be identified within the history of the reception of Marx's *magnum opus*. This tendency, in evidence since the 1970s and 1980s, consists in the practice of sharply foregrounding the specific categorial interconnection between the commodity, value and money in Marx's critique of political economy; in this context, researchers from various regions of the world can be cited, such as Hans-Georg Backhaus and the Marx-interpreters who draw inspiration from him in Germany and Australia, John Milios* in Greece, Young Bin Hahn in South Korea, and Trai Han Hac in France. On the international level, the 'monetary theory of value' has not only emerged as an interpretative current within research into Marx's critique of political economy, but its 'unquestionable power' (in the words of Wolfgang Fritz Haug) has also been recognised by critics of this current (such as Haug himself). Crucially, the historical evolution of the reception of Marx by the interpretative current propounding the 'monetary theory of value' over the last decades has been embedded within the general context of the worldwide development of a reading of *Capital* which is oriented to form-theory or form-critique, or to questions of methodology and social theory.

2 The Problematic of Enquiry and Exposition in the Critique of Political Economy

2.1 A 'Mont Blanc' of Research Material[79]

Of central importance in relation to Marx's understanding of his method is his distinction between enquiry and exposition. A well-known passage in *Capital* on this range of problems can be found in Marx's 1873 postface to the second edition of the first volume. Here, Marx comments as follows: 'Of course the method of presentation must differ in form from that of inquiry. The latter has to appropriate the material in detail, to analyse its different forms of development and to track down their inner connection'. Marx continues that

---

*   John Milios is also known as Yannis/Giannis Milios.

79   In this subchapter, the engagement with Marx's process of enquiry within the history of the reception of Marx's critique of political economy will not be thematised; rather, a brief treatment of Marx's process of enquiry itself will be offered, as this is indispensable on account of the interconnection between Marx's process of enquiry and his exposition. The question as to whether there is a specific method of enquiry in Marx, and as to the features of such a method, cannot be addressed here.

it is only when this has been accomplished that the 'real movement' can be exposited appropriately. If this is done successfully, such that 'the life of the subject-matter is now reflected back in the ideas, then it may appear as if we have before us an *a priori* construction'.[80] Yet this semblance of an '*a priori* construction' is deceptive. With these methodological indications, Marx brings the process of enquiry out from the shadow of the exposition and demonstrates that the former is the precondition of the latter. This passage has frequently been quoted or commented upon in the international discussion of Marx's method. It is worth noting that one of the most important exponents of the Japanese discussion of Marx of the postwar period, Samezō Kuruma, held this methodological passage from the postface to the second edition of the first volume of *Capital* to be a more significant commentary by Marx on his method than the well-known 'chapter on method' from the 1857 *Introduction to the Critique of Political Economy*. The aim of Marx's enquiry is to gain knowledge with regard to the internal interconnection between the various economic categories and relations. It is only when the internal structure and the laws of motion of the capitalist economy have been adequately penetrated and investigated that these can be exposited such that the 'life of the subject-matter' is reflected ideally. For Marx, enquiry signified among other things the critical engagement with political economy – i.e. with this science as it had been elaborated before his time and with the contributions to this discipline to be found in the corresponding contemporary literature. In this process, Marx endeavoured to become acquainted with, and to penetrate conceptually, the widest possible horizon of economic thought. Authors working in connection with the *MEGA*[2] edition have referred to Marx's 'evaluation of a literature so copious as to render an overview scarcely practicable'.[81]

From the beginning of his economic studies to shortly before his death, Marx not only made excerpts from the numerous economists which he categorised under different historical phases and various theoretical orientations: he was also concerned to do justice to the international character of economic theory formation, and constantly to broaden his horizon in this regard. Of course, he was interested first and foremost in the development from William Petty, via John Locke and Dudley North to the mid-eighteenth century, and then via James Steuart to Adam Smith and David Ricardo (the zenith of bourgeois economic thought), and finally to the various orientations which emerged

---

80   Marx 1976, p. 102.

81   Hecker, Jungnickel and Kopf 1991, p. 496. On the source material which formed the foundation of Marx's enquiry, see Syrow 1989.

after Ricardo. Marx also attached great significance to the Francophone development stretching from Boisguillebert, via the Physiocrats around François Quesnay, the 'vulgar economist' Jean-Baptiste Say, and Sismondi (whom Marx held in high esteem), to Bastiat (whom Marx criticised vehemently). However, Marx also devoted attention to economic thinkers from numerous other countries. He praised the American, Benjamin Franklin; he received the work of Galiani, an eighteenth century Italian economist; he rebuked Charles H. Carey, an opponent of Ricardo considered by Marx to be an American counterpart of Bastiat; he commented on Spanish approaches to economic thought; and, in his latter years, he increasingly registered economic literature of Russian origin.[82]

It is likely that Marx did not engage intensively with the science of political economy until after he relocated to Paris.[83] In the course of 1844, the future author of *Capital* studied works by Jean-Baptiste Say; the Polish member of the Smithian School, Skarbek; the Ricardian, McCulloch;[84] the 'vulgar economist', Destutt de Tracy;[85] the Ricardian, James Mill; he also pored over Engels's text, *Outlines of a Critique of Political Economy*. Marx particularly engaged in a reception of the most important British economists of the eighteenth and nineteenth centuries, namely Adam Smith and David Ricardo. 1844 was also the year in which Marx composed his first significant economic and philosophical work, the *Economic and Philosophical Manuscripts* (this text was first published posthumously in 1932).[86]

In 1845 and 1846, Marx expanded and deepened his knowledge of economic literature, both in Brussels, and also during library research undertaken together with Engels in England (in July and August 1845).[87] During this period,

---

82 Marx's formidable skills in foreign languages stood him in good stead for his evaluation of economic literature: see Sperl 2004b, p. 166.

83 On the Paris excerpt notebooks, see Rumjanzewa 1980.

84 Marx would later express the view that McCulloch – for whom he had a profound aversion – had, along with James Mill, contributed to the demise of the Ricardian School.

85 It is likely that Marx first used the term 'vulgar economics' in the so-called 'second draft of *Capital*' of 1861–3.

86 The publication of this previously scarcely known source material opened up a new perspective on the 'young Marx', and provoked 'tremors' which shook the established image of Marx. It can be regarded as a long-term effect of the publication of this work in 1932 that the West German discussion of Marx often revolved around the 'young Marx' until into the 1960s, even if this is not the only explanation for the latter phenomenon. Herbert Marcuse was one of the first commentators on the *Economic and Philosophical Manuscripts* (see Marcuse 2005).

87 On the excerpts taken in the summer of 1845, see Wassina 1989.

one of Marx's concerns was to gain a systematic overview of the history of political economy as a whole. He accordingly devoted his attention to several works dealing with the history of this science.[88] By the time he wrote his polemic against Pierre-Joseph Proudhon, *The Poverty of Philosophy*, in 1847, Marx had to a large extent drawn close to Ricardo's theoretical position, even if he had not taken over this position himself.[89] However, Marx was still a long way from reaching the theoretical level that he would attain in the course of the elaboration of his 'mature' critique of political economy.

New opportunities were opened up to Marx as a result of his move to London in 1849. 'The enormous amount of material relating to the history of political economy assembled in the British Museum, the fact that London is a convenient vantage point for the observation of bourgeois society, and finally the new stage of development which this society seemed to have entered with the discovery of gold in California and Australia, induced me to start again from the very beginning and to work carefully through the new material'.[90] Between the late summer of 1850 and December 1851, Marx filled 18 notebooks with extracts from economic works. Six more notebooks followed in the period up to 1853. These so-called 'London notebooks' contain above all excerpts relating to economic problems in the narrow sense, but also those pertaining to themes which transcend the boundaries of the discipline of political economy in the narrow sense.[91] Among his other research activities, Marx once again embarked on an exhaustive study of the classical political economists: James Steuart, Adam Smith and David Ricardo. He accorded an important status to the theory of money – the object of an intensive engagement by Marx in 1850/1 – particularly in the first London notebooks. In a second stage of processing his excepted material in the spring of 1851, Marx compiled a collection of excerpts on the theory of money that he had made in Paris, Brussels, Manchester and London, and added commentaries. Around the same time, he composed his first self-standing theoretical economic work since the resumption of his systematic studies; this text, which is little-known in the international Marx debate, was entitled *Reflection*.[92] In summary, it can be said that Marx deepened his

---

88   See Marx 1998a, pp. 389 ff., Marx 1998b, pp. 407 ff., and Marx 1998c, pp. 413 ff., among other sources.

89   An attempt to elaborate on the differences between Marx and Ricardo is made in Ōishi 1995.

90   Marx 1987b, pp. 264–5.

91   See Jahn 1987; Wassina 1983; Jahn and Noske 1983.

92   Rolf Hecker reports that there is at least a Spanish translation of *Reflection*, however (see

economic knowledge enormously in the early 1850s, and thus laid a theoretical foundation without which he could not have written *Capital* in its published form. It should not be overlooked that Marx already anticipated some important results of his research in the early 1850s. This is true, for example, in relation to his rejection of the quantity theory of money. The early 1850s are to be regarded as a phase in Marx's creative process, and one which should by no means be underrated. A close textual comparison between passages in *Bullion* (written in 1851) and the first notebook of the *Grundrisse* (written in 1857) reveals that Marx partially drew on his 1851 treatment of the theory of money in composing the latter text.[93]

However, it should be pointed out that in Marx's work the processes of enquiry and exposition are sometimes intertwined, such that it is scarcely possible to clearly demarcate them. This is particularly true of the manuscripts dating from Marx's creative period from 1857 onwards. Thus, in the *Grundrisse* and *Theories of Surplus-Value* it is noticeable that the text still at times exhibits the character of a process of enquiry, in which Marx is continually thinking through the material anew. This also occurs precisely in Marx's critical engagement with political economic thinkers. In the context of Marx's intensive reception of political economy, it should be noted that it was not (or at least not only) the impressive volume of material processed by Marx in his research which paved the way to an understanding of the internal structure of the capitalist economy; rather, it was also the specific questions posed by Marx in relation to the material provided by this science which played a decisive role in enabling him to attain a comprehensive level of knowledge vis-à-vis the internal structure of the capitalist economy and the internal interconnection between economic categories by means of his critical engagement with economic science.

In a letter written to Engels on 20 February 1866, Marx states in relation to the problematic of his exposition that 'the *composition*, the coherence, is a triumph of German science'.[94] Marx presumably considered his manner of exposition to be a specific feature of his own theory formation, constituting a moment which enabled him to distinguish himself from the political economists who preceded him. It should be recalled here that in *Theories of Surplus-Value*, Marx

---

Hecker 1998, p. 15). This text by Marx has also been published in Russian. Investigations of the manuscript, *Reflection*, are undertaken in Wygodski 1978a, Schrader 1980, and Christ 1979.

93   See Schrader 1980, p. 120.

94   Marx 1987e, p. 232.

was extremely critical in his engagement with David Ricardo – specifically with regard to Ricardo's exposition and the architectonic of this exposition.[95]

In *Capital*, Marx is concerned with the specific, internal connection within an organic whole constituted by economic categories – i.e. he focuses on the specific, internal interconnection of these categories within an integral economic system which is articulated in a determinate way. In his logical exposition, Marx aimed to demonstrate this specific, internal interconnection within a whole formed by economic categories by exhibiting their genetic development. Decisively, however, the process of exposition of Marx's critique of political economy presupposed an intensive process of enquiry. Yet, although it is true that Marx first developed the systematic exposition of his 'mature' critique of political economy from 1857 onwards (i.e. at a point in time when his process of enquiry was already at an advanced stage), it should by no means be inferred from this that the period between 1843/4 and 1857 corresponds to a phase of enquiry in Marx's work, with the subsequent period from the *Grundrisse* onwards representing a phase of exposition. From 1857 onwards, enquiry and exposition are tightly interwoven in the history of the elaboration of Marx's critique of political economy, and, regarded as a whole, enquiry could by no means be said to retreat into the background to any great extent during this process. Alongside the drafting of systematic manuscripts on the critique of political economy, in which the dimension of enquiry is also present to some degree, Marx continued to make excerpts, and through his research activity amassed a 'Mont Blanc' of material to be processed. A large proportion of this excerpted material from the period beginning in 1857 remains unpublished, including such extraordinarily important sources as the part devoted to excerpts of Notebook VII, which Marx used for his research between 1859 and 1863, or the eight supplementary notebooks (Notebooks A to H), which chronicle the process whereby Marx was able to gain a deeper level of knowledge of the historical phase of the emergence of political economy, among other things.[96] Finally, the *Theories of Surplus-Value* must also be understood, at least in part, as documenting a process of enquiry. Marx continued to make numerous excerpts relating to economic questions after 1863, including on the topics of the money market, crisis, the financial system, and landed property.

Marx remained an active researcher into the 1870s and 1880s. A relatively short time before his death, he engaged with questions relating to currency,

---

95   See also Marxhausen 1987a.

96   On the material referred to here, see Müller 1977 and Schnickmann 1979. On Marx's reception of Adam Smith in the part of Notebook VII devoted to excerpts, see Schrader 1983.

money, banking and finance, for example. His research activity consisted not only in the reception of various theories of political economy, but also in recording empirical material and statistical analysis. An essay by Carl-Erich Vollgraf demonstrates just how much importance Marx placed on his studies of empirical and statistical material in the late phase of his work on *Capital*.[97] According to Vollgraf, the USA came increasingly into Marx's field of vision as he collected empirical material. In his late correspondence, Marx emphasised that '[t]he most interesting field for the economist is now certainly to be found in the United States, and, above all, during the period of 1873 ... until 1878 – the period of chronic crisis ... The imbeciles in Europe who fancy that theore[ti]cians like myself and others are at the root of the evil, might learn a wholesome lesson by reading the official Yankee reports [here Marx alludes to the material on economic development in the USA which he regularly consulted – J.H.]'.[98]

Marx pursued his research activity until shortly before the end of his life. Even in his final years, Marx was still concerned with collecting immense quantities of material for further work on *Capital*. From 1877 to 1879, for example, at a time when Marx's ability to work had long since been severely impaired, he completed ten excerpt notebooks on economics. Marx's main focus here was the banking and financial system. These notebooks remain as yet unpublished; they are due to appear in *MEGA*[2], Volume IV/25. When he was already more than 50 years old, Marx learned Russian in order to be able to undertake a systematic evaluation of the specialist literature in this language. An index entitled 'Russiches in my bookstall',* which Marx compiled shortly before his death, registers the Russian-language specialist literature which Marx had collected in his own private library.

2.2 The Ascent from the Abstract to the Concrete and the 'Problem of the Beginning'[99] in Marx's Presentation

Marx's method of exposition is often interpreted in the sense of an ascent from the abstract to the concrete. In terms of the methodological dimension of the

---

97 See Vollgraf 2002.

98 Marx 1991a, p. 344.

* ['Russian material in my bookstall'].

99 Michael Krätke has rightly identified an 'asymmetry in terms of the attention' devoted to the beginning of the logical exposition of the Marxian critique of political economy relative to that accorded to its conclusion. Whereas the 'problem of the beginning' has been much discussed in Marx-interpretation, the question of the conclusion has been neglected (see Krätke 2002, p. 8).

Marxian critique of political economy, participants within the international Marx discussion often refer back to an excerpt drafted by Marx in the summer of 1857 (i.e. before he began writing the *Grundrisse*, according to the dating given in *MEGA*², Volume II/1), which thematises, among other things, an ascent from the abstract to the concrete.

The text in question is the famous 'chapter on method', which was not published until after Marx's death. Marx begins his argumentation in the following way: 'When we consider a given country politico-economically, we begin with its population, its distribution among classes, town, country, the coast, the different branches of production, export and import, annual production and consumption, commodity prices etc'.[100] Marx continues: 'It seems to be correct to begin with the real and the concrete, with the real precondition, thus to begin, in economics, with e.g. the population, which is the foundation and the subject of the entire social act of production'.[101] On closer examination, however, it can be ascertained that such a beginning is not the correct one. Population is an abstraction, if, for example, the classes of which it is composed are disregarded. 'These classes in turn are an empty phrase if I am not familiar with the elements on which they rest. E.g. wage labour, capital, etc.'. These latter in turn presuppose 'exchange, division of labour, prices, etc. ... For example, capital is nothing without wage labour, without value, money, price etc.'. Marx writes: 'Thus, if I were to begin with the population, this would be a chaotic representation* of the whole'.[102] By means of further determination, simpler concepts would be attained, from 'the represented concrete towards ever thinner abstractions until I had arrived at the simplest determinations. From there the journey would have to be retraced until I had finally arrived at the population again, but this time not as the chaotic representation of a whole, but as a rich totality of many determinations and relations'.[103] It would appear that the basic thought that Marx has in mind is that of a progression from the concrete to the abstract, and subsequently from the abstract back to the concrete; the latter is now differently determined, however.

Marx draws a parallel between the two 'paths of thought' outlined here and two currents in the history of economic thought. The first path of thought was that traced by early political economy, by the economic thinkers of the seventeenth century. The latter, according to Marx, begin with the living whole,

---

100   Marx 1973, p. 100.
101   Ibid.
*   [*Vorstellung*] – Martin Nicolaus translates *Vorstellung* as 'conception'.
102   Marx 1973, p. 100 [translation modified – N.G.].
103   Ibid [translation modified – N.G.].

with population, the nation, the state, several states, etc., and they always conclude by discovering through analysis a few determinant, abstract, general relations such as division of labour, money, value, etc.[104] However, according to
Marx, the development of economic science did not end there. Marx points
to a later epoch of economic thought when he writes: 'As soon as these individual moments had been more or less firmly established and abstracted, there
began the economic systems, which ascended from the simple relations, such
as labour, division of labour, need, exchange value, to the level of the state,
exchange between nations and the world market'. This is followed by Marx's
assessment that the latter 'is obviously the scientifically correct method'.[105]
Thus it should not be overlooked that Marx considered in the summer of 1857
that this second path – which he attributed to a later historical epoch of economic theory – was entirely germane to his own theoretical development. This
second path, however, presupposes the first. Marx continues his exposition and
writes that the concrete is concrete because 'it is the concentration* of many
determinations, hence unity of the manifold.** It appears in the process of
thinking, therefore, as a process of concentration, as a result, not as a point of
departure, even though it is the point of departure in reality and hence also the
point of departure for intuition*** and representation. Along the first path the
full representation was evaporated to yield an abstract determination; along
the second, the abstract determinations lead towards a reproduction of the
concrete by way of thought'.[106] Hegel had conceived the real as the result of
'thought concentrating itself,**** probing its own depths, and unfolding itself
out of itself, by itself'.[107] For Marx, however, the method of the ascent from the
abstract to the concrete means the appropriation of the concrete by thought,

---

104   Ibid.
105   Marx 1973, p. 101.
*   [*Zusammenfassung*] – here, and in the following sentence, there could be an argument for
       translating *Zusammenfassung* as 'comprehension' (as the term is rendered by Paul Guyer
       and Allen Wood in their translation of Kant's *Critique of Pure Reason* – see Kant 1998, p. 217
       and p. 261).
**   [*des Mannigfaltigen*] – Martin Nicolaus translates this as 'the diverse'.
***   [*Anschauung*] – it seems appropriate to translate *Anschauung* as 'intuition' (the standard
       English translation for the term in Kant, for example) given that Marx deliberately uses a
       philosophical register in this context. In his translation, Martin Nicolaus uses 'observation'
       for *Anschauung*.
106   Marx 1973, p. 101.
****   [*sich in sich zusammenfassenden*] – arguably this should be translated as 'thought com-
       prehending itself within itself' (see above note on the translation of *Zusammenfassung*).
107   Marx 1973, p. 101.

or rather the reproduction of the concrete as the concrete in the mind. This is not to be confused with the real process by which the concrete itself comes into being. The 'chapter on method' has been the subject of much controversy within the discussions around international Marx research in the last decades. However, with the publication in 1994 of a historical and systematic commentary by a Swiss working group on this famous excerpt from Marx's writings, a state of the research has been attained which establishes a benchmark for subsequent interpretations.

A central interpretational premise of Judith Jánoska, Martin Bondeli, Konrad Kindle and Marc Hofer vis-à-vis the methodological reflections which Marx set down in August 1857 is the discrimination between different levels. Thus the group of authors differentiates a 'level of appropriation' from the 'level of reality' and from a 'level of historical reflection'. The 'level of appropriation' corresponds to the process of theoretical cognition. However, between this level and the 'level of reality', which corresponds to the real object itself, the relation is not the one posited by the theory of reflection. The 'level of historical reflection' refers to the theoretical elaboration of the economic object in the history of the science of political economy.

How is the methodological interpretation of Jánoska, Bondeli, Kindle and Hofer delineated in detail? In accordance with the differentiation between a 'level of reality' and a 'level of appropriation', the 'concrete' has different meanings on the different respective levels. Vis-à-vis the 'level of reality', concepts such as 'abstract' and 'concrete', or 'the abstract' and 'the concrete', designate real forms of social existence. In relation to the 'level of appropriation', on the contrary, it should be noted that the terms 'abstract' and 'concrete', or 'the abstract' and 'the concrete', refer to the corresponding stages of the conceptual appropriation of the object in the thought of the theoretician.[108]

According to Marx's 'chapter on method', the movement of the process of knowledge is from the concrete to the abstract, and finally from the abstract to the concrete. In terms of the first of the different meanings of 'the concrete' referred to by the Swiss group of authors, 'the concrete' corresponds to the 'level of reality' and is understood as 'a segment of reality, as the object* of appropriation and object** of scientific work'.[109] This concrete is a real presupposition, which remains outside the process of thought and exists independently of it.

---

108   See Jánoska, Bondeli, Kindle and Hofer 1994, p. 54.

*   [Gegenstand].

**   [Objekt].

109   Jánoska, Bondeli, Kindle and Hofer 1994, p. 61.

The real-concrete is the point of departure for observation* and representation.** 'When it [the real-concrete] is taken up by the cognitive faculty of
sensibility, "representation", a "represented concrete" is yielded, ... a "full" ... but
also, pejoratively, a "chaotic" ... representation'.[110] From this second concrete –
'the concrete of representation' – the simplest categories and thinnest abstractions can be reached by means of further determination. Then, departing from
this point, the movement of the process of cognition leads to the concrete in a
third sense. Here it consists of a thought-concrete in the sense of a rich, conceived totality of many determinations and relations.[111] This second path, as is
underlined by the Swiss commentary, traces the ascent from the abstract to the
concrete.

The Swiss group of authors expands on the correlation indicated by Marx
in the 'chapter on method' between the two methodological paths and various thinkers within the history of economic thought as follows: 'Our attempted
reconstruction shows that there is a background within the history of economic
thought which does indeed exhibit the methodological approaches projected
onto the tradition by Marx. Petty and Steuart *can* in fact be regarded as representatives of the "first path", and Smith and Ricardo as exponents of the
"second"'.[112] On the one hand, Marx refers to the economists of the seventeenth
century, who began with the 'living whole' and discovered 'through analysis a
small number of determinant, abstract, general relations';[113] on the other, he
alludes to the 'economic systems, which ascended from the simple relations,
such as labour, division of labour, need, exchange value, to the level of the state,
exchange between nations and the world market'.[114] To summarise, the observation can be made in relation to the systematic and historical commentary on
the 'chapter on method' by the Swiss working group that these authors' theoretical strength lies in (a) their rigorous analysis of this important methodological
section in Marx's text in terms of the latter's conceptual content in relation to
epistemological questions, and (b) their discussion of this section within the
contexts of the history of science and the history of philosophy.

Marx's 'chapter on method', written in the summer of 1857, represents an
important step within the process of his methodological self-clarification as

---

*   [*Anschauung*] – see note above.
**   [*Vorstellung*] – see note above.
110   Jánoska, Bondeli, Kindle and Hofer 1994, p. 62.
111   Jánoska, Bondeli, Kindle and Hofer 1994, pp. 62 f.
112   Jánoska, Bondeli, Kindle and Hofer 1994, p. 108.
113   Marx 1973, p. 100.
114   Marx 1973, pp. 100–1.

he developed the method he would employ in *Capital*, even if this text cannot be considered the last word on this method as it is exhibited in his *magnum opus*. Indeed, the method employed in *Capital* was the result of a concatenation of processes of enquiry and attempts at exposition over many years. Within the process of Marx's theoretical development, the methodological insights expounded in the 'chapter on method' represent a transitional stage rather than an endpoint.

In 1862, Marx presented important methodological considerations relating to the problem of exposition in the second part of *Theories of Surplus-Value*, where he comments on Ricardo's method. According to Marx, Ricardo takes for granted the principle of the determination of value by labour time, and proceeds to investigate whether 'the other economic relations *contradict* this determination of value or to what extent they modify it'.[115,*] For Marx, the history of political economy reveals not only the scientific necessity of this procedure, but also its 'scientific inadequacy': '[t]his inadequacy not only shows itself in the method of presentation (in a formal sense) but leads to erroneous results because it omits some essential links and *directly* seeks to prove the congruity of the economic categories with one another'.[116]

A decisive feature of the Marxian method consists in the dimension of the mediation of the various economic categories with one another. The latter are at times to be located on completely different levels of abstraction – this was something Marx knew he needed to consider in his conception of the exposition. As the above quotation from *Theories of Surplus-Value* indicates, Marx was able to identify a grave methodological deficit in Ricardo's approach. Yet it is strikingly typical of Marx's procedure that he insists on the historical jus-

---

115   Marx 1989c, p. 390. It should be noted in relation to Marx's reception of Ricardo's theory of value that the adequacy of Marx's interpretation has at times been questioned within research in this area. A particular focus of criticism has been Marx's conception that Ricardo begins his exposition by setting out his labour theory of value, only then to commit the error of equating labour values and prices of production. The neo-Ricardian economist, Ian Steedman, rejects this criticism of Ricardo by Marx: 'Marx persistently misinterprets Ricardo's use of the term value to be his (Marx's) use and then accuses Ricardo of "mistakenly" identifying value and cost [or price of production – J.H.] – terms which for Ricardo were simply synonyms' (Steedman 1989, p. 55). For Steedman, Ricardo reveals himself to be a theorist of prices of production; due to limitations of space, this important problematic cannot be considered in any more detail here.

*   For an extensive overview of recent Marxist debates in relation to the so-called 'transformation problem' (i.e. the problem of the transformation of values into prices of production), see Moseley 2015.

116   Marx 1989c, p. 390.

tification and necessity of Ricardo's method. In his assessment of the scientific achievements of political economists, Marx did not merely pay heed to the criterion of the correctness of their views; he also took account of the respective role that corresponded to them in the historical development of this science. This can be illustrated by referring to Marx's subsequent assessment in relation to the history of the formation of economic theory: Marx judged that Ricardo, within the context of his method, was able to overcome the alleged dualism of Smith, which consisted in an oscillation between an 'esoteric' and an 'exoteric' element of theory.[117] On the one hand, the scientific value of Ricardo's method is evident, according to Marx; on the other hand, however, 'the scientific deficiencies of his procedure are clearly visible'.[118] Marx's line of thought emphasises the necessarily inverted and extremely peculiar architectonic of the British political economist, which, according to Marx, is closely connected to Ricardo's method.[119] The latter consists, on Marx's view, in the confrontation between economic categories and the basic principle of the determination of value by labour time.[120]

Marx expounds his critique of Ricardo's method as follows: in the first chapter of *Principles* (i.e. the chapter on value), 'not only are commodities assumed

---

117   Marx writes that Smith 'moves with great naïveté in a perpetual contradiction. On the one hand he traces the intrinsic connection existing between economic categories or the obscure structure of the bourgeois economic system. On the other, he simultaneously sets forth the connection as it appears in the phenomena of competition and thus as it presents itself to the unscientific observer just as to him who is actually involved and interested in the process of bourgeois production' (Marx 1989c, p. 390).

118   Marx 1989c, p. 392.

119   '[T]he faulty architectonics of the theoretical part [of Ricardo's *Principles of Political Economy and Taxation* – i.e. of the first six chapters of this work – J.H.] is not accidental, rather it is the result of Ricardo's method of investigation itself and of the definite task which he set himself in his work. It expresses the scientific deficiencies of this method of investigation itself' (Marx 1989c, p. 393).

120   'Thus the entire Ricardian contribution is contained in the first two chapters of his work. In these chapters, the developed bourgeois relations of production, and therefore also the developed categories of political economy, are confronted with their principle – the determination of value – and examined in order to determine the degree to which they directly correspond to this principle and the position regarding the apparent discrepancies which they introduce into the value relations of commodities. These chapters contain the whole of his critique of hitherto existing political economy, the categorical break with the contradiction that pervades Adam Smith's work through its esoteric and exoteric modes of consideration, and, at the same time, because of this critique, they produce some quite new and startling results. Hence the great theoretical satisfaction afforded by these first two chapters' (Marx 1989c, p. 394 [translation modified – N.G.]).

to exist – and when considering value as such, nothing further is required – but also wages, capital, profit, the general rate of profit and even ... the various forms of capital as they arise from the process of circulation, and also the difference between "natural and market-price".[121] A similar criticism of Ricardo is to be found in Marx's correspondence. In a letter written in 1868 to Ludwig Kugelmann, Marx raises the critical objection against Ricardo that 'in his first chapter on value, he presupposes *as given* all possible categories which are still to be developed, in order to prove their adequacy vis-à-vis the law of value'.[122] A consequence of Ricardo's procedure is that economic categories which are in fact only to be developed at a later stage of the exposition are already taken as given at a relatively early stage, or even from the outset. A footnote by Marx reveals that he was concerned to avoid similar problems in his own exposition (i.e. in the chapter on the commodity at the beginning of the first volume of *Capital*): 'The reader should note that we are not speaking here of the wages or value the worker receives for (e.g.) a day's labour, but of the value of the commodity in which his day of labour is objectified. At this stage of our presentation, the category of wages does not exist at all'.[123] In *Theories of Surplus-Value*, in the context of his reception of the section of Ricardo's text on the modification of the principle of the determination of value by the quantity of labour, Marx accuses the British economic scientist of lacking the power of abstraction:

> All Ricardo's illustrations only serve him as a means to smuggle in the *presupposition of a general rate of profit*. And this happens in the first chapter 'On Value', while wages are supposed to be developed only in the fifth chapter and profits in the sixth. How from the mere determination of the '*value*' of the commodities their surplus-value, the profit and even a *general rate of profit* are derived remains obscure to Ricardo. In fact the only thing which he proves in the above illustrations is that the *prices* of the commodities, in so far as they are determined by the general rate of profit, are entirely different from their *values*. And he arrives at this difference by postulating the *rate of profit* to be law. One can see that though Ricardo is accused of being too abstract, one would be justified in accusing him of the opposite: lack of the power of abstraction, inability, when dealing with the values of commodities, to forget profits, a factor which confronts him as a result of competition.[124]

---

121   Marx 1989c, p. 393.
122   Marx 1988b, p. 43.
123   Marx 1976, p. 135.
124   Marx 1989c, p. 416 [translation modified – N.G.].

Through his engagement with the chapter on value in Ricardo's major work, *Principles of Economy and Taxation*, Marx gained a clear idea of how an adequate beginning of the exposition should *not* be formulated.

With regard to the 'problem of the beginning' in Marx's own exposition, the question arises as to which title the opening chapter of the exposition should bear. The title of the first chapter of the *Rohentwurf** of 1857–8 reads as follows: 'II. The Chapter on Money';[125,**] as indicated by the editors of the $MEGA^2$ volume containing the *Grundrisse*, Marx inserted the title at a later point and added the numeration at the latest when he began a section entitled 'Value', which was to precede the chapter on money.[126] In relation to the problem of the beginning of the exposition in Marx, Rosdolsky comments that the necessity of correcting the 'idealist manner of the presentation' prompted the Trier-born theorist to choose the commodity as the starting point of his exposition in his text, *A Contribution to the Critique of Political Economy* (which was written between November 1858 and January 1859).[127] In advancing this thesis, Rosdolsky relies on a famous passage from the first notebook of the *Grundrisse*.[128] It is difficult to determine when precisely Marx decided to give the first chapter the title, 'The Commodity', rather than 'Value'. In one of the best-known letters written by Marx in the period shortly before he finished working on the *Rohentwurf* (to Engels on 2 April 1858), it is clear that he still intends the title of the first chapter of the section 'a) Capital in General' to be 'Value'.[129] Marx hoped that his work would be published in the form of serialised notebooks (the first of which was to contain the chapter dealing with value, which he had broken off at an early stage, such that it remained fragmentary in the corresponding version in the *Rohentwurf*); to this end, in June 1858 Marx embarked on an intensive review of his own *Grundrisse*, and

---

*   The German title of the *Grundrisse* is *Grundrisse der Kritik der politischen Ökonomie* (*Rohentwurf*). *1857–1858*. This is rendered in English as 'Outlines of the Critique of Political Economy (Rough Draft), 1857–58'.

125   Marx 1976d, p. 49.

**   This numbering is omitted in the English-language edition of the *Grundrisse* (see Marx 1973, p. 115).

126   See Marx 1976d, p. 776.

127   See Rosdolsky 1977, p. 114.

128   Here, Marx writes: 'It will be necessary later, before this question is dropped, to correct the idealist manner of the presentation, which makes it seem as if it were merely a matter of conceptual determinations and of the dialectic of these concepts. Above all in the case of the phrase: product (or activity) becomes commodity; commodity, exchange value; exchange value, money' (Marx 1973, p. 151).

129   Marx 1983e, p. 298.

compiled an index of everything which he considered important in relation to the range of themes to be handled in the respective instalments of his work. This 'Index to the Seven Notebooks', or its first version, contains a plan for the architectonic of the critique of political economy, extending from the 'beginning' of the exposition to the circulation of capital; in this plan, it is clearly still Marx's intention to have an opening chapter entitled 'Value'.[130]

In the latter half of 1858 (in August, according to the $MEGA^2$ editors), Marx began drafting the *Urtext* of *A Contribution to the Critique of Political Economy*, but broke off work on the manuscript in autumn of the same year. As is well known, only parts of the chapter on money and the beginning of the chapter on capital have been preserved from this manuscript, which was unpublished in Marx's lifetime. The editors of $MEGA^2$, Volume II/2, claim that Marx drafted a chapter on value as the opening chapter of the *Urtext*; this claim cannot be verified.[131]

According to the editors of $MEGA^2$, Marx commenced work in November 1858 on the version of *A Contribution to the Critique of Political Economy* which was subsequently published in 1859.[132] He had taken the decision to entitle the opening chapter 'The Commodity' rather than 'Value' by the end of November 1858 at the latest. This much, at least, can be inferred from Marx's correspondence (specifically, from his letter to Engels of 29 November 1858).[133] It would appear, at any rate, that it was not until he had finished working on the *Grundrisse* that Marx resolved to prepare a draft for an opening chapter with the title 'The Commodity'.

The commodity is also the initial category in *Capital*. The commodity of the beginning of Marx's exposition in this work is a *concretum* – a simple concrete, to borrow Rafael Echeverría's formulation – but simultaneously also an *abstractum* due to its as yet underdetermined form-character. This is so because decisive dimensions of its form-determinacy – its determinate being* as a capitalistically produced commodity, as a component of a commodity capital – remain to be determined in the course of Marx's exposition.

---

130   Marx 1987f, p. 421.

131   The $MEGA^2$ editors base their claim on a text by Marx from the summer of 1861 entitled *'Referate zu meinen eignen Heften'*, where he registers the temporary existence of a 'Notebook C' (see Marx 1987g, p. 518 and Marx 1980, p. 272), which is not extant (at least as a complete notebook). However, there is no direct, unambiguous proof that this notebook contained a chapter of the *Urtext* on value.

132   See Marx 1980, p. 370.

133   See Marx 1983f, p. 358.

*   [*Dasein*] – often translated as 'existence'.

In the *Notes on Adolph Wagner's 'Lehrbuch der politischen Ökonomie'* (a study which constitutes Marx's last text on the critique of political economy), Marx elucidates his own procedure in the first volume of *Capital*. This late text by Marx is particularly revealing with regard to the problem of the beginning of the exposition, and clarifies important aspects of Marx's understanding of his method. Here, Marx writes that he did not choose 'concepts' or the 'concept of value' as his starting point; his point of departure is rather 'the simplest social form in which the product of labour presents itself in contemporary society, and this is the "commodity"'.[134] Marx states that he analyses the commodity initially in its form of manifestation; here, he finds that it is on the one hand a use-value in its natural form, and on the other 'a bearer of exchange-value, and from this point of view it is itself an "exchange-value"'.[135] According to Marx, the analysis of the latter dimension of the commodity shows that exchange-value is a form of manifestation of commodity-value; Marx then 'start[s] on the analysis of the latter'.[136] Marx clearly states how his method is *not* to be understood: 'Thus I do not divide value into use-value and exchange-value as opposites into which the abstraction "value" splits up; rather, I divide the concrete social form of the product of labour, the "commodity": the latter is on the one hand, use-value and on the other, "value," not exchange value, since the mere form of appearance is not its own content'.[137] Marx further argues that his analysis of the commodity at the beginning of his exposition does not merely refer to the dual character of the commodity as the unity of use-value and value, but also to the dual character of the labour objectified in the commodity.

With regard to the 'problem of the beginning' of Marx's exposition, two significant contributions to research from the discussion of the 1980s and 1990s can now be considered. Gerhard Göhler's 1980 habilitation thesis on the structure of Marx's exposition within the respective sections on the commodity and the exchange process revolves around the question of the status of dialectic in Marx's exposition. In this connection, Göhler focuses on the first chapter of *A Contribution to the Critique of Political Economy* on the one hand, and on the sections on the commodity and the exchange process in the first two editions of *Capital* (1867 and 1872/3) on the other. According to Göhler, a distinction between two different types of dialectic can be discerned by comparing Marx's various approaches to his exposition with specific reference to the manner in which money and the exchange process are developed from the category of

---

134 Marx 1989d, p. 544.
135 Ibid.
136 Marx 1989d, pp. 544–5.
137 Marx 1989d, p. 545 [translation modified – N.G.].

the commodity. Göhler considers an 'emphatic dialectic' to be operative in *A Contribution to the Critique of Political Economy*; particularly decisive here, in Göhler's view, is Marx's conception of contradiction. In the case of 'emphatic dialectic', the Berlin-based political scientist argues that an explicative function can be attributed to contradiction within the context of argumentation – i.e. the movement of the contradiction itself is the decisive driving force within the categorial development and the progression of the exposition. Göhler maintains, however, that the execution of the emphatic dialectic is miscarried in the development of commodities, money and exchange process in *A Contribution to the Critique of Political Economy*. 'The failure of the emphatic dialectic which is comprehensively applied in the development of money and the exchange process is ... a result of the fact that elements are placed together which do actually belong together objectively, but which, of a necessity which is equally objective, must be developed separately from one another'.[138] According to Göhler, the universal equivalent is the result of the sequential development of the value-form, whereas the exchange process is conceived of as the result of the development of a contradiction. The execution of this latter development alone would not 'yield the universal equivalent'.[139] Göhler argues as follows:

> Since the development of the value-form is not fully integrated into the development of the exchange process, the development of the contradiction in the exchange process cannot be executed in a continuous and comprehensive way for its relevant elements, and thus cannot be rigorously carried through in an emphatic sense; yet this is what is required in order to sustain this development.[140]

By contrast, the dialectic is 'reduced' – according to Göhler – in both the above-mentioned editions of *Capital*. The Berlin-based political scientist refers in this context to a descriptive (as opposed to explicative) function of contradiction. With regard to *Capital*, Göhler explains that the 'difficulties of the interconnection between forms of value and the exchange process ... are removed from the main development and concentrated within a separate treatment of the exchange process'.[141] Göhler surmises that there was a break in Marx's relation to Hegel between *A Contribution to the Critique of Political Economy* and *Capital*, with Marx turning away from Hegel (although Göhler argues that Marx

---

138   Göhler 1980, p. 166.
139   Göhler 1980, p. 166.
140   Ibid.
141   Göhler 1980, p. 167.

never completely broke free from Hegel's influence). Although Göhler's study represents one of the milestones within the German-language methodological discussion of Marx, there has not been a reception of his approach in other countries that could compare with the reception of the work of Hans-Georg Backhaus, for example. In Germany, however, Göhler represents one of the essential points of reference for the methodological discussion of the critique of political economy, with his approach meeting with both approval (for instance from Christian Iber in relation to the determination of the relation between the structure of the value-form and the chiastic structure of exchange)[142] and criticism. Among the criticisms of Göhler's approach is that levelled by Helmut Brentel at the former's central thesis of 'Marx's reduction of the dialectic', which Brentel finds unpersuasive. Another critique by Dieter Wolf focuses in particular on Göhler's understanding of contradiction in Marx.[143]

An original contribution to the discussion of the 'problem of the beginning' of the critique of political economy is the thesis developed by the Argentinian-Mexican philosopher and theologian, Enrique Dussel, in research carried out in the 1980s and 1990s. In his analysis of the 'chapter on method' in the 1857 *Introduction to the Critique of Political Economy*, Dussel regards the ascent from the simple and abstract to the intellectually concrete, to the complex, to the concrete totality, as a dialectical element.[144] According to Dussel, the structure of categories in the critique of political economy is prescribed by their internal interconnection in modern capitalist society. In the first book in his trilogy, Dussel also investigates Marx's conception of the logic of his exposition from the plan outlined in the 1857 *Introduction* to the 'Index to the Seven Notebooks'[145] compiled by Marx in 1858.[146] As was indicated above, in the second book of his trilogy Dussel refers not only to the *1861–63 Manuscripts*, in which Marx follows up on his text, *A Contribution to the Critique of Political Economy*, but also to the latter text itself. Dussel points out that although Marx indicates his intention to choose 'Value' as the title for his opening section in his letter to Engels of 2 April 1858, as well as in his 'Index to the Seven Notebooks', he then, in a letter to Engels dated 13 January 1859, refers to his opening chapter

---

142 Iber has published a lecture series held at the Institute for Philosophy of the Free University of Berlin in book form (see Iber 2005).

143 On the critical engagement with Göhler, see Brentel 1989, pp. 347 ff. and Wolf 2002, p. 224. Michael Heinrich also criticises Göhler (see Heinrich 1999a, pp. 228 f.).

144 See Dussel 1985, p. 52.

145 The index bears this title because the *Grundrisse* manuscript is contained in seven notebooks.

146 See Dussel 1985, pp. 61 ff.

under the heading of 'The Commodity'.[147,*] (Dussel's research can be supplemented here as follows: Marx already gives 'The Commodity' as the title of his opening chapter in a letter to Engels dated 29 November 1858).[148] According to Dussel, the structure of the *Urtext* of *A Contribution to the Critique of Political Economy* – a text which was drafted in the latter half of 1858 before Marx composed the published version of *A Contribution* – is already anticipated in a letter written to Engels on 2 April 1858; the structure is the following: value – money – capital.[149] As is well known, it is not only *A Contribution to the Critique of Political Economy* that begins with the category of the commodity: this is also true of *Capital*. Dussel interprets the individual commodity as the elementary existence** of bourgeois wealth;[150] as unity of use-value and value, the commodity is the category which forms Marx's starting point.[151] Value is in turn interpreted by the Argentinian as the 'fundamental being' of capital.

Yet there is also a further line of argument in Dussel's search for the category that forms the starting point of Marx's critique of political economy. For Dussel, the most fundamental opposition which Marx establishes in his critique of political economy is not so much that between concrete-useful and abstract-universal labour, nor that between use-value and value. The Argentinian philosopher maintains instead that it is first and foremost the antagonism between 'living labour' and 'objectified labour' which is accorded central significance. Dussel argues that 'living labour' has a decisive function, and advances the conception that, as the source of value and surplus value, it is extrinsic to capital. This source is subsumed by capital, however. The crux of Dussel's interpretation of Marx is that the category of 'living labour' is the actual starting point of the dialectical exposition. For the Argentinian, 'living labour' is actually a primordial category within the structure of categories – in fact it is the very first.[152] In turn, 'living labour' stands in opposition to 'objectified labour', which is thus of a similar relevance for the beginning of the dialectical exposition. The Latin American philosopher and theologian writes: 'The dialectical logical

---

147   See Dussel 1988, p. 27.

*   The first two chapters of Dussel 1988 were not included in the English-language edition (Dussel 2001a).

148   Marx 1983f, p. 358.

149   See Dussel 1985, p. 330.

**   [*Dasein*] – this could also be rendered as 'determinate being'.

150   See Dussel 1988, p. 28.

151   See Dussel 1985, pp. 332 f.

152   See Dussel 1990, p. 421.

movement of *Capital* begins in the radical contradiction of "living labor" and "objectified labor" as capital'.[153]

Nevertheless, this raises the question as to what to make of a beginning of an exposition which has 'the commodity' as its starting point, as is undeniably the case in the first volume of *Capital*. On Dussel's interpretation, there are evidently two 'beginnings', each with a different status. Dussel argues as follows in *El Último Marx*: 'In effect, it was necessary to begin with Chapter One on the commodity and money ... in order to comply with a pedagogical order, or the order of the "exposition"; *logically*, however, it was necessary to start with the absolute contradiction between "money and living labour"'.[154] It is worth taking a closer look at Dussel's line of argument here. The Argentinian considers that the function of Marx's plans for the architectonic of his critique of political economy is to problematise the 'ordering' of economic categories within the context of the development of the concept of capital. Yet Dussel establishes a distinction here: in terms of the 'ordering of the enquiry', which is a matter of a logical, essence-related ordering, the fourth chapter of the second edition of *Capital* or the second chapter of the first edition – i.e. the section of Marx's text containing the transformation of money into capital – is to be located at the beginning. With regard to the 'ordering of the exposition', however, the first chapter of *Capital* represents the beginning; Dussel understands this 'ordering of the exposition' to be 'pedagogical'. The circumstance that the commodity is the first category to be exhibited does not signify for Dussel that it also occupies first place in the essence-related 'internal' ordering of categories.

In fact, 'living labour' constitutes a central categorial point of reference in Marx's work for Dussel. According to the Argentinian philosopher and theologian, it is the creatrix of all value and all wealth, and economic categories such as value, the commodity, money, etc. are its modalities.[155] Dussel also attributes a central significance to the category of 'living labour' within the context of his emphatic reference to the character of Marxian theory as critique, insofar as he regards Marx's *critique* of political economy as one that is undertaken from the perspective of 'living labour'.[156]

Within the Anglo-Saxon discussion, the theory formed by Dussel has been the cause of some controversy. Patrick Murray has voiced criticisms of several aspects of Dussel's theory.[157] A major point of criticism is associated with

---

153   Dussel 2001b, p. 20.
154   Dussel 1990, p. 420.
155   See Dussel 2001a, p. 196.
156   See Dussel 2001a, pp. 190–1.
157   See Murray 2002.

Murray's critical view of so-called 'Ricardian Marxism'. Murray argues that a distinction is to be drawn between Marxian theory on the one hand, and 'Ricardian Marxism' on the other. It is only the former, and not the latter, which theorises the *specific social form* of labour within the capitalist mode of production. Murray places Dussel under the rubric of 'Ricardian Marxism', and defines the latter as follows: 'The hallmark of Ricardian Marxism is that it takes the theory of surplus-value to be the heart and soul of Marx's critique of capitalism'.[158] Murray argues that Dussel underestimates the importance of Marx's exposition of the sphere of simple circulation at the beginning of his exposition in *Capital*, and likewise the problematic of the specific social form which is the object of Marx's exposition. This element of Murray's critique of Dussel is relevant in relation to the problem of the beginning in Marx's exposition, since it is in this context that the question of the significance of Marx's exposition of the categories of the commodity and money – i.e. the categories of the first section of the second edition of *Capital* – can be posed.

A response to Murray's critique of Dussel was formulated by Fred Moseley.[159] The latter takes the view that the 'heart and soul' of Marx's critique of capitalism encompasses both his theory of surplus value and exploitation on the one hand, and his theory of specific forms on the other. Moseley maintains that the category of the commodity is to be considered the logical starting point with regard to Marx's exposition of his theory of capitalism. Moseley also notes that 'an important point of agreement between Murray and myself, and with Dussel as well, is that *Capital* is about capitalism from the very beginning – that is, from chapter 1 of volume 1'.[160] Short shrift is given here to any interpretation which holds that the beginning of Marx's exposition is concerned with a pre-capitalist 'simple commodity production'.

2.3   The Relation of Marx's Critique of Political Economy to Hegel's Philosophy as Reflected in the International Debate

In connection with the international debate on the problematic of Marx's exposition, it is necessary to undertake a closer examination of a theme which has been the subject of intensive discussion in scientific research on Marx's method in his critique of political economy, namely Marx's relation to Hegel. In this context, the central focus is the relation of Marx's 'mature' critique of

---

158   Murray 2002, p. 120.
159   See Moseley 2002. For Moseley's view of Dussel, see also Moseley 2001.
160   Moseley 2002, p. 127.

political economy to Hegel's philosophy, rather than the extensive reception of Hegel undertaken by Marx in his early work.

In the second part of this work, two interpretative orientations (those of the Della Volpean and Althusserian Schools) were considered whose position with regard to Marx's relation to Hegel was characterised above all by the foregrounding of a sharp demarcation between these two thinkers. Although it is obvious that 'anti-Hegelianism' by no means represents a *differentia specifica* of Althusser and Colletti, it should be noted that the Della Volpean School stood at the head of the 'anti-Hegelian' movement within Marxism, at least in Western Europe. Within a number of varieties of Marxism, including Soviet or Eastern European orthodox Marxism, Japanese and Latin American Marxism, there were certain tendencies which were opposed to any 'Hegelianisation' of Marxian theory (in the case of Latin American Marxism, this opposition was mediated by the local reception of Althusser). Also worth noting within this context is the anti-Hegelian orientation of the Anglo-Saxon 'analytical Marxism' of the 1980s. In parts of the debate of the 1960s and 1970s, however, there already existed a current of interpretation of the Hegel-Marx relation which deviated from anti-Hegelian interpretations; an example of this current can be seen in the positive reference to Hegel within the Marx-interpretation of Hans-Jürgen Krahl. It should by no means be assumed, then, that it is legitimate to make unqualified generalisations about an 'anti-Hegelianism' within the Marx debate of the 1960s and 1970s. Since that period, there has been a further development in the state of the discussion internationally. It is worth recalling here various theoretical approaches of the 1990s which distance themselves from the anti-Hegelian discourse, including that of the Iranian, Ali Shamsavari. A 'New Dialectic' approach proposing a positive redefinition of the Hegel-Marx relation has emerged at approximately the same time within the Anglo-Saxon world. Yet 'anti-Hegelianism' cannot be said to have disappeared from the international Marx debate in recent times, as can be demonstrated by reference to the interpretative approach of John Rosenthal (see below).

The relation of the Marxian to the Hegelian method can by no means be reduced to a mere 'application' or 'transfer': the complexity of the Hegel-Marx relation should not be underestimated. Marx engaged critically with Hegel's *Phenomenology of Spirit*, his *Philosophy of Right* and his *Logic* (both the *Science of Logic* and the *Encyclopaedia Logic*). Marx undertook his reception of Hegel both in various theoretical contexts and at different periods in the production of his theoretical works.

Marx adopted different positions vis-à-vis Hegel at different points in time. Within international research on Marx, there is in general a high level of familiarity with the sources documenting his critical engagement with Hegel.

Worthy of mention in this context, alongside the *Critique of Hegel's Philosophy of Right* of 1843 and other writings from this same decade, are Marx's mature works on the critique of political economy, including his 1857 *Introduction* and the postface to the second edition of the first volume of *Capital*, as well as his correspondence. Other sources are less well known, however. With regard to the period from 1857 onwards, in addition to the numerous better-known passages from texts where Marx engages critically with Hegel's philosophy, an excerpt made by Marx from the *Encyclopaedia Logic* has also been preserved (it is difficult to date Marx's excerpt, although it was probably made at the beginning of the 1860s); although the corresponding volume of $MEGA^2$ has not as yet been published, this excerpt has been available to the scientific community for decades, and yet it has thus far received little attention in specialist circles.[161]

In the 1960s, the Czechoslovak philosopher, Jindřich Zelený, distinguished four different stages in Marx's critical engagement with Hegel's philosophy. The first stage identified by Zelený occurs in Marx's 1841 dissertation, *The Difference Between the Democritean and Epicurean Philosophy of Nature*; the second stage corresponds to Marx's 1843 critical reception of Hegel's philosophy of right; the third stage is associated with the *Economic and Philosophical Manuscripts*; the fourth stage comprises *The German Ideology* and *The Poverty of Philosophy*. Zelený considers the latter two stages to be particularly significant; the Czech philosopher regards the period from 1844 to 1847 as the most important and philosophically richest period in Marx's reception of Hegel. Yet how, on this basis, would Zelený classify those of Marx's critical engagements with Hegel that are documented in his 1857 *Introduction*, in his 'mature' work from 1857/8 onwards, and, not least, in his correspondence from his London period? Zelený responds as follows:

> The question whether, in the further development of Marx's thought in relation to Hegel's philosophy, there are any changes or modifications which could be described as constituting a new, specific stage in Marx's critical confrontation with Hegel must be answered in the negative. The relation of Marx to Hegel remains in essence as elucidated in principle by the former following a relatively complicated development in the fourth stage of his reception of Hegel – i.e. in *The German Ideology* and the *Poverty of Philosophy*.[162]

---

161   See O'Malley and Schrader 1977.

162   Zelený 1980, p. 179. [Translation modified – N.G.].

In the 1980s, Andreas Arndt distinguished various phases of Marx's engagement with Hegel from 1857 onwards. Arndt identifies Marx's work on the 1857 *Introduction* as marking the beginning of a period of intensive critical confrontation with Hegel. This was followed, however, by a temporary 'virtual silence' in relation to Hegel on the part of Marx once he had resumed his work on *A Contribution to the Critique of Political Economy* in 1861. While working on his *1861–63 Manuscripts*, and, more precisely, on his *Theories of Surplus-Value* (written during the course of 1862), Marx engaged critically with the problematic of the method of political economy. According to Arndt, Marx reconsidered the category of contradiction at this time. Arndt writes as follows:

> After his intensive experimentation with Hegel during the concluding phase of his enquiry into the systematic interconnection of the categories of bourgeois society and in his first attempt at an exposition (up to 1859), both of which serve to clarify for Marx the outline of the system of the critique of political economy, the programme of dialectic is first concretised through the elucidation of the category of contradiction in his direct critical engagement with the method of bourgeois economics.[163,*]

Arndt discerns a continuous critical engagement by Marx with the problem of dialectic and Hegelian philosophy during the period from 1865 to 1868. Arndt maintains that subsequently – from the late 1860s up to Marx's death in 1883 – this critical engagement rather recedes into the background.[164,**]

In the context of the question as to the theoretical relation between Marx's critique of political economy and Hegel's thought, it is worth indicating, by means of a short excursus on Hegel's treatment of political economy, the fundamental difference between the way in which Hegel and Marx confronted this science. This short excursus on Hegel's engagement with economic theory is also rendered necessary by the emergence in the 1990s of a novel situation in the history of the debate around the reception of Hegel and Marx. An interpretative current has formed within the Anglo-Saxon discussion of the Hegel-Marx relation – at least according to the account given by Ian Fraser and Tony Burns

---

163   Arndt 1985, p. 230.

*   Arndt's study has recently been republished with the addition of a new afterword (see Arndt 2012).

164   In another study, Arndt emphasises a specific concept of objective mediation which he discerns in Marx (see Arndt 2004, pp. 37 ff.). For a recent approach by Arndt to Marx's relation to Hegelian dialectic, see Arndt 2008.

**   See also Arndt 2013 for a subsequent contribution on this theme.

in their historical survey of this debate – which has broken with the previous orientations guiding the exegesis of this theoretical relation. According to Fraser and Burns, this new interpretative tendency takes a radically different path, one which – it might be added – does not so much involve a specific or novel interpretation of Marx, but rather of Hegel. To put it concisely: in this context, Hegel is not construed as an idealist, but as a materialist.

Fraser and Burns point out, however, that the central focus of this interpretative current is not so much Hegel's metaphysics as his economic, social and political thought: 'In so far as he is of significance for the history of Marxism, the true importance of Hegel, on this view, is to be found in his social and political thought, or in what is usually referred to as his *Realphilosophie*, rather than in his general philosophy or his metaphysics'.[165] These two authors expand upon this point as follows: 'From this point of view, then, there is no need for Marxists to *appropriate* a modified, materialist version of Hegel's philosophical idealism into their own thought. For Marx's "materialism" can be derived *directly* from Hegel's own social thought without any such adaptation or modification'.[166] Thus, the 'fundamental claim that is made by this new reading of the Hegel-Marx connection' consists in the assertion 'that Hegel's dialectic and Marx's dialectic are one and the same'.[167] Regardless of the evaluation that might be made in relation to this new approach to the interpretation of the Hegel-Marx relation and of Hegelian thought in particular, it is in any case clear that, given the existence of this new interpretation, an exclusive or one-sided focus on the relation of Marx's critique of political economy to the *Science of Logic* or to the *Phenomenology of Spirit* is no longer permissible, and that Hegel's engagement with economic and social questions merits some attention.

Hegel's relation to the science of political economy is much discussed within research on Hegel. Crucially, Hegel integrated his references to political economy within his philosophy of right and social philosophy, or, to be more precise, within his corresponding theory of civil society.* This is to say that although he recognised political economy as an independent science, it did not have this status in his own treatment. Jürgen Kuczynski has referred to 'Hegel's "philosophisation" of the economy'.[168] Georg Ahrweiler perceives a

---

165   Fraser and Burns 2000, p. 21.

166   Ibid.

167   Fraser and Burns 2000, p. 22.

*   [*bürgerlichen Gesellschaft*] – the convention in English translations of Hegel's philosophy of right is to render *bürgerliche Gesellschaft* as 'civil society', although it should be borne in mind that the term is translated in many other contexts as 'bourgeois society'.

168   Kuczynski 1981, p. 258.

certain 'dilettantism' at work in the way Hegel refers to the economic problematic.[169] A well-known statement by the philosopher in relation to 'political
economy'[170],* is set out in § 189 of *Elements of the Philosophy of Right*. For Hegel,
'political economy' is a science whose development 'is of interest in showing
how *thought* extracts from the endless multitude of details with which it is
initially confronted the simple principles of the thing [*Sache*], the understanding which works within it and controls it (see Smith, Say, and Ricardo)'.[171] A
question arising in relation to this paragraph and its listing of the economists,
Adam Smith, Jean-Baptiste Say and David Ricardo, is that of Hegel's reception of these economic thinkers. It is likely that Hegel was better acquainted
with the Scot's – i.e. Smith's – theory than with that of the other two economists.[172] However, Andreas Arndt suspects that there were considerable omissions in Hegel's reception of Smith. In *Elements of the Philosophy of Right*, Hegel
showed no interest in the Scot's approaches to the theory of value or his distinction between use-value and exchange-value.[173] A further important question for Hegel research is that of his reception of the economic thought of
James Steuart.[174] In his mid-twentieth century study of the young Hegel, György
Lukács alerted a broad readership to an annotated commentary to Steuart's

169　Ahrweiler 1976, p. 101.
170　With regard to Hegel's terminology, Norbert Waszek refers to a science 'which Hegel
　　　designates in his *Elements of the Philosophy of Right* employing the unusual expression
　　　"*Staatsökonomie*" ... but which he also refers to – for the most part synonymously – as
　　　'*politische Ökonomie*" and "*Nationalökonomie*" ' (see Waszek 1995, p. 36).
*　　　All three terms – *Staatsökonomie* (literally: state economics), *politische Ökonomie* and
　　　Nationalökonomie (literally: national economics) – can be rendered in English as 'political
　　　economy' (the latter term can also be translated as 'economics').
171　Hegel 1991, p. 227.
172　Norbert Waszek writes that although it was unlikely that 'Hegel had a noticeable direct
　　　knowledge of Say and Ricardo – that is why there are no other references and no identifi-
　　　able allusions to their writings – he knew of them, probably through the review journals,
　　　he perceived them as independent followers of Smith, and he thus appreciates – and one
　　　need not read more into the reference – that Say and Ricardo (along with Smith) were the
　　　acknowledged leaders of the subject' (Waszek 1988, p. 133). According to Andreas Arndt,
　　　Hegel became acquainted with Ricardo through Say; Arndt points out that Hegel's liter-
　　　ary estate contained Say's 1819 text, *Principes de l'économie politique par Dav. Ricardo* (see
　　　Arndt 1988, p. 327).
173　See Arndt 1988, p. 326. According to Arndt, it is doubtful whether Hegel ever 'read more
　　　than the first chapter in the first volume of *Wealth of Nations*'. Arndt argues that 'otherwise
　　　it would be difficult to explain the fact that Hegel was unable to see the problem of wage
　　　labour and capital despite his references to Smith' (Arndt 1988, p. 326).
174　See Chamley 1965.

1767 *Inquiry into the Principles of Political Economy* written by Hegel between February and May 1799.[175] Since the Steuart commentary itself has not been preserved, and the only available source for this work is a brief report in the biography of Hegel by Rosenkranz, a student of the German philosopher, it has been suggested that 'it would be advisable to refrain from any remarks based on mere speculation'.[176] Ernst Erdös, who has described Hegel as a 'critic of bourgeois society on the terrain of bourgeois society', considers the Stuttgart-born philosopher to be a follower of neither Smith nor Steuart.[177] By contrast, Erdös insists that Hegel's independence is worth emphasising. Other interpreters challenge the idea that Hegel operated on the level of the modern (Anglo-Saxon) political economy of his time.[178]

Finally, it is important to note the fundamental difference between the Hegelian and the Marxian relation to political economy. Hegel clearly marked out a position in relation to political economy in the section on the 'system of needs' in his doctrine on civil society in *Elements of the Philosophy of Right*; however, his doctrine of civil society is thematised within his philosophy of right, which is a component of the philosophy of objective spirit, and thus part of his philosophical system. By contrast, Marx was concerned to provide a fundamental critique of the science of political economy, and simultaneously to revolutionise it theoretically, rather than merely seeking (as did Hegel) to integrate into a philosophical system some of the insights gained as a result of a critical engagement with this discipline. Accordingly, the economic research carried out by Marx, in particular his critical engagement with economic science, was located not only in a totally different theoretical and programmatic context, but was also incomparably more intensive than that undertaken by Hegel. Marx's exposition in *Capital* presupposes the total theoretical penetration of his object, including the internal interconnection between economic categories and relations. Such a project was undertaken by Marx, and not by Hegel.

Before parts of the international discussion of the Hegel-Marx relation can be considered more closely, it is necessary to briefly indicate some passages in Marx's texts and correspondence which afford an insight into Marx's own understanding of his theoretical relation to Hegel. In the famous postface to the second edition of the first volume of *Capital*, Marx writes the following: 'My dialectical method is, in its foundations, not only different from the Hegelian,

---

175   See Lukács 1975, p. 170. See also Riedel 1982, p. 120.

176   Sayama 2004, p. 22.

177   Erdös 1986, p. 76.

178   See Arndt and Lefèvre 1988 and Priddat 1990.

but exactly opposite to it'. According to Marx, Hegel transforms the process of thinking – under the name of the Idea – into an independent subject, and into the 'demiurge of the real', such that the real merely forms the external manifestation of the Idea. Marx contrasts his own position: '[w]ith me the reverse is true: the ideal is nothing but the material world reflected in the mind of man, and translated into forms of thought'. Marx continues as follows: 'I criticized the mystificatory side of the Hegelian dialectic nearly thirty years ago, at a time when it was still the fashion. But just when I was working at the first volume of *Capital*, the ill-humoured, arrogant and mediocre epigones who now talk large in educated German circles began to take pleasure in treating Hegel in the same way as the good Moses Mendelssohn treated Spinoza in Lessing's time, namely as a "dead dog"'. Marx states that this had prompted him to profess himself Hegel's pupil, and that he had occasionally coquetted with Hegel's mode of expression.

> The mystification which the dialectic suffers in Hegel's hands by no means prevents him from being the first to present its general forms of motion in a comprehensive and conscious manner. With him it is standing on its head. It must be inverted, in order to discover the rational kernel within the mystical shell.[179]

Marx's critique is directed at the 'mystification' of dialectic or method at the hands of Hegel. In his letter of 16 January 1858, Marx states that his leafing through of Hegel's *Logic* has been of 'great use' to him 'as regards *method* of treatment',[180] and gives notice of a project which he presumably never realised: 'If ever the time comes when such work is again possible, I should very much like to write 2 or 3 sheets making accessible to the common reader the rational aspect of the method which Hegel not only discovered but also mystified'.[181] No such text was published by Marx or to be found in the materials contained in his literary estate. In a letter to Lassalle dated 31 May 1858, Marx expresses his opinion that Hegelian dialectic is the ultimate word in philosophy, but that it is necessary 'to divest it of the mystical aura given it by Hegel'.[182] Over a decade later, Marx was prompted, in an exchange with Ludwig Kugelmann, to refer critically to the 'mystical form' of the dialectic in Hegel. In his letter of 6 March 1868, Marx writes that the reviewer of *Capital*, Eugen Dühring, knows very well

---

179   Marx 1976a, pp. 102–3.
180   Marx 1983a, p. 249.
181   Ibid.
182   Marx 1983c, p. 316.

that 'my method of exposition is not Hegelian, since I am a materialist, and Hegel an idealist. Hegel's dialectic is the basic form of all dialectic, but only after being stripped of its mystical form, and it is precisely this which distinguishes my method'.[183] Shortly after, on 9 May 1868, Marx advised Joseph Dietzgen as follows: 'When I have cast off the burden of political economy, I shall write a "Dialectic". The true laws of dialectics are already contained in Hegel, though in a mystical form. What is needed is to strip away this form'.[184]

The author of *Capital* recognised that the method of the exposition which was to elucidate and develop the internal interconnections of the capitalist economy was necessarily given by the latter's structure itself. Rather than establishing an '*a priori* construction', as Marx puts it in his postface to the 1873 second edition of the first volume of *Capital*, the 'object' must first be sufficiently penetrated in its specific structure by means of a protracted and detailed process of enquiry in order to make possible an explanation and development of the object's internal interconnections in the exposition. Marx's approach was too differentiated to be considered a mere external 'transfer' or 'application' of Hegelian logic or method to the economy. In his letter of 1 February 1858 to Engels, Marx – referring to Lassalle – had already indicated precisely how *not* to proceed with Hegelian logic: 'It is plain to me from this one note that, in his second grand opus, the fellow intends to expound political economy in the manner of Hegel. He will discover to his cost that it is one thing for a critique to take a science to the point at which it admits of a dialectical presentation, and quite another to apply an abstract, ready-made system of logic to vague presentiments of just such a system'.[185]

Various interpretations of the Hegel-Marx relation will be presented in what follows. No more than a minimal selection of contributions to the international debate on this question can be considered here, however, as it is beyond the scope of the present study to provide anything like an adequate survey of this debate since 1980. With the exception of a brief presentation of the interpretative approach of Fred Schrader, the following exposition focuses on contributions from the Anglo-Saxon discussion, given the prominent role played by the interpretation of the Hegel-Marx relation in the latter context.

In a pioneering study, published in 1980, on Marx's preparatory work for *Capital* in the period from 1850 to 1858, Fred Schrader advanced the thesis that the comments made by Marx on his relation to Hegel's *Logic* while draft-

---

183   Marx 1987h, p. 544.
184   Marx 1988c, p. 31.
185   Marx 1983d, p. 261.

ing the *Grundrisse* – i.e. that he had leafed through Hegel's *Logic*, which had been of great use to him in terms of his own method of treatment –[186] are to be taken literally. 'No significant reception of Hegel occurred, no world spirit was thus revealed to be capital, nor yet was it a matter of deciphering an identity between the movements of an essence and those of value'.[187] According to Schrader, a partial analogy with certain aspects of Hegelian logic in the chapter on money in the *Grundrisse* – Schrader acknowledges that this analogy can be drawn – is given by certain parallels between aspects of Hegelian logic and the material used by Marx in certain places. To what does this 'material' refer? In Schrader's view, it can be argued that there are indeed correspondences to Hegel in the *Grundrisse* in the context of Marx's reception of the economists, Sismondi, Storch and Say – more precisely, these correspondences are given by parallels between certain dimensions of Hegelian logic and aspects of the considerations of these economists with regard to the theories of money and capital. 'Following Marx's references, it can be established that, at decisive junctures in his *Rohentwurf*, and in fact in those very passages which correspond to Hegelian logic, he relied on Sismondi, Storch and Say not only in an economic and factual sense, but also conceptually, and even in terms of his overall conception'.[188]

Schrader has since reassessed the results of his research that he first published in 1980. He now argues that what has to be clarified is whether, when and where Marx relates to Hegelian logic, to Spinoza's concept of substance, or to Leibniz's logic of relations. At stake in this enquiry, according to Schrader, are important findings with regard to Marx's *modus operandi*. Schrader argues that it is conceivable, on the one hand, that Marx proceeded on a completely eclectic and pragmatic basis, that his mode of operation was characterised by unsystematic improvisation, influenced by his current reading at any given point in time, with 'a specific concept "fitting" particularly well at a given juncture'.[189] Schrader recognises that this point of view bears a similarity to his own interpretation in 1980. 'On the other hand', Schrader continues, 'it might be suspected that this usage is not quite so innocent after all, and that, behind the quote, Marx is in fact also establishing a relation to the author quoted. In both cases, the question of the status of conceptuality would have to be posed'.[190] One dimension of Schrader's new intervention on the issue of the Hegel-Marx

---

186 See Marx 1983a, p. 249.

187 Schrader 1980, p. 136.

188 Schrader 1980, p. 134.

189 Schrader 2007, p. 177. See also Schrader 1998, p. 87.

190 Schrader 2007, p. 177.

relation consists in his questioning of the frequent tendency to privilege the *Science of Logic* or the *Philosophy of Right* in interpretations of Marx's method and his relation to the Stuttgart-born philosopher (the *Phenomenology of Spirit* could arguably also be added to the above works). 'Other published works by Hegel which were undoubtedly read by Marx are not taken into consideration. These include ... the *Encyclopaedia*, and not merely the "lesser *Logic*" (§§ 19–244), but also the *Philosophy of Objective Spirit* (§§ 483–552), in which Hegel integrates logic and social theory into a whole system'.[191] Schrader himself deserves credit for having caused slightly more attention to be focused on the 'lesser *Logic*' contained in the *Encyclopaedia*, and particularly on its rather neglected reception by Marx (an excerpt by Marx from this work by Hegel was published by Schrader in collaboration with Joseph O'Malley in the 1970s).

A little more than three decades ago, the Marx-interpreter, Sean Sayers, felt compelled to insist to the Anglo-Saxon readership that dialectic is not a mere absurdity.[192] In the intervening period, the discussion centring around Christopher Arthur, Tony Smith and others – a discussion which is of significance for the debate on dialectic – has become ever more established within Anglo-Saxon research into Marx. It would appear that Arthur identifies a decisive key to an adequate reconstruction of Marx's critique of political economy precisely in his reference to Hegel's logic. An edited volume published in 1993 by Fred Moseley represents a milestone in the development of the Hegel-Marx debate within the Anglo-Saxon reception of Marx; three of the interpretative approaches included in this volume will be presented here.[193,*]

Christopher Arthur's 'Hegelianising' approach has already been referred to in the expositional survey of the Anglo-Saxon discussion of Marx given above.

---

191   Schrader 2007, p. 177.
192   'What then is dialectic? First of all one must see that it is not a mere absurdity, but a philosophy, a logic, a way of seeing the world' (Sayers 1980, p. 2).
193   See Moseley 1993. A follow-up volume featuring contributions from a virtually identical list of authors was published four years later (see Moseley and Campbell 1997). Moseley has also published an important edited volume on Marx's theory of money (see Moseley 2005).
*   The three volumes referred to here (Moseley 1993, Moseley and Campbell 1997, and Moseley 2005) are associated with the International Symposium on Marxian Theory (ISMT), an international forum for researchers with an interest in systematic dialectic and value-form theory established on the initiative of Fred Moseley in 1990. Alongside Moseley, long-standing participants include Christopher Arthur, Riccardo Bellofiore, Patrick Murray, Tony Smith, Martha Campbell, Roberto Fineschi and Geert Reuten. Some 11 edited volumes have so far been published under the auspices of the ISMT (see https://chrisarthur .net/international-symposium-on-marxian-theory-ismt/ for details).

In Arthur's view, the question of how Marx's critique of political economy bene-
fitted from his appropriation of Hegelian logic is to be taken very seriously.
Arthur draws attention to the significance of form-theory (and thus echoes
Helmut Brentel's interventions in the West German Marx discussion of the
1980s): 'It is agreed by all intelligent Marxists that the question of social form
is the key to the Marxian understanding of economic systems'.[194] Accordingly,
Arthur argues that 'Marxist theory needs a science of form'.[195] An important
distinction established by the British philosopher is that between systematic
and historical dialectic: 'On the whole, Marx is trying to use the former, as I
do ...'.[196] Arthur criticises Marx's exposition for its premature introduction of
abstract labour as the substance of value, which causes some readers to see an
'embodied-labour theory of value' in Marx (indeed, for certain form-theorists
within the Anglo-Saxon discussion, such an 'embodied-labour theory of value'
appears to be something of a spectre to be exorcised in any adequate reconstruction of Marx's critique of political economy). It might be asked in this
context whether Arthur might have been influenced by the Uno School, which
likewise considers that Marx introduces abstract labour as the substance of
value prematurely in his exposition. In relation to Hegel's logic, Arthur writes
the following: 'I think that the relationship between Hegel's logic and the value-
form is much closer than that of an external identification of its logical structure, or a methodologically motivated application of its norms of adequacy,
or an expositional strategy that finds it convenient to move from simpler to
more complex structures'.[197] It should be noted that when Arthur uses the term
'value-form' in this context, he refers not merely to the value-form analysis in
the narrow sense, but to a system comprising various moments: the commodity, money and capital. The British philosopher continues as follows: 'I believe
that in some sense the value-form and Hegel's logic are to be identified; we are
not simply applying Hegel's logic to an independent content. It is not that the
value-form happens to generate structures of a complexity mapped by Hegel in
his logical categories; the forms are in effect of such abstract purity as to constitute a real incarnation in the world of the ideas of Hegel's logic'.[198] According to
Arthur, however, it is precisely the proximity to Hegel's logic which casts a critical light on Marx's object. The latter represents, on Arthur's view, an inverted
reality which is systematically alienated from its bearers, it is 'an object that

---

194   Arthur 1993, p. 70.
195   Arthur 1993, p. 71.
196   Arthur 1993, p. 86.
197   Arthur 1993, p. 66.
198   Arthur 1993, p. 66.

in its spiritualisation of material interchange and practical activities into the heaven of pure forms virtually incarnates the Hegelian "Idea".[199] The material abstraction (or 'real abstraction') of the exchange process constitutes a specific reality of 'pure forms'.

With regard to its conceptual content, the peculiar relation which Arthur establishes to Hegel in this context has a specifically socially critical bearing; the significance of this circumstance is underlined by a controversy between Arthur and the Marx-researcher, Tony Smith, which took place in 2003. On that occasion, Arthur observed that the difference between his own approach and that of Smith consisted in the fact that the latter

> criticises capitalism for failing to live up to the demands of Hegel's philo-
> sophy; whereas I think it is to be criticised precisely because it does so.
> I argue this is so because it is a system of self-moving abstraction. Obvi-
> ously, we must be reading Hegel very differently. I agree with the Marx of
> 1843, 1857 and 1872 that Hegel inverts the relation between thought and
> being. My innovation is to argue that capital is also an inverted reality
> with a parallel logic.[200]

In his contribution to the same edited volume of 1993, Tony Smith attempted to identify two different types of dialectical theory in Hegel: 'The first concerns the dialectics of history. Hegel believed that there is a logic of devel-
opment underlying both world history and the history of art, religion, and philosophy. *Dialectics* was the term he used to refer to this logic of development'.

The American interpreter of Hegel and Marx characterises the second type of dialectical theory in Hegel as follows:

> However, the second sort of dialectical theory, found in writings such
> as *The Science of Logic* and *The Philosophy of Right*, is our sole concern
> here. This may be termed systematic dialectics and is concerned with
> the ordering of categories from the simple and abstract to the complex
> and concrete. This ordering does not coincide with the order of events in
> history ...[201]

---

199   Ibid.
200   Arthur 2003a p. 195. On Arthur's critical engagement with Smith, see also Arthur 2003b.
201   Smith 1993, p. 15.

Smith focuses in particular on the second type of dialectical theory in Hegel, and draws on 'systematic dialectic'. The American Marx-researcher argues that 'Marx did indeed make use of a systematic dialectical method similar to that found in Hegel'.[202] Smith's interpretation thus displays a similarity to that of Arthur: Smith, too, distinguishes the systematic dialectic upon which he draws from any 'historical' dialectic. For Smith, the dialectical logic in Marx's critique of political economy consists in the systematic progression from one level of abstraction to the next, and, more precisely, in the circumstance that this occurs on the basis of a 'necessary derivation' of each categorial level from the preceding one. What are the grounds of this necessity? 'The necessity of the derivation is materially grounded in the practice of social agents. Derivations are justified if and only if we can show that social agents operating within one social form would necessarily tend to act in a manner that leads to the introduction of a new social form'.[203] Although without doubt a representative of a kind of 'systematic dialectical' reading of *Capital*, Smith understands Marx's *magnum opus* to be altogether a much more complex work. He expands on this point as follows: '[*Capital*] includes many dimensions that cannot be reduced to the systematic progression of economic categories ... The systematic dialectical reading does not incorporate the whole of the book'.[204] Nonetheless, the American Marx-interpreter maintains that 'systematic dialectic' captures the *leitmotiv* of *Capital*, its underlying theoretical architectonic.

At the beginning of the 1990s, Smith published a monograph presenting his conception of *Capital* as a theory of economic categories that are structured in their relation to one another in accordance with the dialectical logic that Marx appropriated from Hegel. According to Smith, the dialectical method applied by Marx is to be understood as a systematic categorial progression. Smith's interpretative approach is also noteworthy insofar as he attempts to define the criteria that a theory of categories must satisfy 'if it is to capture adequately the immanent unfolding of the subject matter'.[205] Firstly, the theoretical starting point is of decisive importance: the simplest and most abstract category is to be selected as the point of departure, such that the remaining categories can be derived from it. Secondly, a linear progression must be given in the sequence of categories, such that the transition from one category to the next is necessarily grounded in their specific content. Thirdly, 'there is the question

---

202   Smith 1993, p. 16.
203   Smith 1993, p. 25.
204   Ibid.
205   Smith 1990, p. 45.

of *the general categorial/ontological framework* used throughout the theory'.[206] Smith adds that '[w]hen he defined the categories "commodity", "money", "capital", and so on, [Marx] did so in terms of a specific categorial framework found in Hegel's *Logic*, one taken from the level of essence (*Wesen*)'.[207] The American Marx-interpreter argues that the systematic dialectical logic, which is in evidence in *Capital* from beginning to end, displays no methodological ambiguity. Yet, according to Smith, Marx made concessions to his readership: he played down 'the systematic nature of the theory' and emphasised 'the much more accessible historical components of the work'.[208] Smith further comments that an alternative for Marx would have been to anticipate Lenin's famous aphorism: 'It is impossible completely to understand Marx's *Capital*, and especially its first chapter, without having thoroughly studied and understood the *whole* of Hegel's *Logic*. Consequently, half a century later none of the Marxists understood Marx!'[209]

According to the American Marx-researcher, Patrick Murray, a parallel can be drawn between Hegel's Logic of Essence and Marx's theory of value. Murray refers to the problem of essence and manifestation, and observes that Hegel considered that the essence must manifest itself, or, to put it more precisely, 'the essence must appear as something other than itself'. According to Murray, Hegel's Logic of Essence, 'whereby the *essence necessarily appears as something other than itself*, is the pivotal conceptual resource founding Marx's theory of value – value necessarily appears as something other than itself, namely money (price) ...'.[210,*] Murray emphasises the significance for the critique of political economy of Marx's critical engagement with Hegel, by means of which Marx appropriated 'conceptual resources that enabled him to overcome Ricardo's theories of value and capital'. The American interpreter of *Capital* formulates his point as follows: 'I argue that it is precisely the lessons learned from Hegel that make *Capital* great'.[211] Murray opposes the view that Marx merely adopted Ricardo's labour theory of value (there can be no doubt that Murray is correct

---

206 Smith 1990, p. 46.
207 Ibid.
208 Smith 1990, p. 32.
209 Lenin 1976, p. 180.
210 Murray 1993, p. 38.
* See also Murray's monograph on Marx's theory of scientific knowledge (Murray 1988), particularly chapters 11, 13–16, 18, 19, where this argument is situated more broadly within the context of Marx's critical appropriation – within his mature critique of political economy – of Hegelian logic (and Hegelian philosophy more generally).
211 Murray 1993, p. 37.

on this score), and argues that Marx moved beyond the traditional understanding of the problem of essence and manifestation, 'which fails to show that essence (value) must appear (as money)'.[212] According to Murray, Marx himself was able to demonstrate this; Murray develops the point as follows: '*Once we recognize what value is, namely, an abstract, reflective, "social" objectivity, it is evident that it can have no immediate appearance*'.[213] It might be added here that the peculiarity of the concept of value itself (provided this is correctly grasped) necessitates a unity of the theories of value and money. With regard to these latter theories, the American interpreter of Marx develops his argument as follows: 'Because it is an abstraction, a being of reflection, value cannot appear immediately; it must appear as something other than itself. Money proves to be the necessary form of value's appearance – and to be necessary for value's existence – yet money is not value'.[214] Murray's point could be expressed as follows: it is by means of Marx's critique of political economy that the categories abstract labour, value and money can be correctly grasped. Murray's reading of Marx points in a similar direction to that indicated by the current which has emerged in the German-language discussion in connection with the research carried out by Hans-Georg Backhaus, and which can be described as the 'monetary theory of value'.

The interpretative approaches of Tony Smith and Patrick Murray serve to demonstrate, among other things, that a positive reference to Hegel's philosophy has become established within a part of the Anglo-Saxon discussion of the critique of political economy in recent times. After thinkers such as Louis Althusser (who was widely received in the English-speaking world, particularly in the 1970s) and Galvano Della Volpe had established a sharp demarcation between Marx and Hegel, and attempted to distance Marx from Hegel, a completely different interpretative tendency seems to have developed and gathered strength in the Anglo-Saxon Marx debate of the last few decades. Yet this tendency in turn has not remained uncontested; 'anti-Hegelian resistance' has also been offered, as is exemplified by the interpretative approach which will now be outlined.

A further important work of Anglo-Saxon provenance is John Rosenthal's *The Myth of Dialectics*, published in 1998. In this study, Rosenthal is concerned to find a third way beyond the alternative of Hegelian Marxism and analytical Marxism. In this endeavour, he invokes the unity of the theories of value,

---

212   Murray 1993, p. 48.

213   Murray 1993, p. 52.

214   Murray 1993, p. 51.

value-form and money in Marx: 'Marx's so-called "value-theory" is ... from the outset a theory of *money*, and a theory of money, I am suggesting, in a unique sense which finds no exact parallel in either neoclassical economics or classical political economy'.[215] Rosenthal argues that it would also be an error to regard Marx as a Ricardian as far as the theory of value is concerned. On this point, it can be conceded to Rosenthal that he has correctly grasped an essential aspect of Marx's theory of value which is sometimes overlooked in the English-speaking world (and beyond), namely that there is a fundamental difference between Marx's and Ricardo's respective theories of value. Rosenthal further asserts that there is an analogy (although not a homology) between Marx's theory of value and money on the one hand, and Hegel's exposition of the 'Concept' on the other. Rosenthal argues that according to Marx, money is to be grasped as 'a *real universal*: a generality, viz. the common character of all commodities as "exchange-values", which has acquired independent existence in the form of some determinate commodity or "use-value"'.[216] There exists an 'unmistakeable isomorphism' between Hegel's 'Idea' and the 'real form of economic value, viz. money'.[217] Yet Rosenthal takes up an unambiguous position against Hegel and against any 'Hegelianising' reading of Marx.

In Germany, Rosenthal's book has been vehemently criticised. The philosopher, Michael Quante, censures its author for failing to present a treatment of the question of Marx's relation to Hegel free from the interference of political 'positioning': 'Anyone who might have believed that this lamentable feature of Marx-research were now a thing of the past will learn, from reading Rosenthal's book, that this is sadly not the case'.[218] Quante sees Hegel shunted off to the corner of the political Right in Rosenthal's monograph. Quante further argues that Rosenthal's work is characterised by a complete 'lack of familiarity' with and 'prejudiced distortion' of Hegel's philosophy.[219] This critique can be countered, however, by the recognition that Rosenthal's interpretation of Marx's theory of value is a useful reference in relation to a number of important points.

---

215   Rosenthal 1998, p. ix. In addition to his monograph, an essay by Rosenthal on the Hegel-Marx problem has also been the focus of much attention within the English-language debate (see Rosenthal 1999).

216   Rosenthal 1998, p. 139.

217   Ibid.

218   Quante 2002, p. 453.

219   Quante 2002, p. 455.

2.4 *Summary*

Since the 1960s and 1970s, a fundamental characteristic of scientific engagement with Marx's critique of political economy has consisted in the increased focus on Marx's process of enquiry and on his specific exposition. As far as Marx's exposition is concerned, the question of the ascent from the abstract to the concrete and the problem of the beginning have proved to be central points of reference for the reception of Marx. Attention was already devoted to these themes in the 1960s, and the theory which has been formed in relation to these questions also constitutes an important aspect of the period within the history of the reception of Marx stretching back to the 1980s. The insight to be preserved here is that Marx's form of exposition necessarily corresponds to the specific structure of his economic object. With regard to the relation between Hegel's and Marx's method, which is of great relevance for the problematic of the exposition, the key observation to be retained is that this relation is by no means to be reduced to the simple external 'application' or 'transfer' of Hegel's method to an alien 'object'. Furthermore, an important conclusion vis-à-vis the interpretation of the Hegel-Marx relation in general is that it is not only the *Science of Logic* which is to be considered in this context; rather, other texts by the Stuttgart-born philosopher with which Marx engaged critically must also be brought into relation. Since the 1990s in particular, a certain tendency has gained an increasing profile within the international interpretation of the critique of political economy, namely the interpretative current which is characterised by a more open or positive relation to Hegel's philosophy, in marked contrast to the 'anti-Hegelian' positions of Althusser and Colletti. It seems to me that a condition for a productive future debate on the problematic of Marx's 'dialectical exposition' is above all that the question of dialectic be discussed in relation to the specific problems of *economic* theory which Marx attempted to solve in his exposition.[220]

3 The Six-Volume Plan and the Concept of 'Capital in General'

3.1 *The Structure of the Critique of Political Economy in Six Volumes*

An important dimension of Marx's method emerged in the course of his work on the *Grundrisse*, where he outlines the project to expound the internal struc-

---

220   It should be emphasised, however, that the question of dialectic should not be restricted to the problematic of the exposition, since dialectic also exists precisely within the real object of Marx's critique of political economy.

ture and the economic life-process of modern capitalist society in a systematically structured work consisting of six volumes. Within Marx's six-volume plan,
the first volume was to deal with capital, the second with landed property, and
the third with wage labour. These first three volumes in turn form a separate
unity within Marx's six-volume plan, insofar as they were intended to thematise the economic life-conditions of the three great classes of modern bourgeois
society, in contrast to the three following volumes. The fourth and fifth volumes
were to be dedicated to the state and international trade respectively, and the
sixth was to deal with the world market. This six-volume plan, outlined by Marx
in his letter to Lassalle of 22 February 1858 and in his famous letter to Engels of
2 April in the same year,[221] was never to be realised.[222]

Indeed, Marx explains in his letter to Lassalle of 11 March 1858 that he has no
intention of elaborating all six volumes to the same extent; rather, he intends
'to give no more than the broad outline in the last three, whereas in the first
three, which contain the actual nub of the economic argument, some degree of
amplification will be unavoidable'.[223] It is thus safe to assume that Marx aimed
to lay most weight on the volumes on capital, landed property and wage labour.

The first three volumes within the six-volume plan correspond to the class
structure of the capitalist mode of production. However, the population of
those societies in which the capitalist mode of production predominates is not
reducible to the three major classes – the capitalist class, the working class,
and the class of landowners. Marx was of course aware of this circumstance.
In *Theories of Surplus-Value*, he refers to the 'constantly growing number of
the middle classes, those who stand between the workman on the one hand
and the capitalist and landlord on the other'; here Marx points out that '[t]he
middle classes maintain themselves to an ever increasing extent directly out of
revenue, they are a burden weighing heavily on the working base and increase
the social security and power of the upper ten thousand'.[224] Marx represented

---

221   See Marx 1983e, pp. 298 ff.

222   Enrique Dussel has commented that a fraction as small as one seventy-second (!) of Marx's
      planned project is available to readers in the form of works that he himself published.
      Dussel bases his assessment on the following calculation: the volume of *Capital* that Marx
      himself published on the production process of capital represents only one of three parts
      within one of four sections (the sections corresponding to competition, credit and share
      capital are not included) within one of six volumes. Three multiplied by four multiplied
      by six gives 72 (see Dussel 1990, p. 410). It would seem that Dussel includes a dash of Latin
      American humour here.

223   Marx 1983g, p. 287.

224   Marx 1989c, p. 198.

the perspective that 'the mass of the *classe moyenne* should grow and that the proletariat (those who work) should constitute a constantly declining proportion (even though it increases absolutely) of the total population'. According to Marx, '[t]his in fact is the *course* taken by bourgeois society'.[225] Nonetheless, the three major classes are the central focus in Marx's investigation. Despite Marx's thesis of the 'constantly growing number of the middle classes' which stand between the working class on the one hand, and the capitalist class and the class of landowners on the other, it is the latter three classes which form the basic structure of modern capitalist society as far as Marx is concerned. In the third volume of *Capital*, Marx refers to 'all three classes that make up the framework of modern society – wage labourer, industrial capitalist, landowner'.[226]

The question which arises is that of the fate of the six-volume plan in the history of the development of Marx's critique of political economy. Did Marx maintain his original conception of the plan for the architectonic of his critique of political economy?[227] Did this conception undergo changes? Was it ultimately abandoned by Marx? An important part of international research on *Capital* has revolved around such questions for some decades now. A scientific consensus is still a long way from being achieved, however. The thesis that Marx abandoned his six-volume plan could potentially be challenged by dissenters: the latter might appeal to his later indication – in the first volume of *Capital* – of the need for an independent treatment of the complex of problems associated with wage labour:

> Wages themselves again take many forms. This fact is not apparent from the ordinary economic treatises, which, in their crude obsession with the material side [*Stoff*], ignore all differences of form. An exposition of all these forms belongs to the special study of wage-labour, and not, therefore, to this work. Nevertheless, we shall have to give a brief description of the two fundamental forms here.[228]

Does this 'special study of wage-labour' correspond to the previously planned volume on wage labour? It is questionable within this context whether this 'exposition' was still to be carried out within the framework of the original six-

---

225   Marx 1989b, p. 78.

226   Marx 1981a, p. 756.

227   In referring here to the six-volume plan as Marx's original conception of his plan for the architectonic of the critique of political economy, abstraction is made from the plans which he devised in the period before 1858.

228   Marx 1976a, p. 683.

volume structure, and whether this was to be undertaken by Marx himself. Within the context of the problematic of ground rent in the third volume of *Capital*, Marx distinguishes an 'independent treatment of landed property' from his own theoretical approach in *Capital*.[229] Does this imply that Marx planned to undertake such an 'independent treatment of landed property' after completing *Capital*? And would such an 'independent treatment' correspond in the way that it were conceived to the volume on landed property? A further important question is whether the second and third volumes of Marx's original conception were rendered obsolete by the inclusion of a section on wages in the first volume of *Capital* and by the integration of a section on ground rent into the third volume of this work.[230] Inclusions of this kind were certainly not anticipated by Marx within the original six-volume plan, or within the originally planned division of the volume on capital.

One of the most interesting controversies within research on Marx revolves around the question as to whether, and in which form, Marx maintained the six-volume plan, or at least certain of its elements. Research into the problematic of the plan for the architectonic of Marx's project of the critique of political economy was already carried out in the interwar period and in the immediate postwar period by theorists such as Henryk Grossmann, Samezō Kuruma and Fritz Behrens. An important impetus for the discussion was provided by Roman Rosdolsky's monograph, which was to a large extent drafted already in the 1950s, but which was not published until 1968. Since this time, this work has been translated into numerous languages and has even become an international classic. With regard to the first three of the six volumes that Marx's work was to comprise, Rosdolsky comments that the corresponding structure – i.e. the planned division of the categories capital, landed property and wage labour into three separate volumes in this sequence – was by no means devised according to external considerations, but was instead given by the 'inner nature' of the capitalist mode of production itself, by the specific interconnection between these categories which correspond to the class struc-

---

229   Marx 1981a, p. 752.

230   Some qualifications are in order here: although Marx's text in the first edition of the first volume of *Capital* includes a part on wages (see Marx 1983j, pp. 433–56), this does not form a separate section – this change was only made in the second and subsequent editions. In the original manuscript for the third volume of *Capital* contained in the so-called *1863–65 Manuscripts*, which is not yet divided into seven sections and 52 chapters (these divisions were introduced in Engels's edition), but merely into seven chapters, the part of the text on ground rent of course has the status of a separate chapter (rather than a separate section). See Marx 2004.

ture of bourgeois society. In working on the *Grundrisse*, Marx had, according to Rosdolsky, found himself compelled 'not only to disregard the category of landed property ... but also to omit a more detailed examination of the forms of wages in order to work out the concept of capital in its purity'.[231] On Rosdolsky's view, Marx made a transition in 1864–5 from his original plan to a new one, and in this context Rosdolsky establishes a distinction between the first three and the final three volumes of Marx's sextet: 'As far as these last books [the volumes on the state, international trade and the world market respectively – J.H.] are concerned our inquiry suggests the conclusion that they were never really "abandoned". That is to say, the subject matter was never fully assimilated within the second structure of the work, but rather held back for the "eventual continuation" itself'.[232] Rosdolsky argues that the position is different in the case of the respective volumes on landed property and wage labour: 'These had to be incorporated into the new structure because *Capital* would have been inconceivable without a treatment of the questions which they deal with'.[233] The Galician-born scholar suggests that Marx, in accordance with the alterations to his plan (which only concerned the first three volumes of his original plan), integrated what was formerly to be the second volume (on landed property) into the third volume of the work which he produced on the basis of his new conception; by contrast, 'the material for the third book (on wage-labour) was incorporated in the last section but one of Volume I'.[234] According to Rosdolsky, Marx's new planned structure no longer made provision for the independent second and third volumes of the original six-volume plan of 1858. Rosdolsky's interpretation of the problematic of Marx's plans for his critique of political economy prompted subsequent international research questioning, modifying or criticising his theses.

In his 1978 monograph on the historical development of the structure of Marx's *magnum opus*, Winfried Schwarz opposed the conception that 'Marx, by including the forms of wages, or more precisely, the transformation of the form of the value of labour power [in the first volume of *Capital* – J.H.], completely abandoned the volume on wage labour'.[235] According to Schwarz, it was by no means the case that Marx shelved the entire volume on wage labour, instead incorporating it into *Capital*; rather, 'of the original range of themes to be addressed in the volume on wages [i.e. the volume on wage labour – J.H.],

---

231   Rosdolsky 1977, p. 39.
232   Rosdolsky 1977, p. 23.
233   Ibid.
234   Rosdolsky 1977, p. 53.
235   Schwarz 1978, p. 68.

the only one which is dealt with in *Capital* is the transformation of the form of the wage' – i.e. only one aspect of the material which was to be considered for inclusion in the volume on wage labour.[236] In the light of the above-cited passage from Marx, Schwarz's hypothesis that the Trier-born theorist did not integrate all of the content of the volume on wage labour into *Capital* within the context of his new conception might appear to be a reasonable one, given certain premises.[237]

The problematic of the structure and range of Marx's *oeuvre* on the critique of political economy has of course also been the focus of much attention within Japanese research. As early as 1930, Samezō Kuruma expressed the view that *Capital* corresponds in principle to the originally planned section on 'capital in general' within the volume on capital (i.e. the first volume within the six-volume plan). Thus, for Kuruma, the critique of political economy remained unfinished as a complete system.[238] Although the Japanese discussion of the postwar period was marked by the increasing influence of interpretations which were incompatible with the thesis that *Capital* was in principle an elaboration of the originally planned section on 'capital in general', there were still some researchers who advanced similar interpretations in the 1970s and 1980s, as indicated by Iichiro Sekine and Teinosuke Otani.[239] From the 1950s onwards, however, Kinzaburo Sato exerted a significant influence on the discussion. In a text dating from 1954, in which he drew – many years before the great wave of *Grundrisse*-readings in the 'West' – on Marx's 1857/8 *Rohentwurf*, Sato took it that Marx partially incorporated the thematic complexes of wage labour and landed property (as well as those of competition and credit) into the theory developed in *Capital*. According to Sato, this occurred in the form of a 'division' of these respective thematic complexes: each of the latter was partially taken up in *Capital* (although this only applied to their fundamental determinations), and partially reserved for special investigations (beyond the level of their fundamental determinations). Within the discussion of the postwar period (according to the account given by Sekine and Otani), the Marx-researcher and translator of the *Grundrisse*, Kojiro Takagi, advanced the view that *Capital* ought to be considered as a kind of realisation of the first three volumes within the six-volume plan.[240] In 1970, Kiyoshi Matsui considered that Marx had drawn a 'line of demarcation' between the first three and final three

---

236   Schwarz 1978, p. 72.

237   See Marx 1976a, p. 683.

238   See Itoh 1988, p. 56 and Otani and Sekine 1987, p. 250.

239   See Otani and Sekine 1987, p. 250.

240   See Otani and Sekine 1987, p. 250.

themes to be treated in the six-volume plan.[241] In my opinion, this assessment by the Japanese interpreter of Marx is fundamentally accurate.

In the 1980s, Makoto Itoh engaged with the problematic of the exposition from his standpoint as a member of the Uno School. From the perspective of this school, the six-volume plan is scarcely of relevance for any further work on *Capital*. Kōzō Uno's point of view is reproduced by Itoh as follows: 'Uno did not discuss the plan problem in detail by following the formation of Marx's manuscripts from the *Grundrisse*, but treated it from the theoretically wider view of how to locate and complete *Capital* as the system of basic principles for all of Marxian economics'.[242] According to Itoh, the 'basic theories' of wage labour and landed property within the capitalist mode of production must be located at a high level of abstraction. Itoh maintains, however, that the implication of the 'basic theories' of wage labour, competition between capitals, credit, share capital and landed property in the theoretical scope of a theory of the 'basic principles of political economy' such as that given in *Capital* by no means excludes a more concrete investigation of these aspects beyond the level of abstraction which characterises Marx's *magnum opus*.

The problematic of Marx's six-volume plan was also thematised in the Anglo-Saxon world in the 1980s, especially in Allen Oakley's study – a pioneering work within the Anglophone context – on the history of the emergence of Marx's critique of political economy. In this study, a great deal of attention is devoted to Marx's plans for the architectonic of his critique of political economy. Oakley emphasises that *Capital* must be interpreted within the context of its sources and the history of its elaboration as a work. According to Oakley, three major strands of argumentation are to be distinguished in the research with regard to Marx's six-volume plan. Firstly, the interpretation has been advanced that Marx's choice of the title *Capital: A Critique of Political Economy* has no significance vis-à-vis the problematic of the six-volume plan. On this view, this plan was retained in principle. The second conception outlined by Oakley is a modification of the first: 'The view taken is that Marx revised the original Six-Book project by absorbing the material intended for the second and third books on Landed Property and Wage-Labour under the rubric *Capital*'.[243] The Australian Marx-researcher considers that this line of argument implies the point of view that by retaining the respective planned volumes on the state, international trade and the world market, Marx embarked on a four-volume project, and fur-

---

241   See Matsui 1970, p. 33.

242   Itoh 1988, p. 60.

243   Oakley 1983, p. 107.

thermore that *Capital* is to be regarded as the incomplete first volume in a work of this scope. A third reading is identified by Oakley as follows: 'The third interpretation is that beyond the early 1860s, Marx's intention was to work out the four books of *Capital* only'.[244] Oakley's assessment of the situation is that none of the respective advocates of these three strands of argument can claim that their position is completely unassailable. According to the Australian Marx-researcher's interpretation, it by no means necessarily follows from the indications given by Marx in *Capital* relating to economic questions which are not addressed within the scope of his *magnum opus* that Marx planned a treatment of these questions within the framework of a work structured into six volumes.[245] On Oakley's view, Marx's own perspective on *Capital* points in the direction of an interpretation of this work as a self-contained totality.

It should not go unmentioned that within a stream of the Soviet reception of Marx, and specifically that undertaken by the Marx-researcher Albert Kogan, it was suggested that the author of *Capital* had remained committed to the basic methodological idea associated with the six-volume plan. In the 1960s, Kogan had already carried out intensive research into the problematic of the architectonic of the critique of political economy. In 1986, substantial results of Kogan's research into this question were published in German.[246] Here, the Soviet researcher comments that Marx had striven with his six-volume plan to 'provide a scientific structure for the general theory of capitalism'.[247] Kogan's concern is to identify Marx's fundamental methodological idea, and he argues that the latter consists in a dual or two-part exposition of landed property, wage labour, the state, international trade and the world market. What, then, characterises Marx's methodology according to Kogan? On the one hand, the Soviet researcher argues that the above themes were included in *Capital*, and more precisely in the exposition of 'capital in general', but only insofar as their elaboration was necessary within the framework of the theory of surplus value; on the other hand, Kogan maintains that beyond this framework, Marx reserved 'special studies' on landed property, wage labour, the state, international trade and the world market for an exposition which would take place beyond (and subsequent to) *Capital*.

Arguably the most remarkable – or, it might be said, the most fascinating – engagement with Marx's six-volume plan was that undertaken in the 1980s by the *MEGA*² working group around the Marx-researcher, Wolfgang Jahn,

---

244   Ibid.
245   Oakley 1983, p. 108.
246   See Kogan 1986.
247   Kogan 1986, pp. 58 f.

within the Marxism-Leninism Department of the Martin Luther University of Halle/Saale.[248] Jahn took the view that although Marx was unable to fulfil his six-volume plan, he never abandoned it. This was the background to Jahn's critical engagement with Rosdolsky. According to Jahn, Rosdolsky's alleged misinterpretation begins when he regards Marx's 1858 structuring scheme as merely an *a priori* work plan: 'Yet this plan was already based on Marx's initial dialectical elaboration of a vast body of research material which he had collected since beginning his economic studies'. On Jahn's view, Marx's six-volume plan provides the fundamental structuring of the capitalist mode of production in its core moments 'in an initial step of analysis'. These core moments 'formed the principal stages of abstraction for the theoretical exposition of the totality of the objective capitalist mode of production, and for its reproduction as a thought-concrete'. This line of thought brings Jahn to the following conclusion: 'Nor, then, is the main criterion for the correctness of the "six-volume plan" whether and to which extent Marx actually realised this plan; the criterion is rather whether this plan, as a theoretical structure, correctly grasps the main dimensions of reality'.[249] It was this view which determined the approach taken by the group around Jahn to Marx's six-volume plan and which informed the spectacular reconstruction project devised by this team of researchers.

First, however, it is worth further pursuing Jahn's interpretation. According to the latter, Marx never abandoned his comprehensive plan of 1858/9 for his manuscript, *A Contribution to the Critique of Political Economy*.[250] Jahn maintains, however, that new results of Marx's research – first and foremost in relation to the volume on capital – had prompted the Trier-born theorist to undertake drastic modifications. Nevertheless, 'the fundamental structure of the organic whole was retained, regardless of whether Marx later referred to "volumes", "independent studies" or "sections", etc'.[251] According to Jahn, Marx intended to provide a systematic elaboration of the first three volumes, and only a sketch of the final three. In 1862, however, Marx conceded that this project would be more than he could manage. At this time, Marx resolved to 'concentrate all his energy on what was most important: the volume on capital'.[252] Jahn further claims that Marx arrived at new insights from the

---

248 See, among other works, Mohl 2002.

249 Jahn 1992a, p. 128.

250 The title *A Contribution to the Critique of Political Economy* refers here to the overall work as conceived by Marx in his original 1858/9 plan (a work which remained unfinished), rather than merely to the 'first volume' of this work which was published in 1859.

251 Jahn 1992a, p. 129.

252 Ibid.

point of view of content during his work on the *1861–63 Manuscripts*, and that these had implications for his original six-volume structure. According to the Halle/Saale-based researcher, Marx had recognised that 'average profit, interest, ground rent, etc., could not be excluded from the general analysis of capital. If the general concept of capital is grasped as value in process, as self-valorising value, then it cannot be said to be fully developed or "finished" until the concrete forms of surplus-value have also been integrated into the exposition'.[253] Jahn points out that after 1863, Marx no longer used the original structuring concept of 'capital in general': 'The general analysis of capital of the volume on capital was now characterised conceptually as the general concept of capital, the general nature of capital, capital in its core structure, and the like'.[254] Jahn's argument might be stated as follows: the conception of the general analysis of capital in the volume on capital was significantly extended from the point of view of its content. As a result of this change, only those abstract-universal elements were taken over which were necessary for the development of the law of surplus value in the broader sense. The systematic development at a higher level of concretion – i.e. in the context of the structure of the missing sections of the volume on capital and of Volumes Two to Six – remained open.[255] According to Jahn, Marx's modified conception led him to integrate into the book on capital determinate themes which were essential for the development of the law of surplus value in the broader sense, and which he had originally intended to treat in Volumes Two and Three. This by no means implies for Jahn, however, that Marx abandoned these volumes (or the six-volume plan as a whole).

At a symposium in the summer of 1991, Jahn expressed the following view: 'A reception of Marx's economic theory which remained restricted to the general nature* of capital had negative consequences for Marx-related theory and practice'.[256] Jahn emphasised that from the perspective of the interpretation of Marx, the reconstruction and further development of Marx's economic theory had by no means been concluded, and further expanded on this point as follows: 'The consideration of the particular and the singular in addition to the universal, and the development of the more concrete levels of exposition of economic theory which follow *Capital*, can give rise to a more profound

---

253 Jahn 1992a, pp. 130 f.

254 Jahn 1992a, p. 131.

255 Ibid.

* [*allgemeine Wesen*].

256 Jahn 1992b, p. 19.

understanding of Marx's economic theory and provide valuable intellectual stimuli for the economic analysis of the present'.[257]

Jahn by no means stood alone in pursuing his approach to the fundamental reconstruction of Marxian theory. His working group in Halle shared the view that the main criterion for the correctness of the six-volume plan was not the question of its realisation or non-realisation by Marx, but rather its adequacy for the structuring of the theory of the reality of the capitalist mode of production. It was in connection with this perspective that the ambitious project of the Halle-based group around Jahn thrived. This was the project to reconstruct the six-volume plan in terms of its content, and to 'complete' or 'write' the 'incomplete' or 'unwritten' Marx – these researchers intended to continue writing and to complete Marx's planned six-part *magnum opus* themselves, as it were.[258]

Although the planned comprehensive reconstruction of Marx's incomplete *magnum opus* did not come to fruition, 'individual investigations into all the relevant structural components of this work were presented in the form of dissertations' and articles appearing in the journal, *Arbeitsblätter zur Marx-Engels-Forschung*, published by the Department of Marxism-Leninism at the Martin Luther University.[259] The bulk of the material elaborated in Halle/Saale, particularly that which took the form of dissertations (most of which were not published in book form) has not yet been intensively reappraised by the succeeding generation of researchers. It should be recalled that 'more than 40 diploma theses, more than 40 doctoral theses, and more than 10 habilitation theses' were produced within the milieu around the Halle-based Marx-research group until it was 'wound down' following the 'fall of the Iron Curtain'.[260] A portion of these works of research primarily concerns the structural components of the six-volume plan. Despite the attention that the research activities around Jahn gained in the 'West' as in the 'East', Halle's *genius loci* still remains to be tapped systematically; this is perhaps something that could yet be promoted by German and international Marx-research. This is certainly particularly true

---

257 Ibid.

258 On the Halle-based interpretation of the six-volume plan (an interpretation which was considerably influenced by Jahn's research), see Mohl 1991, pp. 125 f. It should perhaps be noted that Fritz Sternberg – a social democrat theorist – voiced the idea, already in 1955, that further work should be devoted to carrying out Marx's six-volume project: 'Marxism must achieve what Marx himself wasn't able to. It is necessary to write the volumes that he left unwritten, and thus to rewrite *Capital* itself on this basis ...' (Sternberg 1955, p. 339).

259 Jahn 1992a, p. 135.

260 Galander 2002, p. 10.

in relation to the thematic areas that Marx, in accordance with his original conception, intended to elaborate in Volumes Two to Six of his six-volume project, as well as in Sections B to D (on the thematic complexes of competition, credit and share capital respectively) of the corresponding volume on capital. A planned collective monograph by members of the Halle-based working group was to thematise the content of the six-volume plan and draw conclusions from the Halle-based methodological research carried out up to that point, but it did not come to fruition; this project could not be realised due to the 'winding down' of academic institutions which followed the upheavals of 1989/90, among other factors. This unwritten monograph would have 'taken the position, on the foundation of Marx's *oeuvre* as a whole, that the six-part plan for the architectonic of his work retained its validity, without qualification, as a methodological guideline for the enquiry into, and exposition of, political economy'.[261]

When, in the immediate period following the fall of the Berlin Wall, an intensive discussion was initiated between those involved in methodologically oriented research in East and West Germany, the Halle-based attempted reconstruction on the basis of the six-volume plan was naturally a central theme. In this context, the problems confronting the working group from Halle/Saale became evident. Ehrenfried Galander, a participant in the Halle-based working group, offered a clear statement at the time: 'increasingly differentiated positions have emerged within our group in relation to the project, and these have rendered unworkable our original intention, which was to write a monograph on the project – i.e. there are differentiated positions which simply do not allow such a monograph to be written'.[262] (Incidentally, a proposal for altering the planned book's conception had also been considered in the meantime; this would have seen the book assuming the form of an edited volume rather than a collectively written monograph).

Another participant in the project, Ulrike Galander, gave the following summary: 'Our original conception, which was that of a classical reconstruction following the principle of the ascent from the abstract to the concrete both within the architectonic of the six volumes and within each individual volume, simply fails in relation to the content. There are divergent views within the group on this score, but that is my opinion'.[263] This did not imply for Ulrike Galander that Marx had himself abandoned the six-volume plan, however.

261   Galander 2002, p. 12.
262   E. Galander 1991.
263   U. Galander 1991.

Gunter Willing, whose specialism within the group was the volume on the state, illustrated the problem with which he saw himself confronted: 'It is just not sufficient for me to ascend from the abstract to the concrete and to attempt a logical derivation of the categories from one another. For in reality there are also breaks there. For example, the breaks in the transition to the volume on the state. I can't make such a derivation'.[264] An additional remark is in order here: Willing's opinion must be regarded against the background of his intensive engagement over several years with the problematic of the volume on the state. In my opinion, Willing touches on an important point: one of the most significant content-related problems which any ambitious project of reconstruction along the lines of the Halle-based undertaking would have to pose is the question of which mediations are possible and meaningful within the exposition of the organic whole in a determinate logical sequence.

By no means was it the political 'transition' alone – an unforeseen external event – which foiled the Halle-based project: evidently, determinate problems of content proved to be insurmountable. Problems were also indicated by West German researchers participating in the discussion. Winfried Schwarz, for example, recalled the historical changes that had occurred in relation to questions of the monetary system and international trade since Marx's lifetime, and posed the following queries: 'It's an unresolved problem for me, then, how is it possible to consider that the internal nature of capital has remained the same, that capital has remained essentially unchanged, whereas its external manifestations have undergone very marked transformations? Are the transformations in the sphere of the world market, for example, merely a problem of the "surface", or do these transformations also affect the "core structure" ... of capital itself?'[265] Schwarz observed that the question arising here was how identity and change were to be thought together in this context.

Jahn's interpretation of the six-volume problematic has been particularly called into question by Michael Heinrich.[266] The line of argument provided by the West German interpreter of Marx implies that the latter subsequently abandoned the six-volume plan he originally conceived in 1858. Heinrich advances the thesis that the inclusion of determinate themes from the problematic of landed property and that of wage labour in *Capital* had rendered it impossible to separate out the exposition of capital, landed property and wage labour into

---

264   Willing 1991.

265   Schwarz 1991.

266   See Heinrich 2002b.

different volumes. Heinrich concedes that in terms of their content, the three volumes of *Capital* do not correspond precisely to the originally planned exposition of the entire material on the ranges of problems associated with capital, landed property and wage labour in the anticipated first three volumes of the six-volume plan. Were this latter exposition to have been carried out, it would have certainly been more comprehensive. According to Heinrich, however, 'it should be taken into account that what is missing in *Capital* in terms of content is located on a completely different *level of abstraction* to the sections and volumes as these were conceived in the original plan'.[267] Heinrich's argument implies that the 'special studies' to which Marx referred while working on *Capital* – studies which Marx considered to lie beyond the purview of that work – are to be located on a totally different level from the exposition in *Capital*, which is (in Heinrich's interpretation) an exposition of the capitalist mode of production in its 'ideal average'.[268]

According to Heinrich, Marx devised his draft plans 'in the course of his work'; these 'expressed determinate insights into the structural interconnections of bourgeois society'.[269] Within the context of his previous six-volume structure, Marx had planned to set out '[t]he economic conditions of existence of the three great classes into which modern bourgeois society is divided'.[270] Heinrich's interpretation of Marx's well-known letter to Kugelmann of 28 December 1862 is that 'Marx merely intended to realise a small part of his six-volume plan in *Capital*: this corresponded to the remainder of the first section of the first volume of *A Contribution to the Critique of Political Economy*'.[271] Heinrich characterises the 'special study of wage-labour'[272] and the 'independent

---

267   Heinrich 2002b, p. 98.

268   The reference to the exposition of the capitalist mode of production in its 'ideal average' is given in a well-known passage from the third volume of *Capital*: 'In presenting the reification of the relations of production and the autonomy they acquire vis-à-vis the agents of production, we shall not go into the form and manner in which these connections appear to them as overwhelming natural laws, governing them irrespective of their will, in the form that the world market and its conjunctures, the movement of market prices, the cycles of industry and trade and the alternation of prosperity and crisis prevails on them as blind necessity. This is because the actual movement of competition lies outside our plan, and we are only out to present the internal organization of the capitalist mode of production, its ideal average, as it were' (Marx 1981a, pp. 969–70).

269   Heinrich 1999a, p. 179.

270   Marx 1987b, p. 261.

271   Heinrich 1999a, p. 180.

272   Marx 1976, p. 683.

treatment of landed property'[273] to which Marx refers in the first and third volumes of *Capital* respectively, and which Marx possibly intended to undertake at a later stage, as special investigations that could not be compared to the expositions previously planned within the framework of the six-volume structure. Heinrich gives the following assessment in relation to *Capital*: 'Through the exposition of the struggle over the limits of the working day, of the effects of machinery on working conditions, of the general law of capitalist accumulation, and of wages and ground rent as forms of revenue', Marx had 'dealt with the fundaments of "[t]he economic conditions of existence of the three great classes"[274] which were to have formed the object of the first three volumes of the six-volume plan'.[275] According to Heinrich, these economic conditions of existence were so closely connected with the laws of capital that a separate exposition would have been impossible for Marx. For the West German interpreter of Marx, it is the 'capitalist mode of production' or the 'economic law of motion of modern societies' (to use Marx's terminology) which forms the object of *Capital*.

Within the Anglo-Saxon discussion, a high-profile study by Michael Lebowitz focused on the absence of Marx's planned volume on wage labour.[276] A more recent Anglo-Saxon contribution on the question of the volumes planned by Marx, but which remained unwritten, is that by Christopher Arthur, who centres his attention on the first three volumes (according to Marx's conception of 1858). Arthur is positively inclined towards the proposition of independent volumes on landed property and wage labour; these would be separate from the volume on capital, but would simultaneously be based on the latter. Within this context, most weight would be attached to the book on capital (thus, in actual fact, to *Capital*, on Arthur's view): 'The central importance of capital, as against wage-labour and landed property, determines the status of the two unwritten books as complementary rather than equal to *Capital*'.[277] Arthur provides the following assessment of the thematic range of *Capital*: '*Capital* studies wage-labour and landed property as they appear *within* capital; in some sense, they are expressions of capital, but there is a need for separate books on them as *themselves*, not just in relation to capital'.[278] According to Arthur, landed property and wage labour each represent an 'other' of capital; thus, there is

---

273   Marx 1981a, p. 752.
274   Marx 1987b, p. 261.
275   Heinrich 1999a, p. 191.
276   Lebowitz 1992.
277   Arthur 2006b, p. 110.
278   Arthur 2006b, p. 106.

certainly room for 'two extra discourses in addition to a study of the form in which capital appropriates these "others" of itself'.[279]

At the end of the 'chapter on method' in the 1857 *Introduction* (i.e. before he had formulated his six-volume plan), Marx drafted an earlier conception of his planned work, and here, in the second point within his structure, he refers to

> [t]he categories which make up the inner structure of bourgeois society and on which the fundamental classes rest. Capital, wage labour, landed property. Their interrelation. Town and country. The three great social classes. Exchange between them. Circulation. Credit system (private).[280]

Marx subsequently stated in the famous 1859 preface to *A Contribution to the Critique of Political Economy* that he planned to undertake an investigation into the '[t]he economic conditions of existence of the three great classes' of modern bourgeois society.[281] Here it should be recalled that Marx had reserved the first three of the six volumes for this purpose. A question arising against this background, then, is the following: in which form could Marx develop his class theory, given that he did not write (or did not complete) the first three volumes of his original plan?

Shortly after the turn of the millennium, Michael Krätke engaged with what he described as the widespread verdict, both within Marxism and within criticisms of Marx, that an explicit exposition of his class theory was nowhere to be found in his work.[282] According to Krätke, the exposition of the 'three classes that make up the framework of modern society – wage-labourer, industrial capitalist, landowner', which are to be found 'together here ... and confronting one another', can only be situated at the conclusion of the course of Marx's exposition – i.e. at the end of the third volume of *Capital*.[283] Krätke thus points out that what Ricardo refers to at the outset of his presentation, namely the tripartite structure of bourgeois society, is located by Marx at the conclusion of his own exposition.[284] Krätke argues that 'even the most adamantly vulgar

279   Arthur 2006b, p. 98.

280   Marx 1973, p. 104.

281   Marx 1987b, p. 261.

282   See Krätke 2003, p. 226.

283   Marx 1981a, p. 756.

284   See Krätke 2003, p. 226. In another text, Krätke writes the following: 'The final section [of the third volume of *Capital* – J.H.] concludes with a chapter on 'Classes', thus with that which the classical economists such as Ricardo took for granted as their starting point. Marx saw things differently: class is a highly complex concept which can only be

among the economists' had considered it self-evident 'to refer to the three great classes into which "society" was quite naturally divided'; the economists named by Krätke in this context include Jean-Baptiste Say, Thomas Robert Malthus, John Ramsay McCulloch and Nassau Senior.[285] One of Krätke's central theses is that Marx intended to go on to provide a critique of the 'accepted "class theory" of the economists, including a critique of the concept of economic classes which was prevalent at the time'.[286] Krätke also refers to Marx's views regarding the increase in the 'middle classes'[287] and the relative decrease of the working proletariat as a proportion of the overall population.[288] For Krätke, however, Marx's references to the 'middle class' are imprecise: the Trier-born theorist takes this category to include '*rentiers*, the "moneyed class" or the class with a fixed income, consisting predominantly of unproductive, "idle capitalists" who only consume, along with the strata appended to them ..., and also minor independent producers, who continually emerge as minor master craftsmen and minor self-working capitalists in "new lines of business", where they begin anew the development of capital and capitalist production'.[289] On Krätke's view, the category of class is neither exclusively associated with the sphere of production, nor with the sphere of circulation, nor is it solely a category of distribution, nor exclusively one of consumption; rather, it is all of these things 'at once, and in connection with one another'.[290] The usual reduction of classes to categories exclusively defined by distribution, as in the conception of 'classes according to income', misses the complexity of the matter.

Yet the question remains as to whether the non-realisation of the 1858 six-volume plan might indeed have impinged in a problematic way on Marx's class theory. If this were to be demonstrated, it would probably apply not least with regard to the working class, whose economic conditions of existence Marx originally intended to thematise in the volume on wage labour. It is likely that a part of the comprehensive range of themes that were to have been treated in the volume on wage labour could not be incorporated into *Capital*;

---

developed on the foundation of the analysis of the capitalist mode of production – it is not to be located prior to the latter in the exposition' (Krätke 2008, p. 15). Ricardo refers to a tripartite class structure of society in the very first paragraph of his preface to *Principles of Political Economy and Taxation* (see Ricardo 2001, p. 5).

285   Krätke 2003, pp. 226 f.
286   Krätke 2003, p. 227.
287   Marx 1989c, p. 198.
288   Marx 1989b, p. 78.
289   Krätke 2003, p. 232.
290   Krätke 2003, pp. 235 f.

furthermore, Marx left behind no 'special study of wage labour' (as he termed it in his well-known formulation in the first volume of *Capital*). Against this background, Michael Lebowitz indeed touches on a sore point with his thesis that a treatment of the problematic of wage labour remains a *desideratum* in Marx.

3.2   *The Problematic of 'Capital in General'*

It was during the course of Marx's work on the *Grundrisse* – at the latest – that the differentiation between various levels of abstraction emerged as a tenet of decisive significance for his project of an exposition of the critique of political economy. A consideration of the structural concept of 'capital in general', which Marx counterposed to the 'competition of many capitals', belongs within this context. Underlying this separation is Marx's reflection that the immanent laws of capital do not ensue from competition; rather, they are merely realised in and through the latter.[291] Marx insists that these laws can by no means be explained by competition itself.[292] Accordingly, he considered that it was first necessary to deduce the immanent laws of capital in abstraction from competition.

In the spring of 1858, Marx planned to subdivide the first volume within his six-volume schedule, the volume on capital, into four sections. The first section was to have 'capital in general' as its object, the second 'competition' or the action of many capitals upon one another; the third section would deal with credit, and the fourth and final section was to treat share capital. The section on 'capital in general' was to include both the production process of capital and the circulation process of capital, along with a further and final moment: 'the unity of the two, or capital and profit; interest'.[293] This, at least, is the division which can be arrived at on the basis of Marx's letters to Ferdinand Lassalle of 11 March 1858 and to Friedrich Engels of 2 April 1858, if these are taken together.[294]

Opinions are divided on the issues of (a) the determination of the content of the structuring concept of 'capital in general' within Marx's critique of political economy, and (b) the effective longevity of this concept within the history of the elaboration of Marx's *oeuvre* on the critique of political economy. A further question arising is whether this structural concept itself underwent

---

291   In the *Grundrisse*, Marx wrote the following: 'Competition generally, this essential loco-
        motive force of the bourgeois economy, does not establish its laws, but is rather their
        executor' (Marx 1973, p. 552).

292   See Marx 1973, p. 752.

293   Marx 1983g, p. 287.

294   See Marx 1983g, p. 287 and Marx 1983e, p. 298.

determinate changes in terms of its content as Marx developed his critique of political economy over time. One of Marx's best-known characterisations of 'capital in general' occurs in the *Grundrisse*:

> *Capital in general*, as distinct from the particular capitals, does indeed appear (1) *only as an abstraction*; not an arbitrary abstraction, but an abstraction which grasps the specific characteristics which distinguish capital from all other forms of wealth – or modes in which (social) production develops. These are the aspects common to every capital as such, or which make every specific sum of values into capital. And the distinctions within this abstraction are likewise abstract particularities which characterize every kind of capital, in that it is their position [*Position*] or negation [*Negation*] (e.g. fixed capital or circulating capital); (2) however, capital in general, *as distinct from* the particular real capitals, is itself a *real* existence.[295]

Although there were isolated studies already in Germany in the 1920s on the problematic of the plan of the critique of political economy as a question of the history of the elaboration of Marx's *oeuvre*, it was only in the wake of the publication of Roman Rosdolsky's famous monograph that a discriminating discussion of this problematic and of the problem of 'capital in general' developed in the FRG.[296] It can even be surmised that it was Rosdolsky's work which first generated – or at least acted to extend – any adequate awareness, on the part of many of those interested in Marx, of problems such as that of the interconnection between the different levels of abstraction in the critique of political economy. Rosdolsky considered that Marx's distinction between 'capital in general' and the 'competition of many capitals' represented an important working model. Rosdolsky argues that the later exposition in *Capital* – provided all three volumes are taken as the basis – points beyond the original concept of 'capital in general'. According to Rosdolsky, *Capital* is by no means restricted to themes that were previously assigned to the section on 'capital in general', since considerations from the sections on 'competition of many capitals', 'the credit system' and 'share capital' had been included in the third volume.[297] The engagement by subsequent researchers with Rosdolsky was partially critical. One of the most ambitious investigations into 'capital in general' to be carried

---

295   Marx 1973, p. 449.
296   See Grossmann 2013.
297   See Rosdolsky 1977, p. 56.

out in the FRG was that presented by Winfried Schwarz in the 1970s.[298] Like Rosdolsky's work, Schwarz's study was also the subject of controversy within the
contemporary Marx debate. Schwarz's main thesis with regard to the decisive
question of whether or not Marx abandoned the concept of 'capital in general'
is that although this concept continues to exist in Marx's conception after 1863,
it no longer constitutes a 'main structural consideration' within Marx's development, but rather persists under what might be termed the dominance of a
new structural principle.

A source of inspiration for the discussion of the 'capital in general' problematic within the GDR was the Soviet research (particularly that of the 1960s)
into the draft plans for the critique of political economy. In the Soviet Union,
Alexander Malysch insisted that Marx had only used the concept of 'capital
in general' until 1863. By contrast, his compatriot, Albert Kogan, advanced the
view that *Capital* was still based on the conception of 'capital in general'. Vitaly
Vygodsky, one of the most significant Soviet Marx-researchers of the 1960s and
1970s, presumed that Marx retained the structural standpoint of 'capital in
general' after 1862; Vygodsky argued, however, that over time Marx came to
include within the exposition of 'capital in general' many of the problems that
he had previously earmarked for subsequent parts of his overall work.[299] From
Vygodsky's thesis it becomes clear that the question as to whether or not Marx
retained the concept of 'capital in general' must be supplemented by a further
one, namely whether, and how, the thematic scope of this concept might have
changed during the course of the development of Marx's critique of political
economy, or, more precisely, whether a thematic 'broadening' of this concept
can be identified. In the GDR, the assessment of Wolfgang Jahn and Roland Nietzold was that 'capital in general' no longer occurred as a structural component
of *Capital*, and that Marx 'no longer employs this concept in its strong sense'.[300]

Nevertheless, a qualification should be added here in relation to the Soviet
engagement with the 'capital in general' problematic. Albert Kogan advanced
the view that Marx had 'carved up' or 'divided up' the thematic domains of competition and credit, and that in their case a twofold exposition was required.
On the one hand, insofar as they were directly related to the theory of surplus
value, they would have to be addressed within *Capital* – more precisely, within
the range of the exposition of 'capital in general'. On the other hand, Kogan
considers that the special investigations (the special studies) into these themes

---

298   See Schwarz 1978. Schwarz had already offered a critique of Rosdolsky a few years previ-
       ously (see Schwarz 1974).
299   See Vygodsky 1974, p. 120.
300   Jahn and Nietzold 1978, p. 168.

would necessarily fall outside *Capital* and the structural heading of 'capital in general'.[301] According to Kogan, this notion of a twofold exposition of themes such as competition and credit – firstly within the framework of the treatment of the theory of surplus value, and later as relatively independent questions – represents a key idea of Marx's methodology.

The engagement with the question of 'capital in general' remained a notable dimension of subsequent Soviet research into Marx. In the second half of the 1980s, Michail Ternovski and Alexander Chepurenko advanced the view that relatively soon, Marx became aware of the restrictedness of the concept of 'capital in general' in its initial, provisional formulation in the *Grundrisse*. Ternovski and Chepurenko do not contend that Marx discarded the category of 'capital in general'; rather, they argue that the specific conceptual content of this category underwent a fundamental alteration in the time following this category's initial determination by Marx. More precisely, they claim that Marx came to appreciate that 'a general concept of capital could not exist beyond the reciprocal relations between individual capitals', and thus revised his position with regard to the concept of 'capital in general' as he had originally outlined it.[302] These authors further argue that Marx had begun 'to turn away from the treatment of "capital in general" as an abstract-universal existing alongside individual capitals. However, this turn initially manifests merely as the conception of "capital in general" as an abstraction of total social capital', which actually occurs in the *Grundrisse* itself.[303]

There was also an engagement with the problematic of Marx's plans for the architectonic of his critique of political economy within the French reception of the latter. Within this context, a study by Paul Boccara dating from the early 1960s has already been referred to above. In 1965, Roger Establet, a member of the Althusserian School, had set out his observations in relation to the problematic of Marx's plan for the critique of political economy in *Lire le Capital*.[304],* A subsequent French contribution, which refers in part to the

---

301   On Kogan, see Schwarz 1978, pp. 276 ff. On the Soviet debate around the draft plans for the critique of political economy, see also Müller 1978a.

302   Ternowski and Tschepurenko 1987, p. 182.

303   Ibid.

304   See Establet 1965. The German edition does not contain this contribution.

*   Establet's contribution – along with those by Jacques Rancière and Pierre Macherey – was omitted from the abridged second edition of *Lire le Capital,* and likewise from the English-language edition, *Reading Capital* (see Althusser and Balibar 1970). An unabridged English-language edition, which restores the original contributions, is forthcoming from Verso.

German-language debate on Marx's plans for the architectonic of his critique of political economy between Rosdolsky, Schwarz and Manfred Müller, dates from 1980. Alongside his consideration of the plan given by Marx in the 1857 *Introduction*, the author of this work, Marc Sagnol, pays particular attention to the problematic of Marx's various plans over the course of his work on the *Grundrisse* manuscript. Within the context of this problematic, the question of the category of 'capital in general' must be posed, as must the query as to whether this category persisted through the history of the origins and elaboration of *Capital*. Sagnol formulates his thesis as follows: '[In *Capital*], there is ... no transition from "capital in general" to "many capitals" – i.e. to competition'; nevertheless, Sagnol argues that the category of 'capital in general' is by no means completely jettisoned in the course of the further development from the *Grundrisse* to *Capital*: rather, this category undergoes an important modification.[305] This occurs, according to Sagnol, in the form of an extension of the concept of 'capital in general': 'In positing wage labour and ground rent as two determinations of capital, Marx expands his initial concept of "capital in general", and endows it with the sense of the internal articulation or internal structure of bourgeois society; originally, however, this internal articulation or structure was only to be posited after the study of the three fundamental categories'.[306] Yet for Sagnol, the development towards *Capital* is not limited to this aspect alone: the French interpreter of Marx argues that the latter's *magnum opus* is in general characterised by a restriction of its object-domain relative to Marx's original, more comprehensive theoretical project.

According to the research undertaken by Michael Heinrich in the 1980s and 1990s, the structural concept of 'capital in general' played a decisive role in Marx's projected exposition from the time of his work on the *Grundrisse* until 1863, after which point it no longer occurred either in Marx's correspondence or in his manuscripts.[307] Thus, for Heinrich, it is not merely the term that disappears, but also the content-structuring concept for which this term stood. Heinrich argues that it is evident that themes are treated in *Capital* which concern competition between capitals, credit, or share capital. The key circumstance for Heinrich is that Marx's systematic distinction between 'capital in general' and the 'competition of many capitals' is informed by a determinate conception with regard to the structural interconnection of bourgeois society. Heinrich explains that in accordance with this conception, Marx regards com-

---

305   Sagnol 1982, p. 21.
306   Sagnol 1982, p. 25.
307   See Heinrich 1999a, pp. 179 ff. See also Heinrich 1986.

petition as the form in which the 'immanent' laws of capital are manifested. According to the West German interpreter of Marx, the latter holds that these immanent laws cannot be explained by competition itself. Heinrich considers the distinction between 'capital in general' and 'the competition of many capitals' to be Marx's first attempt at a categorial definition of his view that the actual movement of individual capitals is merely the realisation of the 'laws of the internal nature of capital'. According to Heinrich, Marx establishes two different requirements which the section on 'capital in general' has to fulfil: on the one hand, its content is to be presented at a determinate *level of abstraction*, at which abstraction is made from competition (which includes both the actual movement of, and all relations between, the many capitals); on the other hand, 'the exposition is to have a *determinate range as regards content –* it is to comprise *all* the determinations which become manifest in competition'.[308] Heinrich argues, however, that the problem of satisfying both criteria for the exposition of 'capital in general' simultaneously proved insoluble. On Heinrich's view, the structural concept of 'capital in general' is exploded in the period after 1863 by Marx's integration into the logic of his exposition of, on the one hand, the presentation of the average rate of profit, and, on the other, the presentation of the reproduction and circulation of total social capital. Yet the question now arises as to which structuring principle takes the place vacated by the strict differentiation between 'capital in general' and 'competition'. Heinrich argues that the previous conception of 'capital in general' on the one hand and 'competition' on the other is replaced in *Capital* by 'the consideration of the *individual capital* and the *constitution of total social capital* on the three successive, ascending levels of exposition corresponding to the immediate process of production, the process of circulation and the total process'.[309]

More recently, Heinrich has proposed a periodisation of the development and elaboration of Marx's work on the critique of political economy in which he identifies two distinct projects: the first of these bore the title *A Contribution to the Critique of Political Economy* and was to comprise six volumes; the second was the *Capital*-project, which was to consist of four volumes. To the first of these projects Heinrich ascribes two earlier drafts (namely the *Grundrisse* and the *1861–63 Manuscripts*), as well as the 1858 *Urtext* and the first volume of *A Contribution to the Critique of Political Economy*, published in 1859 (the *1861–63 Manuscripts* were intended as a continuation of this latter work). The second project (i.e. the *Capital*-project) is regarded by Heinrich as comprising three

---

308   Heinrich 1999a, p. 185.
309   Heinrich 1999a, p. 193.

drafts: the so-called *1863–65 Manuscripts*; Marx's work on *Capital* in the period from 1866–71; and, finally, his work on *Capital* in the period from 1871 until his death, together with the corresponding supplementary studies he carried out during this time. For Heinrich, then, there are ultimately five drafts divided between two distinct projects.[310],[*] In my opinion, this proposed division is novel and represents an alternative to Enrique Dussel's four-part classification (see above). Heinrich locates his thesis that Marx replaced one structural principle by another – such that the earlier structural principle of a distinction between 'capital in general' and 'competition' was replaced by the later structural principle of the consideration of the individual capital on the one hand, and total social capital on the other – within the context of his considerations on the history of the development of Marx's work on the critique of political economy as follows: he attributes the former structural principle to the project entitled *A Contribution to the Critique of Political Economy*, and the latter one to the *Capital*-project.

Since Heinrich published a version of his older theses in English in the 1980s, there is a certain familiarity within specialist circles within the Anglophone world with his perspective on the problematic of 'capital in general'.[311] However, Heinrich encountered two critics in this context, both of whom were concerned to provide an alternative interpretation on this question. This was a notable occurrence from the point of view of the history of the reception of Marx, since the problematic of Marx's plans for the architectonic of his critique of political economy and of the peculiar structure of the critique of political economy had long since been rather neglected within the English-language Marx debate – in contrast to Japan, for example, where an intensive engagement with these questions had been initiated at a far earlier point in time.[312] (As in the case

---

310   See Heinrich 2006.
*   See also Heinrich 2009.
311   See Heinrich 1989.
312   With regard to the Anglo-Saxon interpretation of Marx prior to the wave of readings of the
       Grundrisse of the mid- and late 1970s, it is true, for example, that the US interpreter of Marx,
       Raya Dunayevskaya, engaged in the 1950s with the question of changes to the structure of
       Capital. The focus of Dunayevskaya's engagement with the question of structure was, in
       the first instance, mostly on factors other than the Six-Volume-Plan and the problematic
       of the architectonic of Marx's critique of political economy which revolved around 'capital
       in general' – a problematic which Kuruma had made a central focus of attention already
       in the 1930s. The first true wave of engagement with this problematic within Anglo-Saxon
       research occurred in connection with the wave of reception of the *Grundrisse* of the 1970s.
       For the views advanced by Dunayevskaya in 1958, see Dunayevskaya 1958, pp. 26 ff. Space

of German-language interpretation of Marx, a major stimulus for the discussion of this problematic was Rosdolsky's monograph, an English translation of which was published in 1977). The first critical engagement with Heinrich's theory in this context was that by Paul Burkett, who defended the view that Marx had retained the ordering concept of 'capital in general' while working on *Capital*.[313] The second critical response to Heinrich within the English-language discussion came from Fred Moseley, who argued that Marx maintained the distinction between 'capital in general' and 'competition' throughout – i.e. up to and including his final version of *Capital*.[314] According to Moseley, Marx's theories of the average rate of profit and of prices of production, as well as his theories of interest, mercantile profit and ground rent, are to be considered in connection with this distinction. Moseley's interpretation will be examined in more detail in the following.

On Moseley's reading, the primary purpose of Marx's concepts of 'capital in general' and 'competition' is to establish the distinction between, on the one hand, surplus-value production or the determination of the quantity of total social surplus value, and, on the other, the distribution of surplus value. Moseley argues that the former moment corresponds to the level of abstraction of 'capital in general', and the latter to that of 'competition'.[315] For the American interpreter of Marx, one of the latter's central premises is that *'the total amount of surplus-value is determined prior to and independent of the division of this total amount into individual parts'*.[316] Moseley notes that Marx's distinction between the production of surplus value on the one hand, and its distribution on the other, enabled the author of *Capital* to advance theoretically beyond David Ricardo. On Moseley's view, then, the concept of 'capital in general' relates to total social capital. Like Burkett, Moseley refers to the English-language article Heinrich published in 1989, and engages critically with the definition of 'capital in general' given there; the American interpreter of Marx argues that on Heinrich's definition, 'capital in general' comprises '*all* the common characteristics of individual capitals, including the average rate of profit, as opposed to only the *most essential* common characteristic (the production of surplus-value)'.[317] Moseley thus contrasts Heinrich's interpretation of 'capital in general'

---

does not permit a consideration here of Dunayevskaya's 1978 polemic against Rosdolsky's *The Making of Marx's Capital* (see Dunayevskaya 1978).

313   See Burkett 1991.
314   See Moseley 1995.
315   See also Moseley 2007.
316   Moseley 1995, p. 17.
317   Moseley 1995, p. 24.

with his own, which identifies the moment of surplus-value production as the *most essential* common characteristic defining individual capitals.

With regard to the *1861–63 Manuscripts*, Moseley comments that 'the impression one gets from studying this manuscript is one of Marx's increasing clarity' in relation to both the distinction between 'capital in general' and 'competition' and the central significance of this distinction vis-à-vis themes which were later included in the third volume of *Capital*.[318] To borrow from Winfried Schwarz's interpretation (although this pointed in a somewhat different direction), it could be said that Moseley attempts to demonstrate not only that the concept of 'capital in general' continued to exist in Marx's theory after 1863, but that it did so as an absolutely central and determining element, rather than as a comparatively subordinate one. On Moseley's view, the first volume of *Capital*, which was composed in 1866/7, is marked by the distinction between 'capital in general' and 'competition' – a distinction which Moseley regards as retaining its validity. This distinction 'continued to provide the basic logical structure for the three volumes of *Capital*, and especially for Marx's theory of the average rate of profit and of the other specific forms of surplus-value in Volume 3'.[319] According to Moseley's interpretation, the third volume of *Capital* is located primarily on the level of abstraction corresponding to 'competition', and a major theoretical question here is the distribution of surplus value.

In the mid-1990s, the South Korean, Seung-Wan Han, took the position that Marx no longer used the concept 'capital in general' after finishing work on the *1861–63 Manuscripts*. It would seem that this view has become accepted in various currents of Marx research. According to Han, however, the precise point in time at which Marx abandoned this structural concept is hard to determine. Marx had apparently retained this concept practically until completion of the so-called 'second draft of *Capital*'. A major thesis of Han is that Marx's abandonment of the term 'capital in general' as a structural concept went hand-in-hand with his supposed revision of the principle of a determinate dialectical development in a strong sense. Han comments as follows: ' "Capital in general" was an abstraction, but one which was posited as a starting point of the dialectical development. In this sense, it was a universal which was to unfold its immanent determinations over the course of the dialectical process of development'.[320] These determinations were to have achieved a 'real existence' by the end of the development. Han argues that Marx had planned, through his construction of

318   Moseley 1995, p. 33.

319   Moseley 1995, pp. 39 f.

320   Han 1995, p. 146.

the concept of 'capital in general', to provide a logical exposition demonstrating the development of capital into a totality which 'posits the presuppositions of its formation as its own moments in the course of the dialectical development'.[321] All of the determinations that were supposedly immanent to 'capital in general' were to have been developed from the latter itself. On this view, the repulsion of capitals from one another is already inherent within 'capital in general', and this repulsion develops into competition between real capitals. According to Han, this appears to have been a guiding principle within the context of Marx's project for a dialectical development: Marx had assumed that competition both could and necessarily had to be developed immanently from 'capital in general'. However, as Han points out, if Marx discarded his experimental concept of 'capital in general' and the associated conception of a dialectical development in the strong sense, it must of course be asked which method of exposition prevailed instead. The South Korean Marx-researcher argues that within the context of the alteration to the method of exposition, 'the strategy of *concretisation*, which Marx retained throughout as a further methodological principle, assumes a new form: it no longer consists in a process of the immanent unfolding of determinations, which was the conception associated with the concept of "capital in general"; instead it is now defined by *a process of the extrinsic integration of moments which were previously "disregarded"*'.[322] Han explains that those elements which had been abstracted from on the previous levels of the exposition would now be gradually introduced. The laws which had been elaborated in the preceding exposition would thus be continuously supplemented, corrected, modified.

An investigation into the question not of *whether*, but *when* Marx abandoned the structural concept of 'capital in general' was recently presented by a Japanese researcher. The problematic of 'capital in general' had already been taken up within Japanese research before the Second World War, in the context of an early study on crisis theory by Samezō Kuruma. This discussion was carried on more intensively in the postwar period. The view expressed in Kuruma's early study, namely that Marx remains committed to the structural concept of 'capital in general' in the final version of *Capital*, is contested by Izumi Omura, a member of the *MEGA*² working group in Sendai. For Omura, who establishes a strict differentiation between the 'capital in general' system and the subsequent *Capital*-system, there can be no doubt on this score. Omura takes the view that the two well-known draft plans contained in Notebook XVIII of the

---

321   Han 1995, p. 129.
322   Han 1995, p. 147.

1861–63 Manuscripts[323] represent the final ones corresponding to the 'capital in general' conception. Omura further insists that it would be wrong to associate these draft plans with Marx's new conception after his final abandonment of the structural concept of 'capital in general' and of the content defined by this concept. According to Omura, Marx's later conception – the one corresponding to *Capital* – only emerged during the course of his work on the so-called *1863–65 Manuscripts*, and not during the previous process of drafting the *1861–63 Manuscripts*. The Japanese researcher argues that it was while composing the so-called *Capital* manuscript of 1863–5 that Marx included the analysis relating to three problems – 'i.e. wages, competition (market value and market price) and the exchange value of natural resources (the price of land and differential rent)' – in the volumes on *Capital*; at the time of the two draft plans given in the *1861–63 Manuscripts*,[324] these problems lay beyond the conception of 'capital in general'.[325] Omura points out, however, that Marx did actually intend temporarily to carry out both draft plans which he had outlined in Notebook XVIII *and* to follow this with an exposition of the theory of competition (market value and market price), the credit system (fictitious capital), landed property (differential rent and the price of land) and wage labour (wages). According to Omura, this temporary project was subsequently replaced by the new conception – i.e. the conception corresponding to *Capital*.

Incidentally, it is worth noting that the view advanced by Omura contradicts the understanding of the editors of *MEGA*[2], Volume II/3.1; the latter claim that the new plan delineated in Notebook XVIII essentially anticipates the structure subsequently to be found in *Capital*, and thus that Marx had by this stage already taken the content-related decision to abandon the structural principle of the division between 'capital in general' and 'competition'.[326] It is to be hoped that the debate on the problematic of 'capital in general' – a debate whose intensity has long since abated within the German-language discussion – will continue to be a prominent theme within the Japanese methodological discussion and in Japanese research within this field.

3.3   *Summary*

In his letter of 31 July 1865 to Engels, Marx wrote the following in relation to his manuscript for *Capital*: 'I cannot bring myself to send anything off until I have the whole thing in front of me'. Marx further explains that '[w]hatever

---

323   See Marx 1991b, pp. 346–7.
324   Ibid.
325   Omura 2002, p. 54.
326   See Marx 1976e, p. 12*.

shortcomings they may have, the advantage of my writings is that they are an artistic whole, and this can only be achieved through my practice of never having things printed until I have them in front of me *in their entirety*. This is impossible with Jacob Grimm's method [i.e. publication in successive instalments – J.H.] which is in general better with writings that have no dialectical structure'.[327] The three volumes of *Capital* are certainly to be considered an 'artistic whole' having a 'dialectical structure', even taking into account the fact that Marx was only able to publish the first volume separately (in three different versions) in his lifetime and left behind manuscripts containing working or rough drafts for the second and third volumes which were not yet ready for publication.[328] However, a question to be posed within the context of the debate outlined above (i.e. the debate within international research on Marx over the 'six-volume plan' and the 'capital in general' problematic) is the following: is the 'artistic whole' constituted by the three volumes of *Capital* in fact *the* whole, or merely *a* whole which was in turn to be part of a larger whole, where this larger whole was intended to be a comprehensive and overarching work on the critique of political economy? Over the last few decades, numerous studies have contributed to research into the history of the structure of Marx's *magnum opus*, but as yet no consensus has been achieved with regard to the status of the 'six-volume plan' and 'capital in general' within the development taken by Marx's theory.

4 Crisis Theory in and after Marx

4.1 *Approaches to the Interpretation of Marx's Crisis Theory*
The very dynamic of the capitalist mode of production necessarily generates economic crises. Not only is a crisis-free capitalism impossible, according to Marx, but – it might be added – a peculiar proneness or susceptibility to crisis is immanent within the capitalist mode of production, distinguishing it from all other historical modes of production.

---

327 Marx 1987a, p. 173.

328 Also to be taken into account is Engels's statement, shortly after the death of his friend, that the latter had planned 'to re-write a great part of the text of the first volume, to formulate many theoretical points more exactly, to insert new ones, and to bring historical and statistical materials up to date'; according to Engels, Marx was prevented from carrying out this plan by his poor health and by the pressing need to work on the second volume (Marx 1976a, p. 106).

Marx was by no means the only, or even the first, theorist of crisis: the discussion of this phenomenon had emerged a few decades previously. Most worthy of mention in this context is the so-called 'general glut debate' or 'general glut controversy' around the problematic of a general oversupply of markets – a debate which pitted Jean-Baptiste Say and David Ricardo against Thomas Robert Malthus and Simonde de Sismondi. Say and Ricardo, relying on the thesis of the continuous equilibrium between supply and demand, declared the oversupply of markets to be an impossibility, whereas Malthus and Sismondi questioned the validity of this view.[329] Ricardo, whom Marx considered to be at the zenith of classical economics, denied precisely the possibility of general overproduction: 'Productions are always bought by productions, or by services; money is only the medium by which the exchange is effected. Too much of a particular commodity may be produced, of which there may be such a glut in the market as not to repay the capital expended on it; but this cannot be the case with respect to all commodities'.[330] In his *1861–63 Manuscripts*, Marx engaged critically and at some length with aspects of the 'general glut debate'.

From the position taken by Marx with respect to Ricardo, it would be reasonable to infer that the shortcomings in the latter's theory of crises were in part due to historical factors: 'Ricardo himself did not actually know anything of crises, of general crises of the world market, arising out of the production process itself'.[331] Marx observes that Ricardo had been able to attribute the crises which occurred in the period from 1800 to 1815 to increases in the price of corn due to crop failures, to the devaluation of paper currency, or to the effects of the continental blockade during the war against Napoleon. Marx continues as follows: '[Ricardo] was also able to explain the crises after 1815, partly by a bad year and a shortage of corn, and partly by the fall in corn prices,

---

329   Within the Marxist discussion, reference is made to the different theoretical backgrounds of Malthus and Sismondi, even though both indicate the possibility of general crises: 'In Malthus' hands this tendency towards underconsumption became a reactionary apologetic for feudal land-owners, whose high living and conspicuous consumption was presented as a welcome counter-balance to the tendency of capitalists to over-save' (Shaikh 1978, p. 224). 'Unlike the reactionary parson Malthus, Sismondi was a radical who was deeply impressed by the suffering of the peasants and workers under capitalism. In his time he stood at the head of what Marx called petty-bourgeois socialism, which struggled against the cruelty and destruction engendered by capitalism and sought to reform it so as to ameliorate these conditions' (Shaikh 1978, p. 225). Sismondi cannot be described as a socialist in the strict sense, however.

330   Ricardo 2001, p. 210.

331   Marx 1989c, p. 128.

because those causes which, according to his own theory, had forced up the price of corn during the war when England was cut off from the continent, had ceased to operate; partly by the transition from war to peace which brought about "sudden changes in the channels of trade".[332] Marx concludes by remarking that Ricardo's successors were confronted by the periodicity of crises on the world market – a periodicity which characterised a later stage of historical development – and that it was this very periodicity which prevented these later economists from denying the facts or interpreting them as mere coincidences.

A characteristic feature of Marx's theory of crises consists in the fact that he was able, on the foundation of the monetary dimension of his value theory, to demonstrate the internal connection between economic categories (value, the commodity and money) and the possibility of economic crises. The dimension of the specific form-determinacy of the products of labour within the capitalist mode of production is of decisive significance here. The specific necessity of the doubling of the commodity into commodity and money corresponds to a peculiarity characterising social relations between commodity owners; this peculiarity consists in the fact that the latter bring the products of their labour into relation with one another as commodities. In turn, the necessary doubling of the commodity into commodity and money itself necessarily conditions a separation of sale and purchase into two diverging acts within one and the same process. Sale and purchase are characterised by a relation in which they simultaneously belong together and yet are mutually independent. The possibility of crisis alluded to here does not yet entail the reality of crisis – indeed, the distinction between the possibility and the reality of crisis is of decisive significance within Marx's theory. He makes the point in *Theories of Surplus-Value* as follows: 'the real crisis can only be educed from the real movement of capitalist production, competition and credit' – i.e. the real crisis can only be theorised at a completely different level of abstraction.[333]

Within the context of his crisis theory, Marx made continuous references over a number of years to the separation between sale and purchase which money entails. Such references occur in *Bullion. Das vollendete Geldsystem,** in the *Grundrisse*, in *A Contribution to the Critique of Political Economy*, in *Theories of Surplus-Value*, and finally in *Capital*. In *Bullion*, a compilation of excerpts in

---

332   Marx 1989c, p. 129.
333   Marx 1989c, p. 143.
*   *Bullion. Das vollendete Geldsystem* [*Bullion: The Consummate Monetary System*] (Marx 1986). This text has not yet been published in English translation.

the second stage of processing by Marx and dating from the first half of 1851, the future author of *Capital* argues that with money, 'the act of exchange is decomposed into the two mutually independent actions of purchase and sale ... The necessary consequence of money is thus the divergence between these two actions ... which can be ... in *disharmony*, in *disproportion*. With money, the ground is thus already laid for crises'.[334] In *A Contribution to the Critique of Political Economy*, Marx writes that the separation between purchase and sale in the exchange process is 'the universal form of the splitting apart' of moments which belong together, the universal form 'of their becoming fixed in opposition to one another, in short it contains the general possibility of commercial crises, however only because the antagonism between commodity and money is the abstract and general form of all antagonisms inherent in the bourgeois mode of labour. Although circulation of money can occur therefore without crises, crises cannot occur without circulation of money'.[335] Within German-language research, considerable attention has been devoted since the 1970s (at the latest) to the interconnection between Marx's theories of value, money and crisis at the level of exposition corresponding to simple circulation.[336]

In the second part of *Theories of Surplus-Value*, Marx adduces the above-cited dictum from Chapter 21 of Ricardo's *Principles of Political Economy and Taxation*, according to which products are always bought by products or services, and money is merely the medium through which exchange takes place.[337] Marx criticises this conception, arguing that Ricardo transforms the commodity into a mere product, a mere use-value, and thus transmutes commodity exchange into the mere barter of products or use-values: 'This represents a regression not only behind capitalist production, but even behind simple commodity production itself; and the most complicated phenomenon of capitalist production – the world market crisis – is flatly denied, by denying the first condition of capitalist production, namely, that the product must be a commodity and therefore present itself as money and undergo the process of metamorphosis'.[338] Marx points out that Ricardo's reference to 'services' as opposed to wage labour elides the latter's particular determinacy and that of its use, which consists in the production of surplus value; the particular rela-

---

334   Marx 1986, p. 4 [my translation – N.G.].

335   Marx 1987b, p. 332 [translation modified – N.G.].

336   See, for example, Bader et al. 1975a, p. 138 ff. See also Fahling 1978, pp. 51 ff.

337   See Ricardo 1821, pp. 291–2. On Marx's critique of Ricardo's conception with regard to crises, see Stapelfeldt 2006, pp. 431 ff.

338   Marx 1989c, p. 132 [translation modified – N.G.].

tion through which the commodity and money are transformed into capital is thus disregarded: '"Service" is labour seen only as use-value (which is a side issue in capitalist production) just as the term "productions" fails to express the essence of the commodity and its inherent contradiction'.[339] Ricardo conceives of money as a mere intermediary in the exchange of products, rather than as 'an essential and necessary form of existence of the commodity which must manifest itself as exchange-value, as general social labour. Since the transformation of the commodity into mere use-value (product) obliterates the essence of exchange-value, it is just as easy to deny, or rather it is necessary to deny, that money is an essential form of the commodity, a form which, in the process of metamorphosis, is independent vis-à-vis the original form of the commodity'.[340] Marx emphasises that Ricardo disregards crises by 'forgetting or denying' the form-determinacy of the product *qua* commodity; the doubling of the commodity into commodity and money; the corresponding splitting of purchase and sale into two mutually independent acts; and, finally, 'the relation of money or commodities to wage-labour'.[341] According to Marx, Ricardo thus overlooks the primary presuppositions of capitalist production. To summarise, Marx attempts in this context to demonstrate the deficiencies of Ricardo's approach, which, at least in part, denies crises; the Trier-born theorist does so by identifying the omissions in Ricardo's theories of value and money. Nevertheless, it should be emphasised, as does Marx, that in reality the fundamental separation of purchase and sale into two mutually independent acts within one and the same process merely gives the *possibility* of crisis.

To return to the 1850s: the problematic of economic crisis still constituted a point of reference in Marx's thought some years after he had written *Bullion*, and not only within the context of his journalistic activity. Towards the mid-1850s, Marx assembled excerpt material on the problematic of crisis. During this period, he gathered together previous excerpts referring to this problematic (among other themes) into a compilation of excerpts which had undergone a second stage of processing. This yielded the text entitled '*Citate. Geldwesen. Creditsystem. Crisen*', through which Marx was able to deepen the process of his theoretical self-clarification in relation to these ranges of problems.* An insight

---

339   Ibid [translation modified – N.G.].
340   Ibid [translation modified – N.G.].
341   Marx 1989c, pp. 132–3.
*   Marx's notebook entitled *Citate. Geldwesen. Creditsystem. Crisen* [*Quotations: The Monetary System; The Credit System; Crises*] (Marx 1854/5) remains as yet unpublished.

into this material is afforded by the research carried out by Fred Schrader, the results of which were published in his 1980 monograph (already referred to above).[342]

Towards the end of the 'chapter on method' in his *Introduction to the Critique of Political Economy*, Marx outlines a plan for the architectonic of his work; from this plan, which dates from the summer of 1857, it is evident that Marx considered that he had already found a place for a systematic treatment of the crisis problematic within his conception of a text on the systematic critique of political economy. Marx's view at this time was that the theory of crisis should be approached in a systematic way only at a later stage within the logic of the exposition. In the 'chapter on method' in the 1857 *Introduction*, Marx identifies the problematic of the world market and crises as the final point within the exposition.[343]

It is possible that Marx's decision to begin work on the *Grundrisse* manuscript of 1857/8 was prompted by the impending crisis, or by Marx's expectation of the latter. It can reasonably be assumed that he also harboured political hopes related to this prospect. In 1850, at the beginning of his time in London, he had already outlined a connection between economic crisis and political revolution: 'A new revolution is possible only in consequence of a new crisis. It is, however, just as certain as this crisis'.[344] At a later stage, this connection was presumably dissolved within Marx's thinking, or he came to reject his belief in it; this was certainly not the case before the end of 1857, however. At the time Marx commenced his work on the *Grundrisse*, such insights had not yet occurred to him.

In a letter written on 18 December 1857, Marx gave Engels an account of his work on the *Grundrisse* and informed him of his compilation of empirical material on the economic crisis:

> I am engaged on a twofold task: 1. Elaborating the outlines of political economy. (For the benefit of the public it is absolutely essential to go into the matter *au fond*, as it is for my own, individually, to get rid of this nightmare.)
>
> 2. The *present crisis*. Apart from the articles for the *Tribune*, all I do is keep records of it, which, however, takes up a considerable amount of time. I think that, somewhere about the spring, we ought to do a

---

342   See Schrader 1980.

343   Marx 1973, p. 108.

344   Marx 1978b, p. 135.

pamphlet together about the affair as a reminder to the German public that we are still there as always, and always the same. I have started 3 large record books – England, Germany, France. All the material on the American affair is available in the *Tribune*, and can be collated subsequently.[345]

The corresponding excerpt material has not yet been published, although it is scheduled to appear in *MEGA*², Volume IV/14. A preliminary insight is possible, however, thanks to the research carried out by Klaus-Dieter Block and Rolf Hecker. The latter give an account of three 'crisis notebooks' which are to be published in *MEGA*², and which bear the following titles: '1857. France'; 'Book of the Crisis of 1857'; and 'The Book of the Commercial Crisis'. The first of these is a 'compilation of material containing excerpts from newspapers on the course taken by the crisis of 1857 in France, Italy and Spain'.[346] The 'Book of the Crisis of 1857' records information on the London money market as well as on developments in the stock exchanges in 'Hamburg, Northern Kingdom, Prussia, Austria (Germany)', among other topics. The third notebook contains observations relating to 'the 1857 trade crisis in England, the USA, China, India, Egypt and Australia'.[347] In the course of his systematic processing of these collections of empirical material, Marx evidently came to understand the economic crisis of 1857/8 as being international in its scale, and devoted his attention to the course taken by the crisis in various regions of the world. The economic crisis so eagerly awaited by Marx had indeed spread rapidly across countries and continents since the autumn of 1857. Yet this situation also prompted Marx to set himself the task of writing up his comprehensive theoretical work as expeditiously as possible.

Although arguments and observations relating to the theory of crisis are to be found in various passages within the *Grundrisse*, this manuscript does not contain a self-contained, unified or truly worked out theory of crisis. Although the same can be said in relation to *Theories of Surplus-Value* (contained in the *1861–63 Manuscripts*), Marx did devote ample space in this later text to various considerations relating to crisis theory. One of the arguments advanced by Marx in this context is that capitalist overproduction is conditioned by the general law of the production of capital:

---

345   Marx 1983h, pp. 224–5.

346   Block and Hecker 1991, p. 95.

347   Block and Hecker 1991, p. 96. On Marx's theoretical treatment of the crisis of 1857/8, see also Goldberg 1987.

> Overproduction is specifically conditioned by the general law of the pro-
> duction of capital: to produce to the limit set by the productive forces,
> that is to say, to exploit the maximum amount of labour with the given
> amount of capital, without any consideration for the actual limits of the
> market or the needs backed by the ability to pay; and this is carried out
> through continuous expansion of reproduction and accumulation, and
> therefore constant reconversion of revenue into capital, while on the
> other hand, the mass of the producers remain tied to the average level
> of needs, and must remain tied to it according to the nature of capitalist
> production.[348]

Marx's crisis-theoretical reflections play a further role in the draft for the third
volume of *Capital* contained within the so-called *1863–65 Manuscripts*, for
instance in what is the third chapter according to the arrangement in *MEGA*[2],
Volume II/4.2 – i.e. the chapter on the law of the tendential fall in the general
rate of profit accompanying progress in capitalist production. Some of Marx's
observations here correspond to the theory of overaccumulation: 'Overproduction *of capital* (= plethora of capital) and not of individual commodities –
though this overproduction of capital always involves overproduction of commodities – is nothing other than overaccumulation *of capital*'.[349]

The crisis problematic remained a part of Marx's thinking in later times,
prompting him to gather material. A new phase of excerpting material related
to the theory of crisis can be dated to the late 1860s; in this case, too, the
corresponding material is still awaiting publication in *MEGA*[2]. A letter written
to Engels on 31 May 1873 illustrates the significance Marx continued to attach
as a crisis theorist to his work with statistical material: 'you know about those
graphs in which the movements of prices, discount rates, etc., etc., over the
year, etc., are shown in rising and falling zigzags. I have variously attempted
to analyse crises by calculating these ups and downs as irregular curves and I
believed (and still believe it would be possible if the material were sufficiently
studied) that I might be able to determine mathematically the principal laws
governing crises'.[350] Marx had also consulted his friend, Samuel Moore, on this
score. In his letter of 10 April 1879 to Danielson (a Russian acquaintance), Marx
informed the latter that it would have been inopportune to have published the
second volume of *Capital* before the contemporary English industrial crisis had

---

348   Marx 1989c, pp. 163–4.
349   Marx 1998, p. 250 [translation modified – N.G.]; compare Marx 1993, p. 325.
350   Marx 1989e, p. 504.

reached its climax, and that the phenomena of the crisis were this time quite singular. Marx advised Danielson that '[i]t is therefore necessary to watch the present course of things until their maturity before you can "consume" them "productively", I mean "theoretically"'.[351]

It remains to emphasise the extent to which Marx was concerned to process concrete historical and empirical material alongside his more theoretical and abstract reflections on crisis theory. Michael Krätke reports that Marx had 'assembled an astounding volume of statistical and documentary material on the history of crises and economic cycles'.[352] In a further essay, Krätke suggests that Marx's work as an economic journalist provides important source material for research into his investigations into economic crises.[353]

In the following section, an account is given of the international discussion of research into crisis theory in and after Marx. The Marxist discussion of crisis theory which took place from the interwar period to the 1970s, and which is associated with an older generation of researchers, such as Eugen Varga, Natalie Moszkowska, Henryk Grossmann, Samezō Kuruma and Paul Mattick, is omitted from this account; by contrast, the focus is directed towards international contributions to research by more recent generations of researchers with an orientation towards Marx.[354]

In 1980, a study of crisis theory by Makoto Itoh, one of the leading representatives of the Uno School, was published for an international readership. Itoh defended the thesis that Marx's theory of crisis underwent a development from the *Grundrisse* via *Theories of Surplus-Value*, to *Capital*. Itoh argues that the approaches to crisis theory bequeathed by Marx throughout his work can be attributed to two different types of theory: an 'excess commodity theory' on the one hand, and an 'excess capital theory' on the other; Itoh further claims that within the context of the progressive development in Marx's crisis theory from the *Grundrisse* to *Capital*, it is only in the latter that the theoretical centre of gravity shifts from the first type of theory in the direction of the second.[355] So

---

351   Marx 1991c, p. 354.

352   Krätke 2006b, p. 5.

353   Krätke 1999. For a further account of Marx's investigations into cyclical crises, see Rojas 1989, pp. 133 ff.

354   In 1929, Henryk Grossmann defended the thesis that a theory of collapse could be reconstructed from Marx's work, and that this forms nothing less than a 'cornerstone of the economic system of Marx' (Grossmann 1992, p. 29). In more recent research, by contrast, Marx is rarely treated as a 'theorist of collapse' in the sense advocated by Grossmann.

355   In the German translation of a text by Itoh (compare Itoh 1976, p. 101 and Itoh 1978, pp. 129–30), 'excess commodity theory' is rendered as 'theory of the overproduction of

much for Itoh's general thesis. The Japanese theorist argues that in determinate passages from the *Grundrisse*, Marx holds that 'economic crisis is almost equivalent, or leads directly, to the final collapse of capitalist production, basing himself on an excess commodity theory of an underconsumptionist type'.[356] Itoh considers that Marx diversifies his 'excess commodity theory of crisis' in *Theories of Surplus-Value*, with a disproportionality approach being ranged alongside the underconsumptionist one. Itoh claims that a new type of crisis theory comes to the fore in *Capital*, namely an 'excess capital theory', which focuses on the absolute overproduction of capital. According to Itoh, however, this theory-type is given in *Capital* in an incomplete form.

Generally speaking, the Uno School regards crisis theory as a significant field of research within its overall theoretical approach. This tendency can be traced back to Kōzō Uno himself. According to Tomiichi Hoshino, Uno's theory of crisis focuses on two ranges of problems: on the one hand, Uno is concerned to identify the cause of economic crises in the process of capital accumulation (on Hoshino's account, this demonstration occurs within the framework of the theory of profit). On the other hand, Uno endeavours to detect the concrete mechanisms which can be adduced as an explanation for the outbreak of crises (according to Hoshino, this investigation takes place within the framework of the theory of credit).[357] Hoshino's assessment is that Uno attempts to prove that a 'pure' capitalist society is prone to crisis; yet, as Hoshino makes clear, Uno's theory is by no means to be taken as a theory of collapse. Like Itoh, Hoshino identifies the 'excess commodity theory' and the 'excess capital theory' as two fundamentally distinct types of crisis theory to be found in Marx's *oeuvre*. According to Hoshino, Uno himself was 'the most forceful critic of the excess commodity theory'.[358]

Probably the best-known recent study of Anglo-Saxon origin to focus on the interpretation of Marx's theory of crisis dates from the 1990s.[359] As Makoto Itoh had done previously, and at approximately the same time as Michael Heinrich was engaged in a similar project, the author of this work, Simon Clarke, considered the history of the development of Marx's crisis theory within the context of the latter's various manuscripts on the critique of political theory. According to Clarke, the theory of crisis plays no more than a rather

---

commodities, or theory of overproduction', and 'excess capital theory' is given as 'theory of overaccumulation'.

356   Itoh 1980, p. 96.
357   See Hoshino 1995, p. 65.
358   Hoshino 1995, p. 72.
359   See Clarke 1994, p. 247.

minor role in Marx's analysis within the first volume of *Capital*; nor can it be said to occupy a prominent position within the following two volumes. The crucial point established by Clarke is that the tendency to crisis is 'pervasive' within the capitalist mode of production, 'since the competitive regulation of capital accumulation is not achieved by the smooth anticipation of market adjustments by omniscient capitalists, but by the process of overaccumulation and crisis, as the tendency to overproduction runs into the barrier of the limited market'.[360] Clarke identifies Marx's focus on a tendency to crisis which is immanent within the capitalist mode of production as a defining feature of his theory: 'To insist that Marx had no theory of crisis is to insist that the focus of Marx's work is not the crisis as catastrophic event, but the inherent tendency to crisis that underlies the permanent instability of social existence under capitalism'.[361] For the British interpreter of Marx, overaccumulation and crisis belong to the 'normality' of the capitalist process of accumulation. Several years before his book was published, Clarke proposed some theses on the discussion of the theory of crisis within the debate oriented to Marx's theory.[362] Within the conception that Clarke presents in this earlier context, he indicates that a far-reaching critique of underconsumptionist theoretical approaches ought to be based on considerations relating to the theory of disproportionality, rather than taking as its basis the theory of the tendency of the rate of profit to fall. Clarke understands the tendency to overproduction as being immanent within the social form of capitalist production. On his view, crisis is the form in which the contradictions which are immanent within capital become manifest at surface-level. Clarke writes as follows: 'The Marxist theory of crisis is distinguished from bourgeois theories in the first instance in being concerned with the *necessity* of crisis'.[363] Yet Clarke emphasises that the theory of the necessity of crisis should not be identified with notions of the necessity of the collapse of capitalism.

Within the German-language discussion, Michael Heinrich has established that Marx dealt with problems relating to the theory of crisis in the *Grundrisse*, in the *1861–63 Manuscripts*, and in his work on *Capital* after 1863; Heinrich insists, however, that Marx's writings contain no theory of crisis that could be said to be finished, coherently presented, or unified from the point of view of its content. The West German interpreter of Marx considers that any attempt to merely assemble the various 'passages on crisis theory into a single theory' is

---

360   Ibid.
361   Clarke 1994, p. 279.
362   See Clarke 1990–1.
363   Clarke 1990–1, p. 442.

doomed to fail 'on account of the enormous differences in terms of their content'.[364] Heinrich argues that the notion of a Marxian theory of collapse could best be supported by referring to the *Grundrisse*, where Marx's focus on the theory of crisis hones in on a dynamic of underconsumption. Heinrich sees other aspects as being foregrounded in the *1861–63 Manuscripts*, however. In this context, Marx's considerations on crisis theory are taken up with the critique of the notions of harmony entertained by bourgeois economists. Here, according to Heinrich, the *topos* of the final crisis gives way to the conception of the crisis as a phenomenon accompanying the capitalist mode of production.[365] Heinrich considers that Marx still partially adheres to an underconsumptionist approach in these manuscripts. In the draft for the third volume of *Capital* contained in the so-called *1863–65 Manuscripts*, Heinrich identifies both 'a provisional consideration of the *cycle* as well as approaches to the development of a *general* concept of crisis which is not restricted to the cyclical movement'.[366]

In a more recent essay, Heinrich attempts to construct an approach to the theory of crisis which is based on the third volume of *Capital*, but which does not depend on the law of the tendential fall in the rate of profit (according to Heinrich, this law is not conclusively proved by Marx).[367] Here, Heinrich writes that the approaches to crisis theory which are of interest from the point of view of a monetary theory of value can be detected precisely in those reflections by Marx which are not predicated on the law of the tendential fall in the rate of profit. The West German interpreter of Marx argues that surplus-value production knows no internal limits. He considers that there thus exists a tendency towards the continual expansion of production and of the possibilities for production to take place. Yet, according to Heinrich, the consumptive capacity of society must be deemed limited, and, as such, it allows the realisation of surplus value to occur on no more than a restricted basis. Heinrich argues that the corresponding conceptual approach in Marx is not to be identified with a classical underconsumption theory, since Marx does not focus in this context on a shortfall in demand arising from the low level of wages, but rather on the way that capitals' consumption is limited by the 'drive to accumulation'. Heinrich attempts to pursue the argumentation beyond Marx

364   Heinrich 1999a, p. 342.

365   See Heinrich 1999a, p. 354.

366   Heinrich 1995b. Several years later, the South Korean researcher, Lee Jun Kim, engaged with Marx's theory of crisis (see Kim 1998). In his book, Kim presents an extensive and detailed critique of Heinrich's 1995 essay. Restrictions of space do not permit a closer examination in this context of the various criticisms levelled at Heinrich.

367   See Heinrich 2001.

himself: one of the ways of understanding how such a process plays out is that the capitalist is at liberty to accumulate his previous profits in future in the form of industrial or fictitious capital. In this context, the constellation of high interest rates and low profit expectations push the capitalist to accumulate in the form of fictitious capital, which heats speculation, but which can lead to a 'demand gap' in relation to industrial production – i.e. to a shortfall in productive consumption. Heinrich develops the argument as follows:

> That which was manifested on the level of simple circulation as the general *possibility* of crisis, namely the interruption of C–M–C in order to hold on to money, assumes a concrete form when the capitalist process is considered as a totality which is not merely mediated by money, but by the credit system: the capitalistically produced commodity (commodity capital) is sold not in order to purchase anew the elements of productive capital with the money capital so obtained ..., but rather to invest this money capital in one of the forms of fictitious capital.[368]

According to Heinrich, the consequences are unsold commodities and overcapacity on the side of industrial capital, and the possibility of increased speculation and an ensuing crash on the side of fictitious capital. In general, the following can be established in relation to Heinrich's approach: he considers that Marx's intended exposition of the capitalist mode of production in its 'ideal average' certainly contains the exposition of crisis *tendencies* which are inherent to this mode of production; what Marx's intended exposition does not contain, however, is a 'universal *model* of crisis merely requiring a few more parameters to be entered'.[369]

At around the turn of the millennium, a working group around the Greek theoretical journal, *Theseis*, likewise engaged with Marx's theory of crisis. According to John Milios, Dimitri Dimoulis and George Economakis, economic crisis is to be thought of as a temporary destabilisation of the capitalist reproduction process and simultaneously as a driving force towards the restoration of economic equilibrium. These authors argue that crises are not to be regarded as a permanent phenomenon of the capitalist mode of production. Milios, Dimoulis and Economakis suggest that the rather fragmentary character of Marx's crisis theory may be due in part to the fact that Marx was primarily concerned in *Capital* with permanent structural features of the capitalist mode

---

368   Heinrich 2001, p. 172.
369   Heinrich 2001, p. 174.

of production, with its laws; his treatment of elements such as crises and the economic cycle, which are located on a different level, occupied a subordinate position within his exposition.[370] These authors regard the concept of the overproduction of capital as constituting an essential dimension of Marx's theory of crisis.

According to Milios, this allegedly key concept in Marx's analysis within the context of his theory of crisis is expounded in a more systematic way in the third volume of *Capital* than at any other place in Marx's *oeuvre*.[371] Milios argues that crises are to be regarded as the conjunctural overaccumulation of capital – i.e. as 'a conjunctural production of commodities (means of production and means of consumption) in such quantities and prices, that they temporarily hinder the accumulation process'.[372] Milios writes that '[c]rises constitute a fusion-condensation of all forms of contradictions induced by these external relations, in a way that a fall in the rate of profit and a holdback or even a halt of the capitalist expanded reproduction process occurs'.[373]

A more recent study of the theory of crisis, published in Denmark and authored by Birger Linde, offers an interpretation of Marx's theory of crisis which takes into account how this theory developed over the history of the elaboration of Marx's *oeuvre*.[374] Linde thus retraces the development of the Trier-born theorist's conceptions of crisis theory from his early approaches right up to *Capital*. The results of Linde's research are consonant with the tenor of sections of the international scientific discussion of Marx in two important respects. Firstly, Linde challenges the notion that there is a theoretically consistent, unified theory of crisis in Marx. Instead, the Danish researcher identifies several approaches to the theory of crisis in Marx, which combine to form a heterogeneous overall picture. Secondly, Linde rejects any attempt to rely uncritically on Marx's theory of the tendential fall in the rate of profit and without calling it into question. This critical perspective, which Linde shares with a number of Japanese and German researchers, is thoroughly heterodox vis-à-vis the Marxist theoretical tradition. Also noteworthy is Linde's discrimination between Marx's various crisis-theoretical enquiries according to the two distinct levels of abstraction on which these are undertaken.[375] Linde draws a distinction in Marx between an abstract universal level of theory and the

---

370   See Milios, Dimoulis and Economakis 2002, p. 159.

371   See Milios 1999, p. 3.

372   Milios 1999, p. 1.

373   Milios 1999, p. 11.

374   See Linde 2004.

375   See Linde 2004, pp. 179 f.

level of the investigation into concrete historical processes of crisis. The crux of Linde's argument is that Marx neglected a third level of abstraction which is to be located between these two levels of abstraction – i.e. a kind of 'intermediate level' mediating the other two. According to Linde, this represents an omission within Marx's theory of crisis.

4.2   An Insight into the Marx-Oriented Discussion of Crisis in South Korea following the Asian Financial Crisis of 1997

Attention can now be focused upon recent South Korean approaches to research into Marx's theory of crisis. The interconnection between, on the one hand, money or credit and, on the other, crisis, had previously represented a point of reference for economic research oriented to Marx.[376] This line of enquiry was pursued in an ambitious way in several approaches to research conceived by South Korean researchers during or following the Asian Financial Crisis of 1997 (a crisis which particularly affected South Korea). Incidentally, the Free University of Berlin appears to have been a central node in the development of South Korean crisis theory, since the three theorists presented here all carried out their doctoral research at this university.

The first work to be noted within this context is a study by Dae-Won Park.[377] Here, the South Korean investigates the elements in Marx's crisis theory in the three volumes of *Capital* – i.e. according to the different theoretical levels at which each of the three volumes of *Capital* is located respectively: the level of the immediate process of production, that of the circulation process of capital, and that of the overall process of capitalist production.* Park undertakes this analysis against the background of his critical engagement with various Marxist approaches to the interpretation of the theory of crisis: disproportionality theory; underconsumption theory; the profit squeeze approach (which posits that the increasing strength of the working class within the economic class struggle squeezes the rate of profit and can thus lead to an economic crisis); and a certain version of overaccumulation theory. In his own reconstruction, Park relies on another form of overaccumulation theory which centres on 'explanations of the tendential fall in the rate of profit as a result of changes

---

376   In the 1980s, for example, the economist, James Crotty, emphasised the importance of money and credit for an adequate Marxist theory of accumulation and crisis (see Crotty 1985).

377   See D-W. Park 2002.

*   These subtitles are omitted in the Penguin English-language editions of the three volumes of *Capital*.

in the organic composition of capital'.[378] Furthermore, Park not only takes
into account Marx's distinction between the mere possibility and the reality of
crisis (it can be added here that according to Marx, the former can already be
thematised, at least in part, in connection with the sphere of simple commodity
circulation, whereas 'the real crisis can only be educed from the real movement
of capitalist production, competition and credit');[379] the South Korean theorist
is also concerned to highlight the nexus between the theories of credit and
crisis. Park argues that although Marx's investigation into credit, interest and
financial crisis remained rather fragmentary, certain theoretical insights can be
distilled from Marx's work, and the approaches to the theory of crisis which are
to be found there can be enhanced and/or concretised by taking into account
the credit function in the capitalist accumulation process:

> The most important insight is that credit, while essential for capitalist
> development, is the fundamental means by which crises become gener-
> alised over the whole of the capitalist economy. Credit can expand the
> horizon of capitalist development, but it cannot resolve capitalist contra-
> dictions. Credit continually drives capitalist production beyond its limits,
> thus generating economic crises.[380]

In his doctoral thesis, which draws on the conception of a 'monetary theory of
value' which has been widely disseminated within the German-language Marx
discussion in particular (although it has featured elsewhere), the South Korean
researcher, Young Bin Hahn, focuses on the interconnection between money,
credit and crisis.[381] Hahn perceives a commonality in the approaches of Karl
Marx and John Maynard Keynes – notwithstanding the significant theoretical
differences between them – in that both propagate a 'non-neutrality' of money.
Rather than dismissing the category of money as an economically irrelevant
factor, '[i]n their theories of money and credit, Marx, and later Keynes, showed
that money is by no means neutral in market relations on account of its role
in the process of social reproduction'.[382] Hahn observes that both Marx and
Keynes think of capitalist production as being characterised by instability and
disequilibria. The South Korean researcher argues that although Marx left no
finished theory of crisis, he did emphasise 'the role of money and credit as an

---

378   D-W. Park 2002, p. 68.
379   Marx 1989c, p. 143.
380   D-W. Park 2002, p. 195.
381   See Hahn 1999.
382   Hahn 1999, p. 6.

essential moment of the accumulation process and of crisis'.[383] In Hahn's view, a decisive factor here is the possibility of crisis through the separation of sale and purchase from one another; this possibility is characteristic of the monetary economy. Yet Hahn insists that this mere possibility is not to be identified with real crisis. On the South Korean's interpretation, Marx ultimately derives crisis 'from the contradictions which exist immanently within the capitalist mode of production'.[384]

Several years later, a compatriot of Hahn's would intervene in the discussion on the interconnection between the theories of money, credit and crisis, with the aim of contributing to the development of an epistemology of the monetary theory of crisis. This contribution came from the philosopher, No-Wan Kwack, who has made significant efforts towards a productive further development of Marx's critique of political economy.

In an initial essay, Kwack warns that the moments of crisis were not to be sought in production or in industrial capital alone, and instead locates them 'on every level of total social capital, and thus on every level of *Capital*'.[385] According to Kwack, Marx focused on a specific susceptibility to crisis within capitalism. The South Korean philosopher demonstrates a particular interest in Marx's approaches to a monetary theory of crisis. Kwack notes that although Marx underestimated the monetary crisis and/or the credit crisis, he 'indicated some approaches which would need to be further developed' in this regard.[386]

Kwack has published a sophisticated contribution to the theoretical foundations for a monetary theory of crisis in which he draws on, and simultaneously points beyond, Marx; in this work, Kwack orients his approach in part to the Marx-interpretation of Michael Heinrich, despite specific criticisms that he makes of the latter.[387] The epistemology of this monetary theory of crisis includes a critique of the empiricist and individualist axioms of neoliberal economic theory. In his interpretation of Marx, Kwack is concerned to extract the peculiar theoretical foundations of the approaches to the theory of crisis which are to be found in the critique of political economy. According to Kwack, Marx effects a break with the 'theoretical field' of political economy and establishes a new 'theoretical field'; yet his elaboration of his critique of political economy

---

383   Hahn 1999, p. 152.
384   Hahn 1999, p. 161.
385   Kwack 2003, p. 135.
386   Kwack 2003, p. 142.
387   See Kwack 2006.

was not without its theoretical ambivalences. It is evident within this context that Kwack relies in part on Heinrich's interpretation of Marx.

Kwack argues that the interconnected whole constituted by total social capital cannot be reduced to the movement of the individual capital. He further develops this point as follows: 'And this implies in turn that the conception of the social interrelation as a whole cannot be reduced to the sensory experience of the individual element'.[388] The South Korean philosopher contends that the distinction between the conception of the social interrelation and the sensory experience of the individual element is central to Marx's method. According to Kwack, the latter is oriented towards social relations rather than the individual capital: 'The object of Marx's theory is thus constituted in a different way when compared to classical and neoclassical economics, neoliberalism and modern epistemology; the latter for the most part presuppose the uniformity of the individual and the whole (individualism) and ultimately reduce cognition to the empirical or sensory experience of the individual (empiricism)'.[389] Kwack argues that Marx broke with the empiricist science of his time in two fundamental ways: he made the social relation itself the object of science and rejected the reduction of the social whole to the sum of its individual parts. Neither of these moves on Marx's part were compatible with empiricism: 'For Marx, the singular or the particular ... has to be explained from the interconnection of the whole – i.e. from the relation of the whole. Thus the individual or the particular is only of importance for the investigation if it affects the dynamic of the whole'.[390]

Kwack also identifies tendencies in Marx which he considers indicative of theoretical deficiencies: the South Korean interpreter of Marx refers critically to the latter's supposed inclination towards a reduction of total social capital to industrial capital; Kwack argues that this leads Marx to reduce economic crisis to industrial capital or industrial production.[391] Accordingly, the mere resuscitation of Marx is insufficient: 'What is required instead is a critical engagement with him in order to facilitate the further development and maximisation of the new theoretical field which he founded'.[392]

Kwack's conceptual approach focuses on the interconnection between credit, speculation and crisis. He contends that this interconnection has not been sufficiently taken into account by the traditional orientations within Marxist

---

388   Kwack 2006, p. 74.

389   Ibid.

390   Kwack 2006, p. 139.

391   See Kwack 2006, p. 5.

392   Kwack 2006, p. 140.

crisis theory (underconsumption theory, the theory of collapse and disproportionality theory).[393] A further dimension of Kwack's research contribution consists in his critical understanding of the approaches to crisis theory that Marx contemplated within the context of his reflections on the law of the tendential fall in the rate of profit; Kwack regards these as being provisional and questionable. According to the South Korean philosopher, *Capital* cannot be said to contain a systematic theory of crisis.

Kwack defines economic crisis as a process whose sudden outbreaks (which Marx had also identified) are inexplicable without reference to credit and speculation. Kwack maintains that capital necessarily suffers losses on the level of society as a whole through the credit-mediated collapse in speculation. The South Korean interpreter of Marx draws the following conclusion: 'The inherent susceptibility of capitalism to crisis is accounted for by the circumstance that capitalist speculation necessarily induces its own sudden collapse through the development of the credit system, and by the fact that this speculation is promoted by capitalist accumulation and the development of the credit system'.[394] Needless to say, such a 'collapse' is not to be understood in the sense of a traditional Marxist 'theory of collapse'.

Excursus on the World Market and Crisis

A specificity of the capitalist mode of production consists in the fact that, as a rule, economic crises result from an economic dynamic which is immanent in the capitalist mode of production itself. A further distinguishing feature of the capitalist mode of production is the circumstance that these crises which arise from the immanent dynamic of the capitalist mode of production itself can occur in the form of crises in the world market. In *Theories of Surplus-Value*, Marx notes that in general crises in the world market, all of the contradictions within capitalist production erupt collectively. Marx makes the following trenchant observation:

> World market crises must be regarded as the real concentration and forcible adjustment of all the contradictions within the bourgeois economy. The individual moments which are thus concentrated in these crises must emerge and be developed in each sphere of the bourgeois economy. As we advance in our examination of the latter, new determinations of this antagonism must be developed on the one hand; and on the other, the

---

393 See Kwack 2006, p. 168.
394 Kwack 2006, p. 173.

more abstract forms of this antagonism must be shown to be recurrent and contained in the more concrete forms.[395]

Marx grasps general crises in the world market, which arise from the economic process itself, as a historical novelty which first occurs when the capitalist mode of production has reached a determinate stage of development.

As Marx explains in the third volume of *Capital*, he considers the world market to be 'the very basis ... of the capitalist mode of production'.[396] A connection between the world market and crisis is already indicated in the conception of his work on the critique of political economy that Marx outlined in 1857. In the draft plan given in the *Grundrisse* (a draft plan which predates those contained in Marx's letters to Lassalle and Engels between February and April 1858), Marx refers, among other things, to the themes to be treated in the envisaged parts of the work on the state, external trade and the world market (Marx does not yet allude here to three volumes – i.e. the final three within the framework of a six-volume plan). In this context, Marx ranges crises and other themes within the problematic of the world market. In a letter written to Engels on 8 October 1858, Marx defines the generation of the world market (at least in its fundamental characteristics) and of production on this basis as the historic mission of bourgeois society.

A recent work of research thematising (among other issues) the connection between the theory of the world market and the theory of crisis in Marx was published by Christian Girschner, an adherent of Helmut Reichelt's interpretation of Marx. Girschner argues that for Marx, the dynamic of development of the capitalist world market has a 'developmental and coercive character which is double-sided, but also polarising, discontinuous and reckless; it revolutionises both society and technology; it is spasmodic; it is expansive as an end in itself; and it is mediated by economic crises' – this is a dynamic over which the agents of production exert no communal, conscious control.[397] According to Girschner, Marx criticises Ricardo's theory of external trade, arguing that the latter cannot explain world market crises in principle. As Girschner points out, Marx indicates in *Theories of Surplus-Value* that crises in the capitalist world market 'could not really occur at all as a necessity inherent to modern capital' according to Ricardo's theory.[398] For Marx, by contrast, the ever-recurring crises in the capitalist world market are 'the expression of economically objective and

---

395   Marx 1989c, p. 140 [translation modified – N.G.].
396   Marx 1981a, p. 205.
397   Girschner 1999, p. 9.
398   Girschner 1999, p. 169.

necessary contradictions within modern capital – i.e. of contradictions which are not merely contingent and explicable in terms of intentionality'.[399] Girscher adduces the above-cited passage from *Theories of Surplus-Value* to argue that Marx grasps crisis in the capitalist world market as the real concentration and violent adjustment of the contradictions within the capitalist economy.

4.3   *Summary*

By way of conclusion to the account given here of the way that the perspective on Marx's crisis theory has developed within the history of the reception of his work, it can be ascertained that Marx's crisis theory has tended to be interpreted less as a unified, consistent and completely elaborated theory, and rather more as characterised by the coexistence of various theoretical approaches which point in different directions in terms of their content. It is particularly true in relation to Marx's theory of crisis that he left behind an 'unfinished project' – i.e. a project for which mere interpretation is not sufficient, but which also requires creative further development. It can further be noted that much attention is devoted within modern Marxist crisis theory to the connection between, on the one hand, the theories of money and credit, and, on the other, the theory of crisis. Research into this connection has been further developed since the great Asian Financial Crisis of 1997.

In my opinion, a foundational function can certainly be attributed to the 'monetary theory of value', and the category of money is in turn to be grasped as a central moment of the theory of crisis. Beyond this, however, recent research has demonstrated that it is possible, through innovation, to go beyond the mere interpretation of Marx's approaches to crisis theory, whose elaboration within the critique of political economy remained fragmentary. The insight to be retained above all is that the characteristic susceptibility to crisis of the capitalist mode of production – the fact that it is characteristically crisis-ridden – is conditioned by the latter's own dynamic.

---

399   Girschner 1999, p. 170.

Conclusion

The survey provided here of the development of the reception of Marx's critique of political economy in various regions of the world, in combination with the consideration at a greater depth of some of the key themes within this reception, has revealed a complex of interweaving strands, whereby theories are formed in reference to each other, scientific cooperation is undertaken and theory transfers occur – all of these processes taking place on an international scale. In individual cases, theoretical schools have emerged that transcend national and linguistic boundaries. Overall, it can be emphasised that the engagement with Marx's critique of political economy received an unforeseen impetus in the 1960s and 1970s in particular, in a process that was as variegated as it was fertile.[1] Although the interest in Marxian theory which was aroused in this context has since receded somewhat in terms of its intensity (in particular since the 1980s), it persists to this day in many countries. The 1960s and 1970s represented an important phase in the emergence and development of a fertile theory transfer which extended across linguistic and national boundaries. Nonetheless, attempts to overcome those determinate features which correspond to a certain 'theoretical provincialism' within the formation of theory oriented to Marx's critique of political economy have met with moderate success at best in various countries.

In West Germany, an intensive discussion of the critique of political economy emerged in the mid-1960s in Frankfurt am Main, and subsequently in West Berlin; although this discussion was dominated by the West German debate, which was marked by theorists and theory collectives such as Alfred Schmidt, Hans-Georg Backhaus, Helmut Reichelt, Hans-Jürgen Krahl, the *Projektgruppe Entwicklung des Marxschen Systems*,* interpretative approaches from Eastern and Western Europe were also taken into consideration from the late 1960s onwards. The methodological discussion received a decisive impetus from a German-speaking exile, Roman Rosdolsky, whose death in 1967 prevented him from taking any further part in the debate. Subsequent research (by Brentel, Behrens, Heinrich and Rakowitz) drew at least in part on the reading of Marx by Backhaus and by those within his orbit. More recently, there has

---

1   In order to prevent misunderstandings, I should point out that although I place a particular emphasis on the remarkable theoretical progress made in the international *Capital*-debate since the 1960s in particular, this is in no way to belittle the merits of significant Marxist thinkers in the first half of the twentieth century.

*   'Project Group: Development of Marx's System'.

been an intermittent critical engagement with the Althusserian School, and to a lesser extent with other Western European currents of Marx-interpretation, as well as with corresponding theoretical approaches in Eastern Europe. Much the same can be said in relation to approaches that have been developed in the Anglo-Saxon world, in Asia (including Japan), and in Latin America.

Since the Second World War, an independent, innovative and variegated methodological debate has evolved within Japanese research, although this has been especially marked by the tendency towards the formation of schools of thought. Over a long period, the transfer of Japanese theoretical currents and interpretations of *Capital* to the West was relatively restricted – this was certainly a regrettable circumstance, given the impressive 'theoretical richness' of the Japanese discussion. There has been no more than a scant reception in the West of important thinkers such as Samezō Kuruma, Kinzaburo Sato and Sekisuke Mita, at least until recently.[2] The Marxist philosopher, Shingo Shibata, observed more than three decades ago that 'unjustifiably, there is very little knowledge of Japanese Marxism in Europe'.[3] On the whole, there has been little change in this situation over the last few decades. Although both the Japanese-Canadian branch of the Uno School (grouped around Thomas Sekine) and Makoto Itoh – also a member of the Uno School – have a strong international presence (particularly within the Anglo-Saxon discussion), this would seem to represent something of an exception. There is, however, an ongoing reception in China of the thought of Japanese philosophers and economists who draw on Marx; Wataru Hiromatsu and Makoto Itoh are among those whose work forms a reference within this context.

In South Korea, any engagement with the theory of Karl Marx that deviated from official anti-Marxist indoctrination was for a long period either impossible or driven 'underground'. This situation has since changed. Interest in Marxian theory has receded in the meantime, however. Within the theoretical activity of South Korean researchers with an orientation towards Marx's critique of political economy, there has been a reception of European and Japanese currents of thought and approaches, among others. During and after the Asian Financial Crisis of 1997, South Korean researchers with an orientation to Marx engaged with the interconnection between the theories of money, credit and crisis. The epistemological problematic has also been addressed within the South Korean interpretation of Marx. By contrast, research undertaken in the

---

2   This situation could soon change, not least because the results of research by Kuruma are now also accessible in English thanks to the translations provided by Michael Schauerte, a US citizen.

3   Shibata 1977.

People's Republic of China has been scarcely able until now to have any impact on the international methodological discussion in relation to *Capital*.

In the former Soviet Union, a sophisticated discussion of value theory had already developed around Isaak I. Rubin in the 1920s, although this was to be curtailed by Stalinism. The *Capital*-discussion was revitalised during and after the period of the 'Khrushchev Thaw', and ultimately developed a certain pluralism, as exemplified by the debates around Vladimir Shkredov and Igor Boldyrev. A close cooperation was developed between Soviet and East German researchers within the framework of the $MEGA^2$ project and associated research. While there were heavy restrictions to the penetration of any influences into the Soviet Bloc from the other side of the 'Iron Curtain', works by Soviet, East German and Czechoslovak authors (such as Vitaly Solomonovich Vygodsky, I.I. Rubin, Evald Ilyenkov, W. Tuchscheerer and Jindřich Zelený) had a considerable impact in the non-Socialist countries. It is particularly regrettable, however, that the comprehensive research undertaken within the orbit of the Halle-based 'Six-Volume Reconstruction Project' has not been adequately taken into consideration within the international discussion in the 'West'.

In Western Europe, Italy and France have formed the most important theoretical centres. In Italy, alongside the predominantly 'autochthonous' discussion of the postwar period, which was particularly associated with the approaches of thinkers such as Galvano Della Volpe, Lucio Colletti, Claudio Napoleoni and Cesare Luporini, there has also been a reception of theoretical approaches originating from France, West Germany, Latin America and the former countries of 'actually existing socialism'. Within France, the Althusserian School developed a great influence in the 1960s and 1970s, although Althusser also encountered vehement criticism within the French context; this school of thought also had a notable impact elsewhere, including in other European countries, in Latin America and in the Anglo-Saxon world.[4] Of all the orientations referred to here, Althusserianism would appear to represent the most truly global theoretical current. In Greece, the influence of the West German interpretation of Marx's theory of value as a 'monetary theory of value' proved to be significant, as is illustrated by the processes of theory formation which have occurred within the orbit of the Greek journal, *Theseis*. The Danish 'capital-logic' discourse was developed in the 1970s under the influence of the West German New Marx-Reading and in opposition to Althusserianism.

---

4   Althusser's interpretation of Marx was also received in the Arab world at an early stage (see Mosbah 2006). *Pour Marx* and at least parts of *Lire le Capital* were published in Arabic translation in Damascus already in 1966.

The question of whether to adhere to or to oppose Althusserianism also played an important role in Latin America in the 1960s and 1970s, where this current was relatively influential. Enrique Dussel's 'autochthonous' theoretical approach has been of great significance since the mid-1980s. Dussel has striven to elaborate a specifically Latin American perspective on the critique of political economy from the global 'periphery'. A number of sophisticated approaches have also been developed in Latin America since the 1990s. These relate to Marx's critique of political economy as a critical theory of fetishism (Néstor Kohan), or emphasise the fundamentally critical character of Marx's theory as the critique of political economy (Jorge Grespan), or focus on the form-theoretical dimension in Marx (Rolando Astarita).

With regard to the situation in the Anglo-Saxon world, it can be established that the debate here has proven capable – at least sporadically, and especially since the 1970s and 1980s – of taking into consideration contemporary approaches originating elsewhere. There has been an Anglophone reception of works produced within German-language research, such as Backhaus's form-theoretical approach and also Rosdolsky's path-breaking investigation into the problematic of Marx's plans for the architectonic of his critique of political economy. Important contributions by two South Asian theorists closely associated with the Anglo-Saxon discourse, Banaji and Shamsavari, stimulated thinking in relation to the 'Hegelianising' interpretative orientation. In the 1980s, the influence of the Uno School was manifest, especially in Canada. There was also a reception of Anti-Hegelian approaches: Colletti and Althusser were important figures in this regard. Coinciding approximately with this increased reception of various international approaches since the 1970s was an intensification of the 'autochthonous' methodological discussion of Marx's critique of political economy. A specifically Anglo-Saxon theoretical project came to be developed in the shape of 'analytical Marxism' (even if this project, whose heyday came in the 1980s and early 1990s, was highly contested within the Anglo-Saxon world, and was, in my opinion, theoretically retrograde); on the other hand, largely independent 'Hegelianising' theoretical currents (the 'New Dialectic' approach and related orientations) were formed above all from the 1980s and 1990s onwards. Yet as these developments occurred, there was an increasing tendency for the Anglo-Saxon Marx debate to close itself off from external influences (even if there were, and continue to be, counter-tendencies: contributions by thinkers such as Enrique Dussel, Jacques Bidet and Alfredo Saad-Filho have met with a certain resonance within the Anglophone discussion). Vice versa, 'analytical Marxism' was scarcely able to influence the Marx debate beyond the Anglo-Saxon world.

Reviewing the conceptual approaches within the historical development of the international Marx debate that have been examined in the present study, it is possible to identify several interpretative tendencies which can be ranged under the rubric of the New Marx-Reading which has emerged since the 1960s and 1970s in particular (the precursors to such a reading are disregarded here). Within this context, a fundamental renewal of Marx-oriented thought has been undertaken.

Marx's approach has been grasped more strongly than ever before as an emphatic *critique* of political economy – this is in marked contrast to its reduction to a mere 'alternative' political economy. A significant factor here has been the establishment of an absolutely fundamental demarcation between Marx and the classical economists, and between Marx and Ricardo in particular; a question which has occasionally been raised in this context, however, is that of the possible ambivalences within Marx's 'scientific revolution' vis-à-vis classical political economy. The tendency to attach considerably more value to Marx's critique of political economy than to certain discourses of traditional Marxism, such as the 'dialectics of nature' or a determinate form of historical determinist thought, has been of crucial significance here. In addition, an alternative has been developed to the Marx discourse which relied primarily on the latter's early writings; this has occurred through the switching of the main focus to the 'mature' critique of political economy that Marx elaborated during his time in London. This concentration on Marx's critique of political economy has resulted in the development of a certain sensitivity towards its specifically 'qualitative' dimension, particularly from the 1960s and 1970s onwards. A new interest – one that persists to this day – was awakened in Marx's form-theory, his theory of fetish and mystification (his critique of political economy includes a comprehensive 'disenchantment' or 'demystification' of the 'inverted world' of the economy), and his differentiation between various levels of abstraction and exposition in the critique of political economy. In this latter connection, a discussion has developed internationally within the secondary literature concerning the problematic of Marx's plans for the architectonic of his critique of political economy. Likewise, there has been a serious engagement with epistemological questions. The interpretation of Marx's theory of value as a monetary theory of value has become ever more strongly established. The specifically necessary interconnection between the commodity, value and money has come to be foregrounded. A decidedly form-theoretical and/or form-critical reading of Marx has been developed. In addition, the so-called 'logico-historical' interpretation introduced by Friedrich Engels has been largely superseded within research into Marx. The insight has come to be accepted that the object of the beginning of the exposition of the first volume of *Capital* is by no means to be considered a historical, pre-capitalist 'simple commodity production'. Moreover, the intensive engagement with Marx's value-form analysis has come to play an increasingly prominent role within the reception of his work. In West Germany, for example, this occurred from the 1960s and 1970s onwards, whereas in Japan this was the case significantly earlier.

From the perspective of the history of theory, the emergence and further development of the New Marx-Reading as a current within the international interpretation of *Capital* over the last few decades has contributed to the formation of an adequate image of Marx beyond 'popular' myths and the questionable alternative of the damnation or canonisation of the Trier-born thinker.[5] The period since the 1960s in particular can be considered as constituting a new epoch in the development of Marx-related thought: in this new era, it has been possible to set free an innovative theoretical potential that had formerly been blocked by Stalinism.

Also significant is the interconnection between the publishing history of Marx's *oeuvre* and the historical development of the interpretation of Marx. In the 1950s and 1960s, a mode of reading Marx which was especially prevalent in Western Europe was primarily oriented to his early writings, relying mainly on the *Economic and Philosophical Manuscripts*, which were first published in 1932; in the 1960s and 1970s, by contrast, the increasing interest in the Marx of the 'mature' critique of political economy coincided with an international wave of publication and reception of the *Grundrisse*, which had first appeared in 1939/41.[6] Likewise, a part of the German-language and Japanese *Capital*-debate of the 1990s was closely connected with the progress of the $MEGA^2$ edition, and particularly with the publication in 1992/3 of Marx's original manuscript for the third volume of his so-called *Capital* draft of 1863–5.

On the basis of the present study, it is possible to demonstrate the innovative theoretical potential that has been developed on an international and

---

5   A popular introduction to the critique of political economy by Michael Heinrich is based on the results of the New Marx-Reading and establishes a demarcation between Marx, the critic of political economy, and 'worldview Marxism' (see Heinrich 2012). Given that Heinrich's introduction has been widely disseminated since its publication, it is to be hoped that aspects of this new kind of image of Marx might permeate the consciousness of a wider public beyond the ranks of researchers and specialist circles.

6   This is not to suggest that Marx's 'mature' critique of political economy attracted no scientific interest in the 1950s. It should be recalled that Western European authors such as Maximilien Rubel in France or Giulio Pietranera in Italy also published studies on Marx's 'mature' critique of political economy during that decade.

virtually global scale over the last decades within the interpretation of Marx, and within critical social theory with an orientation to Marx's critique of political economy. Despite the extensive marginalisation of Marxism *in politicis* as a consequence of the political upheavals of 1989/90, the scientific reception of Marx has continued to develop in a productive way to the present day. Marxism in the sense of a comprehensive 'worldview' has been superseded historically. Yet the Marxian theoretical approach, which aims to explain the internal interconnection between economic categories and relations, and at the same time to accomplish a 'disenchantment' or 'demystification' of the 'inverted world' of the economy by means of a critical theory of fetishism and mystification, retains its contemporary relevance and theoretical significance for the understanding of 'societies in which the capitalist mode of production prevails'.[7] It is all the more important, then, to develop an awareness of the complex and (virtually) global history of the interpretation of Marxian theory over the last decades.

7   Marx 1976a, p. 125.

Postface

This work was first published in German in 2009 under the title *Marx global.*
Zur Entwicklung des internationalen Marx-diskurses seit 1965, and has been
very slightly revised for the English-language edition. Thematically, it deals
with the international interpretation of Marx's critique of economics up to
approximately 2007/8. Following the publication of the German edition, six-
teen reviews were published in Germany, Austria, Italy and Switzerland. Most
of these reviews recognised *Marx global* as a positive contribution; the spectrum of reactions ranged from emphatic acclaim to vehement criticism. The
most extensive contribution to the discussion came in the form of an open and
non-polemical critical engagement by the philosopher, Wolfdietrich Schmied-
Kowarzik, who argued that Marx's critique of political economy, while indispensable, should be understood as being bound up within a project of the
'philosophy of social praxis' – a project oriented towards 'human emancipation'.[1] This postface is not the place to engage in a dialogue with Schmied-
Kowarzik, since the decisive issues here refer us to questions of fundamentals. Ultimately, it would be a matter of determining the relation between the
'young', the 'middle-period' and the 'mature' Marx in a differentiated way, and of
posing the question of possible breaks and continuities in his theoretical development. Here, I would merely indicate that, with regard to these questions,
diverging conceptions have also been presented within the German-language
Neue Marx-Lektüre.

As far as the worldwide reception of Marx since the beginning of the twenty-
first century is concerned, the material presented here can be supplemented
by a number of reports and surveys which have appeared since the publication
of the German edition of this work in 2009 – including above all those accounts
which also take the period after 2007/8 into consideration.[2] Given the language
barriers involved, further additions to *Marx Worldwide* would be very welcome,
especially in relation to the engagement with Marx in China and South Korea.
The Japanese Marx-researcher, Kenji Mori, is currently leading a wide-ranging
research project into the history of the reception of Marx with the participation
of international researchers; the aim of this project is to undertake a systematic

---

1 See Schmied-Kowarzik 2010.
2 See, for example, the contributions by Francisco Sobrino, Armando Boito, Luiz Eduardo Mota,
   Paul Blackledge, Jean-Numa Ducange, Jan Hoff, Gianfranco Ragona, Vesa Oittinen, Daping
   Hu, Seongjin Jeong and Hiroshi Uchida in Musto 2010.

compilation and investigation of the ongoing Marx-oriented or Marx-based discussions of crisis theory in various countries, and to present the results to the interested public. The Italian journal, *Il Ponte*, dedicated a 2013 issue to the international reception of Marxian theory, with a particular emphasis on the critique of political economy; this issue took the form of detailed accounts focusing on various countries and encompassing above all the period since the turn of the millennium.[3]

---

3   Fineschi, Redolfi Riva and Sgrò 2013.

Bibliography

Adorno, Theodor W. 1974, *Philosophische Terminologie*, Volume Two, Frankfurt am Main: Suhrkamp.

———— 2000, 'Kritik der Pseudo-Aktivität: Adornos Verhältnis zur Studentenbewegung im Spiegel seiner Korrespondenz: Eine Dokumentation', *Frankfurter Adorno-Blätter*, VI: 42–116.

———— 2001 [1966], *Negative Dialectics*, translated by Dennis Redmond, available at: http://www.efn.org/~dredmond/ndtrans.html

Ahrweiler, Georg 1976, *Hegels Gesellschaftslehre*, Darmstadt: Luchterhand.

Altamira, César 2006, *Los marxismos del nuevo siglo*, Buenos Aires: Biblos.

Albritton, Robert 1984, 'The Dialectic of Capital: A Japanese Contribution', *Capital & Class*, 22: 157–76.

———— 1986, *A Japanese Reconstruction of Marxist Theory*, Basingstoke: Macmillan.

———— 1999, *Dialectics and Deconstruction in Political Economy*, Basingstoke: Macmillan.

———— 2002, 'A Response to Chris Arthur', *Historical Materialism*, 10, 2: 207–18.

———— 2005, 'How Dialectics Runs Aground: The Antinomies of Arthur's Dialectic of Capital', *Historical Materialism*, 13, 2: 167–88.

———— 2007, *Economics Transformed: Discovering the Brilliance of Marx*, London: Pluto.

Albritton, Robert and John R. Bell 1995, 'Introduction', in *A Japanese Approach to Political Economy: Unoist Variations*, edited by Robert Albritton and Thomas Sekine, Basingstoke: Macmillan.

Althusser, Louis 1969, 'Avertissement aux lecteurs du Livre I du *Capital*', in *Le Capital, Livre I*, by Karl Marx, translated by Joseph Roy, Paris: Garnier-Flammarion.

———— 1971 [1964–70], *Lenin and Philosophy: And Other Essays*, translated by Ben Brewster, London: NLB.

———— 1974, 'Projet de Préface pour un recueil de textes qui irait de "Lire le Capital" (1965) à "Lenine et la philosophie" (1968)', in *Théorie et Politique: Louis Althusser*, by Saül Karsz and Louis Althusser, Paris: Fayard.

———— 1978a, 'The Crisis of Marxism', *Marxism Today*, July: 215–27.

———— 1978b, 'Avant-propos', in *Le concept de loi économique dans 'Le Capital'*, by Gérard Duménil, Paris: Maspero.

———— 1979 [1965], *For Marx*, translated by Ben Brewster, London: Verso.

———— 1985 [1971], 'Marxism and Class Struggle', translated by Patrick Lyons, *Radical*, 1: 12–13.

———— 2006 [1994], 'Marx in his Limits', in: *Philosophy of the Encounter: Later Writings, 1978–1987*, by Louis Althusser, edited by François Matheron and Olivier Corpet, translated by G.M. Goshgarian, London: Verso.

Althusser, Louis and Étienne Balibar 1970 [1965], *Reading Capital*, London: NLB.

────── 1972 [1965], *Das Kapital lesen*, two volumes, Reinbek: Rowohlt.

Althusser, Louis, Étienne Balibar, Roger Establet, Pierre Macherey and Jacques Rancière 2014 [1965], *Das Kapital lesen*, translated by Frieder Otto Wolf and Eva Pfaffenberger: Münster, Westfälisches Dampfboot.

Altvater, Elmar 1998, '*Das Kapital* (Bd. 1) von Marx in Schaubildern und Kommentaren', in *Kapital.doc: Das Kapital (Bd. 1) von Marx in Schaubildern und Kommentaren*, edited by Elmar Altvater et al., Münster: Westfälisches Dampfboot.

Amadeo, Javier 2006, 'Mapeando el Marxismo', in *La teoría marxista hoy: problemas y perspectivas*, edited by Atilio Borón, Javier Amadeo and Sabrina González, Buenos Aires: Consejo Latinoamericano de Ciencias Sociales.

Amin, Samir 1978, *The Law of Value and Historical Materialism*, New York, NY: Monthly Review Press.

Anderson, Kevin 1983, 'The "Unknown" Marx's *Capital*, Volume I: The French Edition of 1872–75, 100 Years Later', *Review of Radical Political Economics*, 15, 4: 71–80.

Anderson, Perry 1976, *Considerations on Western Marxism*, London: NLB.

────── 1980, *Arguments within English Marxism*, London: NLB.

────── 1983, *In the Tracks of Historical Materialism*, London: Verso.

Anonymous 1968, 'Marx in Print' [reproduced from *Times Literary Supplement*, 9 May 1968], *Monthly Review*, 20, 5: 65–8.

Antonova, Irina 2006, 'Einige methodologische Aspekte der Wechselwirkung von Sozial- und Naturwissenschaften bei Marx', in *Karl Marx und die Naturwissenschaften im 19. Jahrhundert*, (*Beiträge zur Marx-Engels-Forschung: Neue Folge*, 2006), edited by Rolf Hecker et al., Hamburg: Argument.

Arenz, Horst, Joachim Bischoff and Urs Jaeggi (eds.) 1973, *Was ist revolutionärer Marxismus? Kontroverse über Grundfragen marxistischer Theorie zwischen Louis Althusser und John Lewis*, West Berlin: VSA.

Aricó, José 1980, *Marx y América Latina*, Lima: Centro de Estudios para el Desarrollo y la Participación.

Arndt, Andreas 1985, *Karl Marx: Versuch über den Zusammenhang seiner Theorie*, Bochum: Germinal.

────── 1988, 'Negativität und Widerspruch in Hegels Ökonomie: Voraussetzungen der Hegelschen Kritik der politischen Ökonomie in der Auseinandersetzung mit Fichte', *Hegel-Jahrbuch*, 1988: 315–28.

────── 2004, *Unmittelbarkeit*, Bielefeld: Transcript.

────── 2008, 'Was ist Dialektik? Anmerkungen zu Kant, Hegel und Marx', *Das Argument*, 274: 37–48.

────── 2012 [1985], *Karl Marx: Versuch über den Zusammenhang seiner Theorie*, Berlin: Akademie.

────── 2013, '... unbedingt das letzte Wort aller Philosophie', in *Karl Marx – Per-*

spektiven der Gesellschaftskritik, edited by Daniel Loick and Rahel Jaeggi, Berlin: Akademie.

Arndt, Andreas and Wolfgang Lefèvre 1986, 'System und System-Kritik: Zur Logik der bürgerlichen Gesellschaft bei Hegel und Marx', *Hegel-Jahrbuch*, 1986: 11–25.

Arthur, Christopher J. 1979, 'Dialectic of the Value-Form', in *Value: The Representation of Labour in Capitalism*, edited by Diane Elson, London: CSE Books.

———— 1986, *Dialectics of Labour: Marx and his Relation to Hegel*, Oxford: Blackwell.

———— 1993, 'Hegel's *Logic* and Marx's *Capital*', in *Marx's Method in Capital: A Reexamination*, edited by Fred Moseley, Atlantic Highlands, NJ: Humanities.

———— 1996, 'Engels as Interpreter of Marx', in *Engels Today: A Centenary Appreciation*, edited by Christopher Arthur, Basingstoke: Macmillan.

———— 2000, 'Marx, Orthodoxy, Labour, Value', in *Marx' Ökonomiekritik im Kapital*, (*Beiträge zur Marx-Engels-Forschung: Neue Folge*, 1999), edited by Rolf Hecker et al., Hamburg: Argument.

———— 2002a, *The New Dialectic and Marx's Capital*, Leiden: Brill.

———— 2002b, 'On Robert Albritton's *Dialectics and Deconstruction in Political Economy*', Historical Materialism 10, 1: 251–7.

———— 2003a, 'Once more on the Homology Thesis: A Response to Smith's Reply', *Historical Materialism*, 11, 1: 195–8.

———— 2003b, 'The Hegel-Marx Connection', *Historical Materialism*, 11, 1: 179–83.

———— 2003c, 'Review Article on Enrique Dussel, *Towards an Unknown Marx: A Commentary on the Manuscripts of 1861–3*', Historical Materialism, 11, 2: 247–63.

———— 2006a, 'Money and Exchange', *Capital & Class*, 90: 7–36.

———— 2006b, 'The Inner Totality of Capitalism', *Historical Materialism*, 14, 3: 85–111.

———— 2008, 'USA, Britain, Australia and Canada [Dissemination and reception of the *Grundrisse* in the world]', in *Karl Marx's Grundrisse: Foundations of the Critique of Political Economy 150 Years Later*, edited by Marcello Musto, New York, NY: Routledge.

Artous, Antoine 2004, 'Le marxisme comme théorie critique', available at: http://www.preavis.org/breche-numerique/IMG/pdf/ARTOUS_marxisme-theorie-critique_CC173.pdf

———— 2006, *Marx et le fétichisme: le marxisme comme théorie critique*, Paris: Syllepse.

Astarita, Rolando 2004, *Valor, mercado mundial y globalización*, Buenos Aires: Kaicron.

Avenas, Denise and Alain Brossat 1972, 'Les malsaines "lectures" d'Althusser', *Sur la Méthode*, 9: 64–79.

Backhaus, Hans-Georg 1980 [1969], 'On the Dialectics of the Value-Form', translated by Konstanz-Sydney Research Program, *Thesis Eleven*, 1: 99–120.

———— 1997a, *Dialektik der Wertform: Untersuchungen zur marxschen Ökonomiekritik*, Freiburg: ça ira.

———— 1997b, 'Zuvor: Die Anfänge der neuen Marx-Lektüre', in *Dialektik der Wertform*: *Untersuchungen zur marxschen Ökonomiekritik*, by Hans-Georg Backhaus, Freiburg: ça ira.

———— 1997c, 'Anhang: Theodor Adorno über Marx und die Grundbegriffe der soziologischen Theorie – Aus einer Seminarmitschrift im Sommersemester 1962', in *Dialektik der Wertform*: *Untersuchungen zur marxschen Ökonomiekritik*, by Hans-Georg Backhaus, Freiburg: ça ira.

———— 1998, 'Über die Notwendigkeit einer Ent-Popularisierung des Marxschen Kapitals', in *Kein Staat zu machen: Zur Kritik der Sozialwissenschaften*, edited by Christoph Görg and Roland Roth, Münster: Westfälisches Dampfboot.

———— 2000a, 'Über den Doppelsinn der Begriffe "Politische Ökonomie" und "Kritik" bei Marx und in der Frankfurter Schule', in *Wolfgang Harich zum Gedächtnis. Eine Gedenkschrift in zwei Bänden*, Volume 2, edited by Stefan Dornuf and Reinhard Pitsch, Munich: Müller & Nerding.

———— 2000b, 'Über den Begriff der Kritik im Marxschen Kapital und in der Kritischen Theorie', in *Kritik der Politik: Johannes Agnoli zum 75. Geburtstag*, edited by Joachim Bruhn, Manfred Dahlmann and Clemens Nachtmann, Freiburg im Breisgau: ça ira.

Backhaus, Hans-Georg and Helmut Reichelt 1994, 'Der politisch-ideologische Grundcharakter der Marx-Engels-Gesamtausgabe': eine Kritik an den *Editionsrichtlinien* der IMES, *MEGA-Studien*, 1994, 2: 101–118.

Badaloni, Nicola 1971, *Il Marxismo italiano degli anni sessanta*, Rome: Editore Riuniti.

———— 1972, *Per il comunismo: questioni di teoria*, Torino: Einaudi.

Bader, Veit-Michael et al. 1975a, *Krise und Kapitalismus bei Marx*, Volume One, Frankfurt am Main: Europäische Verlagsanstalt.

———— 1975b, *Krise und Kapitalismus bei Marx*, Volume Two, Frankfurt am Main: Europäische Verlagsanstalt.

Bader, Veit-Michael, Joachim Bischoff, Heiner Ganßmann, Werner Goldschmidt, Burkhard Hoffmann and Lothar Riehn 1970, '"Marxistische Wirtschaftstheorie" – ein Lehrbuch der Politischen Ökonomie?', *Das Argument*, 57: 216–27.

Badia, Gilbert 1981, 'Einige Bemerkungen über die Verbreitung der Werke von Karl Marx und Friedrich Engels in Frankreich', *Marx-Engels-Jahrbuch*, 4: 447–62.

Balibar, Étienne 1974, 'Sur la dialectique historique: Quelques remarques critiques à propos de *Lire le capital*', in *Cinq études du matérialisme historique*, by Étienne Balibar, Paris: Maspero.

———— 1990, 'Actualité d'Althusser à l'étranger', *Actuel Marx*, 7: 164–67.

———— 1995 [1993], *The Philosophy of Marx*, London: Verso.

Balibar, Étienne, and Gérard Raulet (eds.) 2001, *Marx démocrate: le manuscrit de 1843*, Paris: Presses universitaires de France.

Banaji, Jairus 1979, 'From the Commodity to Capital: Hegel's Dialectic in Marx's *Capital*', in *Value: The Representation of Labour in Capitalism*, edited by Diane Elson, London: CSE Books.

Bandyopadhyay, Pradeep 1972, 'The Many Faces of French Marxism', *Science & Society*, 36, 2: 129–57.

Barreda, Andrés 1987, 'Entwicklung der Diskussion und Erforschung der Werke von Marx und Engels in Mexiko während der letzten drei Jahrzehnte', in *Internationale Marx-Engels-Forschung*, (*Marxistische Studien: Jahrbuch des IMSF*, 12), edited by Institut für Marxistische Studien und Forschungen, Frankfurt am Main: IMSF.

Barshay, Andrew E. 2004, *The Social Sciences in Modern Japan: The Marxian and Modernist Traditions*, Berkeley, CA: University of California Press.

Becker, Egon 2005, 'Nachwort', in *Facetten der Warenform: Zur Arbeitswerttheorie von Karl Marx unter besonderer Berücksichtigung der Widerspruchsproblematik*, by Begoña Gutiérrez de Dütsch, Norderstedt: Books on Demand.

Becker, Jens 2002, 'Der Konflikt zwischen dem SDS und der SPD-Führung in den 50er und frühen 60er Jahren', in *Emanzipation als Versöhnung: Zu Adornos Kritik der 'Warentausch'-Gesellschaft und Perspektiven der Transformation*, edited by Iring Fetscher, Alfred Schmidt, Hans-Georg Backhaus et al., Frankfurt am Main: Neue Kritik.

Behrens, Diethard 1993, 'Erkenntnis und Ökonomiekritik', in *Gesellschaft und Erkenntnis: zur materialistischen Erkenntnis- und Ökonomiekritik*, edited by Diethard Behrens, Freiburg im Breisgau: ça ira.

———— 1995, 'Ein Kommentar zum MEGA²-Band II/4.2', in *Engels' Druckfassung versus Marx' Manuskripte zum III. Buch des 'Kapital'*, (*Beiträge zur Marx-Engels-Forschung: Neue Folge*, 1995), edited by Rolf Hecker et al., Hamburg: Argument.

———— 2007, 'Der Anfang und die Methode', in *Geld – Kapital – Wert: Zum 150. Jahrestag der Niederschrift von Marx' ökonomischen Manuskripten 1857/58 'Grundrisse der Kritik der politischen Ökonomie'*, (*Beiträge zur Marx-Engels-Forschung: Neue Folge*, 2007), edited by Rolf Hecker et al., Hamburg: Argument.

Behrens, Diethard and Kornelia Hafner 1993, 'Totalität und Kritik', in *Gesellschaft und Erkenntnis: zur materialistischen Erkenntnis- und Ökonomiekritik*, edited by Diethard Behrens, Freiburg im Breisgau: ça ira.

Behrens, Fritz 1952, *Zur Methode der politischen Ökonomie: ein Beitrag zur Geschichte der politischen Ökonomie*, East Berlin: Akademie.

———— 1953, 'Zur Entwicklung der politischen Ökonomie beim jungen Marx', *Aufbau: Kulturpolitische Monatsschrift*, 9, 5: 444–56.

Bell, John R. 1995, 'Dialectics and Economic Theory', in *A Japanese Approach to Political Economy: Unoist Variations*, edited by Robert Albritton and Thomas Sekine, Basingstoke: Macmillan.

———— 2003, 'From Hegel to Marx to the Dialectic of Capital', in *New Dialectics and Political Economy*, edited by Robert Albritton and John Simoulidis, Basingstoke: Palgrave Macmillan.

Bello, Walden 2004, 'Marx, Gramsci und die Philosophie des Widerstandes', available at: http://praxisphilosophie.de/bellomarx.pdf

Bellofiore, Riccardo 1997, 'Guest Editor's Introduction', *International Journal of Political Economy*, 27, 2: 3–20.

———— 2006, 'Marx dopo Hegel: Il capitale come totalità e la centralità della produzione', in in *Sulle tracce di un fantasma: L'opera di Karl Marx tra filologia e filosofia*, edited by Marcello Musto, Rome: Manifestolibri.

———— (ed.) 2007, *Da Marx a Marx?: un bilancio dei marxismi italiani del Novecento*, Rome: Manifestolibri.

Bellofiore, Riccardo and Roberto Finelli 1998, 'Capital, Labour and Time: The Marxian Monetary Labour Theory of Value as a Theory of Exploitation', in *Marxian Economics: A Reappraisal, Volume One: Method, Value and Money*, edited by Riccardo Bellofiore, Basingstoke: Macmillan.

Bellofiore, Riccardo and Roberto Fineschi (eds.) 2009, *Re-reading Marx: New Perspectives after the Critical Edition*, Basingstoke: Palgrave Macmillan.

Benoit Hector 1996, 'Sobre a crítica (dialética) de *O Capital*', *Crítica marxista*, 3: 14–44.

———— 1999, 'Pensando com (ou contra) Marx? Sobre o método dialético de *O Capital*', *Crítica marxista*, 8: 81–92.

Bensaïd, Daniel 2002 [1995], *Marx for our Times: Adventures and Misadventures of a Critique*, translated by Gregory Elliott, London: Verso.

Bernstein, Gail Lee 1976, *Japanese Marxist: A portrait of Kawakami Hajime, 1879–1946*, Cambridge, MA: Harvard University Press.

Bidet, Jacques 1987, 'Kōzō Uno et son école: une théorie pure du capitalisme', in *Le Marxisme au Japon*, (*Actuel Marx*, 2), edited by Jacques Bidet and Jacques Texier, Paris: L'Harmattan.

———— 1990, *Théorie de la modernité suivi de Marx et le marché*, Paris: Presses universitaires de France.

———— 1991, 'Für eine metastrukturale Theorie der Moderne', *Deutsche Zeitschrift für Philosophie*, 39: 1331–40.

———— 1992, 'Für eine allgemeine Theorie der modernen Gesellschaft', *Dialektik*, 1992/3: 67–86.

———— 1999, *Théorie générale: théorie du droit, de l'économie et de la politique*, Paris: Presses universitaires de France.

———— 2004, *Explication et reconstruction du 'Capital'*, Paris: Presses universitaires de France.

———— 2005a, 'Les nouvelles interprétations du *Capital*', available at: http://perso.orange.fr/jacques.bidet/intercap.htm

———— 2005b, 'The Dialectician's Interpretation of Capital: On Christopher Arthur, *The New Dialectic and Marx's Capital*', *Historical Materialism*, 13, 2: 121–46.

———— 2006, 'Die metastrukturale Rekonstruktion des *Kapital*', in *Das Kapital neu lesen: Beiträge zur radikalen Philosophie*, edited by Jan Hoff, Alexis Petrioli, Ingo Stützle, Frieder Otto Wolf, Münster: Westfälisches Dampfboot.

———— 2007 [1985], *Exploring Marx's Capital: Philosophical, Economic and Political Dimensions*, translated by David Fernbach, Leiden: Brill.

Bihr, Alain 2001, *La reproduction du capital: prolégomènes à une théorie générale du capitalisme*, Lausanne: Page deux.

———— 2007, 'La critique du fétichisme économique, fil rouge du *Capital*' available at: http://netx.u-paris10.fr/actuelmarx/cm5/com/M15_Philo_Bihr.pdf (last retrieved 28 April 2008).

———— 2010, 'La critique de la valeur, fil rouge du *Capital*', *¿Interrogations?*, 10, available at: http://www.revue-interrogations.org/La-critique-de-la-valeur-Fil-rouge

Birwa, 1989, 'Zur Frage der Übersetzung und Herausgabe der Werke von Karl Marx in mongolischer Sprache', *Beiträge Zur Marx-Engels-Forschung*, 28: 133–8.

Bischoff, Joachim 1973, *Gesellschaftliche Arbeit als Systembegriff: über wissenschaftliche Dialektik*, West Berlin: VSA.

Blank, Hans-Joachim 2002, 'Zur Marx-Rezeption des frühen Horkheimer', in *Emanzipation als Versöhnung: Zu Adornos Kritik der 'Warentausch'-Gesellschaft und Perspektiven der Transformation*, edited by Iring Fetscher and Alfred Schmidt, Frankfurt am Main: Neue Kritik.

Bljumin, I.G. 1953, 'Die Mehrwertlehre – der Grundpfeiler der ökonomischen Theorie von Marx', *Sowjetwissenschaft: Gesellschaftswissenschaftliche Abteilung*, 3: 343–61.

Block, Klaus-Dieter and Rolf Hecker 1991, 'Das "Book of the Crisis of 1857" von Karl Marx', in *Studien zum Werk von Marx und Engels*, (*Beiträge zur Marx-Engels-Forschung*: Neue Folge, 1991), edited by Rolf Hecker et al., Hamburg: Argument.

Boccara, Paul 1978, *Sur la mise en mouvement du 'Capital'*, Paris: Editions sociales.

———— 1982, *Studien über 'Das Kapital'*, Frankfurt am Main: Marxistische Blätter.

Bonefeld, Werner 2001, '"Kapital" and its subtitle: a note on the meaning of critique', *Capital & Class*, 75: 53–64.

———— 2014, *Critical Theory and the Critique of Political Economy: On Subversion and Negative Reason*, New York, NY: Bloomsbury Academic.

———— 2016, 'Negative Dialectics and the Critique of Economic Objectivity', *History of the Human Sciences*, 29, 2: 60–76.

Bonefeld, Werner, Richard Gunn, John Holloway and Kosmas Psychopedis 1995, 'Introduction: Emancipating Marx', in *Open Marxism, Volume Three: Emancipating Marx*, edited by Werner Bonefeld, Richard Gunn, John Holloway and Kosmas Psychopedis, London: Pluto.

Bose, Arun 1980, *Marx on Exploitation and Inequality: An Essay in Marxian Analytical Economics*, Delhi: Oxford University Press.

Braunstein, Dirk 2011, *Adornos Kritik der politischen Ökonomie*, Bielefeld: Transcript.

Bravo, Gian Mario 1989, 'Einhundert Jahre Marx-Rezeption in Italien. Triviale Deutungen, überwundene Standpunkte, schöpferische Neuansätze', in *Karl Marx, Friedrich Engels und Italien*, (*Schriften aus dem Karl-Marx-Haus*, 40, 2), edited by Gerhard Kuck, Trier: Studienzentrum Karl-Marx-Haus der Friedrich-Ebert-Stiftung.

———— 1992, *Marx ed Engels in Italia: la fortuna, gli scritti, le relazioni, le polemiche*, Rome: Editori Riuniti.

Brentel, Helmut 1989, *Soziale Form und ökonomisches Objekt: Studien zum Gegenstands- und Methodenverständnis der Kritik der politischen Ökonomie*. Opladen: Westdeutscher Verlag.

Bubner, Rüdiger 1973, 'Logik und Kapital', in *Dialektik und Wissenschaft*, by Rüdiger Bubner, Frankfurt am Main: Suhrkamp.

Buckmiller, Michael 2006, 'Die Marx-Interpretation im Briefwechsel zwischen Karl Korsch und Roman Rosdolsky: (1950–1954)', in *Die Marx-Engels-Werkausgaben in Der UdSSR Und DDR (1945–1968)*, (*Beiträge zur Marx-Engels-Forschung: Neue Folge, Sonderband 5*), edited by Rolf Hecker et al., Hamburg: Argument.

Bueno Martínez, Gustavo 1973, 'Sobre el significado de los "Grundrisse" en la interpretación del marxismo', *Sistema*, 2: 15–39.

Bufalo, Romeo Salvatore and Mario Alcaro (eds.) 1990, *Storia e sapere dell'uomo: marxismo, etica e filosofia in Mario Rossi*, Milan: Angeli.

Burkett, Paul 1991, 'Some Comments on "Capital in General" and the Structure of Marx's *Capital*', *Capital & Class*, 44: 49–72.

Burtin, Juri 1991, 'Die Achillesferse der Marxschen Geschichtstheorie', *Marx-Engels-Jahrbuch*, 13: 170–244.

Buzgalin, Alexander V. and Andrej I. Kolganov 2007, 'Postsowjetischer Marxismus in Russland: Antworten auf die Herausforderungen des XXI. Jahrhunderts – Thesen zur Formierung einer wissenschaftlichen Schule', available at: http://www.rosalux .de/cms/fileadmin/rls_uploads/pdfs/Marxismus_in_Russland_neu/pdf

Callesen, Gerd 1987, 'Über die Verbreitung der Werke von Marx und Engels in Dänemark', *Marx-Engels-Jahrbuch*, 10: 339–78.

Callinicos, Alex 1989, 'Introduction: Analytical Marxism', in *Marxist Theory*, edited by Alex Callinicos, Oxford: Oxford University Press.

———— 2003, *An Anti-Capitalist Manifesto*, Cambridge: Polity.

———— 2004a [1983], *The Revolutionary Ideas of Karl Marx*. London: Bookmarks.

———— 2004b, 'Contours of Anglo-Saxon Marxism', available at: http://www.psa.ac.uk/ spgrp/marxism/online/callinicos.pdf

———— 2005a, 'Against the New Dialectic', *Historical Materialism* 13, 2: 41–59.

———— 2005b, 'I contorni del marxismo anglosassone', in *Sulle tracce di un fantasma: l'opera di Karl Marx tra filologia e filosofia*, edited by Marcello Musto, Roma: Manifestolibri.

———— 2007 [1999], *Social Theory: A Historical Introduction*, Cambridge: Polity.

Cassano, Franco (ed.) 1973, *Marxismo e filosofia in Italia (1958–1971): I dibattiti e le inchieste su Rinascita e il Contemporaneo*, Bari: De Donato.

Cazzaniga, Gian Mario 1987, 'Le centenaire de Marx en Italie', in *L'état du marxisme*, (*Actuel Marx*, 1), edited by Jacques Bidet and Jacques Texier, Paris: L'Harmattan.

Cerroni, Umberto 1972, 'Introduzione', in *Il pensiero di Marx: antologia*, edited by Umberto Cerroni, Rome: Editori Riuniti.

Chai, Fangguo 2006, 'Systematische Übersetzung der Werke von Marx und Engels: Zur zweiten chinesischen Ausgabe der Marx-Engels-Werke', translated by Naoki Hashimoto, *Marx-Engels-Marxismus-Forschung, Japan*, 47.

Chamley, Paul 1965, 'Les origines de la pensée économique de Hegel', *Hegel-Studien*, 3: 225–61.

Chesebro, James William 1972, *The Radical Revolutionary in America: Analysis of a Rhetorical Movement, 1960–1972*, Ann Arbor, MI: University of Michigan Press.

Chou, Li-Quan 1988, 'Great Changes in Marxist Philosophy in China Since 1978', *Philosophy East and West*, 38, 1: 58–63.

Christ, Hella 1979, 'Marx' Smith-Rezeption in den Londoner Exzerptheften (1850–1853) und in den Manuskripten "Reflection" und "Bullion: Das vollendete Geldsystem"', *Arbeitsblätter zur Marx-Engels-Forschung*, 8: 4–17.

Chu, Choeng-Lip 1998, *Ideologie und Kritik*, Regensburg: Roderer.

Chung, Moon-Gil 1999, 'Aktivitäten zur Marx-Engels-Forschung und -Edition in Sud-Korea', in *Geschichtserkenntnis und kritische Ökonomie*, (*Beiträge zur Marx-Engels-Forschung: Neue Folge*, 1998), edited by Rolf Hecker et al., Hamburg: Argument.

Clarke, Simon 1989, 'The Basic Theory of Capitalism: A Critical Review of Itoh and the Uno School', *Capital & Class*, 37: 133–49.

———— 1990–1, 'The Marxist Theory of Overaccumulation and Crisis', *Science & Society*, 54, 4: 442–67.

———— 1994, *Marx's Theory of Crisis*, Basingstoke: Macmillan.

Claussen, Detlev 1998, 'Hans-Jürgen Krahl – ein philosophisch-politisches Profil', in *Von der Flaschenpost zum Molotowcocktail: Frankfurter Schule und Studentenbewegung*, Volume Three, edited by Wolfgang Kraushaar, Hamburg: Rogner & Bernhard bei Zweitausendeins.

Cleaver, Harry 1979, *Reading Capital Politically*, Brighton: Harvester.

———— 1986, 'Karl Marx: Economist or Revolutionary', in *Marx, Schumpeter and Keynes: A Centenary Celebration*, edited by Suzanne W. Helburn and David F. Bramhall, Armonk, NY: M.E. Sharpe.

Cohen, G.A. 2000 [1978], *Karl Marx's Theory of History: A Defence*, Oxford: Clarendon.

Colletti, Lucio 1973 [1969], *Marxism and Hegel*, translated by Lawrence Garner, London: NLB.

———— 1974, 'A Political and Philosophical Interview', *New Left Review*, 86: 3–28.

———— 1975 [1974], 'Marxism and the Dialectic', translated by John Matthews, *New Left Review*, 93: 3–29.

Conert, Hansgeorg 1974, 'Gibt es einen jugoslawischen Sozialismus? Produktionsverhältnisse und Ideologie (2. Teil)', *Das Argument*, 84: 76–103.

Cornu, Auguste 1952–68, *Karl Marx und Friedrich Engels: Leben und Werk*, three volumes, East Berlin: Aufbau.

Corradi, Cristina 2005, *Storia dei marxismi in Italia*, Rome: Manifestolibri.

Crespo, Luís 1977, 'Louis Althusser en Espagne (1966–1976)', *Dialectiques: Revue trimestrielle* 15–16: 57–63.

Crotty, James R. 1985, 'The Centrality of Money, Credit and Financial Intermediation in Marx's Crisis Theory', in: *Rethinking Marxism: Essays in the Honor of Harry Magdoff and Paul Sweezy*, edited by Stephen Resnick and Richard Wolff, New York: Autonomedia.

Dal Pra, Mario 1977 [1965], *La dialettica in Marx: dagli scritti giovanili all' 'Introduzione alle critica dell'economia politica'*, Bari: Laterza.

De Brunhoff, Suzanne 1976 [1967], *Marx on Money*, New York: Urizen Books.

Della Volpe, Galvano 1973 [1956], *Für eine materialistische Methodologie*, translated by Nicolao Merker and Henning Ritter, West Berlin: Merve.

———— 1979a [1956], 'For a materialist methodology of economics and of the moral disciplines in general (on Marx's methodological writings from 1843–1859)', in *Rousseau and Marx: And Other Writings*, by Galvano della Volpe, translated by John Fraser, Atlantic Highlands, NJ: Humanities.

———— 1979b [1956], 'The postumously-published philosophical works of 1843 and 1844', in *Rousseau and Marx: And Other Writings*, by Galvano della Volpe, translated by John Fraser, Atlantic Highlands, NJ: Humanities.

———— 1979c [1956], 'The poverty of philosophy', in *Rousseau and Marx: And Other Writings*, by Galvano della Volpe, translated by John Fraser, Atlantic Highlands, NJ: Humanities.

———— 1979d [1956], 'The introduction (1857) and the preface (1859) to The critique of political economy' *in Rousseau and Marx: And Other Writings*, by Galvano della Volpe, translated by John Fraser, Atlantic Highlands, NJ: Humanities.

———— 1980 [1950], *Logic as a Positive Science*, translated by Jon Rothschild, London: NLB.

Demir, Yakub 1968, 'Das "Kapital" von Karl Marx und der Einfluss des Marxismus-Leninismus auf die türkische Arbeiterbewegung', in *Das Kapital' von Karl Marx und seine internationale Wirkung: Beiträge ausländischer Teilnehmer an der wissenschaftlichen Session '100 Jahre "Das Kapital"'*, veranstaltet vom ZK der SED am 12. und 13. September 1967 in Berlin, edited by the Central Committee of the Socialist Unity Party of Germany, East Berlin: Dietz.

De Moraes, João Quartim et al. 1995–2007, *História do marxismo no Brasil*, six volumes, Campinas: Unicamp.

Denis, Henri 1957, *Valeur et capitalisme*, Paris: Éditions sociales.

———— 1980, *L'Économie de Marx: histoire d'un échec*, Paris: Presses universitaires de France.

Deppe, Frank 1999, 'Was bedeutete es, in den 50er Jahren gesagt zu haben: "Sie dür-
fen niemals vergessen, dass ich Marxist und Sozialist bin"? Leo Kofler und die
"heimatlose Linke" jenseits von Sozialdemokratie und Staatssozialismus', available
at: http://www.leo-kofler.de/texte/deppe.html (last retrieved 8 April 2001).

Deqiang, Han 2003, 'Chinese Cultural Revolution: Failure and Theoretical Originality',
available at: http://www.nodo50.org/cubasigloXXI/congreso04/deqiang_300304.pdf

Derichs, Claudia 1995, *Japans Neue Linke: Soziale Bewegung und außerparlamentar-
ische Opposition, 1957–1994*, Hamburg: Gesellschaft für Natur- und Völkerkunde Ost-
asiens.

De Vicente Hernando, César 2004–5, 'Las lecturas de Althusser: la conflictiva recepción
de su obra en España', *ER: revista de filosofía*, 34–5: 247–75.

Dieterich, Heinz 2006, *Der Sozialismus des 21. Jahrhunderts: Wirtschaft, Gesellschaft und
Demokratie nach dem globalen Kapitalismus*, Berlin: Homilius.

Dimoulis, Dimitri and Jannis Milios 2000, 'Werttheorie, Ideologie und Fetischismus',
in: Rolf Hecker u. a. (Hg.), in *Marx' Ökonomiekritik im Kapital*, (*Beiträge zur Marx-
Engels-Forschung: Neue Folge*, 1999), edited by Rolf Hecker et al., Hamburg: Argument.

Dimoulis, Dimitri and John Milios 2004, 'Commodity Fetishism vs. Capital Fetishism:
Marxist Interpretations vis-à-vis Marx's Analyses in Capital', *Historical Materialism*,
12, 3: 3–42.

Dlubek, Rolf 1992, 'Frühe Initiativen zur Vorbereitung einer neuen MEGA (1955–1858)',
in *Zur Kritik und Geschichte der MEGA²*, (*Beiträge zur Marx-Engels-Forschung: Neue
Folge*, 1992), edited by Rolf Hecker et al., Hamburg, Argument.

———— 1993, Rolf Dlubek, 'Tatsachen und Dokumente aus einem unbekannten
Abschnitt der Vorgeschichte der MEGA² (1961–1965)', in *Marx-Engels-Forschung im
historischen Spannungsfeld*, (*Beiträge zur Marx-Engels-Forschung: Neue Folge*, 1993),
edited by Rolf Hecker et al., Hamburg: Argument.

———— 1994, 'Die Entstehung der zweiten Marx-Engels-Gesamtausgabe im Spannungsfeld von legitimatorischem Auftrag und editorischer Sorgfalt', *MEGA-Studien*,
1994, 1: 60–106.

Dognin, Paul-Dominique 1977, *Les 'sentiers escarpés' de Karl Marx: le chapitre I du
'Capital' traduit et commenté dans trois rédactions successives*, two volumes, Paris:
Éditions du Cerf.

Dozekal, Egbert 1985, *Von der 'Rekonstruktion' der Marxschen Theorie zur 'Krise des
Marxismus': Darstellung und Kritik eines Diskussionsprozesses in der Bundesrepublik
von 1967 bis 1984*, Cologne: Pahl-Rugenstein.

Duménil, Gérard 1978, *Le concept de loi économique dans "Le Capital"*, Paris: Maspero.

Dunayevskaya, Raya 1958, *Marxism and Freedom: From 1776 Until Today*, New York, NY:
Bookman Associates.

———— 1978, 'A Critique of Roman Rosdolsky: Rosdolsky's Methodology and the Missing Dialectic', *in Marx's Capital and Today's Global Crisis*, by Raya Dunayevskaya,
Detroit, MI: News & Letters Committees.

Duncan, Colin A.M. 1983, 'Under the Cloud of *Capital*: History vs. Theory', *Science &
Society*, 47, 3: 300–22.

Dussel, Enrique 1985, *La producción teórica de Marx: un comentario a los Grundrisse*,
Mexico City: Siglo veintiuno.

———— 1988, *Hacía un Marx desconocido: Un comentario de los Manuscritos del 61–63*,
Iztapalapa: Siglo veintiuno.

———— 1990, *El último Marx (1863–1882) y la liberación latinoamericana: un comentario
a la tercera y a la cuarta redacción de 'El capital'*, Iztapalapa: Siglo veintiuno.

———— 1993, *Las metáforas teológicas de Marx*, Estella: Verbo Divino.

———— 2001a [1988], *Towards an Unknown Marx: A Commentary on the Manuscripts of
1861–63*, translated by Yolanda Angulo, edited by Fred Moseley, London/New York,
NY: Routledge.

———— 2001b, 'The Four Drafts of *Capital*: Toward a New Interpretation of the Dialectical Thought of Marx', *Rethinking Marxism*, 13, 1: 10–26.

Dutschke, Rudi 1966, 'Zur Literatur des revolutionären Sozialismus von K. Marx bis in
die Gegenwart', West Berlin, available at: http://www.infopartisan.net/archive/1967/
266764.html

———— 2000, 'Auf der Suche nach einem linken Weg aus der Krise – Brief an den
Genossen und Professor Lukács (1967)', *Das Argument*, 238: 829–58.

Dvořáček, Zdenek 1983, 'Die Werke von Marx und Engels in der Tschechoslowakei (1876
bis 1980)', *Marx-Engels-Jahrbuch*, 6: 367–405.

Ebbinghaus, Angelika 2003, 'Die "andere" Arbeiterbewegung: Operaistische Strömun-
gen in den 1970er Jahren', in *Fluchtpunkte: Das soziale Gedächtnis der Arbeiterbewegung*, edited by Arno Klönne, Karl A. Otto and Karl Heinz Roth, Hamburg: VSA.

Echeverría, Bolívar 1975, 'La revolución teórica comunista en *Las Tesis sobre Feuerbach*',
Historia y Sociedad, 6: 45–63.

———— 1979, 'Comentario sobre el "Punto de Partida" de *El Capital*', in *El Capital: teoría,
estructura y método*, edited by Pedro López Díaz, Mexico City: Ediciones de Cultura
Popular.

Echeverria, Rafael 1989, 'Critique of Marx's 1857 *Introduction*', in *Ideology, Method,
and Marx: Essays from Economy and Society*, edited by Ali Rattansi, London: Routledge.

Elbe, Ingo 2006, 'Holloways "Open Marxism": Bemerkungen zu Formanalyse als Hand-
lungstheorie und Revolutionsromantik', available at: http://www.rote-ruhr-uni
.com/texte/elbe_open_marxism.pdf

———— 2007, 'Die Beharrlichkeit des "Engelsismus": Bemerkungen zum "Marx-Engels-
Problem"', *Marx-Engels-Jahrbuch*, 2007: 92–105.

———— 2008, 'Wertformanalyse und Geld: Zur Debatte über Popularisierungen, Brüche und Versteckspiele in der Marxschen Darstellung', in *Gesellschaftliche Praxis und ihre wissenschaftliche Darstellung: Beiträge zur Kapital-Diskussion*, by Ingo Elbe, Tobias Reichardt and Dieter Wolf, Hamburg: Argument.

———— 2010 [2008], *Marx im Westen: die neue Marx-Lektüre in der Bundesrepublik seit 1965*, Berlin: Akademie.

———— 2013 [2006], 'Between Marx, Marxism and Marxisms – Ways of Reading Marx's Theory', translated by Alexander Locascio, available at: https://viewpointmag.com/2013/10/21/between-marx-marxism-and-marxisms-ways-of-reading-marxs-theory/

Eldred, Michael 1984, *Critique of Competitive Freedom and the Bourgeois-Democratic State: Outline of a Form-Analytic Extension of Marx's Uncompleted System*, Copenhagen: Kurasje.

Eldred, Michael and Marnie Hanlon 1981, 'Reconstructing Value-Form Analysis', *Capital & Class*, 13: 24–60.

Eldred, Michael, Marnie Hanlon, Lucia Kleiber and Volkbert M. Roth 1984, *La forma-valore: Progetto di ricostruzione e completamento del frammento di sistema di Marx*, Manduria: Lacaita.

Elliott, Gregory 1987, *Althusser: The Detour of Theory*, London: Verso.

———— 1998, *Perry Anderson: The Merciless Laboratory of History*, Minneapolis: University of Minnesota Press.

———— 2008, 'Non-traduttore, traditore? Notes on postwar European Marxisms in translation', *Radical Philosophy*, 152: 31–9.

Elster, Jon 1982, 'Marxism, Functionalism, and Game Theory', *Theory & Society*, 11, 4: 453–82.

———— 1985, *Making Sense of Marx*, Cambridge: Cambridge University Press.

———— 1986, 'Reply to Comments on *Making Sense of Marx*', *Inquiry*, 29, 1: 65–77.

Engels, Frederick 1980 [1859], 'Karl Marx, *A Contribution to the Critique of Political Economy*', in *Marx and Engels Collected Works*, Volume 16, London: Lawrence and Wishart.

———— 1985 [1933], *Synopsis of Volume One of Capital by Karl Marx*, in *Marx and Engels Collected Works*, Volume 20, London: Lawrence and Wishart.

Erdös, Ernst 1986, 'Hegels politische Ökonomie im Verhältnis zu Sismondi', *Hegel-Jahrbuch*, 1986: 75–86.

Escuela de Filosofía y Letras, Universidad Autónoma de Puebla 1977, *Dialéctica*, 3.

Establet, Roger 1965, 'Présentation du plan du *Capital*', in *Lire le Capital*, by Louis Althusser, Jacques Rancière, Pierre Macherey, Étienne Balibar and Roger Establet, Paris: Maspero.

Fahling, Ernst 1978, *Die logische Struktur der Krisentheorie bei Karl Marx*, Munich: Minerva.

Fausto, Ruy 1986, *Marx: Logique et Politique: Recherches pour une reconstitution du sens de la dialectique*, Paris: Publisud.

———— 1997, *Dialetica marxista, dialetica hegeliana: A* produção capitalista como circulação *simples*, São Paulo: Paz e Terra.

Favre, Pierre and Monique Favre 1970, *Les Marxismes après Marx*, Paris: Presses universitaires de France.

Fetscher, Iring 2006, 'Karl Marx, Friedrich Engels: Studienausgabe – Überlegungen, die zur Zusammensetzung der Texte zur Studienausgabe in vier Bänden (1966) geführt haben', in *Marx-Engels-Werkausgaben in der UdSSR und DDR (1945 bis 1968)*, (*Beiträge zur Marx-Engels-Forschung: Neue Folge, Sonderband 5*), edited by Rolf Hecker et al., Hamburg: Argument.

Fichter, Tilman and Siegward Lönnendonker 1977, *Kleine Geschichte des SDS: Der Sozialistische Deutsche Studentenbund von 1946 bis zur Selbstauflösung*, West Berlin: Rotbuch.

Fine, Ben and Alfredo Saad-Filho, 2003 [1975], *Marx's Capital*, London: Pluto.

Fine, Robert 2001, 'The Marx-Hegel Relationship: Revisionist Interpretations', *Capital & Class*, 75: 71–82.

Finelli, Roberto 2006, 'La Scienza del Capitale como "circolo del presupposto-posto": Un confronto con il deconstruzionismo', in *Sulle tracce di un fantasma: L'opera di Karl Marx tra filologia e filosofia*, edited by Marcello Musto, Rome: Manifestolibri.

Fineschi, Roberto 1999, 'Marx dopo la nuova edizione storica-critica (MEGA²): un nuovo oggetto di ricerca', *Marxismo oggi*, 1999, 1/2: 199–239.

———— 2001, *Ripartire da Marx: processo storico ed economia politica nella teoria del 'capitale'*, Naples: La città del sole.

———— 2002a, 'Zum Geschichtsbegriff in der marxistischen Debatte Italiens: Teil II und III', in *Neue Texte, neue Fragen: Zur Kapital-Edition in der MEGA*, (*Beiträge zur Marx-Engels-Forschung: Neue Folge*, 2001), edited by Rolf Hecker et al., Hamburg: Argument.

———— 2002b, 'MEGA²: dalla filologia all'interpretazione critica; un resoconto sul dibattito tedesco sulla teoria de valore negli anni '70/'80', in *MEGA²: Marx ritrovato grazie alla nuova edizione critica*, edited by Alessandro Mazzone, Rome: Media Print.

———— 2005, 'The Four Levels of Abstraction of Marx's Concept of "Capital"', available at: http://www.marx-gesellschaft.de/Texte/1005_Fineschi_Four%20Levels_ Abstraction.pdf

———— 2006a, 'In che senso è dialettica la teoria marxiana del capitale?', *Marxismo oggi*, 2006, 1: 70–79.

———— 2006b, *Marx e Hegel: contributi a una rilettura*, Rome: Carocci.

———— 2006c, 'Nochmals zum Verhältnis Wertform – Geldform – Austauschprozess', in *Neue Aspekte von Marx' Kapitalismus-Kritik*, (*Beiträge zur Marx-Engels-Forschung: Neue Folge*, 2004), edited by Rolf Hecker et al., Hamburg: Argument.

———— 2007, 'Novità dalla MEGA [intervista con Manfred Neuhaus e Gerald Hubmann]', *Marxismo oggi*, 2007, 1: 85–96.

———— 2008, *Un nuovo Marx: filologia e interpretazione dopo la nuova edizione storico-critica* (*MEGA²*), Rome: Carocci.

Fineschi, Roberto, Tommaso Redolfi Riva and Giovanni Sgrò (eds.) 2013, *Karl Marx 2013*, (*Il Ponte*, 69, 5/6), Florence: Il Ponte Editori.

Fischer, Anton M. 1978, *Der reale Schein und die Theorie des Kapitals bei Karl Marx*, Zürich: Europa.

Forquin, Jean-Claude 1968, 'Lecture d'Althusser', in *Dialectique marxiste et pensée structurale (à propos des travaux d'Althusser)* by Pierre Vilar et al., Paris: Études et documentation internationales.

Fornet-Betancourt, Raúl 1994, *Ein anderer Marxismus? Die philosophische Rezeption des Marxismus in Lateinamerika*, Mainz: Grünewald.

Fraser, Ian 1997, 'Two of a Kind: Hegel, Marx, Dialectic and Form', *Capital & Class*, 61: 81–106.

Fraser, Ian and Tony Burns 2000, 'Introduction: An Historical Survey of the Hegel-Marx Connection', in *The Hegel-Marx Connection*, by Tony Burns and Ian Fraser, Basingstoke: Macmillan.

Fraser, John 1977, *An Introduction to the Thought of Galvano Della Volpe*, London: Lawrence and Wishart.

Fukuzawa, Hiroomi 1981, Aspekte der Marx-Rezeption in Japan: Spätkapitalisierung und ihre sozioökonomischen Folgen, dargestellt am Beispiel der japanischen Gesellschaft, Bochum: Brockmeyer.

Fulda, Hans Friedrich 1975, 'These zur Dialektik als Darstellungsmethode (im "Kapital" von Marx)', in *Hegel-Jahrbuch 1974: Referate des X. Internationalen Hegel-Kongresses in Moskau, 1974, zu dem Zentralthema 'Dialektik'*, edited by Wilhelm R. Beyer, Cologne: Pahl-Rugenstein.

Furihata, Setsuo 1987, 'Entwicklung des japanischen Kapitalismus und marxistische Wirtschaftswissenschaft in Japan', *Prokla*, 66: 76–90.

Gabel, Joseph 1975, 'Hungarian Marxism', *Telos*, 25: 185–91.

Gajano, Alberto 1979, *La dialettica della merce: introduzione allo studio di 'Per la critica dell'economia politica' di Marx*, Naples: Laboratorio.

Galander, Ehrenfried 1991, [Mündlicher Beitrag zur Diskussionsrunde 4], in *Naturwissenschaften und Produktivkräfte bei Marx und Engels*, (*Marx-Engels-Forschung heute*, 3), edited by Institut für Marxistische Studien und Forschungen, Frankfurt am Main: IMSF.

———— 2002, 'Wolfgang Jahns Forschungen zum Sechs-Bände-Plan', in *In Memoriam Wolfgang Jahn: Der ganze Marx – Alles Verfasste veröffentlichen, erforschen und den 'ungeschriebenen' Marx rekonstruieren*, (*Wissenschaftliche Mitteilungen, Heft 1*), edited by Berliner Verein zur Förderung der MEGA-Edition e. V., Hamburg: Argument.

Galander, Ehrenfried and Ulrike Galander 1979, 'Probleme der Marxschen politischen Ökonomie', *Deutsche Zeitschrift für Philosophie*, 27, 10: 1258–61.

Galander, Ulrike 1991, [Mündlicher Beitrag zur Diskussionsrunde 4], in *Naturwissenschaften und Produktivkräfte bei Marx und Engels*, (*Marx-Engels-Forschung heute*, 3), edited by Institut für Marxistische Studien und Forschungen, Frankfurt am Main: IMSF.

Galander, Ulrike, Thomas Marxhausen and Marion Zimmermann 1983, 'Marx' Analyse philosophischer Aspekte in der Ricardoschen und postricardoschen bürgerlichen politischen Ökonomie', *Wissenschaftliche Zeitschrift der Martin Luther-Universität Halle-Wittenberg*, 32, 2: 31–49.

Galcerán Huguet, Monserrat 1987, 'Beschäftigung mit Marx und Engels in Spanien', in *Internationale Marx-Engels-Forschung*, (*Marxistische Studien: Jahrbuch des IMSF*, 12), edited by Institut für Marxistische Studien und Forschungen, Frankfurt am Main: IMSF.

Gandler, Stefan 2015 [1999], *Critical Marxism in Mexico: Adolfo Sánchez Vázquez and Bolívar Echeverría*, translted by George Ciccariello-Maher and Stefan Gandler, Leiden: Brill.

——— 2000, 'Verdinglichung und Ethos der kapitalistischen Moderne: Zur Lukács-Rezeption in Lateinamerika', in *Lukács 2000*, edited by Frank Benseler and Werner Jung, (*Jahrbuch der Internationalen Georg-Lukács-Gesellschaft*, 2000), Bielefeld: Aisthesis.

——— 2007, 'Moderne und Kapitalismus aus Eurozentrismus-kritischer Perspektive: Aktuelle Beiträge aus Mexiko zur Marxinterpretation', in *Geld – Kapital – Wert: Zum 150. Jahrestag der Niederschrift von Marx' ökonomischen Manuskripten 1857/58 'Grundrisse der Kritik der politischen Ökonomie'*, (*Beiträge zur Marx-Engels-Forschung: Neue Folge*, 2007), edited by Rolf Hecker et al., Hamburg: Argument.

García de la Sienra, Adolfo 1992, *The Logical Foundations of the Marxian Theory of Value*, Dordrecht: Kluwer Academic Publishers.

Gayle, Curtis Anderson 2003, *Marxist History and Postwar Japanese Nationalism*, London: Routledge.

——— 2006, Curtis Anderson Gayle, 'Marxistische Geschichtstheorie im modernen Japan', in *Geschichtswissenschaft in Japan: Themen, Ansätze und Theorien*, edited by Hans Martin Krämer, Tino Schölz and Sebastian Conrad, Göttingen: Vandenhoeck & Ruprecht.

Geerlandt, Robert 1978, *Garaudy et Althusser: Le débat sur l'humanisme dans le Parti Communiste Français et son enjeu*, Paris: Presses universitaires de France.

Geras, Norman 1990, 'Essence and Appearance: Aspects of Fetishism in Marx's *Capital*', in *Karl Marx's Social and Political Thought: Critical Assessments*, Volume Four, edited by Bob Jessop and Charlie Malcolm-Brown, London: Routledge.

Germer, Claus Magno 1997, 'How capital rules money – Marx's theory of money in capitalism', available at: http://copejournal.com/wp-content/uploads/2015/12/Germer-How-Capital-Rules-Money-Marxs-Theory-of-Money-in-Capitalism-1997.pdf

————— 2001, 'The abstract/concrete relation in the method of political economy', available at: http://copejournal.com/wp-content/uploads/2015/12/Germer-The-Abstract-Concrete-Relation-in-the-Method-of-Political-Economy-2001.pdf

Giacometti, Maria et al. (eds.) 1986, *La cognizione della crisi: saggi sul marxismo di Louis Althusser*, Milan: Angeli.

Gianni, Emilio 2007, 'The Diffusion of Marxism in Italy from 1848 to 1926', in *Geld – Kapital – Wert: Zum 150. Jahrestag der Niederschrift von Marx' ökonomischen Manuskripten 1857/58 'Grundrisse der Kritik der politischen Ökonomie'*, (*Beiträge zur Marx-Engels-Forschung: Neue Folge*, 2007), edited by Rolf Hecker et al., Hamburg: Argument.

Girschner, Christian 1999, *Politische Ökonomie und Weltmarkt: allgemeine Weltmarktdynamik in der Marxschen Kritik der politischen Ökonomie*, Cologne: PapyRossa.

Godelier, Maurice 2012 [1966], *Rationality and Irrationality in Economics*, translated by Brian Pearce, London: Verso.

Göhler, Gerhard 1980, *Die Reduktion der Dialektik durch Marx: Strukturveränderungen der dialektischen Entwicklung in der Kritik der politischen Ökonomie*, Stuttgart: Klett-Cotta.

Goldberg, Jörg 1987, 'Die Beobachtung der kapitalistischen Weltwirtschaftskrise von 1857/58 durch Marx und Engels und die Entwicklung der Krisentheorie', in *Internationale Marx-Engels-Forschung*, (*Marxistische Studien: Jahrbuch des IMSF*, 12), edited by Institut für Marxistische Studien und Forschungen, Frankfurt am Main: IMSF.

Golman, Lew 1978, 'Die Herausgabe der Werke von Karl Marx und Friedrich Engels in englischer Sprache', in *Marx-Engels-Jahrbuch*, 1: 435–53.

Golman, Lew and Richard Sperl 1976, 'Zum Erscheinen der ersten Bände der neuen Marx-Engels-Gesamtausgabe', *Deutsche Zeitschrift Für Philosophie*, 24, 1: 58–73.

Goshgarian, G.M. 2006, 'Translator's Introduction', in: *Philosophy of the Encounter: Later Writings, 1978–1987*, translated by G.M. Goshgarian, London: Verso.

Graf, Ruedi 1995, 'Della-Volpe-Schule', in *Historisch-Kritisches Wörterbuch des Marxismus*, Volume Two, edited by Wolfgang Fritz Haug et al., Hamburg: Argument.

Grassi, Enrico 1976, *L' 'esposizione dialettica' nel Capitale di Marx*, Rome: Basilicata.

Grebing, Helga 1977, *Der Revisionismus: Von Bernstein bis zum 'Prager Frühling'*, Munich: Beck.

Grespan, Jorge 2000, 'A crise na crítica à economia política', *Crítica marxista*, 10: 94–110.

————— 2001, 'Marx, crítico da teoria clássica do valor', *Crítica marxista*, 12: 59–76.

————— 2002, 'A dialético do avesso', *Crítica marxista*, 14: 21–44.

Grossmann, Henryk 1992 [1929], *The Law of Accumulation and Breakdown of the Capitalist System, Being Also a Theory of Crises*, translated by Jairus Banaji, London: Pluto.

————— 2013 [1929], 'The Change in the Original Plan for Marx's *Capital* and Its Causes', translated by Geoffrey McCormack, *Historical Materialism*, 21, 3: 138–64.

Guarasci, Richard 1980, *The Theory and Practice of American Marxism, 1957–1970*, Lanham, MD: University Press of America.

Guerrero, Diego 1997, *Historia del pensamiento económico heterodoxo*, Madrid: Trotta.

—— 2008, *Un resumen completo de 'El Capital' de Marx*, Madrid: Maia.

Guibert, Bernard 2006, '"Die Eule der Minerva fliegt in der Dämmerung" – Eine symptomale Lektüre der "symptomalen *Kapital*-Lektüre" in Frankreich', in *Das Kapital neu lesen: Beiträge zur radikalen Philosophie*, edited by Jan Hoff, Alexis Petrioli, Ingo Stützle, Frieder Otto Wolf, Münster: Westfälisches Dampfboot.

Guihéneuf, Robert 1952, *Le probléme de la théorie marxiste de la valeur*, Paris: Colin.

Gutiérrez de Dütsch, Begoña 2005, *Facetten der Warenform: zur Arbeitswerttheorie von Karl Marx unter besonderer Berücksichtigung der Widerspruchsproblematik*, Norderstedt: Books on Demand.

Hac, Tran Hai 2003, *Relire 'Le capital': Marx, critique de l'économie politique et objet de la critique de l'économie politique*, two volumes, Lausanne: Éditions Page Deux.

Hafez, Jacin 1969, 'Arabisierung des Marxismus', in *Die arabische Linke*, edited by Bassam Tibi, Frankfurt am Main: Europäische Verlagsanstalt.

Hafner, Kornelia 1999, 'Diskussionen gegen den Zeitgeist: "Das Marx-Kolloquium"', in *Geschichtsphilosophie oder das Begreifen der Historizität*, edited by Diethard Behrens, Freiburg im Breisgau: ça ira.

—— 2005, '"Daß der Bann sich löse": Annäherungen an Adornos Marx-Rezeption', in *Materialistische Theorie und Praxis: Zum Verhältnis von Kritischer Theorie und Kritik der politischen Ökonomie*, edited by Diethard Behrens, Freiburg: ça ira.

Hafner, Kornelia and Kirsten Huckenbeck 2008, '150 Jahre *Grundrisse* – Eine Revolutionierung der Marx-Lektüre: Tagungsbericht', in *Das Spätwerk von Friedrich Engels: Zur Edition in der Marx-Engels-Gesamtausgabe*, (*Beiträge zur Marx-Engels-Forschung: Neue Folge*, 2008), edited by Rolf Hecker et al., Hamburg: Argument.

Hahn, Young Bin 1999, 'Die Geldtheorie von Marx und Keynes: Ein Vergleich in Bezug auf den Krisenbegriff in der Geldwirtschaft', available at: http://www.diss.fu-berlin .de/1999/26/index.html

Han, Seungwan 1995, *Marx in epistemischen Kontexten: eine Dialektik der Philosophie und der 'positiven Wissenschaften'*, Frankfurt am Main: Lang.

Hardt, Michael and Antonio Negri 2000, *Empire*, Cambridge, MA: Harvard University Press.

Harnecker, Marta 1969, *Los conceptos elementales del materialismo histórico*, Mexico City: Siglo veintiuno.

—— 1999, *La izquierda en el umbral del Siglo XXI: Haciendo posible lo imposible*, Mexico City: Siglo veintiuno.

Harnecker, Marta and Iosif Abramovich Lapidus 1972, *El capital: conceptos fundamentales*, Buenos Aires: Siglo veintiuno.

Hashimoto, Naoki 1991, 'Bericht über die Arbeitsgemeinschaft der Marx-Engels-Forscher in Japan', in *Studien zum Werk von Marx und Engels*, (*Beiträge zur Marx-*

Engels-Forschung: Neue Folge, 1991), edited by Rolf Hecker et al., Hamburg, Argument.

Haug, Wolfgang Fritz 1972, 'Die Bedeutung von Standpunkt und sozialistischer Perspektive für die Kritik der politischen Ökonomie', *Das Argument,* 74: 561–85.

———— 1978, 'Westlicher Marxismus? Kritik eines notwendigen Versuchs, die marxistische Theorie zu historisieren', *Das Argument,* 110: 484–502.

———— 1981, 'Orientierungsversuche materialistischer Philosophie: Ein fragmentarischer Literaturbericht', *Das Argument,* 128: 516–32.

———— 1983, '1883–1983: L' oeuvre de Marx – un siècle après', *Das Argument,* 139: 425–9.

———— 1985 [1974], *Vorlesungen zur Einführung ins 'Kapital',* West Berlin: Argument.

———— 2003, 'Wachsende Zweifel an der Monetären Werttheorie', *Das Argument,* 251: 424–37.

———— 2007, 'Die "Neue *Kapital*-Lektüre" der monetären Werttheorie', *Das Argument,* 272: 560–74.

Hay, Laszlo 1968, 'Das "Kapital" von Karl Marx und der Aufbau des Sozialismus in Ungarn', in *'Das Kapital' von Karl Marx und seine internationale Wirkung: Beiträge ausländischer Teilnehmer an der wissenschaftlichen Session '100 Jahre "Das Kapital"', veranstaltet vom ZK der SED am 12. und 13. September 1967 in Berlin,* edited by the Central Committee of the Socialist Unity Party of Germany, East Berlin: Dietz.

Hecker, Rolf 1979, 'Einige Probleme der Wertformanalyse in der Erstausgabe des "Kapitals" von Karl Marx', *Arbeitsblätter zur Marx-Engels-Forschung,* 8: 76–94.

———— 1982, 'Neue Forschungsergebnisse über die Entwicklung der Marxschen ökonomischen Theorie (Mitteilung über neue sowjetische Dissertationen)', *Beiträge zur Marx-Engels-Forschung,* 13: 95–102.

———— 1987, 'Die Entwicklung der Werttheorie von der 1. zur 3. Auflage des ersten Bandes des "Kapitals" von Karl Marx (1867–1883)', *Marx-Engels-Jahrbuch,* 10: 147–96.

———— 1995, ' "Das Kapital"-Seminar in Tokio, November 1994: Konferenzbericht', in *Engels' Druckfassung versus Marx' Manuskripte zum III. Buch des 'Kapital', (Beiträge zur Marx-Engels-Forschung: Neue Folge,* 1995), edited by Rolf Hecker et al., Hamburg: Argument.

———— 1997, 'Zu den Beziehungen zwischen dem Moskauer Marx-Engels-Institut und dem Ohara-Institut für Sozialforschung in Osaka. Die Marx/Engels-Editionen in Japan von 1918 bis 1937', in *David Borisovic Rjasanov und die erste MEGA, (Beiträge zur Marx-Engels-Forschung: Neue Folge, Sonderband 1),* edited by Rolf Hecker et al., Hamburg: Argument.

———— 1998, 'Internationale Marx/Engels-Forschung und -Edition: Ein Literaturbericht', *z.: Zeitschrift Marxistische Erneuerung,* 33: 8–25.

———— 2001a, 'Editorial', in *Stalinismus und das Ende der ersten Marx-Engels-Gesamtausgabe (1931–1941), (Beiträge zur Marx-Engels-Forschung: Neue Folge, Sonderband 3),* edited by Rolf Hecker et al., Hamburg: Argument.

———— 2001b, Rolf Hecker, 'Unbekannte Geschichte der Erstveröffentlichung des Marxschen ökonomischen Manuskripts von 1857/58 als *Grundrisse der Kritik der politischen Ökonomie* (1939/41) unter den Bedingungen des Stalinismus', available at: http://www.marxforschung.de/docs/010213hecker.pdf

———— 2002, 'Einfache Warenproduktion oder einfache Warenzirkulation – Die Debatte um die Ausgangskategorie des *Kapital*', in *In Memoriam Wolfgang Jahn: Der ganze Marx – Alles Verfasste veröffentlichen, erforschen und den 'ungeschriebenen' Marx rekonstruieren*, (*Wissenschaftliche Mitteilungen, Heft 1*), edited by Berliner Verein zur Förderung der MEGA-Edition e. V., Hamburg: Argument.

———— 2010, 'Rjazanovs Herausgabe der MEGA und oder vs. Marxismus-Leninismus', in *Der sich selbst entfremdete und wiedergefundene Marx*, edited by Helmut Lethen et al., Munich: Fink.

Hecker, Rolf, Jürgen Jungnickel and Eike Kopf 1991, 'Zu einigen Forschungs- und Editionsfragen des ersten Bandes des "Kapitals" in der MEGA', *Prokla*, 84: 496–510.

Hecker, Rolf and Alexander Tschepurenko 1998, 'Nachbemerkung zu Vladimir Petrovic Schkredov, "Über Engels' Historismus in seinem *Kapital*-Verständnis"', in *Marx und Engels: Konvergenzen – Divergenzen*, (*Beiträge zur Marx-Engels-Forschung: Neue Folge*, 1997), edited by Rolf Hecker et al., Hamburg: Argument.

Hecker, Rolf et al. (eds.) 1997, *David Borisovic Rjasanov und die erste MEGA*, (*Beiträge zur Marx-Engels-Forschung: Neue Folge, Sonderband 1*), Hamburg: Argument.

Hecker, Rolf et al. (eds.) 2000, *Erfolgreiche Kooperation: Das Frankfurter Institut für Sozialforschung und das Moskauer Marx-Engels-Institut (1924–1928)*, Hamburg: Argument.

Hegel, Georg Wilhelm Friedrich 1991 [1821], *Elements of the Philosophy of Right*, translated by Allen W. Wood, Cambridge: Cambridge University Press.

———— 1969 [1812], *Hegel's Science of Logic*, translated by A.V. Miller, London: Allen & Unwin.

Heinrich, Michael 1986, 'Hegel, die "Grundrisse" und das "Kapital": Ein Nachtrag zur Diskussion um das "Kapital" in den 70er Jahren', *Prokla*, 65: 145–60.

———— 1989, '"Capital in General" and the Structure of Marx's *Capital*', *Capital & Class*, 38: 63–79.

———— 1995a, 'Edition und Interpretation: Zu dem Artikel von Hans-Georg Backhaus und Helmut Reichelt, "Der politisch-ideologische Grundcharakter der Marx-Engels-Gesamtausgabe"', *MEGA-Studien*, 1995, 2: 111–21.

———— 1995b, 'Gibt es eine Marxsche Krisentheorie? Die Entwicklung der Semantik von "Krise" in den verschiedenen Entwürfen zu einer Kritik der politischen Ökonomie', in *Engels' Druckfassung versus Marx' Manuskripte zum III. Buch des 'Kapital'*, (*Beiträge zur Marx-Engels-Forschung: Neue Folge*, 1995), edited by Rolf Hecker et al., Hamburg: Argument.

———— 1996, 'Engels' Edition of the Third Volume of *Capital* and Marx's Original Manuscript', *Science & Society*, 60, 4: 452–66.

——— 1998, 'Kommentierte Literaturliste zur Kritik der politischen Ökonomie', in *Kapital.doc. Das Kapital (Bd. 1) von Marx in Schaubildern und Kommentaren*, edited by Elmar Altvater et al., Münster: Westfälisches Dampfboot.

——— 1999a [1991], *Die Wissenschaft vom Wert: Die Marxsche Kritik der politischen Ökonomie zwischen wissenschaftlicher Revolution und klassischer Tradition*, Münster: Westfälisches Dampfboot.

——— 1999b, 'Geschichtsphilosophie bei Marx', in *Geschichtsphilosophie oder das Begreifen der Historizität*, edited by Diethard Behrens, Freiburg im Breisgau: ça ira.

——— 2001, 'Monetäre Werttheorie: Geld und Krise bei Marx', *Prokla*, 123: 151–76.

——— 2002a, [Mündlicher Diskussionsbeitrag], in: 'Protokoll der Diskussion des Referats von Dieter Wolf (Abschrift einer Bandaufzeichnung)', unpublished manuscript.

——— 2002b, 'Der 6-Bücher-Plan und der Aufbau des *Kapital*: Diskontinuierliches in Marx' theoretischer Entwicklung', in *In Memoriam Wolfgang Jahn: Der ganze Marx – Alles Verfasste veröffentlichen, erforschen und den 'ungeschriebenen' Marx rekonstruieren, (Wissenschaftliche Mitteilungen, Heft 1)*, edited by Berliner Verein zur Förderung der MEGA-Edition e. V., Hamburg: Argument.

——— 2003, 'Geld und Kredit in der Kritik der politischen Ökonomie', *Das Argument*, 251: 397–409.

——— 2006, 'Deconstructing "Capital": New Insights from Marx's Economic Manuscripts in "MEGA"', available at: http://www.oekonomiekritik.de/312Deconstructing%20Capital.htm

——— 2008, *Wie das Marxsche Kapital lesen? Hinweise zur Lektüre und Kommentar zum Anfang von 'Das Kapital'*, Stuttgart: Schmetterling.

——— 2009, 'Reconstruction or Deconstruction? Methodological Controversies about Value and Capital and New Insights from the Critical Edition', in *Re-reading Marx: New Perspectives after the Critical Edition*, edited by Riccardo Bellofiore and Roberto Fineschi, London: Palgrave Macmillan.

——— 2012 [2003], *An Introduction to the Three Volumes of Karl Marx's Capital*, translated by Alexander Locascio, New York: Monthly Review Press.

Henning, Christoph 2005, *Philosophie nach Marx: 100 Jahre Marxrezeption und die normative Sozialphilosophie der Gegenwart in der Kritik*, Bielefeld: Transcript.

——— 2006, *Narrative der Globalisierung: Zur Marxrenaissance in Globalismus und Globalisierungskritik*, Trier: Studienzentrum Karl-Marx-Haus der Friedrich-Ebert-Stiftung.

Henry, Michel 1976a, *Marx, tome I: Une philosophie de la réalité*, Paris: Gallimard.

——— 1976b, *Marx, tome II: Une philosophie de l'économie*, Paris: Gallimard.

Hirano, Y. 1929, 'K. Fukumoto, Zur Methodologie der "Kritik der Politischen Ökonomie", Tokio 1926, 439 S. [Rezension]', *Archiv für die Geschichte des Sozialismus und der Arbeiterbewegung*, 14: 157–60.

Hiromatsu, Wataru 1987, 'La philosophie de Marx "pour nous"', translated by Takashi Minatomichi, in *Le Marxisme au Japon*, (*Actuel Marx*, 2), edited by Jacques Bidet and Jacques Texier, Paris: L'Harmattan.

Hobsbawm, Eric 1964, 'Introduction', in *Pre-Capitalist Economic Formations*, by Karl Marx, translated by Jack Cohen, edited by Eric Hobsbawm, London: Lawrence and Wishart.

————— 1973 [1966], 'The Structure of Capital', in: *Revolutionaries: Contemporary Essays*, by Eric Hobsbawm, London: Weidenfeld and Nicolson.

————— 1982, 'The Fortunes of Marx's and Engels' Writings', in *The History of Marxism, Volume One: Marxism in Marx's Day*, edited by Eric Hobsbawm et al., Brighton: Harvester.

Hobsbawm, Eric, Georges Haupt, Franz Marek, Ernesto Ragionieri, Vittorio Strada and Corrado Vivanti (eds.) 1978–82, *Storia del Marxismo*, five volumes, Turin: Einaudi.

Hodges, Donald Clarke 1967, 'The Method of *Capital*', *Science & Society*, 31, 4: 505–14.

————— 1970, 'Marx's Concept of Value and Critique of Value Fetishism', *Science & Society*, 34, 3: 342–46.

Hoff, Jan 2004, *Kritik der klassischen politischen Ökonomie: zur Rezeption der werttheoretischen Ansätze ökonomischer Klassiker durch Karl Marx*, Cologne: PapyRossa.

————— 2008, *Karl Marx und die 'ricardianischen Sozialisten': ein Beitrag zur Geschichte der politischen Ökonomie, der Sozialphilosophie und des Sozialismus*, Cologne: Papy-Rossa.

Hoff, Jan, Alexis Petrioli, Ingo Stützle and Frieder Otto Wolf (eds.) 2006a, *Das Kapital neu lesen: Beiträge zur radikalen Philosophie*. Münster: Westfäliches Dampfboot.

Hoff, Jan, Alexis Petrioli, Ingo Stützle and Frieder Otto Wolf 2006b, 'Einleitung', in *Das Kapital neu lesen: Beiträge zur radikalen Philosophie*, edited by Jan Hoff, Alexis Petrioli, Ingo Stützle, Frieder Otto Wolf, Münster: Westfälisches Dampfboot.

Holloway, John, 'Why read *Capital*?', *Capital & Class*, 75: 65–70.

————— 2005 [2002], *Change the World Without Taking Power*, London: Pluto.

Holzkamp, Klaus 1974, 'Die historische Methode des wissenschaftlichen Sozialismus und ihre Verkennung durch J. Bischoff', *Das Argument*, 84: 1–75.

Hoshino, Tomiichi 1995, 'The Theory of Economic Crises: An Unoist Approach', in *A Japanese Approach to Political Economy: Unoist Variations*, edited by Robert Albritton and Thomas Sekine, Basingstoke: Macmillan.

Hoston, Germaine A. 1986, *Marxism and the Crisis of Development in Prewar Japan*, Princeton, NJ: Princeton University Press.

Hountondji, Paulin J. 1984, 'Marxism and the Myth of an "African Ideology"', in *Rethinking Marxism*, edited by Sakari Hänninen and Leena Paldán, Berlin: Argument.

————— 1996 [1976], *African Philosophy: Myth and Reality*, translated by Henri Evans and Jonathan Rée, Bloomington, IN: Indiana University Press.

Hyppolite, Jean 1973 [1955], 'On the Structure and Philosophical Presuppositions of

Marx's Capital', in Studies *on Marx and Hegel*, by Jean Hippolyte, translated by John O'Neill, New York, NY: Harper and Row.

Iacono, Alfonso M. 1987, 'Sul concetto di "feticismo" in Marx', in *Marx e il mondo contemporaneo*, edited by Anna Maria Nassisi et al., Rome: Editori Riuniti.

Iber, Christian 2005, *Grundzüge der Marx'schen Kapitalismustheorie*. Berlin: Parerga.

———— 2006, 'Die Bedeutung der Differenz in der Entwicklung der Wertformen zwischen der ersten und der zweiten Auflage des *Kapital*', in *Das Kapital neu lesen: Beiträge zur radikalen Philosophie*, edited by Jan Hoff, Alexis Petrioli, Ingo Stützle, Frieder Otto Wolf, Münster: Westfälisches Dampfboot.

Iljenkow, Ewald W. 1969 [1960], 'Die Dialektik des Abstrakten und Konkreten im "Kapital" von Marx', in: *Beiträge zur marxistischen Erkenntnistheorie*, edited by Alfred Schmidt, Frankfurt am Main: Suhrkamp.

Ilyenkov, Evald Vasilyevich 1982 [1960], *The Dialectics of the Abstract and the Concrete in Marx's Capital*, translated by Sergei Kuzyakov, Moscow: Progress.

Iñigo Carrera, Juan 2004, *El capital: razón histórica, sujeto revolucionario y conciencia*, Buenos Aires: Imago Mundi.

Iorio, Marco 2005, *Karl Marx interkulturel gelesen*, Nordhausen: Bautz.

Ishibashi, Sadao 1995, 'The Demonstration of the Law of Value and the Uno-Sekine Approach', in *A Japanese Approach to Political Economy: Unoist Variations*, edited by Robert Albritton and Thomas Sekine, Basingstoke: Macmillan.

Ishikura, Masao 2004, 'Marx's Theory of Money and Monetary Production Economy', *Hitotsubashi Journal of Economics*, 45, 2: 81–91.

Ishizuka, Ryoji 2004, 'Hiromatsu-Schule', in *Historisch-Kritisches Wörterbuch des Marxismus*, Volume 6/I, edited by Wolfgang Fritz Haug et al., Hamburg: Argument.

Ito, Narihiko 1994, 'Zur Aktualität von Karl Marx: Eine Tagung in Sapporo (Japan)', *Jahrbuch für historische Kommunismusforschung*, 1994: 323–5.

Itoh, Makoto 1976, 'Die Entwicklung der Krisentheorie bei Marx', *Prokla*, 22: 101–23.

———— 1978, 'The Formation of Marx's Theory of Crisis', *Science & Society*, 42, 2: 129–55.

———— 1980, *Value and Crisis: Essays on Marxian Economics in Japan*, London: Pluto.

———— 1988, *The Basic Theory of Capitalism: The Forms and Substance of the Capitalist Economy*, Basingstoke: Macmillan.

———— 2006, 'Marx's Economic Theory and the Prospects for Socialism', in *Marx for the 21st Century*, edited by Hiroshi Uchida, London: Routledge.

Iwasaki, Chikatsugu 1979, 'Zur Diskussion über die materialistische Dialektik in Japan', *Deutsche Zeitschrift für Philosophie*, 27, 3: 359–63.

———— 1987, 'Zur Entwicklung der marxistischen Dialektik in Japan', in *Marxistische Dialektik in Japan: Beiträge japanischer Philosophen zu aktuellen Problemen der dialektisch-materialistischen Methode*, edited by Siegfried Bönisch et al., East Berlin: Dietz.

Jahn, Wolfgang 1978, 'Die Entwicklung der Ausgangskategorie der politischen Ökonomie des Kapitalismus in den Vorarbeiten zu Marx' "Kapital"', in ... *unsrer Partei einen Sieg erringen: Studien zur Entstehungs- und Wirkungsgeschichte des 'Kapitals' von Karl Marx*, edited by Roland Nietzold, Hannes Skambraks, and Günter Wermusch, East Berlin, Die Wirtschaft.

———— 1987, 'Die "Londoner Hefte 1850–1853" in der Entwicklung der politischen Ökonomie von Karl Marx', in *Internationale Marx-Engels-Forschung*, (*Marxistische Studien: Jahrbuch des IMSF*, 12), edited by Institut für Marxistische Studien und Forschungen, Frankfurt am Main: IMSF.

———— 1992a, 'Ist Das Kapital ein Torso? Über Sinn und Unsinn einer Rekonstruktion des "6-Bücherplanes" von Karl Marx', *Dialektik*, 1992, 3: 125–38.

———— 1992b, 'Die Problemantinomie in der Entwicklung von Ware, Wert und Geld zwischen dem esoterischen und dem exoterischen Werk von Karl Marx und die Folgen', *Marx-Engels-Forschung heute*, 4: 16–26.

Jahn, Wolfgang and Roland Nietzold 1978, 'Probleme der Entwicklung der Marxschen politischen Ökonomie im Zeitraum 1850 bis 1863', *Marx-Engels-Jahrbuch*, 1: 145–74.

Jahn, Wolfgang and Dieter Noske 1983, 'Zu einigen Aspekten der Entwicklung der Marxschen Forschungsmethode der politischen Ökonomie in den Londoner Heften (1850–1853)', *Marx-Engels-Jahrbuch*, 6: 121–47.

Jahn, Wolfgang et al. (eds.) 1983, *Der Zweite Entwurf des 'Kapitals': Analysen, Aspekte, Argumente*, East Berlin: Dietz.

Jánoska, Judith, Martin Bondeli, Konrad Kindle and Marc Hofer 1994, *Das 'Methodenkapitel' von Karl Marx: ein historischer und systematischer Kommentar*, Basel: Schwabe.

Jay, Martin 1984, *Marxism and Totality: The Adventures of a Concept from Lukács to Habermas*, Berkeley, CA: University of California Press.

Jeong, Seongjin 1996, 'Capitalism and Stalinism in South Korea: A Marxist Critique', available at: http://nongae.gsnu.ac.kr/~seongjin/publications/stalinismsk.doc

Joe, Hyeon-Soo 1995, *Politische Ökonomie als Gesellschaftstheorie: Studien zur Marx-Rezeption von Isaak Iljitsch Rubin und Kozo Uno*, Marburg: Phillips-Universität.

Judt, Tony 1986, *Marxism and the French Left*, Oxford: Clarendon.

Jüncke, Christoph 2000, 'Freiheit wozu? Zur Einführung in Leben und Werk von Leo Kofler (1907–1995)', in *Zur Kritik bürgerlicher Freiheit: Ausgewählte politisch-philosophische Texte eines marxistischen Einzelgängers*, by Christoph Jüncke and Leo Kofler, Hamburg: VSA.

———— 2007, *Sozialistisches Strandgut: Leo Kofler – Leben und Werk (1907–1995)*, Hamburg; VSA.

Jungnickel, Jürgen and Carl-Erich Vollgraf 2005, 'Engels' Redaktionsunterlagen zu Marx' Manuskript von 1864/65, das 1894 als Band III des "Kapitals" erschien', in *Engels' Druckfassung versus Marx' Manuskripte zum III. Buch des 'Kapital'*, (*Beiträge zur*

Marx-Engels-Forschung: Neue Folge, 1995), edited by Rolf Hecker et al., Hamburg: Argument.

Kakuta, Shuichi 2009, 'Methodological Differences between Two Marxian Economists in Japan: Kōzō Uno and Sekisuke Mita', *Research in Political Economy*, 25: 277–99.

Kallscheuer, Otto 1986, *Marxismus und Erkenntnistheorie in Westeuropa: eine politische Philosophiegeschichte*, Frankfurt am Main: Campus.

Kandel, J.P. 1960/1, 'Marx-Engels-Forschung in der Sowjetunion', *Sowjetwissenschaft: Gesellschaftswissenschaftliche Beiträge*, 1960/1: 282–304.

Kant, Immanuel 1998 [1781], *Critique of Pure Reason*, translated and edited by Paul Guyer and Allen W. Wood, Cambridge: Cambridge University Press.

Karatani, Kōjin 2005 [2001], *Transcritique: On Kant and Marx*, translated by Iwasaburō Kōso, Cambridge, MA: MIT Press.

Karsz, Saül and Louis Althusser 1974, *Théorie et Politique: Louis Althusser*, Paris: Fayard.

Katsiaficas, George 1987, *The Imagination of the New Left: A Global Analysis of 1968*, Boston, MA: South End.

Kawakami, Hajime 1928, 'Marxist Political Economy as a Science', available at: http://www.marxists.org/subject/japan/kawakami/economy-science.htm

Keane, John and Brian Singer 1974/5, 'On Conceptual Archeology: A Reply to Postone and Reinicke', *Telos*, 22: 148–53.

Kee, Alistair 1990, *Marx and the Failure of Liberation Theology*, London: SCM.

Kern, Bruno 1992, *Theologie im Horizont des Marxismus: zur Geschichte der Marxismus-rezeption in der lateinamerikanischen Theologie der Befreiung*, Mainz: Grünewald.

Kessler, Mario 2002, 'Zwischen Ost und West: Ernst Bloch, Hans Mayer, Leo Kofler, Alfred Kantorowicz', in *Exil und Nach-Exil: Vertriebene Intellektuelle im 20. Jahrhundert*, by Mario Kessler, Hamburg: VSA.

Kha, Saen-Yang 1987, 'La grande mutation actuelle du marxisme chinois', in *L'état du marxisme*, (*Actuel Marx*, 1), edited by Jacques Bidet and Jacques Texier, Paris: L'Harmattan.

Khilnani, Sunil 1995, *Revolutionsdonner: Die französische Linke nach 1945*, Hamburg: Rotbuch.

———— 2003, 'French Marxism – existentialism to structuralism', in *The Cambridge History of Twentieth-Century Political Thought*, edited by Terence Ball and Richard Bellamy, Cambridge: Cambridge University Press.

Kicillof, Axel and Guido Starosta 2007a, 'On Materiality and Social Form: A Political Critique of Rubin's Value-Form Theory', *Historical Materialism*, 15, 3: 9–43.

———— 2007b, 'Value Form and Class Struggle: A Critique of the Autonomist Theory of Value', *Capital & Class*, 92: 13–44.

Kim, Ho-Gyun 2008, South Korea [Dissemination and reception of the *Grundrisse* in the world], in *Karl Marx's Grundrisse: Foundations of the Critique of Political Economy 150 Years Later*, edited by Marcello Musto, New York, NY: Routledge.

Kim, Kyoung-Soo 2007, 'Kapitalismus im 21. Jahrhundert und die alternative Globalis-
    ierung – Kongressbericht über die dritte Marx-Communale 2007 in Seoul', in *Marx-
    Engels-Jahrbuch*, 2007: 170–75.

Kim, Kyung-Mi 1999, *Hilferding und Marx: Geld- und Kredittheorie in Rudolf Hilferdings
    'Das Finanzkapital' und im Marxschen 'Kapital'*. Cologne: PapyRossa.

Kim, Lee Jun 1998, *Krise der Theorie und Theorie der Krise*, Frankfurt am Main: Lang.

Kincaid, Jim 2005a, 'Debating the Hegel-Marx Connection: A Symposium on Chris-
    topher J. Arthur's *The New Dialectic and Marx's "Capital"*: Editorial Introduction',
    Historical Materialism, 13, 2: 27–40.

———— 2005b, 'A Critique of Value-Form Marxism', *Historical Materialism*, 13, 2: 85–119.

Kirchhoff, Christine, Hanno Pahl, Christoph Engemann, Judith Heckel and Lars Meyer
    2004, 'Zuvor', in *Gesellschaft als Verkehrung: Perspektiven einer neuen Marx-Lektüre*,
    edited by Christine Kirchhoff, Hanno Pahl, Christoph Engemann, Judith Heckel,
    Lars Meyer, Freiburg/Br.: ça ira.

Kittsteiner, Heinz-Dieter 1977, '"Logisch" und "Historisch": Differenzen des Marxschen
    und Engelsschen Systems der Wissenschaft', *Internationale wissenschaftliche Korres-
    pondenz zur Geschichte der deutschen Arbeiterbewegung*, 13: 1–47.

Knight, Nick 1996, *Li Da and Marxist Philosophy in China*, Boulder, CO: Westview.

———— 2005, *Marxist Philosophy in China: From Qu Qiubai to Mao Zedong, 1923–1945*,
    Dordrecht: Springer.

Kobayashi, Toshiaki 1998, 'Hiromatsu Wataru – ein marxistischer Philosoph im Nach-
    kriegsjapan', in *'Intelli'*, (*Japan-Lesebuch III*), edited by Steffi Richter, Tübingen:
    Gehrke.

Kocyba, Hermann 1979, *Widerspruch und Theoriestruktur: Zur Darstellungsmethode im
    Marxschen 'Kapital'*, Frankfurt am Main: Materialis.

Kofler, Leo 2000, 'Marxistischer und stalinistischer Marxismus', in *Zur Kritik bürger-
    licher Freiheit: ausgewählte politisch-philosophische Texte eines marxistischen Einzel-
    gängers*, by Leo Kofler, edited by Christoph Jünke, Hamburg: VSA.

Kogan, Albert 1986, 'Zur Frage der Methodologie des Planes der sechs Bücher von Karl
    Marx', *Arbeitsblätter zur Marx-Engels-Forschung*, 20: 56–80.

———— 1991, 'Aktuelle Probleme der Marxschen Geldtheorie in den "Grundrissen der
    Kritik der politischen Ökonomie"', *Marx-Engels-Jahrbuch*, 13: 246–62.

Kohan, Néstor 1998, *Marx en su (tercer) mundo: hacia un socialismo no colonizado*,
    Buenos Aires: Biblos.

———— 2005, *El capital: historia y método – una introducción*, Havana: Editorial de
    Ciencias Sociales.

Kołakowski, Leszek 2008 [1976], *The Main Currents of Marxism*, translated by P.S. Falla,
    New York, NY: Norton.

Kosík, Karel 1967, 'Gesellschaftliches Sein und ökonomische Kategorien', *Folgen einer
    Theorie: Essays über 'Das Kapital' von Karl Marx*, edited by Ernst Theodor Mohl et
    al., Frankfurt am Main: Suhrkamp.

Kouvelakis, Stathis 2003 [2003], *Philosophy and Revolution: From Kant to Marx*, translated by G.M. Goshgarian, London: Verso.

Krahl, Hans-Jürgen 1970, 'Bemerkungen zum Verhältnis von Kapital und Hegelscher Wesenslogik', in *Aktualität und Folgen der Philosophie Hegels*, edited by Oskar Negt, Frankfurt am Main: Suhrkamp.

————— 1971, 'Zur Wesenslogik der Marxschen Warenanalyse', in *Konstitution und Klassenkampf: Zur historischen Dialektik von bürgerlicher Emanzipation und proletarischer Revolution*, by Hans-Jürgen Krahl, Frankfurt am Main: Neue Kritik.

————— 1984, 'Hegels Idealismus und materialistische Erkenntniskritik', in *Vom Ende der abstrakten Arbeit*, by Hans-Jürgen Krahl, Frankfurt am Main: Materialis.

————— 1999, 'Der politische Widerspruch in der Kritischen Theorie Adornos', in *Keine Kritische Theorie ohne Amerika*, edited by Detlev Claussen, Oskar Negt and Michael Werz, Frankfurt am Main: Neue Kritik.

Krämer, Hans Martin, Tino Schölz and Sebastian Conrad 2006, 'Geschichtswissenschaft in Japan: Entwicklung und aktueller Diskussionsstand', in *Geschichtswissenschaft in Japan: Themen, Ansätze und Theorien*, edited by Hans Martin Krämer, Tino Schölz and Sebastian Conrad, Göttingen: Vandenhoeck & Ruprecht.

Krätke, Michael 1996, 'Marxismus als Sozialwissenschaft', in *Materialien zum Historisch-Kritischen Wörterbuch des Marxismus*, edited by Frigga Haug and Michael Krätke, Hamburg: Argument.

————— 1999, 'Kapitalismus und Krisen: Geschichte und Theorie der zyklischen Krisen in Marx' ökonomischen Studien 1857/58', in *Geschichtserkenntnis und kritische Ökonomie, (Beiträge zur Marx-Engels-Forschung: Neue Folge*, 1998), edited by Rolf Hecker et al., Hamburg: Argument.

————— 2002, '"Hier bricht das Manuskript ab." (Engels) Hat das *Kapital* einen Schluss? Teil I', in *Neue Texte, neue Fragen: Zur Kapital-Edition in der* MEGA, (*Beiträge zur Marx-Engels-Forschung: Neue Folge*, 2001), edited by Rolf Hecker et al., Hamburg: Argument.

————— 2003, '"Hier bricht das Manuskript ab" (Engels): Hat das Kapital einen Schluss? Teil II', in *Klassen, Revolution, Demokratie: zum 150. Jahrestag der Erstveröffentlichung von Marx' Der 18. Brumaire des Louis Bonaparte, (Beiträge zur Marx-Engels-Forschung: Neue Folge*, 2002), edited by Rolf Hecker et al., Berlin: Argument.

————— 2005, 'Le dernier Marx et *Le Capital*', *Actuel Marx*, 37: 145–60.

————— 2006a, 'Das Marx-Engels-Problem: Warum Engels das Marxsche *Kapital* nicht verfälscht hat', *Marx-Engels-Jahrbuch*, 2006: 142–70.

————— 2006b, 'Marx als Wirtschaftsjournalist', in: *Die Journalisten Marx und Engels*, (*Beiträge zur Marx-Engels-Forschung: Neue Folge*, 2005), edited by Rolf Hecker et al., Hamburg: Argument.

————— 2008, 'Marx – unser Zeitgenosse', available at: http://www.marxforschung.de/docs/081001kraetke.pdf

Krüger, Horst 1975, 'Die Intelligenz und der soziale Fortschritt im unabhängigen Indien', in *Studien zum Kampf um den sozialen Forschritt in Indien*, edited by Annemarie Hafner, Joachim Heidrich, Petra Heidrich and Horst Krüger, East Berlin: Deutscher Verlag der Wissenschaften.

Kubo, Seijiro 2006, 'Die Bibliographie über die marxistische Literatur (1929) und ihre Bedeutung für die Wirkungsgeschichte des Marxismus in Japan', in *Neue Aspekte von Marx' Kapitalismus-Kritik*, (*Beiträge zur Marx-Engels-Forschung: Neue Folge*, 2004), edited by Rolf Hecker et al., Hamburg: Argument.

Kubota, Ken 2010, 'Die dialektische Darstellung des allgemeinen Begriffs des Kapitals im Lichte der Philosophie Hegels: Zur logischen Analyse der politischen Ökonomie unter besonderer Berücksichtigung Adornos und der Forschungsergebnisse von Rubin, Backhaus, Reichelt, Uno und Sekine', in *Das Kapital und Vorarbeiten – Entwürfe und Exzerpte*, (*Beiträge zur Marx-Engels-Forschung: Neue Folge*, 2010), edited by Rolf Hecker et al., Hamburg: Argument.

Kuczynski, Jürgen 1981, 'Hegel und die politische Ökonomie – ein Brief von J.K. an Manfred Buhr', in *Vom Mute des Erkennens: Beiträge zur Philosophie G.W.F. Hegels*, edited by Manfred Buhr and T.I. Oïzerman, Frankfurt am Main: Marxistische Blätter.

Kuhn, Rick 2007, *Henryk Grossman and the Recovery of Marxism*, Urbana, IL: University of Illinois.

Külow, Volker and Andre Jaroslawski (eds.) 1993, *David Rjasanow: Marx-Engels-Forscher, Humanist, Dissident*, East Berlin: Dietz.

Kundel, Erich 1989, 'Zur Tätigkeit des Wissenschaftlichen Rates für Marx-Engels-Forschung der DDR', *Marx-Engels-Forschung heute*, 1: 24–9.

Kuroda, Kan'ichi 2000, *Engels' Political Economy: On the Difference in Philosophy between Karl Marx and Friedrich Engels*, Tokyo: Akane Books.

Kuruma, Samezō (ed.) 1977, *Marx-Lexikon zur politischen Ökonomie*, five volumes, Vaduz: Topos.

———— 2008 [1957], *Marx's Theory of the Genesis of Money: How, Why and Through What is a Commodity Money?*, translated by E. Michael Schauerte, Denver, CO: Outskirts.

Kwack, No-Wan 2003, 'Marxsche Ansätze zur monetären Krisentheorie und deren Epistemologie', in *Mit Marx ins 21. Jahrhundert: zur Aktualität der Kritik der politischen Ökonomie*, edited by Olaf Gerlach, Stefan Kalmring and Andreas Nowak, Hamburg: VSA.

———— 2006, 'Zur Fundierung der monetären Krisentheorie: Marxsche epistemologische Ambivalenzen der Finanzkrisentheorie – Ein Versuch der Weiterentwicklung', available at: http://www.diss.fu-berlin.de/2006/232/index.html

Labica, Georges 1987, *Karl Marx, les 'Thèses sur Feuerbach'*, Paris: Presses universitaires de France.

Lamo de Espinosa, Emilio 1981, *La teoría de la cosificación: de Marx a la Escuela de Francfort*, Madrid: Alianza Editorial.

Lange, Oskar 1963–8, *Politische Ökonomie*, two volumes, Frankfurt am Main: Europäische Verlagsanstalt.

Lebowitz, Michael A. 1988, 'Is "Analytical Marxism" Marxism?', *Science & Society*, 52, 2: 191–214.

———— 1992, *Beyond Capital: Marx's Political Economy of the Working Class*, Basingstoke: MacMillan.

———— 1994, 'Analytical Marxism and the Marxian Theory of Crisis', *Cambridge Journal of Economics*, 18: 163–79.

Lee, Chai-on 1993, 'Marx's Labour Theory of Value Revisited', *Cambridge Journal of Economics*, 17, 4: 463–78.

Lee, Frederic S. 2001, 'Conference of Socialist Economists and the Emergence of Heterodox Economics in Post-War Britain', *Capital & Class*, 75: 15–40.

Lee, Seong-Paik 1998, *Erneuerungsversuch und Ende der Sowjetphilosophie in der Spätphase der Perestroika*, Wiesbaden: Harrassowitz.

Lefebvre, Henri 1985, *Karl Marx*, Paris: Bordas.

Lefebvre, Jean-Pierre 1985, 'Présentation du corpus', in *L'oeuvre de Marx, un siècle après: 1883–1983*, edited by Georges Labica, Paris: Presses universitaires de France.

Lefèvre, Wolfgang 2005, 'Marcuse, Studentenbewegung, FU-Identität', in *Zur Aktualität der Philosophie Herbert Marcuses: Beiträge einer Veranstaltung an der FU Berlin am 17. Juli 2003*, edited by Detlev Claussen, Berlin: Allgemeiner Studierendenausschuß der Freien Universität Berlin.

Lenin, Vladimir Ilyich 1964 [1917], *Imperialism, The Highest Stage Of Capitalism*, translated by Yuri Sdobnikov, in *Collected Works*, Volume 22, Moscow: Progress.

———— 1976 [1930], 'Conspectus of Hegel's Book *The Science of Logic*', translated by Clemence Dutt, in *Collected Works*, Volume 38, Moscow: Progress.

———— 1977 [1913], 'The Three Sources and Three Component Parts of Marxism', translated by George Hanna, in *Collected Works*, Volume 19, Moscow: Progress.

León del Río, Yohanka 2000, "Avatares del marxismo en la década del sesenta", available online at: http://www.filosofia.cu/contemp/yoe003.htm (last retrieved 21 April 2007).

Levant, Alex and Vesa Oittinen (eds.) 2014, *Dialectics of the Ideal: Evald Ilyenkov and Creative Soviet Marxism*, Leiden: Brill.

Levine, Norman 1975, *The Tragic Deception: Marx Contra Engels*, Santa Barbara: Clio Books.

———— 1984, *Dialogue within the Dialectic*, London: Allen & Unwin.

———— 2002, 'Hegel and the 1861–63 Manuscripts of *Das Kapital*', *Rethinking Marxism* 14, 4: 47–58.

———— 2006–8, *Divergent Paths: Hegel in Marxism and Engelsism*, three volumes, Lanham, MD: Lexington Books.

Ley, Hermann 1954, 'Marx' Einleitung in die Grundrisse der Kritik der politischen Ökonomie', *Deutsche Zeitschrift für Philosophie* 2, 3: 574–600.

Liedman, Sven-Eric 1977, *Motsatsernas spel: Friedrich Engels' filosofi och 1800-talets vetenskaper*, Lund: Bo Cavefors.

———— 1986 [1977], *Das Spiel der Gegensätze: Friedrich Engels' Philosophie und die Wissenschaften des 19. Jahrhunderts*, Frankfurt: Campus.

Lietz, Barbara 2000, 'Die Problematik von Wert und Tauschwert und die "Ergänzungen und Veränderungen zum ersten Band des *Kapital*"', in *Marx' Ökonomiekritik im Kapital*, (*Beiträge zur Marx-Engels-Forschung: Neue Folge*, 1999), edited by Rolf Hecker et al., Hamburg: Argument.

Liguori, Guido 2006, 'Il Marxismo Italiano tra teoria e politica: 'Critica Marxista' 1963–1991', *Critica Marxista*, 1: 27–36.

Likitkijsomboon, Pichit 1992, 'The Hegelian Dialectic and Marx's *Capital*', *Cambridge Journal of Economics*, 16, 4: 405–19.

———— 1995, 'Marxian Theories of Value-Form', *Review of Radical Political Economics* 27, 2: 73–105.

Limoeiro-Cardoso, Miriam 2002, 'Sobre Althusser e a crise do Marxismo', in *A obra teórica de Marx: Atualidade, problemas e interpretações*, edited by Armando Boito Jr. et al., São Paulo: IFCH-UNICAMP.

Lin, Chun 1993, *The British New Left*, Edinburgh: Edinburgh University Press.

Linde, Birger 2004, *De store kriser 1: kriseteori og kriser i 1800-tallet – inspirationen fra Marx*, Roskilde: Internationale Udviklingsstudier, Roskilde Universitetscenter.

Lipietz, Alain 1992, 'Vom Althusserismus zur "Theorie der Regulation"', in *Hegemonie und Staat: kapitalistische Regulation als Projekt und Prozess*, edited by Alex Demirović and Hans-Peter Krebs, Münster: Westfälisches Dampfboot.

Lippert, Wolfgang 1979, *Entstehung und Funktion einiger chinesischer marxistischer Termini: Der lexikalisch-begriffliche Aspekt der Rezeption des Marxismus in Japan und China*, Wiesbaden: Steiner.

Lippi, Marco 1979 [1976], *Value and Naturalism in Marx*, London: NLB.

Litschev, Alexander and Dietrich Kegler 1992, 'Einleitung', in *Abschied vom Marxismus: Sowjetische Philosophie im Umbruch*, edited by Alexander Litschev and Dietrich Kegler, Reinbek: Rowohlt.

Liu, Fangtong, 2004, *China's Contemporary Philosophical Journey: Western Philosophy and Marxism*. Washington, DC: Council for Research in Values and Philosophy.

Lock, Grahame 1977, 'Althusser en Angleterre', *Dialectiques: Revue trimestrielle* 15–16: 64–72.

López Arnal, Salvador 2007, 'Le renversement: Manuel Sacristán critique de Louis Althusser', *ContreTemps*, 20: 82–92.

Löwy, Michael 1992, "Introduction", in *Marxism in Latin America from 1909 to the Present: An Anthology*, edited by Michael Löwy, Atlantic Highlands, New Jersey: Humanities.

———— 2003 [1970], *The Theory of Revolution in the Young Marx*, Leiden: Brill.

Lu, Lu 2006, 'New Chinese Edition of Marx and Engels Collected Works, Regarded from the Perspective of MEGA and the Chinese Reception of Marxism', available at: http://www.psa.ac.uk/spgrp/marxism/online/lulu.pdf

Lukács, Georg 1971 [1923], 'What is Orthodox Marxism?', in *History and Class Consciousness: Studies in Marxist Dialectics*, by Georg Lukács, translated by Rodney Livingstone, London: Merlin.

―――― 1975 [1948], *The Young Hegel: Studies in the Relations between Dialectics and Economics*, translated by Rodney Livingstone, London: Merlin.

―――― 1981, *Gelebtes Denken: Eine Autobiographie im Dialog*, Frankfurt am Main: Suhrkamp.

Lundkvist, Anders 1973, *Introduktion til metoden i Kapitalen*, Århus: Modtryk.

Luporini, Cesare 1976, 'La logica specifica dell'oggetto specifico: sulla discussione di Marx con Hegel', in *Problemi teorici del marxismo*, edited by Critica Marxista, Rome: Editori Riuniti.

―――― 1983, 'La concezione della storia in Marx', in *Marx, un secolo*, edited by Nicolao Merker, Rome: Editori Riuniti.

Macherey, Pierre 2008, *Marx 1845, les 'thèses' sur Feuerbach: traduction et commentaire*, Paris: Éditions Amsterdam.

Maclean, Brian 1981, 'Kōzō Uno's Principles of Political Economy', *Science & Society*, 45, 2: 212–27.

Malysch, Alexander I. 1963, 'Marx' ökonomische Manuskripte von 1857/58 – eine wichtige Etappe in der Entwicklung der marxistischen politischen Ökonomie', in *Beiträge zur Geschichte der deutschen Arbeiterbewegung*, edited by Institut für Marxismus-Leninismus beim ZK der SED, East Berlin: Dietz.

―――― 1971, 'Friedrich Engels' Beitrag zur Ausarbeitung des Gegenstandes und der Methode der politischen Ökonomie', *Friedrich Engels, 1820–1970: Referate, Diskussionen, Dokumente*, edited by Hans Pelger, Hannover: Verlag für Literatur und Zeitgeschehen.

Mandel, Ernest 1962 [1962], *Marxist Economic Theory*, transated by Brian Pearce, London: Merlin.

―――― 1970 [1967], *The Formation of the Economic Thought of Karl Marx: 1843 to Capital*, transated by Brian Pearce, London: NLB.

―――― 1976a [1964], *An Introduction to Marxist Economic Theory*, New York, NY: Pathfinder.

―――― 1976b, 'Introduction', in *Capital*, Volume One, by Karl Marx, Harmondsworth: Penguin.

―――― 1978, 'Introduction', in *Capital*, Volume Two, by Karl Marx, Harmondsworth: Penguin.

―――― 1981, 'Introduction', in *Capital*, Volume Three, by Karl Marx, Harmondsworth: Penguin.

———— 1991 [1976–91], *Kontroversen um 'Das Kapital'*, Berlin: Dietz.

Mandel, Ernest and Johannes Agnoli 1980, *Offener Marxismus: Ein Gespräch über Dogmen, Orthodoxie und die Häresie der Realität*, Frankfurt am Main/New York, NY: Campus.

Mao, Zedong 1977 [1957], 'On the Correct Handling of Contradictions among the People', in *Selected Works*, Volume Five, by Zedong Mao, Peking: Foreign Languages Press.

Marcuse, Herbert 1958, *Soviet Marxism: A Critical Analysis*, New York, NY: Columbia University Press.

———— 1967, 'Ziele, Formen und Aussichten der Studentenopposition', *Das Argument*, 45: 398–408.

———— 2005 [1932], 'New Sources on the Foundation of Historical Materialism', in *Heideggerian Marxism*, edited by Richard Wolin and John Abromeit, Lincoln, NE: University of Nebraska Press.

Markus, György 1969, 'Über die erkenntnistheoretischen Ansichten des jungen Marx', in *Beiträge zur marxistischen Erkenntnistheorie*, edited by Alfred Schmidt, Frankfurt am Main: Suhrkamp.

Marramao, Giacomo 1973, 'Kritische Bemerkungen zur Korsch-Rezeption in Italien', in *Über Karl Korsch* (*Jahrbuch Arbeiterbewegung*, 1), edited by Claudio Pozzoli, Frankfurt am Main: Fischer.

———— 1975, 'Korsch in Italy', *Telos*, 26: 174–184.

Martínez Marzoa, Felipe 1983, *La Filosofía de 'El Capital' de Marx*, Madrid: Taurus.

Marx, Karl 1854/5, 'Citate: Geldwesen, Creditwesen, Crisen' (unpublished manuscript), IISG, Amsterdam, MEN, Sign. B79/75.

———— 1964 [1939], *Pre-Capitalist Economic Formations*, translated by Jack Cohen, edited by Eric Hobsbawm, London: Lawrence and Wishart.

———— 1965, *Theorien über den Mehrwert* (*Vierter Band des "Kapitals"*), *Erster Teil*, in *Marx-Engels-Werke*, Volume 26.1, East Berlin: Dietz.

———— 1967, *Theorien über den Mehrwert* (*Vierter Band des "Kapitals"*), *Zweiter Teil*, in *Marx-Engels-Werke*, Volume 26.2, East Berlin: Dietz.

———— 1968, *Theorien über den Mehrwert* (*Vierter Band des "Kapitals"*), *Dritter Teil*, in *Marx-Engels-Werke*, Volume 26.3, East Berlin: Dietz.

———— 1971 [1939], *Marx's Grundrisse*, edited and translated by David McLellan, London: Macmillan.

———— 1973 [1939], *Grundrisse: Foundations of the Critique of Political Economy* (*Rough Draft*), translated by Martin Nicolaus, Harmondsworth: Penguin.

———— 1976a [1867], *Capital*, Volume One, translated by Ben Fowkes, Harmondsworth: Penguin.

———— 1976b, 'Postface to the Second Edition', in *Capital*, Volume One, translated by Ben Fowkes, Harmondsworth: Penguin.

—————— 1976c, *Value: Studies by Marx*, edited and translated by Albert Dragstedt, London: New Park Publications.

—————— 1976d, *Marx-Engels-Gesamtausgabe*, Volume II/1.1, East Berlin: Dietz.

—————— 1976e, *Marx-Engels-Gesamtausgabe*, Volume II/3.1, East Berlin: Dietz.

—————— 1978a [1867], 'The Value-Form', translated by Mike Roth and Wal Suchting, in *Capital & Class*, 4: 135–50.

—————— 1978b, *The Class Struggles in France, 1848 to 1850*, in *Marx and Engels Collected Works*, Volume 10, London: Lawrence and Wishart.

—————— 1980, *Marx-Engels-Gesamtausgabe*, Volume II/2, East Berlin: Dietz.

—————— 1981a [1894], *Capital*, Volume Three, translated by David Fernbach, Harmondsworth: Penguin.

—————— 1981b, *Marx-Engels-Gesamtausgabe*, Volume II/1.2, East Berlin: Dietz.

—————— 1982a, 'Marx to Joseph Weydemeyer. 27 June 1851', in *Marx and Engels Collected Works*, Volume 38, London: Lawrence and Wishart.

—————— 1982b, *Marx-Engels-Gesamtausgabe*, Volume I/2, East Berlin: Dietz.

—————— 1983a, 'Marx to Engels. 16 January 1858', in *Marx and Engels Collected Works*, Volume 40, London: Lawrence and Wishart.

—————— 1983b, 'Marx to Joseph Weydemeyer. 1 February 1859', in *Marx and Engels Collected Works*, Volume 40, London: Lawrence and Wishart.

—————— 1983c, 'Marx to Ferdinand Lassalle. 31 May 1858', in *Marx and Engels Collected Works*, Volume 40, London: Lawrence and Wishart.

—————— 1983d, 'Marx to Engels. 1 February 1858', in *Marx and Engels Collected Works*, Volume 40, London: Lawrence and Wishart.

—————— 1983e, 'Marx to Engels. 2 April 1858', in *Marx and Engels Collected Works*, Volume 40, London: Lawrence and Wishart.

—————— 1983f, 'Marx to Engels. 29 November 1858', in *Marx and Engels Collected Works*, Volume 40, London: Lawrence and Wishart.

—————— 1983g, 'Marx to Ferdinand Lassalle. 11 March 1858', in *Marx and Engels Collected Works*, Volume 40, London: Lawrence and Wishart.

—————— 1983h, 'Marx to Engels. 18 December 1857', in *Marx and Engels Collected Works*, Volume 40, London: Lawrence and Wishart.

—————— 1983i, 'Marx to Ferdinand Lassalle. 12 November 1858', in *Marx and Engels Collected Works*, Volume 40, London: Lawrence and Wishart.

—————— 1983j [1867], *Marx-Engels-Gesamtausgabe*, Volume II/5, East Berlin: Dietz.

—————— 1983k, 'Marx to Ferdinand Lassalle. 22 February 1858', in *Marx and Engels Collected Works*, Volume 40, London: Lawrence and Wishart.

—————— 1986, *Bullion: Das vollendete Geldsystem*, in *Marx-Engels-Gesamtausgabe*, Volume IV/8, East Berlin: Dietz.

—————— 1987a, 'Marx to Engels. 31 July 1865', in *Marx and Engels Collected Works*, Volume 42, London: Lawrence and Wishart.

———— 1987b, *A Contribution to the Critique of Political Economy*, in *Marx and Engels Collected Works*, Volume 29, London: Lawrence and Wishart.

———— 1987c, 'Marx to Ludwig Kugelmann. 13 October 1866', in *Marx and Engels Collected Works*, Volume 42, London: Lawrence and Wishart.

———— 1987d, 'Marx to Engels. 22 June 1867', in *Marx and Engels Collected Works*, Volume 42, London: Lawrence and Wishart.

———— 1987e, 'Marx to Engels. 20 February 1866', in *Marx and Engels Collected Works*, Volume 42, London: Lawrence and Wishart.

———— 1987f, 'Index to the 7 Notebooks', in *Marx and Engels Collected Works*, Volume 29, London: Lawrence and Wishart.

———— 1987g, 'References to my own Notebooks', in *Marx and Engels Collected Works*, Volume 29, London: Lawrence and Wishart.

———— 1987h, 'Marx to Ludwig Kugelmann. 6 March 1868', in *Marx and Engels Collected Works*, Volume 42, London: Lawrence and Wishart.

———— 1987i, 'Marx to Johann Philipp Becker. 17 April 1867', in *Marx and Engels Collected Works*, Volume 42, London: Lawrence and Wishart.

———— 1988a, 'Marx to Ludwig Kugelmann. 12 October 1868', in *Marx and Engels Collected Works*, Volume 43, London: Lawrence and Wishart.

———— 1988b, 'Marx to Ludwig Kugelmann. 11 July 1868', in *Marx and Engels Collected Works*, Volume 43, London: Lawrence and Wishart.

———— 1988c, 'Marx to Joseph Dietzgen. 9 May 1868', in *Marx and Engels Collected Works*, Volume 43, London: Lawrence and Wishart.

———— 1988d, *Marx-Engels-Gesamtausgabe*, Volume II/4.1, East Berlin: Dietz.

———— 1989a, *Critique of the Gotha Programme*, in Marx *and Engels Collected Works*, Volume 24, London: Lawrence and Wishart.

———— 1989b, *Theories of Surplus-Value*, in *Marx and Engels Collected Works*, Volume 31, London: Lawrence and Wishart.

———— 1989c, *Theories of Surplus-Value*, in *Marx and Engels Collected Works*, Volume 32, London: Lawrence and Wishart.

———— 1989d, 'Marginal Notes on Adolph Wagner's *Lehrbuch der politischer Oekonomie*', in *Marx and Engels Collected Works*, Volume 24, London: Lawrence and Wishart.

———— 1989e, 'Marx to Engels. 31 May 1873', in *Marx and Engels Collected Works*, Volume 44, London: Lawrence and Wishart.

———— 1989f [1872–5], *Marx-Engels-Gesamtausgabe*, Volume II/7, East Berlin: Dietz.

———— 1991a, 'Marx to Nikolai Danielson. 15 November 1878', in *Marx and Engels Collected Works*, Volume 43, London: Lawrence and Wishart.

———— 1991b, 'Economic Manuscript of 1861–63', in *Marx and Engels Collected Works*, Volume 33, London: Lawrence and Wishart.

———— 1991c, 'Marx to Nikolai Danielson. 10 April 1879', in *Marx and Engels Collected Works*, Volume 45, London: Lawrence and Wishart.

———— 1993, 'Manuskript 1863/65 zum 3. Buch des "Kapital"', in *Marx-Engels-Gesamtausgabe*, Volume II/4.2, Berlin: Dietz.

———— 1994 [1867], 'The Value-Form', translated by Mike Roth and Wal Suchting, in *Debates in Value Theory*, edited by Simon Mohun, Basingstoke: Macmillan.

———— 1998a, 'Exzerpte aus Joseph Pecchio: Histoire de l'économie politique en Italie', in *Marx-Engels-Gesamtausgabe*, Volume IV/3, Berlin: Akademie.

———— 1998b, 'Exzerpte aus John Ramsay MacCulloch: Discours sur l'origine, les progrès, les objets particuliers, et l'importance de l'économie politique', in *Marx-Engels-Gesamtausgabe*, Volume IV/3, Berlin: Akademie.

———— 1998c, 'Exzerpte aus Charles Ganilh: Des systèmes d'économie politique ...', in *Marx-Engels-Gesamtausgabe*, Volume IV/3, Berlin: Akademie.

———— 2004 [1894], *Marx-Engels-Gesamtausgabe*, Volume II/15, Berlin: Akademie.

Marxhausen, Thomas 1980, 'Was verstand Marx unter "klassischer politischer Ökonomie"?', *Arbeitsblätter zur Marx-Engels-Forschung*, 12: 36–43.

———— 1987a, 'Aspekte der Marxschen Analyse der "sonderbaren Architektonik" von Ricardos "Principles" im Manuskript 1861–1863', *Beiträge zur Marx-Engels-Forschung*, 23: 97–102.

———— 1987b, 'Zum Zusammenhang von Fetischismus, Entfremdung und Ideologie bei Marx', *Deutsche Zeitschrift für Philosophie*, 35, 12: 1099–109.

———— 1988, 'Die Theorie des Fetischismus im dritten Band des *Kapital*', *Beiträge zur Marx-Engels-Forschung*, 25: 209–44.

———— 2006, '"MEGA-MEGA" und kein Ende', *Utopie kreativ*, 189/190: 596–617.

———— 2008, 'Kapital-Editionen', in *Historisch-Kritisches Wörterbuch des Marxismus*, Volume 7/I, edited by Wolfgang Fritz Haug et al., Hamburg: Argument.

Marxhausen, Thomas and Otto Schattenberg 1978, '"Klassische bürgerliche politische Ökonomie" und "Vulgärökonomie" – Entstehung, Inhalt und Einsatz der Begriffe im ökonomischen Werk von Marx', *Arbeitsblätter zur Marx-Engels-Forschung*, 4: 4–23.

Masaki, Hachiro 1986, 'Marxsche Wertformtheorie als notwendige Kombination zweier Methoden: Eine methodologische Reflexion', *Osaka City University Economic Review*, 21: 19–41.

Matsui, Kiyoshi 1970, 'Marx's Plan in the "Critique of Political Economy" and the Crisis in the World Market', *The Kyoto University Economic Review*, 88: 28–56.

Mattick, Paul 1935, 'The Inevitability of Communism' (Polemic Pamphlet No. 3), edited by S.L. Solon, New York, NY: Polemic Publishers.

———— 1941, 'Man and Society in the Age of Reconstruction', *Living Marxism*, 5, 4: 20–59.

———— 1959, 'Value Theory and Capital Accumulation', *Science & Society*, 23, 1: 27–51.

———— 1962, 'Marxism and the New Physics', *Philosophy of Science*, 29, 4: 350–64.

———— 1967, 'Reflections on Input-Output Economics', *Science & Society*, 31, 2: 202–21.

———— 1968, 'Gunnar Myrdal's Dilemma', *Science & Society*, 32, 4: 421–40.

———— 1969, *Marx and Keynes: The Limits of the Mixed Economy*, London: Merlin.

———— 1972, 'Samuelson's "Transformation" of Marxism into Bourgeois Economics', *Science & Society*, 36, 3: 258–73.

———— 1974, *Kritik der Neomarxisten: Baran, Gillman, Hook, Mandel, Sweezy*, Frankfurt am Main: Fischer.

———— 1978, 'Monopoly Capital', in *Anti-Bolshevik Communism*, by Paul Mattick, London: Merlin.

———— 1981, 'Ernest Mandel's Late Capitalism', in *Economic Crisis and Crisis Theory*, by Paul Mattick, London: Merlin.

Mauke, Michael 1970, *Die Klassentheorie von Marx und Engels*, edited by Klaus Meschkat, Kajo Heymann and Jürgen Werth, Frankfurt am Main: Europäische Verlagsanstalt.

Mawatari, Shoken 1985, 'The Uno School: A Marxian approach in Japan', *History of Political Economy*, 17: 403–18.

Mayer, Günter 2007, 'Nachwort: Zur Situation des postsowjetischen Marxismus in Russland', in *Postsowjetischer Marxismus in Russland: Antworten auf die Herausforderungen des XXI. Jahrhunderts. Thesen zur Formierung einer wissenschaftlichen Schule*, by Aleksandr V. Buzgalin and Andrej I. Kolganov, available at: http://www.rosalux.de/cms/fileadmin/rls_uploads/pdfs/Marxismus_in_Russland_neu/pdf

Mayer, Günter and Wolfgang Küttler 2007, 'Postsowjetische Marxisten in Russland', *Utopie kreativ*, 201/202: 740–63.

Mayer, Thomas 1989, 'In Defense of Analytical Marxism', *Science & Society*, 53, 4: 416–41.

Mazzone, Alessandro 1977, 'Der Kapitalfetischismus: Über Grundfragen einer materialistischen Ideologietheorie (I)', *Sozialistische Politik*, 42: 64–92.

———— 1978a, 'Der Kapitalfetischismus: Über Grundfragen einer materialistischen Ideologietheorie (II)', *Sozialistische Politik*, 43: 84–103.

———— 1978b, 'Der Kapitalfetischismus: Über Grundfragen einer materialistischen Ideologietheorie (III)', *Sozialistische Politik*, 45: 136–49.

———— 1988, 'Die spezifische Zeitlichkeit der kapitalistischen Produktionsweise. Oder: Die historische Mission des Kapitals', in *Philosophie als Verteidigung des Ganzen der Vernunft*, edited by Hans Jörg Sandkühler, Domenico Losurdo, Hans Heinz Holz and Jeroen Bartels, Cologne: Pahl-Rugenstein.

———— 2002a, 'Was heisst "Produzieren"? Überlegungen zum Klassenbegriff im *Kapital*', in *Neue Texte, neue Fragen: Zur Kapital-Edition in der MEGA*, (*Beiträge zur Marx-Engels-Forschung: Neue Folge*, 2001), edited by Rolf Hecker et al., Hamburg: Argument.

———— (ed.) 2002b, *MEGA²: Marx ritrovato grazie alla nuova edizione critica*, Rome: Media Print.

McCormack, Gavan 1971, 'The Student Left in Japan', *New Left Review*, 65: 37–53.

Mchaurab, Sobhye, 1984. 'Marx auf Arabisch: Stand, Probleme und Aufgaben bei der Übersetzung der Werke von Marx und Engels in die arabische Sprache', *Beiträge zur Marx-Engels-Forschung*, 17: 144–57.

McLellan, David 1979, *Marxism after Marx*, London: Macmillan.

Meek, Ronald L. 1967, *Economics and Ideology and Other Essays: Studies in the Development of Economic Thought*, London: Chapman & Hall.

Meikle, Scott 1985, *Essentialism in the Thought of Karl Marx*, London: Duckworth.

Melcher, Dorothea 2005, 'Venezuelas Erdöl-Sozialismus', *Das Argument*, 262: 506–20.

Mepham, John 1979, 'From the *Grundrisse* to *Capital*: The Making of Marx's Method', in *Issues in Marxist Philosophy, Volume 1: Dialectics and Method*, edited by John Mepham and David-Hillel Ruben, Brighton: Harvester.

Mercier-Josa, Solange 1986, *Retour sur le jeune Marx: deux études sur le rapport de Marx à Hegel dans les manuscrits de 44 et dans le manuscrit dit de Kreuznach*, Paris: Méridiens Klincksieck.

Merker, Nicolao 1975, 'Einleitung: Galvano della Volpe als Theoretiker des Marxismus', in *Rousseau und Marx: Beiträge zur Dialektik geschichtlicher Strukturen*, by Galvano della Volpe, Darmstadt: Luchterhand.

Mészáros, István 1970, *Marx's Theory of Alienation*, London: Merlin.

———— 1993, 'Marxism Today: An interview with István Mészáros', *Monthly Review*, 44, 11: 9–24.

———— 1995, *Beyond Capital: Towards a Theory of Transition*, London: Merlin.

———— 2000, 'The Need for a Radical Alternative: Interview with István Mészáros', *Monthly Review*, 51, 8: 26–39.

Milios, Jannis 2006, 'Die Marxsche Werttheorie und das Geld: Zur Verteidigung der These über den endogenen Charakter des Geldes', in *Neue Aspekte von Marx' Kapitalismus-Kritik*, (*Beiträge zur Marx-Engels-Forschung: Neue Folge*, 2004), edited by Rolf Hecker et al., Hamburg: Argument.

Milios, John 1999, 'On Marx's Crisis Theory in the Original Manuscript of the 3rd Volume of *Capital*', available at: https://www.academia.edu/12010416/ON_MARXS _CRISIS_THEORY_IN_THE_ORIGINAL_MANUSCRIPT_OF_THE_3RD_VOLUME_ OF_CAPITAL

Milios, John 2007, '*Capital* after Louis Althusser: Focusing on Value-Form Analysis', in *Rileggere Il Capitale: la lezione di Louis Althusser*, edited by Michele Cangiani and Maria Turchetto, Milan: Mimesis.

Milios, John, Dimitri Dimoulis and George Economakis 2002, *Karl Marx and the Classics: An Essay on Value, Crises and the Capitalist Mode of Production*, Aldershot: Ashgate.

Miskevitsch, Larisa Romanovna 2006, 'Die zweite russische Marx-Engels-Werkausgabe (Sotschinenija): Ihre Prinzipien und Besonderheiten', in *Marx-Engels-Werkausgaben in der UdSSR und DDR (1945 bis 1968)*, (*Beiträge zur Marx-Engels-Forschung:*

Neue Folge, Sonderband 5), edited by Carl-Erich Vollgraf, Richard Sperl and Rolf Hecker, Hamburg: Argument.

Miskewitsch, Larissa, Michail Ternowski, Alexander Tschepurenko and Witali Wygodski 1982, 'Zur Periodisierung der Arbeit von Karl Marx am "Kapital" in den Jahren 1863 bis 1867', *Marx-Engels-Jahrbuch*, 5: 294–322.

Mita, Sekisuke 2006 [1974], 'The Method of *Capital*', translated by E. Michael Schauerte, available at: http://www.marxists.org/subject/japan/mita/method-capital.htm

Mitsunobu, Sugiyama 2002, 'The World Conception of Japanese Social Science: The Koza Faction, the Otsuka School, and the Uno School of Economics', in *New Asian Marxisms*, edited by Tani E. Barlow, Durham, NC: Duke University Press.

Miyakawa, Akira 1994, 'Der gesamtgesellschaftliche Reproduktionsprozess in der Theoriegeschichte: F. Quesnay, A. Smith und K. Marx', in *Quellen und Grenzen von Marx' Wissenschaftsverständnis*, (*Beiträge zur Marx-Engels-Forschung: Neue Folge*, 1994), edited by Rolf Hecker et al., Hamburg: Argument.

———— 1996, 'Eine Wiederaufnahme der Testamentsvollstreckung durch die MEGA? Neuere Tendenzen in japanischen Studien zum zweiten Buch des *Kapital*', MEGA-*Studien*, 1995, 2: 42–53.

———— 1999, 'Japanische Forschungen zu Marx' drittem Buch des *Kapital* durch die MEGA im Aufschwung', in *Geschichtserkenntnis und kritische Ökonomie*, (*Beiträge zur Marx-Engels-Forschung: Neue Folge*, 1998), edited by Rolf Hecker et al., Hamburg: Argument.

Miyake, Yoshio 1993, 'Marx' ökonomisches Manuskript von 1861–1863 und Probleme seiner Edition im MEGA^2-Band II/3: Die Stellung der 23 Hefte von "Zur Kritik der politischen Ökonomie" (Manuskript 1861 bis 1863) in Marx' ökonomischen Arbeiten', in *Marx-Engels-Forschung im historischen Spannungsfeld*, (*Beiträge zur Marx-Engels-Forschung: Neue Folge*, 1993), edited by Rolf Hecker et al., Hamburg: Argument.

Mizuta, Hiroshi 2006, 'The Japanese concept of civil society and Marx's *bürgerliche Gesellschaft*', in *Marx for the 21st Century*, edited by Hiroshi Uchida, London: Routledge.

Mohl, Ernst Theodor 1991, 'Zur Marx-Forschung in Halle', in *Naturwissenschaften und Produktivkräfte bei Marx und Engels*, (*Marx-Engels-Forschung heute*, 3), edited by Institut für Marxistische Studien und Forschungen, Frankfurt am Main: IMSF.

———— 2002, 'Ein Reisebericht', in *In Memoriam Wolfgang Jahn: Der ganze Marx – Alles Verfasste veröffentlichen, erforschen und den 'ungeschriebenen' Marx rekonstruieren*, (*Wissenschaftliche Mitteilungen, Heft 1*), edited by Berliner Verein zur Förderung der MEGA-Edition e. V., Hamburg: Argument.

Mollo, Maria de Lourdes Rollemberg 1991, 'A Relação entre Moeda e Valor em Marx', *Revista de Economia Política*, 42: 40–59.

Montano, Mario 1971, 'On the Methodology of Determinate Abstraction: Essay on Galvano della Volpe', *Telos*, 7: 30–49.

Morales, Cesáreo 1983, 'El althusserianismo en México', *Dialéctica*, 14–15: 173–84.

Morf, Otto 1970 [1951], *Geschichte und Dialektik in der politischen Ökonomie: zum Verhältnis von Wirtschaftstheorie und Wirtschaftsgeschichte bei Karl Marx*, Frankfurt am Main: Europäische Verlagsanstalt.

Morishima, Michio 1973, *Marx's Economics: A Dual Theory of Value and Growth*, Cambridge: Cambridge University Press.

Morris, J. 1966, 'Commodity Fetishism and the Value Concept: Some Contrasting Points of View', *Science & Society*, 30, 2: 206–12.

Morris-Suzuki, Tessa 1989, *A History of Japanese Economic Thought*, London: Routledge.

Mosbah, Salah 2006, 'La scuola del materialismo contemporaneo: Note sulla ricezione di Althusser nel mondo arabo (1960–1990)', in *Althusseriana quaderni, 1. Giornate di studio sul pensiero di Louis Althusser: Venezia, 11 e 12 febbraio 2004: atti del convegno*, edited by Maria Turchetto et al., Milan: Mimesis.

Moseley, Fred (ed.) 1993, *Marx's Method in Capital: A Reexamination*, Atlantic Highlands, NJ: Humanities.

———— 1995, 'Capital in General and Marx's Logical Method: A Response to Heinrich's Critique', *Capital & Class*, 56: 15–48.

———— 2001, 'Introduction to "The Four Drafts of Capital: Towards a New Interpretation of the Dialectical Thought of Marx," By Enrique Dussel', *Rethinking Marxism*, 13, 1: 1–9.

———— 2002, 'The "Heart and Soul" of Marx's Critique of Capitalism: Exploitation or Social Form – or Both? A Reply to Patrick Murray', *Rethinking Marxism*, 14, 3: 122–8.

———— (ed.) 2005, *Marx's Theory of Money: Modern Appraisals*, New York: Palgrave Macmillan.

———— 2006, 'Kapital im Allgemeinen und Konkurrenz der vielen Kapitalien in der Theorie von Marx: Die quantitative Dimension', *Marx-Engels-Jahrbuch*, 2006: 81–117.

———— 2015, *Money and Totality: A Macro-Monetary Interpretation of Marx's Logic in Capital and the End of the 'Transformation Problem'*, Leiden: Brill.

Moseley, Fred, and Martha Campbell (eds.) 1997, *New Investigations of Marx's Method*, Atlantic Highlands, NJ: Humanities.

Mtschedlow, Michail 1978, 'Zu einigen Fragen der Erforschung und Veröffentlichung des theoretischen Nachlasses von Karl Marx und Friedrich Engels in der UdSSR', in *Beiträge zur Geschichte der Marx/Engels-Forschung und -Edition in der Sowjetunion und der DDR*, edited by Institut für Marxismus-Leninismus beim ZK der SED, East Berlin: Dietz.

Mugnai, Massimo 1984, *Il mondo rovesciato: contraddizione e 'valore' in Marx*, Bologna: Il Mulino.

Müller, Klaus 1988, 'Analytischer Marxismus: Technischer Ausweg aus der theoretischen Krise?', *Prokla*, 72: 39–71.

Müller, Manfred 1977, 'Die vorbereitenden Materialien für Marx' ökonomisches Manuskript von 1861–1863', *Beiträge zur Marx-Engels-Forschung*, 1: 95–102.

———— 1978a, 'Zu einigen sowjetischen Forschungsergebnissen über die Entstehungsgeschichte des "Kapitals"', in *Beiträge zur Geschichte der Marx/Engels-Forschung und -Edition in der Sowjetunion und der DDR*, edited by Institut für Marxismus-Leninismus beim ZK der SED, East Berlin: Dietz.

———— 1978b, *Auf dem Wege zum 'Kapital': Zur Entwicklung des Kapitalbegriffs von Karl Marx in den Jahren 1857–1863*, East Berlin: Akademie.

———— 1983, 'Über die Stellung des Manuskripts "Zur Kritik der politischen Ökonomie" (1861–1863) im ökonomischen Nachlass von Karl Marx', *Marx-Engels-Jahrbuch*, 6: 173–208.

Müller, Ulrich 1975, 'Althussers strukturalistische Umdeutung des "Kapital"', *Das Argument*, 89: 85–92.

Müller, Wolfgang 1969a, 'Habermas und die Anwendbarkeit der Arbeitswerttheorie', *Sozialistische Politik*, 1: 39–53.

———— 1969b, 'Marxistische Wirtschaftstheorie und Fetischcharakter der Ware: Kritische Bemerkungen zum Hauptwerk Ernest Mandels', *Neue Kritik*, 51/52: 69–86.

Muntaner, Carles and Francisco Fernández Buey 1998: 'Manuel Sacristán, Spanish Marxist – Breaking the Pact of Silence', *Rethinking Marxism*, 10, 2: 123–37.

Murray, Patrick 1988, *Marx's Theory of Scientific Knowledge*, Atlantic Highlands, NJ: Humanities.

———— 1993, 'The Necessity of Money: How Hegel Helped Marx Surpass Ricardo's Theory of Value', in *Marx's Method in Capital: A Reexamination*, edited by Fred Moseley, Atlantic Highlands, NJ: Humanities.

———— 2002, 'The Trouble with Ricardian Marxism: Comments on "The Four Drafts of *Capital*: Toward a New Interpretation of the Dialectical Thought of Marx," by Enrique Dussel', *Rethinking Marxism*, 14, 3: 114–22.

———— 2005, 'The New Giants Staircase: A Contribution to a Symposium on Christopher Arthur's book, *The New Dialectic and Marx's Capital*', *Historical Materialism*, 13, 2: 61–84.

Musto, Marcello 2004, 'La "Nuova MEGA" e il carteggio di Marx ed Engels del 1858–1859', *Critica Marxista*, 2004, 5: 56–60.

———— (ed.) 2005, *Sulle tracce di un fantasma: L'opera di Karl Marx tra filologia e filosofia*, Rome: Manifestolibri.

———— 2007a, 'Marx in Paris: Manuskripte und Exzerpthefte aus dem Jahr 1844', in *Geld – Kapital – Wert: Zum 150. Jahrestag der Niederschrift von Marx' ökonomischen Manuskripten 1857/58 'Grundrisse der Kritik der politischen Ökonomie'*, (*Beiträge zur Marx-Engels-Forschung: Neue Folge*, 2007), edited by Rolf Hecker et al., Hamburg: Argument.

———— 2007b, 'The Rediscovery of Karl Marx', *International Review of Social History*, 52: 477–98.

———— 2008, 'History, Production and Method in the 1857 "Introduction"', in *Karl Marx's Grundrisse: Foundations of the Critique of Political Economy 150 Years Later*, edited by Marcello Musto, New York, NY: Routledge.

———— (ed.) 2010, 'Marx's Global Reception Today', *Socialism and Democracy*, 24, 3: 147–211.

Nagatani, Kiyoshi 1997, 'Value-form as a Starting Point of Uno Theory', available at: http://homepage2.nifty.com/nagatani-kiyoshi/myworks.htm

Napoleoni, Claudio 1975 [1970], *Smith, Ricardo, Marx: Observations on the History of Economic Thought*, translated by J.M. Alec Gee, Oxford: Blackwell.

———— 1983, 'Il capitale e il pensiero economico di Marx', in *Marx e i marxismi: mostra per il centenario della morte di Karl Marx a cura della Fondazione Giangiacomo Feltrinelli*, edited by Aldo Agosti et al., Milan: Feltrinelli.

Navarro, Fernanda 1992, 'La réception en Amérique latine', *Magazine littéraire*, 304: 55–6.

Naville, Pierre 1968, 'La méthodologie dans l'analyse du "Capital"', in *En partant du 'Capital'*, edited by Victor Fay et al., Paris: Anthropos.

Negri, Antonio 1984, *Marx beyond Marx: Lessons on the Grundrisse*, translated by Michael Ryan, Maurizio Viano and Harry Cleaver, South Hadley, MA: Bergin et Garvey.

Negt, Oskar 1974, 'Einleitung', in *Kontroversen über dialektischen und mechanistischen Materialismus*, by Nikolai Bucharin and Abram Deborin, edited by Oskar Negt, Frankfurt am Main, Suhrkamp.

Nelson, Anitra 1999, *Marx's Concept of Money: The God of Commodities*, London: Routledge.

Nicolaus, Martin 1968, 'The Unknown Marx', *New Left Review*, 48: 41–61.

Niechoj, Torsten 2003, 'Analytischer Marxismus – eine rationale Wahl? Stand und Perspektive eines Forschungsprogramms', in *Mit Marx ins 21. Jahrhundert: zur Aktualität der Kritik der politischen Ökonomie*, edited by Olaf Gerlach, Stefan Kalmring and Andreas Nowak, Hamburg: VSA.

Nietzold, Roland, Hannes Skambraks and Günter Wermusch (eds.) 1978, *... unsrer Partei einen Sieg erringen: Studien zur Entstehungs- und Wirkungsgeschichte des 'Kapitals' von Karl Marx*, East Berlin: Die Wirtschaft.

Niji, Yoshihiro 1983, 'Hegels Theorie vom Urteil und Marx' Theorie von der Wertform', *The Hannan Ronshu* 19, 2: 55–7.

———— 1995, 'Der Formgehalt oder Forminhalt des Wertausdrucks in der Politischen Ökonomie von Karl Marx – die Hegelsche Logik als Quelle des Marxschen Wertbegriffs', *The Hannan Ronshu*, 31, 2: 1–4.

Nikolić, Miloš 1983, 'The Basic Results of the Development of Contemporary Marxism', *Socialism in the World: International Journal of Marxist and Socialist Thought*, 38: 12–61.

Nowak, Leszek 1976, 'Das Problem der Erklärung in Karl Marx' "Kapital"', in *Zur Wissenschaftslogik einer kritischen Soziologie*, edited by Jürgen Ritsert, Frankfurt am Main: Suhrkamp.

———— 1978, 'Weber's Ideal Types and Marx's Abstraction', *Neue Hefte für Philosophie*, 13: 81–91.

Núñez Tenorio, J.R. 1969, *Marx y la economía política*, Caracas: Instituto de Investigaciones, Facultad de Ciencias Económicas y Sociales, Universidad Central de Venezuela.

———— 1985, *Problemas del método de la economía política*, Caracas: Panapo.

Oakley, Allen 1983, *The Making of Marx's Critical Theory: A Bibliographical Analysis*, London: Routledge & Kegan Paul.

Oguro, Masao 1986, 'Zur theoretischen Bedeutung der "Wertform" im "Kapital" von Karl Marx', *Arbeitsblätter zur Marx-Engels-Forschung*, 18: 23–47.

Ōishi, Takahisa 1995, 'Ricardo's Value Theory Re-examined: Marx vs. Ricardo on Value', in *Engels' Druckfassung versus Marx' Manuskripte zum III. Buch des 'Kapital'*, (*Beiträge zur Marx-Engels-Forschung: Neue Folge*, 1995), edited by Rolf Hecker et al., Hamburg: Argument.

———— 2001, The Unknown Marx: Reconstructing a Unified Perspective. London: Pluto.

Oittinen, Vesa 2008, 'Kapitallogik (II)', in *Historisch-Kritisches Wörterbuch des Marxismus*, Volume 7/I, edited by Wolfgang Fritz Haug et al., Hamburg: Argument.

Oittinen, Vesa and Paula Rauhala 2014, 'Evald Ilyenkov's Dialectics of Abstract and Concrete and the Recent Value-Form Debate', in *Dialectics of the Ideal: Evald Ilyenkov and Creative Soviet Marxism*, edited by Alex Levant and Vesa Oittinen, Leiden: Brill.

Okishio, Nobuo 1963, 'A Mathematical Note on Marxian Theorems', *Weltwirtschaftliches Archiv*, 91: 287–99.

Ollman, Bertell 2003, *Dance of the Dialectic: Steps in Marx's Method*, Urbana, IL: University of Illinois Press.

O'Malley, Joseph and Fred E. Schrader 1977, 'Marx's Précis of Hegel's Doctrine on Being in the Minor Logic', *International Review of Social History*, 22: 423–31.

Omiya, Samanosuke 1980, 'Zur Marx-Engels-Forschung und -Edition in Japan', in *Marx-Engels-Jahrbuch*, 3: 365–76.

Omura, Izumi 1995, 'Zum Abschluss der Veröffentlichung der verschiedenen Ausgaben des *Kapital* in der MEGA²: von der 3. deutschen Auflage, der "Auflage letzter Hand von Marx" (1984), zur 3. Auflage, "die dem letzten Willen des Autors zu einem bestimmten Grad entspricht" (1991)', *MEGA-Studien*, 1994, 2: 56–67.

———— 2002, 'Von *Zur Kritik der politischen Ökonomie* zum *Kapital*: Marx' konzeptionelle Überlegungen zum *Kapital* 1862 und 1863 bis 1865', in *Neue Texte, neue Fragen: Zur Kapital-Edition in der MEGA*, (*Beiträge zur Marx-Engels-Forschung: Neue Folge*, 2001), edited by Rolf Hecker et al., Hamburg: Argument.

———— 2005, 'Der Beitrag japanischer Wissenschaftler zur Fertigstellung der MEGA', in *Karl Marx: Neue Perspektiven auf sein Werk*, edited by Beatrix Bouvier, Trier: Studienzentrum Karl-Marx-Haus der Friedrich-Ebert-Stiftung.

———— 2006, 'La ricerca su Marx in Giappone e l'attività del gruppo di lavoro della MEGA di Sendai', in *Sulle tracce di un fantasma: L'opera di Karl Marx tra filologia e filosofia*, edited by Marcello Musto, Rome: Manifestolibri.

Otani, Teinosuke 1989, 'Das Problem der Geldbildung und seine Lösung im "Kapital"', *Beiträge zur Marx-Engels-Forschung*, 27: 177–85.

Otani, Teinosuke and Iichiro Sekine 1987, 'Beschäftigung mit Marx und Engels in Japan: Forschungen über die Methode der politischen Ökonomie und die Entstehungs-geschichte des *Kapitals*', in *Internationale Marx-Engels-Forschung*, (*Marxistische Studien: Jahrbuch des IMSF*, 12), edited by Institut für Marxistische Studien und Forschungen, Frankfurt am Main: IMSF.

Palti, Elias José 2005, *Verdades y saberes del Marxismo: Reacciones de una tradición política ante su 'crisis'*, Buenos Aires: Fondo de Cultura Económica.

Paragenings, Heinz 2006, 'Die Rolle der Grundrisse in der ökonomischen Debatte der fünfziger Jahre in der DDR', in *Marx-Engels-Werkausgaben in der UdSSR und DDR (1945 bis 1968)*, (*Beiträge zur Marx-Engels-Forschung: Neue Folge, Sonderband 5*), edited by Carl-Erich Vollgraf, Richard Sperl and Rolf Hecker, Hamburg: Argument.

Park, Dae-Won 2002, *Struktur der Krisentheorie bei Karl Marx und kritische Analyse der verschiedenen Krisentheorien*, Seoul: Moonwon.

Park, Mi 2002, 'Ideology and Lived Experience: Revolutionary Movements in South Korea, 1980–1995', available at: http://www.edgehill.ac.uk/Research/smg/pdf -Conference/MiPark-Ideology and Lived Experience.pdf (last retrieved 10-05-2007)

———— 2005, 'Organizing Dissent against Authoritarianism: The South Korean Student Movement in the 1980s', available at: http://people.stfx.ca/rbantjes/Soc212/Texts/ Korea-Journal-final.doc

Paulani, Leda Maria 1994, 'Sobre dinheiro e valor: uma critica às posicoes de Brunhoff e Mollo', *Revista de Economia Política*, 55: 67–77.

———— 2002, 'A atualidade da crítica da economia política', in *A obra teórica de Marx: Atualidade, problemas e interpretações*, edited by Armando Boito Jr. et al., São Paulo: IFCH-UNICAMP.

Peña, Milcíades 2000, *Introducción al pensamiento de Marx: notas inéditas de un curso de 1958*, Buenos Aires: Ediciones El Cielo por Asalto.

Peter, Anton 1997, *Enrique Dussel: Offenbarung Gottes im Anderen*, Mainz: Grünewald.

Pietilä, Veikko 1984, 'The Logical, the Historical and the Forms of Value – Once Again', in *Rethinking Marxism*, edited by Sakari Hänninen and Leena Paldán, Berlin: Argu-ment.

Pietranera, Giulio 1973, 'La estructura lógica de *El Capital*', in *Estudios sobre El Capital*, by Maurice Dobb et al., Madrid: Siglo veintiuno de España.

Ping, He 2007, 'On the phenomenon of "Return to Marx" in China', *Frontiers of Philosophy in China*, 2, 2: 219–29.

Porcaro, Mimmo 1986, *I difficili inizi di Karl Marx: contro chi e per che cosa leggere 'Il capitale' oggi*, Bari: Dedalo.

Postone, Moishe 1993, *Time, Labor, and Social Domination: A Reinterpretation of Marx's Critical Theory*, Cambridge: Cambridge University Press.

———— 2003 [1993], *Zeit, Arbeit und gesellschaftliche Herrschaft: eine neue Interpretation der kritischen Theorie von Marx*, translated by Christoph Seidler et al., Freiburg im Breisgau: ça ira.

Postone, Moishe and Helmut Reinicke 1974/5, 'On Nicolaus' "Introduction" to the *Grundrisse*', *Telos*, 22: 130–48.

Potier, Jean-Pierre 1986, *Lectures italiennes de Marx: les conflits d'interprétation chez les économistes et les philosophes, 1883–1983*, Lyon: Presses universitaires de Lyon.

———— 1989, 'Les économistes italiens et la théorie de Marx: le débat de Modène en 1978', in *Marxisme italien. Quelle identité? 1975–1988*, (*Actuel Marx*, 4), edited by Jacques Bidet and Jacques Texier, Paris: Presses universitaires de France.

Pouch, Thierry 2001, *Les économistes français et le marxisme: apogée et déclin d'un discours critique (1950–2000)*, Rennes: Presses universitaires de Rennes.

Poulantzas, Nicos 1968, 'Theorie und Geschichte: Kurze Bemerkungen über den Gegenstand des "Kapitals"', in *Kritik der politischen Ökonomie heute: 100 Jahre 'Kapital'*, edited by Alfred Schmidt and Walter Euchner, Frankfurt am Main, Europäische Verlagsanstalt.

Pozzoli, Claudio 1972, 'Notiz des Herausgebers', in *Spätkapitalismus und Klassenkampf: Eine Auswahl aus den 'Quaderni Rossi'*, edited by Claudio Pozzoli, Frankfurt am Main: Europäische Verlagsanstalt.

Pradella, Lucia 2015, *Globalisation and the Critique of Political Economy: New Insights from Marx's Writings*, Abingdon: Routledge.

Preve, Costanzo 1984, *La filosofia imperfetta: una proposta di ricostruzione del marxismo contemporaneo*, Milan: Angeli.

———— 1993, *Ideologia italiana: saggio sulla storia delle idee marxiste in Italia*, Milan: Vangelista.

———— 2007, *Storia critica del marxismo: dalla nascita di Karl Marx alla dissoluzione del comunismo storico novecentesco, 1818–1991*, Naples: La città del sole.

Priddat, Birger P. 1990, *Hegel als Ökonom*, Berlin: Duncker & Humblot.

Prokla 1979, 'Krise des Marxismus?', *Prokla*, 36.

Prokop, Siegfried 2006, 'Das Karl-Marx-Jahr 1953: Intellektuelle der DDR im Widerstreit zwischen Ideologie, Politik und Wissenschaft', in *Marx-Engels-Werkausgaben in der UdSSR und DDR (1945 bis 1968)*, (*Beiträge zur Marx-Engels-Forschung: Neue Folge, Sonderband 5*), edited by Carl-Erich Vollgraf, Richard Sperl and Rolf Hecker, Hamburg: Argument.

Projektgruppe Entwicklung des Marxschen Systems 1973, *Das Kapitel vom Geld: Interpretation der verschiedenen Entwürfe*, West Berlin: VSA.

———— 1975, *Der 4. Band des 'Kapital'?: Kommentar zu den Theorien über den Mehrwert*. West Berlin: VSA.

———— 1978, *Grundrisse der Kritik der politischen Ökonomie (Rohentwurf): Kommentar*, Hamburg: VSA.

Projektgruppe zur Kritik der politischen Ökonomie 1973, *Zur Logik des Kapitals*, West Berlin: VSA.

Psychopedis, Kosmas 1984, *Geschichte und Methode: Begründungstypen und Interpretationskriterien der Gesellschaftstheorie: Kant, Hegel, Marx und Weber*, Frankfurt am Main: Campus.

———— 2000, 'Das politische Element in der Darstellung dialektischer Kategorien', in *Kritik der Politik: Johannes Agnoli zum 75. Geburtstag*, edited by Joachim Bruhn, Manfred Dahlmann and Clemens Nachtmann, Freiburg im Breisgau: ça ira.

Quante, Michael 2002, 'Zeit für Marx? Neuere Literatur zur Philosophie von Karl Marx', *Zeitschrift für philosophische Forschung*, 56: 449–67.

Rakowitz, Nadja 2000, *Einfache Warenproduktion: Ideal und Ideologie*, Freiburg im Breisgau: ça ira.

Ramsay, Anders 2009 [2008], 'Marx? Which Marx?', translated by Steven Cuzner and Michelle Koerner, available at: http://www.eurozine.com/articles/2009-12-21-ramsay-en.html

Rancière, Jacques 1976 [1965], 'The Concept of "Critique" and the "Critique of Political Economy" (from the 1844 Manuscript to *Capital*)', *Economy and Society*, 5, 3: 352–76.

———— 1989 [1973], 'How to use *Lire le Capital*', translated by Tanya Asad, in *Ideology, Method and Marx: Essays from Economy and Society*, edited by Ali Rattansi, London: Routledge.

———— 2011 [1974], 'On the Theory of Ideology: Althusser's Politics', in *Althusser's Lesson*, by Jacques Rancière, translated by Emiliano Battista, London: Continuum.

Ranganayakamma, N.S. 1999, *An introduction to Marx's 'Capital'*, three volumes, Hyderabad: Sweet Home Publications.

Redaktionskollegium des Marx-Engels-Jahrbuchs 1978, 'Geleitwort', in: *Marx-Engels-Jahrbuch*, 1: 9–16.

Reichelt, Helmut 1969, 'Zur Marxschen Werttheorie und deren Interpretation bei Werner Hofmann', *Sozialistische Politik*, 2: 17–25.

———— 1992, 'Zur strukturalistischen Erneuerung des Marxismus', *Marx-Engels-Forschung heute*, 4: 120–36.

———— 2001 [1970], *Zur logischen Struktur des Kapitalbegriffs bei Karl Marx*, Freiburg im Breisgau: ça ira.

———— 2003, 'Grenzen der dialektischen Darstellungsform – oder Verabschiedung der

Dialektik? Einige Anmerkungen zur These von Dieter Riedel', *MEGA-Studien*, 2000/1: 100–126.

———— 2007, 'Zum Problem der dialektischen Darstellung ökonomischer Kategorien im Rohentwurf des *Kapitals*', in *Geld – Kapital – Wert: Zum 150. Jahrestag der Niederschrift von Marx' ökonomischen Manuskripten 1857/58 'Grundrisse der Kritik der politischen Ökonomie'*, (*Beiträge zur Marx-Engels-Forschung: Neue Folge*, 2007), edited by Rolf Hecker et al., Hamburg: Argument.

Reinicke, Helmut 1973, *Für Krahl*, West Berlin: Merve.

Renault, Emmanuel 2000, 'Marx et les critiques de l'économie politique', *Actuel Marx*, 27: 153–66.

Renxiang, Jiang 1998, 'Zur Herausgabe der Marx-Engels-Werke in China', in *Geschichtserkenntnis und kritische Ökonomie*, (*Beiträge zur Marx-Engels-Forschung: Neue Folge*, 1998), edited by Rolf Hecker et al., Hamburg: Argument.

Resnick, Stephen and Richard D. Wolff 2007, 'A Marxism made in USA: Marx Beyond Althusser? / Un marxisme made in USA: Marx au-delà d'Althusser?' (interview by Jacques Bidet), available at: http://rdwolff.com/content/marxism-made-usa-marx -beyond-althusser-un-marxisme-made-usa-marx-au-delà-d'althusser

Reuten, Geert 1993, 'The Difficult Labor of a Theory of Social Value: Metaphors and Systematic Dialectics at the Beginning of Marx's *Capital*', in *Marx's Method in Capital: A Reexamination*, edited by Fred Moseley, Atlantic Highlands, NJ: Humanities.

———— 1995, 'Conceptual Collapses: A Note on Value-Form Theory', *Review of Radical Political Economics*, 27, 3: 104–10.

Reuten, Geert and Michael Williams 1989, *Value-Form and the State: The Tendencies of Accumulation and the Determination of Economic Policy in Capitalist Society*, London: Routledge.

Ribas, Pedro (ed.) 1994, *Verbreitung und Rezeption der Werke von Marx und Engels in Spanien*, (*Schriften aus dem Karl-Marx-Haus*, 46), Trier: Studienzentrum Karl-Marx-Haus der Friedrich-Ebert-Stiftung.

Ribas, Pedro and Rafael Plá León 2008, 'Cuba, Argentina, Spain and Mexico [Dissemination and reception of the *Grundrisse* in the world]', in *Karl Marx's Grundrisse: Foundations of the Critique of Political Economy 150 Years Later*, edited by Marcello Musto, New York, NY: Routledge.

Ricardo, David 2001 [1817], *On the Principles of Political Economy and Taxation*, Kitchener: Batoche.

Riedel, Dieter 1998, 'Grenzen der dialektischen Darstellungsform', *MEGA-Studien*, 1997, 1: 3–40.

Riedel, Manfred 1982, *Zwischen Tradition und Revolution: Studien zu Hegels Rechtsphilosophie*, Stuttgart: Klett-Cotta.

Ripalda, José María 1978, 'Notiz über die Grenzen der Dialektik', *Das Argument*, 110: 529–34.

———— 1981, 'Marx, Hegel und die Philosophie: Kritik neuerer Untersuchungen', *Das Argument*, 128: 533–39.

Ritsert, Jürgen 1973, *Probleme politisch-ökonomischer Theoriebildung*, Frankfurt am Main: Athenäum.

———— 1998, 'Realabstraktion: Ein zurecht abgewertetes Thema der kritischen Theorie?', in *Kein Staat zu machen: Zur Kritik der Sozialwissenschaften*, edited by Christoph Görg and Roland Roth, Münster: Westfälisches Dampfboot.

Roberts, Marcus 1996, *Analytical Marxism: A Critique*, London: Verso.

Robles Baez, Mario L. 2000, 'La influencia del método "lógico-histórico" de Engels en las interpretaciones sobre el objeto de la sección primera del tomo I de *El Capital* de Marx: critica y propuesta', available at: https://marxismocritico.files.wordpress.com/2011/10/la_influencia_del_mo_logico_historico.pdf

Roces, Wenceslao 1983, 'La Filosofia de "El Capital": En el centenario de Marx', *El Trimestre Economico*, 200: 1861–6.

Rockmore, Tom 2002, *Marx after Marxism: The Philosophy of Karl Marx*, Oxford: Blackwell.

Rodin, Davor 1988, 'Theorie des Warensystems bei Karl Marx', in: *Hegel-Jahrbuch*, 1986: 45–55.

Roemer, John E. 1981, *Analytical Foundations of Marxian Economic Theory*, Cambridge: Cambridge University Press.

———— 1986, '"Rational Choice" Marxism: Some Issues of Method and Substance', in *Analytical Marxism*, edited by John E. Roemer, Cambridge: Cambridge University Press.

Roies, Albert 1974 [1971], *Lectura de Marx por Althusser*, Barcelona: Laia.

Rojahn, Jürgen 1994, 'Und sie bewegt sich doch!: Die Fortsetzung der Arbeit an der MEGA unter dem Schirm des IMES', *MEGA-Studien*, 1994, 1: 5–31.

Rojas, Raúl 1989, *Das unvollendete Projekt: zur Entstehungsgeschichte von Marx' Kapital*, Berlin: Argument.

Rokitjanskij, Jakov 1993, 'Das tragische Schicksal von David Borisovic Rjasanov', in *Marx-Engels-Forschung im historischen Spannungsfeld*, (*Beiträge zur Marx-Engels-Forschung: Neue Folge*, 1993), edited by Rolf Hecker et al., Hamburg: Argument.

———— 2009, *Gumanist oktjabr'skoj ėpochi: Akademik D.B. Rjazanov – social-demokrat, pravozaščitnik, učenyj*, Moscow: Sobranie.

Rosdolsky, Roman 1953, 'Das "Kapital im allgemeinen" und die "Vielen Kapitalien": ein Beitrag zur Methodologie des Marxschen "Kapitals"', *Kyklos*, 6: 153–63.

———— 1974 [1968], 'Comments on the Method of Marx's *Capital* and Its Importance for Contemporary Marxist Scholarship', translated by David Bathrick and Anson Rabinbach, *New German Critique*, 3: 62–72.

———— 1977 [1968], *The Making of Marx's 'Capital'*, translated by Pete Burgess, London: Pluto.

Rosenberg, David I. 1958, *Die Entwicklung der ökonomischen Lehre von Marx und Engels in den vierziger Jahren des 19. Jahrhunderts*, East Berlin: Dietz.

Rosental, Mark M. 1953, 'Die Ausarbeitung des Gesetzes vom Kampf der Gegensätze in Karl Marx's *Kapital*', *Deutsche Zeitschrift für Philosophie*, 1–2: 332–49.

———— 1957, *Die Dialektik in Marx' 'Kapital'*, translated by J. Harhammer, East Berlin: Dietz.

Rosenthal, John 1998, *The Myth of Dialectics: Reinterpreting the Hegel-Marx-Relationship*, Basingstoke: Macmillan.

———— 1999, 'The Escape from Hegel', *Science & Society*, 63, 3: 283–309.

Rossi, Mario 1974, *Da Hegel a Marx, volume III: Il giovane Marx*, Milano: Feltrinelli.

———— 1975, *Da Hegel a Marx, volume IV: La concezione materialistica della storia*, Milano: Feltrinelli.

Rovatti, Pier Aldo, 1972, 'Fetishism and Economic Categories', *Telos*, 14: 87–105.

———— 1973, 'The Critique of Fetishism in Marx's *Grundrisse*', *Telos*, 17: 56–69.

Rubel, Maximilien 1950, 'Contribution a l'Histoire de la Genèse du Capital: Les Manuscrits économico-politiques de Karl Marx (1857–58)', *Revue d'histoire économique et sociale*, 28: 169–85.

———— 1980 [1957], *Marx, Life and Works*, translated by Mary Bottomore, London: Macmillan.

———— 1995, 'Nach hundert Jahren: Plädoyer für Friedrich Engels', *Internationale Wissenschaftliche Korrespondenz zur Geschichte der deutschen Arbeiterbewegung*, 31, 4: 520–31.

Ruben, Peter 1977, 'Über Methodologie und Weltanschauung der Kapitallogik', *Sozialistische Politik*, 42: 40–64.

Rubin, Isaak Il'jič 2010 [1923], 'Die Marx'sche Theorie des Warenfetischismus', in *Kritik der politischen Philosophie: Eigentum, Gesellschaftsvertrag, Staat II*, edited by Devi Dumbadze, Ingo Elbe and Sven Ellmers, Münster: Westfalisches Dampfboot.

———— 2012, 'Studien zur Geldtheorie von Marx', in *Isaak Il'jič Rubin: Marxforscher, Ökonom, Verbannter (1886–1937)*, (*Beiträge zur Marx-Engels-Forschung: Neue Folge, Sonderband 4*), edited by Carl-Erich Vollgraf, Richard Sperl and Rolf Hecker, Hamburg: Argument.

Rubin, Isaak Ill'ich 1972 [1923], *Essays on Marx's Theory of Value*, translated by Fredy Perlman, Detroit: Black and Red.

———— 1979 [1926], *A History of Economic Thought*, translated and edited by Donald Filtzer, London: Ink Links.

———— 1994 [1927], 'Abstract Labour and Value in Marx's System', in *Debates in Value Theory*, edited by Simon Mohun, Basingstoke: Macmillan.

Rumjanzewa, Nelly 1980, 'Zur Veröffentlichung der Pariser Hefte von Karl Marx im Band IV/2 der MEGA', *Marx-Engels-Jahrbuch*, 3: 275–93.

Saad-Filho, Alfredo 1997, 'Re-reading both Hegel and Marx: The "New Dialectics" and the Method of Capital', *Revista de Economia Política*, 17: 107–20.

————— 2001, *The Value of Marx: Political Economy for Contemporary Capitalism*, London: Routledge.

Sacristán Luzón, Manuel 2004, *Escritos sobre El Capital (y textos afines)*, edited by Salvador López Arnal, with a prologue by Alfons Barceló and an epilogue by Óscar Carpintero, Barcelona: El Viejo Topo.

Sagnol, Marc 1982, 'Des "Grundrisse" au "Capital": Sur la modification du plan du "Capital"', *La Pensée: Recherches Marxistes, Sciences, Société, Philosophie*, 228: 17–28.

Sakuramoto, Yoichi 2000, 'Fukumoto Kazuo, ou la naissance de l'intellectuel marxiste au Japon', *Actuel Marx*, 27: 179–87.

Salama, Pierre, and Tran Hai Hac 1992, *Introduction à l'économie de Marx*, Paris: La Découverte.

Salomon, David 2006, 'West-östlicher Marxismus: Entgegnung auf Chenshan Tian', *Das Argument*, 268: 193–4.

Sánchez Vázquez, Adolfo 1977 [1967], *The Philosophy of Praxis*, translated by Michael González, London: Merlin.

————— 1978, *Ciencia y revolución: el marxismo de Althusser*, Madrid: Alianza.

Sandemose, Jørgen 2007, *Totalitet og metode: Tre essays om Marx' hovedverk*, Oslo: Spartacus.

Sayama, Keiji 2004, *Die Geburt der bürgerlichen Gesellschaft: zur Entstehung von Hegels Sozialphilosophie*, Berlin: Philo.

Sayer, Derek 1979, *Marx's Method: Ideology, Science and Critique in Capital*, Hassocks: Harvester.

————— 1987, *The Violence of Abstraction: The Analytic Foundations of Historical Materialism*, Oxford: Blackwell.

Sayers, Sean 1980, 'On the Marxist Dialectic', in *Hegel, Marx and Dialectic: A Debate*, edited by Richard Norman and Sean Sayers, Brighton: Harvester.

Schaff, Adam 1984a, 'Marxismus heute', in *Polen heute*, by Adam Schaff, Vienna: Europaverlag.

————— 1984b, 'Die Aktualität des Marxismus', in *Polen heute*, by Adam Schaff, Vienna: Europaverlag.

————— 1984c, 'Krise des Marxismus oder der Marxisten?', in *Polen heute*, by Adam Schaff, Vienna: Europaverlag.

————— 1984d, 'Den Marxismus propagieren – aber wie?', in *Polen heute*, by Adam Schaff, Vienna: Europaverlag.

Schanz, Hans-Jørgen 1973, *Til rekonstruktion af kritikken af den politiske økonomis omfangslogiske status*, Copenhagen: Modtryk.

Schauerte, E. Michael 2007, 'Samezō Kuruma's Life as a Marxist Economist', *Research in Political Economy*, 24: 281–94.

Schelkshorn, Hans 1992, *Ethik der Befreiung: Einführung in die Philosophie Enrique Dussels*, Vienna: Herder.

Schiavone, Aldo 1976, 'Per una rilettura delle "Formen": teoria della storia, dominio del valore d'uso e funzione dell'ideologia', in *Problemi teorici del marxismo*, edited by Critica Marxista, Rome: Editori Riuniti.

Schkredov, Vladimir Petrovic 1998, 'Über Engels' Historismus in seinem *"Kapital"*-Verständnis', in *Marx und Engels: Konvergenzen – Divergenzen*, (*Beiträge zur Marx-Engels-Forschung: Neue Folge*, 1997), edited by Rolf Hecker et al., Hamburg: Argument.

Schmidt, Alfred (ed.) 1965, *Existentialismus und Marxismus: Eine Kontroverse zwischen Sartre, Garaudy, Hyppolite, Vigier und Orcel*, Frankfurt am Main: Suhrkamp.

——— 1968, 'Zum Erkenntnisbegriff der Kritik der politischen Ökonomie', in *Kritik der politischen Ökonomie heute: 100 Jahre Kapital*, edited by Walter Euchner and Alfred Schmidt, Frankfurt am Main: Europäische Verlagsanstalt.

——— 1969, 'Der strukturalistische Angriff auf die Geschichte', in *Beiträge zur marxistischen Erkenntnistheorie*, edited by Alfred Schmidt, Frankfurt am Main: Suhrkamp.

——— 1981 [1971], *History and Structure: An Essay on Hegelian-Marxist and Structuralist Theories of History*, translated by Jeffrey Herf, Cambridge, MA: MIT Press.

——— 1993 [1962], *Der Begriff der Natur in der Lehre von Marx*, Hamburg: Europäische Verlagsanstalt.

——— 2014 [1962], *The Concept of Nature in Marx*, translated by Ben Fowkes, London: Verso.

Schmidt, Lars-Henrik 1977, *Filosofikritisk Rekonstruktion: Om Althusser og Kapitallogikken*, Copenhagen: Rhodos.

Schmieder, Falko 2005, 'Zur Kritik der Rezeption des Marxschen Fetischbegriffs', *Marx-Engels-Jahrbuch*, 2005: 106–27.

Schmied-Kowarzik, Wolfdietrich 2010, 'Die Herausforderung der Marxschen Philosophie der Praxis und die Misere aktueller Marxinterpretation', in *Von der Systemkritik zur gesellschaftlichen Transformation*, edited by Horst Müller, Norderstedt: Books on Demand.

Schnickmann, Artur 1979, 'Marx' "Beihefte" von 1863', *Beiträge zur Marx-Engels-Forschung*, 5: 99–104.

Schoch, Bruno 1980, *Marxismus in Frankreich seit 1945*, Frankfurt am Main: Campus.

Schrader, Fred 1980, *Restauration und Revolution: Die Vorarbeiten zum 'Kapital' von Karl Marx in seinen Studienheften 1850–1858*, Hildesheim: Gerstenberg.

——— 1983, 'Karl Marxens Smithkommentar von 1861/62 im Heft VII: Zur Rationalität des aporetischen Arbeitsbegriffs', *International Review of Social History*, 28: 50–90.

——— 1998, '"Methode" und "Logik": Zur Integration von (Wert-)Substanz und Rechtssystem bei Hegel (1817–1830) und Marx (1857–1861)', *MEGA-Studien*, 1998, 2: 82–91.

———— 2007, ' "By mere accident": Hegel – Marx, 1857–1861', *Hegel-Jahrbuch*, 2007: 175–81.

Schwarz, Winfried 1974, 'Das "Kapital im allgemeinen" und die "Konkurrenz" im ökonomischen Werk von Karl Marx: Zu Rosdolskys Fehlinterpretation der Gliederung des "Kapital"', *Gesellschaft: Beiträge zur Marxschen Theorie*, 1: 222–47.

———— 1978, *Vom 'Rohentwurf' zum 'Kapital': die Strukturgeschichte des Marxschen Hauptwerkes*, West Berlin: Das Europäische Buch.

———— 1987, 'Die Geldform in der 1. und 2. Auflage des "Kapital": Zur Diskussion um die "Historisierung" der Wertformanalyse', in *Internationale Marx-Engels-Forschung*, (*Marxistische Studien: Jahrbuch des IMSF*, 12), edited by Institut für Marxistische Studien und Forschungen, Frankfurt am Main: IMSF.

———— 1991, [Mündlicher Beitrag zur Diskussionsrunde 4], in *Naturwissenschaften und Produktivkräfte bei Marx und Engels*, (*Marx-Engels-Forschung heute*, 3), edited by Institut für Marxistische Studien und Forschungen, Frankfurt am Main: IMSF.

Schweier, Thomas Lutz 1999, 'Geschichtliche Reflexion bei Marx: Bemerkungen zu seinem Geschichtsverständnis', in *Geschichtsphilosophie oder das Begreifen der Historizität*, edited by Diethard Behrens, Freiburg im Breisgau: ça ira.

Sekine, Thomas 1975, 'Uno-Riron: A Japanese Contribution to Marxian Political Economy', *Journal of Economic Literature*, 13: 847–77.

———— 1980a, 'Translator's Introduction', in *Principles of Political Economy: Theory of a Purely Capitalist Society*, by Kōzō Uno, Brighton: Harvester.

———— 1980b, 'An Essay on Uno's Dialectic of Capital', in: *Principles of Political Economy: Theory of a Purely Capitalist Society*, by Kōzō Uno, Brighton: Harvester.

———— 1984, 'An Uno School Seminar on the Theory of Value', *Science & Society*, 48, 4: 419–32.

———— 1986, *The Dialectic of Capital: A Study of the Inner Logic of Capitalism*, two volumes, Tokyo: Yushindo.

———— 1997, *An Outline of the Dialectic of Capital*, two volumes, Basingstoke: Macmillan.

———— 1998, 'The Dialectic of Capital: An Unoist Interpretation', *Science & Society*, 62, 3: 434–45.

———— 2003, 'The Dialectic, or Logic that Coincides with Economics', in *New Dialectics and Political Economy*, edited by Robert Albritton and John Simoulidis, Basingstoke: Palgrave Macmillan.

Semprún, Jaime 1968, 'Économie politique et philosophie dans les "Grundrisse" de Marx', *L'Homme et la société*, 7: 5–68.

Sève, Lucien 1980, 'Krise des Marxismus?', *Das Argument*, 122: 518–23.

———— 2004, *Penser avec Marx aujourd'hui, tome I: Marx et nous*, Paris: La Dispute.

Shaikh, Anwar 1978, 'An Introduction to the History of Crisis Theories', in *U.S. Capitalism in Crisis*, edited by URPE Crisis Reader Editorial Collective, New York, NY: URPE.

Shamsavari, Ali 1991, *Dialectics and Social Theory: The Logic of Capital*, Braunton: Merlin.

Shaozhi, Su 1983, 'Developing Marxism under Contemporary Conditions: In Commemoration of the Centenary of the Death of Karl Marx', in *Marxism in China*, edited by Su Shaozhi, Wu Dakun, Ru Xin and Cheng Renquian, Nottingham: Spokesman.

———— 1984, 'Neues Marxismusverständnis in China', *Das Argument*, 143: 74–80.

———— 1985, *Some Questions Concerning the Writing of the History of the Development of Marxism*, Beijing: The Institute.

———— 1989, 'Niemand hat das Recht, darüber zu urteilen, wer Marxist ist und wer nicht: Zwei Reden', *Das Argument*, 177: 747–57.

———— 1993a, *Marxism and Reform in China*, Nottingham: Spokesman.

———— 1993b, 'A Decade of Crises at the Institue of Marxism-Leninism-Mao Zedong Thought, 1979–1989', *The China Quarterly*, 134: 335–51.

Shibata, Shingo 1977, *Revolution in der Philosophie: der praktische Materialismus und seine Aufhebung*, Hamburg: VSA.

Shigeta, Sumio 2006, 'Zur Geschichte der Terminologie des "Kapitalismus" im 19. Jahrhundert', in *Neue Aspekte von Marx' Kapitalismus-Kritik*, (*Beiträge zur Marx-Engels-Forschung: Neue Folge*, 2004), edited by Rolf Hecker et al., Hamburg: Argument.

Shin, Gi-Wook 2002, 'Marxism, Anti-Americanism, and Democracy in South Korea: An Examination of Nationalist Intellectual Discourse', in *New Asian Marxisms*, edited by Tani E. Barlow, Durham, NC: Duke University Press.

Siemek, Marek J. 2002, 'Die Gesellschaft als philosophisches Problem bei Marx', in *Von Marx zu Hegel: zum sozialpolitischen Selbstverständnis der Moderne*, by Marek J. Siemek, Würzburg: Königshausen & Neumann.

Skambraks, Johannes and Zuo Haixiang 1991, 'Zur Marx-Engels-Forschung in China', in *Studien zum Werk von Marx und Engels*, (*Beiträge zur Marx-Engels-Forschung: Neue Folge*, 1991), edited by Rolf Hecker et al., Hamburg: Argument.

Smith, Tony 1990, *The Logic of Marx's Capital: Replies to Hegelian criticisms*, Albany: State University of New York Press.

———— 1993, 'Marx's *Capital* and Hegelian Dialectical Logic', in *Marx's Method in Capital: A Reexamination*, edited by Fred Moseley, Atlantic Highlands, NJ: Humanities.

Soldani, Franco 1998, 'Marx and the Scientific Thought of his Time', in *Marx und Engels: Konvergenzen – Divergenzen*, (*Beiträge zur Marx-Engels-Forschung: Neue Folge*, 1997), edited by Rolf Hecker et al., Hamburg: Argument.

———— 2002, *La strada non presa: il marxismo e la conoscenza della realtà sociale*, Bologna: Pendragon.

Sperl, Richard 2000, 'Eine gemeinsame Gesamtausgabe für Marx-Engels – politisch-ideologische Programmatik oder editorisches Erfordernis?', in *Marx-Engels-Edition und biographische Forschung*, (*Beiträge zur Marx-Engels-Forschung: Neue Folge*, 2000), edited by Rolf Hecker et al., Hamburg: Argument.

———— 2004a, 'Das Vollständigkeitsprinzip der Marx-Engels-Gesamtausgabe – editorischer Gigantismus?', in *'Edition auf hohem Niveau': zu den Grundsätzen der Marx-Engels-Gesamtausgabe (MEGA), (Wissenschaftliche Mitteilungen des Berliner Vereins zur Förderung der MEGA-Edition e. V.,* Volume Five), by Richard Sperl, Hamburg: Argument.

———— 2004b, 'Die editorische Dokumentation von Übersetzungen in der Marx-Engels-Gesamtausgabe', in *'Edition auf hohem Niveau': zu den Grundsätzen der Marx-Engels-Gesamtausgabe (MEGA), (Wissenschaftliche Mitteilungen des Berliner Vereins zur Förderung der MEGA-Edition e. V.,* Volume Five), by Richard Sperl, Hamburg: Argument.

Stapelfeldt, Gerhard 1979, *Das Problem des Anfangs in der Kritik der politischen Ökonomie*. Frankfurt am Main: Campus.

———— 2006, *Der Liberalismus: die Gesellschaftstheorien von Smith, Ricardo und Marx*, Freiburg im Breisgau: ça ira.

Starosta, Guido 2008, 'The Commodity-Form and the Dialectical Method: On the Structure of Marx's Exposition in Chapter 1 of *Capital*', *Science & Society*, 72, 3: 295–318.

Steedman, Ian 1989, 'Marx on Ricardo', in *From Exploitation to Altruism*, by Ian Steedman, Oxford: Polity.

Sternberg, Fritz 1955, *Marx und die Gegenwart: Entwicklungstendenzen in der zweiten Hälfte des zwanzigsten Jahrhunderts*, Cologne: Verlag für Politik und Wirtschaft.

Stutje, Jan Willem 2007, *Ernest Mandel: rebel tussen droom en daad, 1923–1995*. Antwerpen: Houtekiet.

Stützle, Ingo 2006, 'Die Frage nach der konstitutiven Relevanz der Geldware in Marx' Kritik der politischen Ökonomie', in *Das Kapital neu lesen: Beiträge zur radikalen Philosophie*, edited by Jan Hoff, Alexis Petrioli, Ingo Stützle and Frieder Otto Wolf, Münster: Westfälisches Dampfboot.

———— 2008, 'Marx' innerer Monolog: vor 150 Jahren schrieb Karl Marx die "Grundrisse"', *z.: Zeitschrift Marxistische Erneuerung*, 73: 113–22.

Sugihara, Kaoru 1987, 'Le débat sur le capitalisme japonais (1927–1937)', in *Le Marxisme au Japon*, (*Actuel Marx*, 2), edited by Jacques Bidet and Jacques Texier, Paris: L'Harmattan.

Suzumura, Kotaro 2006, 'Shigeto Tsuru (1912–2006) – Life, Work and Legacy', *European Journal of the History of Economic Thought*, 13, 4: 613–20.

Světlý, Jaroslav 1993 [1983], 'Marx's Method of Political Economy and the Present Time', in *Karl Marx's Economics: Critical Assessments*, Second Series, Volume Five, edited by John Cunningham Wood, London: Routledge.

Sweezy, Paul 1970 [1942], *The Theory of Capitalist Development: Principles of Marxian Political Economy*, New York, NY: Oxford University Press.

———— 1972 [1942], *Theorie der kapitalistischen Entwicklung: Eine analytische Studie über die Prinzipien der Marxschen Sozialökonomie*, Frankfurt am Main: Suhrkamp.

Swing, Raymond 2006, *Formale und generative Dialektik mit Marx über Marx hinaus*, Copenhagen: Swing.

Sylvers, Malcolm and Roberto Fineschi 2003, 'Novità della Marx-Engels-Gesamtausgabe: La grande edizione storico-critica va avanti', *Marxismo oggi*, 2003, 1: 87–129.

Syrow, Alexander 1989, 'Über die Herausbildung der Ansichten von Marx als Historiker der politischen Ökonomie: Die Erforschung der Quellengrundlage des "Kapitals"', *Beiträge zur Marx-Engels-Forschung*, 27: 98–104.

Tagai, Imre 1989, 'Zur Dialektik der Werttheorie im "Kapital"', *Beiträge zur Marx-Engels-Forschung*, 27: 173–77.

Tairako, Tomonaga 1987, 'Der fundamentale Charakter der Dialektik im "Kapital" von Marx: Zur "Logik der Verkehrung"', in *Marxistische Dialektik in Japan: Beiträge japanischer Philosophen zu aktuellen Problemen der dialektisch-materialistischen Methode*, edited by Siegfried Bönisch et al., East Berlin: Dietz.

———— 1997, 'Materialismus und Dialektik bei Marx', in *Elemente zur Kritik der Werttheorie*, edited by Friedrun Quaas and Georg Quaas, Frankfurt am Main: Lang.

———— 2002, 'Philosophy and Practice in Marx', *Hitotsubashi Journal of Social Studies*, 34: 47–57.

———— 2003, 'Marx on Capitalist Globalization', *Hitotsubashi Journal of Social Studies*, 35:11–6.

———— 2005, 'Contradictions of Contemporary Globalization: How is Socialist Philosophy to Cope with it?', *Hitotsubashi Journal of Social Studies*, 37: 53–62.

———— 2009–12, 'Die neuesten Tendenzen der *Deutschen Ideologie*-Forschung in Asien', *Hitotsubashi Journal of Social Studies*, 41, 2: 49–57.

Takenaga, Susumu 1985, *Valeur, formes de la valeur et étapes dans la pensée de Marx*, Berne: Lang.

———— 2007, 'Sur les révisions de la seconde à la troisième édition des Essais sur la théorie de la valeur de Marx par I.I. Roubine – une phase dans la polémique de la valeur dans l'ex-Union soviétique dans les années 1920', available at: http://netx .u-paris10.fr/actuelmarx/cm5/com/M15_Marx_Takenaga.doc (last retrieved 28 May 2008).

Tarrit, Fabien 2006, 'A Brief History, Scope, and Peculiarities of "Analytical Marxism"', *Review of Radical Political Economics*, 38, 4: 595–618.

Taylor, Nicola and Riccardo Bellofiore 2004, 'Marx's *Capital I*, the Constitution of Capital: General Introduction', in *The Constitution of Capital: Essays on Volume I of Marx's Capital*, edited by Riccardo Bellofiore and Nicola Taylor, Basingstoke: Palgrave Macmillan.

Teixeira, Francisco José Soares 1995, *Pensando com Marx: Uma leitura critico-comentada de O Capital*, São Paulo: Ensaio.

———— 1999, 'Sobre a crítica dialética de *O Capital*: uma anticrítica', *Crítica marxista*, 8: 93–114.

Ternowski, Michail and Alexander Tschepurenko 1987, '"Grundrisse": Probleme des zweiten und dritten Bandes des "Kapitals" und das Schicksal des Begriffs des "Kapital im Allgemeinen"', in *Internationale Marx-Engels-Forschung*, (*Marxistische Studien: Jahrbuch des IMSF*, 12), edited by Institut für Marxistische Studien und Forschungen, Frankfurt am Main: IMSF.

Theunissen, Michael 1975, 'Krise der Macht: Thesen zur Theorie des dialektischen Widerspruchs', in *Hegel-Jahrbuch 1974: Referate des X. Internationalen Hegel-Kongresses in Moskau, 1974, zu dem Zentralthema 'Dialektik'*, edited by Wilhelm R. Beyer, Cologne: Pahl-Rugenstein.

Thompson, E.P. 1978, *The Poverty of Theory and Other Essays*, London: Merlin.

Tian, Chenshan 2006, 'Chinesische Dialektik: die historische Entwicklung des Marxismus in China', *Das Argument*, 268: 184–92.

Tombazos, Stavros 2014 [1994], *Time in Marx: The Categories of Time in Marx's Capital*, Leiden: Brill.

Tomberg, Friedrich 1969, 'Der Begriff der Entfremdung in den "Grundrissen" von Karl Marx', *Das Argument*, 52: 187–223.

Tosel, André 2008a, 'Devenirs du Marxisme 1968–2005: De la Fin du Marxisme-Léninisme aux mille Marxismes', available at: http://www.marxau21.fr/index.php?option =com_content&view=article&id=2:devenirs-du-marxisme-1968-2005-de-la-n-du -marxisme-leninisme-aux-mille-marxismes&catid=59:histoire-du-marxisme& Itemid=82

――― 2008b, 'The Development of Marxism: From the End of Marxism-Leninism to a Thousand Marxisms – France-Italy, 1975–2005', in *Critical Companion to Contemporary Marxism*, edited by Jacques Bidet and Stathis Kouvelakis, Leiden: Brill.

――― 2008c, 'La réception des *Grundrisse* en France', *La Pensée*, 355: 83–92.

Tribe, Keith 1990, 'Remarks on the Theoretical Significance of Marx's *Grundrisse*', in *Karl Marx's Social and Political Thought: Critical Assessments*, Volume One, edited by Bob Jessop and Charlie Malcolm-Brown, London: Routledge.

Trofimow, P.S. 1953, 'Fragen der materialistischen Dialektik und Erkenntnistheorie im "Kapital" von Karl Marx', *Deutsche Zeitschrift für Philosophie*, 1, 3–4: 579–600.

Tronti, Mario 2006 [1965], 'Marx, forza-lavoro, classe operaia', in *Operai e capitale*, by Mario Tronti, Turin: Einaudi.

――― 2008, 'Italy [Dissemination and reception of the *Grundrisse* in the world]', in *Karl Marx's Grundrisse: Foundations of the Critique of Political Economy 150 Years Later*, edited by Marcello Musto, New York, NY: Routledge.

Tschechowski, Valeri 2007, 'Zur Übersetzung des Marxschen Begriffs Wert ins Russische', in *Geld – Kapital – Wert: Zum 150. Jahrestag der Niederschrift von Marx' ökonomischen Manuskripten 1857/58 'Grundrisse der Kritik der politischen Ökonomie'*, (*Beiträge zur Marx-Engels-Forschung: Neue Folge*, 2007), edited by Rolf Hecker et al., Hamburg: Argument.

Tschepurenko, Alexander 1989, 'Der Marx-Engels-Sektor am IML Moskau', *Marx-Engels-Forschung heute*, 1: 30–33.

Tsuru, Shigeto 1993, *Institutional Economics Revisited*, Cambridge: Cambridge University Press.

———— 1994a, 'An Aspect of Marx's Methodology in Economics: "The Fetishism of Commodities"', in *Economic Theory and Capitalist Society: The Selected Essays of Shigeto Tsuru*, Volume One, by Shigeto Tsuru, Aldershot: Elgar.

———— 1994b, 'Marx and the Analysis of Capitalism: A New Stage on the Basic Contradiction?', in *Economic Theory and Capitalist Society: The Selected Essays of Shigeto Tsuru*, Volume One, by Shigeto Tsuru, Aldershot: Elgar.

———— 1994c, 'Mr. Dobb and Marx's Theory of Value', in *Economic Theory and Capitalist Society: The Selected Essays of Shigeto Tsuru*, Volume One, by Shigeto Tsuru, Aldershot: Elgar.

Tsushima, Tadayuki 1956, 'Understanding "Labor Certificates" on the Basis of the Theory of Value – The Law of Value and Socialism', available at: http://www.marxists .org/subject/japan/tsushima/labor-certificates.htm

Tuchscheerer, Walter 1962, 'Zur Marx-Engels-Forschung in der DDR auf dem Gebiet der politischen Ökonomie', in *Beiträge zur Geschichte der deutschen Arbeiterbewegung, 1962 (Sonderband)*, edited by Institut für Marxismus-Leninismus beim ZK der SED, East Berlin: Dietz.

———— 1968, *Bevor 'Das Kapital' entstand: Die Herausbildung und Entwicklung der ökonomischen Theorie von Karl Marx in der Zeit von 1843–1858*, East Berlin: Akademie.

Uchida, Hiroshi 1988, *Marx's Grundrisse and Hegel's Logic*, London and New York, NY: Routledge.

———— 2008, Japan [Dissemination and reception of the Grundrisse in the world], in *Karl Marx's Grundrisse: Foundations of the Critique of Political Economy 150 Years Later*, edited by Marcello Musto, New York, NY: Routledge.

Uno, Kōzō 1980 [1950–2], *Principles of Political Economy: Theory of a Purely Capitalist Society*, translated by Thomas T. Sekine, Brighton: Harvester.

Uroeva, Anna V. 1978, ' "Das Kapital" eroberte sich den Erdball: Zur internationalen Verbreitung des Marxschen Hauptwerkes bis 1895', in *... unsrer Partei einen Sieg erringen: Studien zur Entstehungs- und Wirkungsgeschichte des 'Kapitals' von Karl Marx*, edited by Roland Nietzold, Hannes Skambraks and Günter Wermusch, East Berlin: Die Wirtschaft.

Van Parijs, Philippe 1994, 'Analytischer Marxismus', in *Historisch-kritisches Wörterbuch des Marxismus*, Volume One, edited by Wolfgang Fritz Haug et al., Hamburg: Argument.

Vargas Lozano, Gabriel 1976, 'La introducción a la crítica de la economía política de 1857', *Dialéctica*, 1: 29–52.

———— 1988, 'Marxismo y filosofía hoy en Latinoamerica', *Dialéctica*, 19: 63–75.

Vasina, Ljudmila 1994, 'I.I. Rubin – Marxforscher und Politökonom', in *Quellen und Grenzen von Marx' Wissenschaftsverständnis*, (*Beiträge zur Marx-Engels-Forschung: Neue Folge, 1994*), edited by Rolf Hecker et al., Hamburg: Argument.

———— 2002, 'Wolfgang Jahn und Vitalij Vygodskij – Freunde und MEGA-Forscher', in *In Memoriam Wolfgang Jahn: Der ganze Marx – Alles Verfasste veröffentlichen, erforschen und den 'ungeschriebenen' Marx rekonstruieren*, (*Wissenschaftliche Mitteilungen, Heft 1*), edited by Berliner Verein zur Förderung der MEGA-Edition e. V., Hamburg: Argument.

Vasina, Lyudmila L. 2008, 'Russia and the Soviet Union [Dissemination and reception of the *Grundrisse* in the world]', in *Karl Marx's Grundrisse: Foundations of the Critique of Political Economy 150 Years Later*, edited by Marcello Musto, New York, NY: Routledge.

———— 2010, 'Vitalij Solomonovic Vygodskij – eine biographische Skizze', in *Quellen- und 'Kapital'-Interpretation: Erinnerungen*, (*Beiträge zur Marx-Engels-Forschung: Neue Folge, 2009*), edited by Rolf Hecker et al., Hamburg: Argument.

Vazjulin, Viktor 1987, 'Das Historische und Logische in der Methodologie von Karl Marx', translated by Gert Meyer, in *Internationale Marx-Engels-Forschung*, (*Marxistische Studien: Jahrbuch des IMSF*, 12), edited by Institut für Marxistische Studien und Forschungen, Frankfurt am Main: IMSF.

———— 2005a, 'Entwicklung systematisch denken: Ein Vergleich des Systems der dialektischen Logik bei Hegel und Marx', *Deutsche Zeitschrift für Philosophie*, 53, 2: 203–18.

———— 2005b, *Die Logik des Kapitals von Karl Marx*, translated by Gudrun Havemann, Norderstedt: Books on Demand.

Veca, Salvatore 1971, 'Value, Labour and the Critique of Political Economy', *Telos*, 9: 48–64.

———— 1977, *Saggio sul programma scientifico di Marx*, Milano: Il Saggiatore.

Veljak, Lino 2008, 'Yugoslavia [Dissemination and reception of the *Grundrisse* in the world]', in *Karl Marx's Grundrisse: Foundations of the Critique of Political Economy 150 Years Later*, London: Routledge.

Vincent, Jean-Marie 1973, *Fétichisme et societe*, Paris: Anthropos.

———— 1991, *Abstract Labour: A Critique*, Basingstoke: Macmillan.

———— 2001, *Un autre Marx: après les marxismes*, Lausanne: Page deux.

Vollgraf, Carl-Erich 1991, 'Zuerst die Nr. 349 im Vereinsregister – dann unbekannt; zunächst wohlbetucht, dann auf Spenden aus: Das launische Schicksal des Vereins "MEGA-Stiftung e. V." im deutschen Einigungsprozess', *Studien zum Werk von Marx und Engels*, (*Beiträge zur Marx-Engels-Forschung: Neue Folge*, 1991), edited by Rolf Hecker et al., Hamburg: Argument.

———— 2002, 'Marx' Arbeit am dritten Buch des *Kapital* in den 1870/80er Jahren', in *In Memoriam Wolfgang Jahn: Der ganze Marx – Alles Verfasste veröffentlichen, erforschen und den 'ungeschriebenen' Marx rekonstruieren*, (*Wissenschaftliche Mitteilungen, Heft 1*), edited by Berliner Verein zur Förderung der MEGA-Edition e. V., Hamburg: Argument.

———— 2006, 'Engels' Kapitalismus-Bild und seine inhaltlichen Zusätze zum dritten Band des *Kapital*, in *Neue Aspekte von Marx' Kapitalismus-Kritik, (Beiträge zur Marx-Engels-Forschung: Neue Folge*, 2004), edited by Rolf Hecker et al., Hamburg: Argument.

Vollgraf, Carl-Erich and Jürgen Jungnickel 1994, '"Marx in Marx' Worten"? Zu Engels' Edition des Hauptmanuskripts zum dritten Buch des *Kapital*, MEGA-*Studien* 1994, 2: 3–55.

Vollgraf, Carl-Erich, Richard Sperl and Rolf Hecker (eds.) 2012, *Isaak Il'jič Rubin. Marxforscher – Ökonom – Verbannter (1886–1937), (Beiträge zur Marx-Engels-Forschung: Neue Folge, Sonderband 4)*, Hamburg: Argument.

Von Holt, Dirk, Ursula Pasero and Volkbert Roth 1974, *Aspekte der Marxschen Theorie, 2: Zur Wertformanalyse*, Frankfurt am Main: Suhrkamp.

Von Wroblewsky, Vincent 1977, 'Diskussionen in Frankreich um die Logik bei Marx', *Deutsche Zeitschrift für Philosophie*, 25, 9: 1123–7.

Vranicki, Predrag 1971 [1961], *Historija marksizma*, Zagreb: Naprijed.

———— 1985 [1961], *Geschichte des Marxismus*, two volumes, Frankfurt am Main: Suhrkamp.

Vrtačič, Ludvik 1975, *Der jugoslawische Marxismus: Die jugoslawische Philosophie und der eigene Weg zum Sozialismus*, Freiburg im Breisgau: Walter.

Vygodski, Vitali 1993, 'Überlegungen zu einigen Dogmen der Marx-Interpretation', in *Marx-Engels-Forschung im historischen Spannungsfeld, (Beiträge zur Marx-Engels-Forschung: Neue Folge*, 1993), edited by Rolf Hecker et al., Hamburg: Argument.

Vygodsky, Vitaly 1974 [1965], *The Story of a Great Discovery: How Karl Marx Wrote 'Capital'*, translated by Christopher Salt, Tunbridge Wells: Abacus.

Warnke, Camilla 2000, '"Ich lasse auf Hegel nicht scheißen!" Wolfgang Harichs Vorlesungen zur Geschichte der Philosophie 1951–1954', in *Wolfgang Harich zum Gedächtnis: Eine Gedenkschrift in zwei Bänden*, Volume Two, edited by Stefan Dornuf and Reinhard Pitsch, Munich: Müller & Nerding.

———— 2001, '"Das Problem Hegel ist längst gelöst": Eine Debatte in der DDR-Philosophie der fünfziger Jahre', in *Anfänge der DDR-Philosophie: Ansprüche, Ohnmacht, Scheitern*, edited by Volker Gerhardt and Hans-Christoph Rauh, Berlin: Links.

Wassina, Ljudmila 1983, 'Die Ausarbeitung der Geldtheorie durch Karl Marx in den Londoner Heften (1850–1851)', *Marx-Engels-Jahrbuch*, 6: 148–72.

———— 1989, 'Zur Veröffentlichung der Manchester-Hefte von Marx in der Vierten Abteilung der MEGA', *Marx-Engels-Jahrbuch*, 11: 230–41.

Waszek, Norbert 1988, *The Scottish Enlightenment and Hegel's Account of 'Civil Society'*, Dordrecht: Kluwer Academic Publishers.

———— 1991, *Eduard Gans (1797–1839): Hegelianer, Jude, Europäer – Texte und Dokumente*, Frankfurt am Main: Lang.

———— 1995, 'Hegels Lehre von der "bürgerlichen Gesellschaft" und die politische Ökonomie der schottischen Aufklärung', *Dialektik*, 1995, 3: 35–50.

Wiggershaus, Rolf 1995 [1986], *The Frankfurt School: Its History, Theories, and Political Significance*, Cambridge, MA: MIT Press.

Willing, Gunter 1991, [Mündlicher Beitrag zur Diskussionsrunde 4], in *Naturwissenschaften und Produktivkräfte bei Marx und Engels*, (*Marx-Engels-Forschung heute*, 3), edited by Institut für Marxistische Studien und Forschungen, Frankfurt am Main: IMSF.

Wippermann, Wolfgang 2008, *Der Wiedergänger: Die vier Leben des Karl Marx*, Wien: Kremayr & Scheriau.

Wolf, Dieter 2002 [1985], *Der dialektische Widerspruch im 'Kapital': ein Beitrag zur Marxschen Werttheorie*, Hamburg: VSA.

———— 2004, 'Kritische Theorie und Kritik der Politischen Ökonomie', in *Zur Konfusion des Wertbegriffs: Beiträge zur 'Kapital'-Diskussion*, (*Wissenschaftliche Mitteilungen des Berliner Vereins zur Förderung der MEGA-Edition e. V., Heft 3*), edited by Dieter Wolf and Heinz Paragenings, Hamburg: Argument.

———— 2007, 'Zum Übergang vom Geld ins Kapital in den *Grundrissen*, im *Urtext* und im *Kapital*: Warum ist die "dialektische Form der Darstellung nur richtig, wenn sie ihre Grenzen kennt"?', in *Geld – Kapital – Wert: Zum 150. Jahrestag der Niederschrift von Marx' ökonomischen Manuskripten 1857/58 'Grundrisse der Kritik der politischen Ökonomie'*, (*Beiträge zur Marx-Engels-Forschung: Neue Folge*, 2007), edited by Rolf Hecker et al., Hamburg: Argument.

———— 2008, 'Zur Methode in Marx' *Kapital* unter besonderer Berücksichtigung ihres logisch-systematischen Charakters: Zum "Methodenstreit" zwischen Wolfgang Fritz Haug und Michael Heinrich', in *Gesellschaftliche Praxis und ihre wissenschaftliche Darstellung: Beiträge zur Kapital-Diskussion*, edited by Ingo Elbe, Tobias Reichardt and Dieter Wolf, Hamburg: Argument.

Wolf, Frieder Otto 1983, 'Am "Kapital" arbeiten! Einführende Notizen zu Althussers *Kapital*-Text', *Prokla*, 50: 127–29.

———— 1994, 'Althusser-Schule', in *Historisch-kritisches Wörterbuch des Marxismus*, Volume One, edited by Wolfgang Fritz Haug et al., Hamburg: Argument.

———— 2006, 'Marx' Konzept der "Grenzen der dialektischen Darstellung"', in *Das Kapital neu lesen: Beiträge zur radikalen Philosophie*, edited by Jan Hoff, Alexis Petrioli, Ingo Stützle and Frieder Otto Wolf, Münster: Westfälisches Dampfboot.

Wolff, Richard D. 2006, 'Die überdeterministische und klassentheoretische *Kapital*-Lektüre in den USA', in *Das Kapital neu lesen: Beiträge zur radikalen Philosophie*, edited by Jan Hoff, Alexis Petrioli, Ingo Stützle and Frieder Otto Wolf, Münster: Westfälisches Dampfboot.

———— 2007, 'The New Reading of Karl Marx's *Capital* in the United States', *History of Economics Review*, 45: 26–40.

Woods, Alan 2008, *Reformism or Revolution: Marxism and Socialism of the 21st Century*, London: Wellred.

Wright, Steve 2002, *Storming Heaven: Class Composition and Struggle in Italian Auto-nomist Marxism*, London: Pluto.

Wygodski, W.S. 1976 [1965], *Wie 'Das Kapital' entstand*, East Berlin: Die Wirtschaft.

—— 1978a, 'Zum Manuskript "Reflection" von Karl Marx in Heft VII der Londoner Exzerpte', in ... *unsrer Partei einen Sieg erringen: Studien zur Entstehungs- und Wir-kungsgeschichte des 'Kapitals' von Karl Marx*, edited by Roland Nietzold, Hannes Skambraks, and Günter Wermusch, East Berlin, Die Wirtschaft.

—— 1978b, *Das Werden der ökonomischen Theorie von Marx und der wissenschaft-liche Kommunismus*, Berlin: Dietz.

Xiaoping, Wei 2006, 'Lo stato attuale della ricerca su Marx in Cina', in *Sulle tracce di un fantasma: L'opera di Karl Marx tra filologia e filosofia*, edited by Marcello Musto, Rome: Manifestolibri.

Yagi, Kiichiro 2004, 'History-Oriented Economics in Kyoto', *The Kyoto Economic Review*, 73, 1: 11–22.

—— 2005, 'Emergence of Marxian Scholarship in Japan: Kawakami Hajime and his Two Critics', available at: http://www.econ.kyoto-u.ac.jp/~yagi/yagi2005/linkfiles/ EMERGENCEMARXIAN.doc

—— 2011, 'Was "*Sozialforschung*" an Aesopian term? Marxism as a link between Japan and the West', in *The Dissemination of Economic Ideas*, edited by Heinz D. Kurz et al., Cheltenham: Elgar.

Yang, Haifeng 2006, 'Critique of Metaphysics, Capital Logic and Totality, and Social Critique Theory – The Three Critical Dimensions of Marx's Philosophy', *Frontiers of Philosophy in China*, 1, 2: 269–78.

Yang, Jinhai 2006, 'Introduction to Marxism Research in China', available at: http://www .psa.ac.uk/spgrp/marxism/online/jinhai.pdf

Yamada, Toshio 1987, 'Les tendances du marxisme japonais contemporain', in *Le Marx-isme au Japon*, (*Actuel Marx*, 2), edited by Jacques Bidet and Jacques Texier, Paris: L'Harmattan.

Zelený, Jindřich 1980 [1962], *The Logic of Marx*, translated and edited by Terrell Carver, Oxford: Blackwell.

Zhang, Zhongpu 2008, 'China [Dissemination and Reception of the *Grundrisse* in the World]', in *Karl Marx's Grundrisse: Foundations of the Critique of Political Economy 150 Years Later*, edited by Marcello Musto, New York, NY: Routledge.

Zimmerli, Walther Ch. 1984, 'Die Aneignung des philosophischen Erbes: Eine Analyse der Diskussion "Über das Verhältnis des Marxismus zur Philosophie Hegels" in der DDR 1952/53 bis 1956/57', in *Ein kurzer Frühling der Philosophie: DDR-Philosophie in der 'Aufbauphase'*, edited by Clemens Burrichter, Munich: Schöninghausen.

Zimmermann, Marion 1979, 'Marx' Ricardo-Rezeption im Heft VIII der Londoner Exzerpthefte (1850–1853)', *Arbeitsblätter zur Marx-Engels-Forschung*, 8: 18–31.

Index

Abendroth, Wolfgang   76
Adorno, Theodor W.   9, 28, 29, 64, 77n9, 79
Achundov, G.   125
Ahrweiler, Georg   252
Albiac, Gabriel   181
Albritton, Robert   104n116, 190, 191, 113n155,
    114, 190, 191
Althusser, Louis   11, 16, 33–36, 38, 53,
    54, 69, 83, 89, 116, 144, 154–159, 163,
    167, 168, 169n412, 175, 181, 185, 207,
    208n24, 209, 249, 263, 265, 316,
    317
Altvater, Elmar   86n42
Amadeo, Javier   14
Amin, Samir   59n134
Anderson, Kevin   195
Anderson, Perry   9–11, 36–38, 196–199
Antonova, Irina   135n256
Aricó, José   58n131
Aristoteles   189
Arndt, Andreas   251, 253
Arthur, Christopher   6, 71, 172n427, 189–191,
    218, 224–226, 258–261, 270
Artous, Antoine   160
Astarita, Rolando   177, 178, 317

Backhaus, Hans-Georg   6, 13, 16n38, 29,
    30n35, 70, 77–82, 83n28, 86, 91, 115, 116,
    122, 131n240, 132n244, 152, 163, 166n398,
    186, 187, 194, 203, 204, 223, 224, 227, 245,
    263, 314, 317
Badaloni, Nicola   148
Bader, Veit-Michael   86
Bailey, Samuel   112, 214
Balibar, Etienne   155, 157
Banaji, Jairus   115, 116, 186, 317
Barreda, Andres   167, 168n408
Barshay, Andrew E.   47, 100, 101
Bastiat, Frédéric   229
Becker, Egon   179n457
Behrens, Diethard   203, 314
Behrens, Fritz   163n260, 268
Bell, John R.   114
Bello, Walden   66n156
Bellofiore, Riccardo   146n293, 150, 151, 194
Benoit, Hector   176

Bensaid, Daniel   71
Berlusconi, Silvio   53
Bidet, Jacques   13, 157, 158, 160–162, 198, 199,
    317
Bihr, Alain   160
Bischoff, Joachim   84–86
Blyumin, I.   20
Bloch, Ernst   8, 13
Block, Klaus-Dieter   299
Boccara, Paul   158, 285
von Böhm-Bawerk, Eugen   93
Boldyrev, Igor   125, 134, 135, 316
Bolivar, Simon   71
Bondeli, Martin   164, 236
Bonefeld, Werner   70n179
Brentano, Lujo   92, 93
Brentel, Helmut   6, 89, 198, 203, 205, 206, 223,
    224, 226, 245, 259, 314
Brill, Hermann   79
de Brosses, Charles   149
de Brunhoff, Suzanne   158
Bubner, Rüdiger   87
Buckmiller, Michael   75
Burkett, Paul   289
Burns, Tony   251, 252
Buzgalin, Alexander V.   65, 66

Callinicos, Alex   71
Cardoso, Fernando Henrique   166
Carey, Henry Charles   229
Carrera, Juan Inigo   180
Cassano, Franco   146n294
Castoriadis, Cornelius   33n48
Cerroni, Umberto   148
Chavez, Hugo   69, 71
Cheng, Enfu   121
Chepurenko, Alexander   131, 134, 135, 285
Chesebro, James William   38
Chessin, N.   130, 131
Chou, Li-Quan   61, 62
Chu, Choeng-Lip   122
Chung, Monn Gil   60
Clarke, Simon   113n156, 302, 303
Claussen, Detlev   29n34
Cleaver, Harry   55
Cohen, Gerald A.   191, 193n531

Colletti, Lucio   31, 52–54, 58, 116, 142–146, 151,
        152, 185, 249, 265, 316, 317
Conert, Hansgeorg   50
Cornu, Auguste   154n334
Crespo, Luis   181
Crotty, James R.   307n376

Da, Li   24
Danielson, Nikolai   300, 301
Darimon, Alfred   212
Debord, Guy   33n48
Demir, Yakub   49n104
Denis, Henri   157n350
Deqiang, Han   67, 68
Destutt de Tracy, A.L.C.   229
Deutscher, Isaac   38n66
Dieterich, Heinz   69
Dietzgen, Joseph   256
Dimoulis, Dimitri   165, 166, 207, 305
Dlubek, Rolf   128, 129
Dobb, Maurice   96
Dognin, Paul-Dominique   159
Dozekal, Egbert   87
Dühring, Eugen   255
Duménil, Gérard   159
Dunayevskaya, Raya   38n66, 288n312
Duncker, Franz   215
Dussel, Enrique   6, 13, 14, 39n69, 57, 58, 69,
        168, 170–174, 198, 207, 245–248, 266n222,
        288, 317
Dutschke, Rudi   28

Echeverria, Bolivar   5, 167, 168, 175, 207
Echeverria, Rafael   169, 170, 242
Economakis, George (Georgios)   165, 305
Elbe, Ingo   14–16, 142n283
Eldred, Michael   186, 187
Elliott, Gregory   185n490
Elster, Jon   191n524, 192, 193
Establet, Roger   154, 155, 285

Fangtong, Liu   61
Fausto, Ruy   176
Fetscher, Iring   80
Feuerbach, Ludwig   22n9, 41, 144, 155, 169, 170
Fichte, Johann Gottlieb   22n9
Fine, Ben   189
Fine, Robert   189
Finelli, Roberto   150, 151

Fineschi, Roberto   150n319, 151, 152, 220
Fischer, Anton M.   164
Fornet-Betancourt, Raúl   39
Franklin, Benjamin   88, 229
Fraser, Ian   189, 251, 252
Fukuda, Tokuzo   93
Fukumoto, Kazuo   11, 73, 94, 95
Fukuyama, Francis   64
Fukuzawa, Hiroomi   46
Fulda, Hans Friedrich   87
Furihata, Setsuo   42, 49

Gajano, Alberto   148, 149
Galander, Ehrenfried   276
Galander, Ulrike   138, 276, 277
Galceran Huguet, Monserrat   36, 180
Galiani, Ferdinando   229
Gandler, Stefan   5, 40, 41, 167n204
Garaudy, Roger   35, 153
Garcia Bacca, Juan David   167n404
Germer, Claus Magno   176
Geymonat, Ludovico   142
Giannotti, José Artur   166
Girschner, Christian   312, 313
Glucksmann, André   52
Godelier, Maurice   154
Göhler, Gerhard   80, 88, 243–245
Goldmann, Lucien   8, 33n48
Golman, Lew   59
Gramsci, Antonio   8, 9, 15, 25, 142n284
Grespan, Jorge   177, 317
Grimm, Jacob   293
Grlic, Danko   50
Grossmann, Hendrik   73, 75n5, 268, 301
Grünberg, Carl   124
Guerrero, Diego   182
Guevara, Ernesto (Che)   71
Guiterrez de Dütsch, Begona   179, 180

Habermas, Jürgen   83
Hahn, Young Bin   122, 227, 308, 309
Hai Hac, Tran   159, 206, 207
Haifeng, Yang   120, 121
Han, Seungwan   122, 123, 149, 290, 291
Hanlon, Marnie   186
Hardt, Michael   55n119
Harich, Wolfgang   22
Harnecker, Marta   69, 167, 168, 175, 181
Hartmann, Klaus   30n35

Haug, Wolfgang Fritz   41, 50n104, 58, 85, 86, 92, 227
Hayden, Tom   38
Hecker, Rolf x,   19, 20, 96, 97n93, 125, 131, 133, 139n271, 230n92, 299
Hegel, G.W.F.   1n2, 21, 22, 30, 34, 76, 82, 86, 87, 108, 109, 111, 112, 114–117, 122, 123, 127, 140–145, 147–152, 155, 156, 158, 169, 170–173, 176, 185, 186, 188, 189, 191, 193n530, 202, 235, 244, 245, 248–265
Heinrich, Michael x,   6, 12, 13, 30n37, 80, 89, 90, 92, 156, 165, 209–211, 219, 220, 277–279, 286–289, 302, 305, 309, 310, 314, 319n5
Heller, Agnes   51
Henning, Christoph   5, 6
Henry, Michel   159
Hinkelammert, Franz Josef   175
Hirata, Kiyoaki   44
Hiromatsu, Wataru   98, 99, 100n105, 121, 144, 315
Hitler, Adolf   75
Hobsbawm, Eric   115n166, 183, 184
Hofer, Marc   164, 236
Hoff, Jan   83, 165n390
Holloway, John   70, 138, 174
Holzkamp, Klaus   86
Horkheimer, Max   77n9, 124
Hoshino, Tomiichi   302
Hountondji, Paulin J.   59, 60
Hubmann, Gerald   150n319
Hyppolite, Jean   153

Iacono, Alfonso M.   149
Iber, Christian   145
Ilyenkov, Evald   127, 151, 175, 316
Iorio, Marco   5n5
Ishikura, Masao   109n138
Itoh, Makoto   93, 101, 113, 271, 301, 302, 315
Iwasaki, Chikatsugu   95n84, 108
Iwata, Hiroshi   99, 106

Jahn, Wolfgang   83, 132, 137, 194, 272–275, 277, 284
Janoska, Judith   149, 164, 236, 237
Jay, Martin   142n283
Jeong, Seongjin   61n139
Jeong, Woon-Young   122
Joe, Hyeon-Soo   122

Kandel, J.P.   126
Kant, Immanuel   21n9, 111, 112, 145
Karatani, Kojin   111, 112
Karsz, Saül   138n412
Katsiaficas, George   30n38, 38
Kautsky, Karl   22n9
Kawakami, Hajime   8, 24, 73, 93–95
Kegler, Dietrich   65
Keynes, John Maynard   308
Kicillof, Axel   180
Kim, Kyung-Mi   122
Kim, Lee Jun   122, 304n366
Kim, Soo-Haeng   121, 122
Kincaid, Jim   183n478
Kindle, Konrad   164, 236
Kittsteiner, Heinz-Dieter   224
Kleiber, Lucia   186
Knight, Nick   23, 24
Kofler, Leo   27
Kogan, Albert   134, 272, 284, 285
Kohan, Néstor   174, 207, 317
Kolakowski, Leszek   8
Kolganov, Andrej I.   65
Korsch, Karl   8–10, 15, 28, 52, 75, 95, 153
Kosik, Karel   140
Krahl, Hans-Jürgen   28–30, 249, 314
Krätke, Michael   12, 160n369, 224n71, 233n99, 280, 281, 301
Kuczynski, Jürgen   252
Kugelmann, Ludwig   209n30, 215, 240, 255, 278
Kundel, Erich   139
Kuroda, Kan'ichi   47, 48, 107, 108
Kuruma, Samezo   8, 73, 95, 97, 98, 100, 101, 115, 218, 220, 221, 228, 268, 270, 288n312, 291, 301, 315
Kushin, I.A.   22
Kushida, Tamizo   93–96
Kwack, No-Wan   122, 156, 309–311

La Grassa, Gianfranco   142
Lamo de Espinosa, Emilio   181
Lassalle, Ferdinand   1, 177, 255, 256, 266, 282, 312
Lebowitz, Michael   187, 193, 282
Lee, Chai-on   122
Lee, Seong-Paik   65
Lefébvre, Henri   33n48
Lefebvre, Jean-Pierre   160

Leibniz, Gottfried Wilhelm 257

Lenin, W.I. 5, 7, 19, 35, 48, 61, 62, 103, 114, 119, 120, 262

Leontjew, Lew 125

Lessing, Gotthold Ephraim 255

Levinas, Emmanuel 58, 173

Levine, Norman 188, 194n538, 195, 224n74

Lévy, Bernard-Henry 52

Lewis, John 36n56

Liedman, Sven-Eric 163n383

Likitkijsomboon, Pichit 117, 118

Limoeiro-Cardoso, Miriam 54n117

Linde, Birger 306, 307

Lippert, Wolfgang 24, 93n74

Lippi, Marco 149

Litschev, Alexander 65

Locke, John 228

Löwy, Michael 39, 71, 175

Lukacs, Georg 8, 9, 13, 15, 22, 28, 37, 51, 95, 200, 253

Lundquist, Anders 161n379

Luporini, Cesare 147, 148, 151, 316

Luxemburg, Rosa 71

Macherey, Pierre 154, 155, 159

MacLean, Brian 114n162

Malthus, Thomas Robert 281, 294

Malysch, Alexander I. 125, 225n73, 284

Mandel, Ernest 70n180, 83

Markovic, Mihailo 50

Mariategui, José Carlos 39, 71

Marramao, Giacomo 32

Marcuse, Herbert 8, 28, 38, 39

Markus, György 51

Martinez Marzoa, Felipe 181

Marxhausen, Thomas 113, 138

Masaki, Hachiro 221–223

Matsui, Kiyoshi 270, 271

Mattick, Paul 38n66, 301

Mauke, Michael 28n26

Mawatari, Shoken 103, 106, 114n159

Mayer, Thomas 193

Mazzone, Alessandro 150

McLellan, David 19n1, 184

Meek, Ronald 182

Meikle, Scott 189

Melcher, Dorothea 68

Mendelsohn, Moses 255

Mepham, John 186n492

Merker, Nicolao 143n285

Merleau-Ponty, Maurice 9

Mészáros, István 68, 69

Miki, Kiyoshi 97n92

Milios, John (Jannis) 18, 63, 165, 166, 207, 208n24, 227, 305, 306

Mita, Sekisuke 108

Miyakawa, Akira 108, 110–112

Mizuta, Hiroshi 42

Mohl, Ernst Theodor 27n9, 137

Monal, Isabel 166n399

Montano, Mario 142n282

Moore, Samuel 300

Morishima, Michio 100n103

Morris-Suzuki, Tessa 42, 43, 94

Moseley, Fred 190, 194, 248, 258, 289, 290

Moszkowska, Natalie 301

Mugnai, Massimo 149

Müller, Manfred 137, 194, 286

Müller, Ulrich 156n346

Murray, Patrick 190, 247, 248, 262, 263

Musto, Marcelo 145n291, 150n319

Nagatani, Kiyoshi 97, 98

Napoleon I. 294

Napoleoni, Claudio 146, 152, 316

Navarro, Fernanda 168

Naville, Pierre 154n335

Negri, Antonio (Toni) 54, 55

Nelson, Anitra 216

Neuhaus, Manfred 150n319

Nikolaus, Martin 183, 184n484

Nietzold, Roland 284

Niji, Yoshihiro 109

Nikolic, Milos 26, 27

Nishida, Kitaro 97n92

North, Dudley 228

Noske, Dieter 237

Nowak, Leszek 141n278

Oakley, Allen 271, 272

Oguro, Masao 220

Ohara, Magosaburo 95

Oishi, Takahisa 111, 230n89

Oittinen, Vesa 161n379

Okishio, Nobuo 100n103

Ollman, Bertell 190, 191

O'Malley, Joseph 258

Omiya, Samanosuke   49n103
Omura, Izumi   96, 116, 291, 292
Otani, Teinosuke   220, 270

Palti, Elias José   11
Panzieri, Raniero   32
Park, Dae-Won   122, 307, 308
Park, Young-Ho   122
Paschukanis, Eugen   15, 16
Pena, Milciades   167
Petrioli, Alexis   83
Petrovic, Gajo   50, 51
Petty, William   258
Pietranera, Giulio   146, 147
Ping, He   119
Pinochet, Augusto   69
Plekhanow, G.W.   22n9
Porfirio Miranda, José   168n408
Postone, Moishe   188
Pozzoli, Claudio   32
Preve, Costanzo   143n284
Proudhon, Pierre-Joseph   212, 230
Psychopedis, Kosmas   166n398

Quante, Michael   264
Quesnay, Francois   110, 229
Qiubai, Qu   24, 25

Rakowitz, Nadja   91, 203, 314
Rancière, Jacques   16, 36, 154, 155, 159
Reichelt, Helmut   6, 13, 16n38, 30n35, 70, 77,
   81, 82, 86, 91, 92, 152, 162, 166n398, 194,
   203, 204, 222, 312, 314
Renault, Emmanuel   160n369
Reuten, Geert   118n178, 188, 190
Ricardo, David   111, 112, 137, 138n266,
   140, 165, 178, 207–211, 214, 216, 228–
   230, 232, 237–241, 253, 262, 264,
   280, 281n284, 289, 294–297, 312,
   318
Ricci, Francois   158
Riedel, Dieter   91, 92
Ripalda, José Maria   181
Rjazanov, David B.   124, 126
Robles Baez, Mario L.   168
Roces, Wenceslao   167n404
Rockmore, Tom   189
Rodin, Davor   141
Roemer, John E.   191n524, 192, 193

Roies, Albert   181
Rojas, Raul   146n296, 175
Rosdolsky, Roman   10, 74–76, 84, 136n260,
   152, 153, 162, 184n487, 185, 186n492, 194,
   241, 268, 269, 273, 283, 284, 286, 289, 314,
   317
Rosenberg, D.I.   126
Rosenkranz, Karl   254
Rosental, Marc M.   20, 22, 126
Rosenthal, John   186, 249, 263, 264
Rossi, Mario   147
Roth, Volkbert (Michael, Mike)   86, 186
Rovatti, Pier Aldo   184n303
Rubel, Maximilien   153, 154, 319n6
Ruben, Peter   163n382
Rubin, Isaak Iljitsch   15, 16, 22, 73, 74, 122,
   124–126, 131, 135, 152, 176, 180, 185, 226,
   216

Saad-Filho, Alfredo   175, 176, 317
Sacristán Luzón, Manuel   36, 37
Sagnol, Marc   286
Sakisaka, Itsuro   42, 43, 97
Salama, Pierre   206n18
Salomon, David   25
Sanchez Vazquez, Adolfo   5, 8, 11, 40, 41, 167,
   168, 171
Sartre, Jean-Paul   33n48, 153
Sato, Kinzaburo   270, 315
Say, Jean-Baptiste   229, 253, 281, 294
Sayers, Sean   258
Schaff, Adam   56
Schanz, Hans-Joergen   162, 163
Schauerte, E. Michael   315n2
Schelling, F.W.   22n9, 172
Schkredov, Vladimir Petrovic   130–132, 134,
   316
Schmidt, Alfred   13, 27, 77, 78, 80, 81, 112n149,
   140, 156n346, 194, 204n11, 314
Schmieder, Falko   188n505
von Schmoller, Gustav   92
Schrader, Fred   88, 256–258
Schwarz, Winfried   80, 87, 88, 194, 269, 270,
   277, 284, 286, 290
Schweier, Thomas Lutz   90
Sekine, Iichiro   270
Sekine, Thomas (Tomohiko) x,   46, 98n95,
   101, 102n108, 103, 104, 107, 113, 114, 117, 191,
   315

Senior, Nassau   281
Sève, Lucien   54, 157
Shaikh, Anwar   294n329
Shamsavari, Ali   116, 117, 185, 249, 317
Shaozhi, Su   11, 12, 61n142, 62, 63, 67
Shibata, Shingo   315
Shigeta, Sumio   202
Siemek, Marek J.   140, 141
Simonde de Sismondi, J.C.L.   294
Siqi, Ai   24, 25
Skarbek, F.   229
Smith, Adam   110, 111, 212, 216, 228–230,
      232n96, 237, 239, 253, 254
Smith, Tony   190, 191, 258, 260–263
Sperl, Richard   129n230, 139n271
Soldani, Franco   149, 150
de Spinoza, Baruch   255, 257
Sraffa, Piero   149, 192
Stalin, Josef   19–23, 44, 45, 47, 61, 74, 75, 107,
      119, 120, 126, 131, 135
Stapelfeldt, Gerhard   87, 88
Starosta, Guido   180
Steedman, Ian   116, 149
Sten, Jan   21n9
Sternberg, Fritz   275n258
Steuart, James   228, 230, 237, 253, 254
von Storch, Heinrich Friedrich   257
Stutje, Jan-Willem   70n180
Stützle, Ingo   83
Suzumura, Kotaro   96n91
Sweezy, Paul   38n66, 96, 182, 183

Tagai, Imre   141, 142
Tairako, Tomonaga   66, 67, 110, 119n182
Takagi, Kojiro   270
Takano, Iwasaburo   96
Takenaga, Susumu   109, 124n203
Taylor, Nicola   194
Teixeira, Francisco   176
Ternowski, Michail   285
Theunissen, Michael   87
Thompson, E.P.   9, 36n56, 38
Tian, Chenshan   25
Timpanaro, Sebastiano   142
Togliatti, Palmiro   31
Tombazos, Stavros   166n398
Tosaka, Jun   97n92
Tosel, André   13, 14
Tribe, K.   184

Trofimow, P.S.   20
Tronti, Mario   32, 33, 148n303
Trotsky, Leo   10, 71
Tsuru, Shigeto   96
Tsushima, Tadayuki   44
Tuchscheerer, Walter   83, 136, 137, 152, 316

Uchida, Hiroshi   109, 158
Uno, Kozo   11, 13, 45–49, 97–108, 113, 114, 117,
      118, 122, 190, 191, 217–220, 259, 271, 301,
      302, 315, 317

Vadée, Michel   158
Varga, Eugen   301
Vargas Lozano, Gabriel   169
Veca, Salvatore   148
de Vicente Hernando, César   181
Vincent, Jean-Marie   159
Vollgraf, Carl-Erich   139n271, 233
Volkogonov, D.   21n9
della Volpe, Galvano   11, 31, 37, 52, 53, 142–
      147, 151, 152, 185, 249, 263, 316
Vranicki, Predrag   7, 8, 11, 17, 50

Wagner, Adolph   92, 155, 156, 216, 243
Warnke, Camilla   21, 22
Wasjulin (Vazjulin), Wiktor A.   6, 127, 133
Waszek, Norbert   253n170, 253n172
Weber, Marx   141n278
Weller, Paul   125
Williams, Michael   188
Willich, August   23n12
Willing, Gunter   277
Wippermann, Wolfgang   16, 17
Wolf, Dieter   82n26, 92
Wolf, Frieder Otto   83
Wolff, Richard D.   185
Woods, Allan   69n172
Wygodski (Vygodski), Witali Solomonowitsch
      83, 126, 127, 130, 134, 135, 284, 316

Xiaoping, Deng   61, 65, 72, 118, 251
Xiaoping, Wei   118, 119

Yamada, Moritaro   42
Yamada, Toshio   98–100
Yamakawa Hitoshi   42
Yaobang, Hu   62
Yibing, Zhang   121

Zapata, Emiliano   66n157
Zedong, Mao   12, 24, 25, 62, 67, 68
Zeleny, Jindrich   83, 140, 210, 250, 316

Zhang, Zhongpu   120
Zimmermann, Marion   138